PEARSON ALWAYS LEARNING

Multicultural Film:
An Anthology

Fall 2013

Selected by Kathryn Karrh Cashin and Lauren C. Martilli

Introduction by Lauren C. Martilli

Cover Art: Courtesy of Eyewire/Getty Images

Pearson Learning Solutions, 501 Boylston Street, Suite 900, Boston, MA 02116
A Pearson Education Company
www.pearsoned.com

Printed in the United States of America

1 2 3 4 5 6 7 8 9 10 V0ZN 17 16 15 14 13

000200010271762436

BW/TB

ISBN 10: 1-269-21682-1
ISBN 13: 978-1-269-21682-1

Contents

Introduction to Multicultural Film: An Anthology, Fall 2013

Cinematic Representations of Race, Class, Gender, Religion, and Sexuality in American Film

When was the last time a Hollywood movie inspired you or captivated your attention? Were you particularly drawn to the actors, imagery, storyline, or special effects? Each of us likely has preferences about the cultural products we consume, especially movies—whether we prefer comedy to horror, drama over musicals, or any variety of film genres, the movies impact our lives in profound ways. In addition to entertainment value, Hollywood movies teach us valuable lessons; they portray images of the nation that inform our understanding of American culture and what constitutes ideal citizenship. Movies tell us how to behave, what to wear, and what constitutes good or bad behavior, style, or character. To participate meaningfully in our communities, we must have tools to analyze, interpret, and negotiate the many messages and meanings in Hollywood film.

I remember watching the political thriller *Blood Diamond* (2006) starring Leonardo DiCaprio, Jennifer Connelly, and Djimon Hounsou. When American journalist Maddie Bowen (Connelly) exclaims, "Americans wouldn't buy a diamond if they knew it cost someone their hand," it resonated with me, yet the final courtroom scene implies a resolution to the corruption and terror of the conflict diamond trade. It provoked further research into the issue of conflict diamonds as well as child soldiers, both are highly complex issues that are far more widespread than I initially imagined, but very few Hollywood movies seem to adequately confront these issues.

Given the structure and commercial imperatives of the Hollywood feature film, the omissions are understandable, but our awareness of social issues must not cease when the movie ends. We must remain cognizant of the formal techniques and devices filmmakers choose in their construction of meaning. Mise en scène elements such as lighting, scenery, props, and wardrobe are intentional choices that must be considered in the context of each film. Moreover, the construction of meaning in film extends to socially accepted (and contested) meanings such as nationality, race, class, gender, and sexuality.

For example, consider a few exemplars of Hollywood drama: *Forrest Gump* (1994), *The Blind Side* (2009), or *The Help* (2011). Each story involves a main character, an American individual who pursues equal rights for all citizens regardless of race, class, physical or mental ability. Symbolic of progress and equanimity, Forrest (Tom Hanks), the Touhy family (Sandra Bullock et al.), and Skeeter (Emma Stone) portray presumably ideal qualities of American citizenship—they aspire to help others through compassionate acts of courage and generosity. Yet, when we examine the representation of race, ethnicity, class, gender, or sexuality in each film, what more might we uncover? In movies that tell stories about triumph and empowerment in the face of racism and prejudice, why are leading protagonists almost always white? We might also consider which individuals and social groups appear privileged at the expense of those marginalized or exploited? The concept of white privilege and, what critics refer to as, the "white savior film" offer useful conceptual tools to facilitate a critical exploration of cultural representation.

Furthermore, Hollywood movies often follow established patterns. We frequently see familiar character types and similar narrative structure across a wide variety of films. For example, the "happily ever after" ending is a Hollywood favorite, especially in comedy and romance films. A comparison of the popular Disney animated film *Cinderella* (1950) with *Sex and the City* (2008), for instance, offers some insight.

Cinderella represents the quintessential "fair maiden" and "damsel in distress" character type. Endowed with beauty (portrayed as thin, fair-skinned, with blond hair, and blue eyes) and charming compassion, she overcomes oppression with elegance and grace, and by winning the heart of Prince Charming. The glass slipper fits, followed by a royal wedding, and, *naturally,* the couple lives happily ever after. Are we convinced? Do we believe in the fairytale love story? We may even imagine ourselves in one of these roles.

Fast-forward several decades to the movie *Sex and the City* (2008) based on the popular television series which recycles familiar patterns. Blonde-haired, blue-eyed Carrie Bradshaw (Sara Jessica Parker) is a modern Cinderella—she is a writer living in New York City who socializes and shops with friends. In the movie, Carrie plans the wedding of her dreams to her version of Prince Charming, Mr. Big who has (finally) divorced his wife. Like Cinderella, she overcomes obstacles to "live happily ever after," albeit the social conditions have changed, but ultimately the shoe fits, only this time it's a Manolo Blahnick (a very expensive designer brand).

While *Cinderella* (1950) and *Sex and the City* (2008) are merely two examples from a plethora of Hollywood feature films, they follow similar formulas. Arguably, they perpetuate a myth that happiness involves love and wealth, more specifically heterosexual marriage and an upper-class lifestyle. Both leading characters—Cinderella and Carrie—are white, wealthy, 'feminine' heterosexual women who pursue white, wealthy 'masculine' heterosexual men. While social conditions have significantly changed, both stories feature similar narrative patterns and convey similar messages about American identities that are often accepted as natural. Yet, how might these narratives underrepresent or silence certain individuals or social groups in American culture?

Approaching cinematic representations through the lens of cultural studies provides the tools necessary for these types of analyses. A cultural studies framework offers meaningful conceptual tools for interpreting and evaluating the construction of American identities in Hollywood film. This course and the articles in this edition of *Multicultural Film: An Anthology* aim to broaden your awareness of and engagement with multicultural meanings in Hollywood film. In an age of unprecedented technological advancement, our ability to respond critically to the visual texts we encounter regularly is paramount to living a productive life within our individual communities, and as members of a the global audience.

Lauren C. Martilli

1

Cultural Studies, Multiculturalism, and Media Culture

Douglas Kellner

Radio, television, film, and the other products of media culture provide materials out of which we forge our very identities; our sense of selfhood; our notion of what it means to be male or female; our sense of class, of ethnicity and race, of nationality, of sexuality; and of "us" and "them." Media images help shape our view of the world and our deepest values: what we consider good or bad, positive or negative, moral or evil. Media stories provide the symbols, myths, and resources through which we constitute a common culture and through the appropriation of which we insert ourselves into this culture. Media spectacles demonstrate who has power and who is powerless, who is allowed to exercise force and violence, and who is not. They dramatize and legitimate the power of the forces that be and show the powerless that they must stay in their places or be oppressed.

We are immersed from cradle to grave in a media and consumer society and thus it is important to learn how to understand, interpret, and criticize its meanings and messages. The media are a profound and often misperceived source of cultural pedagogy: They contribute to educating us how to behave and what to think, feel, believe, fear, and desire—and what not to. The media are forms of pedagogy that teach us how to be men and women. They show us how to dress, look, and consume; how to react to members of different social groups; how to be popular and successful and how to avoid failure; and how to conform to the dominant system of norms, values, practices, and institutions. Consequently, the gaining of critical media literacy is an important resource for individuals and citizens in learning how to cope with a seductive cultural environment. Learning how to read, criticize, and resist socio-cultural manipulation can help empower oneself in relation to dominant forms of media and culture. It can enhance individual sovereignty vis-à-vis media culture and give people more power over their cultural environment.

In this chapter, I will discuss the potential contributions of a cultural studies perspective to media critique and literacy. In recent years, cultural studies has emerged as a set of approaches to the study of culture and society. The project was inaugurated by the University of Birmingham Centre for Contemporary Cultural Studies, which developed a variety of critical methods for the analysis, interpretation,

Reprinted from *Gender, Race, and Class in Media,* Second Edition, edited by Jean M. Humez and Gail Dines (2002), by permission of Sage Publications.

and criticism of cultural artifacts.[1] Through a set of internal debates, and responding to social struggles and movements of the 1960s and the 1970s, the Birmingham group came to focus on the interplay of representations and ideologies of class, gender, race, ethnicity, and nationality in cultural texts, including media culture. They were among the first to study the effects of newspapers, radio, television, film, and other popular cultural forms on audiences. They also focused on how various audiences interpreted and used media culture differently, analyzing the factors that made different audiences respond in contrasting ways to various media texts.

Through studies of youth subcultures, British cultural studies demonstrated how culture came to constitute distinct forms of identity and group membership. For cultural studies, media culture provides the materials for constructing views of the world, behavior, and even identities. Those who uncritically follow the dictates of media culture tend to "mainstream" themselves, conforming to the dominant fashion, values, and behavior. Yet cultural studies is also interested in how subcultural groups and individuals resist dominant forms of culture and identity, creating their own style and identities. Those who obey ruling dress and fashion codes, behavior, and political ideologies thus produce their identities within the mainstream group, as members of specific social groupings (such as white, middle-class conservative Americans). Persons who identify with subcultures, like punk culture, or black nationalist subcultures, look and act differently from those in the mainstream, and thus create oppositional identities, defining themselves against standard models.

Cultural studies insists that culture must be studied within the social relations and system through which it is produced and consumed and that thus study of culture is intimately bound up with the study of society, politics, and economics. Cultural studies shows how media culture articulates the dominant values, political ideologies, and social developments and novelties of the era. It conceives of U.S. culture and society as a contested terrain with various groups and ideologies struggling for dominance (Kellner, 1995). Television, film, music, and other popular cultural forms are thus often liberal or conservative, although they occasionally articulate more radical or oppositional positions and are often ideologically ambiguous, combining various political positions.

Cultural studies is valuable because it provides some tools that enable one to read and interpret one's culture critically. It also subverts distinctions between "high" and "low" culture by considering a wide continuum of cultural artifacts ranging from novels to television and by refusing to erect any specific cultural hierarchies or canons. Previous approaches to culture tended to be primarily literary and elitist, dismissing media culture as banal, trashy, and not worthy of serious attention. The project of cultural studies, by contrast, avoids cutting the field of culture into high and low, or popular against elite. Such distinctions are difficult to maintain and generally serve as a front for normative aesthetic valuations and, often, a political program (i.e., either dismissing mass culture for high culture, or celebrating what is deemed "popular" while scorning "elitist" high culture).

Cultural studies allows us to examine and critically scrutinize the whole range of culture without prior prejudices toward one or another sort of cultural text, institution, or practice. It also opens the way toward more differentiated political, rather than aesthetic, valuations of cultural artifacts in which one attempts to distinguish critical and oppositional from conformist and conservative moments in a cultural artifact. For instance, studies of Hollywood film show how key 1960s films promoted the views of radicals and the counterculture and how film in the 1970s was a battleground between liberal and conservative positions; late 1970s films, however, tended toward conservative positions that helped elect Ronald Reagan as president (see Kellner & Ryan, 1988).

There is an intrinsically critical and political dimension to the project of cultural studies that distinguishes it from objectivist and apolitical academic approaches to the study of culture and society. British cultural studies, for example, analyzed culture historically in the context of its societal origins effects. It situated culture within a theory of social production and reproduction, specifying the ways that cultural forms served either to further social domination or to enable people to resist and struggle against domination. It analyzed society as a hierarchical and antagonistic set of social relations characterized by the oppression of subordinate class, gender, race, ethnic, and national strata. Employing Gramsci's (1971) model of hegemony and counterhegemony, it sought to analyze "hegemonic," or ruling, social and cultural forces of domination and to seek "counterhegemonic" forces of resistance and struggle. The project as aimed at social transformation and attempted to specify forces of domination and resistance in order to aid the process of political struggle and emancipation from oppression and domination.

For cultural studies, the concept of ideology is of central importance, for dominant ideologies serve to reproduce social relations of domination and subordination.[2] Ideologies of class, for instance, celebrate upper-class life and denigrate the working class. Ideologies of gender promote sexist representations of women and ideologies of race utilize racist representations of people of color and various minority groups. Ideologies make inequalities and subordination appear natural and just, and thus induce consent to relations of domination. Contemporary societies are structured by opposing groups who have different political ideologies (liberal, conservative, radical, etc.) and cultural studies specifies what, if any, ideologies are operative in a given cultural artifact (which could involve, of course, the specification, of ideological contradictions). In the course of this study, I will provide some examples of how different ideologies are operative in media cultural texts and will accordingly provide examples of ideological analysis and critique.

Because of its focus on representations of race, gender, and class, and its critique of ideologies that promote various forms of oppression, cultural studies lends itself to a multiculturalist program that demonstrates how culture reproduces certain forms of racism, sexism, and biases against members of subordinate classes, social groups, or alternative lifestyles. Multiculturalism affirms the worth of different types of culture and cultural groups, claiming, for instance, that black, Latino, Asian, Native American, gay and lesbian, and other oppressed and marginal voices have their own validity and importance. An insurgent multiculturalism attempts to show how various people's voices and experiences are silenced and omitted from mainstream culture and struggles to aid in the articulation of diverse views, experiences, and cultural forms, from groups excluded from the mainstream. This makes it a target of conservative forces who wish to preserve the existing canons of white male, Eurocentric privilege and thus attack multiculturalism in cultural wars raging from the 1960s to the present over education, the arts, and the limits of free expression.

Cultural studies thus promotes a multiculturalist politics and media pedagogy that aims to make people sensitive to how relations of power and domination are "encoded" in cultural texts, such as those of television or film. But it also specifies how people can resist the dominant encoded meanings and produce their own critical and alternative readings. Cultural studies can show how media culture manipulates and indoctrinates us, and thus can empower individuals to resist the dominant meanings to media cultural products and to produce their own meanings. It can also point to moments of resistance and criticism within media culture and thus help promote development of more critical consciousness.

A critical cultural studies—embodied in many of the chapters collected in this reader—thus develops concepts and analyses that will enable readers to analytically dissect the artifacts of contemporary media culture and to gain power over their cultural environment. By exposing the entire field of culture to knowledgeable scrutiny, cultural studies provides a broad, comprehensive framework to undertake studies of culture, politics, and society for the purposes of individual empowerment and social and political struggle and transformation. In the following pages, I will therefore indicate some of the chief components of the type of cultural studies that I find most useful.

Components of a Critical Cultural Studies

At its strongest, cultural studies contains a threefold project of analyzing the production and political economy of culture, cultural texts, and the audience reception of those texts and their effects. This comprehensive approach avoids too narrowly focusing on one dimension of the project to the exclusion of others. To avoid such limitations, I would thus propose a multiperspectival approach that (a) discusses production and political economy, (b) engages in textual analysis, and (c) studies the reception and use of cultural texts.[3]

Production and Political Economy

Because it has been neglected in many modes of recent cultural studies, it is important to stress the importance of analyzing cultural texts within their system of production and distribution, often referred to as the political economy of culture.[4] Inserting texts into the system of culture within which they are produced and distributed can help elucidate features and effects of the texts that textual analysis alone might miss or downplay. Rather than being antithetical approaches to culture, political economy can actually contribute to textual analysis and critique. The system of production often determines what sort of artifacts will be produced, what structural limits there will be as to what can and cannot be said and shown, and what sort of audience effects the text may generate.

Study of the codes of television, film, or popular music, for instance, is enhanced by studying the formulas and conventions of production. These cultural forms are structured by well-defined rules and conventions, and the study of the production of culture can help elucidate the codes actually in play. Because of the demands of the format of radio or music television, for instance, most popular songs are three to five minutes, fitting into the frames of the distribution system. Because of their control by giant corporations oriented primarily toward profit, film and television production in the United States is dominated by specific genres such as talk and game shows, soap operas, situation comedies, action/adventure series, reality TV, and so on. This economic factor explains why there are cycles of certain genres and subgenres, sequelmania in the film industry, crossovers of popular films into television series, and a certain homogeneity in products constituted within systems of production marked by rigid generic codes, formulaic conventions, and well-defined ideological boundaries.

Likewise, study of political economy can help determine the limits and range of political and ideological discourses and effects. My study of television in the United States, for instance, disclosed that takeover of the television networks by major transnational corporations and communications conglomerates was part of a "right turn" within U.S. society in the 1980s whereby powerful corporate groups won control of the state and the mainstream media (Kellner, 1990). For example, during the 1980s all three networks were taken over by major corporate conglomerates: ABC was bought out in 1985 by Capital Cities, NBC was absorbed by GE, and CBS was purchased by the Tisch Financial Group. Both ABC and NBC sought corporate mergers and this motivation, along with other benefits derived from Reaganism, might well have influenced them to downplay criticisms of Reagan and to generally support his conservative programs, military adventures, and simulated presidency.

Corporate conglomeratization has intensified further and today AOL and Time Warner, Disney, and other global media conglomerates control ever more domains of the production and distribution of culture (McChesney, 2000). In this global context, one cannot really analyze the role of the media in the Gulf war, for instance, without analyzing the production and political economy of news and information, as well as the actual text of the Gulf war and its reception by its audience (see Kellner, 1992). Likewise, the ownership by conservative corporations of dominant media corporations helps explain mainstream media support of the Bush administration and their polities, such as the 2000 U.S. presidential election (Kellner, 2001).

Looking toward entertainment, one cannot fully grasp the Madonna phenomenon without analyzing her marketing strategies, her political environment, her cultural artifacts, and their effects (Kellner, 1995). In a similar fashion, younger female pop music stars and groups such as Mariah Carey, Britney Spears, Jennifer Lopez, or N'Sync also deploy the tools of the glamour industry and media spectacle to make certain stars the icons of fashion, beauty, style, and sexuality, as well as purveyors of music. And in appraising the full social impact of pornography, one needs to be aware of the sex industry and the production process of, say, pornographic films, and not just dwell on the texts themselves and their effects on audiences.

Furthermore, in an era of globalization, one must be aware of the global networks that produce and distribute media culture in the interests of profit and corporate hegemony. Yet political economy alone does not hold the key to cultural studies and important as it is, it has limitations as a single approach. Some political economy analyses reduce the meanings and effects of texts to rather circumscribed and reductive ideological functions, arguing that media culture merely reflects the ideology of the ruling economic elite that controls the culture industries and is nothing more than a vehicle for capitalist ideology. It is true that media culture overwhelmingly supports capitalist values, but it is also a site of intense struggle between different races, classes, gender, and social groups. Thus, in order to fully grasp the nature and effects of media culture, one needs to develop methods to analyze the full range of its meanings and effects.

Textual Analysis

The products of media culture require multidimensional close textual readings to analyze their various forms of discourses, ideological positions, narrative strategies, image construction, and effects. There have been a wide range of types of textual criticism of media culture, ranging from quantitative content analysis that dissects the number of, say, episodes of violence in a text, to qualitative study that examines images of women, blacks, or other groups, or that applies various critical theories to unpack the meanings of the texts or to explicate how texts function to produce meaning. Traditionally, the qualitative analysis of texts has been the task of formalist literary criticism, which explicates the central meanings, values, symbols, and ideologies in cultural artifacts by attending to the formal properties of imaginative literature texts—such as style, verbal imagery, characterization, narrative structure and point of view, and other formal elements of the artifact. From the 1960s on, however, literary-formalist textual analysis has been enhanced by methods derived from semiotics, a critical approach for investigating the creation of meaning not only in written languages but also in other, nonverbal codes, such as the visual and auditory languages of film and TV.

Semiotics analyzes how linguistic and nonlinguistic cultural "signs" form systems of meanings, as when giving someone a rose is interpreted as a sign of love, or getting an A on a college paper is a sign of mastery of the rules of the specific assignment. Semiotic analysis can be connected with genre criticism (the study of conventions governing established types of cultural forms, such as soap operas) to reveal how the codes and forms of particular genres follow certain meanings. Situation comedies, for instance, classically follow a conflict/ resolution model that demonstrates how to solve certain social problems by correct actions and values, and thus provide morality tales of proper and improper behavior. Soap operas, by contrast, proliferate problems and provide messages concerning the endurance and suffering needed to get through life's endless miseries, while generating positive and negative models of social behavior. And advertising shows how commodity solutions solve problems of popularity, acceptance, success, and the like.

A semiotic and genre analysis of the film *Rambo* (1982) for instance, would show how it follows the conventions of the Hollywood genre of the war film that dramatizes conflicts between the United States and its "enemies" (see Kellner, 1995). Semiotics describes how the images of the villains are constructed according to the codes of World War II movies and how the resolution of the conflict and happy ending follows the traditional Hollywood classical cinema, which portrays the victory of good over evil. Semiotic analysis would also include study of the strictly cinematic and formal elements of a film like *Rambo*, dissecting the ways that camera angles present Rambo as a god, or slow-motion images of him gliding through the jungle code him as a force of nature. Semiotic analysis of the 2001 film *Vanilla Sky* could engage how Cameron Crowe's film presents a remake of a 1997 Spanish film, and how the use of celebrity stars Tom Cruise and Penelope Cruz, involved in a real-life romance, provides a spectacle of modern icons of beauty, desire, sexuality, and power. The science fiction theme and images present semiotic depictions of a future in which techno-science can make everyone beautiful and we can live out our culture's dreams and nightmares.

The textual analysis of cultural studies thus combines formalist analysis with critique of how cultural meanings convey specific ideologies of gender, race, class, sexuality, nation, and other ideological dimensions. Ideological textual analysis should deploy a wide range of methods to fully explicate each dimension and to show how they fit into textual systems. Each critical method focuses on certain features of a text from a specific perspective: The perspective spotlights some features of a text while ignoring others. Marxist methods tend to focus on class, for instance, while feminist approaches will highlight gender, critical race theory spotlights race and ethnicity, and gay and lesbian theories explicate sexuality.

More sophisticated critical Marxism, feminisms, or semiotics articulate their own method with the other approaches to develop multiperspectivist positions. Yet each critical method on its own has its particular strengths and limitations, with specific optics and blindspots. Traditionally, Marxian ideology critiques have been strong on class and historical contextualization and weak on formal analysis, while some versions are highly "reductionist," reducing textual analysis to denunciation of ruling class ideology. Feminism excels in gender analysis and in some versions is formally sophisticated, drawing on such methods as psychoanalysis and semiotics, although some versions are reductive and early feminism often limited itself to analysis of images of gender. Psychoanalysis in turn calls for the interpretation of unconscious contents and meaning, which can articulate latent meanings in a text, as when Alfred Hitchcock's dream sequences in films like *Spellbound* (1945) or *Vertigo* (1958) project cinematic symbols that illuminate his characters' dilemmas, or when the image of the female character in *Bonnie and Clyde* (1967) framed against the bars of her bed suggests her sexual frustration, imprisonment in lower-middle-class family life, and need for revolt.

Of course, each reading of a text is only one possible reading from one critic's subject position, no matter how multiperspectival, and may or may not be the reading preferred by audiences (which themselves will be significantly different according to their class, race, gender, ethnicity, ideologies and so on). Because there is a split between textual encoding and audience decoding, there is always the possibility of a multiplicity of readings of any text of media culture (Hall, 1980b). There are limits to the openness or polysemic nature of any text, of course, and textual analysis can explicate the parameters of possible readings and delineate perspectives that aim at illuminating the text and its cultural and ideological effects. Such analysis also provides the materials for criticizing misreadings, or readings that are one-sided and incomplete. Yet to further carry through a cultural studies analysis, one must also examine how diverse audiences actually read media texts, and attempt to determine what effects they have on audience thought and behavior.

Audience Reception and Use of Media Culture

All texts are subject to multiple readings depending on the perspectives and subject positions of the reader. Members of distinct genders, classes, races, nations, regions, sexual preferences, and political ideologies are going to read texts differently, and cultural studies can illuminate why diverse audiences interpret texts in various, sometimes conflicting, ways. It is indeed one of the merits of cultural studies to have focused on audience reception in recent years and this focus provides one of its major contributions, though there are also some limitations and problems with the standard cultural studies approaches to the audience.[5]

A standard way to discover how audiences read texts is to engage in ethnographic research, in an attempt to determine how texts affect audiences and shape their beliefs and behavior. Ethnographic cultural studies have indicated some of the various ways that audiences use and appropriate texts, often to empower themselves. Radway's (1983; see also her chapter in this volume) study of women's use of Harlequin novels, for example, shows how these books provide escapism for women and could be understood as reproducing traditional women's roles, behavior, and attitudes. Yet they can also empower women by promoting fantasies of a different life and may thus inspire revolt against male domination. Or they may enforce, in other audiences, female submission to male domination and trap women in ideologies of romance, in which submission to Prince Charming is seen as the alpha and omega of happiness for women.

Media culture provides materials for individuals to create identities and meanings and cultural studies detects specific ways that individuals use cultural forms. Teenagers use video games and music television as an escape from the demands of a disciplinary society. Males use sports as a terrain of fantasy identification, in which they feel empowered as "their" team or star triumphs. Such sports events also generate a form of community, currently being lost in the privatized media and consumer culture of our time. Indeed, fandoms of all sorts, ranging from *Star Trek* fans ("Trekkies") to devotees of *Buffy the Vampire Slayer*, or various soap operas, also form communities that enable people to relate to others who share their interests and hobbies. Some fans, in fact, actively recreate their favorite cultural forms, such as rewriting the scripts of preferred shows, sometimes in the forms of "slash," which redefine characters' sexuality, or in the forms of music poaching or remaking such as "filking" (see examples in Lewis, 1992, and Jenkins, 1992).

This emphasis on audience reception and appropriation helps cultural studies overcome the previous one-sided textualist orientations to culture. It also directs focus on the actual political effects that texts have and how audiences use texts. In fact, sometimes audiences subvert the intentions of the producers or managers of the cultural industries that supply them, as when astute young media users laugh at obvious attempts to hype certain characters, shows, or products (see de Certeau, 1984, for more examples of audiences constructing meaning and engaging in practices in critical and subversive ways). Audience research can reveal how people are actually using cultural texts and what sort of effects they are having on everyday life.

Yet there are several problems that I see with reception studies as they have been constituted within cultural studies, particularly in the United States. First, there is a danger that class will be downplayed as a significant variable that structures audience decoding and use of cultural texts. Cultural studies in England were particularly sensitive to class differences—as well as subcultural differences—in the use and reception of cultural texts, but I have noted many dissertations, books, and articles in cultural studies in the United States where attention to class has been downplayed or is missing altogether. This is not surprising as a neglect of class as a constitutive feature of culture and society is an endemic deficiency in the American academy in most disciplines.

There is also the reverse danger, however, of exaggerating the constitutive force of class, and downplaying, or ignoring, such other variables as gender or ethnicity. Staiger (1992) notes that Fiske (1989a, 1989b), building on Hartley, lists seven "subjectivity positions" that are important in cultural reception, "self, gender, age-group, family, class, nation, ethnicity," and proposes adding sexual orientation. All of these factors, and no doubt more, interact in shaping how audiences receive and use texts and must be taken into account in studying cultural reception, for audiences decode and use texts according to the specific constituents of their class, race or ethnicity, gender, sexual preferences, and so on.

Furthermore, I would warn against a tendency to romanticize the "active audience," by claiming that all audiences produce their own meanings and denying that media culture may have powerful manipulative effects. Some individuals who do cultural studies (tradition of) reception research distinguish between dominant and oppositional readings (Hall, 1980b), a dichotomy that structures much of Fiske's work. "Dominant" readings are those in which audiences appropriate texts in line with the interests of the hegemonic culture and the ideological intentions of a text, as when audiences feel pleasure in the restoration of male power, law and order, and social stability at the end of a film like *Die Hard*, after the hero and representatives of authority eliminate the terrorists who had taken over a high-rise corporate headquarters. An "oppositional" reading, by contrast, celebrates the resistance to this reading in audience appropriation of a text; for example, Fiske (1993) observes resistance to dominant readings when homeless individuals in a shelter cheered the destruction of police and authority figures, during repeated viewings of a videotape of *Die Hard*.

Although this can be a useful distinction, there is a tendency in cultural studies to celebrate resistance per se without distinguishing between types and forms of resistance (a similar problem resides with indiscriminate celebration or audience pleasure in certain reception studies). For example, resistance to social authority by the homeless evidenced in their viewing of *Die Hard* could serve to strengthen brutal masculist behavior and encourage manifestations of physical violence to solve social problems. Jean-Paul Sartre, Frantz Fanon, and Herbert Marcuse, among others, have argued that violence can be either emancipatory, when directed at forces of oppression, or reactionary, when directed at popular forces struggling against oppression. Many feminists, by contrast, or those in the Gandhian tradition, see all violence as forms of brute masculist behavior and many people see it as a problematical form of conflict resolution. Resistance and pleasure cannot therefore be valorized per se as progressive elements of the appropriation of cultural texts, but difficult discriminations must be made as to whether the resistance, oppositional reading, or pleasure in a given experience is progressive or reactionary, emancipatory or destructive.

Thus, while emphasis on the audience and reception was an excellent correction to the one-sidedness of purely textual analysis, I believe that in recent years cultural studies has overemphasized reception and textual analysis, while underemphasizing the production of culture and its political economy. This type of cultural studies fetishizes audience reception studies and neglects both production and textual analysis, thus producing populist celebrations of the text and audience pleasure in its use of cultural artifacts. This approach, taken to an extreme, would lose its critical perspective and would lead to a positive gloss on audience experience of whatever is being studied. Such studies also might lose sight of the manipulative and conservative effects of certain types of media culture and thus serve the interests of the cultural industries as they are presently constituted.

A new way, in fact, to research media effects is to use the databases that collect media texts such as Nexis/Lexis, or search engines like Google, and to trace the effects of media artifacts like *The X-Files*, *Buffy the Vampire Slayer*, or advertising corporations like Nike and McDonald's, through analysis of references to them in the media. Likewise, there is a new terrain of Internet audience research that studies how fans act in chat rooms devoted to their favorite artifacts of media culture, create their own fan-sites, or construct artifacts that disclose how they are living out the fantasies and scripts of the culture industries. Previous studies of the audience and the reception of media privileged ethnographic studies that selected slices of the vast media audiences, usually from the site where researchers themselves lived. Such studies are invariably limited and broader effects research can indicate how the most popular artifacts of media culture have a wide range of effects. In my book *Media Culture* (1995), I studied some examples of popular cultural artifacts that clearly influenced behavior in audiences throughout the globe. Examples include groups of kids and adults who imitated Rambo in various forms of asocial behavior, or fans of *Beavis and Butt-Head* who started fires or tortured animals in the modes practiced by the popular MTV cartoon characters. Media effects are complex and controversial and it is the merit of cultural studies to make their study an important part of its agenda.

Toward a Cultural Studies Approach That Is Critical, Multicultural, and Multiperspectival

To avoid the one-sidedness of textual analysis approaches, or audience and reception studies, I propose that cultural studies itself be multiperspectival, getting at culture from the perspectives of political economy, text analysis, and audience reception, as outlined above. Textual analysis should utilize a multiplicity of perspectives and critical methods, and audience reception studies should delineate the wide range of subject positions, or perspectives, through which audiences appropriate culture. This requires a multicultural approach that sees the importance of analyzing the dimensions of class, race and ethnicity, and gender and sexual preference within the texts of media culture, while studying as well their impact on how audiences read and interpret media culture.

In addition, a critical cultural studies attacks sexism, racism, or bias against specific social groups (i.e., gays, intellectuals, and so on), and criticizes texts that promote any kind of domination or oppression. As an example of how considerations of production, textual analysis and audience readings can fruitfully intersect in cultural studies, let us reflect on the Madonna phenomenon. Madonna first appeared in the moment of Reaganism and embodied the materialistic and consumer-oriented ethos of the 1980s ("Material Girl"). She also appeared in a time of dramatic image proliferation, associated with MTV, fashion fever, and intense marketing of products. Madonna was one of the first MTV music video superstars who consciously crafted images to attract a mass audience. Her early music videos were aimed at teenage girls (the Madonna wanna-be's), but she soon incorporated black, Hispanic, and minority audiences with her images of interracial sex and multicultural "family" in her concerts. Madonna also appealed to gay and lesbian audiences, as well as to feminist and academic audiences, as her videos became more complex and political (i.e., "Like a Prayer," "Express Yourself," "Vogue," and so on).

Thus, Madonna's popularity was in large part a function of her marketing strategies and her production of music videos and images that appealed to diverse audiences. To conceptualize the meanings and effects in her music, films, concerts, and public relations stunts requires that her artifacts be interpreted within the context of their production and reception, which involves discussion of MTV, the music industry, concerts, marketing, and the production of images (see Kellner, 1995). Understanding Madonna's popularity also requires focus on audiences, not just as individuals but as members of specific groups, such as teenage girls, who were empowered in their struggles for individual identity by Madonna, or gays, who were also empowered by her incorporation of alternative images of sexuality within popular mainstream cultural artifacts. Yet appraising the politics and effects of Madonna also requires analysis of how her work might merely reproduce a consumer culture that defines identity in terms of images and consumption. It would make an interesting project to examine how former Madonna fans view the evolution and recent incarnations of the superstar, such as her second marriage and 2001 Drowned World tour, as well as to examine how contemporary fans view Madonna in an age that embraces younger teen pop singers like Britney Spears or Mariah Carey.

In short, a cultural studies that is critical and multicultural provides comprehensive approaches to culture that can be applied to a wide variety of artifacts from pornography to Madonna, from MTV to TV news, or to specific events like the 2000 U.S. presidential election (Kellner, 2001), or media representations of the 2001 terrorist attacks on the United States and the U.S. response. Its comprehensive perspectives encompass political economy, textual analysis, and audience research and provide critical and political perspectives that enable individuals to dissect the meanings, messages, and effects of dominant cultural forms. Cultural studies is thus part of a critical media pedagogy that enables individuals to resist media manipulation and to increase their freedom and individuality. It can empower people to gain sovereignty over their culture and to be able to struggle for alternative cultures and political change. Cultural studies is thus not just another academic fad, but can be part of a struggle for a better society and a better life.

Notes

1. For more information on British cultural studies, see Hall (1980b), Hall et al. (1980), Johnson (1986/1987), Fiske (1986), O'Conner (1989), Turner (1990), Grossberg (1989), Agger (1992), and the articles collected in Grossberg, Nelson, and Triechler (1992), During (1992, 1998), and Durham and Kellner (2000). I might note that the Frankfurt school also provided much material for a critical cultural studies in their works on mass culture from the 1930s through the present; on the relation between the Frankfurt school and British cultural studies, see Kellner (1997).

2. On the concept of ideology, see Kellner (1978, 1979), Centre for Contemporary Cultural Studies (1980), Kellner and Ryan (1988), and Thompson (1990).

3. This model was adumbrated in Hall (1980a) and Johnson (1986/1987) and guided much of the early Birmingham work. Around the mid-1980s, however, the Birmingham group began to increasingly neglect the production and political economy of culture (some believe that this was always a problem with their work) and much of their studies became more academic, cut off from political struggle. I am thus trying to recapture the spirit of the early Birmingham project, reconstructed for our contemporary moment. For a fuller development of my conception of cultural studies, see Kellner (1992, 1995, 2001).

4. The term *political economy* calls attention to the fact that the production and distribution of culture take place within a specific economic system, constituted by relations between the state and economy. For instance, in the United States a capitalist economy dictates that cultural production is governed by laws of the market, but the democratic imperatives of the system mean that there is some regulation of culture by the state. There are often tensions within a given society concerning how many activities should be governed by the imperatives of the market, or economics, alone and how much state regulation or intervention is desirable, to assure a wider diversity of broadcast programming, for instance, or the prohibition of phenomena agreed to be harmful, such as cigarette advertising or pornography (see Kellner, 1990).

5. Cultural studies that have focused on audience reception include Brunsdon and Morley (1978), Radway (1983), Ang (1985, 1996), Morley (1986), Fiske (1989a, 1989b), Jenkins (1992), and Lewis (1992).

References

Agger, B. (1992). *Cultural studies*. London: Falmer.

Ang, I. (1985). *Watching Dallas*. New York: Methuen.

Ang, I. (1996). *Living room wars: Rethinking media audiences for a postmodern world*. London and New York: Routledge.

Brunsdon, C., & Morley, D. (1978). *Everyday television: "Nationwide."* London: British Film Institute.

Centre for Contemporary Cultural Studies. (1980). *On ideology*. London; Hutchinson.

de Certeau, M. (1984). *The practice of everyday life*. Berkeley: University of California Press.

Durham, M. G., & Kellner, D. (Eds.). (2001). *Media and cultural studies: Keyworks.* Malden, MA, and Oxford, UK: Basil Blackwell.

During, S. (1992). *Cultural studies.* London and New York: Routledge.

During, S. (1998). *Cultural studies.* (2nd ed.). London and New York: Routledge.

Fiske, J. (1986). British cultural studies and television. In R. C. Allen (Ed.), *Channels of discourse* (pp. 254–289). Chapel Hill: University of North Carolina Press.

Fiske, J. (1987). *Television culture.* New York and London: Routledge.

Fiske, J. (1989a). *Reading the popular.* Boston: Unwin Hyman.

Fiske, J. (1989b). *Understanding popular culture.* Boston: Unwin Hyman.

Fiske, J. (1993). *Power plays, power works.* London: Verso.

Gramsci, A. (1971). *Selections from the prison notebooks.* New York; International.

Grossberg, L. (1989). The formations of cultural studies: An American in Birmingham. *Strategies, 22,* 114–149.

Grossberg, L., Nelson, C., & Treichler, P. (1992). *Cultural studies.* New York: Routledge.

Hall, S. (1980a). Cultural studies and the Centre: Some problematics and problems. In S. Hall et al., *Culture, media, language* (pp. 15–47). London: Hutchinson.

Hall, S. (1980b). Encoding/decoding. In S. Hall et al., *Culture, media, language* (pp. 128–138). London: Hutchinson.

Hall, S. et al. (1980). *Culture, media, language.* London: Hutchinson.

Jenkins, H. (1992). *Textual poachers.* New York: Routledge.

Johnson, R. (1986/1987). What is cultural studies anyway? *Social Text, 16,* 38–80.

Kellner, D. (1978, November-December). Ideology, Marxism, and advanced capitalism. *Socialist Review, 42,* 37–65.

Kellner, D. (1979, May-June). TV, ideology, and emancipatory popular culture. *Socialist Review, 45,* 13–53.

Kellner, D. (1990). *Television and the crisis of democracy.* Boulder, CO: Westview.

Kellner, D. (1992). *The Persian Gulf TV war.* Boulder, CO: Westview.

Kellner, D. (1995). *Media culture. Cultural studies, identity, and politics between the modern and the postmodern.* London and New York: Routledge.

Kellner, D. (1997). Critical theory and British cultural studies: The missed articulation. In J. McGuigan (Ed.), *Cultural methodologies* (pp. 12–41). London: Sage.

Kellner, D. (2001). *Grand theft 2000.* Lanham, MD: Rowman & Littlefield.

Kellner, D., & Ryan, M. (1988). *Camera politica: The politics and ideology of contemporary Hollywood film.* Bloomington: Indiana University Press.

Lewis, L. A. (1992). *Adoring audience: Fan culture and popular media.* New York: Routledge.

McChesney, R. (2000). *Rich media, poor democracy: Communications politics in dubious times.* New York: New Press.

Morley, D. (1986). *Family television.* London: Comedia.

O'Connor, A. (1989, December), The problem of American cultural studies. *Critical Studies in Mass Communication,* pp. 405–413.

Radway, J. (1983). *Reading the romance.* Chapel Hill: University of North Carolina Press.

Staiger, J. (1992). Film, reception, and cultural studies. *Centennial Review, 26*(1), 89–104.

Thompson, J. (1990). *Ideology and modern culture.* Cambridge, UK, and Stanford, CA: Polity Press and Stanford University Press.

Turner, G. (1990). *British cultural studies: An introduction.* New York: Unwin Hyman.

2 | A Conceptual Framework for Understanding Race, Class, Gender, and Sexuality

Lynn Weber

Since the mid-1980s, scholarship and college courses that address multiple dimensions of inequality under the rubric of race, class, gender, and (recently) sexuality studies have grown rapidly. Most courses now employ a set of readings, many of which are drawn from a growing number of anthologies. A strength of this approach is its presentation of the diversity of human experiences and the multiplicity of critical perspectives. A weakness is its failure to convey the commonalities in race, class, gender, and sexuality analyses of social reality. To aid in teaching and research on race, class, gender, and sexuality, this article presents six common themes that characterize this scholarship. Race, class, gender, and sexuality are historically and globally specific, socially constructed power relations that simultaneously operate at both the macro (societal) and micro (individual) levels of society. Scholarship in this tradition emphasizes the interdependence of knowledge and activism.

People's real life experiences have never fit neatly into the boundaries created by academic disciplines: Lives are much more complex and far reaching. Just as the social, political, economic, and psychological dimensions of everyday life are intertwined and mutually dependent, so too are the systems of inequality—race, class, gender, and sexuality— that limit and restrict some people while privileging others. Increasingly, interdisciplinary studies, including Women's Studies and multicultural studies, are extending the range of the curriculum; such programs are critical sites for the development of meaningful commentaries on human social and psychological realities that reflect such complexities (Magner, 1996).

It is in Women's Studies—not in racial or ethnic studies, not in social stratification (class) studies in sociology, not in psychology or in other traditional disciplines—that race, class, gender, and sexuality studies first emerged.[1] Because of its critical stance toward knowledge in the traditional

Reprinted from *Psychology of Women Quarterly* 22, no. 1 (1998).

disciplines, its interdisciplinary approach, and its orientation toward social change and social betterment, Women's Studies has been most open to self-critique for its exclusion of multiple oppressed groups, such as women of color, working-class women, and lesbians (Baca Zinn, Weber Cannon, Higginbotham, & Dill, 1986; Weber Cannon, Higginbotham, & Leung, 1988).

Since these initial writings, scholarship and college courses that simultaneously address these multiple dimensions of inequality under the rubric of race, class, gender, and, increasingly, sexuality studies have grown rapidly. Texts in most courses now consist of a set of readings selected by individual faculty and/or of one of a growing number of anthologies on the topic (Andersen & Collins, 1995; Anzaldúa, 1987a, 1987b; Baca Zinn & Dill, 1994; Chow, Wilkinson, & Baca Zinn, 1996; Cyrus, 1993; Rothenberg, 1995). The strength of these anthologies is that they demonstrate the significance of race, class, gender, and sexuality by presenting a wide array of diverse human experiences and analyses across these dimensions. Students are encouraged to move beyond thinking about major social and personal issues solely from their own viewpoints or from dominant group perspectives. The major limitation is that anthologies provide little direction in identifying the themes and assumptions that pull these diverse perspectives together. We are given little guidance about what constitutes a race, class, gender, and sexuality analysis of social reality. In part, this omission parallels the development of the field of race, class, gender, and sexuality studies, which began by revealing diverse experiences across these dimensions to counter the monolithic views of the social world put forth in both mainstream and Women's Studies scholarship.

Now, however, scholars are beginning to search for and to identify common themes and approaches that characterize the work in race, class, gender, and sexuality studies (cf. Baca Zinn & Dill, 1996). This process should invite debate and critique, further the development of the scholarship, and help provide one or more frameworks for teaching about this work. This article presents six themes that currently characterize this scholarship. By reminding us of some questions that need to be asked in any analysis of human society, these themes can guide the race, class, gender and sexuality analyses we conduct for our research, our teaching, and our social activism.

A Brief History of Race, Class, Gender, and Sexuality Studies

In the 1970s and 1980s, women of color, the majority of whom were poor or working class, were especially vehement in voicing their opposition to theories of and perspectives on social reality that focused on a single dimension—especially on gender, but also on race, class, or sexuality. They argued that the multidimensionality and interconnected nature of race, class, gender, and sexuality hierarchies are especially visible to those who face oppression along more than one dimension of inequality. Patricia Hill Collins (1990), author of *Black Feminist Thought,* identifies the "interlocking nature of oppression" as one of three recurring themes in the work of Black feminists. Collins notes that this theme dates back at least to Sojourner Truth, who in the mid-19th century said: "There is a great stir about colored men getting their rights, and not colored women theirs. You see the colored men will be masters over the women, and it will be just as bad as before" (cited in Loewenberg & Bogin, 1976, p. 238).

When Black women began to critique recent gender scholarship for its exclusionary practices, they focused on conducting analyses that began from the experiences of Black women, putting them at center stage. *The Black Woman* (Cade, 1970), *Ain't I a Woman* (Hooks, 1981), *The Black Woman* (Rodgers-Rose, 1980), "The Dialectics of Black Womanhood" (Dill, 1979), and "Race, Class, and Gender: Prospects for an All Inclusive Sisterhood" (Dill, 1983) were among the first critical perspectives on Black women published as books or articles in major feminist journals.

The irony of ignoring groups whose experiences typically reflected the confluence of multiple major dimensions of inequality was captured in the often-cited title of one of the first anthologies in Black Women's Studies: *All the Women Were White, All the Blacks Were Men, But Some of Us Are Brave: Black Women's Studies* (Hull, Scott, & Smith, 1982). Since that time, the critique of the White middle-class bias in Women's Studies has been joined by a critique of the male bias in racial ethnic studies, harkening back to the words of Sojourner Truth. And the study of race, class, gender, and sexuality has been expanded by studies of other groups of women of color (cf. Amaro & Russo, 1987; Anzaldúa, 1987b; Baca Zinn & Dill, 1994); of other oppressed groups, such as gays and lesbians (cf. Barale & Halperin, 1993; D'Emilio & Freedman, 1988; Greene, 1994); and, more recently, of privilege itself: for example, studies of the social construction of whiteness (cf. Frankenberg, 1993; McIntosh, 1995; Roediger, 1991) or of masculinity (cf. Brod & Kaufman, 1994; Connell, 1995; Messner, 1992).

As a recently developing field, race, class, gender, and sexuality studies has not yet produced a wide range of competing theories about the nature of race, class, gender, and sexual hierarchies. Rather, it has begun to generate debates about the most productive ways of conceptualizing race, class, gender, and sexuality; about the nature of their relationships to one another; and about their manifestations in everyday life (see, e.g., Collins et al., 1995, pp. 491–513; West & Fenstermaker, 1995, pp. 8–37).

The scholarship has been characterized more by diversity of content and commonalities in perspective than by competing or conflicting interpretations. Perhaps these common themes arise because the field is young and the research and writing has come primarily from women of color and other marginalized groups who share an "outsider within" perspective (Collins, 1991). Although inside the academy by virtue of their status as professors, writers, researchers, and scholars, these groups also have an outsider's view of the knowledge that the academy has produced because they are women of color, come from working-class backgrounds, and/or are gays and lesbians. Much of the new scholarship follows the tradition established by early writers who made women of color the center of attention, describing their everyday lives. Seeing the world through the eyes of oppressed groups raises new questions about our preconceived notions of many aspects of social reality—from the social relations of domestic work to what it takes to be a "good" mother to the American Dream that talent and hard work will produce material success (Dill, 1988; Glenn, 1992; Hochschild, 1995; Rollins, 1985).

At the same time that it questions traditional scholarship and interpretations of the lives of oppressed as well as dominant groups, the scholarship on race, class, gender, and sexuality also tends to avoid grand theorizing about the essential natures of these hierarchies. Scholars instead emphasize that these social constructs cannot be understood outside of their context in the real lives of real people. And, in part, because examining race, class, gender, and sexuality simultaneously forces one to acknowledge the multiple angles of vision that are brought to bear in any social situation, scholars in the field are reluctant to put forth a single unifying theory of the dynamics of these processes (Collins, 1990).

Some of the dominant themes in the new scholarship, which are also emerging in gender, sexuality, and race scholarship, can be broadly subsumed under the label of social constructionist theories and in recent work on "multiracial feminism" (Baca Zinn & Dill, 1996). They emphasize the historical and social contingencies of these dimensions and, to some extent, their macro social structural character and their basis in power relations (cf. Brod & Kaufman, 1994; Connell, 1985, 1995; Frankenberg, 1993; Omi & Winant, 1994; Thorne, 1993; West & Fenstermaker, 1995; West & Zimmerman, 1987).

Common Themes in Race, Class, Gender, and Sexuality Scholarship

I have identified six common themes in this new scholarship. Five of them describe the way that race, class, gender, and sexuality are conceptualized as systems of oppression; the sixth is an epistemological assumption.

1. Contextual. Race, class, gender, and sexuality are contextual. Although they persist throughout history, race, class, gender, and sexuality hierarchies are never static and fixed, but constantly undergo change as part of new economic, political, and ideological processes, trends, and events. Their meanings vary not only across historical time periods, but also across nations and regions during the same period. Because race, class, gender, and sexuality must always be understood within a specific historical and global context, research tends to avoid the search for common meanings that would apply to all times and all places.

For example, in the post-Civil Rights era in the United States, the racial signifiers "Latino/a," "Asian American," "People of Color," and "Native American" developed when people from different cultures, tribes, and national origins were treated as a single racial group by a dominant culture that failed to recognize differences among "racial" ethnic groups. Many members of these groups subsequently organized politically to resist their joint oppressions, and out of those political movements new racial identities were forged (Omi & Winant, 1994). These labels did not exist before the 1960s, and even today some people identify with them and others do not, signifying the fluid, political, historically specific, and social meaning of race.

Additionally, during the mid-19th century, dominant cultural conceptions of femininity became associated with the warm, personal, "private" sphere of home, whereas masculinity became associated with the cold, "public" sphere of the labor market. As Carol Tavris (1992, p. 265) notes:

> *People began to attribute to inherent male and female characteristics what were actually requirements of their increasingly separate domains. Thus, women were expected to provide warmth, nurturance, and care, and forgo achievement; men were expected to provide money and success, and forgo close attachments. The masculine ideal, tailored to fit the emerging economy, was to be an independent, self-made, financially successful man. Masculinity now required self-control: no gaudy displays of emotion; no weakness; no excessive self-indulgence in feelings. Femininity required, and soon came to embody, the opposite.*

Despite the pervasiveness of these images, numerous race, class, and gender scholars have noted that not *all* women and men were included in these ideals of masculinity and femininity. Men of color were not extended a family wage, and women of color were already in the paid labor market, doing domestic work, other low-wage service work, or agricultural work. Further, the ideal traits held up for men and women of color contrasted sharply with those for White women and men. For example, after Reconstruction the ideal dominant culture image of the "good" African American man was the Sambo image: a happy-go-lucky, silly, and stupid person who was often afraid of the dark (Goings, 1994). The image provided a justification for slavery and at the same time reduced the perceived physical and sexual threat posed by real African American men. The Mammy image was the female parallel to Sambo: A happy asexual slave who so loved the master's family—and slavery itself—that she would willingly give over her life to the care and nurturance of slave-owning White families (Collins, 1990; Goings, 1994). As the ideal White man was strong, independent, and emotionless, Sambo—like White women—was weak, dependent, and full of emotion. White women were to nurture their families, whereas emotionally strong Mammies could have no families of their own, just as they could have no sexuality. In sum, the meanings of masculinity and femininity are differently constructed throughout history for different social groups through social processes that produce and maintain a racialized, class-bound, heterosexist patriarchy.

2. Socially constructed. Race, class, gender, and sexuality are social constructs whose meaning develops out of group struggles over socially valued resources. The dominant culture defines the categories within race, gender, and sexuality as polar opposites—White and

Black (or non-White), men and women, heterosexual and homosexual—to create social rankings: good and bad, worthy and unworthy, right and wrong (Lorber, 1994). It also links these concepts to biology to imply that the rankings are fixed, permanent, and embedded in nature. That is, dominant groups define race, gender, and sexuality as ranked dichotomies, where Whites, men, and heterosexuals are deemed superior. Dominant groups justify these hierarchies by claiming that the rankings are a part of the design of nature—not the design of those in power. Subordinate groups resist the binary categories, the rankings associated with them, and the biological rationales used to justify them. Critical examination of either process—polarizing or biologizing—reveals that race, gender, and sexuality are based neither in polar opposites nor in biology but are social constructs whose meanings evolve out of group struggles (Garnets & Kimmel, 1991; King, 1981; Lorber, 1994; Omi & Winant, 1994).

When we say that race, gender, and sexuality are social constructs, not fixed biological traits, we also mean that we cannot *fully* capture their meaning in everyday life in the way that social scientists often attempt to do by employing them as variables in traditional quantitative research. When race, gender, and sexuality are treated as discrete variables, individuals are typically assigned a single location along each dimension, which is defined by a set of presumably mutually exclusive and exhaustive categories. This practice reinforces the view of race, gender, and sexuality as permanent characteristics of individuals, as unchangeable, and as polarities—people can belong to one and only one category. The practice cannot grasp the relational character, the historical specificity, or the conflicting meanings that arise in everyday life (Omi & Winant, 1994). "Mixed race" people, for example, often have no place in the schemas provided. And what of the people who see themselves as bisexual or as heterosexual at one time of life and gay or lesbian at another?

The case of social class provides an instructive contrast to race, gender, and sexuality ideologies. The dominant ideology of social class is that it is not binary, polarized, or biological. Instead, the United States is seen as having an open economic system where talent and hard work—not inherited physical traits—are the primary determinants of one's economic location (Hochschild, 1995). Our system is not seen as polarized between rich and poor, capitalists and workers, or middle and working classes. Rather, it is viewed as a continuous ladder of income and resources, where people can slide up and down based on their own efforts and abilities—not on their biology (Vanneman & Weber Cannon, 1987). In the final analysis, the real power of the middle and upper classes is reinforced through this ideology as well as through the race, gender, and sexuality ideologies because all obscure the forces that underlie the social hierarchy. In the case of social class, however, unfair hierarchy is obscured by referring to ability and effort rather than by referring to biological superiority. Social class ideology disavows biology and categorical binaries, yet justifies hierarchy and dominance nonetheless. The case of social class makes very clear that ideologies are created to justify hierarchies and need not be based in binaries or biology, nor need they be internally consistent or logical. To justify the power and control of the dominant group, ideologies of dominance develop in different ways over time and in different social contexts and can rest on fundamentally very different—even seemingly contradictory—beliefs.

For over a century, social expectations of women's work and family roles, for example, has been rationalized by the biological fact that women can bear children. Middle-class mothers who stay at home to care for their children are often viewed by the dominant culture as "good mothers," yet poor women who do the same are viewed as lazy or "welfare queens." How can women's reproductive capacities prescribe their roles as mothers when we have different expectations for mothers of different classes, races, and sexual orientations?

Furthermore, the biological relationship of women to children is far more complex than ever before and is even now being challenged as a basis for legally defining motherhood. Today, when women and men have so many different biological and social relationships to their children, the courts are increasingly being asked to mediate questions of who should rear children. Consider the following "mothers":

✦ *traditional mothers:* women who have a genetic, gestational, and legally sanctioned social relationship to the child

✦ *lesbian mothers:* women whose biological relationship may be the same as that of traditional mothers, yet whose legal status as mothers is often challenged because of their sexual orientation

✦ *surrogate mothers:* either genetic mothers who provide an egg, but do not bear the child; or gestational mothers (as in the case of Baby M) who have no genetic relationship to it, but bear the child

✦ *social mothers:* foster mothers, adoptive mothers, or "other" mothers who have no direct genetic or gestational relationship to the child, but play a significant role in raising the child (cf. Collins, 1990).

Each of these ways of mothering is constructed in race, class, gender, and sexual hierarchies that prescribe the meanings attached to them and shape the legally prescribed rights of these mothers to rear children. Chesler (1986, p. 280) discusses why we have the phenomenon of surrogate mothers at all:

> *Racism is the issue, and why thousands of babies are "unsuitable" (for adoption). Ownership is the issue, and the conceit of patriarchal genetics. "Barren women" are the issue, and why some women must come to feel an excruciating sense of failure because they cannot bear a child. . . . And guilt and money, and how women can earn both, are the issues that need honest attention.*

Race, class, gender, and sexuality are social constructions that are constantly undergoing change both at the level of social institutions and at the level of personal identity. They are not fixed, static traits of individuals, as is implied when they are treated either as biological facts or as categorically fixed variables in a research model. They are, however, deeply embedded in the practices and beliefs that make up our major social institutions. The permanence and pervasiveness they exhibit illustrate their significance as major organizing principles of society and of personal identity.

3. Systems of power relationships. Perhaps the single most important theme is that race, class, gender, and sexuality are historically specific, socially constructed hierarchies of domination—they are power relationships. They do not merely represent different lifestyle preferences or cultural beliefs, values, and practices. They are power hierarchies in which one group exerts control over another, securing its position of dominance in the system, and in which substantial material and nonmaterial resources—such as wealth, income, or access to health care and education—are at stake (Baca Zinn & Dill, 1996; Connell, 1987, 1995; Glenn, 1992; Vanneman & Weber Cannon, 1987; Weber, 1995; Weber, Hancock, & Higginbotham, 1997; Wyche & Graves, 1992). Race, class, gender, and sexuality are thus fundamental sources of social conflict among groups.

The centerpiece of these systems is the exploitation of one group by another for a greater share of society's valued resources. That they are based in social relationships between dominant and subordinate groups is key to understanding these systems. There can be no controlling males without women whose options are restricted; there can be no valued race without races that are defined as "other"; there can be no owners or managers without workers who produce the goods and services that the owners own and the managers control; and there can be no heterosexual privilege without gays and lesbians who are identified as "abnormal" or as "other."

Race, class, gender, and sexuality are not just rankings of socially valued resources—who has more income or prestige. They are power relationships—who exerts power and control over whom (Baca Zinn & Dill, 1996; Connell, 1987, 1995; Glenn, 1992; Griscom, 1992; Kahn & Yoder, 1992; Vanneman & Weber Cannon, 1987; Weber, 1995; Weber et al., 1997; Yoder &

Kahn, 1992). The groups that have power in a social system influence the allocation of many types of resources. In one sense, then, the procurement of socially valued resources can be seen as the end product—the spoils to the victors—of struggles for power. To maintain and extend their power and control in society, dominant groups can and do use the resources that they command. So socially valued resources, such as money and prestige, accrue to those in power and, once procured, serve as tools for maintaining and extending that power into future social relations.

Although scholars studying race, class, gender, and sexuality tend to see them as power relations, this perspective is not universally accepted. Ethnic approaches to race (cf. Glazer & Moynihan, 1975), gradational perspectives on class (reviewed in Vanneman & Weber Cannon, 1987), sex/gender differences, and gender roles (for a review, see West & Fenstermaker, 1995), and moral or biological approaches to sexual orientation all conceive of these dimensions as differences that are not ultimately power based. Differences between women and men, gays and straights, and among racial and ethnic groups are taken as primarily centered in women's and men's social roles and in cultural variations in traditions such as food, clothing, rituals, speech patterns, leisure activities, child-rearing practices, and sexual practices.

These perspectives often downplay or ignore the very real struggles over scarce resources that accompany location in these different groups. A similar tradition in the field of stratification—the gradational approach—sees class inequality as represented by relative rankings along a scale of prestige or income (a ladder image), not by the struggle between opposing groups for scarce resources (for reviews see Lucal, 1994; Vanneman & Weber Cannon, 1987). In the gradational perspective, no oppositional relationships exist between positions on a scale; it is a continuum along which some people simply have more than others.

Perhaps because race, class, gender, and sexuality studies primarily emerged from the experiences and analyses of groups who face multiple dimensions of oppression, and perhaps because power relationships are simply much more apparent when more than one dimension of inequality is addressed, the cultural difference, gradational, or ranking perspective is almost nonexistent in race, class, gender, and sexuality studies. The view that power relations are central is almost universal.

Looking at the relational nature of these systems of inequality rather than the differences in rankings of resources that accompany these systems forces us to focus on privilege as well as on oppression. Because the one cannot exist without the other, any analysis of race, class, gender, and sexuality must incorporate an understanding of the ways in which the privilege of dominant groups is tied to the oppression of subordinate groups. Consequently, the scholarship in this field has begun to explore the social constructions of Whiteness (cf. Frankenberg, 1993; McIntosh, 1995; Roediger, 1991), of masculinity (cf. Brod & Kaufman, 1994; Connell, 1995; Messner, 1992), and of heterosexual privilege (Giuffre & Williams, 1994; Rich, 1980).

4. Social structural (macro) and social psychological (micro). Race, class, and gender relations are embedded and have meaning at the micro level of individuals' everyday lives as well as the macro level of community and social institutions. To grasp the significance of race, class, gender, and sexuality in society, we must examine their meaning in both contexts. In fact, a key aspect of such analyses involves explicating the linkages between broad societal level structures, trends, and events and the ways in which people in different social locations live their lives. In the last 25 years, for example, U.S. society has undergone major shifts in the distribution of wealth, income, jobs, and housing and in the health status of its people. Race, class, gender, and sexuality power relations structure the ways in which these societal trends develop and play out among different groups of people.

Macro social structural trends are often represented analytically as a set of lifeless statistics about different populations. When we look at statistics summarizing national trends in economic or health indicators, for example, it is difficult to know exactly what they mean for the way people live their lives. But when we closely follow the everyday lives of a group of people, we can learn how they live with financial constraints, how they feed their families, how they deal with the stresses they face, how they manage work and family life, how they stay healthy.

It is in families and individual lives where race, class, gender, and sexuality scholarship has made perhaps its most important contributions. This work has begun to identify the ongoing struggles of subordinate groups to resist negative and controlling images of their group—to resist internalizing the limits to self-esteem, self-valuation, and collective identity imposed by the dominant group (cf. Bookman & Morgen, 1987; Collins, 1990; Comas-Díaz & Greene, 1994; Weber et al., 1997).

Because of the distorted images of subordinate groups that pervade society's institutions such as education and the media, subordinate groups are viewed by many as weak human beings who passively accept—and even deserve—a lesser share of society's valued resources. However, subordinate groups actively resist oppression and devaluation in numerous ways every day. Although, as a consequence of their location in subordinate social locations, they often lack institutional power, subordinate group members can and do use other forms of personal power and collective action to resist unfair treatment and to struggle for group power. Daily acts of resistance can range from the individual psychological process of rejecting negative group images and affirming positive group images to group activities designed to produce social change. Acts of resistance also range from passive forms such as work slow-downs or excessive and carefully planned use of sick leave (to ensure maximum disruption of the workplace) to active measures such as public protests, marches on Washington, strikes, or violence (Bookman & Morgen, 1987). For example, through public protest and persistent demand for civil rights laws, which made racial discrimination in education, housing, employment, and other areas of society illegal, African Americans were able to shift greater educational and economic opportunity and earning power in their direction.

Although the barriers of oppression are material and ideological, the resources associated with one's social location in the matrix of dominance and subordination are both material and psychological (Collins, 1990; Weber et al., 1997). Nonmaterial psychosocial resources have important consequences for social and psychological well-being that in turn affect one's ability to secure material resources. Psychosocial resources associated with one's social location include positive feelings of well-being and self-respect that result from a strong connection to and identity with a group of people who share a common history and life experiences (Comas-Díaz & Greene, 1994). Developing a positive identity and feelings of self-respect is easier for dominant groups whose own experiences serve as the public model for how all people should live their lives. Because social institutions such as schools are structured to support the White middle class, such children are usually raised in families with greater access to resources to help them succeed in school. They enter school with greater expectations for success; teachers expect their success and, therefore, give them more attention. Teachers' positive orientations enhance the children's sense of self-worth, thus further improving their performance and their chances for school success (Oakes, 1985; Ornstein & Levine, 1989; Polakow, 1993).

Occupying a subordinate location in the race, class, gender, and sexuality systems, however, does not necessarily equate with a lack of psychosocial resources (Comas-Díaz & Greene, 1994). Working-class, Latino/a children, for example, growing up in the barrio may develop such intangible resources if they are surrounded by loving family members and neighbors who convey a sense of each child's special worth as an individual and as a Latino/a. And this psychosocial resource can serve as the function for a healthy defense against negative or rejecting messages from the dominant society. Resistance to the pressures of structured inequality within subordinate group communities can, in fact, be a psychosocial resource that can be used in a collective struggle against oppression and in a personal journey toward self-appreciation and good mental health.

The key aspect of dominance, then, is not whether people have access to psychosocial resources but whether the social order supports or constrains people's development. The concept of hegemonic ideologies refers to beliefs about what is right and proper, which reflect the dominant group's stance and pervade society. Controlling images refer to dominant culture beliefs about subordinate groups; these images serve to restrict their options and to constrain them. Although society has many conceptions of working women, for example, only one is hegemonic, taking precedence over other conceptions and serving as the standard against which the value or worth of all other conceptions of working women is measured.

When you hear the phrase "today's working woman" mentioned in the media or in a popular magazine, what kind of woman comes to mind? In all likelihood, no matter what your race, class, gender, or sexual orientation, you think of a White, heterosexual, professional woman working hard in a position of some power in the labor force. She is most likely married, but if she is single, she is certainly young. This image of today's working woman is not only atypical, it is antithetical to the reality of work for most women today. Only 28.7% of working women are in professional, managerial, or administrative positions, and many of those hold little real power in the workplace (U.S. Bureau of Labor Statistics, 1995).

Why would such an atypical image come to mind? Because this image is the dominant, hegemonic conception of working women. It represents the image of the most powerful race, class, and sexual orientation group of women. It is grossly over-represented in the media, because it is set up as the model, the ideal against which other working women are to be judged. By its repeated presentation in the media (e.g., most women seen on television are White, middle-class, professional women), the image distorts the public perception, leaving the impression that the attainment of positions of power among women is far more possible than is actually the case. By masking the true nature of race, class, gender, and sexuality oppression, the image helps to preserve the status quo. The image further sets up a standard for judgment that most women cannot attain. If they come to believe that their failure to measure up is a result of their personal limitations—lack of talent, desire, or effort—they internalize the oppression. If, on the other hand, they are aware of the dominant belief system nature of and the structural barriers to attaining the "ideal," they resist internalizing the oppression and have the potential for self-definition and self-valuation, a process critical to the survival of oppressed groups.

To comprehend the human agency, resilience, creativity, and strength of oppressed group members, one must view the actions and motivations of subordinate group members through their own lenses, not through the lenses of the controlling images of the dominant culture. Recognition of the history of subordinate group resistance helps to counter the cultural myths and beliefs in the dominant culture that the subordinate place of these groups is a "natural" aspect of society.

Race, class, gender, and sexuality scholarship has clarified the notion of internalized oppression, as well as the processes within communities that enable them to survive and the individuals within them to define themselves, value themselves, and build community solidarity (Collins, 1990; Weber et al., 1997). The Civil Rights Movement, racial and ethnic pride, gay pride, and women's movements are collective manifestations of resistance to negative and controlling images of and structures constricting oppressed groups. Interestingly, the American labor movement has been too weak and invisible to provide a positive counterimage that workers can employ to resist oppression.

5. *Simultaneously expressed.* Race, class, gender, and sexuality simultaneously operate in every social situation. At the societal level, these systems of social hierarchies are connected to each other and are embedded in all social institutions. At the individual level, we each experience our lives and develop our identities based on our location along all dimensions, whether we are in dominant groups, subordinate groups, or both.

That almost all of us occupy both dominant and subordinate positions and experience both advantage and disadvantage in these hierarchies means that there are no pure oppressors or oppressed in our society. Thus, race, class, gender, and sexuality are not reducible to immutable personality traits or other seemingly permanent characteristics. Instead, they are social constructions that often give us power and options in some arenas while restricting our opportunities in another.

From this principle we cannot argue that we are all oppressed or that our oppressions can simply be added up and ranked to identify the most oppressed group or the most victimized individuals. We cannot say that disadvantage on any two dimensions is the same as on any other two. No simple mathematical relationship can capture the complexity of the interrelationships of these systems. And yet recognizing that each of us simultaneously experiences all of these dimensions—even if one is foregrounded in a particular situation—can help us see the often obscured ways in which we benefit from existing race, class, gender, and sexuality social arrangements, as well as the ways in which we are disadvantaged. Such an awareness can be key in working together across different groups to achieve a more equitable distribution of society's valued resources.

The final characteristic describes a common epistemology of race, class, gender, and sexuality scholarship.

6. Interdependence of knowledge and activism. Race, class, gender, and sexuality scholarship emphasizes the interdependence of knowledge and activism (Baca Zinn & Dill, 1994, 1996; Collins, 1990). These analyses developed as a means of understanding oppression and of seeking social change and social justice. The "truth value" or merit of this knowledge depends on its ability to reflect back to social groups their experiences in such a way that they can more effectively define, value, and empower themselves to seek social justice.

When we think of race, class, gender, and sexuality as historically specific, socially constructed power relations that simultaneously operate at both macro and micro levels, a more complex set of questions arises than from analyses of a single dimension. The following is an example from everyday life that illustrates the simultaneous impact of these hierarchies on a fundamental social identity in the United States today.

Race, Class, Gender, Sexuality and the Construction of Masculinity

Consider how masculinity is differently defined by and for heterosexual, White, middle-class males and for other groups of men, such as gays, working-class White men, and men of color. When you hear about such groups as the Michigan Militia or the Ku Klux Klan, you likely think of White working-class men. If you hear of the Crips or the Bloods, you likely think of Black or Latino, working-class, male gang members. Research by Kathleen Blee (1991) on *Women of the Ku Klux Klan* and by Karen Joe and Meda Chesney-Lind (1995) on female gang members has clearly documented that women are active participants in both worlds. Nonetheless, in the dominant culture ideology, these worlds are almost exclusively associated with working-class men.

How is masculine identity socially constructed for working-class males? The dominant culture portrays men in these groups as valuing physical strength, aggressive behavior, and dominance over women and as devaluing emotional sensitivity and intellectual development.

Consider now the dominant image of White professional/middle-class males. These men are deemed superior based on their positions of power and authority in the labor force, by their financial or material wealth, by their intellectual prowess and knowledge, and, increasingly today, by their emotional sensitivity—but *not* by their physical strength or aggressiveness.

In the popular documentary *Hoop Dreams* (Marx, Gilbert, Gilbert, & James, 1994) and in Michael Messner's (1992) *Power at Play: Sport and the Problem of Masculinity,* we see the difference in how schools steer athletically talented working-class men toward careers in athletics. Sports represent a career that fits with racialized conceptions of what is suitable for working-class men. And because they represent one of the few legitimate avenues for upward social mobility, sports careers are sought by working-class and lower-class men—despite the almost insurmountable odds against making a lifelong career in sports. Only 6% or 7% of high school football players ever play in college, and only 2% of eligible college football or basketball athletes ever sign a professional contract. The chances of attaining professional status in a sport are 4 in 100,000 for a White man, 2 in 100,000 for a Black man, and 3 in 1,000,000 for a U.S.-born Latino (Messner, 1992, p. 45).

Athletically talented, White, middle-class men, in contrast, are steered into college to achieve the academic credentials to work in the middle class—as professionals, owners, managers, or administrators. Athletics are seen as a way of building positive character traits, such as competitiveness, camaraderie, and determination, and of providing valuable avenues for social networking in the middle class. Sports are almost never considered as a career in themselves.

The dominant conception of masculinity in capitalist economies portrays "real men" as those who have power in the economic realm, where ownership, authority, competitiveness, and mental—not physical—labor are valued. Physical strength or physically aggressive behavior is not a valued method of maintaining power and control.

Sports do, however, serve an important role in constructing masculine identities for the many men who play them. As Messner's (1992) research shows, sport is an institution created by and for men. Misogyny and homophobia, as exhibited in extremely derogatory language toward women and gay men in the context of sports, serve as bonding agents for heterosexual men by separating them from anything "feminine." Expressing strong antigay sentiments enables men to be intimate without being sexual. And objectifying women through derogatory language enables men to be sexual without being intimate, a process that fits with maintaining a position of control over women and men of lower status in the race, class, gender, and sexuality hierarchies (Messner, 1992).

In sum, many masculinities operate in the United States today. What it means to be a man—or a woman, a husband or a wife, a father or a mother—depends on one's *simultaneous* location in the race, class, gender, and sexuality hierarchies.

Conclusions

This conceptual framework for understanding race, class, gender, and sexuality can support our teaching by guiding the content we select for classes, the questions we bring to the analysis of course readings and materials, and the ways in which we promote positive interaction across race, class, gender, and sexuality hierarchies in the classroom. First, it provides a framework for conceptualizing and assessing the diverse readings that currently constitute courses on gender and diversity. To convey the complexities of these intersections we need to select course content—readings, lectures, films—that highlight the intersections of multiple dimensions of oppression. Providing students with a set of themes to help them review the diverse materials they read can be a useful pedagogical tool.

Second, rather than providing a set of answers, I hope these themes raise some questions and issues to consider in our analyses of social reality. I am increasingly convinced that the most important tools we bring to the analytical process are the questions we ask.

Race, class, gender, and sexuality are contextually rooted in history and geography. Ask how the dynamics we study might vary in different places and at different times. It is important to take account of the histories and global context of particular groups to understand their current situations. Taking a broad historical and global view also enables us to see the tremendous changes that have taken place in each of these systems over time and the diversity across social geography and thus to recognize the potential for change in situations we face every day.

These systems are socially constructed, not biologically determined. Ask if gender and race are taken to determine how people should act out of some notion of biological or social imperative. Is seeing gender or race as an immutable fact of people's lives either privileging them or relegating them to certain inferiority? How might we view a situation differently if someone of a different race, class, gender, or sexual orientation were in it?

The race, class, gender, and sexuality systems operate at the social structural (macro) and the social psychological (micro) levels. When we analyze a particular social event, the interpersonal and psychological manifestations of oppression are often more readily apparent. The broad macro-level forces that shape events are more remote and abstract and are, therefore, more difficult to see. Ask about those structures.

In looking at the case of White male backlash against affirmative action, for example, we can easily see angry White men out to push back gains made by women and people of color and to maintain their position of power and control. We can dismiss them as "oppressors" or bad people. When we ask about the broader race, class, gender, and sexuality forces that shape this situation, however, we also see that the recent decline in our economy has rendered many White men vulnerable to loss of jobs, income, and health. White men's anger in part comes out of their different expectations—out of their sense of privilege. If we are to collaborate to achieve economic change that benefits most people, we must recognize the ways in which many White men, as well as other people, are vulnerable in the present economy.

These systems are simultaneously experienced. All operate to shape everyone's lives at all times. Ask about all of the systems in every situation. Although one dimension may appear to be in the foreground, go beyond the obvious and ask about the less visible dimensions.

Make the connection between activism for social justice and the analyses you conduct. Ask about the implications for social justice of the perspectives you employ, the questions you ask, and the answers you obtain. Does the analysis provide insights that in a political context would likely serve to reinforce existing power relations? Or does it illuminate processes of resistance or avenues for self-definition or self-valuation that could transform the race, class, gender, and sexuality hierarchies? How might people in different social locations react to and employ this analysis? To what ends?

Race, class, gender, and sexuality hierarchies are power relationships. Always ask who has the socially sanctioned power in this situation. What group gains and what group loses? Try not to confuse personal power with social power. Individuals can be powerful by virtue of their insight, knowledge, personalities, and other traits. They can persuade others to act in ways they want. But personal power can be achieved in spite of a lack of socially sanctioned power. It is the power that accrues from occupying a position of dominance in the race, class, gender, and sexuality hierarchies that enables large numbers of people in similar locations to have privileges/advantages in a situation. And it is their systematic and pervasive embeddedness in all our major institutions that makes race, class, gender, and sexuality such critical systems to understand.

Finally, when we change the content that we teach to be more inclusive and to address the complexities of race, class, gender, and sexuality, we need to change our pedagogy as well. Learning about diversity is most likely to take place when classroom interactions and activities promote positive intergroup interaction across race, class, gender, and sexuality. Themes in the scholarship suggest some strategies for shaping positive classroom dynamics across difference.

That race, class, gender, and sexuality are socially constructed, not fixed traits of individuals, means that we cannot accept group membership as a guarantee of the privileged knowledge or experience of any dominant or subordinate group member in our classes. The socially constructed nature of these dimensions means that the experiences and perspectives that students have—for example, even in the same racial group—vary by their age and the region and community they grew up in, as well as by their gender, class, and sexual orientation.

Acknowledging the diversity of experiences among our students need not, however, lead to an unfettered relativism that denies the significance of group membership or the greater impact of some dimensions than others on life chances and options. Because we recognize that power is the foundation on which these systems rest, we must acknowledge the differential power that dominant and subordinate groups wield in the classroom as well as in society at large. Members of dominant groups are less likely to know about subordinate groups and are more likely to rely on stereotypes (Fiske, 1993), speak in class, receive eye contact, have their opinions correctly attributed, and have their contributions shape group responses to tasks (cf. Webster & Foschi, 1988). Teaching strategies that acknowledge these tendencies and contradict them can upset the normative balance of power in the classroom and can increase understanding. They include ground rules to guide classroom discussion; introductions of students that acknowledge their race, ethnicity, and other statuses while identifying them as unique individuals; equal time for talking; and group projects (see Weber Cannon, 1990, for discussion).

Having students address the simultaneity of race, class, gender, and sexuality can help them to understand that there are no pure oppressors nor oppressed people, and that each of them must reflect on their own privilege as well as on their experiences of oppression. They cannot deny their privilege or claim absolute victim status. Recognizing their own multiple locations can open them to the complexities in the lived realities and experiences of others.

And finally, the interdependence of knowledge and activism that is central to race, class, gender, and sexuality scholarship suggests that certain kinds of learning activities can be especially effective. Active learning projects, particularly those that involve students in working together toward solutions to social problems, are especially likely to engage students and to facilitate positive group interaction.

Note

1. Although many scholars still refer to this growing field of study as race, class, and gender studies, I include sexuality because, as I argue, these structures of inequality and the meanings they engender are socially constructed in historically specific time frames and regional locations. Their meanings are not fixed, immutable, or universal but instead arise out of group struggles over socially valued resources, self-determination, and self-valuation. In recent years, the mass movement of gays, lesbians, and bisexuals for social power and self-determination has precipitated significant scholarly attention to sexuality. Our growing awareness and understanding of the pervasiveness and comprehensiveness of the system of compulsory heterosexuality has begun to place it at the center of political and intellectual attention along with race, class, and gender as essential elements in a comprehensive understanding of contemporary human social relationships and psychological processes. To date, however, the scholarship on sexuality is much less developed than work addressing the other dimensions, and race, class, and gender research is only beginning to integrate this new dimension.

References

Amaro, H., & Russo, N. F. (Eds.). (1987). Hispanic women and mental health: Contemporary research and practice [Special issue]. *Psychology of Women Quarterly,* 11(4).

Andersen, M., & Collins, P. H. (1995). *Race, class, and gender: An anthology.* Belmont, CA: Wadsworth.

Anzaldúa, G. (1987a). *Borderlands/la frontera: The new mestiza.* San Francisco: Spinsters/ Aunt Lute.

Anzaldúa, G. (Ed.). (1987b). *Making faces, making soul/haciendo caras: Creative and critical perspectives by women of color.* San Francisco: Spinsters/Aunt Lute.

Baca Zinn, M. & Dill, B. T. (1994). *Women of Color in U.S. Society*. Philadelphia: Temple University Press.

Baca Zinn, M., & Dill, B. T. (1996). Theorizing difference from multiracial feminism. *Feminist Studies, 22*, 321–331.

Baca Zinn, M., Weber Cannon, L., Higginbotham, E., & Dill, B. T. (1986). The costs of exclusionary practices in women's studies. *Signs: Journal of Women in Culture and Society, 11*, 290–303.

Barale, M., & Halperin, D. M. (Eds.). (1993). *The lesbian and gay studies reader*. New York: Routledge.

Blee, K. M. (1991). *Women of the klan: Racism and gender in the 1920s*. Berkeley: University of California Press.

Bookman, A., & Morgen, S. (1987). *Women and the politics of empowerment: Perspectives from the workplace and the community*. Philadelphia: Temple University Press.

Brod, H., & Kaufman, M. (1994). *Theorizing masculinities*. Thousand Oaks, CA: Sage.

Cade, T. (Ed.). (1970). *The Black woman*. New York: Signet.

Chesler, P. (1986). *Mothers on trial: The battle for children and custody*. New York: McGraw-Hill.

Chow, E. N., Wilkinson, D., & Baca Zinn, M. (1996). *Race, class, and gender: Common bonds, different voices*. Thousand Oaks, CA: Sage.

Collins, P. H. (1990). *Black feminist thought: Knowledge, consciousness and the politics of empowerment*. New York: Routledge.

Collins, P. H. (1991). Learning from the outsider within: The sociological significance of Black feminist thought. In M. M. Fonow & J. A. Cook (Eds.), *Beyond methodology: Feminist scholarship as lived research* (pp. 35–39). Bloomington, IN: Indiana University Press.

Collins, P. H., Maldonado, L. A., Takagi, D. Y., Thorne, B., Webber, L., & Winant, H. (1995). Symposium on West and Fenstermaker's "Doing difference." *Gender & Society, 9*, 491–513.

Comas-Díaz, L., & Greene, B. (1994). *Women of color: Integrating ethnic and gender identities in psychotherapy*. New York: Guilford.

Connell, R. W. (1985). Theorising gender. *Sociology, 19*, 260–272.

Connell, R. W. (1987). *Gender and power: Society, the person, and sexual politics*. Stanford, CA: Stanford University Press.

Connell, R. W. (1995). *Masculinities*. Berkeley: University of California Press.

Cyrus, V. (1993). *Experiencing race, class, and gender in the United States*. Mountain View, CA: Mayfield.

D'Emilio, J., & Freedman, E. (1988). *Intimate matters: A history of sexuality in America*. New York: Harper & Row.

Dill, B. T. (1979). The dialectics of Black womanhood. *Signs: Journal of Women in Culture and Society, 4*, 543–555.

Dill, B. T. (1983). Race, class and gender: Prospects for an all-inclusive sisterhood. *Feminist Studies, 9*, 131–150.

Dill, B. T. (1988). Our mother's grief: Racial ethnic women and the maintenance of families. *Journal of Family History, 13*, 415–431.

Fiske, S. T. (1993). Controlling other people: The impact of power on stereotyping. *American Psychologist, 48*, 621–628.

Frankenberg, R. (1993). *The social construction of whiteness: White women, race matters*. Minneapolis, MN: University of Minnesota Press.

Garnets, L., & Kimmel, D. (1991). Lesbian and gay male dimensions in the psychological study of human diversity. In J. Goodchilds (Ed.), *Psychological perspectives on human diversity in America* (pp. 143–189). Washington, DC: American Psychological Association.

Giuffre, P. A., & Williams, C. L. (1994). Boundary lines: Labeling sexual harassment in restaurants. *Gender & Society, 8,* 378–401.

Glazer, N., & Moynihan, D. P. (Eds.). (1975). *Ethnicity: Theory and experience.* Cambridge, MA: Harvard University Press.

Glenn, E. N. (1992). From servitude to service work: Historical continuities in the racial division of paid reproductive labor. *Signs: Journal of Women in Culture and Society, 18,* 1–43.

Goings, K. (1994). *Mammy and Uncle Moses: Black collectibles and American stereotyping.* Bloomington, IN: Indiana University Press.

Greene, B. L. (1994). Lesbian and gay sexual orientations: Implications for clinical training, practice, and research. In B. Greene & G. M. Herek (Eds.), *Lesbian and gay psychology: Theory, research, and clinical applications* (pp. 1–24). Thousand Oaks, CA: Sage.

Griscom, J. L. (1992). Women and power: Definition, dualism, and difference. *Psychology of Women Quarterly, 16,* 389–414.

Higginbotham, E., & Weber, L. (1992). Moving up with kin and community: Upward social mobility for Black and White women. *Gender & Society, 6,* 416–440.

Hooks, B. (1981). *Ain't I a woman.* Boston: South End Press.

Hochschild, J. (1995). *Facing up to the American dream: Race, class, and the soul of the nation.* Princeton, NJ: Princeton University Press.

Hull, G., Scott, P. B., & Smith, B. (Eds.) (1982). *All the women were White, all the Blacks were men, but some of us are brave: Black women's studies.* Old Westbury, NY: Feminist Press.

Joe, K. A., & Chesney-Lind, M. (1995). "Just every mother's angel": An analysis of gender and ethnic variations in youth gang membership. *Gender & Society, 9,* 408–431.

Kahn, A. S., & Yoder, J. D. (Eds.). (1992). Women and power [Special issue]. *Psychology of Women Quarterly, 16,* Whole No. 4.

King, J. (1981). *The biology of race.* Berkeley: University of California Press.

Lorber, J. (1994). *Paradoxes of gender.* New Haven, CT: Yale University Press.

Lowenberg, B. J., & Bogin, R. (Eds.). (1976). *Black women in the nineteenth-century life.* University Park: Pennsylvania State University.

Lucal, B. (1994). Class stratification in introductory textbooks: Relational or distributional models? *Teaching Sociology, 22,* 139–150.

Magner, D. (1996, September 16). Fewer professors believe western culture should be the cornerstone of the college curriculum. *Chronicle of Higher Education,* pp. A12–A15.

Marx, F., Gilbert, J., Gilbert, P. [Producers], & James, S. [Director]. (1994). *Hoop dreams* [Film]. (Available from Facets Video, 1518 W. Fullerton, Chicago, IL 60614)

McIntosh, P. (1995). White privilege and male privilege: A personal account of coming to see correspondences through work in women's studies. In M. Andersen & P. H. Collins (Eds.), *Race, class, and gender: An anthology* (pp. 76–86). Belmont, CA: Wadsworth.

Messner, M. (1992). *Power at play: Sports and the problem of masculinity.* Boston: Beacon.

Oakes, J. (1985). *Keeping track: How schools structure inequality.* New Haven, CT: Yale University Press.

Omi, M., & Winant, H. (1994). *Racial formation in the United States from the 1960s to the 1990s.* New York: Routledge.

Ornstein, A. C., & Levine, D. U. (1989). Social class, race, and school achievement: Problems and prospects. *Journal of Teacher Education, 40,* 17–23.

Polakow, V. (1993). *Lives on the edge: Single mothers and their children in the other America.* Chicago: University of Chicago Press.

Rich, A. (1980). Compulsory heterosexuality and lesbian existence. *Signs: Journal of Women in Culture and Society, 5,* 631–660.

Rodgers-Rose, L. (Ed.). (1980). *The black woman*. Beverly Hills, CA: Sage.

Roediger, D. (1991). *The wages of whiteness: Race and the making of the American working class*. London: Verso.

Rollins, J. (1985). *Between women: Domestics and their employers*. Philadelphia: Temple University Press.

Rothenberg, P. S. (1995). *Race, class, and gender in the United States: An integrated study*. New York: St. Martin's Press.

Tavris, C. (1992). *The mismeasure of woman*. New York: Touchstone.

Thorne, B. (1993). *Gender play: Girls and boys in school*. New Brunswick, NJ: Rutgers University Press.

U.S. Bureau of Labor Statistics (1995). *Employment and earnings* (Vol. 45). Washington, DC: U.S. Government Printing Office.

Vanneman, R., & Weber Cannon, L. (1987). *The American perception of class*. Philadelphia: Temple University Press.

Weber Cannon, L. (1990). Fostering positive race, class, and gender dynamics in the classroom. *Women's Studies Quarterly, 17*, 126–134.

Weber Cannon, L. Higginbotham, E., & Leung, M. (1988). Race and class bias in qualitative research on women. *Gender & Society, 2*, 449–462.

Weber, L. (1995). Comment on "Doing difference." *Gender & Society, 9*, 499–503.

Weber, L., Hancock, T., & Higginbotham, E. (1997). Women, power, and mental health. In S. Ruzek, V. Olesen & A. Clark (Eds.), *Women's health: Complexities and differences* (pp. 380–396). Columbus, OH: Ohio State University Press.

Webster, M., Jr. and Foschi, M. (1988). Status generalization: New theory and research. Palo Alto, CA: Stanford University Press.

West, C., & Fenstermaker, S. (1995). Doing difference. *Gender & Society, 9*, 8–37.

West, C., & Zimmerman, D. H. (1987). Doing gender. *Gender & Society, 1*, 125–151.

Wyche, K. F., & Graves, S. B. (1992). Minority women in academia: Access and barriers to professional participation. *Psychology of Women Quarterly, 16*, 429–438.

Yoder, J. D., & Kahn, A. S. (1992). Toward a feminist understanding of women and power. *Psychology of Women Quarterly, 16*, 381–388.

3 Representation, Meaning and Language

Stuart Hall

I n this chapter we will be concentrating on one of the key processes in the 'cultural circuit'—the practices of *representation*. The aim of this chapter is to introduce you to this topic, and to explain what it is about and why we give it such importance in cultural studies.

The concept of representation has come to occupy a new and important place in the study of culture. Representation connects meaning and language to culture. But what exactly do people mean by it? What does representation have to do with culture and meaning? One common-sense usage of the term is as follows: 'Representation means using language to say something meaningful about, or to represent, the world meaningfully, to other people.' You may well ask, 'Is that all?' Well, yes and no. Representation is an essential part of the process by which meaning is produced and exchanged between members of a culture. It does involve the use of language, of signs and images which stand for or represent things. But this is a far from simple or straightforward process, as you will soon discover.

How does the concept of representation connect meaning and language to culture? In order to explore this connection further, we will look at a number of different theories about how language is used to represent the world. Here we will be drawing a distinction between three different accounts or theories: the *reflective,* the *intentional* and the *constructionist* approaches to representation. Does language simply reflect a meaning which already exists out there in the world of objects, people and events *(reflective)*? Does language express only what the speaker or writer or painter wants to say, his or her personally intended meaning *(intentional)*? Or is meaning constructed in and through language *(constructionist)*? You will learn more in a moment about these three approaches.

Most of the chapter will be spent exploring the *constructionist* approach, because it is this perspective which has had the most significant impact on cultural studies in recent years. This chapter chooses to examine two major variants or models of the constructionist approach—the *semiotic* approach, greatly influenced by the great

Reprinted from *Representation: Cultural Representations and Signifying Practices* (1997), by permission of Sage Publications.

Swiss linguist, Ferdinand de Saussure, and the *discursive* approach, associated with the French philosopher and historian, Michel Foucault. Now, we turn to the principle of representation.

Making Meaning, Representing Things

What does the word **representation** really mean, in this context? What does the process of representation involve? How does representation work?

To put it briefly representation is the production of meaning through language. *The Shorter Oxford English Dictionary* suggests two relevant meanings for the word:

1. To represent something is to describe or depict it, to call it up in the mind by description or portrayal or imagination, to place a likeness of it before us in our mind or in the senses; as for example, in the sentence, 'This picture represents the murder of Abel by Cain.'
2. To represent also means to symbolize, stand for, to be a specimen of, or to sub-stitute for; as in the sentence, 'In Christianity, the cross represents the suffering and crucifixion of Christ.'

The figures in the painting *stand in the place of,* and at the same time, *stand for* the story of Cain and Abel. Likewise, the cross simply consists of two wooden planks nailed together; but in the context of Christian belief and teaching, it takes on, symbolizes or comes to stand for a wider set of meanings about the crucifixion of the Son of God, and this is a concept we can put into words and pictures.

Activity I

Here is a simple exercise about representation. Look at any familiar object in the room. You will immediately recognize what it is. But how do you *know* what the object is? What does 'recognize' mean?

Now try to make yourself conscious of what you are doing—observe what is going on as you do it. You recognize what it is because your thought-processes decode your visual perception of the object in terms of a concept of it which you have in your head. This must be so because, if you look away from the object, you can still *think* about it by con-juring it up, as we say, 'in your mind's eye'. Go on—try to follow the process as it hap-pens: There is the object . . . and there is the concept in your head which tells you what it is, what your visual image of it *means.*

Now, tell me what it is. Say it aloud: 'It's a lamp'—or a table or a book or the phone or whatever. The concept of the object has passed through your mental representation of it to me *via* the word for it which you have just used. The word stands for or represents the concept, and can be used to reference or designate either a 'real' object in the world or indeed even some imaginary object, like angels dancing on the head of a pin, which no one has ever actually seen.

This is how you give meaning to things through language. This is how you 'make sense of' the world of people, objects and events, and how you are able to express a complex thought about those things to other people, or communicate about them through language in ways which other people are able to understand.

Why do we have to go through this complex process to represent our thoughts? If you put down a glass you are holding and walk out of the room, you can still *think* about the glass, even though it is no longer physically there. Actually, you can't think with a glass. You can only think with *the concept of the* glass. As the linguists are fond of saying, 'Dogs bark. But the concept of "dog" cannot bark or bite.' You can't speak with the actual glass, either. You can only speak with the *word* for glass—GLASS—which is the linguistic sign which we use in English to refer to objects which you drink water out of. This is where *representation* comes in. Representation is the production of the meaning of the concepts in our minds through language. It is the link between concepts and language which enables us to *refer to* either the 'real' world of objects, people or events, or indeed to imaginary worlds of fictional objects, people and events.

So there are *two* processes, two **systems of representation** involved. First, there is the 'system' by which all sorts of objects, people and events are correlated with a set of concepts or *mental representations* which we carry around in our heads. Without them, we could not interpret the world meaningfully at all. In the first place, then, meaning depends on the system of concepts and images formed in our thoughts which can stand for or 'represent' the world, enabling us to refer to things both inside and outside our heads.

Before we move on to look at the second 'system of representation', we should observe that what we have just said is a very simple version of a rather complex process. It is simple enough to see how we might form concepts for things we can perceive—people or material objects, like chairs, tables and desks. But we also form concepts of rather obscure and abstract things, which we can't in any simple way see, feel or touch. Think, for example, of our concepts of war, or death, or friendship or love. And, as we have remarked, we also form concepts about things we never have seen, and possibly can't or won't ever see, and about people and places we have plainly made up. We may have a clear concept of, say, angels, mermaids, God, the Devil, or of Heaven and Hell, or of Middlemarch (the fictional provincial town in George Eliot's novel), or Elizabeth (the heroine of Jane Austen's *Pride and Prejudice*).

We have called this a *'system* of representation'. That is because it consists, not of individual concepts, but of different ways of organizing, clustering, arranging and classifying concepts, and of establishing complex relations between them. For example, we use the principles of similarity and difference to establish relationships between concepts or to distinguish them from one another. Thus I have an idea that in some respects birds are like planes in the sky, based on the fact that they are similar because they both fly—but I also have an idea that in other respects they are different, because one is part of nature whilst the other is man-made. The mixing and matching of relations between concepts to form complex ideas and thoughts is possible because our concepts are arranged into different classifying systems. In this example, the first is based on a distinction between flying/not flying and the second is based on the distinction between natural/man-made. There are other principles of organization like this at work in all conceptual systems: for example, classifying according to sequence—which concept follows which—or causality—what causes what—and so on. The point here is that we are talking about, not just a random collection of concepts, but concepts organized, arranged and classified into complex relations with one another. That is what our conceptual system actually is like. However, this does not undermine the basic point. Meaning depends on the relationship between things in the world—people, objects and events, real or fictional—and the conceptual system, which can operate as *mental representations* of them.

Now it could be the case that the conceptual map which I carry around in my head is totally different from yours, in which case you and I would interpret or make sense of the world in totally different ways. We would be incapable of sharing our thoughts or expressing ideas about the world to each other. In fact, each of us probably does understand and interpret the world in a unique and individual way. However, we are able to communicate because we share broadly the same conceptual maps and thus make sense of or interpret the world in roughly similar ways. That is indeed what it means when we say we 'belong to the same culture'. Because we interpret the world in roughly similar ways, we are able to build up a shared culture of meanings and thus construct a social world which we inhabit together. That is why 'culture' is sometimes defined in terms of 'shared meanings or shared conceptual maps' (see du Gay, Hall et al., 1997).

However, a shared conceptual map is not enough. We must also be able to represent or exchange meanings and concepts, and we can only do that when we also have access to a shared language. Language is therefore the second system of representation involved in the overall process of constructing meaning. Our shared conceptual map must be translated into a common language, so that we can correlate our concepts and ideas with certain written words, spoken sounds or visual images. The general term we use for words, sounds or images which carry meaning is *signs*. These signs stand for or represent the concepts and the conceptual relations between them which we carry around in our heads and together they make up the meaning-systems of our culture.

Signs are organized into languages and it is the existence of common languages which enable us to translate our thoughts (concepts) into words, sounds or images, and then to use these, operating as a language, to express meanings and communicate thoughts to other people. Remember that term 'language' is being used here in a very broad and inclusive way. The writing system or the spoken system of a particular language are both obviously 'languages'. But so are visual images, whether produced by hand, mechanical, electronic, digital or some other means, when they are used to express meaning. And so are other things which aren't 'linguistic' in any ordinary sense: the 'language' of facial expressions or of gesture, for example, or the 'language' of fashion, of clothes, or of traffic lights. Even music is a 'language', with complex relations between different sounds and chords, though it is a very special case since it can't easily be used to reference actual things or objects in the world (a point further elaborated in du Gay, ed., 1997, and Mackay, ed., 1997). Any sound, word, image or object which functions as a sign, and is organized with other signs into a system which is capable of carrying and expressing meaning is, from this point of view, 'a language'. It is in this sense that the model of meaning which I have been analysing here is often described as a 'linguistic' one; and that all the theories of meaning which follow this basic model are described as belonging to 'the linguistic turn' in the social sciences and cultural studies.

At the heart of the meaning process in culture, then, are two related 'systems of representation'. The first enables us to give meaning to the world by constructing a set of correspondences or a chain of equivalences between things—people, objects, events, abstract ideas, etc.—and our system of concepts, our conceptual maps. The second depends on constructing a set of correspondences between our conceptual map and a set of signs, arranged or organized into various languages which stand for or represent those concepts. The relation between 'things', concepts and signs lies at the heart of the production of meaning in language. The process which links these three elements together is what we call 'representation'.

Language and Representation

Just as people who belong to the same culture must share a broadly similar conceptual map, so they must also share the same way of interpreting the signs of a language, for only in this way can meanings be effectively exchanged between people. But how do we know which concept stands for which thing? Or which word effectively represents which concept? How do I know which sounds or images will carry, through language, the meaning of my concepts and what I want to say with them to you? This may seem relatively simple in the case of visual signs, because the drawing, painting, camera or TV image of a sheep bears a resemblance to the animal with a woolly coat grazing in a field to which I want to refer. Even so, we need to remind ourselves that a drawn or painted or digital version of a sheep is not exactly like a 'real' sheep. For one thing, most images are in two dimensions whereas the 'real' sheep exists in three dimensions.

Visual signs and images, even when they bear a close resemblance to the things to which they refer, are still signs: they carry meaning and thus have to be interpreted. In order to interpret them, we must have access to the two systems of representation discussed earlier: to a conceptual map which correlates the sheep in the field with the concept of a 'sheep'; and a language system which in visual language, bears some resemblance to the real thing or 'looks like it' in some way. This argument is clearest if we think of a cartoon drawing or an abstract painting of a 'sheep', where we need a very sophisticated conceptual and shared linguistic system to be certain that we are all 'reading' the sign in the same way. Even then we may find ourselves wondering whether it really is a picture of a sheep at all. As the relationship between the sign and its referent becomes less clear-cut, the meaning begins to slip and slide away from us into uncertainty. Meaning is no longer transparently passing from one person to another. . . .

So, even in the case of visual language, where the relationship between the concept and the sign seems fairly straightforward, the matter is far from simple. It is even more difficult with written or spoken language, where words don't look or sound anything like the things to which they refer. In part, this is because there are different kinds of signs. Visual signs are what are called *iconic* signs. That is, they bear, in their form, a certain resemblance to the object, person or event to which they refer. A photograph of a tree reproduces some of the actual conditions of our visual perception in the visual sign. Written or spoken signs, on the other hand, are what is called *indexical*.

They bear no obvious relationship at all to the things to which they refer. The letters T,R,E,E, do not look anything like trees in Nature, nor does the word 'tree' in English sound like 'real' trees (if indeed they make any sound at all!). The relationship in these systems of representation between the sign, the concept and the object to which they might be used to refer is entirely *arbitrary*. By 'arbitrary' we mean that in principle any collection of letters or any sound in any order would do the trick equally well. Trees would not mind if we used the word SEERT—'trees' written backwards—to represent the concept of them. This is clear from the fact that, in French, quite different letters and a quite different sound is used to refer to what, to all appearances, is the same thing—a 'real' tree—and, as far as we can tell, to the same concept—a large plant that grows in nature. The French and English seem to be using the same concept. But the concept which in English is represented by the word, TREE, is represented in French by the word, ARBRE.

Sharing the Codes

The question, then, is: how do people who belong to the same culture, who share the same conceptual map and who speak or write the same language (English) know that the arbitrary combination of letters and sounds that makes up the word, TREE, will stand for or represent the concept 'a large plant that grows in nature'? One possibility would be that the objects in the world themselves embody and fix in some way their 'true' meaning. But it is not at all clear that real trees *know* that they are trees, and even less clear that they know that the word in English which represents the concept of themselves is written TREE whereas in French it is written ARBRE! As far as they are concerned, it could just as well be written COW or VAGHE or indeed XYZ. The meaning is *not* in the object or person or thing, nor is it *in* the word. It is we who fix the meaning so firmly that, after a while, it comes to seem natural and inevitable. The meaning is *constructed by the system of representation*. It is constructed and fixed by the *code,* which sets up the correlation between our conceptual system and our language system in such a way that, every time we think of a tree, the code tells us to use the English word TREE, or the French word ARBRE. The code tells us that, in our culture—that is, in our conceptual and language codes—the concept 'tree' is represented by the letters T,R,E,E, arranged in a certain sequence, just as in Morse code, the sign for V (which in World War II Churchill made 'stand for' or represent 'Victory') is Dot, Dot, Dot, Dash, and in the 'language of traffic lights', Green=Go! and Red=Stop!

One way of thinking about 'culture', then, is in terms of these shared conceptual maps, shared language systems and the *codes which govern the relationships of translation between them.* Codes fix the relationships between concepts and signs. They stabilize meaning within different languages and cultures. They tell us which language to use to convey which idea. The reverse is also true. Codes tell us which concepts are being referred to when we hear or read which signs. By arbitrarily fixing the relationships between our conceptual system and our linguistic systems (remember, 'linguistic' in a broad sense), codes make it possible for us to speak and to hear intelligibly, and establish the translatability between our concepts and our languages which enables meaning to pass from speaker to hearer and be effectively communicated within a culture. This translatability is not given by nature or fixed by the gods. It is the result of a set of social conventions. It is fixed socially, fixed in culture. English or French or Hindi speakers have over time, and without conscious decision or choice, come to an unwritten agreement, a sort of unwritten cultural covenant that, in their various languages, certain signs will stand for or represent certain concepts. This is what children learn, and how they become, not simply biological individuals but cultural subjects. They learn the system and conventions of representation, the codes of their language and culture, which equip them with cultural 'know-how' enabling them to function as culturally competent subjects. Not because such knowledge is imprinted in their genes, but because they learn its conventions and so gradually *become* 'cultured persons'—i.e. members of their culture. They unconsciously internalize the codes which allow them to express certain concepts and ideas through their systems of representation—writing, speech, gesture, visualization, and so on—and to interpret ideas which are communicated to them using the same systems.

You may find it easier to understand, now, why meaning, language and representation are such critical elements in the study of culture. To belong to a culture is to belong to roughly the same conceptual and linguistic universe, to know how concepts and ideas translate into different languages, and how language can be interpreted to refer to or *reference* the world. To share these things is to see the world from within the same conceptual map and to make sense of it through the same language systems. Early anthropologists of language, like Sapir and Whorf, took this insight to its logical extreme when they argued that we are all, as it were, locked into our cultural perspectives or 'mind-sets', and that language is the best clue we have to that conceptual universe. This observation, when applied to all human cultures, lies at the root of what, today we may think of as cultural or linguistic *relativism*.

Activity 2

You might like to think further about this question of how different cultures conceptually classify the world and what implications this has for meaning and representation.

The English make a rather simple distinction between sleet and snow. The Inuit (Eskimos) who have to survive in a very different, more extreme and hostile climate, apparently have many more words for snow and snowy weather. Consider the list of Inuit terms for snow from the Scott Polar Research Institute in Table 1. There are many more than in English, making much finer and more complex distinctions. The Inuit have a complex classificatory conceptual system for the weather compared with the English. The novelist Peter Hoeg, for example, writing about Greenland in his novel, *Miss Smilla's Feelings for Snow* (1994, pp. 5–6), graphically describes 'frazzil ice' which is 'kneaded together into a soapy mash called porridge ice, which gradually forms free-floating plates, pancake ice, which one, cold, noonday hour, on a Sunday, freezes into a single solid sheet'. Such distinctions are too fine and elaborate even for the English who are always talking about the weather! The question however, is—do the Inuit actually experience snow differently from the English? Their language system suggests they conceptualize the weather differently. But how far is our experience actually bounded by our linguistic and conceptual universe?

Table 1 Inuit Terms for Snow and Ice

snow		ice	siku
blowing—	piqtuluk	—pan, broken—	siqumniq
is snowstorming	piqtuluktuq	—ice water	immiugaq
falling—	qanik	melts—to make water	immiuqtuaq
—is falling:—is snowing	qaniktuq	candle—	illauyiniq
light falling—	qaniaraq	flat—	qaimiq
light—is falling	qaniaraqtuq	glare—	quasaq
first layer of—in fall	apilraun	piled—	ivunrit
deep soft—	mauya	rough—	iwuit
packed—to make water	aniu	shore—	tugiu
light soft—	aquluraq	shorefast—	uvaq
sugar—	pukak	slush—	quna
waterlogged. mushy—	masak	young—	sikuliaq
—is turning into masak	masaguqtuaq		
watery—	maqayak		
wet—	misak		
wet falling—	qanikkuk		
wet—is falling	qanikkuktuq		
—drifting along a surface	natinivik		
—is drifting along a surface	natiruviktuaq		
—lying on a surface	apun		
snowflake	qanik		
is being drifted over with—	apiyuaq		

One implication of this argument about cultural codes is that, if meaning is the result, not of something fixed out there, in nature, but of our social, cultural and linguistic conventions, then meaning can never be *finally* fixed. We can all 'agree' to allow words to carry somewhat different meanings—as we have for example, with the word 'gay', or the use, by young people, of the word 'wicked!' as a term of approval. Of course, there must be some fixing of meaning in language, or we would never be able to understand one another. We can't get up one morning and suddenly decide to represent the concept of a 'tree' with the letters or the word VYXZ, and expect people to follow what we are saying. On the other hand, there is no absolute or final fixing of meaning. Social and linguistic conventions do change over time. In the language of modern managerialism, what we used to call 'students', 'clients', 'patients' and 'passengers' have all become 'customers'. Linguistic codes vary significantly between one language and another. Many cultures do not have words for concepts which are normal and widely acceptable to us. Words constantly go out of common usage, and new phrases are coined: think, for example, of the use of 'down-sizing' to represent the process of firms laying people off work. Even when the actual words remain stable, their connotations shift or they acquire a different nuance. The problem is especially acute in translation. For example, does the difference in English between *know* and *understand* correspond exactly to and capture exactly the same conceptual distinction as the French make between *savoir* and *connaitre?* Perhaps; but can we be sure?

The main point is that meaning does not inhere *in* things, in the world. It is constructed, produced. It is the result of a signifying practice—a practice that *produces* meaning, that *makes things mean.*

Theories of Representation

There are broadly speaking three approaches to explaining how representation of meaning through language works. We may call these the reflective, the intentional and the constructionist or constructivist approaches. You might think of each as an attempt to answer the questions, 'where do meanings come from?' and 'how can we tell the "true" meaning of a word or image?'

In the **reflective approach**, meaning is thought to lie in the object, person, idea or event in the real world, and language functions like a mirror, to *reflect* the true meaning as it already exists in the world. As the poet Gertrude Stein once said, 'A rose is a rose is a rose'. In the fourth century BC, the Greeks used the notion of *mimesis* to explain how language, even drawing and painting, mirrored or imitated Nature; they thought of Homer's great poem, *The Iliad,* as 'imitating' a heroic series of events. So the theory which says that language works by simply reflecting or imitating the truth that is already there and fixed in the world is sometimes called 'mimetic'.

Of course there is a certain obvious truth to mimetic theories of representation and language. As we've pointed out, visual signs do bear some relationship to the shape and texture of the objects which they represent. But, as was also pointed out earlier, a two-dimensional visual image of a *rose* is a sign—it should not be confused with the real plant with thorns and blooms growing in the garden. Remember also that there are many words, sounds and images which we fully well understand but which are entirely fictional or fantasy and refer to worlds which are wholly imaginary—including, many people now think, most of *The Iliad!* Of course, I can use the word 'rose' to *refer* to real, actual plants growing in a garden as we have said before. But this is because I know the code which links the concept with a particular word or image. I cannot *think* or *speak* or *draw* with an actual rose. And if someone says to me that there is no such word as 'rose' for a plant in her culture, the actual plant in the garden cannot resolve the failure of communication between us. Within the conventions of the different language codes we are using, we are both right—and for us to understand each other, one of us must learn the code linking the flower with the word for it in the other's culture.

The second approach to meaning in representation argues the opposite case. It holds that it is the speaker, the author, who imposes his or her unique meaning on the world through language. Words mean what the author intends they should mean. This is the **intentional approach**. Again, there is some point to this argument since we all, as individuals, do use language to convey or communicate things which are special or unique to us, to our way of seeing the world. However, as a general theory of representation through language, the intentional approach is also flawed. We cannot be the sole or unique source of meanings in language, since that would mean that we could express ourselves in entirely private languages. But the essence of language is communication and that, in turn, depends on shared linguistic conventions and shared codes. Language can never be wholly a private game. Our private intended meanings, however personal to us, have to *enter into the rules, codes and conventions of language* to be shared and understood. Language is a social system through and through. This means that our private thoughts have to negotiate with all the other meanings for words or images which have been stored in language which our use of the language system will inevitably trigger into action.

The third approach recognizes this public, social character of language. It acknowledges that neither things in themselves nor the individual users of language can fix meaning in language. Things don't *mean:* we *construct* meaning, using representational systems—concepts and signs. Hence it is called the constructivist or **constructionist approach** to meaning in language. According to this approach, we must not confuse the *material* world, where things and people exist, and the *symbolic* practices and processes through which representation, meaning and language operate. Constructivists do not deny the existence of the material world. However, it is not the material world which conveys meaning: it is the language system or whatever system we are using to represent our concepts. It is social actors who use the conceptual systems of their culture and the linguistic and other representational systems to construct meaning, to make the world meaningful and to communicate about that world meaningfully to others.

Of course, signs may also have a material dimension. Representational systems consist of the actual *sounds* we make with our vocal chords, the *images* we make on light-sensitive paper with cameras, the *marks* we make with paint on canvas, the digital *impulses* we transmit electronically. Representation is a practice, a kind of 'work', which uses material objects and effects. But the *meaning* depends, not on the material quality of the sign, but on its *symbolic function*. It is because a particular sound or word *stands for, symbolizes or represents a* concept that it can function, in language, as a sign and convey meaning—or, as the constructionists say, signify (sign-i-fy).

The Language of Traffic Lights

The simplest example of this point, which is critical for an understanding of how languages function as representational systems, is the famous traffic lights example. A traffic light is a machine which produces different coloured lights in sequence. The effect of light of different wavelengths on the eye—which is a natural and material phenomenon—produces the sensation of different colours. Now these things certainly do exist in the material world. But it is our culture which breaks the spectrum of light into different colours, distinguishes them from one another and attaches names—Red, Green, Yellow, Blue—to them. We use a way of *classifying* the colour spectrum to create colours which are different from one another. We *represent* or symbolize the different colours and classify them according to different colour-concepts. This is the conceptual colour system of our culture. We say 'our culture' because, of course, other cultures may divide the colour spectrum differently. What's more, they certainly use different actual *words* or *letters* to identify different colours: what we call 'red', the French call 'rouge' and so on. This is the linguistic code—the one which correlates certain words (signs) with certain colours (concepts), and thus enables us to communicate about colours to other people, using 'the language of colours'.

But how do we use this representational or symbolic system to regulate the traffic? Colours do not have any 'true' or fixed meaning in that sense. Red does not mean 'Stop' in nature, any more than Green means 'Go'. In other settings, Red may stand for, symbolize or represent 'Blood' or 'Danger' or 'Communism'; and Green may represent 'Ireland' or 'The Countryside' or 'Environmentalism'. Even these meanings can change. In the 'language of electric plugs', Red used to mean 'the connection with the positive charge' but this was arbitrarily and without explanation changed to Brown! But then for many years the producers of plugs had to attach a slip of paper telling people that the code or convention had changed, otherwise how would they know? Red and Green work in the language of traffic lights because 'Stop' and 'Go' are the meanings which have been assigned to them in our culture by the code or conventions governing this language, and this code is widely known and almost universally obeyed in our culture and cultures like ours—though we can well imagine other cultures which did not possess the code, in which this language would be a complete mystery.

Let us stay with the example for a moment, to explore a little further how, according to the constructionist approach to representation, colours and the 'language of traffic lights' work as a signifying or representational system. Recall the *two* representational systems we spoke of earlier. First, there is the conceptual map of colours in our culture—the way colours are distinguished from one another, classified and arranged in our mental universe. Secondly, there are the ways words or images are correlated with colours in our language—our linguistic colour-codes. Actually, of course, a *language* of colours consists of more than just the individual words for different points on the colour spectrum. It also depends on how they function in relation to one another—the sorts of things which are governed by grammar and syntax in written or spoken languages, which allow us to express rather complex ideas. In the language of traffic lights, it is the sequence and position of the colours, as well as the colours themselves, which enable them to carry meaning and thus function as signs.

Does it matter which colours we use? No, the constructionists argue. This is because what signifies is not the colours themselves but (a) the fact that they are different and can be distinguished from one another; and (b) the fact that they are organized into a particular sequence—Red followed by Green, with sometimes a warning Amber in between which says, in effect, 'Get ready! Lights about to change'. Constructionists put this point in the following way. What signifies, what carries meaning—they argue—is not each colour in itself nor even the concept or word for it. It is *the difference between Red and Green* which signifies. This is a very important principle, in general, about representation and meaning, and we shall return to it on more than one occasion in the chapters which follow. Think about it in these terms. If you couldn't differentiate between Red and Green, you couldn't use one to mean 'Stop' and the other to mean 'Go'. In the same way, it is only the difference between the letters P and T which enable the word SHEEP to be linked, in the English language code, to the concept of 'the animal with four legs and a woolly coat', and the word SHEET to 'the material we use to cover ourselves in bed at night'.

In principle, any combination of colours—like any collection of letters in written language or of sounds in spoken language—would do, provided they are sufficiently different not to be confused. Constructionists express this idea by saying that all signs are 'arbitrary'. 'Arbitrary' means that there is no natural relationship between the sign and its meaning or concept. Since Red only means 'Stop' because that is how the code works, in principle any colour would do, including Green. It is the code that fixes the meaning, not the colour itself. This also has wider implications for the theory of representation and meaning in language. It means that signs themselves cannot fix meaning. Instead, meaning depends on *the relation between* a sign and a concept which is fixed by a code. Meaning, the constructionists would say, is 'relational'.

Activity 3

Why not test this point about the arbitrary nature of the sign and the importance of the code for yourself? Construct a code to govern the movement of traffic using two different colours—Yellow and Blue—as in the following:

When the yellow light is showing, . . .

Now add an instruction allowing pedestrians and cyclists only to cross, using Pink.

Provided the code tells us clearly how to read or interpret each colour, and everyone agrees to interpret them in this way, any colour will do. These are just colours, just as the word SHEEP is just a jumble of letters. In French the same animal is referred to using the very different linguistic sign MOUTON. Signs are arbitrary. Their meanings are fixed by codes.

As we said earlier, traffic lights are machines, and colours are the material effect of light-waves on the retina of the eye. But objects—things—can also function as signs, provided they have been assigned a concept and meaning within our cultural and linguistic codes. As signs, they work symbolically —they represent concepts, and signify. Their effects, however, are felt in the material and social world. Red and Green function in the language of traffic lights as signs, but they have real material and social effects. They regulate the social behaviour of drivers and, without them, there would be many more traffic accidents at road intersections.

Summary

We have come a long way in exploring the nature of representation. It is time to summarize what we have learned about the constructionist approach to representation through language.

Representation is the production of meaning through language. In representation, constructionists argue, we use signs, organized into languages of different kinds, to communicate meaningfully with others. Languages can use signs to symbolize, stand for or reference objects, people and events in the so-called 'real' world. But they can also reference imaginary things and fantasy worlds or abstract ideas which are not in any obvious sense part of our material world. There is no simple relationship of reflection, imitation or one-to-one correspondence between language and the real world. The world is not accurately or otherwise reflected in the mirror of language. Language does not work like a mirror. Meaning is produced within language, in and through various representational systems which, for convenience, we call 'languages'. Meaning is produced by the practice, the 'work', of representation. It is constructed through signifying—i.e. meaning-producing—practices.

How does this take place? In fact, it depends on two different but related systems of representation. First, the concepts which are formed in the mind function as a system of mental representation which classifies and organizes the world into meaningful categories. If we have a concept for something, we can say we know its 'meaning'. But we cannot communicate this meaning without a second system of representation, a language. Language consists of signs organized into various relationships. But signs can only convey meaning if we possess codes which allow us to translate our concepts into language —and vice versa. These codes are crucial for meaning and representation. They do not exist in nature but are the result of social conventions. They are a crucial part of our culture—our shared 'maps of meaning'—which we learn and unconsciously internalize as we become members of our culture. This constructionist approach to language thus introduces the symbolic domain of life, where words and things function as signs, into the very heart of social life itself.

4 Hegemony

James Lull

Hegemony is the power or dominance that one social group holds over others. This can refer to the "asymmetrical interdependence" of political-economic-cultural relations between and among nation-states (Straubhaar, 1991) or differences between and among social classes within a nation. Hegemony is "dominance and subordination in the field of relations structured by power" (Hall, 1985). But hegemony is more than social power itself; it is a method for gaining and maintaining power.

Classical Marxist theory, of course, stresses economic position as the strongest predictor of social differences. Today, more than a century after Karl Marx and Friedrich Engels wrote their treatises about capitalist exploitation of the working class, economic disparities still underlie and help reproduce social inequalities in industrialized societies. In that important, basic sense, Marxism and Marxist critical theory, which have been so badly maligned in the rhetoric surrounding the recent political transformation of communist nations, remain fundamentally on target. Technological developments in the twentieth century, however, have made the manner of social domination much more complex than before. Social class differences in today's world are not determined solely or directly by economic factors. Ideological influence is crucial now in the exercise of social power.

The Italian intellectual Antonio Gramsci—to whom the term hegemony is attributed—broadened materialist Marxist theory into the realm of ideology. Persecuted by his country's then fascist government (and writing from prison), Gramsci emphasized society's "super structure," its ideology-producing institutions, in struggles over meaning and power (1971, 1973, 1978; see also Boggs, 1976; Sassoon, 1980; and Simon, 1982). A shift in critical theory thus was made away from a preoccupation with capitalist society's "base" (its economic foundation) and towards its dominant dispensaries of ideas. Attention was given to the structuring of authority and dependence in symbolic environments that correspond to, but are not the same as, economically determined class-based structures and processes of industrial production. Such a theoretical turn seems a natural and necessary development in an era when communications technology is such a pervasive and potent ideological medium. According to Gramsci's theory of ideological hegemony, mass media are tools that ruling elites use to "perpetuate their power, wealth, and status [by popularizing] their own philosophy, culture and morality" (Boggs, 1976: 39). The mass media uniquely "introduce elements into individual consciousness that would not otherwise appear there, but will not be rejected by consciousness because they are so commonly shared in the cultural community" (Nordenstreng, 1977: 276). Owners and managers of media industries can produce and reproduce the content, inflections, and tones of ideas favorable to them far more easily than other social groups because they manage key socializing institutions, thereby guaranteeing that their points of view are constantly and attractively cast into the public arena.

Mass-mediated ideologies are corroborated and strengthened by an interlocking system of efficacious information-distributing agencies and taken-for-granted social practices that permeate every aspect of social and cultural reality. Messages supportive of the status quo emanating from schools, businesses, political organizations, trade unions, religious groups, the military, and the mass media all dovetail together ideologically. This inter-articulating, mutually reinforcing process of ideological influence is the essence of hegemony. Society's most entrenched and powerful institutions—which all depend in one way or another on the same sources for economic support—fundamentally agree with each other ideologically.

Hegemony is not a *direct* stimulation of thought or action, but, according to Stuart Hall, is a "framing [of] all competing definitions of reality within [the dominant class's] range, bringing all alternatives within their horizons of thought. [The dominant class] sets the limits—mental and structural—within which subordinate classes 'live' and make sense of their subordination in such a way as to sustain the dominance of those ruling over them" (1977: 333). British social theorist Philip Elliott suggested similarly that the most potent effect of mass media is how they subtly influence their audiences to perceive social roles and routine personal activities. The controlling economic forces in society use the mass media to provide a "rhetoric [through] which these [concepts] are labeled, evaluated, and explained" (1974: 262). Television commercials, for example, encourage audiences to think of themselves as "markets rather than as a public, as consumers rather than citizens" (Gitlin, 1979: 255).

But hegemony does not mature strictly from ideological articulation. Dominant ideological streams must be subsequently reproduced in the activities of our most basic social units—families, workplace networks, and friendship groups in the many sites and undertakings of everyday life. Gramsci's theory of hegemony, therefore, connects ideological representation to culture. Hegemony requires that ideological assertions become self-evident cultural assumptions. Its effectiveness depends on subordinated peoples accepting the dominant ideology as "normal reality or common sense . . . in active forms of experience and consciousness" (Williams, 1976: 145). Because information and entertainment technology is so thoroughly integrated into the everyday realities of modern societies, mass media's social influence is not always recognized, discussed, or criticized, particularly in societies where the overall standard of living is relatively high. Hegemony, therefore, can easily go undetected (Bausinger, 1984).

Hegemony implies a willing agreement by people to be governed by principles, rules, and laws they believe operate in their best interests, even though in actual practice they may not. Social consent can be a more effective means of control than coercion or force. Again, Raymond Williams: "The idea of hegemony, in its wide sense, is . . . especially important in societies [where] electoral politics and public opinion are significant factors, and in which social practice is seen to depend on consent to certain dominant ideas which in fact express the needs of a dominant class" (1976: 145). Thus, in the words of Colombian communication theorist Jesús Martín-Barbero, "one class exercises hegemony to the extent that the dominating class has interests which the subaltern classes recognize as being in some degree their interests too" (1993: 74).

Relationships between and among the major information-diffusing, socializing agencies of a society and the interacting, cumulative, socially accepted ideological orientations they create and sustain is the essence of hegemony. The American television industry, for instance, connects with other large industries, especially advertising companies but also national and multinational corporations that produce, distribute, and market a wide range of commodities. So, for example, commercial TV networks no longer buy original children's television shows. Network executives only want new program ideas associated with successful retail products already marketed to children. By late 1990 more than 20 toy-based TV shows appeared on American commercial TV weekly. Television also has the ability to absorb other major social institutions—organized religion, for instance—and turn them into popular culture. The TV industry also connects with government institutions, including especially the federal agencies that are supposed to regulate telecommunications. The development of American commercial broadcasting is a vivid example of how capitalist economic forces assert their power. Evacuation of the legislatively mandated public service ideal could only have taken place because the Federal Communications Commission stepped aside while commercial interests amassed power and expanded their influence. Symptomatic of the problem is the fact that government regulators typically are recruited from, and return to, the very industries they are supposed to monitor.

Transmedia and transgenre integrations with mutually reinforcing ideological consequences are also commonplace. Popular radio and video songs, for example, can also be commercials. . . . Commercial logos become products themselves and are reproduced on tee-shirts, posters, beach towels, and other informal media. The rhetoric of TV commercials and programs is recycled in the lyrics of rap music and in the routines of stand-up comedians performing live and on television. . . . There are films made for television, magazines published about television, and television news magazines. The most well-known national newspaper in the United States, *USA Today*, is sold nationwide in vending boxes that resemble TV sets. Television commercials appear on Channel One, an educational news channel shown to students in American elementary school classrooms. Logos that advertise only national gasoline, food, and motel chains appear on government highway signs, advising travelers of their availability at upcoming freeway exits. Expensive public relations campaigns of major corporations distribute "informational" supplementary textbooks to elementary and secondary school systems. Major business organizations send digests of their annual reports and other promotional materials to college instructors, hoping this biased information will be incorporated into teaching and research. Similar materials are sent to political and religious leaders so they will pass the information along to their constituencies and congregations.

In the United States, advocacy of alternative political ideologies, parties, and candidates, or suggestions of viable consumer alternatives to the commercial frenzy stimulated and reinforced by advertising and other marketing techniques, are rarely seen on the popular media. Radical ideas typically appear only on underfinanced, non-commercial radio and TV stations and in low-budget print media. These media have tiny public followings compared to commercial television and video outlets, metropolitan daily newspapers, and national magazines. When genuinely divergent views appear on mainstream media, the information is frequently shown in an unfavorable light or is modified and co-opted to surrender to the embrace of mainstream thought. . . . The mass media help create an impression that even society's roughest edges ultimately must conform to the conventional contours of dominant ideologies.

Hegemony has been central to the management of ideology in communist nations too, though it develops differently. Central ideological planning and the creation of propaganda to advise "the people" represent the same intention—to protect the interests of ruling elites. . . .

The collapse of political authority in Eastern and Central Europe and the former Soviet Union was a breakdown in communist ideological hegemony. Conflict between culture producers and young audiences in East Germany and Hungary is typical of what happened in the Soviet bloc (Wicke, 1992; Szemere, 1985). Young rock musicians and their enthusiastic audiences led a cultural and political struggle against the repressive institutions and the ideology behind them. Trying to contain and control rebellious youth, the former communist governments attempted in sinister ways to defuse the politically charged musical and cultural activity of youth by incorporating and sponsoring them. Young people and other dissenters saw through the strategy, however, challenged the hegemony, and stimulated policy changes that later contributed to the dramatic downfall of the European communist governments. In China, the extraordinary student and worker uprising in 1989 is but the most visible sign of wide-spread resistance among that country's disaffected urban population.[1] Recent popular revolutions in communist countries developed from widespread discontent with an interacting spectrum of economic, political, and cultural conditions. Ironically, the workers' uprising that Marx and Engels theorized would take place in repressive, class-based capitalist economies developed instead in communist nations which had proven in many respects to be even more repressive.

Hegemony as an Incomplete Process

Two of our leading critical theorists, Raymond Williams and Stuart Hall, remind us that hegemony in any political context is indeed fragile. It requires renewal and modification through the assertion and reassertion of power. Hall suggests that "it is crucial to the concept that hegemony is not a 'given' and permanent state of affairs, but it has to be actively won and secured; it can also be lost" (1977: 333). Ideological work is the winning and securing of hegemony over time. . . . Ideology is composed of "texts that are not closed" according to Hall, who also notes that ideological "counter-tendencies" regularly appear in the seams and cracks of dominant forms (Hall, 1985). Mediated communications ranging from popular television shows to rap and rock music, even graffiti scrawled over surfaces of public spaces, all inscribe messages that challenge central political positions and cultural assumptions.

Counter-hegemonic tendencies do not inhere solely in texts. They are formulated in processes of communication—in the interpretations, social circulation, and uses of media content. As with the American soldiers' use of military gas masks as inhaling devices to heighten the effect of marijuana smoke, or the homeless's transformation of supermarket shopping carts into personal storage vehicles, ideological resistance and appropriation frequently involve reinventing institutional messages for purposes that differ greatly from their creators' intentions. Expressions of the dominant ideology are sometimes reformulated to assert alternative, often completely resistant or contradictory messages. . . .

Furthermore, resistance to hegemony is not initiated solely by media consumers. Texts themselves are implicated. Ideology can never be stated purely and simply. Ways of thinking are always reflexive and embedded in a complex, sometimes contradictory, ideological regress. . . .

Audience interpretations and uses of media imagery also eat away at hegemony. Hegemony fails when dominant ideology is weaker than social resistance. Gay subcultures, feminist organizations, environmental groups, radical political parties, music-based formations such as punks, B-boys, Rastafarians, and metal heads all use media and their social networks to endorse counter-hegemonic values and lifestyles. Indeed, we have only just begun to examine the complex relationship between ideological representation and social action.

Note

1. It's important to realize that the military suppression of the student-worker uprising in Beijing in 1989 did not stop the Chinese revolutionary movement. It made possible the dramatic and far-reaching (if less visually spectacular) economic and cultural changes that characterize the People's Republic today.

References

Bausinger, H. (1984). Media, technology, and everyday life. *Media, Culture & Society*, 6, 340–52.

Boggs, C. (1976). *Gramsci's Marxism.* London: Pluto.

Elliott, P. (1974). Uses and gratifications research: A critique and a sociological alternative. In J. G. Blumler and E. Katz (eds.), *The Uses of Mass Communications: Current Perspectives on Gratifications Research.* Beverly Hills, CA; Sage.

Gitlin, T. (1979). Prime-time ideology: the hegemonic process in television entertainment. *Social Problems*, 26, 251–66.

Gramsci, A. (1971). *Selections from the Prison Notebooks.* New York: International.

Gramsci, A. (1973). *Letters from Prison.* New York: Harper and Row.

Gramsci, A. (1978). *Selections from Cultural Writings.* Cambridge, MA: Harvard University Press.

Hall, S. (1977). Culture, media, and the "ideological effect." In J. Curran, M. Gurevitch, and J. Woollacott (eds.), *Mass Communication and Society.* London: Edward Arnold.

Hall, S. (1985). Master's session. International Communication Association. Honolulu, Hawaii.

Martin-Barbero, J. (1993). *Communication, Culture and Hegemony.* Newbury Park, CA: Sage.

Nordenstreng, K. (1977). From mass media to mass consciousness. In G. Gerbner (ed.), *Mass Media Policies in Changing Cultures.* New York: Wiley.

Sassoon, A. S. (1980). *Gramsci's Politics.* New York: St. Martin's.

Simon, R. (1982). *Gramsci's Political Thought.* London: Lawrence and Wishart.

Straubhaar, J. (1991). Beyond media imperialism: asymmetrical interdependence and cultural proximity. *Critical Studies in Mass Communication*, 8, 39–59.

Szemere, A. (1985). Pop music in Hungary. *Communication Research*, 12, 401–11.

Wicke, P. (1992). The role of rock music in the political disintegration of East Germany. In J. Lull (ed .), *Popular Music and Communication.* Newbury Park, CA: Sage.

Williams, R. (1976). *Key Words: A Vocabulary of Culture and Society.* New York: Oxford University Press.

5

Ideology and Ideological State Apparatuses (Notes toward an Investigation)

Louis Althusser

On the Reproduction of the Conditions of Production[1]

I must now expose more fully something which was briefly glimpsed in my analysis when I spoke of the necessity to renew the means of production if production is to be possible. That was a passing hint. Now I shall consider it for itself.

As Marx said, every child knows that a social formation which did not reproduce the conditions of production at the same time as it produced would not last a year.[2] The ultimate condition of production is therefore the reproduction of the conditions of production. This may be "simple" (reproducing exactly the previous conditions of production) or "on an extended scale" (expanding them). Let us ignore this last distinction for the moment.

What, then, is *the reproduction of the conditions of production?*

Here we are entering a domain which is both very familiar (since *Capital* Volume Two) and uniquely ignored. The tenacious obviousnesses (ideological obviousnesses of an empiricist type) of the point of view of production alone, or even of that of mere productive practice (itself abstract in relation to the process of production) are so integrated into our everyday "consciousness" that it is extremely hard, not to say almost impossible, to raise oneself to the *point of view of reproduction.* Nevertheless, everything outside this point of view remains abstract (worse than one-sided: distorted)—even at the level of production, and, *a fortiori,* at that of mere practice.

Let us try and examine the matter methodically.

To simplify my exposition, and assuming that every social formation arises from a dominant mode of production, I can say that the process of production sets to work the existing productive forces in and under definite relations of production.

Reprinted from *Lenin and Philosophy and Other Essays* (1991), by permission of Monthly Review Magazine.

It follows that, in order to exist, every social formation must produce the conditions of its production at the same time as it produces, and in order to be able to produce. It must therefore reproduce:

1. the productive forces,
2. the existing relations of production.

Reproduction of the Means of Production

Everyone (including the bourgeois economists whose work is national accounting, or the modern "macro-economic" "theoreticians") now recognizes, because Marx compellingly proved it in *Capital* Volume Two, that no production is possible which does not allow for the reproduction of the material conditions of production: the reproduction of the means of production.

The average economist, who is no different in this than the average capitalist, knows that each year it is essential to foresee what is needed to replace what has been used up or worn out in production: raw material, fixed installations (buildings), instruments of production (machines), etc. I say the average economist = the average capitalist, for they both express the point of view of the firm, regarding it as sufficient simply to give a commentary on the terms of the firm's financial accounting practice.

But thanks to the genius of Quesnay who first posed this "glaring" problem, and to the genius of Marx who resolved it, we know that the reproduction of the material conditions of production cannot be thought at the level of the firm, because it does not exist at that level in its real conditions. What happens at the level of the firm is an effect, which only gives an idea of the necessity of reproduction, but absolutely fails to allow its conditions and mechanisms to be thought.

A moment's reflection is enough to be convinced of this: Mr. X, a capitalist who produces woollen yarn in his spinning-mill, has to "reproduce" his raw material, his machines, etc. But *he* does not produce them for his own production—other capitalists do: an Australian sheep-farmer, Mr. Y, a heavy engineer producing machine-tools, Mr. Z, etc., etc. And Mr. Y and Mr. Z, in order to produce those products which are the condition of the reproduction of Mr. X's conditions of production, also have to reproduce the conditions of their own production, and so on to infinity—the whole in proportions such that, on the national and even the world market, the demand for means of production (for reproduction) can be satisfied by the supply.

In order to think this mechanism, which leads to a kind of "endless chain," it is necessary to follow Marx's "global" procedure, and to study in particular the relations of the circulation of capital between Department I (production of means of production) and Department II (production of means of consumption), and the realization of surplus-value, in *Capital,* Volumes Two and Three.

We shall not go into the analysis of this question. It is enough to have mentioned the existence of the necessity of the reproduction of the material conditions of production.

Reproduction of Labour Power

However, the reader will not have failed to note one thing. We have discussed the reproduction of the means of production—but not the reproduction of the productive forces. We have therefore ignored the reproduction of what distinguishes the productive forces from the means of production, i.e. the reproduction of labour power.

From the observation of what takes place in the firm, in particular from the examination of the financial accounting practice which predicts amortization and investment, we have been able to obtain an approximate idea of the existence of the material process of reproduction, but we are now entering a domain in which the observation of what happens in the firm is, if not totally blind, at least almost entirely so, and for good reason: the reproduction of labour power takes place essentially outside the firm.

How is the reproduction of labour power ensured?

It is ensured by giving labour power the material means with which to reproduce itself: by wages. Wages feature in the accounting of each enterprise, but as "wage capital,"[3] not at all as a condition of the material reproduction of labour power.

However, that is in fact how it "works," since wages represent only that part of the value produced by the expenditure of labour power which is indispensable for its reproduction: sc. indispensable to the reconstitution of the labour power of the wage-earner (the wherewithal to pay for housing, food and clothing, in short to enable the wage-earner to present himself again at the factory gate the next day—and every further day God grants him); and we should add: indispensable for raising and educating the children in whom the proletarian reproduces himself (in n models where n = 0, 1, 2, etc. . . .) as labour power.

Remember that this quantity of value (wages) necessary for the reproduction of labour power is determined not by the needs of a "biological" Guaranteed Minimum Wage (*Salaire Minimum Interprofessionnel Garanti*) alone, but by the needs of a historical minimum (Marx noted that English workers need beer while French proletarians need wine)—i.e. a historically variable minimum.

I should also like to point out that this minimum is doubly historical in that it is not defined by the historical needs of the working class "recognized" by the capitalist class, but by the historical needs imposed by the proletarian class struggle (a double class struggle: against the lengthening of the working day and against the reduction of wages).

However, it is not enough to ensure for labour power the material conditions of its reproduction if it is to be reproduced as labour power. I have said that the available labour power must be "competent," i.e. suitable to be set to work in the complex system of the process of production. The development of the productive forces and the type of unity historically constitutive of the productive forces at a given moment produce the result that the labour power has to be (diversely) skilled and therefore reproduced as such. Diversely: according to the requirements of the socio-technical division of labour, its different "jobs" and "posts."

How is this reproduction of the (diversified) skills of labour power provided for in a capitalist regime? Here, unlike social formations characterized by slavery or serfdom, this reproduction of the skills of labour power tends (this is a tendential law) decreasingly to be provided for "on the spot" (apprenticeship within production itself), but is achieved more and more outside production: by the capitalist education system, and by other instances and institutions.

What do children learn at school? They go varying distances in their studies, but at any rate they learn to read, to write and to add—i.e. a number of techniques, and a number of other things as well, including elements (which may be rudimentary or on the contrary thoroughgoing) of "scientific" or "literary culture," which are directly useful in the different jobs in production (one instruction for manual workers, another for technicians, a third for engineers, a final one for higher management, etc.). Thus they learn "know-how."

But besides these techniques and knowledges, and in learning them, children at school also learn the "rules" of good behaviour, i.e. the attitude that should be observed by every agent in the division of labour, according to the job he is "destined" for: rules of morality, civic and professional conscience, which actually means rules of respect for the sociotechnical division of labour and ultimately the rules of the order established by class domination. They also learn to "speak proper French," to "handle" the workers correctly, i.e. actually (for the future capitalists and their servants) to "order them about" properly, i.e. (ideally) to "speak to them" in the right way, etc.

To put this more scientifically, I shall say that the reproduction of labour power requires not only a reproduction of its skills, but also, at the same time, a reproduction of its submission to the rules of the established order, i.e. a reproduction of submission to the ruling ideology for the workers, and a reproduction of the ability to manipulate the ruling ideology correctly for the agents of exploitation and repression, so that they, too, will provide for the domination of the ruling class "in words."

In other words, the school (but also other State institutions like the Church, or other apparatuses like the Army) teaches "know-how," but in forms which ensure *subjection to the ruling ideology* or the mastery of its "practice." All the agents of production, exploitation and repression, not to speak of the "professionals of ideology" (Marx), must in one way or another be "steeped" in this ideology in order to perform their tasks "conscientiously"—the tasks of the exploited (the proletarians), of the exploiters (the capitalists), of the exploiters' auxiliaries (the managers), or of the high priests of the ruling ideology (its "functionaries"), etc.

The reproduction of labour power thus reveals as its *sine qua non* not only the reproduction of its "skills" but also the reproduction of its subjection to the ruling ideology or of the "practice" of that ideology, with the proviso that it is not enough to say "not only but also," for it is clear that *it is in the forms and under the forms of ideological subjection that provision is made for the reproduction of the skills of labour power.*

But this is to recognize the effective presence of a new reality: *ideology.*

Here I shall make two comments.

The first is to round off my analysis of reproduction.

I have just given a rapid survey of the forms of the reproduction of the productive forces, i.e., of the means of production on the one hand, and of labour power on the other.

But I have not yet approached the question of the *reproduction of the relations of production.* This is a *crucial question* for the Marxist theory of the mode of production. To let it pass would be a theoretical omission—worse, a serious political error.

I shall therefore discuss it. But in order to obtain the means to discuss it, I shall have to make another long detour.

The second comment is that in order to make this detour, I am obliged to re-raise my old question: what is a society?

The State

The Marxist tradition is strict, here: in the *Communist Manifesto* and the *Eighteenth Brumaire* (and in all the later classical texts, above all in Marx's writings on the Paris Commune and Lenin's on *State and Revolution*), the State is explicitly conceived as a repressive apparatus. The State is a "machine" of repression, which enables the ruling classes (in the nineteenth century the bourgeois class and the "class" of big landowners) to ensure their domination over the working class, thus enabling the former to subject the latter to the process of surplus-value extortion (i.e. to capitalist exploitation).

The State is thus first of all what the Marxist classics have called *the State apparatus.* This term means: not only the specialized apparatus (in the narrow sense) whose existence and necessity I have recognized in relation to the requirements of legal practice, i.e. the police, the courts, the prisons; but also the army, which (the proletariat has paid for this experience with its blood) intervenes directly as a supplementary repressive force in the last instance, when the police and its specialized auxiliary corps are "outrun by events"; and above this ensemble, the head of State, the government and the administration.

Presented in this form, the Marxist-Leninist "theory" of the State has its finger on the essential point, and not for one moment can there be any question of rejecting the fact that this really is the essential point. The State apparatus, which defines the State as a force of repressive execution and intervention "in the interests of the ruling classes" in the class struggle conducted by the bourgeoisie and its allies against the proletariat, is quite certainly the State, and quite certainly defines its basic "function."

The State Ideological Apparatuses

Thus, what has to be added to the "Marxist theory" of the State is something else.

Here we must advance cautiously in a terrain which, in fact, the Marxist classics entered long before us, but without having systematized in theoretical form the decisive advances implied by their experiences and procedures. Their experiences and procedures were indeed restricted in the main to the terrain of political practice.

In fact, i.e., in their political practice, the Marxist classics treated the State as a more complex reality than the definition of it given in the "Marxist theory of the State," even when it has been supplemented as I have just suggested. They recognized this complexity in their practice, but they did not express it in a corresponding theory.[4]

I should like to attempt a very schematic outline of this corresponding theory. To that end, I propose the following thesis.

In order to advance the theory of the State it is indispensable to take into account not only the distinction between *State power* and *State apparatus,* but also another reality which is clearly on the side of the (repressive) State apparatus, but must not be confused with it. I shall call this reality by its concept: *the ideological State apparatuses.*

What are the ideological State apparatuses (ISAs)?

They must not be confused with the (repressive) State apparatus. Remember that in Marxist theory, the State Apparatus (SA) contains: the Government, the Administration, the Army, the Police, the Courts, the Prisons, etc., which constitute what I shall in future call the Repressive State Apparatus. Repressive suggests that the State Apparatus in question "functions by violence"—at least ultimately (since repression, e.g. administrative repression, may take non-physical forms).

I shall call Ideological State Apparatuses a certain number of realities which present themselves to the immediate observer in the form of distinct and specialized institutions. I propose an empirical list of these which will obviously have to be examined in detail, tested, corrected and reorganized. With all the reservations implied by this requirement, we can for the moment regard the following institutions as Ideological State Apparatuses (the order in which I have listed them has no particular significance):

✦ the religious ISA (the system of the different Churches),

✦ the educational ISA (the system of the different public and private "Schools"),

✦ the family ISA,[5]

✦ the legal ISA,[6]

✦ the political ISA (the political system, including the different Parties),

✦ the trade-union ISA,

✦ the communications ISA (press, radio and television, etc.),

✦ the cultural ISA (Literature, the Arts, sports, etc.).

I have said that the ISAs must not be confused with the (Repressive) State Apparatus. What constitutes the difference?

As a first moment, it is clear that while there is *one* (Repressive) State Apparatus, there is a *plurality* of Ideological State Apparatuses. Even presupposing that it exists, the unity that constitutes this plurality of ISAs as a body is not immediately visible.

As a second moment, it is clear that whereas the—unified—(Repressive) State Apparatus belongs entirely to the public domain, much the larger part of the Ideological State Apparatuses (in their apparent dispersion) are part, on the contrary, of the *private* domain. Churches, parties, trade unions, families, some schools, most newspapers, cultural ventures, etc., etc., are private.

We can ignore the first observation for the moment. But someone is bound to question the second, asking me by what right I regard as Ideological *State* Apparatuses, institutions which for the most part do not possess public status, but are quite simply *private* institutions. As a conscious Marxist, Gramsci already forestalled this objection in one sentence. The distinction between the public and the private is a distinction internal to bourgeois law, and valid in the (subordinate) domains in which bourgeois law exercises its "authority." The domain of the State escapes it because the latter is "above the law": the State, which is the State *of* the ruling class, is neither public nor private; on the contrary, it is the precondition for any distinction between public and private. The same thing can be said from the starting-point of our

State Ideological Apparatuses. It is unimportant whether the institutions in which they are realized are "public" or "private." What matters is how they function. Private institutions can perfectly well "function" as Ideological State Apparatuses. A reasonably thorough analysis of any one of the ISAs proves it.

But now for what is essential. What distinguishes the ISAs from the (Repressive) State Apparatus is the following basic difference: the Repressive State Apparatus functions "by violence," whereas the Ideological State Apparatuses *function "by ideology."*

I can clarify matters by correcting this distinction. I shall say rather that every State Apparatus, whether Repressive or Ideological, "functions" both by violence and by ideology, but with one very important distinction which makes it imperative not to confuse the Ideological State Apparatuses with the (Repressive) State Apparatus.

This is the fact that the (Repressive) State Apparatus functions massively and predominantly *by repression* (including physical repression), while functioning secondarily by ideology. (There is no such thing as a purely repressive apparatus.) For example, the Army and the Police also function by ideology both to ensure their own cohesion and reproduction, and in the "values" they propound externally.

In the same way, but inversely, it is essential to say that for their part the Ideological State Apparatuses function massively and predominantly *by ideology,* but they also function secondarily by repression, even if ultimately, but only ultimately, this is very attenuated and concealed, even symbolic. (There is no such thing as a purely ideological apparatus.) Thus Schools and Churches are suitable methods of punishment, expulsion, selection, etc., to "discipline" not only their shepherds, but also their flocks. The same is true of the Family. . . . The same is true of the cultural IS Apparatus (censorship, among other things), etc.

It is necessary to add that this determination of the double "functioning" (predominantly, secondarily) by repression and by ideology, according to whether it is a matter of the (Repressive) State Apparatus or the Ideological State Apparatuses, makes it clear that very subtle explicit or tacit combinations may be woven from the interplay of the (Repressive) State Apparatus and the Ideological State Apparatuses. Everyday life provides us with innumerable examples of this, but they must be studied in detail if we are to go further than this mere observation.

Nevertheless, this remark leads us towards an understanding of what constitutes the unity of the apparently disparate body of the ISAs. If the ISAs "function" massively and predominantly by ideology, what unifies their diversity is precisely this functioning, insofar as the ideology by which they function is always in fact unified, despite its diversity and its contradictions, *beneath the ruling ideology,* which is the ideology of "the ruling class." Given the fact that the "ruling class" in principle holds State power (openly or more often by means of alliances between classes or class fractions), and therefore has at its disposal the (Repressive) State Apparatus, we can accept the fact that this same ruling class is active in the Ideological State Apparatuses insofar as it is ultimately the ruling ideology which is realized in the Ideological State Apparatuses, precisely in its contradictions. Of course, it is a quite different thing to act by laws and decrees in the (Repressive) State Apparatus and to "act" through the intermediary of the ruling ideology in the Ideological State Apparatuses. We must go into the details of this difference—but it cannot mask the reality of a profound identity. To my knowledge, *no class can hold State power over a long period without at the same time exercising its hegemony over and in the State Ideological Apparatuses.* I only need one example and proof of this: Lenin's anguished concern to revolutionize the educational Ideological State Apparatus (among others), simply to make it possible for the Soviet proletariat, who had seized State power, to secure the future of the dictatorship of the proletariat and the transition to socialism.[7]

One ideological State apparatus certainly has the dominant role, although hardly anyone lends an ear to its music: it is so silent! This is the school.

It takes children from every class at infant-school age, and then for years, the years in which the child is most "vulnerable," squeezed between the family State apparatus and the educational State apparatus, it drums into them, whether it uses new or old methods, a certain amount of "know-how" wrapped in the ruling ideology (French, arithmetic, natural history, the sciences, literature) or simply the ruling ideology in its pure state (ethics, civic instruction, philosophy). Somewhere around the age of sixteen, a huge mass of children are ejected "into production": these are the workers or small peasants. Another portion of scholastically adapted youth carries on: and, for better or worse, it goes somewhat further, until it falls by the wayside and fills the posts of small and middle technicians, white-collar workers, small and middle executives, petty bourgeois of all kinds. A last portion reaches the summit, either to fall into intellectual semi-employment, or to provide, as well as the "intellectuals of the collective labourer," the agents of exploitation (capitalists, managers), the agents of repression (soldiers, policemen, politicians, administrators, etc.) and the professional ideologists (priests of all sorts, most of whom are convinced "laymen").

Each mass ejected *en route* is practically provided with the ideology which suits the role it has to fulfill in class society: the role of the exploited (with a "highly-developed" "professional," "ethical," "civic," "national" and a-political consciousness); the role of the agent of exploitation (ability to give the workers orders and speak to them: "human relations"), of the agent of repression (ability to give orders and enforce obedience "without discussion," or ability to manipulate the demagogy of a political leader's rhetoric), or of the professional ideologist (ability to treat consciousnesses with the respect, i.e. with the contempt, blackmail, and demagogy they deserve, adapted to the accents of Morality, of Virtue, of "Transcendence," of the Nation, of France's World Role, etc.).

Of course, many of these contrasting Virtues (modesty, resignation, submissiveness on the one hand, cynicism, contempt, arrogance, confidence, self-importance, even smooth talk and cunning on the other) are also taught in the Family, in the Church, in the Army, in Good Books, in films and even in the football stadium. But no other ideological State apparatus has the obligatory (and not least, free) audience of the totality of the children in the capitalist social formation, eight hours a day for five or six days out of seven.

But it is by an apprenticeship in a variety of know-how wrapped up in the massive inculcation of the ideology of the ruling class that the *relations of production* in a capitalist social formation, i.e. the relations of exploited to exploiters and exploiters to exploited, are largely reproduced. The mechanisms which produce this vital result for the capitalist regime are naturally covered up and concealed by a universally reigning ideology of the School, universally reigning because it is one of the essential forms of the ruling bourgeois ideology: an ideology which represents the School as a neutral environment purged of ideology (because it is . . . lay), where teachers respectful of the "conscience" and "freedom" of the children who are entrusted to them (in complete confidence) by their "parents" (who are free, too, i.e. the owners of their children) open up for them the path to the freedom, morality and responsibility of adults by their own example, by knowledge, literature and their "liberating" virtues.

I ask the pardon of those teachers who, in dreadful conditions, attempt to turn the few weapons they can find in the history and learning they "teach" against the ideology, the system and the practices in which they are trapped. They are a kind of hero. But they are rare and how many (the majority) do not even begin to suspect the "work" the system (which is bigger than they are and crushes them) forces them to do, or worse, put all their heart and ingenuity into performing it with the most advanced awareness (the famous new methods!). So little do they suspect it that their own devotion contributes to the maintenance and nourishment of this ideological representation of the School, which makes the School today as "natural," indispensable, useful and even beneficial for our contemporaries as the Church was "natural," indispensable and generous for our ancestors a few centuries ago.

In fact, the Church has been replaced today *in its role as the dominant Ideological State Apparatus* by the School. It is coupled with the Family just as the Church was once coupled with the Family. We can now claim that the unprecedentedly deep crisis which is now shaking the education system of so many States across the globe, often in conjunction with a crisis (already proclaimed in the *Communist Manifesto*) shaking the family system, takes on a political meaning, given that the School (and the School-Family couple) constitutes the dominant Ideological State Apparatus, the Apparatus playing a determinant part in the reproduction of the relations of production of a mode of production threatened in its existence by the world class struggle.

Ideology Is a "Representation" of the Imaginary Relationship of Individuals to Their Real Conditions of Existence

In order to approach my central thesis on the structure and functioning of ideology, I shall first present two theses, one negative, the other positive. The first concerns the object which is "represented" in the imaginary form of ideology, the second concerns the materiality of ideology.

THESIS I: Ideology represents the imaginary relationship of individuals to their real conditions of existence.

We commonly call religious ideology, ethical ideology, legal ideology, political ideology, etc., so many "world outlooks." Of course, assuming that we do not live one of these ideologies as the truth (e.g., "believe" in God, Duty, Justice, etc. . . .), we admit that the ideology we are discussing from a critical point of view, examining it as the ethnologist examines the myths of a "primitive society," that these "world outlooks" are largely imaginary, i.e., do not "correspond to reality."

However, while admitting that they do not correspond to reality, i.e. that they constitute an illusion, we admit that they do make allusion to reality, and that they need only be "interpreted" to discover the reality of the world behind their imaginary representation of that world (ideology = *illusion/allusion*).

There are different types of interpretation, the most famous of which are the *mechanistic* type, current in the eighteenth century (God is the imaginary representation of the real King), and the *"hermeneutic"* interpretation, inaugurated by the earliest church Fathers, and revived by Feuerbach and the theologico-philosophical school which descends from him, e.g., the theologian Barth (to Feuerbach, for example, God is the essence of real Man). The essential point is that on condition that we interpret the imaginary transposition (and inversion) of ideology we arrive at the conclusion that in ideology "men represent their real conditions of existence to themselves in an imaginary form."

Unfortunately, this interpretation leaves one small problem unsettled: why do men "need" this imaginary transposition of their real conditions of existence in order to "represent to themselves" their real conditions of existence?

The first answer (that of the eighteenth century) proposes a simple solution: Priests or Despots are responsible. They "forged" the Beautiful Lies so that, in the belief that they were obeying God, men would in fact obey the Priests and Despots, who are usually in alliance in their imposture, the Priests acting in the interests of the Despots or *vice versa,* according to the political positions of the "theoreticians" concerned. There is therefore a cause for the imaginary transposition of the real conditions of existence: that cause is the existence of a small number of cynical men who base their domination and exploitation of the "people" on a falsified representation of the world which they have imagined in order to enslave other minds by dominating their imaginations.

The second answer (that of Feuerbach, taken over word for word by Marx in his Early Works) is more "profound," i.e. just as false. It, too, seeks and finds a cause for the imaginary transposition and distortion of men's real conditions of existence, in short, for the alienation in the imaginary of the representation of men's conditions of existence. This cause is no longer Priests or Despots, nor their active imagination and the passive imagination of their victims. This cause is the material alienation which reigns in the conditions of existence of men themselves. This is how, in *The Jewish Question* and elsewhere, Marx defends the Feuerbachian idea that men make themselves an alienated (= imaginary) representation of their conditions of existence because these conditions of existence are themselves alienating (in the *1844 Manuscripts*: because these conditions are dominated by the essence of alienated society—*alienated labour*).

All these interpretations thus take literally the thesis which they presuppose, and on which they depend, i.e. that what is reflected in the imaginary representation of the world found in an ideology is the conditions of existence of men, i.e. their real world.

Now I can return to a thesis which I have already advanced: it is not their real conditions of existence, their real world, that "men" "represent to themselves" in ideology, but above all it is their relation to those conditions of existence which is represented to them there. It is this relation which is at the centre of every ideological, i.e. imaginary, representation of the real world. It is this relation that contains the "cause" which has to explain the imaginary distortion of the ideological representation of the real world. Or rather, to leave aside the language of causality it is necessary to advance the thesis that it is the *imaginary nature of this relation* which underlies all the imaginary distortion that we can observe (if we do not live in its truth) in all ideology.

To speak in a Marxist language, if it is true that the representation of the real conditions of existence of the individuals occupying the posts of agents of production, exploitation, repression, ideologization, and scientific practice, does in the last analysis arise from the relations of production, and from relations deriving from the relations of production, we can say the following: all ideology, represents in its necessarily imaginary distortion not the existing relations of production (and the other relations that derive from them), but above all the (imaginary) relationship of individuals to the relations of production and the relations that derive from them. What is represented in ideology is therefore not the system of the real relations which govern the existence of individuals, but the imaginary relation of those individuals to the real relations in which they live.

If this is the case, the question of the "cause" of the imaginary distortion of the real relations in ideology disappears and must be replaced by a different question: why is the representation given to individuals of their (individual) relation to the social relations which govern their conditions of existence and their collective and individual life necessarily an imaginary relation? And what is the nature of this imaginariness? Posed in this way, the question explodes the solution by a "clique,"[8] by a group of individuals (Priests or Despots) who are the authors of the great ideological mystification, just as it explodes the solution by the alienated character of the real world. We shall see why later in my exposition. For the moment I shall go no further.

I can now come to my central thesis.

Ideology Interpellates Individuals as Subjects

This thesis is simply a matter of making my last proposition explicit: there is no ideology except by the subject and for subjects. Meaning, there is no ideology except for concrete subjects, and this destination for ideology is only made possible by the subject: meaning, *by the category of the subject* and its functioning.

By this I mean that, even if it only appears under this name (the subject) with the rise of bourgeois ideology, above all with the rise of legal ideology,[9] the category of the subject (which may function under other names: e.g., as the soul in Plato, as God, etc.) is the constitutive category of all ideology, whatever its determination (regional or class) and whatever its historical date—since ideology has no history.

I say: the category of the subject is constitutive of all ideology, but at the same time and immediately I add that *the category of the subject is only constitutive of all ideology insofar as all ideology has the function (which defines it) of "constituting" concrete individuals as subjects.* In the interaction of this double constitution exists the functioning of all ideology, ideology being nothing but its functioning in the material forms of existence of that functioning.

In order to grasp what follows, it is essential to realize that both he who is writing these lines and the reader who reads them are themselves subjects, and therefore ideological subjects (a tautological proposition), i.e. that the author and the reader of these lines both live "spontaneously" or "naturally" in ideology in the sense in which I have said that "man is an ideological animal by nature."

That the author, insofar as he writes the lines of a discourse which claims to be scientific, is completely absent as a "subject" from "his" scientific discourse (for all scientific discourse is by definition a subject-less discourse, there is no "Subject of science" except in an ideology of science) is a different question which I shall leave on one side for the moment.

As St. Paul admirably put it, it is in the "Logos," meaning in ideology, that we "live, move and have our being." It follows that, for you and for me, the category of the subject is a primary "obviousness" (obviousnesses are always primary): it is clear that you and I are subjects (free, ethical, etc. . . . .). Like all obviousnesses, including those that make a word "name a thing" or "have a meaning" (therefore including the obviousness of the "transparency" of language), the "obviousness" that you and I are subjects—and that that does not cause any problems—is an ideological effect, the elementary ideological effect.[10] It is indeed a peculiarity of ideology that it imposes (without appearing to do so, since these are "obviousnesses") obviousnesses as obviousnesses, which we cannot *fail to recognize* and before which we have the inevitable and natural reaction of crying out (aloud or in the "still, small voice of conscience"): "That's obvious! That's right! That's true!"

At work in this reaction is the ideological *recognition* function which is one of the two functions of ideology as such (its inverse being the function of *misrecognition—méconnaissance*).

To take a highly "concrete" example, we all have friends who, when they knock on our door and we ask, through the door, the question "Who's there?," answer (since "it's obvious") "It's me." And we recognize that "it is him," or "her." We open the door, and it's true, it really was she who was there. To take another example, when we recognize somebody of our (previous) acquaintance *((re)-connaissance)* in the street, we show him that we have recognized him (and have recognized that he has recognized us) by saying to him "Hello, my friend," and shaking his hand (a material ritual practice of ideological recognition in everyday life—in France, at least; elsewhere, there are other rituals).

In this preliminary remark and these concrete illustrations, I only wish to point out that you and I are *always already* subjects, and as such constantly practice the rituals of ideological recognition, which guarantee for us that we are indeed concrete, individual, distinguishable and (naturally) irreplaceable subjects. The writing I am currently executing and the reading you are currently[11] performing are also in this respect rituals of ideological recognition, including the "obviousness" with which the "truth" or "error" of my reflections may impose itself on you.

But to recognize that we are subjects and that we function in the practical rituals of the most elementary everyday life (the hand-shake, the fact of calling you by your name, the fact of knowing, even if I do not know what it is, that you "have" a name of your own, which means that you are recognized as a unique subject, etc.)—this recognition only gives us the "consciousness" of our incessant (eternal) practice of ideological recognition—its consciousness, i.e. its *recognition*—but in no sense does it give us the (scientific) *knowledge* of the mechanism of this recognition. Now it is this knowledge that we have to reach, if you will, while speaking in ideology, and from within ideology we have to outline a discourse which tries to break with ideology, in order to dare to be the beginning of a scientific (i.e. subjectless) discourse on ideology.

Thus in order to represent why the category of the "subject" is constitutive of ideology, which only exists by constituting concrete subjects as subjects, I shall employ a special mode of exposition: "concrete" enough to be recognized, but abstract enough to be thinkable and thought, giving rise to a knowledge.

As a first formulation I shall say: *all ideology hails or interpellates concrete individuals as concrete subjects,* by the functioning of the category of the subject.

This is a proposition which entails that we distinguish for the moment between concrete individuals on the one hand and concrete subjects on the other, although at this level concrete subjects only exist insofar as they are supported by a concrete individual.

I shall then suggest that ideology "acts" or "functions" in such a way that it "recruits" subjects among the individuals (it recruits them all), or "transforms" the individuals into subjects (it transforms them all) by that very precise operation which I have called *interpellation* or hailing, and which can be imagined along the lines of the most commonplace everyday police (or other) hailing: "Hey, you there!"[12]

Assuming that the theoretical scene I have imagined takes place in the street, the hailed individual will turn round. By this mere one-hundred-and-eighty-degree physical conversion, he becomes a *subject*. Why? Because he has recognized that the hail was "really" addressed to him, and that "it was *really him* who was hailed" (and not someone else). Experience shows that the practical telecommunication of hailings is such that they hardly ever miss their man: verbal call or whistle, the one hailed always recognizes that it is really him who is being hailed. And yet it is a strange phenomenon, and one which cannot be explained solely by "guilt feelings," despite the large numbers who "have something on their consciences."

Naturally for the convenience and clarity of my little theoretical theatre I have had to present things in the form of a sequence, with a before and an after, and thus in the form of a temporal succession. There are individuals walking along. Somewhere (usually behind them) the hail rings out: "Hey, you there!" One individual (nine times out of ten it is the right one) turns round, believing/suspecting/knowing that it is for him, i.e. recognizing that "it really is he" who is meant by the hailing. But in reality these things happen without any succession. The existence of ideology and the hailing or interpellation of individuals as subjects are one and the same thing.

I might add: what thus seems to take place outside ideology (to be precise, in the street), in reality takes place in ideology. What really takes place in ideology seems therefore to take place outside it. That is why those who are in ideology believe themselves by definition outside ideology: one of the effects of ideology is the practical *denegation* of the ideological character of ideology by ideology: ideology never says, "I am ideological." It is necessary to be outside ideology, i.e. in scientific knowledge, to be able to say: I am in ideology (a quite exceptional case) or (the general case): I was in ideology. As is well known, the accusation of being in ideology only applies to others, never to oneself (unless one is really a Spinozist or a Marxist, which, in this matter, is to be exactly the same thing). Which amounts to saying that ideology *has no outside* (for itself), but at the same time *that it is nothing but outside* (for science and reality).

Spinoza explained this completely two centuries before Marx, who practiced it but without explaining it in detail. But let us leave this point, although it is heavy with consequences, consequences which are not just theoretical, but also directly political, since, for example, the whole theory of criticism and self-criticism, the golden rule of the Marxist-Leninist practice of the class struggle, depends on it.

Thus ideology hails or interpellates individuals as subjects. As ideology is eternal, I must now suppress the temporal form in which I have presented the functioning of ideology, and say: ideology has always-already interpellated individuals as subjects, which amounts to making it clear that individuals are always-already interpellated by ideology as subjects, which necessarily leads us to one last proposition: *individuals are always-already subjects.* Hence individuals are "abstract" with respect to the subjects which they always-already are. This proposition might seem paradoxical.

That an individual is always-already a subject, even before he is born, is nevertheless the plain reality, accessible to everyone and not a paradox at all. Freud shows that individuals are always "abstract" with respect to the subjects they always-already are, simply by noting the ideological ritual that surrounds the expectation of a "birth," that "happy event." Everyone knows how much and in what way an unborn child is expected. Which amounts to saying, very prosaically, if we agree to drop the "sentiments," i.e. the forms of family ideology (paternal/maternal/conjugal/fraternal) in which the unborn child is expected: it is certain in advance that it will bear its Father's Name, and will therefore have an identity and be irreplaceable. Before its birth, the child is therefore always-already a subject, appointed as a subject in and by the specific familial ideological configuration in which it is "expected" once it has been conceived. I hardly need add that this familial ideological configuration is, in its uniqueness, highly structured, and that it is in this implacable and more or less "pathological" (presupposing that any meaning can be assigned to that term) structure that the former subject-to-be will have to "find" "its" place, i.e., "become" the sexual subject (boy or girl) which it already is in advance. It is clear that this ideological constraint and preappointment, and all the rituals of rearing and then education in the family, have some relationship with what Freud studied in the forms of the pre-genital and genital "stages" of sexuality, i.e., in the "grip" of what Freud registered by its effects as being the unconscious. But let us leave this point, too, on one side.

Let me go one step further. What I shall now turn my attention to is the way the "actors" in this *mise en scène* of interpellation, and their respective roles, are reflected in the very structure of all ideology.

Notes

1. This text is made up of two extracts from an ongoing study. The sub-title "Notes toward an Investigation" is the author's own. The ideas expounded should not be regarded as more than the introduction to a discussion.

2. Marx to Kugelmann, 11 July 1868, *Selected Correspondence,* Moscow, 1955, p. 209.

3. Marx gave it its scientific concept: *variable capital.*

4. To my knowledge, Gramsci is the only one who went any distance in the road I am taking. He had the "remarkable" idea that the State could not be reduced to the (Repressive) State Apparatus, but included, as he put it, a certain number of institutions from *"civil society"*: the Church, the Schools, the trade unions, etc. Unfortunately, Gramsci did not systematize his institutions, which remained in the state of acute but fragmentary notes (cf. Gramsci, *Selections from the Prison Notebooks,* International Publishers, 1971, pp. 12, 259, 260–3); see also the letter to Tatiana Schucht, 7 September 1931, in *Lettre del Carcere,* Einaudi, 1968, p. 479. English-language translation in preparation.

5. The family obviously has other "functions" than that of an ISA. It intervenes in the reproduction of labour power. In different modes of production it is the unit of production and/or the unit of consumption.

6. The "Law" belongs both to the (Repressive) State Apparatus and to the system of the ISAs.

7. In a pathetic text written in 1937, Krupskaya relates the history of Lenin's desperate efforts and what she regards as his failure.

8. I use this very modern term deliberately. For even in Communist circles, unfortunately, it is a commonplace to "explain" some political deviation (left or right opportunism) by the action of a "clique."

9. Which borrowed the legal category of "subject in law" to make an ideological notion: man is by nature a subject.

10. Linguists and those who appeal to linguistics for various purposes often run up against difficulties which arise because they ignore the action of the ideological effects in all discourses—including even scientific discourses.

11. NB: this double "currently" is one more proof of the fact that ideology is "eternal," since these two "currentlys" are separated by an indefinite interval; I am writing these lines on 6 April 1969, you may read them at any subsequent time.

12. Hailing as an everyday practice subject to a precise ritual takes a quite "special" form in the policeman's practice of "hailing" which concerns the hailing of "suspects."

6

The Meritocracy Myth

Stephen J. McNamee and Robert K. Miller, Jr.

According to the ideology of the American Dream, America is the land of limitless opportunity in which individuals can go as far as their own merit takes them. According to this ideology, you get out of the system what you put into it. Getting ahead is ostensibly based on individual merit, which is generally viewed as a combination of factors including innate abilities, working hard, having the right attitude, and having high moral character and integrity. Americans not only tend to think that is how the system should work, but most Americans also think that is how the system does work (Huber and Form 1973, Kluegel and Smith 1986, Ladd 1994).

In our book *The Meritocracy Myth* (Rowman & Littlefield, 2004), <http://www.rowmanlittlefield.com/isbn/0742510565>, we challenge the validity of these commonly held assertions, by arguing that there is a gap between how people think the system works and how the system actually does work. We refer to this gap as "the meritocracy myth," or the myth that the system distributes resources—especially wealth and income—according to the merit of individuals. We challenge this assertion in two ways. First, we suggest that while merit does indeed affect who ends up with what, the impact of merit on economic outcomes is vastly overestimated by the ideology of the American Dream. Second, we identify a variety of nonmerit factors that suppress, neutralize, or even negate the effects of merit and create barriers to individual mobility. We summarize these arguments below. First, however, we take a brief look at what is at stake. That is, what is up for grabs in the race to get ahead?

There are a variety of ways to depict America's unequal distributions of income and wealth. Income refers to how much one earns and wealth refers to how much one owns. Although Americans tend to think of income as coming from wages and salaries, there are actually two sources of income. In addition to income from wages and salaries, income also includes sources of revenue that are unrelated to jobs, such as income from capital gains, dividends, interest payments, and some forms of government aid ("welfare" including food stamps and the like). In some cases, these sources of income are related to prior but not current employment (e.g. social security payments, pensions). Wealth does not refer to a revenue stream, but to assets that one owns such as houses, cars, personal belongings, businesses, nonresidential real estate, stocks and bonds, trusts, and other financial assets. These

Reprinted by permission from *Sociation Today,* spring 2004.

TABLE 1. SHARE OF TOTAL AVAILABLE HOUSEHOLD INCOME, 2002*

Income Group	Share of Income
Top Fifth	49.7%
Second Fifth	23.3%
Third Fifth	14.8%
Fourth Fifth	8.8%
Bottom Fifth	3.5%
Total	100.0%
Top 5 Percent	21.7%

*Source: DeNavas-Walt et al. 2003. See U.S. Current Population Reports for details.

TABLE 2. SHARE OF TOTAL AVAILABLE HOUSEHOLD NET WORTH, 2001*

Wealth Group	Share of Net Worth
99–100th percentile	32.7%
95–99th percentile	25.0%
90–95th percentile	12.1%
50th–90th percentile	27.1%
0–50th percentile	2.8%
Total	100.0%

*Source: Kennickell, 2003. See data from the Federal Reserve Board for details.

assets can further be distinguished between those that tend to depreciate in value (e.g. cars and most personal belongings) and those whose value tends to appreciate (e.g. business, real estate, stocks, etc.). In general, the more wealth one has, the more likely that wealth derives from sources of ownership that tend to appreciate in value. Net worth refers to the difference between assets (what one owns) and liabilities (what one owes). Net worth is an accurate measure of what one is really "worth." Table 1 depicts the distributions of income and Table 2 depicts distributions of net worth.

These tables show that the distributions of income and especially wealth are highly skewed. The top 20 percent of American households, for instance, receive a large portion of the total amount of available income (49.7%) while the lowest 20 percent of American households receive a much smaller portion of available income (3.5%). The top 5% percent of households alone receive 21.7 percent of all available income. The distribution of wealth measured by net worth is even more highly skewed. The richest 1% of households (99th–100th percentile) account for nearly a third of all available net worth while the bottom half of households (0–50th percentile) account for only 2.8% of all available net worth. In other words, the American distributions of income and wealth are "top heavy" (Wolff 2002) and represent a level of economic inequality that is the highest among industrial countries of the world.

These distributions are relevant to the myth of meritocracy in several ways. First, despite the widely held perception that America is a "middle class" society, most of the money is highly concentrated at the top of the system. Second, many of the arguments suggesting that "merit" is behind the distribution of income and wealth also make the case that merit is distributed "normally" in the population. That is, that the shape of the distribution of merit resembles a "bell curve" with small numbers of incompetent people at the lower end, most people of average abilities in the middle and small numbers of talented people at the upper end. The highly skewed distribution of economic outcomes, however, appears quite in excess of any reasonable distribution of merit. Something that is distributed "normally" cannot be the direct and proportional cause of something with such skewed distributions. There has to be more to the story than that.

On Being Made of the Right Stuff

When factors associated with individual "merit" are related to income and wealth, it turns out that these factors are often not as uniquely individual or as influential as many presume. Most experts point out, for instance, that "intelligence," as measured by IQ tests, is partially a reflection of inherent intellectual capacity and partially a reflection of environmental influences. It is the combination of capacity and experience that determines "intelligence." Even allowing for this "environmental" caveat, IQ scores only account for about 10% of the variance in income differences among individuals (Fisher et al. 1996). Since wealth is less tied to achievement than income, the amount of influence of intelligence on wealth is much less. Other purportedly innate "talents" cannot be separated from experience, since any "talent" must be displayed to be recognized and labeled as such (Chambliss 1989). There is no way to determine for certain, for instance, how many potential world-class violinists there are in the general population but who have never once picked up a violin. Such "talents" do not spontaneously erupt but must be identified and cultivated.

Applying talents is also necessary. Working hard is often seen in this context as part of the merit formula. Heads nod in acknowledgment whenever hard work is mentioned in conjunction with economic success. Rarely is this assumption questioned. But what exactly do we mean by hard work? Does it mean the number of hours expended in the effort to achieve a goal? Does it mean the amount of energy or sheer physical exertion expended in the completion of tasks? Neither of these measures of "hard" work is directly associated with economic success. In fact, those who work the most hours and expend the most effort (at least physically) are often the most poorly paid in society. By contrast, the really big money in America comes not from working at all but from owning, which requires no expenditure of effort, either physical or mental. In short, working hard is not in and of itself directly related to the amount of income and wealth that individuals have.

What about attitudes? Again, the story here is mixed. First, it is not clear which particular mix of attitudes, outlooks, or frames of mind are associated with economic success. The kind of mental outlook that would be an advantage in one field of endeavor, may be a disadvantage in another field of endeavor. A different set of "proper attitudes," for instance, may be associated with being a successful artist than being a successful accountant. Second, the direction of influence is not always clear. That is, are certain attitudes a "cause" of success or are certain attitudes the "effect" of success?

An example of the difficulty in discerning the impact and direction of these influences is reflected in the "culture of poverty" debate. According to the culture of poverty argument, people are poor because of deviant or pathological values that are then passed on from one generation to the next, creating a "vicious cycle of poverty." According to this perspective, poor people are viewed as anti-work, anti-family, anti-school, and anti-success. Recent evidence reported in this journal (Wynn, 2003) and elsewhere (Barnes, 2002; Gould, 1999; Wilson, 1996), however, indicates that poor people appear to value work, family, school, and achievement as much as other Americans. Instead of having "deviant" or "pathological" values, the evidence suggests that poor people adjust their ambitions and outlooks according to realistic assessments of their more limited life chances.

An example of such an adjustment is the supposed "present-orientation" of the poor. According to the culture of poverty theory, poor people are "present-oriented" and are unable to "defer gratification." Present orientation may encourage young adults to drop out of school to take low wage jobs instead staying in school to increase future earning potential. However, the present orientation of the poor can be an "effect" of poverty rather than a "cause." That is, if you are desperately poor, you may be forced to be present oriented. If you do not know where your next meal is coming from, you essentially have no choice but to be focused on immediate needs first and foremost. By contrast, the rich and middle class can "afford" to be more future oriented since their immediate needs are secure. Similarly, the poor may report more modest ambitions than the affluent, not because they are unmotivated, but because of a realistic assessment of limited life chances. In this sense, observed differences in outlooks between the poor and the more affluent are more likely a reflection of fundamentally different life circumstances than fundamentally different attitudes or values.

Finally, we challenge the idea that moral character and integrity are important contributors to economic success. Although "honesty may be the best policy" in terms of how one should conduct oneself in relations with others, there is little evidence that the economically successful are more honest than the less successful. The recent spate of alleged corporate ethics scandals at such corporations as Enron, WorldCom, Arthur Andersen, Adelphia, Bristol-Myers Squibb, Duke Energy, Global Crossing, Xerox as well as recent allegations of misconduct in the vast mutual funds industry reveal how corporate executives often enrich themselves through less than honest means. White-collar crime in the form of insider trading, embezzlement, tax fraud, insurance fraud and the like is hardly evidence of honesty and virtue in practice. And neither is the extensive and sometimes highly lucrative so-called "irregular" or "under the table" economy—much of it related to vice in the form of drug trafficking, gambling, pornography, loan sharking, or smuggling. Clearly, wealth alone is not a reflection of moral superiority. To get ahead in America, it no doubt helps to be bright, shrewd, to work hard, and to have the right combination of attitudes that maximize success within given fields of endeavor. Playing by the rules, however, probably works to suppress prospects for economic success since those who play by the rules are more restricted in their opportunities to attain wealth and income than those who choose to ignore the rules.

Nonmerit Barriers to Mobility

There are a variety of social forces that tend to suppress, neutralize, or even negate the effects of merit in the race to get ahead. We might collectively refer to these forces as "social gravity." These forces tend to keep people in the places they already occupy, regardless of the extent of their individual merit.

First and foremost among these nonmerit factors is the effect of inheritance, broadly defined as the effects of initial class placement at birth on future life chances. Inheritance is not just bulk estates that are transferred upon the death of parents. Inheritance refers more broadly to unequal starting points in the race to get ahead. The race to get ahead is like a relay race in which we inherit an initial starting point from parents. For a while, we run alongside our parents as the baton is passed, and then we take off on our own. In this relay race, those born into great wealth start far ahead of those born to poor parents, who have a huge deficit to overcome if they are to catch up. Indeed, of all the factors that we might consider, where we start out in life has the greatest effect on where we end up. In the race to get ahead, the effects of inheritance come first and merit second, not the other way around.

Inheritance provides numerous cumulative nonmerit advantages that are available in varying degrees to all those born into at least some relative advantage, excluding only those at the very bottom of the system. Included among these nonmerit advantages are high standards of living from birth, inter vivos gifts (gifts between the living) such as infusions of cash and property bestowed by parents on their children at critical junctures in the life course (going to college, getting married, buying a home, having children, starting a business, etc.), insulation from downward mobility (family safety nets which prevent children from skidding in times of personal crises, setbacks, or as the result of personal failures), access to educational opportunities as well as other opportunities to acquire personal merit or to have merit identified and cultivated, better health care and consequently longer and healthier lives (which increases earning power and the ability to accumulate assets during the life course).

Another advantage of inheritance is access to high-powered forms of social and cultural capital. Social capital is one's "social resources" and refers essentially to the value of whom you know. Cultural capital is one's cultural resources and refers essentially to the social value of what you know. Everyone has friends, but those born into privilege have friends in high places with resources and power. Everyone possesses culture—bodies of knowledge and information needed to navigate through social space. Full acceptance into the highest social circles, however, requires knowledge of the ways of life of a particular group, a kind of "savoir faire" that includes expected demeanor, manners, and comportment associated with the upper class. Those born into these high powered circles are trained from an early age in the cultural ways of the group, which allows them to travel comfortably in these circles and to "fit in." Outsiders who aspire to become part of these high-powered circles must learn these cultural ways of life from the outside in a more difficult and daunting task that continually carries the risk of being exposed as an imposter or pretender.

Besides the nonmerit effects of inheritance, just plain bad luck can suppress the effects of merit. Bad luck can take many forms but two very common forms of bad luck are to be laid off from a job that you are good at or to spend many years preparing for a job for which demand either never materializes or declines. In looking at jobs and job opportunities, Americans tend to focus on the "supply" side of markets for labor; that is, the pool of available people in the labor force. Much less attention is paid to the "demand" side, or the number and types of jobs available. In the race to get ahead, it is possible and all too common for meritorious individuals to be "all dressed up with no place to go." For the past twenty years, the "growth" jobs in America have disproportionately been in the low wage service sector of the economy. At the same time, more Americans are getting more education, especially higher education. Simply put, these trends are running in opposite directions: the economy is not producing as many high-powered jobs as the society is producing highly qualified people to fill them (Collins 1979, Livingstone 1998).

In addition to the number and types of jobs available, the locations of jobs both geographically and within different sectors of the economy also represent non-merit factors in the prospects for employment. For instance, a janitor who works for a large corporation in New York City may get paid much more for doing essentially the same job as a janitor who works for a small family business in a small town in Mississippi. These effects are independent of the demands of the jobs or the qualifications or merit of the individuals holding them. Differences in benefits and wages between such jobs are often substantial and may mean the difference between a secure existence and poverty.

If poverty were exclusively due to individual differences, we would expect rates of poverty to be randomly distributed throughout the country. Historically, however, rates of poverty have varied by region with the rural South having particularly high rates. These differences have been reduced in recent decades as Northern and Midwest states in the so-called "rust belt" have experienced plant closings and "deindustrialization" while Southern and Southwest states in the so-called "sun belt" have experienced greater economic diversity and development. Despite these trends, research recently reported in this journal (Wimberley and Morris, 2003) shows that rates of poverty in the United States continue to vary by region and locations within regions suggesting that geography is still a major factor in the distribution of economic opportunity.

Education is another factor widely seen as responsible for where people end up in the system. The role of education in getting ahead in America, however, is not as simple as is often assumed. On the one hand, those with more education, on average, have higher income and wealth. Education is thus often seen as the primary means of upward social mobility. In this context, education is widely perceived as a gatekeeper institution which sifts and sorts individuals according to individual merit. Grades, credits, diplomas, degrees, and certificates are clearly "earned," not purchased or appropriated. But, as much research has demonstrated, educational opportunity is not equally distributed in the population (Bowles and Gintis 1976, 2002, Bourdieu and Passeron 1990, Aschaffenburg and Maas 1997, Kozol 1991, Sacks 2003, Ballantine 2001). Upper class children tend to get upper class educations (e.g. at elite private prep schools and ivy league colleges), middle class children tend to get middle class educations (e.g. at public schools and public universities), and working class people tend to get working class educations (e.g. public schools and technical or community colleges), and poor people tend to get poor educations (e.g. inner city schools that have high drop out rates and usually no higher education). Educational attainment clearly depends on family economic standing and is not simply a major independent cause of it. The quality of schools and the quality of educational opportunity vary according to where one lives, and where one lives depends on familial economic resources and race. Most public schools, for instance, are supported by local property taxes. The tax base is higher in wealthy communities and proportionally lower in poorer areas. These discrepancies give rise to the perpetual parental scramble to locate in communities and neighborhoods that have reputations for "good schools," since parents want to provide every possible advantage to their children that they can afford. To the extent that parents are actually successful in passing on such advantages, educational attainment is primarily a reflection of family income. In sum, it is important to recognize that individual achievement occurs within a context of unequal educational opportunity.

Besides education, self-employment is popularly perceived as a major route to upward mobility. Opportunities to get ahead on the basis of being self-employed or striking out on one's own to start a new business, however, have sharply declined. In colonial times, about three fourths of the non-slave American population was self-employed most as small family farmers. Today, only seven percent of the labor force is self employed (U.S. Census Bureau 2002). The "family farm," in particular, is on the brink of statistical extinction. As self-employment has declined, the size and dominance of corporations has increased. This leaves many fewer opportunities for "self-made" individuals to enter existing markets or to establish new ones. America has witnessed the sharp decline of "mom and pop" stores, restaurants, and retail shops and the concomitant rise of Wal-Marts, Holiday Inns, and McDonalds. As more Americans work for someone else in increasingly bureaucratized settings, the prospects of rapid "rags to riches" mobility decline.

In addition to the decline of self-employment, manufacturing has also experienced drastic workforce reduction as production facilities have increasingly moved to foreign countries in efforts to reduce costs of production. This is a significant trend since the United States became a world power based on its industrial strength, which supported a large and relatively prosperous working and middle class. Some service jobs, such as customer service and computer programming, are also being moved to foreign countries in increasing numbers. All of these trends are occurring quite independent of the merit of individuals but nevertheless profoundly impact the opportunities of individuals to get ahead.

The most obvious and widely recognized nonmerit barrier to achievement is discrimination. Discrimination not only suppresses merit; it is the antithesis of merit. Race and sex discrimination have been the most pervasive forms of discrimination in America. The good news is that such discrimination is declining. The bad news is that these forms of discrimination are down but not out. Besides ongoing discrimination, there are still inertial effects of past discrimination that create disadvantage in the present. The divisive debate over affirmative action in America highlights the continuing disagreements about the size and importance of these residual effects and how to best address them.

Most Americans agree that race and sex discrimination are wrong and that a "level playing field" should be established. Indeed, it is often assumed that we would have true equality of opportunity in American if only these forms of discrimination were eliminated. This position is naïve, however, because it overlooks the effects of other nonmerit factors identified here (especially inheritance). Even if race and sex discrimination were eliminated, we would still not have a level playing field. This position also overlooks other forms of discrimination that, while less pervasive in America, nevertheless suppress or neutralize the affects of merit: discrimination on the basis of sexual orientation, religion, age, physical disability (unrelated to job performance), physical appearance, and region (discrimination against Southerners and preference for Yankees). That these forms of discrimination affect fewer people than sex and race discrimination is little comfort to those who are victimized by it. For them, the effective rate of discrimination is 100 percent.

Some of these forms of discrimination are not well-recognized or generally acknowledged. "Lookism," for instance, is a subtle form of discrimination in which attractive people get numerous nonmerit advantages over less attractive people (e.g., more attention, more help, more recognition and credit for accomplishments, more positive evaluation of performance and the like) (Etcoff 1999). These nonmerit advantages have profound and independent effects on life chances and individual merit.

What Now?

In *The Meritocracy Myth,* we do not suggest that "merit" is a myth. Rather, we argue that meritocracy, the idea that societal resources are distributed exclusively or primarily on the basis of individual merit, is a myth. It is a myth because of the combined effects of nonmerit factors such as inheritance, social and cultural advantages, unequal educational opportunity, luck and the changing structure of job opportunities, the decline of self-employment, and discrimination in all of its forms. If meritocracy is a myth, how can the system be made to operate more closely according to meritocratic principles that Americans so uniformly endorse?

We suggest four ways in which American society could be made more genuinely meritocratic.

1. Current forms of discrimination could be reduced or eliminated.

2. The wealthy could be encouraged to redistribute greater amounts of their accumulated wealth through philanthropy in ways that would provide greater opportunity for the less privileged.

3. The tax system could be redesigned to be genuinely progressive in ways that would close the distance between those at the top and the bottom of the system.

4. More government resources could be allocated to provide more equal access to critical services such as education and health care.

All of these measures would reduce the overall extent of inequality in society and at the same time allow individual merit to have a greater effect on economic outcomes. Such fundamental change in the distribution of societal resources and opportunity, however, are predicated on the assumption that these goals would be widely seen as both desirable and politically feasible.

It is generally acknowledged that a pure meritocracy is probably impossible to achieve. What is less generally acknowledged is that such a system may not be entirely desirable. The limits and dangers of a system operating purely on the basis of merit were dramatically portrayed in *The Rise of the Meritocracy* (1961), a novel by British sociologist Michael Young. Young envisioned a society in which those at the top of the system ruled autocratically with a sense of righteous entitlement while those at the bottom of the system were incapable of protecting themselves against the abuses leveled against them from the merit elite above. Instead of a fair and enlightened society, the meritocracy became cruel and ruthless.

One possible advantage of a nonmeritocratic society is that at any point in time there are, for whatever combination of reasons, at least some of those at the top of the system who are less capable and competent than at least some of those at the bottom. Such discrepancies should render humility for those at the top and hope and dignity for those at the bottom. But this can only happen if it is widely acknowledged that inheritance, luck, and a variety of other circumstances beyond the control of individuals are important in affecting where one ends up in the system. While meritocracy may be neither possible nor even desirable, we argue that the myth of meritocracy is itself harmful because by discounting the most important causes of inequality, it leads to unwarranted exaltation of the rich and unwarranted condemnation of the poor. We may always have the rich and poor among us, but we need neither exalt the former nor condemn the latter.

References

Aschaffenburg, Karen, and Ineke Maas. 1997. "Cultural and Educational Careers: The Dynamics of Social Reproduction." *American Sociological Review* 62: 573–87.

Ballantine, Jeanne H. 2001. *The Sociology of Education*. Upper Saddle River, NJ: Prentice Hall.

Barnes, Sandra L. 2002. "Achievement or Ascription Ideology? An Analysis of Attitudes about Future Success for Residents in Poor Urban Neighborhoods." *Sociological Focus*. 35:207–25.

Bourdieu, Pierre, and Jean-Claude Passeron. 1990. *Reproduction in Education, Society, and Culture*. London: Sage.

Bowles, Samuel, and Herbert Gintis. 1976. *Schooling in Capitalist America*. NY: Basic Books.

———. 2002. "Schooling in Capitalist America Revisited." *Sociology of Education* 75: 1–18.

Chambliss, William. 1989. "The Mundanity of Excellence." *Sociological Theory* 7:70–86.

Collins, Randall. 1979. *The Credential Society*. NY: Academic Press.

DeNavas-Walt, Carmen, Robert Cleveland, and Bruce H. Webster, Jr. 2003. "Income In the United States, 2002" in *Current Population Reports*, U.S. Census Bureau, P60–221. Washington, D.C.: U.S. Government Printing Office.

Etcoff, Nancy. 1999. *Survival of the Prettiest: The Science of Beauty*. NY: Doubleday.

Fischer, Claude S., Michael Hout, Martin Sanchez Jankowski, Samuel R. Lucas, Ann Swidler, and Kim Voss. 1996. *Inequality by Design: Cracking the Bell Curve Myth*. Princeton, NJ: Princeton University Press.

Gould, Mark, 1999. "Race and Theory: Adaptation to Discrimination." In *Sociological Theory*. Wilson and Ogbu, eds. 17:171–20.

Huber, Joan, and William Form. 1973. *Income and Ideology: An Analysis of the American Political Formula*. NY: Free Press.

Kennickell, Arthur B. 2003. *A Rolling Tide: Changes in the Distribution of Wealth in the U.S. 1989–2001*. Washington, D.C.: Federal Reserve Board.

Kluegel, James R., and Eliot R. Smith. 1986. *Beliefs about Inequality: Americans' Views of What Is and What Ought to Be*. NY: de Gruyter.

Kozol, Jonathan. 1991. *Savage Inequalities: Children in America's Schools*. NY: Harper-Perennial.

Ladd, Everett Carll. 1994. *The American Ideology*. Storrs, CT: The Roper Center for Public Opinion Research.

Livingstone, D. W. 1998. *The Education-Jobs Gap: Underemployment or Economic Democracy*. Boulder, CO: Westview.

McNamee, Stephen J. and Robert K. Miller, Jr. 2004. *The Meritocracy Myth*. Lanham, MD: Rowman & Littlefield.

Sacks, Peter. 2003. "Class Rules: The Fiction of Egalitarian Higher Education." *The Chronicle of Higher Education* 49 (July 25): B7–10.

U.S. Department of Labor. 2002. "Self Employed in 2000." *Monthly Labor Review*. January 28, 2002.

Wilson, William Julius. 1996. *When Work Disappears: The World of the New Urban Poor.* New York: Knopf.

Wimberley, Ronald C. and Libby V. Morris. *U.S. Poverty in Space and Time: Its Persistence in the South. Sociation Today.* Volume 1, Number 2, Fall 2003.

Wolff, Edward N. 2002. *Top Heavy: The Increasing Inequality of Wealth in America and What Can Be Done About It.* NY: The New Press.

Wynn, Lyndelia Burch. 2003. *The Attitude of AFDC Recipients Towards Work. Sociation Today.* Volume 1, Number 2, Fall 2003.

Young, Michael. 1961. *The Rise of the Meritocracy, 1870–2033: An Essay on Education and Equality.* Baltimore, MD: Penguin Books.

7

The Social Network:
The Contemporary Pursuit of Happiness through Social Connections

Robert Alpert

"We hold these truths to be self-evident, that all men are created equal, that they are endowed by their Creator with certain unalienable rights, that among these are life, liberty and the pursuit of happiness."
— United States *Declaration of Independence* (1776)

"**Q:** *How has your management style changed since last spring [when you hired a $170,000 consultant for your family-owned business of stringed musical instruments]?*"
"**Eric:** We just started looking at the business in a different way. You're not here to have fun. It's to make a living, you know. Nobody's really your friend. You've got to make money, and if you're doing something that's not making money, why are you doing it? It's just looking at everything with an objective point of view and doing our best to take the emotion out of it."
— Deciding to Hire a $170,000 Consultant, *The New York Times*, January 18, 2011.[1]

The United States' myth of opportunity holds that those who work hard may achieve, and that history is a progressive, forward movement in which the country betters itself through such hard work. Yet such optimism has consistently been tempered by a sense that "life, liberty and the pursuit of happiness" inadequately define a satisfied life. Thus, the myth of individual success also frequently becomes a story about loss and failure. For example, based on the life of William Randolph Hearst, the owner of a nationwide chain of "yellow journalism" newspapers, Orson Welles' *Citizen Kane* (1941) portrays Charles Foster Kane as having achieved material success at the cost of a life of dissatisfaction. Forcibly exiled from his childhood home, he remains consistently angry and alone as an adult. Even that champion of historical progress, John Ford, late in life enunciated the myth's failure in *The Man Who*

Reprinted from *Jump Cut: A Review of Contemporary Media* 53 (summer 2011).

Shot Liberty Valance (1962). "When the legend becomes fact, print the legend," grandly announces the newspaper editor. The successful lawyer, governor, senator and ambassador to Britain, played by James Stewart, is ashen-faced, however, when he realizes that the material progress he has cultivated on behalf of his country has masked the fact that Vera Miles, the love of his life whom he married, has never loved him. The myth maker Ford eulogizes instead the primitive John Wayne who has died penniless and alone in order to make way for that dream of "progress."

This same disillusionment also runs through U.S. literature. For example, F. Scott Fitzgerald's *The Great Gatsby* (1925) is the story of Jay Gatsby, who believed in the myth of achieving material success and thereby the promise of a better future only to learn the futility of his quest and his loss of a more Edenic past. Thus, the novel concludes:

> *"Gatsby believed in the green light, the orgastic future that year by year recedes before us. It eluded us then, but that's no matter—tomorrow we will run faster, stretch out our arms farther…And one fine morning—So we beat on, boats against the current, borne back ceaselessly into the past."[2]*

The Social Network deals with that myth of material success and an historical shift in values in which that myth has come to be accepted as fact. It is a bleak portrayal of a male, adolescent-dominated world in which connections, not relationships, are all. The director, David Fincher, has worked with different screenwriters on all of his movies, and his movies prior to *The Social Network*—such as *Se7en* (1995), *The Game* (1997), *Fight Club* (1999), *Zodiac* (2007) and *The Curious Case of Benjamin Button* (2008)—have in common that nearly all have at their center a young man lost and wandering through a series of episodes in which he seeks to define a place for himself. For each of these characters the search is obsessively personal, and in each the character is mistakenly confident that his skills will enable him to triumph. For example, the newly married Brad Pitt as Detective David Mills in *Se7en* taunts killer Kevin Spacey only to become Spacey's seventh victim. Michael Douglas, a wealthy financier in *The Game*, remains certain that he can outsmart those who run the Game only to "succeed" by the grace of those who control the game. Fincher's characters are lost and angry, adolescents in the bodies of grown men. Even *Panic Room* (2002), whose main character is played by Jodie Foster, focuses on her illusion that she can acquire security through her ex-husband's money. Aaron Sorkin, the creator of the TV series *West Wing* and the screenwriter of *The Social Network*, places Fincher's central character in an historical context. As such, he elevates the individual failure of Fincher's character to a cultural failure.

The Social Network bases its story on Mark Zuckerberg (Jesse Eisenberg), who, while an undergraduate student at Harvard University, developed Facebook. Through deposition testimony in two lawsuits brought against Mark — by Eduardo Savarin (Andrew Garfield) and by the Winkelvoss twins, Cameron and Tyler (both played by Armie Hammer) — the movie recounts how what is today a worldwide phenomenon began in Mark's dorm room. Like other Fincher characters, Mark is no less brainy, no less confident that he can outsmart those around him, and yet he fails in the end to find any personal satisfaction in his seeming success. *The Social Network* is especially bleak in that Mark's personal failures gain him financial rewards in a world in which Facebook is everywhere, including Bosnia where, as a young associate at the law firm defending Mark remarks in disbelief, there are not even any roads.

Mark's obsessive creation of Facebook results in a worldwide network of "friending," an exchange of electronic data by persons who are physically and emotionally at a distance from one another. As such, this kind of friending offers a parallel to Mark, who becomes increasingly isolated from those physically surrounding him. Mark Zuckerberg's contemporary success in business, measured in billions of dollars, results in his personal failure to achieve anything of value. Ironically, it was never about the money for Mark; as a high school student, for example, he uploaded for free his idea of an application for an MP3 player, notwithstanding an offer from Microsoft. Later, in his quest for success, he is oblivious to and uncaring about the consequences to others of his commercial success. As a result, by the end of the film, his success has cost him personal growth, his friendship with his one friend, and the loss of an idealized love of his life. While inventing an online "social network," Mark is consistently visually framed as a young man alone, whether in his law firm's large conference room on the night that a settlement will be reached in the two lawsuits or in the loft-like space of the Facebook office on the night Facebook achieves one million members and its entire staff is out celebrating.

The Social Network deals with male adolescents, such as Mark, who should be in transition to manhood but never progress beyond their adolescence. Taught that individual achievement of "life, liberty and the pursuit of happiness" is all, they lack any genuine empathy with others and hence any sense of social obligation or responsibility for its own sake. While Harvard University has long been co-ed, the movie portrays the college as an historic relic: the exclusive domain of its male students. It equates the exclusivity of its "final clubs," fraternity-like clubs, with the busloads of women brought in by those clubs to *Animal House*-like parties. Mark's failed quest was to become a member of a final club at Harvard, which, in Mark's view, would lead to a "better life," the contours of which, though, were unknown to him. Likewise, both in Facebook's early stage when housed in a rented, suburban home in Palo Alto and later when ensconced in its high tech office space, adolescent males run the organization plugged into their computers with women as sexually available and often intoxicated or drugged objects. Women exist solely for the pleasure of these male adolescents who feel nothing beyond themselves and who thereby are inevitably alone in the midst of their noisy, crowded clubs.

It is the film's women, however, who highlight the stunted growth and failings of these adolescent males. No scene better illustrates this than the opening, pre-credit scene in a coffee house where Mark engages in a rapid, nearly incomprehensible dialogue with his date, Erica Albright (Rooney Mara). Talking nonstop about the number of Chinese geniuses and whether he can ever stand out at Harvard, a school filled with perfect score, 1600-SAT-achieving students such as himself, Mark ends up chasing away Erica. He is too solipsistic to understand her anger at his condescension and too self-absorbed in his own supposed worth to offer anything but a half-hearted attempt at apologizing to a woman who is a student at what Mark views as a lesser school. He knows only the rejection he feels. Exiting the coffee house, running through Cambridge and the Harvard campus and retreating to his dorm room, with "hauntingly quiet" music playing under the movie credits, Mark wreaks his revenge. Through his blog he attacks Erica's bra size (which he attributes to help from Victoria's Secret) and her family's Anglicizing of its name from Albrecht to Albright. He also creates his Facemash site. He copies images of Harvard's female students and then degrades those students, a project which is made visually parallel through intercutting to the scenes of women shown partying at one of Harvard's final clubs.

An adolescent male unable to communicate other than through the currency of his ego, Mark is attuned only to the physical attributes of women, remarking that Erica has a "nice face" even as he continues to attack her through his blog. Sexuality for Mark means a blow job in a bathroom stall of a local club. Ironically, at that same club Mark by chance again meets Erica. She refuses to leave her friends with whom she is having dinner in order to speak alone with Mark and then she dismisses his new Facebook site as a "video game." Her response to him makes it clear that Facebook will do nothing to achieve Mark's goals, to the extent he even understands what those goals are. Just as Erica's rejection in the opening scene led to Mark's blog postings and Facemash site, Mark now decides to expand the Facebook site to other universities, Yale and Columbia, and insists that one of his roommates make certain that there is a write-up about Facebook in the Boston University student newspaper, the college which Erica attends. Mark's supposed relationships are founded on his need to be acknowledged as better than anyone else, including sadly the woman whom he had dated and is still in his own mind courting.

Tellingly, Mark idolizes Sean Parker (Justin Timberlake), the founder of Napster. In the film, Sean is introduced to us as a successful celebrity sleeping with a blond Stanford student; he symbolically learns about Mark by shouting that there is a snake in that Stanford student's bed. Indeed, when meeting Mark, Eduardo, and Eduardo's girlfriend, Christy (Brenda Song), at a hip NYC restaurant, Sean is at ease with the attractive women hostesses. Later at a Palo Alto nightclub he is accompanied by two women, whose familiarity he attributes to their modeling for Victoria's Secret, an ironic reference to Mark's putdown of Erica's bra size. Yet Sean also represents a warning to Mark. Sean tells Mark how the founder of Victoria's Secret committed suicide after selling out his interest in the company too early and hence for too little to the adults of this world represented by The Limited. However, during their conversation Mark focuses on how Sean invented Napster during high school to win over a girl who was then dating a lacrosse player. While Mark sarcastically queries Sean whether the Victoria's Secret story is a "parable," ironically Mark fails to recognize that the "parable" for Mark lies in Sean's answer to whether Sean ever thinks about his high school crush. "What girl?" Sean dismissively replies. The difference between Sean and Mark is that Mark has not forgotten Erica. The Mephistophelean-like seduction of this scene—where the overly loud noise nearly drowns out the characters' dialogue in the same way as in the opening scene between Mark and Erica—results in the corruption of a creative imagination into a business success story.

The movie offers the audience some empathy for Mark through Marilyn Delpy (Rashida Jones), the second year associate in the law firm defending Mark in the two lawsuits. Largely silent, she observes all of the depositions and listens to all of the testimony of the players in the Facebook story. Indeed, Sorkin has commented that she is a stand-in for the audience.[3] The only young person in the room besides Mark, the Winkelvosses and Eduardo, she is genuinely amazed at the 22,000 hits to Mark's Facemash site and can laugh at the chicken story in which Eduardo is accused of animal cruelty. The conscience of the movie, her face shows the horror she feels on hearing how Mark duped his only—and trusting—friend Eduardo into signing documents which diluted Eduardo's shares in Facebook to virtually nothing. While Marilyn declines in the movie's last scene Mark's offer to get something to eat, she seemingly offers him the partial comfort of qualifying Erica's comment in the movie's first scene that Mark will be disliked not because he is a nerd but simply because he is an asshole. In her view, Mark is instead "just trying so hard to be an asshole." Clearly in that context, the principle asshole is Sean Parker. He is the entrepreneur who inspires Mark to print up "I'm CEO, Bitch" business cards, which make explicit the misogyny of these adolescent males. Thus, Mark tells Marilyn that he was "drunk and angry and stupid," even as he begins refreshing on his computer his request to "friend" Erica.

Yet the movie remains disquieting and unsettling even as we come to understand Mark. While qualifying Erica's comment, Marilyn, too, leaves Mark alone—in the large law firm conference room. And Mark's conduct is legally punished only by a large fine comparable to a "speeding ticket," to quote Marilyn's comment, so that he becomes the world's youngest billionaire. The lawyers will have their steak dinner following the day-long depositions which have been about events that have been the story of this movie, will return that evening to explain to Mark why he must settle, and will then draft settlement papers and reach terms which will provide no sense of justice to cure the wrongs that have been committed throughout the film. Cash will exchange hands, but friendships have been lost and the possibility, howsoever remote, of an adult relationship between Mark and Erica is foreclosed.

In this respect, a movie about the failure of one individual also reflects the historical failure of a culture. If the opening scene between Erica and Mark explains Mark's personal failing, the scene with Larry Summers (Douglas Urbanski),[4] the president of Harvard, explains how that failing reflects the collective failing in which Mark is himself but a bit player, notwithstanding—or perhaps because of—his commercial success.

The Winkelvoss twins set up the context in which Mark's success represents the new historical order of business. His repeated attacks on them—"If you guys were the inventors of Facebook, you'd have invented Facebook" and "I think that if your clients want to sit on my shoulders and call themselves tall, they have the right to give it a try"—comes with an understanding that his success represents an historical change—"They're suing me because for the first time in their lives things didn't work out exactly the way they were supposed to." A stand-in for "old Harvard"—white, Protestant, moneyed, athletically strong and competitive—the Winkelvosses are both on the crew team and members of one of the final clubs. They maintain an historically quaint sense that the world entitles them to a life which, in their self-serving view, is fundamentally fair. They may exclude others from their club or neglect or even abuse women. For example, they never bother to ask whether their girlfriends were hurt by Mark's Facemash site and belong to a club which brings in women by the busload for their personal entertainment. Nevertheless, "these gentlemen of Harvard" believe in a certain code of behavior. That code is embodied in the Harvard student handbook, which one of them dubs "Harvard law."

But that "Harvard law," as Harvard's president makes clear in his meeting with the Winkelvoss twins, no longer exists in the contemporary world defined by the Mark Zuckerbergs and Facebook. The building in which the meeting occurs is 100 years older than the US republic, as the president's secretary pointedly tells the twins, thereby lending an historical gravitas to this meeting. Yet immediately we see that the Winkelvoss' trust in "Harvard law" is misplaced. For example, the president's secretary makes cautionary note about the near sanctity of the chairs in which the Winkelvoss sit; her words, however, cannot help but remind us of Mark's differing view—that no one can own the rights to all chairs simply because he or she was the first to invent the design of a particular chair. At the meeting, President Larry Summers, who touts his knowledge as the former Secretary of the U.S. Treasury, immediately mocks the Winkelvosses as students who have come to sell a Brooks Brothers clothing franchise. In an exchange of words nearly as fast as Mark's opening one with Erica, Summers brushes aside their reliance on "Harvard law," disclaiming any responsibility on the part of Harvard to intervene. He suggests that they come up with a new idea and ultimately informs them that their recourse is to be found in the anonymity of the court system, which comes to occupy the film through the depositions recounting the story of Facebook. Indeed, Summers pointedly deflects their question about knowing the difference between right and wrong, and he ironically ends the meeting by accusing them of abusing their position by the very arrangement of the meeting through their father. "Anne, punch me," Summers tells his assistant, the same term used by the final clubs in admitting new members.

Larry Summers, like Mark Zuckerberg, is himself the president of a final club, namely Harvard University. Harvard and Facebook are alike in that they both tout their self-serving exclusivity and both impose an isolation on their presidents, placing them in socially acceptable "panic rooms." There is no "Harvard law," only a social Darwinism in which all the spoils go to the winner. As Eduardo later observes in despair to Mark as their friendship deteriorates and in a reference to Sean Parker's earlier speech about success as consisting of catching the huge marlin, "Don't fish eat other fish?" The successful individual feeds on others in order to achieve the success of a presidency. Cannibalism is each individual's "unalienable right."

President Summers' rejection of the Winkelvoss' petition is but one way in which the plot indicates the shifting definition of fairness. For example, the Winkelvoss twins later accept as fair the results by which they lose the Royal Regatta at Henley, but their loss is dismissed by Prince Albert, an insider to an older, still more exclusive club to which they do not belong. In a similar way we see the helplessness of the Winkelvoss' father in the face of a changing world. He has his in-house lawyer send a useless "cease and desist" letter, which Mark readily answers with the assistance of a third-year, Harvard law student. The elder Winkelvoss is still later at a loss for words when the family learns that Facebook has expanded to England so that the twins' loss at Henley has already been broadcast over Facebook.

Historical context defines fairness, and only Napster's Sean Parker seems aware of the latest shift in values, repeatedly announcing that "it's our time." Symbolically, the sponsoring logo to the Winkelvoss' crew boat is the Polaroid logo, a once premiere, Boston-based company which failed to keep pace with the progressive advances of technology. Ironically, as we learn through the end credits, the Winkelvoss twins eventually placed sixth in the Olympics then held in China, the very country in which there are more genius IQs than there are people in the United States. Mark's $65 million settlement check to the Winkelvoss twins is indeed only a "speeding ticket" for what in 2010 was a $25 billion business. Mark's success represents an historical change in which "old Harvard" and its sense of fairness has been rendered as irrelevant as Prince Albert, whom the Winkelvosses mock, because his country, Monaco, is the size of Rhode Island. The athletic Winkelvoss twins have themselves been outsized.

If Mark represents the future and the Winkelvosses the past, then Eduardo represents the present torn between the two and the moral center of the film. His connections with Mark are obvious. He is Mark's friend. He is the only person who expresses concern about Mark's breakup with Erica (which Mark seemingly ignores) and later ironically tells the Facebook lawyers that Mark needs to be protected (even as those lawyers on behalf of Mark are having Eduardo sign corporate papers which will lead to Eduardo's disenfranchisement from Facebook). He is also the technologically savvy student whose algorithm enables Mark to set up the Facemash site, eventually resulting in Mark's introduction to the Winkelvoss twins who disclose to him the idea for the "Harvard connection." Not incidentally, Eduardo is also the person who suggests to Mark that Facebook needs to expand not only to Yale and Columbia, as proposed by Mark, but also to Stanford. He thereby advances the interests of his friend Mark but also dooms himself in the process, since it is through that California connection that Sean Parker learns of Facebook, inevitably leading to Eduardo's being forced out.

Eduardo, however, is also not Mark. He is not so "plugged in" as Mark, evidenced by his lack of enchantment with the supposedly visionary Sean Parker, with whom Mark wholly identifies, and also by his admitted inability to change his relationship status on Facebook, an admission he makes to his then-paranoid girlfriend. Thus, Eduardo is also, in part, "old Harvard" and, as such, connected to the Winkelvoss twins and their world. He acknowledges his desire to become a member of one of the final clubs, and the obsessive development by Mark of Facebook is paralled by Eduardo's obsessive steps in becoming accepted by, and his gradual induction into, one such final club, the Phoenix Club. Tellingly, the two narratives converge when Mark prevails upon Eduardo to disclose to Mark the members of the Phoenix Club so that Mark can launch Facebook through the email addresses of those members. Of course, Mark has only contempt for a club from which he has been excluded, mocking the email address of the Phoenix Club's president and its reference to Lewis Carroll's *Through the Looking Glass*.

That parallel is made explicit in other ways. For example, as a result of his seeking admission to the Phoenix Club, Eduardo is accused of an animal rights violation by supposedly torturing a chicken, namely feeding chicken meat to a chicken. That story, in turn, leads to the revelation of how Mark used Facebook to find answers for his art history essay. Our sympathies in this instance are wholly with Eduardo. The young law associate, Marilyn Delpy, laughs at the silliness of the chicken episode, which the *Harvard Crimson* wrote about (implicitly at Mark's instigation) and which thereby embarrassed Eduardo in the eyes of his father. On the other hand, Mark's use of Facebook to find answers for his art class essay is not excused by any such laughter and is thereby acknowledged for what it is—cheating. Until he accidently found the Winkelvoss' cease and desist letter in Mark's dorm room, Eduardo knew nothing about the Winkelvoss' "Harvard connection" idea, an idea which Mark consistently has disdained because he copied none of their code and hence, in his view, violated no laws.

Indeed, that intellectual property law, which is repeatedly referred to by each of the characters, would likely not recognize the Winkelvoss' contribution for what was merely an "idea." As Mark correctly observes—echoed in Fincher's commentary to the movie—no one can own the rights to the concept of a "chair." Nevertheless, it is Eduardo who understands that law and morality are not one and the same. The former is based on logic, codes, while latter is based on relationships, emotion. While Sean Parker introduces Mark to venture capitalists for whom Facebook is merely a vehicle for making money, without emotional content, Eduardo lends his own money to Mark out of friendship, which Mark himself acknowledges in explaining why he chose to accept his money rather than from the Winkelvoss family. Eduardo also tries to "monetize" the Facebook site through old school advertisers for whom there are real products. That Fincher cast Sorkin to play one such advertising executive expresses Fincher's view as to where Sorkin's sympathies lie. Sorkin harks back to a United States which once made products, such as railroads—and which today might still make products, such as solar panels—rather than primarily engage in the financial wizardry of hedge funds and the virtual realities of Internet communications through Facebook. The connection for Eduardo between relationships and morality is symbolized by his emotionally driven decision to freeze Facebook's funds and his confession to Mark that he did so in order to gain Mark's attention.

While money is of no importance to Mark other than for the social notoriety it provides, relationships are equally of no importance to Mark. They are only social currency providing entry into an exclusive final club where he will be the president. Thus, in response to Eduardo's confession about his anger and need to gain his friend's attention, Mark retaliates by claiming that he needs his CFO, coldly inviting Eduardo to Facebook's new offices; there he "ambushes" Mark through both the company's lawyers and Sean Parker. In fact, Fincher has commented with approval on Mark's need to discard his Harvard roommates, such as Eduardo, if Facebook is to achieve its creative potential. Such words express where Fincher's sympathies lie. Fincher applauds the members of the "millennial generation" in the United States for whom virtual communications render individual success emotionally removed; hence making it becomes less problematic even when one's personal success hurts others.

In the confrontational scene between Mark and Eduardo at the Facebook offices, in which the same "hauntingly quiet" music plays as under the movie's opening credits, Mark is dressed in his "fuck-you" flip-flops and hoodie while Eduardo is dressed in black. Mark is the street kid from *The Wire* with his new electronic toy which will make him billions while addicting its millions of members ("freakishly addictive" to quote the Stanford student's observation to Sean Parker). In contrast to Eduardo (and the Winkelvosses), Mark is the fatherless adolescent and remains always in rebellion against the "adult" world. Eduardo is the Johnny Cash-like figure in black, the rebel of an earlier generation who eventually grew up and became known as husband and father to other country western singers.

Erica rejects Mark for his immaturity, his inability to sustain a genuine relationship with anyone. In contrast to her scene with Mark at a local club in which she wears the classic, black beret, the stereotypical image of a young woman in rebellion, she appears on Facebook in the final scene as an older woman who has outgrown her adolescent self. While Fincher has commented that Erica is not the love of Mark's life, Sorkin in contrast describes as heartbreaking the movie's opening scene. Angry at her rejection of him, Mark tells Erica in the opening scene, "I don't want friends," and she replies, "I have no intention of being friends with you." The scripted, final shot of the movie returns, however, to the image of Erica on Facebook as an adult and Mark's futile quest to friend her, which Sorkin has compared to the nearly final shot in *Citizen Kane* and its disclosure as to the meaning of "rosebud."[5]

At the end of the film, Mark's quest to achieve and his commercial success have inevitably led to his being alone in the large conference room of his adult lawyers. The last image of the inventor of Facebook shows him addictively refreshing his computer trying to "friend" Erica. The patriarchal and exclusionary world embodied by the Winkelvoss twins has been overridden by technology, which makes winners of those with the brains to imagine and implement the demands of the many. Bill Gates and now Mark Zuckerberg are our robber barons. In place of a sexist and ethnically determined society, ours is a far more democratic and merit-based world. Yet it is also a world with little or no moral compass other than the degree of notoriety captured by those who succeed. It moves ahead without regard for the consequences to the many and fosters "relationships" consisting of only immediate connections without any depth, let alone caring.

The personal is political, but it is also now the case that the private is public. That Facebook has routinely captured data on its members—and that its members accede to that—suggests how far the world has come in monetizing people. The movie expresses little sympathy for the Winkelvoss family, except as historic relics. It ultimately condemns Mark Zuckerberg, mourning his failings, including his continued adolescent state and self-love. The movie expresses sympathy for Eduardo, the one character who cares about others. However, he is rewarded by betrayal by his closest friend. In that context, Eduardo's settlement consisting of a listing on a masthead and an undisclosed sum of money is an afterthought of the end credits. The movie's bleakness resides in its sense of waste and lost opportunities. That the characters' story is told through deposition transcripts is apt in a world in which, as Sean Parker foresees, having lived on farms and then in cities, we will now live on the Internet, though alone with our "social networks."

Notes

1. http://boss.blogs.nytimes.com/2011/01/18/deciding-to-hire-a-170000-consultant/. [return to text]

2. F. Scott Fitzgerald, *The Great Gatsby* (1925), Scribner Paperback Fiction, 1995 edition, published by Simon & Schuster, at page 189.

3. Unless otherwise noted, this and all other comments by David Fincher and Aaron Sorkin are from the commentary accompanying the 2011 DVD release of *The Social Network*.

4. Tellingly, Fincher describes Douglas Urbanski in his commentary as a talent manager, identifying the actor Gary Oldman as one such talent. In contrast, Sorkin describes Ubanski as a conservative radio commentator who has filled in on occasion for Rush Limbaugh.

5. *Sight and Sound*, January 2011, *Aaron Sorkin in Conversation* by Joe Fraser, http://www.bfi.org.uk/sightandsound/reviews/specials/aaron-sorkin-jan-2011.php.

   The complete interview of Sorkin by Francine Stock may be found at http://www.bfi.org.uk/live/video/580.

   Mark Zuckerberg's obsessive attempt to friend Erica is also reminiscent of the speech in *Citizen Kane* by the solitary Mr. Bernstein about the girl in a white dress he saw for a moment in 1896 on a Jersey ferry: "I'll bet a moment hasn't gone by since that I haven't thought of that girl."

8

Stereotypes: Conceptual and Normative Considerations

Judith Andre

A familiar battle is raging. The current skirmish involves a comic strip character, Miss Buxley, in "Beetle Bailey." Her portrayal has been called sexist: she's a dumb blonde, physically well-endowed, whose every move leaves her boss panting and unable to think. The author of the strip admits that the situation is stereotypical, but claims that "Miss Buxleys do get preferential treatment. I'm just telling the truth."[1]

Both the attack ("This is an offensive stereotype") and the defense ("I'm just telling the truth") are familiar.[2] The same battle is fought over illustrations in schoolbooks, characters in commercials, situations in sitcoms. Sometimes the battle is an inner one: realizing how blacks have been victimized by stereotypes, one may be reluctant to state some simple truth about, say, blacks and welfare.

Sometimes the question is best resolved by looking at the specific situation. The Miss Buxley character raises many interesting questions: Why is the sexual power of women over men considered funny? Why is the power of men over women—physical, economic, emotional, and political—never considered funny? What is life really like for a buxom young woman in the contemporary United States? Is it true that the Miss Buxleys of the world are treated preferentially in an office? Many stereotypes have fallen once the social scientists examined them.

In this paper, however, I will be interested in the broader question: Is there something in the nature of a stereotype that makes it objectionable, even when it (roughly) represents the truth? My discussion begins with the concept of a stereotype. How does it differ, say, from other generalizations?

The word "stereo" first meant a metal printing plate. The Greek prefix "stereo" means "solid, hard, firm." As Rosemary Gordon points out, "The idea of unchangeability, of monotonous regularity and formalisation was very soon abstracted from the material object itself and applied in a more metaphorical sense . . . The use of 'stereotype' as a verb in the sense of fixing something and perpetuating it in an unchanging form can be traced back to the nineteenth century."[3] Today

Reprinted by permission of the author.

the term means: "a conventional, formulaic, and usually oversimplified conception, opinion, or belief; a person, group, event or issue considered to typify or conform to an unvarying pattern. . . ."[4] As psychologists use the term, the central characteristic of a stereotype is its rigidity: it persists in spite of evidence.[5] Like most beliefs it filters the evidence, so that inconsistent information is less likely to be assimilated. But why do some beliefs have the particular inflexibility that makes them stereotypes?[6] Because stereotypes as I will define them are commonly held (rather than simply individually held) beliefs, discussion of subconscious motivation is particularly problematic. Inflexible opinions in the general public might result from conscious inflexibility on the part of relatively few opinion-makers (in other words, from deliberate indoctrination). But I will assume otherwise: my discussion here will be valid to the extent that general stereotypes are a function of individual resistance to changes of mind.

An unwillingness to face something is a form of self-deception; it results from a sense of danger to oneself: a fear that the unfaced fact itself will turn out to be unpleasant, or at least that the facing of it will be. Thinking is work; an unpredictable world is frightening. Stereotypes, like other generalizations, protect us from both effort and fear. But stereotypes differ from other generalizations in their greater immunity to revision; they are not just handy but disposable rules of thumb. Why are we so particularly unwilling to think about some things? Both logical and psychological reasons are possible. As Quine describes the web of belief, privileged beliefs are those whose denial would bring about the most change in our conceptual scheme. A principle of economy leads us, when beliefs conflict, to keep those which are more fundamental. Psychologically, some beliefs are privileged because they keep us happy (or less unhappy). Their denials are threatening. Now there are only a few kinds of situations where a belief as such makes us happy *overall*; ordinarily it is true beliefs which, in the long run, help us. Flame burns, and burns are painful, soup nourishes; gravity is constant. Believing these true things will make our lives better. But some beliefs make life better whether or not they are true: self-esteem is the central case. My belief that I am attractive, intelligent, and honest makes my life pleasant even if I am wrong on all counts. In fact, I may be much happier than the objectively attractive, intelligent and honest person who doesn't know her own worth. Here the content of the belief is more important than its congruence with reality (although even here that congruence also matters).

In two other areas the content of a belief is more important than its well foundedness: where the belief itself changes the world around me, and where the world around me is invulnerable to any attempt to cope. Our beliefs about other people, for instance, shape their behavior; and our lack of awareness of impending inexorable doom is a blessing if there's nothing we could do about it anyway. (Only rarely would that be true; we might at least want to get our affairs in order. But this is nevertheless a logically possible category.)

This analysis suggests that a stereotype—which we retain in the face of contradictory evidence—must function in one of the following ways: it may be relatively fundamental to our conceptual scheme; it may protect our self-esteem; it may help bring about some desirable situation; or it may shield us from facing an unchangeable, unpleasant fact, when facing it would accomplish nothing. (I'm assuming here quite a rational subconscious; it might be safer to say that the belief *appears* to us, feels to us, important in one of the ways just mentioned, and so we resist questioning it.)

But even among rigid, logically or psychologically privileged beliefs, stereotypes form a subset. To begin with, they concern classes of people rather than the whole human race. Rigid beliefs about human beings in general are not stereotypes (except perhaps in science fiction, where "heroic Terrans" confront extraterrestrials); nor are inflexible beliefs about individuals—about celebrities or historical figures. These are myths, perhaps, but not stereotypes. This may explain why there are relatively few stereotypes about white men; white men are, in this culture, unreflectively taken to be the standard human being from whom women and other races deviate. What stereotypes there are concern not men as such, but men in relation to women: men are naturally polygamous or domestically clumsy.

In addition, stereotypes concern behavioral or psychological attributes. Fat people are believed to be jolly *and* to be bad health risks, but only the belief about their personality counts as a stereotype. A stereotype is usually a belief that members of a group will behave in certain ways—it's an expectation that something observable will happen.

A stereotype is also simple and general. The more complex and specific a statement, the less likely it is to express a stereotype. Compare, for instance, "Most great jazz musicians have been black" (a nonstereotypical claim) with "Blacks are so musical" (a stereotypical claim). This characteristic of a stereotype—generality—complements the first characteristic (rigidity); for a general statement is hard to falsify. If this particular black child is tone-deaf, he may still be good on the drums—or an inspired dancer. If he fails at all these activities, well, he's "the exception that proves the rule"—the original belief may refer to all blacks, almost all, or just a majority of them.

Simplicity is a related characteristic. The categories invoked are not only broad, they are few. Fat people are jolly, priests are dedicated, the Irish are garrulous and hard-drinking.

Finally, stereotypes ignore, or falsify, or oversimplify the causes of this behavior. Because of this, a stereotype at least suggests that the attributed behavior is inevitable; this, too, contributes to the rigidity of the belief. When a cause for the behavior is mentioned, claims gain empirical content and become falsifiable. Thus, beliefs or portrayals that include beliefs about the causes of the behavior are less likely to count as stereotypes. A nagging wife is a stereotype; a wife who nags because her only route to success is through her husband is less so. Even a false or farfetched causal claim—sociobiological speculation, for instance—at least calls attention to the question of cause, and is to that extent better than a free-floating claim such as "women are monogamous, men polygamous; they just are." But unfounded claims about genetic causes are only slightly better than what I have called "free-floating" claims (those which make no reference to cause at all). Stereotypes, in one way or the other, suggest that the behavior in question is an unalterable given. Stereotypes, then, are a subset of commonly believed generalizations about the way certain kinds of people feel and act. Stereotypes are inflexible beliefs; they involve a few broad categories only; and they imply that what they describe is inevitable.

Stereotypes as Undesirable

"Stereotype" is pejorative; there is always something objectionable in the beliefs and images to which the word refers. Once the concept of stereotype has been analyzed, the nature of that objectionableness is clearer. To begin with, a stereotype is particularly resistant to change; it keeps us from seeing the truth, should the truth be at odds with our beliefs. The truth is a good thing to know, ordinarily, since we can deal more effectively with what we see than with what we don't. The habit of seeking the truth is therefore also a good thing; it's useful, and—I will not try to defend this here—morally preferable. Ceteris paribus, then, a stereotype is a bad thing because it is unfriendly to truth.

The analysis in Part I also helps illuminate the role of stereotypes in unjust social arrangements. Remember that a stereotypical portrayal reinforces two beliefs at once: that X's are Y, and that X's are inevitably Y. If these beliefs are particularly privileged, then they must (at least seem to our subconscious) do one of the following: protect our self-esteem; underlie many other significant beliefs; help perpetual situations pleasing to us; shield us from knowledge which is better not known. Stereotypes about minorities do all of this. They protect the self-esteem of the majority in two ways. First, some assure the majority of its superiority. ("Blacks are ignorant.") Secondly, they protect the ruling class from seeing its moral turpitude. ("Blacks are like happy children. They don't need what we need." Or, "Women haven't succeeded because they're naturally frivolous.") The realization that something could and should be changed is a moral burden. Once enlightened, I cannot think well of myself *and* remain inactive. What makes the burden worse is that stereotypes about minorities often do have a central place in our conceptual scheme. The possibility of their falsehood or mutability threatens our beliefs about many other things. When stereotypes fall, beliefs about myself—in particular, about my worth—may fall; as may beliefs about how society actually works, why it works that way, and what alternatives are available. Finally, of course, stereotypes about the disadvantaged are self-fulfilling prophecies. People act as they are expected to act, for a variety of familiar reasons.

Stereotypes concerning minorities, then, may well help perpetuate injustices. Interesting questions remain, however: are all stereotypes about minorities objectionable? For that matter, are all stereotypes as such morally objectionable? Or instead must each be examined for its possible role in perpetuating injustice?

As mentioned earlier, at least one thing counts against all stereotypes: their inflexibility. Truth is endangered, and truth is a good thing. But truth isn't the only good thing; its sacrifice is sometimes justified. And as there are arguments to be given in favor of stock figures in literature, so there are advantages to culturally shared expectations about people. These expectations make the world more predictable and hence more manageable; since they are commonly shared, they make communication easier. A stereotype may even enshrine an attribute of which the people in question are truly and proudly the possessors. Perhaps most Irish *are* religious, most nurses dedicated, most Italians warm and loving.

But "stereotype" remains a pejorative. When, then, would a portrayal of, say, a dedicated physician become objectionable? The objection might be aesthetic rather than moral; stale writing fails to do what literature should do: make us see more clearly. The aesthetic criticism, however, leads directly to the moral one. Stereotypes prevent us from seeing clearly, not only in the sense that they filter out conflicting information, but also in the sense that they keep us from understanding what they do allow us to see. This is true even of positive stereotypes about nonminorities. Suppose most physicians are in fact dedicated. What is the harm in the portrayal of one more selfless doctor? The portrayal keeps us from attending to the uniqueness of each individual. He may be heroic in some respects, conscientious in others, but occasionally imperfect. He, and we, are reluctant to admit the imperfection, and unduly shocked when we do see it; in either case we will not cope well with the problem. We are, ironically, less likely to appreciate his heroism, too—for it is simply expected. All doctors are like that.

Stereotypes, then, are bad things even when the image they convey is a positive one. Their patronizing romanticism keeps us from coping with reality, and from appreciating the individual troubles and successes of the people we meet.

What Is to Be Done?

Stereotypes are avoidable. There are many ways to portray ordinary conventional people without descending into stereotype. We need not be afraid of telling the truth. The guidelines for doing so are found in the description of a stereotype given in Part I. Stereotypes are simple, general, and causally agnostic. A portrayal of a carping mother-in-law is not stereotypical if her individuality shows. What does she complain about? What doesn't she complain about? What other characteristics does she have? Most importantly, why is she so unpleasant? A stereotyped portrayal would focus on just two facts: she is a mother-in-law; she carps. *That* picture reinforces the connection which most people make already and automatically. But even a portrayal that is congruent with a stereotype can challenge that stereotype by calling attention to its limited, specific applicability, and by encouraging thought about the origins of the behavior. The criminals on the TV show *Hill Street Blues* are primarily black and Hispanic. But each is shown as an individual; blacks are seen in many noncriminal roles; and the social factors that promote criminality are obvious. Only for the least discerning of viewers would the show encourage the identification: "young black" = "thug."

To answer the questions which began this paper: there's a great difference between a true generalization and a stereotype. And there's nothing wrong with telling the truth; just make sure it's the whole truth. Responsible portrayals encourage us to see in one another both our individuality and our roles in a social system. Stereotypes blind us to the first, and keep us enlightened about the second. The world of the stereotype is a world of free-floating stock figures, whose behavior has no explanation (except, perhaps, in their genes). It may be a humorous world (although that's a subject for a different paper) but it is not a happy world. Nor is it a true one.

Notes

1. Mort Walker, quoted by Sheryl Jones, "Sexism Draws Some New Battle Lines," *The Ledger-Star* (Norfolk, Virginia), December 28, 1982.

2. Another line of defense is equally familiar: "Your attempt at censorship is worse than anything I've done." However common, the defense is confused. Attempts to influence editorial discretion through reason are not censorship. If legal threats are used (say, the threat of a boycott) the question becomes more complicated. See my "'Censorship': Some Distinctions," in *The International Journal of Applied Philosophy,* vol. 1, no. 4 (Fall 1983), pp. 25–37.

3. Rosemary Gordon, *Stereotypy of Imagery and Belief as an Ego Defense* (Cambridge: University Press, 1962), pp. 2–3.

4. *American Heritage Dictionary* (Boston: Houghton Mifflin, 1979).

5. Gordon, p. 4.

6. The dictionary speaks of community stereotypes, and does not include inflexibility as a defining characteristic. The psychologists are speaking of individually held stereotypes, and give inflexibility as their major defining characteristic. I discuss in this paper those commonly held stereotypes which are relatively inflexible; I assume that most are. Some of the objections I will make, however, apply only to those formulaic beliefs which are relatively rigid; others apply to all formulaic beliefs (about the behavior and feelings of classes of people).

9

Gender Stereotypes: An Analysis of Popular Films and TV

Dr. Stacy L. Smith and Crystal Allene Cook

Introduction

The following four diverse studies on gender and children's entertainment prove the need for more females and more diverse portrayals of females and males in movie and television entertainment aimed at children. No one can argue that viewing again and again an imbalanced fictional "world" where females are often underrepresented or unmotivated can be good for young females or young males. Females take up half the space in society, yet, especially in films aimed at children, they appear much less frequently than do males. Nevertheless, when they do make it onto the silver or small screen, their portrayals can undermine their presence by being "hyper-attractive" or "hypersexual" and/or passive. It is certainly not the intent of this research to suggest that all female portrayals be uplifting or inspirational nor that "pretty" females not be depicted. Rather, the findings from all four studies point to the need for a shift: away from creating females as adornment, enticement, or with inclination to romance as the main or exclusive personality trait or motivator. These four studies open the area of female character-development to an important possible antidote to female under representation as well as overemphasis on physical appearance: the creation of diverse, complicated females who initiate and/or actively participate in their destinies.

Although the main focus of these four studies is entertainment aimed at children, children's entertainment is not the only area with imbalance at issue. The results of one of the following four studies reveal that little change has occurred in the prevalence of single speaking female characters in G, PG, PG-13, and R rated films over the last 16 years. While a few executive women can be commended for breaking through the glass ceiling in the entertainment industry, their influence has had limited results with respect to gender parity and portrayal. Maybe the answer is that for change to occur even more women are needed in the creative process (i.e., producers, writers), where key decision making occurs at the pitch and story development level. In fact, research on television reveals that the participation of women writers and producers increases the percentage of females on screen.[1] Accordingly, another suggestion may be that more women also are needed to

Reprinted from *www.seejane.org* (2008).

join the ranks of casting directors, cinematographers, and show runners so that gender sensitive decisions can be made in the hiring and presentation of female actors in television and film.

Additionally, animators are encouraged to think outside-the-box about the types of characters they construct. Many of the females in animated fare are depicted as hypersexualized and thin. Story artists can incorporate more women as primary and secondary characters to the plot so that a full range of females and males (short and tall, thin and heavy, attractive and unattractive) can be drawn or computer-generated.

Clearly, along the entire creative and marketing process, participants can develop, design, and engage in practical solutions to the problem of gender under representation and flat portrayal in entertainment aimed at children. As balance and portrayals improve, children now and the next generations of children will be the winners. They will be exposed to entertainment in which females take up half the space and both females and males are active, diverse, and complex.

For your reference, according to the U.S. Census, in 2006, females made up 51% and males made up 49% of the population of the United States.

Below, we overview a series of studies conducted by Dr. Stacy Smith and her research team. The studies were not conducted chronologically. Rather, each investigation addressed different research questions and employed different approaches and measures.

Study 1: G-rated Films, 1990-2005

The aim of the first study was a comprehensive examination of gender portrayals in general audience films. Not one study has rigorously content-analyzed G-rated films in both live and animated formats across a variety of distributors. This investigation filled that void. We analyzed the amount and the nature of portrayals of male and female characters in 101 of the top-grossing G-rated movies from 1990 to January 31st, 2005 based on Nielsen EDI© estimates. In total, we tracked over 3,000 individual speaking characters, roughly 1,000 characters who spoke in all male or all female groups, and more than 40 narrators.

The key findings from this study included: fewer than one out of three (28%) of the speaking characters (both real and animated) are female. Fewer than one in five in this sample (17%) of characters in crowd scenes are female, though this finding should be interpreted with caution.[2] In this sample, more than four out of five (83%) of the films' narrators are male.

Gender was not the only aspect of imbalance in these films. We evaluated the apparent ethnicity as characters as well. A full 85.5% of the characters in G-rated films are white, 4.8% are black, and 9.7% are from "other" ethnicities. No differences emerged by character gender.

Study 2: G-, PG-, PG-13, R-Rated Prevalence & Portrayal, 1990-2006

The purpose of study 2 was to examine quantitatively the prevalence and portrayal of single, speaking characters in popular motion pictures. Based on Nielsen EDI© estimates, we content-analyzed 400 of the top-grossing G, PG, PG-13, and R-rated theatrically-released films in North America between January 1, 1990 and September 4th, 2006.[3] It is important to note that this study employed a somewhat different set of G-rated movies from the first study (only 100 films, and including movies through much of 2006). This second study also included 100 movies in each of the other rating categories. Additionally, some of the criteria for coding were changed from the first study. Below, we report our results for the prevalence and portrayal of male and female characters.

Prevalence. Our complete study examined over 15,000 single-speaking characters in four rating categories of films. The results across these four ratings reveal that 73% of the characters are male (n=11,371) and 27% are female (n=4,197). This translates into a ratio of 2.71 males to every 1 female. Significant but trivial deviation[4] occurred by rating (G=2.5 to 1; PG=2.6 to 1; PG-13=2.8 to 1, R=2.9 to 1).

An analysis was also undertaken to see if the proportion of males to females changed over time. Films were categorized by release dates in one of three epochs: 1990 to 1995; 1996 to 2000; and 2001 to 2006. Re-released films were removed from the analysis. The results showed no change over time across the entire sample of films or within a rating. Thus, in this study, the prevalence of females in films has neither increased nor decreased over the last 16 years.

Portrayal. It has been argued that exposure to a thin, attractive, sex-saturated culture may be having a negative effect on youngsters' socio-emotional development.[5] On one hand, viewing these types of portrayals may overemphasize the importance of appearance norms among developing youth. With time and repeated viewing, girls may become dissatisfied with how they look or who they are. Indeed, psychologist Sarah Murnen[6] recently stated, "The promotion of the thin, sexy ideal in our culture has created a situation where the majority of girls and women don't like their bodies... And body dissatisfaction can lead girls to participate in very unhealthy behaviors to try to control weight." Given this concern as well as the recent release of the report of American Psychological Association Task Force on the Sexualization of Girls,[7] it became important to examine how frequently children may be seeing these attractive and sexy characters, particularly females, in popular films.

We also wanted to see if other stereotypes dominate motion picture content. In particular, we are interested in the traditionality surrounding males and females. According to one parent,[8] "Though it's been more than 30 years since feminists first drew attention to the stereotyped gender messages delivered by mainstream television, movies, and books, men and women are still often portrayed in very traditional roles." Another writer points out that media such as television, commercials, and parenting magazines[9] "still show mom with the babies and kids. Most domicile publications still show women vacuuming, cleaning and cooking."

Examining over 4,000 characters across 400 G, PG, PG-13, and R-rated movies, our data reveal that two types of females frequent film: the traditional and the hypersexual. Traditionality was a function of the character's relational and parental status. Females are more likely than males to be depicted as parents (52.2% vs. 40.4%) and in a committed relationship (59.9% vs. 47.4%) in motion pictures. Interestingly, rating had an influence on these distributions. G and PG females were more likely than G and PG males to be shown as parents. A similar trend is observed for relational status across G, PG, and PG-13 films. No gender differences in parental status or relational status were observed in R rated films, however. Over half of the female characters children see in movie content are depicted in a nurturing and stereotypical manner.

In stark contrast, another significant proportion of the females in film are shown in a hypersexualized fashion. Hypersexuality refers to an overemphasis on attractiveness and sexuality by way of clothing (i.e., alluring attire) and body proportions (i.e. uncharacteristically small waist, hourglass figure, thinness). We examined characters to see if males and females vary in hypersexuality. Our results show that they do (see Figure 1).

Females were over five times as likely as males to be shown in sexually revealing clothing, which was defined as attire that enhances, exaggerates, or calls attention to any part of the body from neck to knees. Alluring apparel was often draped on a female with a distorted thin ideal. Nearly a quarter of the females in film had particularly small waists, leaving little room for a womb or any other internal organs. Yet only 8% of males were featured with such a comparatively misshapen midsection. Rounding out these results, females were nearly three times as likely as males (10.6% vs. 3.4%) to be shown with a thin (and in the case of females, an hourglass-shaped) figure. No differences emerged for chest size (males=14.8%, females=15.2%).

Hypersexuality of Males and Females in Popular Films
Figure 1

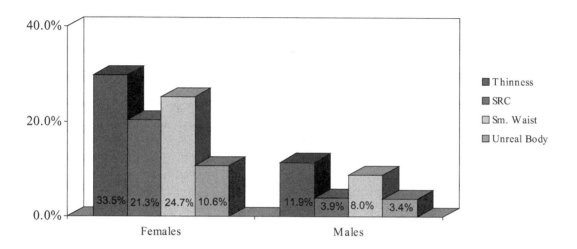

The Hypersexualization of Females Varies by Rating

Given the above findings, we examined the prevalence of female hypersexualization by rating. Rating had a significant impact on how females are portrayed. A few of the differences were between G- and R-rated films.[10] R-rated females are more likely than G-rated females to be depicted as thin (42.9% vs. 33.1%). G-rated females are more likely than their R-rated counterparts to be shown with a small waist (34.6% vs. 23.7%), a large chest (20.6% vs. 13.8%), and an unrealistic body shape (16.3% vs. 10.3%).

Hypersexuality of Females By Film Rating
Figure 2

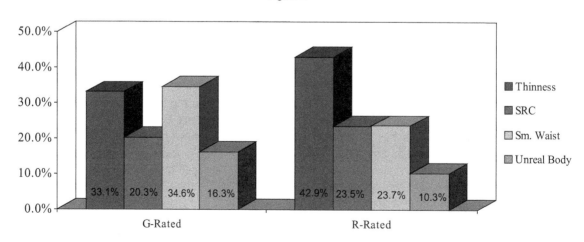

Animated Females Often are Abnormal in Shape, Sexy in Appearance

In addition to rating, we also evaluated how style of presentation affects hypersexualization. To this end, we analyzed females presented in live vs. animated action. We then looked for differences on the hypersexuality measures listed above. There are three reasons for this analysis. First, young children are often reared on general audience films. For example, over half of 0- to 6-year olds have at least 20 videos or DVDs in the home[11] and 46% of the children in this age bracket watch one video or DVD on a "typical" day. Thus, some of children's earliest media memories and favorite characters may come from G-rated motion picture content. Content in videos and DVDs may have a particular influence on children's social learning about gender because they tend to watch the same movies innumerable times.

Second, since females are less likely than males to appear in G-rated silver screen content, when they do appear, the impact of their portrayal may be stronger (that is, since there are fewer females with which to sympathize or to emulate, those that do appear may find their impact overly weighted). Third, animated females are creative constructions of animators and story artists. As a result, these types of characters may be the easiest to alter and change over time.

Style of presentation affects how females are featured in G-rated films. As shown in Table 1, the format females are presented in affects hypersexualization. Animated females are more likely to be shown in a thin and sexy light than are live action females.

Study 3: Qualitative Analysis: An In-Depth Look at 13 Female Leads in G-rated Films

Moving away from a solely quantitative approach, the third study took an in-depth look at how females are presented in G-rated films. In deciding how to approach this qualitative analysis, we had to identify a list of films to evaluate. First, we examined the top-grossing films that featured a female lead. Second, a selection of movies that depicted human or human-like females was desired, given that realistic portrayals seem to have a notable impact on viewers.[12] Third, we questioned whether the qualitative representations of females in G-rated films had changed over time. Our sample includes numerous re-releases of movies, which enabled us to select films distributed between 1937 and 2006.

Fourth, given the popularity of royalty-inspired toys and products,[13] we wanted some of the primary characters to be portrayed as sovereigns. Films about princesses are very profitable. And last but not least, we chose films in which the lead was, at the least, teenaged, as culturally children and pre-teens generally have less decision-making power than do teens and adults. We wanted to clear the path for the female leads to be of an age to make some decisions for themselves.[14]

Based on these criteria, the process yielded a total of 13 films for analysis, featuring live action and animated action, princesses and non princesses, and recent releases as well as timeless classics. Specifically, we assessed the protagonists' aspirations, romantic inclinations, and appearance norms within the context of the plot. Table 2 lists the movies in the

TABLE I. HYPERSEXUALITY INDICATORS BY STYLE OF PRESENTATION FOR G-RATED FILM FEMALES

Measure	Animated Characters	Live Action Characters
SRC	23.4% (n=85)	16.8% (n=52)
Small Waist	45.2% (n=152)	22.4% (n=66)
Large Chest	27.7% (n=96)	12.5% (n=38)
Thinness	39.1% (n=136)	26.3% (n=80)
Unrealistic Ideal	24.6% (n=86)	6.6% (n=20)

qualitative analysis as well as year of release and name of female protagonist. Four key findings are discussed below.

#1 Valued for their Appearance

Almost all of the females in this sample were praised for their appearance or physical beauty. Some of the movies depict the male love interest engaging in affirmation whereas other movies show friends, acquaintances, and even narrators extolling the exteriors of leading females. Social cognitive theory[15] suggests that reinforcements delivered to media characters can function as vicarious incentives to viewers. As such, positive reinforcements can *increase* the likelihood of learning whereas negative reinforcements can *decrease* such effects.[16] Therefore, a child viewer watching these films may vicariously learn that beauty is an essential part of being female.

In and of itself, appearance praise may not be problematic. Appearance praise becomes disconcerting when it is given only to characters that adhere to a narrow ideal of physical attractiveness, which is the formula for many of these females. Over half of the animated female leads in this study are shown with an unrealistic or exaggerated physique. And more than three fourths of live and animated females are depicted in sexually revealing attire. Thus, the beauty ideal reinforced in many of the films is an unattainable standard of sexiness and perfection.

Another aspect which suggests that appearance is valued in these films has to do with social presentations and extreme makeovers. A social presentation refers to putting the protagonist on display for the gaze and evaluation of one or more characters. More than two-thirds of the female protagonists are put on exhibition in these films. The possible motivations behind a social presentation are numerous, such as a royal engagement, nuptials, or a skill-based activity.

Although a few characters in the sample are appraised for their physical abilities, others are evaluated solely for their appearance and demure behavior. If a protagonist is introduced to the audience as less than ideal, then she may need to undergo a metamorphosis prior to her introduction to society. More than a third of the females had an overhaul of their outer shell somewhere in the film. A social presentation, particularly after an extreme makeover, encourages the gaze of other characters and viewers and can reinforce the idea that females are most important in their function as adornments.

TABLE 2			
Title of Film	*Year Released*	*Year Re-released*	*Protagonist*
Snow White and the Seven Dwarfs	1937	1993	Snow White
The Wizard of Oz	1939	1998	Dorothy
Cinderella	1950	1987	Cinderella
Sleeping Beauty	1959	2002	Aurora
The Little Mermaid	1989	1998	Ariel
Beauty and the Beast	1991	2002	Belle
FernGully	1992		Crysta
Pocahontas	1995	2005	Pocahontas
Anastasia	1997		Anastasia
Mulan	1998		Mulan
The Princess Diaries	2001		Mia
The Princess Diaries II	2004		Mia
Ice Princess	2005		Casey

#2 Often Females' Aspirations are Short Sighted

We assessed the goals or wishes of the female protagonists across the 13 films. Our analysis showed that G-rated females can have a distinct set of desires. Some long for romantic love. Others wish for family, adventure, or even an attempt to discover who they are or what they want out of life. We can categorize their character cravings in one of three ways: as *daydreamers*; as those that get *derailed* from their initial ambition; or as *daredevils* that risk it all to achieve a particular goal.

The Daydreamers. Daydreamers are those characters that possess no particular goal or dream only of romantic love. In films with daydreamers, the female lead is more passive, i.e. unlikely to set a chain of events into motion or take action to seek her goals. Instead, the protagonist may respond to changes in her environment while other characters propel the action. A few females are shown with no explicit aspiration. These females are simply reactive to external forces impinging upon the course of their life.

The Derailed. Some leading females express a desire for one thing and are broadsided by romantic love. When this occurs, it can be said that the protagonist is *derailed* from her initial ambition. Characters evidencing this theme may desire adventure or express an urge to explore, yet they fixate their entire intention on romantic involvement with another person. As a result, the derailed females often make unimaginable sacrifices in the name of love.

The Daredevils. Protagonists in this category express a goal or make choices that will move them toward their ambition. Unlike the derailed, daredevils may encounter romantic love but are not willing to relinquish their initial pursuits or accept romance as their only prize.

Overall, in the sample, love seems to be in an integral part of female protagonists' aspirations. Love may be an end state of, an interruption to, or an enhancement in the leading female's life.

#3 A Longing for One-Dimensional Love

Almost all of the films in this sample depict a female lead pursuing a romantic relationship. In some of the movies, the females' romance is the primary focus of the plot, whereas in others it is secondary. The films in which it is secondary often show females capable of having a relationship as well as achieving other life goals.

We examined the process of young love, with three general trends emerging across the plotlines. Some of the heroines fall in love at first sight, which is often dramatically accentuated with song and/or dance.[17] The introduction is sometimes followed by little or no cultivation of the courtship. Despite this, the young couple may be shown declaring their undying love, journeying off into the sunset together, or even getting married. It must be noted that this type of love is grounded in a character's physical appearance, thereby reinforcing the attractiveness norm discussed above.

Many of the female heroines' romantic relationships are formed on deceptive foundations. The leading lady or her romantic partner is dishonest by way of outright lying or strategic omission of important information. Remarkably, the duplicitous actions of one character are likely to be forgiven quickly or remain completely unacknowledged by the relational partner.

A third pathway to love is through communication. This relational component may be found when two characters are shown verbally interacting over the duration of the film. Although it may seem obvious that conversation and quality time spent with one's potential life-partner are important, such negotiations are not always illustrated in general audience romances.[18]

Together, young viewers are not presented with a particularly healthy or realistic portrait of romance in the films reviewed here. Young love is often grounded in artificial or deceptive relationships. Nevertheless, two of the films in our study did show young women negotiating trials, with romance playing a nonexistent to minimal role.

#4 Not Damsels in Distress

A positive finding of the study is that the stereotypical damsel in distress was observed in fewer films than might be expected. Several films do depict male and female characters engaging in reciprocal relational rescues from grave threats.[19] Only one film from our study depicts a female protagonist who saves her love interest but is not shown in a reciprocal rescue.

The female protagonists are sometimes shown engaging in heroic acts to save friends, family members, and society. These acts involve costs that may range from minor inconveniences to major life-course impediments or even death. Several major rescues include: Dorothy saving the scarecrow from burning to death;[20] Ariel rescuing Flounder from being eaten by a shark; Belle sacrificing her freedom for Maurice's release from captivity; Mulan taking her father's place in the draft and becoming a soldier in the Imperial Army; and Crysta destroying Hexxus to save all living creatures in the forest.

Clearly, it seems that the completely helpless damsel in distress is no longer a popular choice for content creators. Instead, some female protagonists are shown in physically active roles with the ability to act heroically. The style of presentation is likely to influence the presence of risk and rescue scenarios. Animated content may depict scenes involving war, magic, or other dangers making them particularly suitable for altruistic behavior.

The purpose of this study was to take an in depth look at female protagonists in G-rated films. Four key themes were identified across the movies. Appearance is heavily focused upon in these films, potentially contributing to negative effects. However, the aspirations and heroic actions of certain general audience female leads should be commended. The latter is important—as such portrayals depict females in a compelling light to both males and females in the viewing audience.

Study 4: TV for Kids 11 and Under: Prevalence, Portrayal, Appearance

In the fourth analysis, we assessed gender roles in television content made for children. To this end, we randomly sampled 1,034 shows from 12 network, public broadcast, and cable outlets including 534 hours of programming between June 12 and August 18th, 2005 to assemble a typical week of children's television programming. We examined the prevalence of males and females, as well as the nature of their demography, appearance, personality, and likeability.

Prevalence. Male characters occur roughly at twice the rate of female characters in television created for children. Sample-wide, the ratio of males to females was 1.67 to 1, including characters presented alone, in groups,[21] or as narrators. Animated programs in particular are more likely to show males. In live-action formats, however, the landscape is a bit more promising: Females occur more frequently in groups than males. However, an almost equal portrayal appears with single-speaking male and female live action characters (ratio = 1.24 males to 1 female).

TV ratings were other criteria by which children's TV was evaluated. Children's shows can be rated TVY (suitable content for all children) or TVY7 (suitable content for age 7 and above, may contain fantasy violence or elements causing fear). Many programs rated TVG (suitable for all ages, little or no sexual content, violence, or strong language) are also targeted to young audiences. Out of the 1,034 shows in the sample, 48.4% were rated TVY, 34.1% were rated TVY7, and 17.5% were rated TVG.

The results indicated that shows rated TVY or TVY7 are more likely to feature males, while almost half of the single-speaking characters in TVG rated shows are female (44.7%).

For TVY, there are 1.64 males to every 1 female that appears in group situations. In TVY7 shows, the ratio is 1.91 males to every 1 female. The ratio of females to males in TVG groups is 1.48 to 1. Only 25 TVG stories portrayed a narrator and the majority were female (72%). This suggests that gender representation indeed varies depending on the target audience. For those shows aimed directly at the youngest audiences, there are still more males on screen. The most equitable portrayals seem to take place in shows rated TVG.

The research also addressed how style of presentation and rating influences the context for gender representation. Not surprisingly, more humans are found in live action shows than animated ones. Live action stories depict more non white males (26.8%) than do animated stories (19.9%). No meaningful difference emerged for females, however. Males and females are less likely to be depicted as parents or relational partners in live as opposed to animated contexts.

For the rating analysis, it was found that TVY7 features the highest proportion of human males; TVG and TVY7 shows had the highest numbers of human male children. Adult females are more likely to be found in shows rated TVY than those rated TVY7 or TVG. TVG featured more non white male and female characters in general, and TVY had more non white female characters than TVY7. TVY-rated males and females have a higher chance of being depicted as parents and in romantic relationships than TVG– or TVY7–rated males and females.

TV G: More Diverse, More Gender-Balanced

The research suggests that the "healthiest" balance of male and female representation is found in shows rated TVG. These programs present a more balanced treatment of characters by gender and in roles of familial responsibility (e.g., parent, romantic relationship). Further, TVG shows depict the highest proportion of non white, ethnic minority characters. A conclusion can be drawn that in G-rated fare, gender-balanced programming is profitable. An additional extrapolation from the near balance in G-rated television is that there is a high likelihood that both males and females are watching.

Portrayal. We also wanted to find out if the format of entertainment (e.g., live action or animated) and rating (e.g., TVY, TVY7, or TVG) affected the presentation of gender roles. In terms of style of presentation, animated males are more likely to be bad and strong and live-action males are more likely to be smart and funny. Live-action females are presented with more humor than those in animation.

In terms of rating, notable differences also emerged across the sample. Males in TVG– and TVY-rated shows are more likely to be depicted as good than are males in TVY7–rated shows. Males in TVY7 contexts are more likely to be strong than are males in TVG or TVY contexts. TVG males are more likely to be featured as smart than TVY males, while TVY7 females are most likely to be the ones with the brains. TVY7 seems to show its share of bad and strong characters independent of gender, perhaps attributed to the quintessential antisocial agents in cartoon type programming.TVG females possess more traditionally feminine attributes than do females of the other ratings. TVG and TVY7 males are more traditionally masculine than are TVY males.

Appearance. Similar to our other studies, we examined hypersexualized attributes of males and females. Sample wide, we observed significant deviation in alluring attire and body shape variables. See Figure 3. Females are almost four times as likely as males to be shown in sexy attire. Further, females are nearly twice as likely as males to be shown with a diminutive waist line. Unrealistic figures are more likely to be seen on females than males.

Looking at style of presentation, the format that females appear in affects their level of sexualization. Females in animated contexts are more likely to be shown in sexually revealing attire than are females in live action contexts (24.5% vs. 17.4%). Females in animated stories are more likely to have small waists (36.9% vs. 6.9%) and have an unrealistic body shape (22.7% vs. 1.2%) than are females in live action stories. Males are also assessed for style of presentation differences. No differences emerged for sexually revealing clothing. However, animated action males are more likely than their live action counterparts to have a large chest (15.4% vs. 4.9%), small waist (18.4% vs. 4.3%), and unrealistically muscularized physique (12.5% vs. .5%). Clearly, animation appears to favor highly sexualized female characters with unrealistic body ideals. For males, animation seems to heighten their muscularity.

Rating also affects hypersexuality norms. The next two figures portray how a few hypersexuality measures differ by rating. As shown in Figure 4, the most problematic depiction of females occurs in TVY7.

We also examined the distribution of hypersexuality variables for males. No differences emerged for sexually revealing clothing or unrealistic body shape. However, chest size and waist size varied by rating.

Hypersexuality of Males and Females in Children's Shows
Figure 3

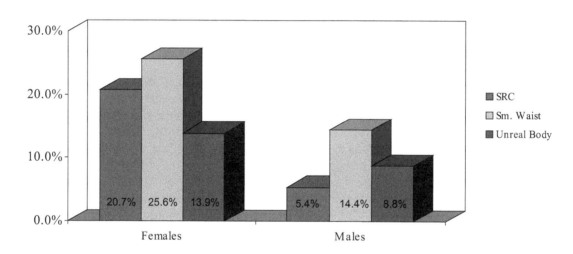

Hypersexuality of Females in Children's Shows by Rating
Figure 4

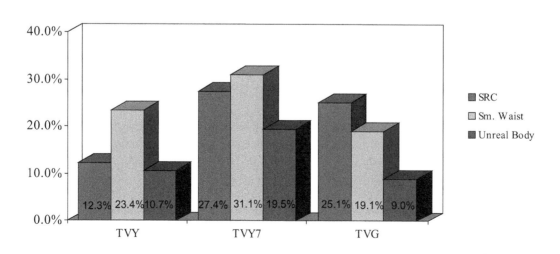

Hypersexuality of Males in Children's Shows by Rating
Figure 5

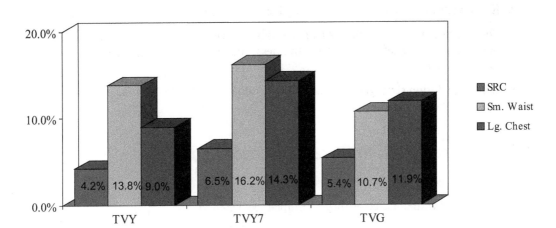

Conclusion

Although differing in samples and approach, the results from these four studies clearly point out that gender inequality is prevalent in both film and television aimed at children. The results from these investigations reveal that much work is needed to be done to achieve gender parity and improved portrayal in film and in children's television. Despite the Civil Rights Movement in the 1950/60s and the rise of second wave Feminism in the 1970s, on screen gender equality still does not exist.

Recommendations for Entertainment Executives and Creators:

1. Include more females as main characters, secondary characters, in crowds, and as narrators.

2. Provide female characters with aspirations beyond romance.

3. Develop the inner character of female characters, too.

Recommendations for Scholars
Other key areas of study

1. The reasons why domestically-released G-rated television programs are far more gender-balanced than domestically-released G-Rated films.

2. Effects of gender-specific marketing on domestic male or female audience prevalence.

3. Key aspects of domestic and international market success of US-conceptualized G-rated films that are more gender-balanced and feature complex female characters.

4. Domestic and international product marketing for US-conceptualized G-rated television and G-rated films.

5. Effects of key international marketing demands on domestic G-rated film releases as well as domestic television programming aimed at children.

6. Content patterns and effects on children associated with stereotypical gender portrayals, both domestically and internationally.

7. Correlation between hiring patterns and on-screen gender balance.

8. Prevalence of males and females in domestic media tracked longitudinally over time.

9. Key aspects of financially successful (top box office) gender-balanced PG-rated films

10. The role of exposure to hypersexual portrayals on girls and boys' short- and long-term perceptions and beliefs about beauty, thinness, and physical attraction, domestically and internationally.

11. Gender inclusion strategies in other multi-national/global industries for possible application to the entertainment industry.

Recommendations for Parents & Teachers

1. Co-view media content with children.

2. Spend time with children as they consume media content.

3. Critically engage and discuss what is present <u>and</u> absent in modern media-based stories.

4. Ask children who is missing in the story and whether the depiction looks like their family, social, or school environment.

For your review. gender imbalance in other key positions of power and influence:

The National Association of Corporate Directors reports women occupy only 16.2 percent of Fortune 100 board seats.
From, Heidrick & Struggles article, 2006.

According to Govspot.com, in the 107th Congress, there are 74 women members: 61 women in the House out of 435 members (14%) and 13 in the Senate (26%).

Here are **The Animation Guild's** most recent statistics, in 2006.
Percentage of Women, 399 out of 2308, or 17.3% in these capacities:
Producers, 8%; Directors 14.9%; Writers 10.8%; Art Directors, 11.1%; Visual Development, 13.1%; Story Art, 13.8%; Layout, 17.8%; Model Designers, 21.4%; Background 25.6%; 2D Animation 21.3%; 3D Animators and Modellers, 13.0%; Compositors, 29.2%; Tech directors, 13.8%; Checkers, etc. 34.0%.

According to **WGA**, west's report, *Catching Up with a Changing America*:
In 2004, the total number of employed film writers was 1770. 18%, or 318, were women. The total number of TV writers for the same year was 3015. 27% of these, or 822, were women.

Endnotes

1. Lauzen, M. M., & Dozier, D. M. (1999). The role of women on screen and behind the scenes in the television and film industries: Review and a program of research. Journal of Communication Inquiry, 23(4), 355-373.

2. The assessment of group characters proved to be an extremely difficult task in study 1. Coders had to determine that two or more characters were 1) speaking simultaneously or 2) looked similar (i.e., the male guards in Aladdin) but were overlapping in speech such that distinct characters could not be identified. For example, the opening scene of

Beauty and the Beast features dozens of characters crisscrossing in and out of frame saying only one or two words. Once coders identified that a group met the definition, they were then expected to estimate using values from a scaled item (e.g., 5-10, 11-25, etc.) the highest number of males, females, and/or characters with an unknown gender in each group.

Given this complexity, our data set initially revealed that the coders were using values that were not valid when assessing mixed gendered groups (e.g., collectives with both males, females, and/or those with unidentifiable gender) and groups with only characters whose gender was not identifiable. Because of this, we only reported the results of groups with same-sex characters. A later reanalysis of reliability judgments of group size revealed that coders had difficulty with estimating the number of males (reliability coefficient over .38) and females (reliability coefficient over .80) in same sex and mixed-gendered groups.

The high reliability for females was largely a function of coders accurately assessing that there were no women or girls in three out of four reliability tests involving same sex groups. Some of the low reliability for estimating males in same sex groups can be attributed to 1) true differences in estimating size or 2) simply entering the wrong numeric value (i.e., entering a "5" instead of a "10" to represent the same level "5-10 characters") from a specified interval level in excel. When correcting for the later source of error, reliability for same sex groups reaches a more acceptable level. Based on this and the small number of decisions used to calculate reliability for estimating group size (n=7 total groups, across four tests), the data presented in the text on same-sex groups are to be interpreted with caution. Clearly, the coding of groups is a fertile ground for future researchers interested in content analytic studies investigating gender balance in motion pictures.

3. Two large groups of students evaluated the film content at the University of Southern California during the 2006/07 academic year. Students were taught to unitize characters as well as apply the conceptual and operational definitions of the variables to film content. A series of diagnostics were undertaken to ensure reliability in the coders' unitizing and variable-level judgments. Post training, these tests revealed consistency in unitizing characters and assigning levels (above .70%) across all the variables. Thus, the consistency of the coders' judgments across all of the measures in the scheme was acceptable.

Additionally, the G, PG, and PG-13 study was commissioned as a result of funds raised by Geena Davis. The R-rated study was funded by the Annenberg School for Communication.

4. Significance is defined in two ways. First, the statistical test must be significant at the $p < .05$ level. Second, the percentages between any two or more categories must differ by at least 5%. Trivial was defined as a statistically significant finding that demonstrated less than a five percent difference between percentages.

5. MacPherson, K. (2005, ¶7-10). Is childhood becoming oversexed? Retrieved March 8, 2007 from http://www. post-gazette.com/pg/05128/500945.stm

6. Hellmich, N. (2006, ¶9). Do thin models warp girls' body image? Retrieved March 8, 2007 from http://www. usatoday.com/news/health/2006-09-25-thin-models_x.htm

7. Report of the APA Task Force on the Sexualization of Girls. (2007). Washington DC: Author.

8. Mithers, C. L. (2001, ¶18). Sugar & spice. Parenting, 15, 7, 90-95.

9. Cohen, E. (2006, June 18, ¶23). Daddy's home: And as a stay-at-home father, he's been there all day. Press & Sun- Bulletin, p. Lifestyle.

10. Some notable deviation occurred with the other ratings as well: Looking at females, the percentages are as follows: sexually revealing clothing (PG=15.6%, PG-13=24.5%), chest size (PG=13.9%, PG-13=14.3%), waist size (PG=20.7%, PG-13=22.8%), body realism (PG=6.3%, PG-13=11.1%), and thinness (PG=27.5%, PG-13=29.5%).

11. Kaiser Family Foundation. (2003). Zero to six: Electronic media in the lives of infants, toddlers, and preschoolers. Menlo Park, CA: Author.

12. Atkin, C. (1983). Effects of realistic TV violence vs. fictional violence on aggression. Journalism Quarterly, 60, 615-621. Thomas, M.H., & Tell, P.M. (1974). Effects of viewing real versus fantasy violence upon interpersonal aggression. Journal of Research in Personality, 8, 153-160.

13. Strauss, G. (2004). Princesses rule the hearts of little girls. USA Today. Retrieved November 11, 2005, from http://www.usatoday.com/life/lifestyle/2004-03-02-princess_x.htm; Disney Consumer Products. (n.d.). Disney princess. Retrieved December 15th, 2007, from https://licensing.disney.com/Home/display.jsp? contentId=dcp_home_ ourfranchises_disney_princess&forPrint=false&language=en&preview=false&region=0

14. Additionally, films with a "buddy plot" or movies depicting a leading lady as a villain were not included in the qualitative analysis.

15. Bandura, A. (1986). Social foundations of thought and action. Englewood Cliffs, NJ: Prentice-Hall.

16. Bandura, A. (1965). Influence of models' reinforcement contingencies on the acquisition of imitative responses. Journal of Personality and Social Psychology, 1, 589-595.

17. To illustrate, Snow White longs for love at first sight when she sings "Someday my prince will come." At that moment, Prince Charming arrives. Though she is serenaded by the young man, Snow White and the Prince never converse. Snow White later informs the dwarves that it was easy to fall in love with the prince because he was very charming. In Cinderella and Sleeping Beauty, each heroine has a brief encounter with the man of her dreams which is hastily characterized as love in song or dialogue with other characters. Finally, Ariel catches a glimpse of Prince Eric from the side of his ship, rescues him from drowning, and sacrifices her entire life course to be "part of his world." Ariel is silent during her three day courtship with Eric; the two marry and sail off into the sunset.

18. Dimitri and Anastasia have an antagonistic relationship, but both parties feel free to express their true feelings to one another. In Princess Diaries II, Mia is shown bickering and competing with Nicholas in their clash for the crown. Their attraction grows along the course of the film. In Ice Princess, Casey and Teddy's relationship develops slowly across the entire context of the plot. At first, the two are acquaintances and become friends, and finally share their first kiss after Casey's skating competition.

19. It could be argued that reciprocal rescues are not evidenced in FernGully due to the nature of the hazardous circumstances in the plot. Multiple characters save Crysta from danger in FernGully, including Zak. Although it is true that Crysta saves Zak, she rescues multiple characters simultaneously. Crysta leads the charge to destroy Hexxus and saves all living creatures in the forest.

20. As Dorothy throws a bucket of water on the scarecrow, she also soaks the wicked witch and causes her demise. This action inadvertently frees all from the witch's oppressive dominion.

21. Groups, in the TV study, included both mixed and same sex collectives.

10

Men, Masculinity, and Manhood Acts

Douglas Schrock[1] and Michael Schwalbe[2]

Abstract

In the 1980s research on men shifted from studying the "male sex role" and masculinity as a singular trait to studying how men enact diverse masculinities. This research has examined men's behavior as gendered beings in many contexts, from intimate relationships to the workplace to global politics. We consider the strengths and weaknesses of the multiple masculinities approach, proposing that further insights into the social construction of gender and the dynamics of male domination can be gained by focusing analytic attention on manhood acts and how they elicit deference from others. We interpret the literature in terms of what it tells us about how males learn to perform manhood acts, about how and why such acts vary, and about how manhood acts reproduce gender inequality. We end with suggestions for further research on the practices and processes through which males construct the category "men" and themselves as its members.

Introduction

Feminism has taught sociology that no account of social life is complete if it ignores gender inequality. Sociologists of course wrote about sex roles, and about masculinity and femininity, before second-wave feminism impacted the discipline in the 1960s and 1970s. But much of this prefeminist writing, done under the influence of functionalism, treated sex roles as complementary and necessary—not as stemming from unequal power relations between women and men. Masculinity and femininity were likewise seen as sex-specific and sex-appropriate personality traits that were expressed behaviorally, rather than as attributions elicited by acts of domination and

[1]Department of Sociology, Florida State University, Tallahassee, Florida 32306-2270; email: dschrock@fsu.edu
[2]Department of Sociology, North Carolina State University, Raleigh, North Carolina 27695-8107; email: michael_schwalbe@ncsu.edu

Annu. Rev. Sociol. 2009. 35:277–95. First published online as a Review in Advance on April 6, 2009. The *Annual Review of Sociology* is online at soc.annualreviews.org
This article's doi: 10.1146/annurev-soc-070308-115933. Copyright © 2009 by Annual Reviews. All rights reserved. 0360-0572/09/0811-0277$20.00

subordination. By the early 1980s, these old views had largely been superseded among sociologists of gender.

Since that time, gender scholars have created an enormous body of theory and research that goes under the rubric of "critical studies of men and masculinities." We acknowledge that defining intellectual eras by reference to decades is an oversimplification and that the emergence of this new strain in gender studies was not a discrete event. Significant changes in sociological thinking about gender, and about men and masculinity in particular, were under way before 1980 (see, e.g., Kessler & McKenna 1978, Pleck & Sawyer 1974, Tolson 1977). Yet it is possible in this case to identify a point at which the terms of the discussion shifted and the study of men and masculinity entered the mainstream. We mark this point as the publication of Carrigan et al.'s 1985 article "Toward a New Sociology of Masculinity."

Carrigan et al. debunked sex-role theory for its blindness to power, showed how masculinity was about power relations among men, not only between women and men, illuminated the link between masculinity and heterosexuality by taking gay sexuality seriously, treated masculinity not as a trait but as a form of collective male practice that has as its effect the subordination of women, and formulated the concepts of hegemonic and subordinated masculinities. Each of these ideas can be traced to earlier works (e.g., Connell 1983), but by integrating them into a coherent analysis, Carrigan et al. put the study of men and masculinities on its contemporary track.

By some measures, that track has been fruitful. Our initial search of *Sociological Abstracts* turned up 2999 articles (78.6% of them published since 1995) that listed "masculinity" or "masculinities" as a key word. There are now several textbooks and edited volumes offering overviews of the field (e.g., Clatterbaugh 1996, Messner & Kimmel 2007), four encyclopedias or handbooks on studies of men and masculinity (Flood et al. 2007, Kimmel & Aronson 2004, Kimmel et al. 2005, Whitehead 2006), and two massive bibliographies (Flood 2008, Janssen 2008). The important question, however, is not how much has been published, but, as we ask here, what has been accomplished?

It could be said that we know a great deal about men and every conventional category of social life. There are literatures on men and work, men and war, men and sports, men and race, men and health, men and aging, men and crime, men and sexuality, men and violence, men and family, and men and friendship. Viewed in these terms, the landscape of our knowledge appears vast. Yet the tendency for sociologists to embrace the men-and-(fill in the blank) pattern when studying men and masculinity has, in our view, become limiting. As we will argue, moving forward depends on reclaiming key insights from Carrigan et al. (1985) and from interactionist analyses of gender.

Our approach here is to avoid the *men and* pattern and instead look at what the literature tells us about what men do, individually and collectively, such that women as a group are subordinated to men as a group and such that some men are subordinated to others. This is meant to reassert the importance of studying practices and processes. Our approach accords with current sociological theory that sees gender not as an attribute of individuals but as the name we give to cultural practices that construct women and men as different and that advantage men at the expense of women (Lorber 1994, Martin 2003, West & Zimmerman 1987). We thus focus primarily on qualitative studies that provide insight into how males construct the category "men" and themselves as its members.[1]

---

[1]We focus primarily on qualitative research for three reasons: (*a*) Qualitative methods are those most often used in studies of masculinity; (*b*) survey-based approaches tend to reify masculinity, treating it as a static psychological trait; and (*c*) qualitative methods provide the best insight into how men present themselves as gendered beings (which is our concern here). Though beyond the scope of this paper, sociologists interested in methodological dilemmas that arise when conducting qualitative research on men have a burgeoning literature to draw on (see, for example, Butera 2006, Gatrell 2006, Hearn 2007, Messner 1990, Schwalbe & Wolkomir 2001, Schacht 1997).

Definitions

Much of the contention and confusion in the field stems from vague definitions of key concepts, inconsistent use of key concepts, or both. Although it is impossible to impose, post hoc, a set of definitions on a body of literature, it is possible to offer a set of definitions that can be used to interpret the literature. Our definitions are anchored in a social constructionist perspective, and as such might not be congenial to all. Definitions are necessary, however, for any attempt at sense-making and for sorting out disagreements. So we begin with the basics: males, men, and masculinity.

Based on differences in reproductive anatomy, humans are sorted into the categories "male" and "female," reflecting a belief that males and females are or should become different kinds of people. Males are taught and expected to identify themselves not only as biological males, but, depending on age, as either boys or men. Females are taught and expected to identify themselves not only as biological females, but, depending on age, as either girls or women. This distinction between reproductive anatomy and gender identity is crucial for understanding what men are and how to study them.

In this view, the category "males" is not equivalent to the category "men." Men are (usually) biological males claiming rights and privileges attendant to membership in the dominant gender group. For an individual male to enjoy the benefits that derive from membership in the dominant gender group, he must present himself to others as a particular kind of social being: a man. This is, as Goffman (1977) and West & Zimmerman (1987) remind us, a dramaturgical task. To be credited as a man, what an individual male must do, in other words, is put on a convincing manhood act (Schwalbe 2005). This requires mastering a set of conventional signifying practices through which the identity "man" is established and upheld in interaction.

The dramaturgical task of establishing creditability as a man and thus as a member of the dominant gender group is aided by having a male body. Because of the conventional association between maleness and manhood, a male body is a symbolic asset. It is normally taken as a sign of qualification for membership in the category "men." However, it is neither necessary (females can mask their secondary sex characteristics, appear to be male, and attempt to put on a manhood act; see, e.g., Dozier 2005) nor sufficient (males can fail to muster the other signifiers necessary to establish themselves as creditable men worthy of full manhood status).

Distinguishing between sex and gender is conventional wisdom in sociology, yet the distinction is worth reiterating, as it remains common to mistake males for men. Even more trouble arises in defining masculinity. Carrigan et al. (1985; see also Connell 1995) define masculinity as a "configuration of practices"—practices that have the effect of subordinating women. Although this definition usefully highlights what men do to maintain dominance, it is not without problems. It is not clear, for instance, precisely which of men's practices constitute masculinity (Martin 1998). The definition also tends to take the category "men" for granted, rather than treating the category as constructed by practices and the meanings given to those practices.

To avoid this problem, our definitional strategy is to say that males—if they are to do their part in maintaining men as the dominant gender group and if they wish to enjoy the privileges that come from membership in that group—must signify possession of a masculine self. This self is, however, only a virtual reality, a dramatic effect, or a consequence of how an actor's appearance and behavior are interpreted by others (Goffman 1959). In this view, as opposed to the commonsense view, a masculine self is not a psychological entity, nor a built-in feature of male bodies. It is, rather, a self imputed to an individual based on information given and given off in interaction, but it is an imputation that matters greatly.

The qualities seen as constituting a masculine self can vary historically and culturally. The practices that are interpreted as signs of a masculine self can also vary depending on other features of the actor (age, race, ethnicity, class), the audience, and the situation. In Western cultures, and in the contemporary United States especially, the essential element is a capacity to exert control or to resist being controlled (Johnson 2005). To elicit the attribution of possessing a masculine self thus requires signifying—with or without conscious awareness—that one possesses the capacities to make things happen and to resist being dominated by others.

Two further notes may be helpful here. First, to observe that males strive to claim membership in the dominant gender category by signifying a masculine self is not a moral critique. All humans learn where they are supposed to fit in a set of preexisting cultural categories, some of which are hierarchically arranged. So just as North Americans of European descent learn to think of and present themselves as white, which is the dominant racial category in U.S. culture, males learn to think of and present themselves as men, which is the dominant gender category. The root of the problem, then, if one opposes racial or gender inequality, lies in a system of privilege, not in individuals. Examining how gender is interactionally constructed, as many scholars have done and as we do here, is a matter of trying to understand how the system is reproduced, not a matter of leveling moral judgment.

Second, we acknowledge that efforts to exert control over the environment—efforts that might be part of manhood acts—can yield positive results. Survival and the quality of human life indeed depend on controlling things in the world. Thus, it is not our claim that attempts to signify a masculine self through acts of control have nothing but oppressive consequences. Our claim is that, whatever other consequences they might have, and regardless of what individual males consciously intend, manhood acts have the effect of reproducing an unequal gender order. Again, the point of taking this analytic view is not to evaluate categories of actors but to arrive at a better understanding of how the gender order works.

Problems with Plurality

Current thinking in the field treats masculinity not as singular but as plural. There is not just one form of masculinity, it is said, but rather there are multiple masculinities. This notion grew out of the distinction between hegemonic masculinity—the kind of manhood act most revered in a culture (Connell 1987, 1995, 2000)—and lower-status ways that manhood is enacted by males with fewer resources. Thinking of masculinity as plural usefully sensitizes us to differences and inequalities among groups of men, but it can also make it hard to see what it is that masculinities have in common, other than enactment by male bodies. We propose that the common theme should be seen not as a type of body but as a type of act: one that signifies a masculine self.

The multiple masculinities concept reflects a laudable desire to value diversity. It is ironic, then, that this concept has fostered a kind of categorical essentialism in studies of men. To invoke, for example, the existence of Black masculinity, Latino masculinity, gay masculinity, Jewish masculinity, working-class masculinity, and so on is to imply that there is an overriding similarity in the gender enactments of males who are Black, Latino, gay, Jewish, or working class. The implicit claim is that all members of the category practice an identifiably unique form of masculinity. This strategy of using conventional categories of race, ethnicity, sexuality, religion, or class to define masculinities into existence is dubious. It can cause us to lose sight of what these allegedly diverse gender-signifying practices have in common (again, other than enactment by male bodies) that makes them masculinity. It can also obscure important within-group variations.

The discourse of multiple masculinities has also had the effect of detaching men from their actions. Despite the ritual defining of masculinities as forms of practice, it is not uncommon to see masculinity invoked to explain men's behavior, as if masculinity were an independent variable that caused men to behave in more or less oppressive ways. This is, as some have pointed out (e.g., MacInnes 1998), circular. If the behavior in question—some form of practice being studied—is what constitutes masculinity, then masculinity cannot be used to explain that behavior. Attributing men's behavior to masculinity also tends to discount men's agency. Our preference for referring to manhood acts arises from a desire to discourage the reification of masculinity and to redirect analytic attention to what males actually do to achieve dominance.

All manhood acts, as we define them, are aimed at claiming privilege, eliciting deference, and resisting exploitation. As suggested earlier, body types are irrelevant, except inasmuch as a male body is a symbolic asset and a female body a liability, when trying to signify possession of a masculine self and put on a convincing manhood act. The view we take here also focuses attention on what males do to create, maintain, and claim membership in a dominant gender group. Our organization and discussion of the literature reflects this concern with practices and processes. We thus turn to considering what the literature tells us about (a) how males learn to signify masculine selves, (b) themes and variations in the construction of manhood acts, and (c) how manhood acts reproduce gender inequality.

Learning to Signify Masculine Selves

Children are born into a world in which males/boys/men are differentiated from females/girls/women. Children must learn to categorize themselves and others in these terms and learn to convey to others that they understand this system of categorization and their place within it. For young males, this means learning to identify themselves as boys and signify masculine selves. They must master, in other words, the "identity codes" (Schwalbe & Mason-Schrock 1996) that are symbolic constituents of the gender order. A great deal of research has examined how this aspect of symbolic culture is learned through childhood interaction and through exposure to media imagery.

Young males' initial adoption of the identity "boy" is micropolitical. Based on 18 months of fieldwork at a preschool, Cahill (1986) found that children and adults use the term "baby" to stigmatize children's socially immature behavior, whereas they reward more mature acts by bestowing the term "boy" or "girl." Such responses do not merely affirm that males are boys and females are girls. More than this, such responses link grown-up status and approval from others with doing gender properly.

Young males also learn that gender identities are signified by using appropriate props. Initially, much of this identity work is done by parents, as newborns and toddlers are equipped with gendered names, clothes, and toys (Pomerleau et al. 1990). Preschool boys who fail to grasp the pattern and wear dresses or pink ribbons are scolded by their peers for misbehavior (Cahill 1989). Based on 42 interviews with diverse parents of preschoolers, Kane (2006) shows that parents—especially heterosexual fathers—often censure preschool sons who play with Barbies or wear fingernail polish or pink clothing. Such policing leads young males to, as Cahill (1989, p. 290) put it, "reject and devalue . . . symbols of female identity" in order to "confirm their identities as boys."

Boys and girls are often sorted or, later, sort themselves into segregated groups. Lever's (1978) field study of 181 fifth graders revealed how girls tend to play in small groups that stress cooperation and intimacy, whereas boys play in larger groups that are more competitive, goal-directed, and rule-guided. Even when boys and girls play together, they often do so in ways that imply essential differences between boys and girls and, usually, the superiority of boys (Thorne 1993). Lever argues that this gender-segregated play can lead to differential skill development that may account for some gender inequality among adults. Our point is that participation in segregated activities comes to be understood as part of how gender identities are signified. Playing or watching sports—violent sports in particular (McBride 1995)—can thus be a way for boys and men to signify masculine selves (Messner 1992).

Another lesson for young males is that emotional display must be regulated, lest it undermine a manhood act. In their ethnographic study of a summer camp, McGuffey & Rich (1999) found that high-status boys ostracized boys who cried. Males involved in sports similarly police the expression of emotion, affirming the principle that boys should not express fear or pain (Curry 1993, Messner 1992). Parents are often complicit in this gendered training because they feel accountable—for their sons' behavior—to other adults (Kane 2006). Parents who believe that their son's masculinity is threatened may be especially inclined to encourage stoicism. For example, during one of McGuffey's (2008, p. 212) 389 interviews with 62 parents of sexually abused sons, one father said of his victimized son, "He's already been made into a woman sexually. I can't let him turn into one emotionally, too!"

Boys also learn that they should feel, or at least express, sexual desire for girls. Among preadolescent and adolescent boys, this desire is signified mainly through talk about the sexual appeal of girls and women, through sharing pin-ups and pornography, and by presenting themselves as heterosexually active and knowledgeable (Fine 1987, Thorne 1993). As Pascoe (2007, p. 114) documented in her ethnography of a high school, boys use language and sometimes violence to turn girls and women into props for signifying heterosexuality. The boys she studied sexually harassed girls with unwanted comments and touching, and talked and joked about rape (see also Renold 2007). Boys' homophobic taunting of other boys who are deemed feminine is also a means of signifying heterosexuality (Pascoe 2007).

One of the most important lessons about signifying manhood concerns aggression and violence. Young boys' play often reflects popular warrior narratives in which violence is "legitimate and justified when it occurs within a struggle between good and evil" (Jordan & Cowan 1995, p. 728). Fathers and older male relatives often encourage (subtly, if not overtly) boys to fight, and reward them for doing so (Athens 1992, Messerschmidt 2000). The importance of signifying manhood through displays of fighting spirit is reinforced in sports, as coaches and teammates celebrate aggressive play while demeaning nonaggressive play as feminine (Fine 1987, Messner 1992). The pervasiveness of bullying has been attributed to this valorization of aggression and violence (Phillips 2007). A common cultural script also portrays effective resistance to bullying as a way to assert a masculine self (Kimmel & Mahler 2003).

Learning to signify a masculine self entails learning how to adjust to audiences and situations and learning how one's other identities bear on the acceptability of a performance. Males in marginalized social groups may face special challenges in this regard (Majors & Billson 1992, Staples 1982). Research on schools shows that teachers and administrators often stereotype African American and Latino boys as unruly, prompting increased surveillance and discipline (Ferguson 2000, Morris 2005). Boys learn, however, that they can impress peers if they break rules, talk back to teachers, and disdain academics (Ferguson 2000, Fordham & Ogbu 1986, Mac an Ghaill 1994, Willis 1977). Boys socialized into urban gangs (Stretesky & Pogrebin 2007) or white supremacist groups (Kimmel 2007) learn that they can achieve manhood status through actual or symbolic acts of intimidation. The lesson—for boys who are marginalized because of class or race—is that a masculine self can be signified, and deference elicited, by evoking fear in others.

The process of learning how to signify a masculine self in situationally appropriate ways continues throughout life. Men in manual labor jobs may learn that signifying a masculine self requires displays of strength and endurance, as well as resistance to being bossed (Collinson 1992). Men training for professional jobs, such as students in traditional MBA programs (Sinclair 1995), learn to signify masculine selves by appearing to be instrumentally oriented, rational, and able to manage subordinates. Men in the military learn that toughness, in-group loyalty, and the sexual objectification of women are the marks of manhood (Higate 2007). Men entering new jobs must thus learn to signify masculine selves in ways that accord with the organization's culture and gender politics.

Media Imagery

Media imagery provides a repertoire of signifying practices that males can draw on to craft manhood acts. For example, in their fieldwork studies, Dyson (1994) shows how boys in elementary school enact superhero narratives, and Milkie (1994) shows how middle school boys discuss, identify with, exaggerate, and imitate the male heroes of Hollywood movies.

More is learned, however, than simply which models to emulate or how to do so. Media imagery also provides a shared symbolic language for identifying certain practices as signs of masculine character.

Research on children's media reveals that it often glorifies men's power. Hamilton et al. (2006) analyzed 200 of the most popular children's books and found that male characters were typically portrayed as assertive and aggressive, rarely nurturing, and more likely than female characters to work outside the home. Research on educational software for preschool children (Sheldon 2004) and comic books (Pecora 1992) similarly finds that male characters are more likely than female characters to be athletic, aggressive, and heroic. Similarly, grade school texts still overwhelmingly depict males as argumentative and competitive (Evans & Davies 2000). And whereas video games depict female characters as "victims or sexual objects," they portray male characters as "heroes and violent perpetrators" (Dietz 1998, p. 438). A lesson conveyed by much of this children's media is thus that males naturally command the attention and deference of others by virtue of their greater strength, daring, and capacity for violence.

Media targeting adolescent and adult men also create signifiers of masculine selves. Popular low-brow men's magazines (e.g., *Stuff*, *Maxim*) root manhood in displays of heterosexual appetite and virtuosity (Ezzell 2008, Taylor 2005). As McCaughey (2008) shows, popular culture often frames men's sexual infidelity and violence against women as biologically determined and thus inevitable. In mainstream magazines aimed at male audiences, men are most often portrayed as at work (Vigorito & Curry 1998), thus affirming productivity and breadwinning as signs of a masculine self. Even television portrayals that depart from these stereotypes, such as news stories about "Mr. Moms," typically underscore heterosexuality as a sign of genuine manhood beneath a veneer of domesticity (Vavrus 2002). The theme of the peaceful, gentle male who turns into a death-dealing warrior after suffering an unbearable outrage has been recycled often in Hollywood films (Sparks 1996). Such imagery affirms the value of a male body as a baseline signifier of a masculine self.

Media imagery also shapes the value of other signifiers. Males in marginalized groups are often represented in derogatory ways. White working-class men are often portrayed on television as "dumb, immature, irresponsible, or lacking in common sense" (Butsch 2003, p. 576). Gay men, although less disparaged in recent years, are often shown as acceptable targets of others' disapproval (Linneman 2008). Black men are often portrayed as lazy, violent, criminal, hypersexual, or naturally athletic (Entman & Rojecki 2000). Latinos too are often depicted as criminal or as illegal immigrants who cause social problems (Dixon & Linz 2002). Arab men are often depicted as decadent sheiks, religious fanatics, or terrorists (Shaheen 2001). Such imagery implicitly affirms the hegemonic ideal as white, monied, and self-possessed. It also provides symbolic resources for crafting conformist and oppositional presentations of masculine selves.

Manhood Acts: Themes and Variations

All manhood acts imply a claim to membership in the privileged gender group. To present one's self as a man is to make this claim, whether the presentation emphasizes or deemphasizes the capacity to exert control. As this point suggests and as research has shown, males can construct and present themselves as men in various ways. It is this variation that has come to be taken as evidence of multiple masculinities. A concern that has guided much research in this genre is for showing how males compensate—that is, how they modify their manhood acts—when they are unable or unwilling to enact the hegemonic ideal.

Research on transsexuals is particularly instructive. These studies have shown how adults must relearn to use their bodies, clothing, speech, and gestures to signify alternate gender identities. Female-to-male transsexuals, or transmen, flatten their chests, take hormones to grow facial hair and muscle tissue, deepen their voices, and cultivate gestures (e.g., giving firm handshakes) to publicly claim their chosen identities as men (Dozier 2005, Johnson 2007). Transwomen likewise mask secondary sex characteristics through surgery, makeup, and vocal alteration and adopt submissive gestures and speech styles (Schrock et al. 2005). Being identified as a member of a gender category, these studies show, depends on mastering the requisite bodily, gestural, sartorial, and vocal signifiers.

Research on transsexuals also shows how the elicitation of deference depends on the type of man one is perceived to be. Based on in-depth interviews with 29 transmen, Schilt (2006) found that whereas white transmen beginning to work as men were taken more seriously, had their requests readily met, and were evaluated as more competent than they were as women, young, small Black, Latino, and Asian transmen did not gain similar advantages. Similarly, in her interview study of 18 transmen, Dozier (2005) found that, as men, white transmen reported being given more respect and more conversational space and being included in men's banter. They also experienced less public harassment. Transmen of color, on the other hand, reported being more frequently treated as criminals, and short and effeminate transmen reported being publicly harassed as gay. Gaining the full privileges of manhood is thus shown to depend not merely on being recognized as male, but on the whole ensemble of signs that are conventionally taken as evidence of a masculine self.

The multiple masculinities concept, despite its problems, has been helpful for seeing how various groups of men, using the material and symbolic resources available to them, are able to emphasize different aspects of the hegemonic ideal as means to construct effective manhood acts. For men in heterosexual relationships, occupational status and income are particularly important for eliciting deference from their partners. Middle- and upper-middle-class men can invoke job demands to avoid childcare and housework (Hochschild 1989, Pyke 1996). Based on 70 in-depth interviews with divorced and remarried men and women, Pyke (1996) showed that middle-class women's deference stems from accepting the idea that men's careers are primary. Even when women earn more than men, women "often defer to their husbands in the decision-making process" to affirm the belief that men should be in control (Tichenor 2005, p. 200). When the male is the primary breadwinner, the threat of leaving can also be used to leverage deference, as Ortiz (2006) showed in his interview-based study of 48 wives of professional athletes.

Men with fewer economic resources may use other strategies to maintain relationship control. Research shows a pattern of more frequent use of overtly coercive behavior, including verbal abuse and physical force, among poor and working-class men (Benson et al. 2004, Pyke 1996, Strauss et al. 1980). Based on in-depth interviews with 122 batterers, Cavanagh and associates (2001) show that males are more likely to be violent when they see their female partners as insufficiently submissive and not servicing their emotional and sexual desires (see also Hearn 1998). Men of all social classes may also use emotional withdrawal as a control strategy (Sattel 1976). The status of being the dominant partner can thus be achieved in different ways. Lacking one kind of resource for eliciting deference often leads to employing another kind of resource in exaggerated fashion. It is also worth noting that no control strategy is guaranteed to succeed.

Close attention to how manhood acts are actually performed shows variation in response to situations. Men in management positions, for example, can use institutional authority to elicit deference, but they must also demonstrate the qualities of rationality, resolve, and competitiveness (Collinson & Hearn 1994), and show loyalty to the male hierarchy (Jackall 1988, Martin 2001). They may sometimes adopt a paternalistic demeanor, playing the role of benevolent guide, and at other times use humiliation and threats (Kerfoot & Whitehead 1998). Professional men may also demonstrate capability by emphasizing their special knowledge (Haas & Shaffir 1977). And as Dellinger (2004) shows in her comparative ethnography of organizations that produce feminist and pornographic magazines, organizational culture influences how men present themselves at work. Manhood acts are thus strategically adapted to the realities of resource availability, individual skill, local culture, and audience expectations.

Manhood acts often entail the sexualization of women as a way to signify heterosexuality, to demarcate gender boundaries, and to challenge women's authority. A great deal of research has looked at how this occurs in workplaces (Prokos & Padavic 2002, Quinn 2002, Uggen & Blackstone 2004). Although the targets of gratuitous sexualization and harassment are often women of lower status, men also sexualize and harass women who are organizational superiors (Rospenda et al. 1998). The same phenomena can be found outside the workplace (Grazian 2007, Schacht 1996). Sexualizing women serves not only to signify heterosexuality and mark the boundary between gender groups, but it also protects males from homophobic abuse by their peers.

Men who publicly identify as gay reject heterosexuality as part of their manhood acts, yet the power of the hegemonic ideal is reflected in the creation of gay male subcultures that valorize large bodies and muscularity (Hennen 2005), sexual risk-taking and voracity (Green & Halkitis 2006), and macho fashion (Mosher et al. 2006). The subtext of these signifying acts can be read as, "Despite conventional societal standards by which we would be judged unmanly, we are indeed men and thus deserving of manhood status." Feminist analysts have suggested that misogyny among some gay men is similarly related to a desire on the part of gay men to distance themselves from women and retain a grip on male privilege (Frye 1983).

Research on men in low-status jobs shows another form of compensation: Instead of trying to control others, these men try to show that they cannot be controlled. These manhood acts rely on joking, verbal jousting, sexist talk, and sometimes sabotage to assert autonomy vis-à-vis bosses (Collinson 1992). Resistance may be heightened when men are expected to perform tasks conventionally associated with women. As Henson & Rogers (2001, p. 233) found when conducting participation observation and in-depth interviews with 68 male temporary clerical workers in Chicago and Los Angeles, despite their relative powerlessness in the workplace, the men resisted "demands for deference [such as] smiling, waiting, taking orders, and tolerating the bad moods of their supervisors." And, as Leidner (1993) shows in her field study of insurance salesmen, when work requires interactional deference with customers, the interaction is redefined as a contest for control so that men will be willing to do it.

The hegemonic ideal pervades the culture and sets a standard against which all manhood acts are measured. Because it is impossible, however, for all men to meet the hegemonic ideal, adjustments must be made, not only individually, but also subculturally. We thus find some working-class men creating bar and music cultures in which they signify masculine selves through heavy drinking and aggressive posturing (Eastman & Schrock 2008, Tilki 2006); economically marginalized men of color relying on sports, fighting, and sexual conquests (Anderson 1999, Wacquant 2003); college men turning to binge drinking and high-risk behavior (Peralta 2007); and others using crime to show that they are fearless and indomitable (Messerschmidt 1993).

Research on male subcultures has documented both wide variation in what are defined as signifiers of a masculine self and consistency in what it means to possess such a self. For example, the politically liberal, middle-class white males who populated the mythopoetic men's movement of the 1990s drew on Jungian psychology to redefine qualities conventionally associated with women—emotional expressivity, nurturance, and gentleness—as evidence of the "deep masculine" residing within all men (Schwalbe 1996). Likewise, the politically conservative Promise Keepers drew on Christian theology to validate similar qualities as masculine (Newton 2005). In both cases, however, the claim was that whereas the masculine self might need cultivation, it is naturally present in males, and its other elements—strength, courage, fierceness, and willingness to sacrifice—suit males to being warriors, leaders, and benevolent fathers.

Subcultural and historical variation in how manhood acts are performed demonstrates the fluidity of what are defined as signifiers of manhood (Kimmel 1996). Variation also arises because not all males are equally well equipped—by virtue of body type, skill, or social location—to enact the locally prevailing hegemonic ideal, thus making compensation and improvisation necessary. There remains, nonetheless, a common theme: the desire to claim an identity as a member of the privileged gender group, a desire that can be satisfied only by putting on a creditable manhood act. In competitive, hierarchical societies, especially those that are classically or vestigially patriarchal, this means signifying a capacity to exert control over one's self, the environment, and others.

The Reproduction of Gender Inequality

The original impetus for studying masculinity was to better understand the reproduction of gender inequality. Carrigan et al. (1985) were expressly concerned with masculinity as configurations of practice that have the effect of subordinating women. More recently, however, some theorists have retreated from the idea that masculinity necessarily produces inequality (see Connell & Messerschmidt 2005, p. 853). Other gender theorists have questioned the detachment of masculinity from gender inequality (Hanmer 1990, Flood 2002, Hearn 2004), arguing that the study of masculinity must remain part of a feminist project aimed at ending men's domination of women.

One reason for the loss of connection to the issue of gender inequality may be the success of the multiple masculinities concept. Eager embrace of this concept led researchers to document the diverse ways males style themselves as men, but with a loss of attention to what these styles have in common. Partly in response to this development, more critically inclined gender scholars (e.g., Jeffreys 2005, McCarry 2007) have urged a shift from the endless cataloging of masculinities to examining *how men's practices create inequality*. This is the path we take in this review. In keeping with the terms set out earlier, we consider what the literature tells us about the consequences of the practices we call manhood acts.

Differentiation is, before all else, basic to the creation and reproduction of gender inequality (Lorber 1994). Manhood acts are how males distinguish themselves from females/women and thus establish their eligibility for gender-based privilege. Indeed, the existence of the category "men" depends on the collective performance and affirmation of manhood acts. And, as argued earlier, successful manhood acts elicit deference from others in concrete situations. In these ways, manhood acts are inherently about upholding patriarchy and reproducing gender inequality. We can, however, look at research that shows how specific elements of manhood acts operate to advantage men at women's expense.

In the workplace, occupational segregation depends, first, on the manhood acts that make it possible to identify and channel different kinds of people toward different kinds of jobs (Reskin 1988). Manhood acts also have the effect of legitimating occupational segregation by upholding the illusion that men are more fit for certain kinds of jobs, especially those that involve the exercise of command. As Jackall's (1988) field study of corporate managers shows, managers must cultivate images of themselves as winners, as able to "get the job done," and as morally flexible and emotionally tough. Among defense intellectuals, a manhood act that features cold rationality may be necessary to be taken seriously (Cohn 1987). Men in some female-dominated occupations are put on a "glass escalator" toward greater authority and reward (Cognard-Black 2004, Williams 1992), whereas others are segregated horizontally in more highly valued specialties (Snyder & Green 2008, Williams 1992). Putting on a manhood act is part of how one establishes similarity to those already at the top of the hierarchy and gets through what others experience as a glass ceiling (Kanter 1977). And to the extent that jobs are designed by those who imagine the ideal occupant to be a male who fits the hegemonic ideal, those whose manhood acts come closest to the ideal are likely to be advantaged (Acker 1990).

Striving to emulate the hegemonic ideal may serve one well when seeking managerial power, but even compensatory manhood acts can make a difference for obtaining economic rewards. If the hegemonic ideal is out of dramaturgical reach, it may be possible to craft a manhood act that emphasizes self-sacrificial endurance to achieve organizational goals. Cooper (2000) shows how this was the case for the 20 computer programmers she interviewed. Much like athletes who signify a masculine self through a willingness to suffer pain

(Curry 1993), these programmers claimed manhood status by practicing "nerd masculinity" that involved suffering long hours of work to meet production goals and to establish a reputation for unique expertise.

In the political sphere, manhood acts approximating the hegemonic ideal may be crafted to achieve or consolidate power (Messner 2007). In the case of the presidency, the act must also serve an iconic function for the nation; that is, the act must represent the collectively imagined, idealized character of the nation (Hall 1979). George W. Bush, for example, refashioned his persona after the 2001 terrorist attacks to underscore his self-proclaimed role as a "war president" leading a great and powerful nation (Coe et al. 2007). Disrespecting the manhood acts of political opponents is also common. During the 2004 U.S. presidential election, the Bush campaign and much of the media framed the losing Democratic candidate, John Kerry, as feminine and French-like (Fahey 2007). Inasmuch as manhood acts are conducive to achieving positions of power—by eliciting deference over the course of a career of status-seeking—and inasmuch as executive positions are reserved for those who can serve as icons of collective power (whether of the corporation or the nation), gender inequality will be the outcome. Women who vie with men for such positions are often compelled to put on a compensatory manhood act or, as it is sometimes said, to "out-macho the boys."

Research on men in social movements, as noted in the previous section, shows that manhood acts often involve collaboration among men. This is true more generally. Even men who reject hegemonic ideals may feel compelled, when in all-male groups, to appear emotionally detached, competitive, and willing to objectify women (Bird 1996). In college fraternities, young men mutually affirm their manhood by collectively defining women as "servers" and as sexual "bait" or "prey" (Martin & Hummer 1989). In cases where men's oppressive behavior is challenged, such as batterer intervention programs (Schrock & Padavic 2007) or prison antiviolence groups (Fox 1999), men often collaborate to outwit social workers and assert a right to control women. Inequality is thus reproduced when males uncritically affirm oppressive elements of other males' manhood acts or conspire to resist challenges to those acts.

Eliciting deference by signifying a capacity to dominate can also affect the division of domestic labor. This is not to say that manhood acts always elicit compliance from female partners when the division of domestic labor is being negotiated. The acts that matter most may be those performed in the public sphere. When a manhood act yields career success, this may tip the balance of power in the household. Gender inequality created through manhood acts in the workplace can thus be translated into gender inequality—in terms of decision-making power and work distribution—within the home (Coltrane 2000). In some cases, a lack of power in the public sphere might lead to a compensatory manhood act in the home, an act that involves a refusal to do what is defined as women's work (Brines 1994). Compensatory manhood acts might also involve the use of violence to subjugate female partners (Hearn 1998).

As noted earlier, manhood acts that involve displays of heterosexual appetite and prowess often entail the sexual objectification and harassment of women. In these acts, which are often competitive and tend to escalate (Quinn 2002), women become props that men use to affirm a heterosexual identity. Gender inequality is reproduced when sexual harassment, or the threat thereof, limits women's public mobility (Gardner 1995) or undermines perceptions of women's competence as workers and professionals (Padavic & Reskin 2002). Sexual activity undertaken as part of a manhood act may also result in unwanted pregnancies that decrease young women's chances for upward mobility (Anderson 1999).[2] Even after relationships end,

---

[2]There is, of course, more to fatherhood than our brief treatment implies. Whereas our concern is mainly with fatherhood as it relates to manhood acts and the reproduction of gender inequality, others have examined the complexities of fatherhood in considerable depth. For examples, see Gavanas (2004), LaRossa (1996), and Marsiglio & Hutchinson (2002).

males may signify their uncontrollability by refusing to pay alimony and child support (Arendell 1992), acts that hurt exes economically.

Claiming a heterosexual identity as part of a manhood act may also involve homophobic taunting, especially among boys and young men. As Pascoe (2007) shows, high school boys use "fag" as an epithet to police the boundaries of acceptable manhood acts (see also Mac an Ghaill 1994). The same phenomenon has been observed among prison inmates (Thurston 1996), mental hospital patients (Leyser 2003), and athletes (Anderson 2002). Whereas this taunting mainly establishes a hierarchy among boys and men, it also reinforces sexist ideology, because the implicit insult is that a man who wants to have sex with men is like a woman—which is to say, less than a man. Homophobic taunting thus helps reproduce gender inequality by devaluing women.

Individual Liabilities and Gender-Class Advantages

The consequences of manhood acts for the reproduction of gender inequality can be contradictory. Men as a gender class can benefit from the collective upholding of sexist ideology and of images of males as possessing essential qualities that suit them for the exercise of power. Yet compensatory manhood acts can sometimes reproduce inequalities in ways that disadvantage subgroups of men. For example, a number of studies (e.g., Willis 1977, MacLeod 1995, Anderson 1999) have shown how self-protective displays of toughness by poor and working-class young men lead to disinvestment in academic work and failure in school. Young men may also distance themselves from intellectual work, which is defined as feminine, and embrace physical work, which is defined as masculine, and thus limit their chances for upward mobility via success in school (Fine et al. 1997).

Beyond school, compensatory manhood acts can undermine employment relationships. Young men who signify a capacity to resist control by others may find it difficult to get and hold jobs in the mainstream economy (Bourgois 1995). The use of crime to signify a masculine self carries the risk of getting caught and losing opportunities for conventional economic success (Messerschmidt 1993). Compensatory manhood acts that are adaptive in some contexts can thus be self-destructive in others. Much depends on who is presenting what kind of masculine self to whom and under what conditions. This suggests a need to examine how the consequences of manhood acts are shaped by racism and the class structure.

Whereas manhood acts that emphasize the defiance of authority can undermine the mobility prospects of individual men, men as a gender class may continue to enjoy privilege because of the collective image fostered by manhood acts that involve crime, violence, and interpersonal intimidation. (The use of state violence in manhood acts undertaken by elite males is also consequential in this regard.) To the extent that such acts imply the innate dangerousness of males, women may feel compelled to seek protection from males deemed safe—protection for which they exchange subservience (Schwalbe et al. 2000, pp. 426–27). Nonviolent males can thus derive privilege from the violent manhood acts of other males.

Males can also incur health damage as a consequence of manhood acts. Research has linked men's higher rates of morbidity and mortality to failure to seek help early (O'Brien et al. 2005); to higher levels of risk-taking behavior, including drinking, smoking, and reckless driving (Verbrugge 1985); and to poor social support networks (House et al. 1988). Men's sports injuries, death by violence, and suicide have also been linked to gender enactment (Sabo 2005). As with crime, much of this health-damaging behavior may be symbolic, intended to signify capacities to control one's own life, to be invulnerable and needless of help, and to be fearless and hence not easily intimidated by others. The effort to signify a masculine self, as some analysts have suggested (Courtenay 2000), can be toxic.

Conclusion

The trends noted at the outset of this review continue apace. Research continues in the men-and-(fill in the blank) pattern. New studies regularly appear that examine masculinity in still more contexts. Although these traditions of research have produced a considerable body of knowledge about the diversity of men's behavior, there has been a tendency to lose sight of the goals of trying to understand (*a*) the social construction of gender in general and (*b*) the reproduction of gender inequality. We have suggested that these problems stem in part from a tendency to reify masculinity, to erroneously see it as an essential quality of male bodies, and to treat it as if it had explanatory power.

Moving forward will require, we have suggested, reclaiming and revamping some of the basic insights of a critical sociology of gender that emphasizes practices and processes. This means maintaining distinctions between anatomy, sex and gender categories, and the identity work that both locates individuals within categories and reproduces the categories themselves. Documenting and analyzing manhood acts—the identity work that males do to claim membership in the dominant gender group, to affirm the social reality of the group, to elicit deference from others, and to maintain privileges vis-à-vis women—may prove to be more useful, we have argued, than merely cataloging more masculinities.

Refocusing our attention on practices and processes—those constitutive of what we have called manhood acts—can generate new empirical challenges. Future research might examine, for example, how males use the interaction order collaboratively to construct manhood acts, how they police and support each other's acts, and how they create and share the material and symbolic resources that enable various kinds of manhood acts. This would mean studying how manhood acts are both institutionalized and, in the face of changing conditions and threats to male supremacy, improvised. Further investigation into how subjectivity is conditioned—that is, how habits of thought and feeling are formed by and implicated in manhood acts—would also be useful.

Another challenge is to examine how the elicitation of deference in face-to-face interaction produces large-scale patterns of male domination. Such research might examine, for example, how manhood acts play a part in network formation and in maintaining regimes of organizational control. Media studies are another avenue for research, especially if attention is shifted from the consumption of images to examining how manhood acts are implicated in the production of gendered images. There is, finally, a need to study both individual and collective resistance to manhood acts, no matter who performs them, presuming an enduring concern with understanding the social processes through which gender inequality can be overcome.

Disclosure Statement

The authors are not aware of any biases that might be perceived as affecting the objectivity of this review.

Acknowledgments

The authors wish to thank Jeff Hearn, Daphne Holden, Sherryl Kleinman, Patricia Yancey Martin, and Christian Vaccaro for helpful comments on an earlier draft.

Literature Cited

Acker J. 1990. Hierarchies, jobs, bodies: a theory of gendered organizations. *Gend. Soc.* 4:139–58

Anderson E. 1999. *Code of the Street: Decency, Violence, and the Moral Life of the Inner City*. New York: W.W. Norton

Anderson ED. 2002. Openly gay athletes: contesting hegemonic masculinity in a homophobic environment. *Gend. Soc.* 16:860–77

Arendell T. 1992. After divorce: investigations into father absence. *Gend. Soc.* 6:562–86

Athens L. 1992. *The Creation of Dangerous Violent Criminals*. Urbana: Univ. Ill. Press

Benson ML, Wooldredge J, Thistlethwaite AB. 2004. The correlation between race and domestic violence is confounded with community context. *Soc. Probl.* 51:326–42

Bird SR. 1996. Welcome to the men's club: homosociality and the maintenance of hegemonic masculinity. *Gend. Soc.* 10:120–32

Bourgois P. 1995. *In Search of Respect: Selling Crack in El Barrio*. Cambridge, UK: Cambridge Univ. Press

Brines J. 1994. Economic dependency, gender, and the division-of-labor at home. *Am. J. Sociol.* 100:652–88

Butera KJ. 2006. Manhunt: the challenge of enticing men to participate in a study on friendship. *Qual. Inq.* 12:1262–82

Butsch R. 2003. Ralph, Fred, Archie and Homer: why television keeps recreating the white male working class buffoon. In *Gender, Race, and Class in the Media*, ed. G Dines, JM Humez, pp. 575–88. Thousand Oaks, CA: Sage

Cahill SE. 1986. Language practices and self definition: the case of gender identity acquisition. *Sociol. Q.* 27:295–311

Cahill SE. 1989. Fashioning males and females: appearance management and the social reproduction of gender. *Symb. Interact.* 12:281–98

Carrigan T, Connell B, Lee J. 1985. Toward a new sociology of masculinity. *Theory Soc.* 14:551–604

Cavanagh K, Dobash RE, Dobash RP, Lewis R. 2001. "Remedial work": men's strategic responses to their violence against intimate female partners. *Sociology* 35:695–714

Clatterbaugh K. 1996. *Contemporary Perspectives on Masculinity: Men, Women and Politics in Modern Society*. Boulder, CO: Westview

Coe K, Domke D, Bagley MM, Cunningham S, Van Leuven N. 2007. Masculinity as political strategy: George W. Bush, the "war on terrorism," and an echoing press. *J. Women Polit. Policy* 29:31–55

Cognard-Black AJ. 2004. Will they stay, or will they go? Sex-atypical work among token men who teach. *Sociol. Q.* 45:113–39

Cohn C. 1987. Sex and death in the rational world of defense intellectuals. *Signs.* 12:687–718

Collinson D, Hearn J. 1994. Naming men as men: implications for work, organizations and management. *Gend. Work Organ.* 1:2–22

Collinson DA. 1992. *Managing the Shopfloor: Subjectivity, Masculinity and Workplace Culture*. New York: Walter de Gruyter

Coltrane S. 2000. Research on household labor: modeling and measuring the social embeddedness of routine family work. *J. Marriage Fam.* 62:1208–33

Connell RW. 1983. *Which Way Is Up? Essays on Sex, Class and Culture*. Sydney: Allen & Unwin

Connell RW. 1987. *Gender and Power: Society, the Person, and Sexual Politics*. Sydney: Allen & Unwin

Connell RW. 1995. *Masculinities*. Sydney: Allen & Unwin

Connell RW. 2000. *The Men and the Boys*. St Leonards, NSW: Allen & Unwin

Connell RW, Messerschmidt JW. 2005. Hegemonic masculinity: rethinking the concept. *Gend. Soc.* 19:829–59

Cooper M. 2000. Being the "go-to guy": fatherhood, masculinity, and the organization of work in Silicon Valley. *Qual. Sociol.* 23:379–405

Courtenay WH. 2000. Constructions of masculinity and their influence on men's well-being: a theory of gender and health. *Soc. Sci. Med.* 50:1385–401

Curry TJ. 1993. A little pain never hurt anyone: athletic career socialization and the normalization of sports injury. *Symb. Interact.* 16:273–90

Dellinger K. 2004. Masculinities in "safe" and "embattled" organizations: accounting for pornographic and feminist magazines. *Gend. Soc.* 18:545–66

Dietz TL. 1998. An examination of violence and gender role portrayals in video games: implications for gender socialization and aggressive behavior. *Sex Roles* 38:425–42

Dixon RL, Linz D. 2002. Overrepresentation and underrepresentation of African Americans and Latinos as lawbreakers on television news. *J. Commun.* 52:131–54

Dozier R. 2005. Beards, breasts, and bodies: doing sex in a gendered world. *Gend. Soc.* 19:297–316

Dyson AH. 1994. The ninjas, the X-Men, and the ladies: playing with power and identity in an urban primary school. *Teach. Coll. Rec.* 96:219–39

Eastman J, Schrock DP. 2008. Southern rock musicians' construction of white trash. *Race Gend. Class.* 15:205–19

Entman RM, Rojecki A. 2000. *The Black Image in the White Mind: Media and Race in America.* Chicago: Univ. Chicago Press

Evans L, Davies K. 2000. No sissy boys here: a content analysis of the representation of masculinity in elementary school reading textbooks. *Sex Roles* 41:255–70

Ezzell MB. 2008. Pornography, lad mags, video games, and boys: reviving the canary in the cultural coal mine. In *The Sexualization of Childhood*, ed. S Olfman, pp. 7–32. Westport, CT: Praeger

Fahey AC. 2007. French and feminine: hegemonic masculinity and the emasculation of John Kerry in the 2004 presidential race. *Crit. Stud. Mass Commun.* 24:132–50

Ferguson AA. 2000. *Bad Boys: Public Schools in the Making of Black Masculinity.* Ann Arbor: Univ. Mich. Press

Fine GA. 1987. *With the Boys: Little League Baseball and Preadolescent Culture.* Chicago: Univ. Chicago Press

Fine M, Weis L, Addelston J, Marusza J. 1997. (In)secure times: constructing white working-class masculinities in the late 20th century. *Gend. Soc.* 11:52–68

Flood M. 2002. Between men and masculinity: an assessment of the term "masculinity" in recent scholarship on men. In *Manning the Next Millennium: Studies in Masculinities,* ed. S Pearce, V Muller, pp. 203–13. Bentley, WA: Black Swan

Flood M. 2008. *The men's bibliography: a comprehensive bibliography of writing on men, masculinities, gender, and sexualities,* 18th ed. http://mensbiblio.xyonline.net/

Flood M, Gardiner JK, Pease B, Pringle K, ed. 2007. *International Encyclopedia of Men and Masculinities.* London/New York: Routledge

Fordham S, Ogbu JU. 1986. Black students' school success: coping with the "burden of 'acting white.'" *Urban Rev.* 18:176–206

Fox KJ. 1999. Changing violent minds: discursive correction and resistance in the cognitive treatment of violent offenders in prison. *Soc. Probl.* 46:88–103

Frye M. 1983. *The Politics of Reality: Essays in Feminist Theory.* Trumansburg, NY: Crossing

Gardner CB. 1995. *Passing By: Gender and Public Harassment.* Berkeley: Univ. Calif. Press

Gatrell C. 2006. Interviewing fathers: feminist dilemmas in fieldwork. *J. Gend. Stud.* 15:237–51

Gavanas A. 2004. *Fatherhood Politics in the United States.* Urbana: Univ. Ill. Press

Goffman E. 1959. *The Presentation of Self in Everyday Life.* New York: Doubleday

Goffman E. 1977. The arrangement between the sexes. *Theory Soc.* 4:301–31

Grazian D. 2007. The girl hunt: urban nightlife and the performance of masculinity as collective activity. *Symb. Interact.* 30:221–43

Green AI, Halkitis PN. 2006. Crystal methamphetamine and sexual sociality in an urban gay subculture: an elective affinity. *Cult. Health Sex.* 8:317–33

Haas J, Shaffir W. 1977. The professionalization of medical students: developing competence and a cloak of competence. *Symb. Interact.* 1:71–88

Hall PM. 1979. The presidency and impression management. *Stud. Symb. Interact.* 2:283–305

Hamilton MC, Anderson D, Broaddus M, Young K. 2006. Gender stereotyping and under-representation of female characters in 200 popular children's picture books: a twenty-first century update. *Sex Roles* 55:557–65

Hanmer J. 1990. Men, power, and the exploitation of women. *Women's Stud. Int. Forum.* 13:443–56

Hearn J. 1998. *The Violences of Men.* London: Sage

Hearn J. 2004. From hegemonic masculinity to the hegemony of men. *Fem. Theory.* 5:49–72

Hearn J. 2007. Methods, methodology, and research. See Flood et al. 2007, pp. 433–38

Hennen P. 2005. Bear bodies, bear masculinity: recuperation, resistance, or retreat? *Gend. Soc.* 19:25–43

Henson KD, Rogers JK. 2001. "Why Marcia you've changed!" male clerical temporary workers doing masculinity in a feminized occupation. *Gend. Soc.* 15:218–38

Higate P. 2007. Peacekeepers, masculinities, and sexual exploitation. *Men Masc.* 10:99–119

Hochschild A. 1989. *Second Shift: Working Parents and the Revolution at Home.* New York: Viking Penguin

House JS, Landis KR, Umberson D. 1988. Social relationships and health. *Science.* 241:540–45

Jackall R. 1988. *Moral Mazes: The World of Corporate Managers.* New York: Oxford Univ. Press

Janssen DF. 2008. *International Guide to Literature on Masculinity.* Harrison, TN: Men's Studies Press

Jeffreys S. 2005. *Beauty and Misogyny.* New York: Routledge

Johnson AG. 2005. *The Gender Knot: Unraveling our Patriarchal Legacy.* Philadelphia: Temple Univ. Press

Johnson K. 2007. Changing sex, changing self: theorizing transitions in embodied subjectivity. *Men Masc.* 10:54–70

Jordan E, Cowan A. 1995. Warrior narratives in the kindergarten classroom: renegotiating the social-contract. *Gend. Soc.* 9:727–43

Kane EW. 2006. "No way my boys are going to be like that!" parents' responses to children's gender nonconformity. *Gend. Soc.* 20:149–76

Kanter RM. 1977. *Men and Women of the Corporation.* New York: Basic Books

Kerfoot D, Whitehead S. 1998. "Boys own" stuff: masculinity and the management of further education. *Sociol. Rev.* 46:436–57

Kessler S, McKenna W. 1978. *Gender: An Ethnomethodological Approach.* New York: John Wiley

Kimmel M. 1996. *Manhood in America: A Cultural History.* New York: Free Press

Kimmel M. 2007. Racism as adolescent male rite of passage: ex-Nazis in Scandinavia. *J. Contemp. Ethnogr.* 36:202–18

Kimmel M, Aronson A, ed. 2004. *A Social, Cultural, and Historical Encyclopedia.* New York: ABC-CLIO

Kimmel M, Hearn J, Connell RW, eds. 2005. *Handbook of Studies on Men and Masculinities.* Thousand Oaks, CA: Sage

Kimmel MS, Mahler M. 2003. Adolescent masculinity, homophobia, and violence: random school shootings, 1982–2001. *Am. Behav. Sci.* 46:1439–58

Kimmel MS, Messner MA. 2007. *Men's Lives.* Boston: Allyn & Bacon. 7th ed.

LaRossa R. 1996. *The Modernization of Fatherhood: A Social and Political History.* Chicago: Univ. Chicago Press

Leidner R. 1993. *Fast Food, Fast Talk.* Berkeley: Univ. Calif. Press

Lever J. 1978. Sex differences in the complexity of children's play and games. *Am. Sociol. Rev.* 43:471–83

Leyser H. 2003. Doing masculinity in a mental hospital. *J. Contemp. Ethnogr.* 32:336–59

Linneman TJ. 2008. How do you solve a problem like Will Truman? The feminization of gay masculinities on Will & Grace. *Men Masc.* 10:583–603

Lorber J. 1994. *Paradoxes of Gender.* New Haven, CT: Yale Univ. Press

Mac an Ghaill M. 1994. *The Making of Men: Masculinities, Sexualities and Schooling.* Buckingham, UK: Open Univ. Press

MacInnes J. 1998. *The End of Masculinity: The Confusion of Sexual Genesis and Sexual Difference in Modern Society.* Philadelphia: Open Univ. Press

MacLeod J. 1995. *Ain't No Makin' It: Aspirations and Attainment in a Low-Income Neighborhood.* Boulder, CO: Westview

Majors R, Billson JM. 1992. *Cool Pose: The Dilemmas of Black Manhood in America.* New York: Lexington

Martin PY. 1998. Why can't a man be more like a woman? Reflections on Robert Connell's Masculinities. *Gend. Soc.* 13:472–74

Martin PY. 2001. "Mobilizing masculinities": women's experiences of men at work. *Organization* 8:587–618

Martin PY. 2003. "Said and done" versus "saying and doing": gendering practices, practicing gender at work. *Gend. Soc.* 17:342–66

Martin PY, Hummer RA. 1989. Fraternities and rape on campus. *Gend. Soc.* 3:457–73

Marsiglio W, Hutchinson S. 2002. *Sex, Men, and Babies: Stories of Awareness and Responsibility.* New York: New York Univ. Press

McBride J. 1995. *War, Battering, and Other Sports: The Gulf Between American Men and Women.* New Jersey: Humanities Press

McCarry M. 2007. Masculinity studies and male violence: critique or collusion? *Women's Stud. Int. Forum.* 30:404–15

McCaughey M. 2008. *The Caveman Mystique: Pop-Darwinism and the Debates Over Sex, Violence, and Science.* New York: Routledge

McGuffey CS. 2008. "Saving masculinity": gender reaffirmation, sexuality, race, and parental responses to male child sexual abuse. *Soc. Probl.* 55:216–37

McGuffey CS, Rich BL. 1999. Playing in the gender transgression zone: race, class, and hegemonic masculinity in middle childhood. *Gend. Soc.* 13:608–27

Messerschmidt JW. 1993. *Masculinities and Crime: Critique and Reconceptualization of Theory.* Lanham, MD: Rowman & Littlefield

Messerschmidt JW. 2000. *Nine Lives: Adolescent Masculinities, the Body, and Violence.* Boulder, CO: Westview

Messner MA. 1990. Men studying masculinity: some epistemological issues in sport sociology. *Soc. Sport J.* 7:136–53

Messner MA. 1992. *Power at Play: Sports and the Problem of Masculinity.* Boston: Beacon

Messner MA. 2007. The masculinity of the governator: muscle and compassion in American politics. *Gend. Soc.* 21:461–80

Milkie MA. 1994. Social world approach to cultural-studies: mass-media and gender in the adolescent peer group. *J. Contemp. Ethnogr.* 23:354–80

Morris EW. 2005. "Tuck in that shirt!" race, class, gender and discipline in an urban school. *Sociol. Perspect.* 48:25–48

Mosher CM, Levitt HM, Manley E. 2006. Layers of leather: the identity formation of leather-men as a process of transforming meanings of masculinity. *J. Homosex.* 51:93–123

Newton J. 2005. *From Panthers to Promise Keepers: Rethinking the Men's Movement.* Lanham, MD: Rowman & Littlefield

O'Brien R, Hunt K, Hart G. 2005. "It's caveman stuff, but that is to a certain extent how guys still operate": men's accounts of masculinity and help seeking. *Soc. Sci. Med.* 61:503–16

Ortiz SM. 2006. Using power: An exploration of control work in the sport marriage. *Sociol. Perspect.* 49:527–57

Pascoe CJ. 2007. *Dude, You're a Fag: Masculinity and Sexuality in High School.* Berkeley: Univ. Calif. Press

Pecora N. 1992. Superman/superboys/supermen: the comic book hero as socializing agent. In *Men, Masculinity, and the Media,* ed. S Craig, pp. 61–77. Newbury Park, CA: Sage

Peralta RL. 2007. College alcohol use and the embodiment of hegemonic masculinity among European American men. *Sex Roles* 56:741–56

Phillips DA. 2007. Punking and bullying: strategies in middle school, high school, and beyond. *J. Interpers. Violence.* 22:158–78

Pleck JP, Sawyer J, eds. 1974. *Men and Masculinity.* Englewood Cliffs, NJ: Prentice-Hall

Pomerleau A, Bloduc D, Cossette L, Malcuit G. 1990. Pink or blue: environmental gender stereotypes in the first two years of life. *Sex Roles* 22:359–67

Prokos A, Padavic I. 2002. 'There oughtta be a law against bitches': masculinity lessons in police academy training. *Gend. Work Organ.* 9:439–59

Pyke KD. 1996. Class-based masculinities: the interdependence of gender, class, and interpersonal power. *Gend. Soc.* 10:527–49

Quinn BA. 2002. Sexual harassment and masculinity: the power and meaning of "girl watching." *Gend. Soc.* 16:386–402

Renold E. 2007. Primary school "studs": (de)constructing young boys' heterosexual masculinities. *Men Masc.* 9:275–97

Reskin BF. 1988. Bringing the men back in: sex differentiation and the devaluation of women's work. *Gend. Soc.* 2:58–81

Reskin BF, Padavic I. 2002. *Women and Men at Work.* Thousand Oaks, CA: Pine Forge

Rospenda KM, Richman JA, Nawyn SJ. 1998. Doing power: the confluence of gender, race, and class in contrapower sexual harassment. *Gend. Soc.* 12:40–60

Sabo D. 2005. The study of masculinities and men's health: an overview. In *Handbook of Studies on Men & Masculinities,* ed. MS Kimmel, J Hearn, RW Connell, pp. 326–52. Thousand Oaks, CA: Sage

Sattel JW. 1976. The inexpressive male: tragedy or sexual politics? *Soc. Probl.* 23:469–77

Schacht SP. 1996. Misogyny on and off the "pitch": the gendered world of male rugby players. *Gender Soc.* 10:550–65

Schacht SP. 1997. Feminist fieldwork in the misogynist setting of the rugby pitch: temporarily becoming a sylph to survive and personally grow. *J. Contemp. Ethnogr.* 26:338–63

Schilt K. 2006. Just one of the guys? How transmen make gender visible at work. *Gend. Soc.* 20:465–90

Schrock D, Padavic I. 2007. Negotiating hegemonic masculinity in a batterer intervention program. *Gend. Soc.* 21:625–49

Schrock D, Reid L, Boyd EM. 2005. Transsexuals' embodiment of womanhood. *Gend. Soc.* 19:317–35

Schwalbe ML. 1996. *Unlocking the Iron Cage: The Men's Movement, Gender Politics, and American Culture.* New York: Oxford Univ. Press

Schwalbe ML. 2005. Identity stakes, manhood acts, and the dynamics of accountability. In *Studies in Symbolic Interaction,* ed. N Denzin, pp. 65–81. New York: Elsevier

Schwalbe ML, Mason-Schrock D. 1996. Identity work as group process. In *Advances in Group Processes,* ed. B Markovsky, M Lovaglia, R Simon, pp. 113–47. Greenwich, CT: JAI

Schwalbe ML, Godwin S, Holden D, Schrock D, Thompson S, Wolkomir M. 2000. Generic processes in the reproduction of inequality: an interactionist analysis. *Soc. Forces* 79:419–52

Schwalbe ML, Wolkomir M. 2001. The masculine self as problem and resource in interview studies of men. *Men Masc.* 4:90–103

Shaheen JG. 2001. *Reel Bad Arabs: How Hollywood Vilifies a People.* New York: Olive Branch

Sheldon JP. 2004. Gender stereotypes in educational software for young children. *Sex Roles* 51:433–44

Sinclair A. 1995. Sex and the MBA. *Organization* 2:295–317

Snyder KA, Green AI. 2008. Revisiting the glass escalator: the case of gender segregation in a female dominated occupation. *Soc. Probl.* 55:271–99

Sparks R. 1996. Masculinity and heroism in the Hollywood "blockbuster": the culture industry and contemporary images of crime and law enforcement. *Br. J. Criminol.* 36:348–60

Staples R. 1982. *Black Masculinity: The Black Man's Blues in American Society.* San Francisco: Black Scholars'

Straus MA, Gelles RJ, Steinmetz SK. 1980. *Behind Closed Doors: Violence in the American Family.* Garden City, NY: Doubleday

Stretesky PB, Pogrebin MR. 2007. Gang-related gun violence: socialization, identity, and self. *J. Contemp. Ethnogr.* 36:85–114

Taylor LD. 2005. All for him: articles about sex in American lad magazines. *Sex Roles* 52:153–63

Thorne B. 1993. *Gender Play: Girls and Boys in School.* New Brunswick, NJ: Rutgers Univ. Press

Thurston R. 1996. Are you sitting comfortably? Men's storytelling, masculinities, prison culture and violence. In *Understanding Masculinities: Social Relations and Cultural Arenas,* ed. M Mac an Ghaill, pp. 139–52. Philadelphia: Open Univ. Press

Tichenor V. 2005. Maintaining men's dominance: negotiating identity and power when she earns more. *Sex Roles* 53:191–205

Tilki M. 2006. The social contexts of drinking among Irish men in London. *Drugs* 13:247–61

Tolson A. 1977. *The Limits of Masculinity.* London: Tavistock

Uggen C, Blackstone A. 2004. Sexual harassment as a gendered expression of power. *Am. Sociol. Rev.* 69:64–92

Vavrus MD. 2002. Domesticating patriarchy: hegemonic masculinity and television's "Mr. Mom." *Crit. Stud. Mass Commun.* 19:352–75

Verbrugge LM. 1985. Gender and health: an update on hypotheses and evidence. *J. Health Soc. Behav.* 26:156–82

Vigorito AJ, Curry TJ. 1998. Marketing masculinity: gender identity and popular magazines. *Sex Roles* 39:135–52

Wacquant L. 2003. *Body and Soul: Notebooks of An Apprentice Boxer.* New York: Oxford

West C, Zimmerman D. 1987. Doing gender. *Gend. Soc.* 1:125–51

Whitehead S, ed. 2006. *Men and Masculinities: Critical Concepts in Sociology.* New York: Routledge

Williams CL. 1992. The glass escalator: hidden advantages for men in the "female" professions. *Soc. Probl.* 39:253–67

Willis P. 1977. *Learning to Labor: How Working Class Kids Get Working Class Jobs.* New York: Columbia Univ. Press

11 *Introduction*

Benedict Anderson

Perhaps without being much noticed yet, a fundamental transformation in the history of Marxism and Marxist movements is upon us. Its most visible signs are the recent wars between Vietnam, Cambodia and China. These wars are of world-historical importance because they are the first to occur between regimes whose independence and revolutionary credentials are undeniable, and because none of the belligerents has made more than the most perfunctory attempts to justify the bloodshed in terms of recognizable *Marxist* theoretical perspective. While it was still just possible to interpret the Sino-Soviet border clashes of 1969, and the Soviet military interventions in Germany (1953), Hungary (1956), Czechoslovakia (1968), and Afghanistan (1980) in terms of—according to taste—'social imperialism,' 'defending socialism,' etc., no one, I imagine, seriously believes that such vocabularies have much bearing on what has occurred in Indochina.

If the Vietnamese invasion and occupation of Cambodia in December 1978 and January 1979 represented the first *large-scale conventional war* waged by one revolutionary Marxist regime against another,[1] China's assault on Vietnam in February rapidly confirmed the precedent. Only the most trusting would dare wager that in the declining years of this century any significant outbreak of inter-state hostilities will necessarily find the USSR and the PRC—let alone the smaller socialist states—supporting, or fighting on, the same side. Who can be confident that Yugoslavia and Albania will not one day come to blows? Those variegated groups who seek a withdrawal of the Red Army from its encampments in Eastern Europe should remind themselves of the degree to which its overwhelming presence has, since 1945, ruled out armed conflict between the region's Marxist regimes.

Such considerations serve to underline the fact that since World War II every successful revolution has defined itself in *national* terms—the People's Republic of China, the Socialist Republic of Vietnam, and so forth—and, in so doing, has grounded itself firmly in a territorial and social space inherited from the prerevolutionary past. Conversely, the fact that the Soviet Union shares with the United Kingdom of Great Britain and Northern Ireland the rare distinction of refusing nationality in its naming suggests that it is as much the legatee of the prenational dynastic states of the nineteenth century as the precursor of a twenty-first century internationalist order.[2]

Reprinted from *Imagined Communities* (1983), by permission of Verso Books.

Eric Hobsbawm is perfectly correct in stating that 'Marxist movements and states have tended to become national not only in form but in substance, i.e., nationalist. There is nothing to suggest that this trend will not continue.'[3] Nor is the tendency confined to the socialist world. Almost every year the United Nations admits new members. And many 'old nations,' once thought fully consolidated, find themselves challenged by 'sub'-nationalisms within their borders—nationalisms which, naturally, dream of shedding this subness one happy day. The reality is quite plain: the 'end of the era of nationalism,' so long prophesied, is not remotely in sight. Indeed, nation-ness is the most universally legitimate value in the political life of our time.

But if the facts are clear, their explanation remains a matter of long-standing dispute. Nation, nationality, nationalism—all have proved notoriously difficult to define, let alone to analyze. In contrast to the immense influence that nationalism has exerted on the modern world, plausible theory about it is conspicuously meagre. Hugh Seton-Watson, author of far the best and most comprehensive English-language text on nationalism, and heir to a vast tradition of liberal historiography and social science, sadly observes: 'Thus I am *driven* to the conclusion that no "scientific definition" of the nation can be devised; yet the phenomenon has existed and exists.'[4] Tom Nairn, author of the path-breaking *The Break-up of Britain,* and heir to the scarcely less vast tradition of Marxist historiography and social science, candidly remarks: 'The theory of nationalism represents Marxism's great historical failure.'[5] But even this confession is somewhat misleading, insofar as it can be taken to imply the regrettable outcome of a long, self-conscious search for theoretical clarity. It would be more exact to say that nationalism has proved an uncomfortable *anomaly* for Marxist theory and, precisely for that reason, has been largely elided, rather than confronted. How else to explain Marx's failure to explicate the crucial adjective in his memorable formulation of 1848: 'The proletariat of each country must, of course, first of all settle matters with *its own* bourgeoisie'?[6] How else to account for the use, for over a century, of the concept 'national bourgeoisie' without any serious attempt to justify theoretically the relevance of the adjective? What is *this* segmentation of the bourgeoisie—a world-class insofar as it is defined in terms of the relations of production—theoretically significant?

The aim of this chapter is to offer some tentative suggestions for a more satisfactory interpretation of the 'anomaly' of nationalism. My sense is that on this topic both Marxist and liberal theory have become etiolated in a late Ptolemaic effort to 'save the phenomena'; and that a reorientation of perspective in, as it were, a Copernican spirit is urgently required. My point of departure is that nationality, or, as one might prefer to put it in view of that word's multiple significations, nation-ness, as well as nationalism, are cultural artifacts of a particular kind. To understand them properly we need to consider carefully how they have come into historical being, in what ways their meanings have changed over time, and why, today, they command such profound emotional legitimacy. I will be trying to argue that the creation of these artefacts towards the end of the eighteenth century[7] was the spontaneous distillation of a complex 'crossing' of discrete historical forces; but that, once created, they became 'modular,' capable of being transplanted, with varying degrees of self-consciousness, to a great variety of social terrains, to merge and be merged with a correspondingly wide variety of political and ideological constellations. I will also attempt to show why these particular cultural artefacts have aroused such deep attachments.

Concepts and Definitions

Before addressing the questions raised above, it seems advisable to consider briefly the concept of 'nation' and offer a workable definition. Theorists of nationalism have often been perplexed, not to say irritated, by these three paradoxes: (1) The objective modernity of nations to the historian's eye vs. their subjective antiquity in the eyes of nationalists. (2) The formal universality of nationality as a socio-cultural concept—in the modern world everyone can, should, will 'have' a nationality, as he or she 'has' a gender—vs. the irremediable particularity of its concrete manifestations, such that, by definition, 'Greek' nationality is sui generis. (3) The 'political' power of nationalisms vs. their philosophical poverty and even incoherence. In other words, unlike most other isms, nationalism has never produced its own grand thinkers; no Hobbeses, Tocquevilles, Marxes, or Webers. This 'emptiness' easily gives rise, among cosmopolitan and polylingual intellectuals, to a certain condescension. Like Gertrude Stein in the face of Oakland, one can rather quickly conclude that there is 'no there there'. It is characteristic that even so sympathetic a student of nationalism as Tom Nairn can nonetheless write that: '"Nationalism" is the pathology of modern developmental history, as inescapable as "neurosis" in the individual, with much the same essential ambiguity attaching to it, a similar built-in capacity for descent into dementia, rooted in the dilemmas of helplessness thrust upon most of the world (the equivalent of infantilism for societies) and largely incurable.'[8]

Part of the difficulty is that one tends unconsciously to hypostasize the existence of Nationalism-with-a-big-N (rather as one might Age-with-a-capital-A) and then to classify 'it' as *an* ideology. (Note that if everyone has an age, Age is merely an analytical expression.) It would, I think, make things easier if one treated it as if it belonged with 'kinship' and 'religion', rather than with 'liberalism' or 'fascism'.

In an anthropological spirit, then, I propose the following definition of the nation: it is an imagined political community—and imagined as both inherently limited and sovereign.

It is *imagined* because the members of even the smallest nation will never know most of their fellow-members, meet them, or even hear of them, yet in the minds of each lives the image of their communion.[9] Renan referred to this imagining in his suavely back-handed way when he wrote that 'Or l'essence d'une nation est que tous les individus aient beaucoup de choses en commun, et aussi que tous aient oublié bien des choses.'[10] With a certain ferocity Gellner makes a comparable point when he rules that 'Nationalism is not the awakening of nations to self-consciousness: it *invents* nations where they do not exist.'[11] The drawback to this formulation, however, is that Gellner is so anxious to show that nationalism masquerades under false pretences that he assimilates 'invention' to 'fabrication' and 'falsity', rather than to 'imagining' and 'creation'. In this way he implies that 'true' communities exist which can be advantageously juxtaposed to nations. In fact, all communities larger than primordial villages of face-to-face contact (and perhaps even these) are imagined. Communities are to be distinguished, not by their falsity/genuineness, but by the style in which they are imagined. Javanese villagers have always known that they are connected to people they have never seen, but these ties were once imagined particularistically—as indefinitely stretchable nets of kinship and clientship. Until quite recently, the Javanese language had no word meaning the abstraction 'society.' We may today think of the French aristocracy of the *ancien régime* as a class; but surely it was imagined this way only very late.[12] To the question "Who is the Comte de X?' the normal answer would have been, not 'a member of the aristocracy,' but 'the lord of X,' 'the uncle of the Baronne de Y,' or 'a client of the Duc de Z.'

The nation is imagined as *limited* because even the largest of them, encompassing perhaps a billion living human beings, has finite, if elastic, boundaries, beyond which lie other nations. No nation imagines itself coterminous with mankind. The most messianic nationalists do not dream of a day when all the members of the human race will join their nation in the way that it was possible, in certain epochs, for, say, Christians to dream of a wholly Christian planet.

It is imagined as *sovereign* because the concept was born in an age in which Enlightenment and Revolution were destroying the legitimacy of the divinely-ordained, hierarchical dynastic realm. Coming to maturity at a stage of human history when even the most devout adherents of any universal religion were inescapably confronted with the living *pluralism* of such religions, and the allomorphism between each faith's ontological claims and territorial stretch, nations dream of being free, and, if under God, directly so. The gage and emblem of this freedom is the sovereign state.

Finally, it is imagined as a *community*, because, regardless of the actual inequality and exploitation that may prevail in each, the nation is always conceived as a deep, horizontal comradeship. Ultimately it is this fraternity that makes it possible, over the past two centuries, for so many millions of people, not so much to kill, as willingly to die for such limited imaginings.

These deaths bring us abruptly face to face with the central problem posed by nationalism: what makes the shrunken imaginings of recent history (scarcely more than two centuries) generate such colossal sacrifices? I believe that the beginnings of an answer lie in the cultural roots of nationalism.

Notes

1. This formulation is chosen simply to emphasize the scale and the style of the fighting, not to assign blame. To avoid possible misunderstanding, it should be said that the December 1978 invasion grew out of armed clashes between partisans of the two revolutionary movements going back possibly as far as 1971. After April 1977, border raids, initiated by the Cambodians, but quickly followed by the Vietnamese, grew in size and scope, culminating in the major Vietnamese incursion of December 1977. None of these raids, however, aimed at overthrowing enemy regimes or occupying large territories, nor were the numbers of troops involved comparable to those deployed in December 1978. The controversy over the causes of the war is most thoughtfully pursued in: Stephen P. Heder, 'The Kampuchean–Vietnamese Conflict,' in David W. P. Elliott, ed., *The Third Indochina Conflict,* pp. 21–67; Anthony Barnett, 'Inter-Communist Conflicts and Vietnam,' *Bulletin of Concerned Asian Scholars,* 11: 4 (October–December 1979), pp. 2–9; and Laura Summers, 'In Matters of War and Socialism Anthony Barnett would Shame and Honour Kampuchea Too Much,' ibid., pp. 10–18.

2. Anyone who has doubts about the UK's claims to such parity with the USSR should ask himself what nationality its name denotes: Great Brito-Irish?

3. Eric Hobsbawm, 'Some Reflections on "The Break-up of Britain" ', New Left Review, 105 (September–October 1977), p. 13.

4. See his *Nations and States,* p. 5. Emphasis added.

5. See his 'The Modern Janus', *New Left Review,* 94 (November–December 1975), p. 3. This essay is included unchanged in *The Break-up of Britain* as chapter 9 (pp. 329–63).

6. Karl Marx and Friedrich Engels, *The Communist Manifesto,* in the *Selected Works,* 1, p. 45. Emphasis added. In any theoretical exegesis, the words 'of course' should flash red lights before the transported reader.

7. As Aira Kemiläinen notes, the twin 'founding fathers' of academic scholarship on nationalism, Hans Kohn and Carleton Hayes, argued persuasively for this dating. Their conclusions have, I think, not been seriously disputed except by nationalist ideologues in particular countries. Kemiläinen also observes that the word 'nationalism' did not come into wide general use until the end of the nineteenth century. It did not occur, for example, in many standard nineteenth century lexicons. If Adam Smith conjured with the wealth of 'nations,' he meant by the term no more than 'societies' or 'states.' Aira Kemiläinen, *Nationalism,* pp. 10, 33, and 48–49.

8. *The Break-up of Britain,* p. 359.

9. Cf. Seton-Watson, *Nations and States,* p. 5: 'All that I can find to say is that a nation exists when a significant number of people in a community consider themselves to form a nation, or behave as if they formed one.' We may translate 'consider themselves' as 'imagine themselves.'

10. Ernest Renan, 'Qu'est-ce qu'une nation?' in *Œuvres Complètes,* 1, p. 892. He adds: 'tout citoyen français doit avoir oublié la Saint-Barthélemy, les massacres du Midi au XIIIe siècle. Il n'y a pas en France dix familles qui puissent fournir la preuve d'une origine franque . . .'

11. Ernest Gellner, *Thought and Change,* p. 169. Emphasis added.

12. Hobsbawm, for example, 'fixes' it by saying that in 1789 it numbered about 400,000 in a population of 23,000,000. (See his *The Age of Revolution,* p. 78). But would this statistical picture of the noblesse have been imaginable under the *ancien régime*?

12 | *Reel Bad Arabs: How Hollywood Vilifies a People*

Jack G. Shaheen

L̲ive images on big screen and television go beyond a thousand words in perpetuating stereotypes and clichés. This article surveys more than a century of Hollywood's projection of negative images of the Arabs and Muslims. Based on the study of more than 900 films, it shows how moviegoers are led to believe that all Arabs are Muslims and all Muslims are Arabs. The moviemakers' distorted lenses have shown Arabs as heartless, brutal, uncivilized, religious fanatics through common depictions of Arabs kidnapping or raping a fair maiden; expressing hatred against the Jews and Christians; and demonstrating a love for wealth and power. The article compares the stereotype of the hook-nosed Arab with a similar depiction of Jews in Nazi propaganda materials. Only five percent of Arab film roles depict normal, human characters.

Introduction

> Al tikrar biallem il hmar *(By repetition even the donkey learns).*

This Arab proverb encapsulates how effective repetition can be when it comes to education: how we learn by repeating an exercise over and over again until we can respond almost reflexively. A small child uses repetition to master numbers and letters of the alphabet. Older students use repetition to memorize historical dates and algebraic formulas.

For more than a century Hollywood, too, has used repetition as a teaching tool, tutoring movie audiences by repeating over and over, in film after film, insidious images of the Arab people. I ask the reader to study in these pages the persistence of this defamation, from earlier times to the present day, and to consider how these slanderous stereotypes have affected honest discourse and public policy.

Reprinted by permission from *Annals of the American Academy of Political and Social Science* 588 (July 2003).

Genesis

In [my book *Reel Bad Arabs*], I document and discuss virtually every feature that Hollywood has ever made—more than 900 films, the vast majority of which portray Arabs by distorting at every turn what most Arab men, women, and children are really like. In gathering the evidence for this book, I was driven by the need to expose an injustice: cinema's systematic, pervasive, and unapologetic degradation and dehumanization of a people.

When colleagues ask whether today's reel Arabs are more stereotypical than yesteryear's, I can't say the celluloid Arab has changed. That is the problem. He is what he has always been—the cultural "other." Seen through Hollywood's distorted lenses, Arabs look different and threatening. Projected along racial and religious lines, the stereotypes are deeply ingrained in American cinema. From 1896 until today, filmmakers have collectively indicted all Arabs as Public Enemy #1—brutal, heartless, uncivilized religious fanatics and money-mad cultural "others" bent on terrorizing civilized Westerners, especially Christians and Jews. Much has happened since 1896—women's suffrage, the Great Depression, the civil rights movement, two world wars, the Korean, Vietnam, and Gulf wars, and the collapse of the Soviet Union. Throughout it all, Hollywood's caricature of the Arab has prowled the silver screen. He is there to this day—repulsive and unrepresentative as ever.

What is an Arab? In countless films, Hollywood alleges the answer: Arabs are brute murderers, sleazy rapists, religious fanatics, oil-rich dimwits, and abusers of women. "They [the Arabs] all look alike to me," quips the American heroine in the movie *The Sheik Steps Out* (1937). "All Arabs look alike to me," admits the protagonist in *Commando* (1968). Decades later, nothing had changed. Quips the U.S. Ambassador in *Hostage* (1986), "I can't tell one [Arab] from another. Wrapped in those bed sheets they all look the same to me." In Hollywood's films, they certainly do.

Pause and visualize the reel Arab. What do you see? Black beard, headdress, dark sunglasses. In the background—a limousine, harem maidens, oil wells, camels. Or perhaps he is brandishing an automatic weapon, crazy hate in his eyes and Allah on his lips. Can you see him?

Think about it. When was the last time you saw a movie depicting an Arab or an American of Arab heritage as a regular guy? Perhaps a man who works ten hours a day, comes home to a loving wife and family, plays soccer with his kids, and prays with family members at his respective mosque or church. He's the kind of guy you'd like to have as your next door neighbor, because—well, maybe because he's a bit like you.

But would you want to share your country, much less your street, with any of Hollywood's Arabs? Would you want your kids playing with him and his family, your teenagers dating them? Would you enjoy sharing your neighborhood with fabulously wealthy and vile oil sheikhs with an eye for Western blondes and arms deals and intent on world domination, or with crazed terrorists, airplane hijackers, or camel-riding bedouins?

Real Arabs

Who exactly are the Arabs of the Middle East? When I use the term "Arab," I refer to the 265 million people who reside in, and the many more millions around the world who are from, the 22 Arab states.[1] The Arabs have made many contributions to our civilization. To name a few, Arab and Persian physicians and scientists inspired European thinkers like Leonardo da Vinci. The Arabs invented algebra and the concept of zero. Numerous English words—algebra, chemistry, coffee, and others—have Arab roots. Arab intellectuals made it feasible for Western scholars to develop and practice advanced educational systems.

In astronomy Arabs used astrolabes for navigation, star maps, celestial globes, and the concept of the center of gravity. In geography, they pioneered the use of latitude and longitude. They invented the water clock; their architecture inspired the Gothic style in Europe. In agriculture, they introduced oranges, dates, sugar, and cotton, and pioneered water works and irrigation. And, they developed a tradition of legal learning, of secular literature and scientific and philosophical thought, in which the Jews also played an important part.

There exists a mixed ethnicity in the Arab world—from 5000 BC to the present. The Scots, Greeks, British, French, Romans, English, and others have occupied the area. Not surprisingly, some Arabs have dark hair, dark eyes, and olive complexions. Others boast freckles, red hair, and blue eyes.

Geographically, the Arab world is one-and-a-half times as large as the United States, stretching from the Strait of Hormuz to the Rock of Gibraltar. It's the point where Asia, Europe, and Africa come together. The region gave the world three major religions, a language, and an alphabet.

In most Arab countries today, 70 percent of the population is under age 30. Most share a common language, cultural heritage, history, and religion (Islam). Though the vast majority of them are Muslims, about 15 million Arab Christians (including Chaldean, Coptic, Eastern Orthodox, Episcopalian, Roman Catholic, Melkite, Maronite, and Protestant), reside there as well.

. . . Their dress is traditional and Western. The majority are peaceful, not violent; poor, not rich; most do not dwell in desert tents; none are surrounded by harem maidens; most have never seen an oil well or mounted a camel. Not one travels via "magic carpets." Their lifestyles defy stereotyping.

. . . Through immigration, conversion, and birth, . . . Muslims are America's fastest growing religious group; about 500,000 reside in the greater Los Angeles area. America's six to eight million Muslims frequent more than 2,000 mosques, Islamic centers, and schools. They include immigrants from more than 60 nations, as well as African-Americans. In fact, most of the world's 1.1 billion Muslims are Indonesian, Indian, or Malaysian. Only 12 percent of the world's Muslims are Arab. Yet, moviemakers ignore this reality, depicting Arabs and Muslims as one and the same people. Repeatedly, they falsely project all Arabs as Muslims and all Muslims as Arabs. As a result, viewers, too, tend to link the same attributes to both peoples.

. . . Hollywood's past omission of "everyday" African-Americans, American Indians, and Latinos unduly affected the lives of these minorities. The same holds true with the industry's near total absence of regular Arab-Americans. Regular Mideast Arabs, too, are invisible on silver screens. Asks Jay Stone, "Where are the movie Arabs and Muslims who are just ordinary people?"[2]

Why is it important for the average American to know and care about the Arab stereotype? It is critical because dislike of "the stranger," which the Greeks knew as xenophobia, forewarns that when one ethnic, racial, or religious group is vilified, innocent people suffer. History reminds us that the cinema's hateful Arab stereotypes are reminiscent of abuses in earlier times. Not so long ago—and sometimes still—Asians, American Indians, blacks, and Jews were vilified.

Ponder the consequences. In February 1942, more than 100,000 Americans of Japanese descent were displaced from their homes and interred in camps; for decades blacks were denied basic civil rights, robbed of their property, and lynched; American Indians, too, were displaced and slaughtered; and in Europe, six million Jews perished in the Holocaust.

This is what happens when people are dehumanized.

Mythology in any society is significant. And, Hollywood's celluloid mythology dominates the culture. No doubt about it, Hollywood's renditions of Arabs frame stereotypes in viewer's minds. The problem is peculiarly American. Because of the vast American cultural reach via television and film—we are the world's leading exporter of screen images—the all-pervasive Arab stereotype has much more of a negative impact on viewers today than it did thirty or forty years ago.

Nowadays, Hollywood's motion pictures reach nearly everyone. Cinematic illusions are created, nurtured, and distributed worldwide, reaching viewers in more than 100 countries, from Iceland to Thailand. Arab images have an effect not only on international audiences, but on international movie makers as well. No sooner do contemporary features leave the movie theaters than they are available in video stores and transmitted onto TV screens. Thanks to technological advances, old silent and sound movies impugning Arabs, some of which were produced before I was born, are repeatedly broadcast on cable television and beamed directly into the home.

Check your local guides and you will see that since the mid-1980s, appearing each week on TV screens, are fifteen to twenty recycled movies projecting Arabs as dehumanized caricatures: *The Sheik* (1921), *The Mummy* (1932), *Cairo* (1942), *The Steel Lady* (1953), *Exodus* (1960), *The Black Stallion* (1979), *Protocol* (1984), *The Delta Force* (1986), *Ernest in the Army* (1997), and *Rules of Engagement* (2000). Watching yesteryear's stereotypical Arabs on TV screens is an unnerving experience, especially when pondering the influence celluloid images have on adults and our youth.

. . . Arabs, like Jews, are Semites, so it is perhaps not too surprising that Hollywood's image of hook-nosed, robed Arabs parallels the image of Jews in Nazi-inspired movies such as *Robert and Bertram* (1939), *Die Rothschilds Aktien von Waterloo* (1940), *Der Ewige Jude* (1940), and *Jud Süss* (1940). Once upon a cinematic time, screen Jews boasted exaggerated nostrils and dressed differently—in yarmulkes and dark robes—than the films' protagonists. In the past, Jews were projected as the "other"—depraved and predatory money-grubbers who seek world domination, worship a different God, and kill innocents. Nazi propaganda also presented the lecherous Jew slinking in the shadows, scheming to snare the blonde Aryan virgin.

Yesterday's Shylocks resemble today's hook-nosed sheikhs, arousing fear of the "other." Reflects William Greider, "Jews were despised as exemplars of modernism," while today's "Arabs are depicted as carriers of primitivism—[both] threatening to upset our cozy modern world with their strange habits and desires."[3]

. . . Because of Hollywood's heightened cultural awareness, producers try not to demean most racial and ethnic groups. They know it is morally irresponsible to repeatedly bombard viewers with a regular stream of lurid, unyielding, and unrepentant portraits of a people. The relation is one of cause and effect. Powerful collages of hurtful images serve to deepen suspicions and hatreds. Jerry Mander observes, screen images "can cause people to do what they might otherwise never [have] thought to do."[4]

One can certainly make the case that movie land's pernicious Arab images are sometimes reflected in the attitudes and actions of journalists and government officials. Consider the aftermath of the 19 April 1995 bombing of the federal building in Oklahoma City. Though no American of Arab descent was involved, they were instantly targeted as suspects. Speculative reporting, combined with decades of harmful stereotyping, resulted in more than 300 hate crimes against them.[5]

A Basis for Understanding

. . . [I have reviewed] more than 900 feature films displaying Arab characters. Regrettably, in all these I uncovered only a handful of heroic Arabs; they surface in a few 1980s and 1990s scenarios. In *Lion of the Desert* (1981), righteous Arabs bring down invading fascists. Humane Palestinians surface in *Hanna K* (1983) and *The Seventh Coin* (1992). In *Robin Hood, Prince of Thieves* (1991), a devout Muslim who "fights better than twenty English knights," helps Robin Hood get the better of the evil Sheriff of Nottingham. In *The 13th Warrior* (1999), an Arab Muslim scholar befriends Nordic warriors, helping them defeat primitive cavemen. And in *Three Kings* (1999), a movie celebrating our commonalities and differences, we view Arabs as regular folks, with affections and aspirations. This anti-war movie humanizes the Iraqis, a people who for too long have been projected as evil caricatures.

Most of the time I found moviemakers saturating the marketplace with all sorts of Arab villains. Producers collectively impugned Arabs in every type of movie you can imagine, targeting adults in well-known and high-budgeted movies such as *Exodus* (1960), *Black Sunday* (1977), *Ishtar* (1987), and *The Siege* (1998); and reaching out to teenagers with financially successful schlock movies such as *Five Weeks in a Balloon* (1962), *Things Are Tough All Over* (1982), *Sahara* (1983), and *Operation Condor* (1997). One constant factor dominates all the films: Derogatory stereotypes are omnipresent, reaching youngsters, baby boomers, and older folk.

I am not saying an Arab should never be portrayed as the villain. What I am saying is that almost all Hollywood depictions of Arabs are bad ones. This is a grave injustice. Repetitious and negative images of the reel Arab literally sustain adverse portraits across generations. The fact is that for more than a century producers have tarred an entire group of people with the same sinister brush.

Villains

. . . Beginning with *Imar the Servitor* (1914), up to and including *The Mummy Returns* (2001), a synergy of images equates Arabs from Syria to the Sudan with quintessential evil. In hundreds of movies "evil" Arabs stalk the screen. We see them assaulting just about every imaginable foe—Americans, Europeans, Israelis, legionnaires, Africans, fellow Arabs, even— for heaven's sake—Hercules and Samson.

Scores of comedies present Arabs as buffoons, stumbling all over themselves. Some of our best known and most popular stars mock Arabs: Will Rogers in *Business and Pleasure* (1931); Laurel and Hardy in *Beau Hunks* (1931); Bob Hope and Bing Crosby in *Road to Morocco* (1942); the Marx Brothers in *A Night in Casablanca* (1946); Abbott and Costello in *Abbott and Costello in the Foreign Legion* (1950); the Bowery Boys in *Bowery to Bagdad* (1955); Jerry Lewis in *The Sad Sack* (1957); Phil Silvers in *Follow That Camel* (1967); Marty Feldman in *The Last Remake of Beau Geste* (1977); Harvey Korman in *Americathon* (1979); Bugs Bunny in *1001 Rabbit Tales* (1982); Dustin Hoffman and Warren Beatty in *Ishtar* (1987); Pauly Shore in *In the Army Now* (1994); and Jim Varney in *Ernest in the Army* (1997).

Some protagonists even refer to Arabs as "dogs" and "monkeys." As a result, those viewers laughing at bumbling reel Arabs leave movie theaters with a sense of solidarity, united by their shared distance from these peoples of ridicule.

In dramas, especially, Hollywood's stars contest and vanquish reel Arabs. See Emory Johnson in *The Gift Girl* (1917); Gary Cooper in *Beau Sabreur* (1928); John Wayne in *I Cover the War* (1937); Burt Lancaster in *Ten Tall Men* (1951); Dean Martin in *The Ambushers* (1967); Michael Caine in *Ashanti* (1979); Sean Connery in *Never Say Never Again* (1983); Harrison Ford in *Frantic* (1988); Kurt Russell in *Executive Decision* (1996); and Brendan Frasier in *The Mummy* (1999).

Perhaps in an attempt to further legitimize the stereotype, as well as to attract more viewers, in the mid-1980s studios presented notable African-American actors facing off against, and ultimately destroying, reel Arabs. Among them, Eddie Murphy, Louis Gossett Jr., Robert Guillaume, Samuel Jackson, Denzel Washington, and Shaquille O'Neal.[6]

In the Disney movie *Kazaam* (1996), O'Neal pummels three Arab Muslims who covet "all the money in the world." Four years later, director William Friedkin has actor Samuel Jackson exploiting jingoistic prejudice and religious bigotry in *Rules of Engagement* (2000). The effects of ethnic exploitation are especially obvious in scenes revealing egregious, false images of Yemeni children as assassins and enemies of the United States.

To my knowledge, no Hollywood WWI, WWII, or Korean War movie has ever shown America's fighting forces slaughtering children. Yet, near the conclusion of *Rules of Engagement*, US marines open fire on the Yemenis, shooting 83 men, women, and children. During the scene, viewers rose to their feet, clapped and cheered. Boasts director Friedkin, "I've seen audiences stand up and applaud the film throughout the United States."[7] Some viewers applaud Marines gunning down Arabs in war dramas not necessarily because of cultural insensitivity, but because for more than 100 years Hollywood has singled out the Arab as our enemy. Over a period of time, a steady stream of bigoted images does, in fact, tarnish our judgment of a people and their culture.

Rules of Engagement not only reinforces historically damaging stereotypes, but promotes a dangerously generalized portrayal of Arabs as rabidly anti-American. Equally troubling to this honorably discharged US Army veteran is that *Rules of Engagement*'s credits thank for their assistance the Department of Defense (DOD) and the US Marine Corps. More than fourteen feature films, all of which show Americans killing Arabs, credit the DOD for providing needed equipment, personnel, and technical assistance. Sadly, the Pentagon seems to condone these Arab-bashing ventures, as evidenced in *True Lies* (1994), *Executive Decision* (1996), and *Freedom Strike* (1998).

On November 30, 2000, Hollywood luminaries attended a star-studded dinner hosted by Defense Secretary William Cohen in honor of Motion Picture Association President Jack Valenti, for which the Pentagon paid the bill—$295,000. Called on to explain why the DOD personnel were fraternizing with imagemakers at an elaborate Beverly Hills gathering, spokesman Kenneth Bacon said: "If we can have television shows and movies that show the excitement and importance of military life, they can help generate a favorable atmosphere for recruiting."

The DOD has sometimes shown concern when other peoples have been tarnished on film. For example, in the late 1950s, DOD officials were reluctant to cooperate with moviemakers attempting to advance Japanese stereotypes. When *The Bridge over the River Kwai* (1957) was being filmed, Donald Baruch, head of the DOD's Motion Picture Production Office, cautioned producers not to overemphasize Japanese terror and torture, advising:

> In our ever-increasing responsibility for maintaining a mutual friendship and respect among the people of foreign lands, the use of disparaging terms to identify ethnic, national or religious groups is inimical to our national interest, particularly in motion pictures sanctioned by Government cooperation.[8]

Arabs are almost always easy targets in war movies. From as early as 1912, decades prior to the 1991 Gulf War, dozens of films presented allied agents and military forces—American, British, French, and more recently Israeli—obliterating Arabs. In the World War I drama *The Lost Patrol* (1934), a brave British sergeant (Victor McLaughlin) guns down "sneaky Arabs, those dirty, filthy swine." An American newsreel cameraman (John Wayne) helps wipe out a "horde of [Arab] tribesmen" in *I Cover the War* (1937).

In *Sirocco* (1951), the first Hollywood feature film projecting Arabs as terrorists, Syrian "fanatics" assail French soldiers and American arms dealer Harry Smith (Humphrey Bogart). *The Lost Command* (1966) shows French Colonel Raspeguy's (Anthony Quinn) soldiers killing Algerians. And, Israelis gun down sneaky bedouins in two made-in-Israel films, *Sinai Guerrillas* (1960) and *Sinai Commandos* (1968).

Arabs trying to rape, kill, or abduct fair-complexioned Western heroines is a common theme, dominating scenarios from *Captured by Bedouins* (1912), to *The Pelican Brief* (1993). In *Brief*, an Arab hit man tries to assassinate the protagonist, played by Julia Roberts. In *Captured*, desert bandits kidnap a fair American maiden, but she is eventually rescued by a British officer. As for her bedouin abductors, they are gunned down by rescuing US Cavalry troops.

Arabs enslave and abuse Africans in about ten films, including *A Daughter of the Congo* (1930), *Drums of Africa* (1963), and *Ashanti* (1979). Noted African-American filmmaker Oscar Micheaux, who made "race movies" from 1919 to 1948, also advanced the Arab-as-abductor theme in his *A Daughter of the Congo*. Though Micheaux's movies contested Hollywood's Jim Crow stereotypes of blacks, *A Daughter of the Congo* depicts lecherous Arab slavers abducting and holding hostage a lovely Mulatto woman and her maid. The maiden is eventually rescued by the heroic African-American officers of the 10th US Cavalry.

Anti-Christian Arabs appear in dozens of films. When the US military officer in *Another Dawn* (1937) is asked why Arabs despise Westerners, he barks: "It's a good Moslem hatred of Christians." Islam is also portrayed as a violent faith in *Legion of the Doomed* (1959). Here, an Arab is told, "Kill him before he kills you." Affirms the Arab as he plunges a knife into his foe's gut, "You speak the words of Allah." And, in *The Castilian* (1963), Spanish Christians triumph over Arab Muslim zealots. How? By releasing scores of squealing pigs! Terrified of the pigs, the reel Arabs retreat.

Arabs invade the United States and terrorize innocents in *Golden Hands of Kurigal* (1949), *Terror Squad* (1988), *True Lies* (1994), and *The Siege* (1998). *The Siege* is especially alarming. In it, Arab immigrants methodically lay waste to Manhattan. Assisted by Arab-American auto mechanics, university students, and a college teacher, they blow up the city's FBI building, kill scores of government agents, blast theatergoers, and detonate a bomb in a crowded bus.

. . . Oily Arabs and robed thugs intent on acquiring nuclear weapons surface in roughly ten films. See *Fort Algiers* (1958) and *Frantic* (1988).

At least a dozen made-in-Israel and Golan-Globus movies, such as *Eagles Attack at Dawn* (1970), *Iron Eagle* (1986), and *Chain of Command* (1993), show Americans and/or Israelis crushing evil-minded Arabs, many of whom are portrayed by Israeli actors.

More than 30 French Foreign Legion movies, virtually a sub-genre of boy's-own-adventure films, show civilized legionnaires obliterating backward desert bedouin. These legion formula films cover a span of more than 80 years, from *The Unknown* (1915) to *Legionnaire* (1998). Scenarios display courageous, outnumbered legionnaires battling against, and ultimately overcoming, unruly Arabs. Even Porky Pig as a legionnaire and his camel join in the melee, beating up bedouins in the animated cartoon, *Little Beau Porky* (1936).

. . . Observes William Greider of the Washington Post, "Much of what Westerners 'learned' about Arabs sounds similar to what nineteenth-century Americans 'discovered' about Indians on this continent . . . acceptable villains make our troubles so manageable." In the past, imagemakers punctuated "anti-human qualities in these strange people," American Indians. They projected them as savages, not thinking like us, "not sharing our aspirations." Once one has concluded that Indians thrive on violence, disorder, and stealth, it becomes easier to accept rather than challenge "irrational" portraits. Today, says Greider, "The Arab stereotypes created by British and French colonialism are still very much with us."[9]

Film producers, broadcast journalists, and military leaders echo Greider's Arab-as-Indian analogy. Seeing marauding desert Arabs approach, the American protagonist in the war movie *The Steel Lady* (1953) quips, "This is bandit area, worse than Arizona Apache." In talking up his film *Iron Eagle* (1986), producer Ron Samuels gushed: Showing an American teen hijacking a jet and wiping out scores of Arabs "was just the kind of story I'd been looking for. . . . It reminded me of the old John Wayne westerns."

Sheikhs

The word "sheikh" means, literally, a wise elderly person, the head of the family, but you would not know that from watching any of Hollywood's "sheikh" features, more than 160 scenarios, including the Kinetoscope short *Sheik Hadj Tahar Hadj Cherif* (1894) and the Selig Company's *The Power of the Sultan* (1907)—the first movie to be filmed in Los Angeles. Throughout the Arab world, to show respect, people address Muslim religious leaders as sheikhs.

Moviemakers, however, attach a completely different meaning to the word. As Matthew Sweet points out, "The cinematic Arab has never been an attractive figure . . . in the 1920s he was a swarthy Sheik, wiggling his eyebrows and chasing the [Western] heroine around a tiled courtyard. After the 1973 oil crisis . . . producers revitalized the image of the fabulously wealthy and slothful sheikh, only this time he was getting rich at the expense of red-blooded Americans; he became an inscrutable bully—a Ray-Ban-ed variation of the stereotypes of the Jewish money lender."[10]

Instead of presenting sheikhs as elderly men of wisdom, screenwriters offer romantic melodramas portraying them as stooges-in-sheets, slovenly, hook-nosed potentates intent on capturing pale-faced blondes for their harems. Imitating the stereotypical behavior of their lecherous predecessors—the "bestial" Asian, the black "buck," and the "lascivious" Latino—slovenly Arabs move to swiftly and violently deflower Western maidens. Explains Edward Said, "The perverted sheikh can often be seen snarling at the captured Western hero and blonde girl . . . [and saying] 'My men are going to kill you, but they like to amuse themselves before.' "[11]

Early silent films, such as *The Unfaithful Odalisque* (1903), *The Arab* (1915), and *The Sheik* (1921), all present bearded, robed Arab rulers as one collective stereotypical lecherous cur. In *The Unfaithful Odalisque*, the sheikh not only admonishes his harem maiden, he directs a Nubian slave to lash her with a cat-o'-nine-tails. In *The Sheik* (1921), Sheikh Ahmed (Valentino) glares at Diana, the kidnapped British lovely and boasts: "When an Arab sees a woman he wants, he takes her!"

Flash forward 33 years. Affirms the sheikh in *The Adventures of Hajji Baba* (1954): "Give her to me or I'll take her!"

Moving to kidnap and/or seduce the Western heroine, clumsy moneyed sheikhs fall all over themselves in more than 60 silent and sound movies, ranging from *The Fire and the Sword* (1914) to *Protocol* (1984). Sheikhs disregard Arab women, preferring instead to ravish just one Western woman.

But Hollywood's silent movies did not dare show Western women bedding sheikhs. Why? Because America's movie censors objected to love scenes between Westerners and Arabs. Even producers experiencing desert mirages dared not imagine such unions.

Some viewers perceived Valentino's *The Sheik* (1921) to be an exception to the rule. Not true. Valentino's Sheikh Ahmed, who vanquishes Diana, the Western heroine in the movie, is actually a European, not an Arab. This helps explain why the European lover-boy dressed in Arab garb was viewed so positively by his essentially female audience. Note the dialogue, revealing Ahmed to be a European:

Diana, the heroine: "His [Ahmed's] hand is so large for an Arab."

Ahmed's French friend: "He is not an Arab. His father was an Englishman, his mother a Spaniard."

Other desert scenarios followed suit, allowing the hero and heroine to make love, but only after revealing they were actually Western Christians!

In Europe, it was otherwise. As early as 1922, a few European movies such as *The Sheikh's Wife* (1922) countered fixed themes, showing Western heroines embracing dashing Arab sheikhs.

Both good and evil sheikhs battle each other in about 60 Arabian Nights fantasies, animated and non-animated. A plethora of unsavory characters, wicked viziers, slimy slavers, irreverent magicians, and shady merchants contest courageous princes, princesses, lamp genies, and folk heroes such as Ali Baba, Sinbad, Aladdin and, on occasion, the benevolent caliph. You can see some of them in the four Kismet fantasies (1920, 1930, 1944, 1955), *Prisoners of the Casbah* (1955), and *Aladdin* (1992).

Even animated cartoon characters thump Arabs. My childhood hero, Bugs Bunny, clobbers nasty Arabs in *1001 Rabbit Tales* (1982). Bugs trounces an ugly genie, a dense sheikh, and the ruler's spoiled son. My other cartoon hero, Popeye, also trounces Arabs. In the early

1930s, Fleischer Studios' lengthy Popeye cartoons presented Arab folk heroes as rogues, not as champions. Popeye clobbers, not befriends, Ali Baba and Sinbad in *Popeye the Sailor Meets Ali Baba's Forty Thieves*, and *Popeye the Sailor Meets Sinbad the Sailor.*

Beginning in the mid-1970s, fresh directors also projected Arab leaders through warped prisms. Emulating their predecessors' stereotypes they, too, displayed Western heroines fending off over-sexed desert sheikhs.

Yet, there are dramatic differences in sheikh images. Once-upon-a-time Arabian Nights movies, such as *Ali Baba Goes to Town* (1937) and *Aladdin and His Lamp* (1952), show indolent sheikhs lounging on thrones. But, contemporary films present oily, militant, ostentatious sheikhs reclining in Rolls Royces, aspiring to buy up chunks of America.

Today's films present anti-Christian, anti-Jewish Arab potentates perched atop missile bases, armed with nuclear weapons, plenty of oil, and oodles of cash. Using Islam to justify violence, today's reel mega-rich hedonists pose a much greater threat to the West, to Israel, and to fellow Arabs than did their predecessors. You can catch a few of their kind in *Rollover* (1981), *Wrong Is Right* (1982), *The Jewel of the Nile* (1985), and *American Ninja 4: The Annihilation* (1991).

Scantily clad harem maidens attend sheikhs in more than 30 scenarios. The rulers shrug off some, torture others, and enslave the rest. Enslaving international beauties in the X-rated movie, *Ilsa: Harem Keeper of the Oil Sheikhs* (1976), is a depraved Arab ruler and his cohort—Ilsa, the "She-Wolf of the S.S." Depraved sheikhs also subjugate dwarfs and Africans; see *Utz* (1992) and *Slavers* (1977).

Often, producers falsify geopolitical realities. During WWII many Arab nations actively supported the Allies. Moroccan, Tunisian, and Algerian soldiers, for example, fought alongside French troops in North Africa, Italy, and France. Also, Jordanian and Libyan troops assisted members of the British armed services. And, late in the conflict, Egypt, Saudi Arabia, and Iraq declared war on Germany.[12]

Yet, most movies fail to show Arabs fighting alongside the good guys. Instead, burnoosed pro-Nazi potentates, some belonging to the "Arabian Gestapo," appear in more than ten sheikh movies; see, for example, *A Yank in Libya* (1942), *Action in Arabia* (1944), and *The Steel Lady* (1953). As early as 1943, about fifty years before the Gulf War, *Adventure in Iraq* (1943) depicts the US Air Force bombing the pro-German Iraqi ruler's "devil-worshiper" minions into oblivion.

From the start, protagonists ranging from Samson to 007 have battled burnoosed chieftains. Flashback to the 1900s. Two 1918 films, *Tarzan of the Apes* and *Bound in Morocco*, show Tarzan and Douglas Fairbanks, respectively, trouncing shifty sheikhs.

Cut to the 1940s. Abbott and Costello, Bing Crosby, and Bob Hope follow suit by belittling Arabs in *Lost in a Harem* (1944) and *Road to Morocco* (1942).

Advance to the 1950s. The Bowery Boys and Tab Hunter thrash robed rulers in *Looking for Danger* (1957) and *The Steel Lady* (1953), respectively.

Flash forward to the 1960s and the 1970s. Elvis Presley, Pat Boone, and Jerry Lewis deride Arabs in: *Harum Scarum* (1965), *The Perils of Pauline* (1967), and *Don't Raise the Bridge, Lower the River* (1968). Other stars bashing sheikhs were Ron Ely in *Slavers* (1977), Michael Douglas in *The Jewel of the Nile* (1985), Cheech and Chong in *Things Are Tough All Over* (1982), and Eddie Murphy in *Best Defense* (1984). And I almost forgot—Burt Braverman drubs two of movie land's ugliest sheikhs in *Hollywood Hot Tubs 2: Educating Crystal* (1990).

The movies of the 1980s are especially offensive. They display insolent desert sheikhs with thick accents threatening to rape and/or enslave starlets: Brooke Shields in *Sahara* (1983), Goldie Hawn in *Protocol* (1984), Bo Derek in *Bolero* (1984), and Kim Basinger in *Never Say Never Again* (1986).

Finally, five made-in-Israel films lambast sheikhs. Particularly degrading is Golan and Globus' *Paradise* (1981). A combination of Western teenagers and chimpanzees finish off the "jackal," a Christian-hating bedouin chieftain, and his cohorts.

Maidens

Arab women, meanwhile, are humiliated, demonized, and eroticized in more than 50 feature films.

Half-Arab heroines as well as mute enslaved Arab women appear in about sixteen features, ranging from foreign legion films to Arabian Nights fantasies. "The Arabian Nights never end," writes William Zinsser. It is a place where young slave girls lie about on soft couches, stretching their slender legs, ready to do a good turn for any handsome stranger who stumbles into the room. Amid all this décolletage sits the jolly old Caliph, miraculously cool to the wondrous sights around him, puffing his water pipe. . . . This is history at its best.[13]

Stereotypical idiosyncrasies abound, linking the Arab woman to several regularly repeated "B" images:

1. They appear as bosomy bellydancers leering out from diaphanous veils, or as disposable "knick-knacks," scantily-clad harem maidens with bare midriffs, closeted in the palace's women's quarters.

2. Background shots show them as Beasts of Burden, carrying jugs on their heads. Some are "so fat, no one would touch them."

3. In films such as *The Sheltering Sky* (1990) they appear as shapeless Bundles of Black, a homogeneous sea of covered women trekking silently behind their unshaven mates.

4. Beginning in 1917 with Fox's silent *Cleopatra*, starring Theda Bara, studios labeled Arab women "serpents" and "vampires." Subsequently, the word "vamp," a derivation of that word, was added to English dictionaries. Advancing the vampire image are movies such as *Saadia* (1953) and *Beast of Morocco* (1966). Both display Arab women as Black magic vamps, or enchantresses "possessed of devils."

5. In *The Leopard Woman* (1920) and *Nighthawks* (1981) they are Bombers intent on killing Westerners.

When those dark-complexioned femmes fatales move to woo the American/British hero, they are often disappointed. The majority of movies, such as *Outpost in Morocco* (1949), posit that an Arab woman in love with a Western hero must die.

A few films allow Arab maidens to embrace Western males. In *A Café in Cairo* (1925) and *Arabesque* (1966), actresses Priscilla Dean and Sophia Loren appear as bright and lovely Arab women. Only after the women ridicule and reject Arab suitors, does the scenario allow them to fall into the arms of Western protagonists.

Regrettably, just a handful of movies—*Anna Ascends* (1922), *Princess Tam Tam* (1935), *Bagdad* (1949), *Flame of Araby* (1951), and *Flight from Ashiya* (1964), present brave and compassionate Arab women, genuine heroines. There are also admirable queens and princesses in several Cleopatra films and Arabian fantasy tales.

. . . Taken together, her mute on-screen non-behavior and black-cloaked costume serve to alienate the Arab woman from her international sisters, and vice versa. Not only do the reel Arab women never speak, but they are never in the work place, functioning as doctors, computer specialists, school teachers, print and broadcast journalists, or as successful, well-rounded electric or domestic engineers. Movies don't show charitable Arab women such as those who belong to the Mosaic Foundation, which donates millions to American hospitals. Points out Camelia Anwar Sadat, Syria and Egypt gave women the right to vote as early as Europe did—and much earlier than Switzerland. Today, women make up nearly one-third of the Egyptian parliament. You would never guess from Hollywood's portrayal of Arab women that they are as diverse and talented as any others. Hollywood has not yet imagined a woman as interesting as Ivonne Abdel-Baki, the daughter of Lebanese immigrants and Ecuador's ambassador to Washington. Abdel-Baki, a specialist in conflict resolution, graduated from

Harvard University's Kennedy School of Government and is fluent in five languages. Or De' Al-Mohammed, the University of Missouri's blind fencing star.[14] And many, many more.

Egyptians

... Egyptian caricatures appear in more than 100 films, from mummy tales to legends of pharaohs and queens to contemporary scenarios. Reel Egyptians routinely descend upon Westerners, Israelis, and fellow Egyptians. Interspersed throughout the movies are souk swindlers as well as begging children scratching for baksheesh. An ever-constant theme shows devious Egyptians moving to defile Western women; see Cecil B. DeMille's *Made for Love* (1926) and *Sphinx* (1981).

Stephen Spielberg's films *Raiders of the Lost Ark* (1981), *Young Sherlock Holmes* (1986), and *Indiana Jones and the Last Crusade* (1989) merit special attention, as do Golan-Globus' 1960s scenarios, made-in-Israel: *Cairo Operation* (1965) and *Trunk to Cairo* (1965). The producers paint Egyptians as nuclear-crazed and pro-Nazi. Their scenarios are particularly objectionable given the real-life heroics of the Arab Brotherhood of Freedom, a group of brave Egyptians who sided with the Allies during World War II.

Imagemakers are not so harsh with Queen Cleopatra. Beginning with Helen Gardner's *Cleopatra* (1912), Hollywood enlisted stars such as Ava Gardner, Theda Bara, Vivian Leigh, Sophia Loren, Claudette Colbert, and Elizabeth Taylor to portray Egypt's seductive queen. Approximately fifteen movies show Egypt's queen, encircled by stereotypical maidens, pining over Roman leaders. Only four movies display Egyptian queens romancing Egyptians. The majority display Egyptian royals feuding with fellow Egyptians as well as Rome's soldiers.

A few movies, such as Cecil B. DeMille's *The Ten Commandments* (1923) and Dream-Works' Jeffrey Katzenberg's *The Prince of Egypt* (1998), feature Egyptian rogues trying to crush heroic Israelites. I found the animated *Prince of Egypt* to be less offensive than DeMille's scenarios. Though Katzenberg's movie displays plenty of Egyptian villains, *Prince of Egypt* offers more humane, balanced portraits than do DeMille's 1923 and 1956 versions of *The Ten Commandments*. DeMille's 1923 film shows Egyptian guards beating "the dogs of Israel" and Pharaoh's ten-year-old son whipping Moses.

From the start, moviemakers linked Egypt with the undead. In Georges Méliès's film *The Monster* (1903), the camera reveals a bearded Egyptian magician removing a skeleton from its casket. Presto! He transforms the bony thing into a lovely maiden. But, not for long. The cunning magician changes the woman back into a skeleton.

Say "Egypt" and producers think "Mummies" and "Money." Beginning with Vitagraph's *The Egyptian Mummy* (1914) and *Dust of Egypt* (1915), Hollywood presented about 26 mummy films. In order to spook viewers, cinematographers placed gauze over the camera's lens, creating chilling, dreamlike, and exotic moods. Topping the list is Universal's *The Mummy* (1932). Due to a fine screenplay and Boris Karloff's performance as the mummy Imhotep, this classic stands the test of time as the mummy film. Other popular mummy movies are *The Mummy's Hand* (1940), *The Mummy's Tomb* (1942), and *The Mummy's Revenge* (1973).

Mummy plots are relatively simple: Revived mummies and their caretaker "priests" contest Western archaeologists. In most scenarios, the ambitious gravediggers ignore tomb curses. So of course they suffer the consequences for daring to reawaken Egypt's sleeping royals. Meanwhile, the Westerners dupe ignorant, superstitious, and two-timing Egyptians.

Once fully revived, the bandages-with-eyes mummy lusts after the archaeologist's fair-skinned daughter. And, the mummy crushes panicked Egyptian workers and all crypt violators—"infidels," "unbelievers," and "heretics." Occasionally, movies like *The Awakening* (1980) pump up the action by offering decomposed horrors; also in this one, a queen's evil spirit so contaminates the Western heroine, she kills her father.

Obviously, there's more to the state of Egypt, the most heavily populated of all Arab countries, than pyramids and curses. Egypt is comprised of a people who take pride in their culture and their long and honorable history. Moving to modernize its economy and to improve the living standards of its population, Egypt now boasts more than fourteen state universities. The likes of scholarly students or noted Egyptian archaeologists, men like the celebrated Kamal El Malakh, are absent from movie screens.

Nor do screenwriters present scenarios patterned after Egypt's renowned journalists and authors, like Rose El-Yousef and Nobel Laureate Naguib Mahfouz. Egyptians, like most other Arabs, are deeply religious and are noted for their warm hospitality. In villages and throughout cosmopolitan cities like Cairo and Alexandria, *Ahlan wa Sahlan* (Welcome, this is your home) is spoken as often as "good morning."

Palestinians

. . . Observed Mark Twain, "We are all ignorant, just about different things." When it comes to the Middle East, many Americans are ignorant about the history and plight of the Palestinian people. One reason is that moviegoers may mistakenly believe reel Palestinians, those ugly make-believe film "terrorists," are real Palestinians. Should this be true, then what must viewers think of Palestinians after exiting movie theaters?

To assume viewers acquire some true knowledge of Palestinians after watching the 45 Palestinian fiction films that I discuss here is both dangerous and misleading. It's the same as thinking that you could acquire accurate knowledge of Africans by watching Tarzan movies, or that you would know all about Americans after watching movies about serial killers.

More than half of the Palestinian movies were released in the 1980s and 1990s; nineteen from 1983–1989; nine from 1990–1998. Absent from Hollywood's Israeli-Palestinian movies are human dramas revealing Palestinians as normal folk—computer specialists, domestic engineers, farmers, teachers, and artists. Never do movies present Palestinians as innocent victims and Israelis as brutal oppressors. No movie shows Israeli soldiers and settlers uprooting olive orchards, gunning down Palestinian civilians in Palestinian cities. No movie shows Palestinian families struggling to survive under occupation, living in refugee camps, striving to have their own country and passports stating "Palestine." Disturbingly, only two scenarios present Palestinian families.

. . . One year after the state of Israel was born, the film, *Sword of the Desert* (1949), presented Palestine according to the popular Zionist slogan, as a land without a people—even though the vast majority of people living in Palestine at the time were, in fact, Palestinians. This myth—no-Palestinians-reside-in-Palestine—is also served up in *Cast a Giant Shadow* (1966) and *Judith* (1966).

A decade after *Sword of the Desert* Paul Newman declared war on the Palestinians in *Exodus* (1960). Hollywood's heroes followed suit. In *Prisoner in the Middle* (1974), David Janssen links up with Israeli forces; together they gun down Palestinian nuclear terrorists. Films from the 1980s such as *The Delta Force* (1986) and *Wanted: Dead or Alive* (1987) present Lee Marvin, Chuck Norris, and Rutger Hauer blasting Palestinians in the Mideast and in Los Angeles. In the 1990s, Charlie Sheen and Kurt Russell obliterate Palestinians in Lebanon and aboard a passenger jet, in *Navy SEALs* (1990) and *Executive Decision* (1996).

In *Ministry of Vengeance* (1989) filmmakers dishonor Palestinians and American military chaplains as well. In lieu of presenting the chaplain, a Vietnam veteran, as a devout, non-violent man, the minister exterminates Palestinians. The minister's parishioners approve of the killings, applauding him.

Seven films, including *True Lies* (1994) and *Wanted: Dead or Alive* (1987), project the Palestinian as a nerve-gassing nuclear terrorist. In more than eleven movies, including *Half-Moon Street* (1986), *Terror in Beverly Hills* (1988), and *Appointment with Death* (1988), Palestinian evildoers injure and physically threaten Western women and children.

The reader should pay special attention to *Black Sunday* (1977), Hollywood's first major movie showing Palestinians terrorizing and killing Americans on US soil. Telecast annually the week of Super Bowl Sunday, the movie presents Dahlia, a Palestinian terrorist, and her cohort Fasil. They aim to massacre 80,000 Super Bowl spectators, including the American President, a Jimmy Carter look-alike.

Dictating numerous Palestinian-as-terrorist scenarios is the Israeli connection. More than half (28) of the Palestinian movies were filmed in Israel. Nearly all of the made-in-Israel films, especially the seven Cannon movies, display violent, sex-crazed Palestinian "bastards [and] animals" contesting Westerners, Israelis, and fellow Arabs.

I believe Cannon's poisonous scenarios are not accidental, but rather propaganda disguised as entertainment. Even in the early 1900s studio moguls knew that motion pictures could serve propagandists. Following WWI, Adolph Zukor, the head of Paramount Pictures affirmed this film-as-propaganda fact, saying fiction films should no longer be viewed as simply "entertainment and amusement." The war years, he said, "register[ed] indisputably the fact that as an avenue of propaganda, as a channel for conveying thought and opinion, the movies are unequaled by any form of communication."[15]

Why the Stereotype?

. . . Ask a film industry executive, director, or writer whether it is ethical to perpetuate ethnic or racial stereotypes and you can expect a quick negative response. How then, to explain that since 1970, these very same individuals produced, directed, and scripted more than 350 films portraying Arabs as insidious cultural "others"?

Either filmmakers are perpetuating the stereotype unknowingly, and would immediately disassociate themselves from such activities were they to realize the implications of their actions, or they are doing so knowingly and will only stop when sufficient pressure is brought to bear on them.

It is difficult to imagine that screenwriters who draft scenes of fat, lecherous sheikhs ogling Western blondes, or crazed Arab terrorists threatening to blow up America with nuclear weapons, are not precisely aware of what they are doing. But we sometimes forget that one of the elements that makes stereotyping so powerful, and so hard to eliminate, is that it is self-perpetuating. Filmmakers grew up watching Western heroes crush hundreds of reel "bad" Arabs. Some naturally repeat the stereotype without realizing that, in so doing, they are innocently joining the ranks of the stereotypes' creators.

Huge inroads have been made toward the elimination of many racial and ethnic stereotypes from the movie screen, but Hollywood's stereotype of Arabs remains unabated. Over the last three decades stereotypical portraits have actually increased in number and virulence.

The Arab stereotype's extraordinary longevity is the result, I believe, of a collection of factors. For starters, consider print and broadcast "if it bleeds it leads" news reports. Like most Americans, creators of popular culture (including novelists, cartoonists, and filmmakers), form their opinions of a people, in part, based on what they read in print, hear on the radio, and see on television. Like the rest of us, they are inundated and influenced by a continuous flow of "seen one, seen 'em all" headlines and sound bites.

. . . The image began to intensify in the late 1940s when the state of Israel was founded on Palestinian land. From that preemptive point on—through the Arab-Israeli wars of 1948, 1967, and 1973, the hijacking of planes, the disruptive 1973 Arab oil embargo, along with the rise of Libya's Muammar Qaddafi and Iran's Ayatollah Khomeini—shot after shot delivered the relentless drum beat that all Arabs were and are Public Enemy No. 1.

Right through the 1980s, the 1990s, and into the twenty-first century, this "bad people" image prevailed, especially during the Palestinian intifada and the Israeli invasion of Lebanon. In 1980, the rabid followers of Iran's Ayatollah Khomeini held 52 Americans hostage at the US Embassy in Teheran for 444 days. Nightly, TV cameras blazoned across the planet Khomeini's supporters chanting "Death to America!" and calling our country "the Great Satan" as they burned our flag and, in effigy, Uncle Sam himself.

At the height of the Iranian hostage crisis anti-Arab feelings intensified, as 70 percent of Americans wrongly identified Iran as an Arab country. Even today, most Americans think of Iranians as Arabs. In fact, Iranians are Persians, another people altogether.

. . . It got worse in the 1990s. Two major events, the Iraqi invasion of Kuwait that led to the Gulf War, and the bombing of New York City's World Trade Center, combined to create misguided mindset, leading some Americans to believe all Arabs are terrorists and that Arabs do not value human life as much as we do. As a result, some of us began even perceiving our fellow Americans of Arab descent as clones of Iraq's Saddam Hussein and the terrorist Osama bin Laden. Well, I think you get the picture.

. . . Not only do these violent news images of extremists reinforce and exacerbate already prevalent stereotypes, but they serve as both a source and excuse for continued Arab-bashing by those filmmakers eager to exploit the issue. In particular, the news programs are used by some producers and directors to deny they are actually engaged in stereotyping. "We're not stereotyping," they object. "Just look at your television set. Those are real Arabs."

Such responses are disingenuous and dishonest. As we know, news reports by their very nature cover extraordinary events. We should not expect reporters to inundate the airwaves with the lives of ordinary Arabs. But filmmakers have a moral obligation not to advance the news media's sins of omission and commission, not to tar an entire group of people on the basis of the crimes and the alleged crimes of a few.

. . . Why would anyone take part in the denigration of a people knowingly? I think one answer is the Arab-Israeli conflict. Though the majority of moviemakers are fair-minded professionals, there are some who, in the interests of pursuing their own political or personal agenda, are willing to perpetuate hate. These individuals may be expected to continue to indict Arabs on movie screens for as long as unjust images are tolerated.

New York Times columnist Maureen Dowd offers another answer: "[S]tereotypes are not only offensive [but] they are also comforting. They . . . exempt people from any further mental or emotional effort. They wrap life in the arch toastiness of fairy tale and myth. They make complicated understandings unnecessary."[16] Convenient stereotypes make everyone's job easier. Rather than having to pen a good joke, the writer inserts a stumbling, bumbling sheikh. Looking for a villain? Toss in an Arab terrorist—we all know what they look like from watching movies and TV. No thought required. As for the audience? Well, it also makes some of us feel better to see ourselves as superior to someone else. If one is no longer allowed to feel superior to Asians, Jews, Latinos, or blacks, at least we can feel superior to those wretched Arabs.

. . . Certainly, the Department of Defense's rubber-stamping of motion pictures that lambaste Arabs plays a role. The fact is, the government has a history of playing a role in what movies do and don't get made. As early as 1917, the federal government not only acknowledged the power of film to influence political thought, it took on the wrongful role of censor. As soon as the United States declared war on Germany, the government declared that no Hollywood movie could arouse prejudice against friendly nations. The 1917 film *The Spirit of '76* reveals heroic American revolutionaries such as Patrick Henry and Paul Revere. But, some frames show British soldiers committing acts of atrocities. As England was our World War I ally, the government protested; a judge declared producer Robert Goldstein's movie advanced anti-British sentiments. Calling the film "potent German propaganda,"[17] the judge sentenced Goldstein to prison.

Greed, too, is an incentive. Bash-the-Arab movies make money. Thus, some producers exploit the stereotype for profit.

. . . The absence of vibrant film criticism is another cause. A much-needed recourse against harmful Arab images would be more vigorous criticism emanating from industry executives and movie critics. I recall, still, Bosley Crowther's *New York Times* review of *Adventure in Sahara* (1938). Instead of criticizing stereotypes, Crowther advanced them, writing: "We know the desert is no picnic and you can't trust an Arab very far."

Another factor is silence. No significant element of public opinion has yet to oppose the stereotype; even scholars and government officials are mum. If we are ever to illuminate our common humanity, our nation's leaders must challenge all hateful stereotypes. Teachers need to move forward and incorporate, at long last, discussions of Arab caricatures in schools, colleges, military, and government classrooms.

Ethnic stereotypes do not die off on their own, but are hunted down and terminated by those whom the stereotypes victimize. Other groups, African-Americans, Asian-Americans and Jewish-Americans, have acted aggressively against discriminatory portraits. Arab-Americans as a group, however, have been slow to mobilize and, as a result, their protests are rarely heard in Hollywood and even when heard, are heard too faintly to get the offenders to back off.

Another reason is lack of presence. With the exception of a few movies, *Party Girl* (1995) and *A Perfect Murder* (1998), Arab-Americans are invisible on movie screens. One reason, simply put, is that there are not many Arab-Americans involved in the film industry; not one is a famous Hollywood celebrity.

What does their absence have to do with contesting stereotypes? Well, one answer is that movie stars have clout. Consider how Brad Pitt altered the scenario, *The Devil's Own* (1996). After reading the initial script, Pitt protested, telling the studio the screenplay made him "uneasy" because it was loaded with stereotypes—"full of leprechaun jokes and green beer." The dialogue, he argued, unfairly painted his character as a stereotypical Irish "bad" guy. Explains Pitt, "I had the responsibility to represent somewhat these [Irish] people whose lives have been shattered. It would have been an injustice to Hollywood-ize it." Unless changes were made to humanize the Irish people, especially his character, Pitt "threatened to walk." The studio acquiesced, bringing in another writer to make the necessary changes.

Also, when it comes to studio moguls, not one Arab American belongs to the media elite. The community boasts no communication giants comparable to Disney's Michael Eisner, DreamWorks' Jeffrey Katzenberg, Fox's Rupert Murdoch, or Time-Warner's Ted Turner.

The lack of an Arab-American presence impacts the stereotype in another way. The industry has a dearth of those men and women who would be the most naturally inclined to strive for accurate and balanced portrayals of Arabs. But a number of high-level Arab Americans in the industry over the course of time would rectify the situation. It's difficult to demean people and their heritage when they're standing in front of you, especially if those persons are your bosses.

. . . Regrettably, America's Arabs do not yet have an organized and active lobby in Los Angeles. To bring about fundamental changes in how motion pictures project Arabs, a systematic lobbying effort is needed. Though the Arab-American and Muslim-American presence is steadily growing in number and visibility in the United States, only a few Arab-Americans meet with and discuss the stereotype with filmmakers. When dialogue does occur, some discriminatory portraits are altered. Declares a February 3, 2001, Council on American-Islamic Relations (CAIR) fax: "The villains in Paramount's upcoming film, The Sum of All Fears, were changed to European neo-Nazis." CAIR officials acknowledged Paramount for this important change, as Tom Clancy's book, on which the movie is based, presents Arab Muslims detonating a nuclear device at the Super Bowl in Denver. In a letter to CAIR, the film's director, Phil Alden Robinson, wrote: "I hope you will be reassured that I have no intention of portraying negative images of Arabs or Muslims."

Ongoing informal and formal meetings with movie executives are essential. Such sessions enable community members to more readily explain to producers the negative effects misperceptions of Arabs have on their children as well as on American public opinion and policy. Also, Arab-Americans need to reach out and expand their concerns with well-established ethnic and minority lobbying groups—with Asians, blacks, Jews, Latinos, gays and lesbians, and others.

Positives

To see is to make possible new ways of seeing. . . . I have tried to be uncompromisingly truthful, and to expose the Hollywood stereotype of Arabs for all to see. While it is true that most filmmakers have vilified the Arab, others have not. Some contested harmful stereotypes, displaying positive images—that is, casting an Arab as a regular person.

In memorable well-written movies, ranging from the Arabian Nights fantasy *The Thief of Bagdad* (1924), to the World War II drama *Sahara* (1943), producers present Arabs not as a threateningly different people but as "regular" folks, even as heroes. In *Sahara,* to save his American friends, a courageous Arab soldier sacrifices his life.

Note this father and son exchange from the film *Earthbound* (1980):

Son: "Why do they [the police] hate us so?"

Father: "I guess because we're different."

Son: "Just because somebody's different doesn't mean they have to hate 'em. It's stupid."

Father: "It's been stupid for a long time."

At first, I had difficulty uncovering "regular" and admirable Arab characters—it was like trying to find an oasis in the desert. Yet, I discovered more than 50 motion pictures sans Arab villains, five percent of the total number reviewed here. Refreshingly, the movies debunk stale images, humanizing Arabs.

As for those Arabian Nights fantasies of yesteryear, only a few viziers, magicians, or other scalawags lie in ambush. Mostly fabulous Arabs appear in *The Desert Song* (1929), *Ali Baba and the Forty Thieves* (1944), *Son of Sinbad* (1955), and *Aladdin and His Magic Lamp* (1969). The movies present viewers with brave and moral protagonists: Aladdin, Ali Baba, and Sinbad. Emulating the deeds of Robin Hood and his men of Sherwood Forest, Arabs liberate the poor from the rich, and free the oppressed from corrupt rulers.

Worth noting is the presence of glittering Arabs in non-fantasy movies. A heroic Egyptian princess appears in the movie serial, *Chandu the Magician* (1932). A courageous Egyptian innkeeper assists British troops in *Five Graves to Cairo* (1943). *Gambit* (1966) displays a compassionate Arab entrepreneur. In *King Richard and the Crusaders* (1954), Saladin surfaces as a dignified, more humane leader than his counterpart, Richard.

Some independent Israeli filmmakers, notably those whose movies were financed by the Fund for the Promotion of Israeli Quality Films, allow viewers to empathize with Palestinians, presenting three-dimensional portraits. To their credit, producers of *Beyond the Walls* (1984) and *Cup Final* (1992) contest the self-promotional history and Palestinian stereotypes spun out by most other filmmakers. Both movies show the Palestinian and the Israeli protagonist bonding; the two men are projected as soul-mates, innocent victims of the Arab-Israeli conflict.

Notes

1. The 22 Arab states are Algeria, Bahrain, Chad, Comoros, Djibouti, Egypt, Iraq, Jordan, Lebanon, Libya, Mauritania, Morocco, Oman, Palestine, Qatar, Saudi Arabia, Somalia, Sudan, Syria, Tunisia, United Arab Emirates, and Yemen.

2. Jay Stone, *Ottawa Citizen* 16 March 1996.

3. William Greider, "Against the Grain," *Washington Post* 15 July 1979: 4E.

4. Jerry Mander, *Four Arguments for the Elimination of Television* (New York: William Morrow, 1978).

5. See ADC, "The Anti-Discrimination Hate Crimes," (Washington, DC, 1996).

6. For movies featuring African-American actors destroying reel Arabs, see *Best Defense* (1984), *Iron Eagle* (1986), *The Delta Force* (1986), *Wanted: Dead or Alive* (1987), *Firewalker* (1986), *Kazaam* (1996), *The Siege* (1998), and *Rules of Engagement* (2000).

7. Matthew Sweet, "Movie Targets: Arabs Are the Latest People to Suffer the Racial Stereotyping of Hollywood," *The Independent* 30 July 2000.

8. Lawrence Suid, *Sailing on the Silver Screen: Hollywood and the U.S. Navy* (Annapolis, MD: Naval Institute Press, 1996): 151.

9. Greider 1E.

10. Sweet.

11. Edward W. Said, *Orientalism* (New York: Pantheon, 1978): 125.

12. I.C.B. Dear and M.R.D. Foot, eds., *The Oxford Companion to World War II* (Oxford: Oxford University Press, 1995).

13. William Zinsser, "In Search of Lawrence of Arabia," *Esquire* June 1961: 72.

14. "Fencing by Ear," *Missou* Fall 1997: 11.

15. Adolph Zukor, "Most Important Events of the Year," *Wid's Year Book* 1918. For more on Palestinian portraits, see my essay "Screen Images of Palestinians in the 1980s," *Beyond the Stars, Volume 1: Stock Characters in American Film*, ed. Paul Loukides and Linda K. Fuller (Bowling Green, OH: Bowling Green State University Press, 1990).

16. Maureen Dowd, "Cuomos vs. Sopranos," *New York Times* 22 April 2001.

17. *Censored!*, documentary, American Movie Classics, 7 December 1999.

Jack G. Shaheen is a professor emeritus of mass communications at Southern Illinois University. Dr. Shaheen is the world's foremost authority on media images of Arabs and Muslims. He regularly appears on national programs such as Nightline, Good Morning America, 48 Hours, *and* The Today Show. *He is the author of* Arab and Muslim Stereotyping in American Popular Culture, Nuclear War Films, *and the award-winning* TV Arab. Los Angeles Times *TV critic Howard Rosenberg calls* Reel Bad Arabs: How Hollywood Vilifies a People *"a groundbreaking book that dissects a slanderous history dating from cinema's earliest days to contemporary Hollywood blockbusters that feature machine-gun wielding and bomb-blowing 'evil' Arabs."*

NOTE: "Reel Bad Arabs" by Jack G. Shaheen was first published in *Reel Bad Arabs: How Hollywood Vilifies a People*, published by Olive Branch Press, an imprint of Interlink Publishing Group, Inc. Text copyright © Jack G. Shaheen 2001. Reprinted with permission.

13 | *Women in Film Noir*

Janey Place

Place discusses film noir as a movement (e.g., German Expressionism, Soviet Formalism, Italian Neo-Realism) rather than genre and as a national myth that secures the existence of the social structure within the precise polemics of WWII. She describes the visual stylization and motifs of two gender scripts in film noir: "spider woman" (independence via a particularly sexual self-knowledge and masquerade) and "nurturing woman" (offering integration for alienated, lost men into stable "values," "roles" and "identities"). This article is pedagogically useful because it considers a number of films, is careful to note atypical examples and explores the continuing popularity of film noir on college campuses, television and film retrospectives due to its "sensuality."

The dark lady, the spider woman, the evil seductress who tempts man and brings about his destruction is among the oldest themes of art, literature, mythology and religion in western culture. She is as old as Eve, and as current as today's movies, comic books and dime novels. She and her sister (or *alter ego*), the virgin, the mother, the innocent, the redeemer, form the two poles of female archetypes.

Film noir is a male fantasy, as is most of our art. Thus woman here as elsewhere is defined by her sexuality: the dark lady has access to it and the virgin does not. That men are not so deterministically delineated in their cultural and artistic portrayal is indicative of the phallocentric cultural viewpoint; women are defined *in relation* to men, and the centrality of sexuality in this definition is a key to understanding the position of women in our culture. The primary crime the "liberated" woman is guilty of is refusing to be defined in such a way, and this refusal can be perversely seen (in art, or in life) as an attack on men's very existence. Film noir is hardly "progressive" in these terms—it does not present us with role models who defy their fate and triumph over it. But it does give us one of the few periods of film in which women are active, not static symbols, are intelligent and powerful, if destructively so, and derive power, not weakness, from their sexuality.

Myth

Our popular culture functions as myth for our society: it both expresses and reproduces the ideologies necessary to the existence of the social structure. Mythology is remarkably responsive to changing needs in the society: in sex roles for example—when it was necessary for women to work in factories during World War II and then necessary to channel them back into the home after the war.

We can look at our historic film heroines to demonstrate these changing attitudes: the strong women of 40s films such as Katharine Hepburn and Rosalind Russell (whose strength was none the less often expressed by their willingness to stand *behind* their men in the last reel) were replaced by the sex goddesses (Marilyn Monroe), virtuous wife types (Jane Wyman), and professional virgins (Doris Day) of the 50s as the dominant cultural heroines. This is not to assert that these were the *only* popular movie stars of their times, but by the shift in relative importance of an archetype can be observed the corresponding change in the needs of the culture which produced them all.

Myth not only expresses dominant ideologies, it is also responsive to the *repressed* needs of the culture. It gives voice to the unacceptable archetypes as well; the myths of the sexually aggressive woman (or criminal man) first allows sensuous expression of that idea and then destroys it. And by its limited expression, ending in defeat, that unacceptable element is controlled. For example, we can see pornography as expressing unacceptable needs which are created by the culture itself, and allowed limited (degraded) expression to prevent these socially induced tensions from erupting in a more dangerous form.

Two aspects of the portrayal of women in film noir are remarkable. First, the particular mix and versions of the more general archetypes that recur in films noirs; and second the style of that expression. Visually, film noir is fluid, sensual, extraordinarily expressive, making the sexually expressive woman, which is its dominant image of woman, extremely powerful. It is not their inevitable demise we remember but rather their strong, dangerous and, above all, exciting sexuality. In film noir we observe both the social action of myth which damns the sexual woman and all who become enmeshed by her, and a particularly potent stylistic presentation of the sexual strength of woman which man fears. This operation of myth is so highly stylised and conventionalised that the final "lesson" of the myth often fades into the background and we retain the image of the erotic, strong, unrepressed (if destructive) woman. The style of these films thus overwhelms their conventional narrative content, or interacts with it to produce a remarkably potent image of woman.

This expression of the myth of man's "right" or need to control women sexually is in contrast to the dominant version of it in "A" films of the 30s, 40s, and 50s, which held that women are so weak and incapable that they need men's "protection" to survive. In these films, it is the woman who is portrayed benefiting from her dependence on men; in film noir, it is clear that men need to control women's sexuality in order not to be destroyed by it. The dark woman of film noir had something her innocent sister lacked: access to her own sexuality (and thus to men's) and the power that this access unlocked.

Movement and Genre

Any claims for film noir's special significance in portraying fear of women (which is both ancient and newly potent, today and during the period which produced film noir) must account for the particularly valid ties between film noir and the cultural obsessions of the United States during the 40s and early 50s. Film noir has been considered a genre, but it has more in common with previous film movements (e.g., German Expressionism, Soviet Socialist Realism, Italian neo-realism) and, in fact, touches every genre. For a consideration of women in film noir, this is more than a semantic dispute. Film movements occur in specific historical periods—at times of national stress and focus of energy. They express a consistency

142

of both thematic and formal elements which makes them particularly expressive of those times, and are uniquely able to express the homogeneous hopes (Soviet Socialist Realism and Italian Neo-Realism) and fears (German Expressionism and film noir) brought to the fore by, for example, the upheaval of war.

The attitudes towards women evidenced in film noir—i.e., fear of loss of stability, identity and security—are reflective of the dominant feelings of the time.

Genres, on the other hand, exist through time: we have had Westerns since the early 1900s and, in spite of rises and falls in their popularity, Westerns are with us today. Genres are characterised more by their subject matter and their iconography than movements, and they can express a wide and changing range of ideologies. The convention of the railroad in the Western, for example, has changed radically from 1924 (*The Iron Horse*) when it symbolised man's hopes for progress, the uniting of the continent, and the building of a peaceful community in the West, to 1972 (Sergio Leone's *Once Upon a Time in the West*), when it was the economic imperative causing exploitation of the poor. Many gangster pictures now champion the criminals, and Westerns depict the West as corrupt and lawless instead of an innocent refuge from corrupt Eastern values and a pure environment in which to build a virtuous society.

Unlike genres, defined by objects and subjects, but like other film movements, film noir is characterised by the remarkably homogeneous visual style with which it cuts across genres: this can be seen in the film noir influence on certain Westerns, melodramas (even musicals) and particularly the detective genre. This style indicates a similarly homogeneous cultural attitude, and is only possible within an isolated time period, in a particular place, in response to a national crisis of some kind.

The characteristics of film noir style, however, are not "rules" to be enforced,[1] nor are they necessarily the most important aspects of each film in which they appear; and no attempt to fix and categorise films will be very illuminating if it prescribes strict boundaries for a category. This leads to suppression of those elements which do not "fit," and to exclusion of films which have strong links but equally strong differences from a particular category. Often the most exceptional examples of these films will be exceptional *because* of the deviations from the general "norms" of the movement.

For example, in the classic film noir, *They Live By Night*, the strain of romanticism is far more important than that of the spider woman, who is in this film a minor character. The "evil" Mattie who turns Bowie over to the police is even psychologically sympathetic—through love and loyalty to her imprisoned husband she is "trading" Bowie for him. On the other hand, in an equally central a film, *Kiss Me Deadly*, no one, male or female, enjoys any of the transcending benefits of the romantic aspects of film noir. Only the victims Christina (Cloris Leachman) and Nick (the mechanic) are sympathetic: the rest are doomed only by their own greed. But after acknowledging that *every* film worth discussing is going to be "exceptional" in *some* way and that their visual styles are going to vary, we can then go on to identify the visual and narrative themes that dominate film noir and influence countless other films made during the 40s and early to mid-50s in the United States.

The detective/thriller genre, whose subjects are generally the lawless underworld, the fringes of society, crimes of passion and of greed, is particularly well suited to the expression of film noir themes. The movement affected other genres: melodrama particularly, but there are Westerns and even musicals that have distinctly noir elements. When the themes of the genre are not conducive to the noir mood, an interesting and confused mix results. *Ramrod* (1947, directed by André de Toth) is one such Western. Veronica Lake plays the typically aggressive, sexual "dark lady" of film noir who causes the murders; Arleen Whelan is her opposite, the nurturing, stay-at-home good woman. The usual stable moral environment of the typical Western is lacking, and the noir influence is evident in the murky moral confusion of the male characters and in their inability to control the direction of the narrative. *Ramrod* has the open, extreme long shots characteristic of the genre, but the clarity they generally signify is undercut by the noir ambiguity.

The dominant world view expressed in film noir is paranoid, claustrophobic, hopeless, doomed, predetermined by the past, without clear moral or personal identity. Man has been inexplicably uprooted from those values, beliefs and endeavours that offer him meaning and stability, and in the almost exclusively urban landscape of film noir (in pointed contrast to the pastoral, idealised, remembered past) he is struggling for a foothold in a maze of right and wrong. He has no reference points, no moral base from which to confidently operate. Any previous framework is cut loose and morality becomes relative, both externally (the world) and internally (the character and his relations to his work, his friends, his sexuality). Values, like identities, are constantly shifting and must be redefined at every turn. Nothing—especially woman—is stable, nothing is dependable.

The visual style conveys this mood through expressive use of darkness: both real, in predominantly underlit and night-time scenes, and psychologically through shadows and claustrophobic compositions which overwhelm the character in exterior as well as interior settings. Characters (and we in the audience) are given little opportunity to orient themselves to the threatening and shifting shadowy environment. Silhouettes, shadows, mirrors and reflections (generally darker than the reflected person) indicate his lack of both unity and control. They suggest a *doppelganger,* a dark ghost, *alter* ego or distorted side of man's personality which will emerge in the dark street at night to destroy him. The sexual, dangerous woman lives in this darkness, and she is the psychological expression of his own internal fears of sexuality, and his need to control and repress it.

The characters and themes of the detective genre are ideal for film noir. The moral and physical chaos is easily expressed in crime: the doomed, tortured souls seem to be at home in the violent, unstable milieu of the underworld. The dark woman is comfortable in the world of cheap dives, shadowy doorways and mysterious settings. The opposite archetype, the woman as redeemer, as agent of integration for the hero into his environment and into himself, is found in the innocent victim who dies for the hero (*The Big Combo*), the longsuffering and faithful lover of the loser hero (*Pick-up on South Street, They Live By Night, Night and the City*) or as a contrast to the fringe world itself (*The Big Heat, On Dangerous Ground, Out of the Past*).

The Spider Woman

The meaning of any film image is a complex function of its visual qualities (composition, angle, lighting, screen size, camera movement, etc.), the content of the image (acting, stars, iconography, etc.), its juxtaposition to surrounding images, and the context of the narrative. Even more broadly, meaning is affected by ever-enlarging contexts, such as the conventions of a particular genre, of film generally, and of the time in which the film is made and in which it is viewed. It would be presumptuous and an impossible undertaking to attempt to establish a "dictionary" of meanings within a system which is so bound for specific meaning to such complex elements and their interaction. Nevertheless, film noir is a movement, and as such is remarkably stylistically consistent. It thus becomes possible to identify recurrent visual motifs and their general range of meanings. Within these recurrent patterns, some drawn from conventions not specifically filmic, others specific to film generally, and still others to film noir or the detective film genre, the source and operation of the sexual woman's dangerous power is expressed visually.

The following illustrations are all made up of these visual motifs, but the consistent meaning is not necessarily the entire meaning in any single image. A director—consciously or unconsciously—can use a convention against its usual meaning for expressive effect, as for example in *Laura*. The power to incite murder which is visually ascribed to Laura's magnificent portrait is revealed to be a product of the neuroses of the men around her, not of the power she wields. Norma Desmond in *Sunset Boulevard* is the most highly stylised "spider woman" in all of film noir as she weaves a web to trap and finally destroy her young victim, but even as she visually dominates him, she is presented as caught by the same false value system. The huge house in which she controls camera movement and is constantly centre frame is also a hideous trap which requires from her the maintenance of the myth of her stardom: the contradiction between the reality and the myth pull her apart and finally drive her mad. The complete meaning of any single image is complex and multidimensional, but we can identify motifs whose meaning proceeds initially from common origins.

The source and the operation of the sexual woman's power and its danger to the male character is expressed visually both in the iconography of the image and in the visual style. The iconography is explicitly sexual, and often explicitly violent as well: long hair (blond or dark), make-up, and jewellery. Cigarettes with their wispy trails of smoke can become cues of dark and immoral sensuality, and the iconography of violence (primarily guns) is a specific symbol (as is perhaps the cigarette) of her "unnatural" phallic power. The *femme fatale* is characterised by her long, lovely legs: our first view of the elusive Velma in *Murder My Sweet* (*Farewell My Lovely*) and of Cora in *The Postman Always Rings Twice* is a significant, appreciative shot of their bare legs, a *directed* glance (so directed in the latter film that the shot begins on her calves, cuts to a shot of her whole body, cuts back to the man looking, then finally back to Lana Turner's turban-wrapped angelic face) from the viewpoint of the male character who is to be seduced. In *Double Indemnity* Phyllis's legs (with a gold anklet significantly bearing her name) dominate Walter's and our own memory of her as the camera follows her descent down the stairs, framing only her spike heels and silk-stockinged calves. Dress—or lack of it—further defines the woman: Phyllis first is viewed in *Double Indemnity* wrapped in a towel, and the sequinned, tight, black gown of the fantasy woman in *Woman in the Window* and the nameless "dames" of film noir instantly convey the important information about them and their role in the film.

The strength of these women is expressed in the visual style by their dominance in composition, angle, camera movement and lighting.[2] They are overwhelmingly the compositional focus, generally centre frame and/or in the foreground, or pulling focus to them in the background. They control camera movement, seeming to direct the camera (and the hero's gaze, with our own) irresistibly with them as they move. (In contrast, the "good" women of film noir and many of the seduced, passive men are predominantly static, both within the frame and in their ability to motivate camera movement and composition.) The *femme fatale* ultimately loses physical movement, influence over camera movement, and is often actually or symbolically imprisoned by composition as control over her is exerted and expressed visually: sometimes behind visual bars (*The Maltese Falcon*), sometimes happy in the protection of a lover (*The Big Sleep*), often dead (*Murder My Sweet, Out of the Past, Gun Crazy, Kiss Me Deadly, Double Indemnity*), sometimes symbolically rendered impotent (*Sunset Boulevard*). The ideological operation of the myth (the absolute necessity of controlling the strong, sexual woman) is thus achieved by first demonstrating her dangerous power and its frightening results, then destroying it.

Often the original transgression of the dangerous lady of film noir (unlike the vamp seductress of the 20s) is ambition expressed metaphorically in her freedom of movement and visual dominance. This ambition is inappropriate to her status as a woman, and must be confined. She wants to be the owner of her own nightclub, not the owner's wife (*Night and the City*). She wants to be a star, not a recluse (*Sunset Boulevard*). She wants her husband's insurance money, not her comfortable, middle-class life (*Double Indemnity*). She wants the "great whatsit," and ends up destroying the world (*Kiss Me Deadly*). She wants independence, and sets off a chain of murders (*Laura*). She wants to win an uninterested lover, and ends up killing him, herself, and two other people (*Angel Face*). She wants money, and succeeds only in destroying herself and the man who loves her (*Gun Crazy, The Killers*). She wants freedom from an oppressive relationship, and initiates events that lead to murder (*The Big Combo, The Postman Always Rings Twice*). Whether evil (*Double Indemnity, Gun Crazy, Kiss Me Deadly, Night and the City, The Maltese Falcon, The Postman Always Rings Twice*), or innocent (*Laura, The Big Combo*), her desire for freedom, wealth or independence ignites the forces which threaten the hero.

Independence is her goal, but her nature is fundamentally and irredeemably sexual in film noir. The insistence on combining the two (aggressiveness and sensuality) in a consequently dangerous woman is the central obsession of film noir, and the visual movement which indicates unacceptable activity in film noir women represents the man's own sexuality, which must be repressed and controlled if it is not to destroy him.

The independence which film noir women seek is often visually presented as self-absorbed narcissism: the woman gazes at her own reflection in the mirror, ignoring the man she will use to achieve her goals.[3] This attention to herself instead of the man is the obvious narrative transgression of Norma Desmond whose images—both reflected and pictures— dominate her mansion in *Sunset Boulevard.* She hires Joe Gillis to work on her script for her comeback, and she continues to insist he participate in her life rather than being interested in his. He dreams he is her pet chimp, and he actually becomes a victim of her Salome. Joe finds an acceptable lover in Betty, the young woman who types while he dictates, smells like soap instead of perfume, dreams of *his* career, and is content to be behind the camera instead of in front. Self-interest over devotion to a man is often the original sin of the film noir woman and metaphor for the threat her sexuality represents to him.

Another possible meaning of the many mirror shots in film noir is to indicate women's duplicitous nature. They are visually split, thus not to be trusted. Further, this motif contributes to the murky confusion of film noir: nothing and no one is what it seems. Compositions in which reflections are stronger than the actual woman, or in which mirror images are seen in odd, uncomfortable angles, help to create the mood of threat and fear.

In some films the "spider women" prove not to be so and are thus redeemed. Gilda and Laura are validated as individuals (Gilda was simply acting out the paranoid fantasies of her true love, Johnny, and Laura was an innocent catalyst for men's idealisations), but the images of sexual power they exhibit are more powerful than the narrative "explanation." The image of Gilda we remember is the close-up introduction to her, with long hair tossed back over her head to reveal her beautiful face. Her song, "Put the Blame on Mame, Boys" (for every natural and economic disaster to hit the world), is ironic, but stripping as she performs, the power she possesses as a sexually alive woman seems almost up to the task. Laura's beautiful, dominating portrait that haunts the characters and determines the action of the film when she is believed dead is the strongest visual image even when she reappears alive.

The framed portrait of a woman is a common motif in film noir. Sometimes it is contrasted with the living woman: in *Night and the City* Helen is a nagging, ambitious, destructive bitch, but her husband gazes longingly at her "safe" incarnation in the framed portrait— under control, static and powerless. Laura's portrait is compositionally dominating, inciting Mark's fantasies and giving visual expression to Waldo's idealised vision of her, but only when she unexpectedly turns up alive does further trouble ensue as she refuses to conform to the fantasies inspired by the portrait. In *Woman in the Window,* an elderly, respectable professor puts his wife and children on a train and, longing for adventure, dreams a beautiful portrait comes to life and involves him in murder. He is about to take his own life when he wakes up, cured of his longing for adventure. The lesson is obvious: only in a controlled, impotent, powerless form, powerless to move or act, is the sexual woman no threat to the film noir man.

On the rare occasions that the normal world of families, children, homes and domesticity appears in film noir it is either so fragile and ideal that we anxiously anticipate its destruction (*The Big Heat*), or, like the "good" but boring women who contrast with the exciting, sexy *femme fatales,* it is so dull and constricting that it offers no compelling alternative to the dangerous but exciting life on the fringe.

The Nurturing Woman

The opposite female archetype is also found in film noir: woman as redeemer. She offers the possibility of integration for the alienated, lost man into the stable world of secure values, roles and identities. She gives love, understanding (or at least forgiveness), asks very little in return (just that he come back to her) and is generally visually passive and static. Often, in order to offer this alternative to the nightmare landscape of film noir, she herself must not be a part of it. She is then linked to the pastoral environment of open spaces, light, and safety characterised by even, flat, high-key lighting. Often this is an idealised dream of the past and she exists only in memory; but sometimes this idealisation exists as a real alternative.

Out of the Past is one of the best of the latter type: one woman (Ann) is firmly rooted in the pastoral environment, static, undemanding and rather dull, while the other (Kathie) is exciting, criminal, very active and sexy. In this film the lack of excitement offered by the safe woman is so clearly contrasted with the sensual, passionate appeal of the other that the detective's destruction is inevitable. Kathie appears out of the misty haze of late afternoon in a little Mexican town, walking towards the detective hero as he sits in a bar, waiting for this woman whose image has already been setup for him by the man she shot and ran away from, who wants her back at any cost. They later embrace against the tumultuous sea, a sudden rainstorm, and the dark, rich textures created by low-key lighting.

The independent, active woman is often the primary noir element of noir-influenced films in other genres. In *Ramrod*, a Western, and *Beyond the Forest*, a melodrama, the initial cause of the drama which results in death is a woman who will not "stay at home"—Connie (Veronica Lake) on her father's ranch and Rosa (Bette Davis) in her small town with her doctor husband. Each woman is characterised sexually as aggressive and dangerous by the iconography and by the results of her actions. But because neither is centrally film noir, in *Ramrod* the quiet, waiting woman gets the man instead of aggressive Connie, and in *Beyond the Forest* Rosa's "unnatural" ambition is powerful enough to cause only her own destruction. The intersection of the Western and its noir influence is particularly interesting because in Westerns women are generally genre objects representing home and stability rather than actors in the drama. Other examples of noir-influenced Westerns are also characterised by active women and noir visual style: *Johnny Guitar, Rancho Notorious,* and *Forty Guns.*

The redemptive woman often represents or is part of a primal connection with nature and/or with the past, which are safe, static states rather than active, exciting ones, but she can sometimes offer the only transcendence possible in film noir. *They Live By Night* and *On Dangerous Ground* (both directed by Nicholas Ray, 1949 and 1951) are characterised by the darkly romantic element that can exist with the cynical. In the former, the young lovers are doomed, but the possibility of their love transcends and redeems them both, and its failure criticises the urbanised world that will not let them live. Their happiest moments are outdoors in the sunlight, with "normalcy" an ideal they can never realise because there is no place for them in the corrupt world. Mary (*On Dangerous Ground*) is not only cut off from the corruption of greed, money and power of the urban environment by living in a rural setting, she is further isolated (and purified) by her blindness. She teaches the badly disturbed and violent Jim to feel, and her reliance on him releases him from his emotional prison. Both characters are crippled—he emotionally and she physically—and need each other to achieve the wholeness of health. This interdependence keeps both characters and their relationship exciting, while other "innocents" of film noir who exist only to contrast with the dangerous woman simply fade into forgetfulness.

Film noir contains versions of both extremes of the female archetypes, the deadly seductress and the rejuvenating redeemer. Its special significance lies in the combination of sensuality with activity and ambition which characterises the *femme fatale,* and in the mode of control that must be exerted to dominate her. She is not often won over and pacified by love for the hero, as is the strong heroine of the 40s who is significantly less sexual than the film noir woman. Indeed, her strength is emphasised by the general passivity and impotence which characterises the film noir male, making her a far greater threat to him than the career woman of the 40s was, and thus only actual or symbolic destruction is an effective control. Even more significant is the form in which the "spider woman's" strength and power is expressed: the visual style gives her such freedom of movement and dominance that it is her strength and sensual visual texture that is inevitably printed in our memory, not her ultimate destruction.

The tendency of popular culture to create narratives in which male fears are concretised in sexually aggressive women who must be destroyed is not specific to the 40s to mid-50s in the United States, but is seen today to a degree that might help to account for the sudden popularity of these films on college campuses, on television, and in film retrospectives. But despite their regressive ideological function on a strictly narrative level, a fuller explanation for the current surge of interest in film noir must acknowledge its uniquely sensual visual style which often overwhelms (or at least acts upon) the narrative so compellingly that it stands as the only period in American film in which women are deadly but sexy, exciting and strong.

Notes

1. Often it is the films made from Raymond Chandler's novels, or films made by a director such as Fritz Lang, that have the most characteristic visual and narrative themes. Indeed, a film noir made by a strong director such as Nicholas Ray may have more in common with one of his films that is not squarely in the film noir style than with other films noirs.

2. Lighting and chiaroscuro can express the moral relationship between characters; in the still of Phyllis Dietrichson and her stepdaughter from *Double Indemnity* (p. 94) the women are contrasted and morally characterised.

3. See, for example, the still from *Double Indemnity* (p. 93) where Phyllis is putting on her lipstick.

14 | Fatal Attractions: "Place," the Korean War, and Gender in Niagara

Merrill Schleier

Abstract: *Niagara* features a landscape or "place" as a star. Focusing especially on Niagara Falls' multilayered and traumatic history helps us understand the film's exploration of mental instability, eroticism, death, and even the ongoing Korean War. Yet the film's conventional plot structure is unable to resolve its gender, class, and other tensions, which reflect the fissures of midcentury America.

The film *Niagara* (Henry Hathaway, 1953) concerns a majestic landscape and its surrounding, conflicted urban environs. Michel de Certeau claims that a sense of place is associated with a specific location or something fixed, such as a city, neighborhood, street, or, in the case of Niagara Falls, a tourist site that includes waterfalls and various points of interest.[1] Yet geographic locations are also mediated by the inhabitants who create various spatial practices, thereby imbuing these settings over time with layered or embedded histories, from which they become inextricable.[2] Landscapes are not natural but human constructions replete with myth and memory that lie beneath the surface and require excavation.[3] Writing specifically about Niagara Falls, sociologist Rob Shields asserts that the physical and built environment around it bear the "sedimented traces of the history of visitors."[4] As I argue, place is depicted in the film to reveal Niagara's multifaceted and troubled past while reflecting something about America's conflicted present. Various points of interest in and around the cataract are underscored, often relating by analogy to characters and their subjective states. The landscape's meaning is further highlighted by means of cinema's formal vocabulary, including camera angles, lighting, framing, and so on. My analysis not only considers the Niagara landscape's significance within the film's narrative but also uncovers the fuller, more complex array of historical references in the film, some of which are already contained within the site itself. Recognizing the dramatic potential of the place,

Merrill Schleier is a Professor in the Department of Visual Arts at the University of the Pacific. Her articles have appeared in Film Studies, Journal of the Society of Architectural Historians, Mosaics, *and* Journal of Architecture, *and a forthcoming article will appear in* QRFV. *Her most recent book is* Skyscraper Cinema: Architecture and Gender in American Film *(University of Minnesota Press, 2009).*

Reprinted from *Cinema Journal* 51, no. 4 (summer 2012), by permission of University of Texas Press.

space, and history of Niagara, screenwriters Charles Brackett, Richard Breen, and Walter Reisch, director Henry Hathaway, and Twentieth Century Fox chief Darryl F. Zanuck were very explicit about their desire to showcase the famous landmark, intent on making an unparalleled film that simulated a tourist journey "seen through the eyes of quite ordinary visitors."[5]

Surprisingly, *Niagara* has prompted little serious scholarly attention save for cursory discussions included in articles and books about Marilyn Monroe and historical studies of the falls.[6] This article considers archival sources to shed new light on the film's genesis, to document the contributions of its three screenwriters, and to point to Zanuck's role in fashioning the story and its characters. Previous analyses have focused largely on the erotic spectacle of Monroe and her conflation with the falls, a strategy originally employed by the studio's publicity department.[7] In 1953, *Newsweek* noted, "The billboards for the current picture, 'Niagara' . . . show her [Monroe] poised titanically if uncomfortably at the very brink of the falls, clad only in a rushing torrent," thereby equating hyperbolic female sexuality with the landscape's unrestrained character.[8] Although the dual spectacle of Monroe and the falls is an important aspect of the film's thematic, reinforcing its caveat against unchecked, illicit passion, its iconography is replete with Niagara's lofty, tawdry, and sometimes repressed past. In addition to their mythic and historical dimensions, cinematic and real landscapes such as *Niagara* and the falls are often ciphers for a broader history of economic and social relations, revealing the connection between classes and modes of production, which form part of the film's economic and political unconscious. Corporate interests prevailed, and the conflicts among various characters were employed prescriptively to valorize middle-class values and midcentury hegemonic gender positions.[9] As I demonstrate, the disturbing specter of the Korean War in *Niagara*, exemplified by the battle-fatigued Loomis, is enlisted to support those ideals. Ultimately, the layers of tension situated in this troubled landscape and enacted by its characters remain unresolved by the film's conventional narrative structure, and reflect gender and class fissures in 1950s America.

The filmmakers' intention to underscore landscape as sublime cinematic spectacle is seen early in the close-up of the roiling waters of Horseshoe Falls at daybreak, Niagara's most dramatic attraction, accompanied by the deafening sound of an aquatic avalanche breaking over the rocks. These effects are employed similarly throughout the film to punctuate scenes and highlight the cataract's importance in the narrative. Cutting to the infinitesimal figure of George Loomis (Joseph Cotten), the camera provides a bird's-eye view of a fog-laden landscape and barely legible figure clamoring helplessly amid the primeval crags, which conjures up the idea of geological time and human mortality, thus imbuing the scene with the place's traumatic past, including mental derangement, suicide, and death. One is initially led to believe that in this setting "this man is going to commit suicide," according to the script, but soon one realizes that he is still embattled, and he is there to confront rather than succumb to Niagara's seeming omnipotence.[10] Challenging it angrily while underscoring his own feelings of smallness and inadequacy, he reveals a wounded masculinity—the result of Korean War "battle fatigue" and the sexual escapades of his much younger wife Rose (Marilyn Monroe), who is carrying on an illicit affair. His condition is exacerbated, we later learn, by the landscape's mentally destabilizing character.[11]

This scene and others like it, which pit humans against nature, also demonstrate the myriad ways that Niagara's physical geography and multifaceted history leave their mark on the film. In addition to George's mental instability and self-destructiveness, his confrontation with the falls echoes those of numerous nineteenth-century daredevils such as the successful jumper Sam Patch and the aerialist Charles Blondin. Like previous adventurers, stunt men, and stunt women who lost their lives challenging the falls, George is impulsive, believing erroneously that he can outwit the powerful cataract, an assumption that ultimately proves fatal. His lonely defiance, which hints that he is contemplating taking his own life, also references the many suicides that have haunted the landscape since the mysterious and reclusive Francis Abbott, "The Hermit of the Falls," arrived in 1829; Abbott was often seen performing daredevil stunts dangerously near the precipice. Because he failed to return to his primitive cabin, which he had emptied of its contents before disappearing, many surmised that Abbott committed suicide; the story appeared in most mid-twentieth-century tourist guides and became part of the site's folklore.[12] According to historian Patrick McGreevey, Niagara Falls is associated with fatality because of the imminent dangers that surround it. Its special geography—the brink, plunge, abyss, rising mists, and rainbows—have all been interpreted in terms of death and a possible afterlife. Indeed, Niagara has been the locale for more suicides than any other single location in North America, ostensibly because of its putative hypnotic effect and iconic status. Rescuers have pulled more than five hundred corpses from the lower river during the twentieth century alone.[13]

Horseshoe Falls is only the first of many stops in the film's choreographed sightseeing journey around the landmark. Indeed, one might say that the film evokes a "tourist gaze."[14] Yet *Niagara* suggests far more than a gaze; it enlists all the senses, especially the auditory and the tactile, in an effort to prompt the viewer to vicariously experience the falls' scenic beauty and dark underbelly, which are both part of its lore. The viewer is taken on a comprehensive scenic tour of the falls' major attractions. It is a tour that is laced with disturbance, as seen in George's initial insomnia-induced challenge, provoked, in part, by the calculating Rose and her lover (Richard Allen). Planning to murder George and make it look like a suicide, they debase the various preordained sites, even converting the bells of the wartime Carillon Tower into a postmortem signal and a perverse inferno-like funerary prison. This also leads to the forbidding morgue, antiseptic hospital, seedy boarding house, and bus station.[15] Hence, the cinematic tour recreates the terror and angst experienced by battle-fatigued George, and his states of mind are subsequently displaced onto Rose and Polly (Jean Peters) so that the viewer may also vicariously feel the falls' destabilizing effects.

Concept and Genesis. In July 1951, after a memorable trip to the falls, Brackett, the film's producer, and one of its screenwriters urged Zanuck to give the "go-ahead on NIAGARA," cognizant that shooting the film on location would involve advance planning. Perhaps more important, Brackett sought permission from Zanuck to revisit Buffalo and the falls with Reisch to "do some intensive research as soon as possible."[16] By early September, after the requisite authorization by Zanuck and lengthy discussions among the three screenwriters, each wrote a separate "step sheet," or film treatment, employing the same general plot outline.[17] Two weeks later, the Twentieth Century Fox Publicity Department had already received a reply from the Greater Niagara Chamber of Commerce offering assistance to Breen and Reisch, who were planning their visit, followed by director Henry Hathaway, who arrived at the beginning of 1952 to survey the setting.[18] Enlisting the help of the Chamber of Commerce not only ensured free publicity for Twentieth Century Fox, but, more important, also aligned the film with the chamber's interests, celebrating Niagara Falls' majestic natural wonders, advertising its various tours and points of interest, highlighting it as a honeymoon destination, and criticizing its lowbrow visitors. At the same time, the filmmakers may have sought to exploit the drama created by such undesirable elements, to capitalize on the fear that adulterers, psychopaths, and murderers might be inhabiting the cabin next door.[19]

Brackett was very explicit about his desire to cast Niagara Falls as one of the film's main attractions.[20] Just prior to Niagara's release in January 1953, Brackett wrote:

> *There was one Old Beauty who had been a top box office attraction in America for almost two hundred years, and a pin-up beauty for the rest of the world. She had hardly been touched by motion pictures—an occasional bow in a newsreel or a travelogue was all she'd been granted—but whose brief glimpse had been handsome beyond belief. I sent a note to Mr. Zanuck asking if it might not be a good idea to make a feature-length picture with Niagara Falls for a star, and got his instant approval.[21]*

Lauding the film's potential for "showmanship," Michael Abel, a producer at Fox, concurred, adding that featuring an iconic landmark would ensure profitability. Writing enthusiastically to Zanuck, he asserted that millions who had heard of Niagara's wonders could vicariously experience it, whereas millions who had already visited, would have an opportunity "to relive that experience by seeing the highlights of Niagara Falls once again on film."[22] Zanuck agreed, suggesting to Brackett that the film heighten the spectacle with a "violent, tumultuous, nerve-assaulting sequence on the rapids," demonstrating his knowledge of Niagara's history while also recognizing the appeal of a "thrill picture."[23] Zanuck, Abel, and Brackett understood that making a Technicolor film that was both a simulated travelogue and a sexualized melodrama enhanced by Monroe's star power would attract fans, movie lovers, and tourists alike, thereby tapping into multiple audience pools. To guarantee its success, gala public events were staged in the twin cities of Niagara Falls, New York, and Niagara Falls, Ontario, at the film's premiere to garner maximum publicity.[24] As a testament to their adept use of the media, the film grossed almost $2.5 million by the end of 1953.[25]

By making Niagara Falls one of the main attractions of the film, Brackett claimed that he aimed to surpass films such as *The Adventurous Sex* (Charles Giblyn, 1925) and *Niagara Falls* (Gordon Douglas, 1941).[26] Hoping to make Niagara's myriad visual, auditory, and suggested tactile aspects integral parts of the story rather than simply background elements, Brackett was explicit about his desire to incorporate its major sites, such as "the roaring cup of Horseshoe Falls, invaded every day by the tiny *Maid of the Mist*; the spidery bridges of the Cave of the Winds; the dark tunnels under Table Rock House; and the whirlpool below the Falls."[27] In this way, his vision accorded with the tourist industry's, which had segmented the falls beginning in the 1830s, through the construction of numerous "gates, turnstiles, stairways, walkways, towers and boats" that separated them into numerous points of interest, staging the various tourist attractions to generate excitement.[28] Rob Shields notes that guide books even prompted visitors with "prescriptions on how to react" to each stopping point along the way.[29]

Romance Tours and Gender Dysfunction. Niagara Falls has been inextricably linked to the honeymoon ritual since the early nineteenth century. It was, in fact, the first such resort in the world, a designation that commenced with the bridal tours of Aaron Burr's daughter Theodosia and her husband in 1801, followed by Jerome Bonaparte (brother of Napoléon) and his wife in 1803, although some scholars claim that private, romantic honeymoons began in the 1830s after the construction of the Erie Canal.[30] By the post–World War II era, Niagara Falls was in the midst of one of its many periods of expansion, accompanied by a massive publicity campaign, spawned by returning GIs and the increase in marriages. More than a billion dollars was pumped into Niagara tourist development during the 1950s, leading to what Dubinsky refers to as a further "sexualization of the place through tourism."[31]

Second honeymooners were also encouraged to visit, often attracted by contests initiated by hotels, businesses, and the Chamber of Commerce. This explains the appearance of *Niagara*'s more conventional tourists, Ray Cutler (Casey Adams), a Shredded Wheat Company junior executive from Toledo, and his wife, Polly, who have been married for three years. They are supposed to represent the wholesome, middle-class heterosexual couple who visited the falls during the postwar era, although their relationship lacks romantic enthusiasm—indeed, they never had a first honeymoon. They are in Niagara because Ray has won a company-sponsored trip for his cereal-stuffed turkey recipe, which in 1950s terms may suggest a feminized masculinity.[32] Pragmatic and nurturing Polly is the only "normal" primary character in the film; her point of view dominates, and her gender identity serves as an antidote to Rose's and George's. Yet the Cutlers' efforts at a marital getaway are marred by Ray's go-getter spirit—he has even brought books by Winston Churchill, prompting a disapproving glance from a customs agent. In spite of Niagara's reputation as a site for newlyweds and repeat honeymooners, neither of *Niagara*'s main married protagonists seems capable of romance; both couples are in a provisional state of destabilization, a ploy recommended by Zanuck to increase the tension and enhance the dramatic rescue of Polly and the reconciliation of the Cutlers at the conclusion.[33]

Ray is so preoccupied with success that he even ignores the falls, more excited to see the Shredded Wheat Company headquarters across the river. One of the script's first treatments has Ray choosing Niagara "for his wedding trip, since the Shredded Wheat Company there is a showplace."[34] The plant, built by the Norcross brothers in 1901, was considered a model factory, a rebuke to all of America's crowded, smoke-belching industrial buildings; it included a stunning view of the rapids, modern ventilation, clean electricity, a hotel-like lobby, and luxurious bathing facilities for its employees.[35] To advertise its product, the building doubled as a tourist destination, claiming one hundred thousand visitors per year as early as 1915.[36] However, the policies of this exceptional, untarnished corporation did not reflect general industrial practices in Niagara Falls during the postwar era, when the chemical and electrometallurgical industries were producing toxic smoke and dumping poisonous waste materials, which the film represses. Although Shredded Wheat's progressive aims might have been lost on contemporary viewers, they would have recognized that the very product associated Ray with wholesomeness and clean living. An article on Niagara Falls written in 1947 reported on the city's "chemically-saturated haze" and stench, which was "happily sniffed by the industrially minded" in contrast to the pleasant odor emanating from the Shredded Wheat factory.[37]

Ray's middle-class masculinity may be understood partly in light of the atypical corporate ethos forged by Shredded Wheat Company founder Henry Perky, who favored self-improvement through salubrious eating and who equated health with morality; Ray sometimes appears dispassionate, obsessed with self-betterment. Even his more positive attributes are mitigated by a conformist spirit and an ingratiating demeanor, which he employs with his boss Mr. Kettering (Don Wilson) at the expense of Polly's safety. He leaves her unattended at the Cave of the Winds and later Chippewa, for example, which enables George to put her at risk. At times Ray seems a caricature of the midcentury executive, so intent on success that he has to be reminded about romance; he disbelieves his wife's well-founded fears, and he frequently treats her condescendingly. In response to Loomis's praise of her warm generosity, he responds sarcastically, "She'll do." On another occasion, tourist photographer Ray encourages her to assume a pin-up pose that resembles the more seductive demeanor of Rose Loomis. And when Loomis returns to Rainbow Cabin B after murdering Rose, prompting Polly to scream in horror, Ray accuses her of being delusional. Rather than soothing his frightened spouse, he declares mockingly, "Take a look. Where is he? Under the icebox?" This depiction of Ray is consonant with the ideas of midcentury social critics such as William H. Whyte Jr., who, in *The Organization Man*, envisioned a management force of conformists lacking common sense and creativity.[38] Zanuck may be credited with the fashioning of Ray as an unlikable, know-it-all type, quipping to Brackett: "I hope I never meet his ilk anywhere!"[39]

The aspiring Ray and his decent wife Polly are depicted in sharp contrast to George and Rose, as seen in the debris and disarray that accompany the latter couple throughout. Rather than blaming Niagara's industries, the cause of pollution is displaced onto the lower-class Loomises, a strategy that would not have displeased the Chamber of Commerce. On his way back to the modest motel complex where he is staying with Rose, George encounters street trash left by tourists like him.[40] Cutting to the darkened noir-inspired interior of Rainbow Cabin B, which displays a "startling lack of neatness," with newspapers, cigarette butts, and clothing strewn everywhere, the camera focuses on the silently plotting Rose, whose legs are spread suggestively under a sheet, underscoring her crassness and predatory sexuality.[41] Later when she seduces George in this room, she does so only to incite his jealousy. Rose is again equated with trash when she tries to escape from Loomis's lethal rage after he murders her lover in self-defense at the Scenic Tunnels.[42] Frantically climbing a set of stairs in the Carillon

Tower, she stops at a pay phone, where everything is disgorged from her purse, reiterating her disordered life. From the beginning of its designation as a tourist site, Niagara was associated with refuse and the behavior of unsavory human beings, such as the exploitive entrepreneurs and hucksters who preyed on visitors. Mark Twain wrote how the littering of the "whole estate with execrable names and offensive signs" marred its Edenic character.[43] Dubinsky argues that after World War II, spurred on by the intensive promotion for honeymooners, Niagara was once again reinvented as "sleazy and 'honky-tonk,'" which attracted lowbrow tourists like George, Rose, and her anonymous lover, who inhabits a cheap boarding house.[44]

The Loomises' chaotic lives even prevent the Cutlers from checking into Rainbow Cabin B upon their arrival at the motel complex, thus impeding the consummation of their honeymoon. Still inhabiting their reserved room, Rose informs the couple that they are unable to leave because the formerly institutionalized George has finally fallen asleep after a restless night at Horseshoe Falls. Trying to recoup their plans, the Cutlers rush to catch the famed *Maid of the Mist* boat excursion, which is to leave in two minutes, thus creating a sense of urgency that adds to the excitement of their first and only transitory erotic encounter. The camera work and the final script's descriptions demonstrate that screenwriters Brackett, Reisch, and Breen wished for this trip to conjure the erotic mythos of Niagara. One of Niagara's principal tours, initiated in 1846, the *Maid of the Mist* was designed to bring spectators in close proximity to Horseshoe Falls to evoke conflicting feelings of awe, wonderment, and fear—or the sublime, the most common way of perceiving them. A close-up shot of the couple shows them subsumed in mist and spray, further rendering them subject to Niagara's power; and "the strange excitement of that terrifying place makes them cling to each other" and "brings their lips together in a kiss."[45]

A reason offered for the falls' appeal to lovers is that its myriad properties are supposedly capable of stimulating passion, its overwhelming character causing couples to become breathless, prompted by inexorable forces beyond their control; in some cases, this causes temporary and partial mental instability. Screenwriter Reisch was aware of this aspect of Niagara's lore, claiming: "The magic of the thundering water casts a spell upon its beholders, a spell they can not free themselves from even if they wished to."[46] Succumbing to these altered states of mind, couples are further shielded by Niagara's mists and numerous distractions, which afford them a degree of anonymity and privacy. Some even believe that positive ions in Niagara Falls' air are the invisible culprits of these passionate interludes.[47] Notwithstanding the falls' power to prompt these short-lived romantic occurrences, the Cutlers' efforts at simulating a honeymoon are interrupted repeatedly by the Loomises' difficulties, which literally "loom" over everything they do, and over Ray's own efforts to improve his business prospects at the Shredded Wheat Company.

The Cutlers' singular erotic moment is later contrasted with the illicit kiss enjoyed by Rose and her lover at the Scenic Tunnels, a scene witnessed from Polly's point of view. The famed subterranean passageways contain various viewing promontories and lookout points which allow for additional visual, tactile, and auditory encounters with the falls from below. Ray encourages Polly to move further out onto an observation plaza so that he may photograph her in front of the dramatic cataract. Glancing to her left, she makes a startling discovery; Rose is passionately kissing a strange young man. Not only is the illicit couple dressed in nondescript rain gear, unlikely to be recognized, but the mist-laden underground setting also serves as a spatial reminder of their sinister motives. Installed in the falls' underbelly to steal an erotic moment and concretize a nefarious plot, Rose and her lover are planning to murder George in this selfsame hellish location.

The Femme Fatale, the Battle-Fatigued Veteran, and the Good Wife. Darkened or cloistered interiors, especially those of the Rainbow Cabins, are Rose's principal spaces, the settings of her numerous states of undress, connivance, and finally mental destabilization. In one scene, the seminude femme fatale is in the shower behind a translucent curtain, the watery motif employed to echo the cascading falls.[48] André Bazin claimed in a review of the film that the motif of rushing water and, more specifically, the falls' humidity steep *Niagara*'s suffering protagonists in its grip.[49] Rose is humming the song "Kiss," a continuation of the Scenic Tunnels' passionate encounter and later a murderous signal which will be played at the Carillon Tower if all goes as planned.[50] When George asks for the cigarettes she has purchased, the plotting Rose instructs him to fetch them from her pocket, where he finds two admission tickets for the tourist attraction, purposely left there to enrage him. Simultaneously seducing and inciting him further, she asks George to dry her back and "light her up too," thereby melding his anger with sexual passion.

George's destabilized and wounded masculinity—exacerbated by Rose's provocations— is the result of his Korean War service; the film thus highlights the unpopular conflict that was still being waged when the film was released. By that time, the war was at a two-year stalemate, with news coverage often relegated to a secondary position in the press, leaving veterans feeling forgotten and unappreciated. During the writing of the screenplay, from late 1951 through mid-1952, however, Korean War imagery still received broad coverage, thus providing *Niagara*'s creators with evocative source material, particularly for their depiction of George. Venues such as *Life* and *Look* employed experienced photojournalists like Carl Mydans, David Douglas Duncan, and Margaret Bourke-White to chronicle the conflict, which resulted in more still photography, proportionally, than had been produced during World War II. At least three book-length photojournalistic accounts were published in 1951, and an exhibition curated by Edward Steichen entitled *Faces of Korea* opened at New York's Museum of Modern Art in the spring.[51] Unlike the World War II soldier, who was pictured as a hero fighting for platoon, country, and universal democratic principles, the soldier in Korea was "depicted as a changed man" who often begged journalists to tell the American public the truth—that they were struggling with inadequate weapons in harsh, sometimes frozen terrain where atrocities were prevalent, and that they were suffering crushing casualties in a wholly useless war.[52] While claiming to simply present the "facts" in an objective fashion, *Life* magazine's Duncan pointed to the emotional toll the conflict was taking on soldiers in his 1951 book *This Is War! A Photo-Narrative in Three Parts*. He asserted that he wished "to show something of the agony, the suffering, and the terrible confusion, the heroism which is an everyday currency among those men who pull the triggers of rifles aimed at other men known as 'the enemy'".[53]

Visual documentarians focused more on the private psychological travails during wartime than had ever been seen before, as historian Andrew Heubner claims; indeed, two of the most prominent images of the Korean conflict are portraits of fatigued and sorrowful soldiers.[54] This depiction accords with the first and perhaps the most disturbing cinematic rendition of Korean War battle-fatigue in *The Steel Helmet* (Samuel Fuller, 1951), the story of hard-bitten Sergeant Zack (Gene Evans), who appears mentally out of touch after he sees half of his comrades blown to bits.[55] By the end of the film, he is an empty shell of his former self, suffering from severe associative disorders, who believes himself to be on his way to the beaches of Normandy rather than the Far East.

The accounts of news reporters and photojournalists were corroborated by the elevated occurrence of battle fatigue on the front. From January to April 1950, during the first four months of the Korean War, when the army avoided providing psychiatrists for the troops, the incidence of "psychiatric casualties was at the high rate of 250 per 1000."[56] This may have been prompted by early devastating fatalities, coupled with the fact that the Korean War veteran was more likely to have suffered from, witnessed, or participated in atrocities and abusive violence than his World War II predecessor.[57] The situation improved when Dr. Albert J. Glass arrived in the Far East and introduced division-level psychiatrists to provide training to medical officers near the front, mobile psychiatric detachments during heavy combat, and a nine-month troop-rotation system, all of which led to a reduction in psychiatric war casualties.[58] Glass believed that it was in a soldier's best interest to rejoin his combat unit, "for in no other way can the patient regain confidence and mastery of the situation and prevent chronic tension and guilt" or a "disabling neurotic compromise."[59]

One surmises that, in spite of improved therapeutic treatment for Korean War soldiers, Loomis has been discharged prematurely with his psychiatric malady still intact, thus demonstrating the acuteness of his condition and the danger he still poses. He suffers from insomnia, depression, and uncontrolled outbursts of anger; typical shots of Loomis show him brooding, raking his hair nervously, or experiencing rapidly shifting moods often provoked or exacerbated by Rose. Moreover, his Korean War experience is recapitulated at the falls: he is taken to a location that he detests; he cannot differentiate between friend and foe; and he is under attack and wounded anew by unseen enemies (Rose and her lover), one of whom he must kill in self-defense. Rather than "Reds," Chinese peasant "hordes," or "gooks," typical xenophobic appellations applied to America's foes, the specter of evil in the film has been transferred to female sexuality.

The pivotal scene that explores the extent of George's battle fatigue and loss of masculinity begins in the motel patio, where a group of youthful guests have gathered to listen to music and dance. He is older than the others (a detail suggested by Zanuck to make George seem an unlikely criminal), which sets him apart from the motel revelers while reflecting the actual age of many Korean War soldiers or World War II "retreads" called up again to serve their country.[60] His age also furthers Rose's disdain; she informs the Cutlers derisively that George prefers a "rocking chair and a corny old tune" to trendy music. Knowing just how to goad him, she emerges from the cabin in an extremely revealing, fire-engine-red dress which George later remarks is "cut down so low in front you can see her knee caps!" Striding purposively to the phonograph, she requests the song "Kiss" as George spies on her from behind the blinds.[61] She sings as if in an amorous trance and throws her head back seductively for the song's chorus, driving her husband into a frenzy that rouses him to stomp over to the group, seize the record, and smash it to bits. Yet this outburst also causes the beaten-down, masochistic veteran to wound himself with the broken record's jagged edge. In accord with media depictions of Korean War soldiers, he is "shaken and exhausted" from this self-inflicted ordeal and evinces the signs of his mental condition. He returns to the cabin angrily and slams the door.[62]

Rose chooses not to follow him, which prompts the nurturing Polly to volunteer to bring bandages and antiseptic to the khaki-and-gray-clad former soldier. Clothed in white like a wartime nurse, Polly goes in for the purpose of "treating the wound."[63] Subsequently George divulges his emasculated, castrated condition: "I suppose *she* sent you in to find out if I cut it off! Well, tell her I didn't." Polly even reaches for the unfastened bandage, a cipher of his impotence, and offers to fasten it, temporarily restoring his manhood. For the first time in the film, they form a temporary couple; this occurs again at two subsequent tourist stops, suggesting an appropriate postwar femininity for the midcentury audience and demonstrating what might have been if George had selected the right woman. A reverse angle shot shows George and Polly in the darkened interior watching Niagara's colorful nocturnal light show, posed in the picture window together like tourist honeymooners, until her husband interrupts their reverie.

The importance of a supportive, secure environment for postwar sufferers of "psychoneurosis" reflected the prevalent wisdom of the psychiatric community, a theme explored in both documentary and narrative films after World War II. In *Let There Be Light* (John Huston, 1946), a documentary about battle fatigue, recovering World War II veterans are told that, to enjoy living again, it was necessary they be "worthwhile and important to someone" who made them "feel safe."[64] Although it may not have been seen widely, the documentary featured the most up-to-date views on the treatment of battle fatigue. A similar message was proffered by *The Best Years of Our Lives* (William Wyler, 1946), which concerns the psychological ailments and adjustment problems of three returning veterans. Much like George, Captain Fred Derry (Dana Andrews) is plagued by nightmares and flashbacks, but his acquisitive, two-timing, and unsympathetic wife, the dance-hall "floozy" Marie (Virginia Mayo), only exacerbates his anxiety. His masculinity can be restored only by marrying the compassionate Peggy Stephenson (Teresa Wright), a hospital nurse and a veteran's daughter.[65] According to Robert

Eberwein, "the woman who helps the veteran with severe psychological problems fight back to normalcy and the promise of a heterosexual union" is explored in a number of films concerning the aftereffects of World War II, and in *Niagara* we see it served up as a solution for the disturbed Korean veteran as well.[66]

In contrast to Polly, Rose is the cause of George's bad luck. After meeting her in a Duluth beer hall and marrying her, he reports that his sheep farm began to fail. He went to Korea to prove his virility by showing her that he is still young enough, although his masculinity had already been compromised, and was further ruined by the war. Depicted here as an adolescent hobbyist, he is reduced to making model cars in his motel room as part of his occupational therapy, rather than driving a real automobile. *Let There Be Light* explores the use of occupational therapy at some length and includes a similar scene of model-car construction; men choose various activities that involve "building rather than destroying" in an effort to undo their war experience. Those who select model cars find relief in "precision work," which answers a "need for order and certainty." Yet this treatment does not stabilize George, perhaps because it is actively undermined by Rose. He even relates his unbalanced passion to a rock subjected to the falls' currents and eventually carried inexorably over the edge, a metaphor that augurs his own fate. Thinking of Korea, the plotting Rose, his infantilizing treatment, and the churning waters induces a renewed outburst, causing him to kick over his work table and wreck his "little" 1907 Maxwell, thereby sabotaging his prescribed therapy and demonstrating the continued volatility of his temper.[67]

The Monument, Wartime Redemption, and Punishment. The Carillon Tower on the Canadian side of the Rainbow Bridge is the film's architectural centerpiece and serves multiple functions. It is transformed by the Loomises from a church-like tower into both an ominous and mentally destabilizing musical cue and a killer's prison, before being restored as a wartime commemorative monument. Viewers are introduced to the tower's import at the onset of the film through the lengthy tolling of its bells that accompanies the Cutlers to their motel; Rose is later led there after hearing the song "Kiss" played from the belfry. It is the site of Rose and George's final confrontation (accompanied by several close-ups of its then-silent bells). A tour guide leading a group through the building informs them with some irony, "The tower is under the control of both countries. Just the same, a lot of Americans claim them [*sic*] bells don't play 'The Star Spangled Banner' as good as they do 'God Save the Queen,'" the reference to the latter song possibly foreshadowing Rose's imminent murder.

Construction of the 165-foot-tall, Deco-inspired white bell tower began in 1941; it literally and figuratively bears the imprimatur of World War II, as it was both a commemorative monument and the site of a protracted conflict between nations. The filmmakers would certainly have learned about its conflicted past when they were considering staging Rose's murder in the belfry; there was a prohibition against photography there, which prompted the studio to build elaborate replicas. Unlike Hitchcock, who often selected dramatic tourist monuments and altered their original dedicatory functions, constructing them anew as sites of disturbance, here trauma is embedded in the tower's actual history.[68] The largest of its fifty-five bronze bells, the ten-ton Bourdon has an inscription that caused a major controversy. Roosevelt, Churchill, and Prime Minister King's names were meant to be inscribed on the giant bell to commemorate the wartime alliance of their respective nations, but for some unknown reason, the Canadian leader's name was omitted.[69] Viewing this as a purposeful and sinister plot to discredit him and as an affront to his wartime leadership, King had Chairman McQuesten of the Niagara Falls Bridge Commission fired.[70] As a result of his humiliating dismissal, the chairman's physical and psychological health deteriorated, and he died shortly thereafter. Many believed that the firing led to his demise, which occurred ominously before the tower's inauguration and the first tolling of its bells in 1948. Thus, the tower was associated with conflict, mental instability, defeat, and death in local legend for years to come.

The military metaphor is explored atop the wartime tower when George achieves a new-found demonic potency by strangling Rose to death before sharp, daggerlike shadows and a backdrop of red and black, temporarily transforming the tower into an infernolike prison before it is reclaimed by a uniformed officer. Unable to escape because the doors are locked, George is forced to spend an evening with Rose's corpse, to which he appeals lovingly. In the morning, the tower is liberated by a soldierly worker who arrives and takes out the trash, symbolically purging the building of the human detritus that George and Rose represent. He somberly ascends the elevator to place the flag at the tower's crest, thereby reclaiming the territory from evil.[71] A close-up shot of the elevator dial indicator reaching the top story supplemented by jarring, extradiegetic music indicates that the soldier stand-in has discovered the body. A bird's-eye view echoes his downward glance, showing the tiny figure of George on the street below, thus setting an intensive manhunt in motion. The worker's discovery and the flag's restitution imply that the Carillon Tower itself will be restored as a location of wartime remembrance, unity, and hope, a place at which tourists might once again hear music from its churchlike bells.

The film's exploration of military trauma is furthered by the representation of the Canadian town of Chippewa, the site of numerous historical conflicts between colonists and indigenous peoples, and later between the Americans and the British in the Revolutionary War and the War of 1812. Kettering's comments concerning the historical town where he takes the Cutlers on a fishing trip underscore its meaning: "This little Canadian town of Chippewa—great Revolutionary War battle—the British whipped us. It's OK now." This dialogue recalls the forgotten military combat, defeat, and resolution that parallel the film's thematic trajectory. Its setting is designed to afford George a last act of courage and sacrifice, and even a partial restoration of his masculinity—which eluded him during the Korean dispute. Chippewa also provides for a final encounter between the provisional couple of George and Polly, thereby facilitating his courage and limited honor.

Once the small cabin craft docks, Kettering and his protégé Ray go for gasoline and tell Polly to get some beer, leaving her alone and unprotected yet again, and illustrating her husband's inadequacy as a leader in times of strife, his study of Churchill notwithstanding. George is also coincidentally in Chippewa. Observing the unattended boat, he hatches a plan to escape by distracting the attendant and scrambling over the side, but he is forced to hide when he hears someone approaching. Unaware that George is on the craft, Polly returns with the refreshments and steps aboard. A few seconds later, they discover each other, prompting George to order her to get off the boat to avoid imminent danger, an act that recalls how she had helped him earlier through her compassionate treatment of his wound. Polly grabs his arm and refuses to desert the injured and defeated soldier, but George casts her aside aggressively, causing her to hit her head accidentally, thus rendering her unconscious. When she awakens and learns of Rose's murder, Polly addresses him as one might a soldier, demanding that he turn himself in to the police: "Are you afraid to stand up and defend yourself?" she challenges.

The boat is now headed toward Grand Island with an American flag conspicuously flapping from its stern—signifying George's patriotism—with the US River Patrol in pursuit. A blaring marine siren reinforces his role as both hero and villain. "He's not crazy enough to head downstream, is he?" his pursuers ask. Soon he has no choice because the boat has run out of gas. The camera tracks the river where the water is calm to "the raging rapids of the upper Niagara," where "the river breaks off and plunges two hundred feet down." The scene thus points to George's inexorable descent and to the landscape's almost animistic desire to exact its revenge for his crime.[72]

Two paradigms of midcentury masculinity are now contrasted. The impotent Ray Cutler looks from a speeding police car toward the vulnerable craft and cries out desperately, "Scuttle it! Scuttle it!" Simultaneously, Loomis has the same idea and seizes a hammer to bang the petcocks violently, allowing torrents of water into the boat and causing it to ground. George's forceful beating of the petcocks affords him a final potency, the symbolic culmination of the earlier encounter with Polly in Rainbow Cabin B. His resourceful action causes the boat to hover precariously near a rocky outcrop at the falls' lip, permitting the now-heroic George to usher Polly to stable ground and ultimately to safety. Struggling to gain her balance, she looks skyward, where a Coast Guard rescue helicopter is seen lowering a chair to hoist her aloft. Not only does this reference the rescue and recovery missions of past daredevils; more important, helicopters of this type were employed for the first time during the Korean conflict to lift the wounded from the battlefield. Before she is saved and reunited with Ray, Polly looks on in horror as George's now-tiny craft is hurtled over the falls. Reduced to an infinitesimal speck just as he began, he is punished for both his crime and his audacious and foolhardy challenge to Niagara's omnipotence, and he descends into the maelstrom to join Rose.

Conclusion. *Niagara* is ultimately a conflicted film that combines conventional genre categories; it is at once a simulated tourist travelogue and a noir-influenced melodrama. Previous critics have viewed the film in terms of the iconic star power of Monroe and her character's unrestrained passions, but I have tried to expand on such readings of the film by situating it within discourses concerning landscape, geography, and historical memory while also attending to the way it reflects mid-twentieth-century North American political and economic fissures. Privileging identification with a white middle-class viewer, the film celebrates vacation travel while blaming lowbrow tourists for Niagara Falls' pollution and debasement. The troubled cinematic landscape is also related to the actual site and embedded with traces of its past, including heightened eroticism, mental instability, suicide, and numerous casualties. Hence, discord emerges from the place itself, where natural wonders and architectural monuments already come freighted with trauma, some of which were acknowledged by Zanuck and the three screenwriters.

Thus, the already-troubled landscape serves as a fertile ground for the exploration of the adverse effects of Korean War battle fatigue, which haunt both George's and the nation's psyche in the years 1951 to 1953. In spite of changes in military policy toward psychiatric casualties, it is too late for George, who is never able to recover, in part because of his scheming wife. In contrast to most film noir, *Niagara* provides neither a strong male protagonist nor a restoration of masculine authority. Even though the Cutlers' reconciliation leads to the provisional reinstatement of heteronormativity and the valorization of the loyal and courageous Polly Cutler, masculinity still remains in deficit, stuck between the Korean War and the new management culture.

Errata

In the Summer 2012 issue (51, no. 4), the clinical term "dissociative disorder" was inadvertently changed to "associative disorders" in Merril Schleier's essay, "Fatal Attractions: 'Place,' the Korean War, and Gender in Niagara." In addition, Prof. Schleier's biographical note stated that her work had previously appeared in the journal *Mosaics*; the correct journal title is *Mosaic*.

Notes

1. Michel de Certeau, *The Practice of Everyday Life*, trans. Steven F. Rendall (Berkeley: University of California Press, 1984), 117–119.

2. Henri Lefebvre, *The Production of Space*, trans. Donald Nicholson-Smith (Oxford, UK: Blackwell, 1999), 38–40.

3. Simon Schama, *Landscape and Memory* (New York: Alfred A. Knopf, 1995), 14. See also Martin Lefebvre, introduction to *Landscape and Film* (London: Routledge, 2006), xii, who sees landscape in relation to cinematic narrative rather than as an aspect of narrative itself, as is the case with *Niagara*.

4. Rob Shields, *Places on the Margin: Alternative Geographies of Modernity* (London: Routledge, 1991), 118.

5. Charles Brackett, "Niagara," January 19, 1953, 1, box 4, file 40, Charles Brackett Papers, Margaret Herrick Library of the Academy of Motion Picture Arts and Sciences, Beverly Hills, CA (hereafter CBP).

6. See Karen Dubinsky, *The Second Greatest Disappointment: Honeymooning and Tourism at Niagara Falls* (Toronto: Between the Lines, 1999), 198–201. See also Elizabeth McKinsey, *Niagara Falls: Icon of the American Sublime* (Cambridge: Cambridge University Press, 1985), 186–187; Pierre Burton, *Niagara: A History of the Falls* (New York: Kodansha, 1997), 274–275; Ginger Strand, *Inventing Niagara: Beauty, Power, Lies* (New York: Simon and Schuster, 2008), 198–200, 214–215. On Monroe and *Niagara*, see Jock Carroll, *Falling for Marilyn: The Lost Niagara Collection* (Toronto: Friedman/Fairfax, 1996); George Bailey, *Marilyn Monroe and the Making of "Niagara"* (Niagara Falls, ON: George Bailey and Company, 1998); C. M. Douglas, "Natural Wonders: Marilyn Monroe and *Niagara*," *Scarlet Street* no. 31, 1998, 32–36, 74.

7. The idea of casting Monroe as Rose Loomis was Zanuck's. See Darryl F. Zanuck to Lew Schreiber, January 22, 1952, interoffice correspondence, box 4, file 33, CBP.

8. "SR Goes to the Movies the Girl on the Calendar," *Newsweek*, February 2, 1953, 78. For other reviewers which concurred with this assessment, see clippings on *Niagara* in box 4, file 41, CBP. See also Howard Thompson, review of *Niagara*, *New York Times*, January 28, 1953.

9. Denis E. Cosgrove, *Social Formations and Symbolic Landscape* (Madison: University of Wisconsin Press, 1998); W. J. T. Mitchell, *Landscape and Power* (Chicago: University of Chicago Press, 1997); Graeme Harper and Jonathan Rayner, eds., *Cinema and Landscape: Film, Nation and Cultural Geography* (Chicago: University of Chicago Press, 2010).

10. Conference on writer's working script of January 17, 1952, box 1228, Twentieth Century Fox Collection, Special Collections, University of California, Los Angeles (hereafter TCF).

11. Cotten's angry lines were suggested, in part, by Zanuck but did not appear in the final shooting script of May 15, 1952. See Charles Brackett to Darryl F. Zanuck, August 19, 1952, box 4, file 42, CBP.

12. Raymond F. Yates, *The Niagara Story* (Buffalo, NY: Foster and Stewart, 1947), 9–10.

13. Patrick McGreevy, *Imagining Niagara: The Meaning and Making of Niagara Falls* (Amherst: University of Massachusetts Press, 1994), 42, 46–47. For a further discussion of the specter of death haunting the falls, see also Claudia Wall and John Wall, *The Accelerated Sublime: Landscape, Tourism and Identity* (Westport, CT: Praeger, 2002), 23. Midcentury articles include John Kobler, "The Fatal Game at Niagara Falls," *Saturday Evening Post*, March 22, 1952, 22–23, 81, 84–85, 88–90, 92, 94–95; and Stephen Cain, "Tragedy at Niagara," *Reader's Digest*, May 1958, 138–144.

14. John Urry, *The Tourist Gaze*, 2nd ed. (London: Sage Publications, 2002).

15. The Carillon Tower is now known as the Rainbow Tower.

16. Charles Brackett to Darryl F. Zanuck, July 9, 1951, box 4, file 34, CBP. Brackett visited the falls in the autumn of 1950.

17. Walter Reisch, "The Niagara Story," September 1, 1951 (51 pages), box 4, file 25; Richard Breen, "The Niagara Story," September 4, 1951 (17 pages), box 4, file 26; Charles Brackett, "The Niagara Story," September 6, 1951 (19 pages), box 4, file 27, CBP.

18. A. W. S. Bennett (manager, Greater Niagara Chamber of Commerce) to Ralph Waycott Jr., assistant to director of public relations, Twentieth Century Fox, September 14, 1951, box 4, file 37, CBP. Charles Brackett to C. B. Kesco, February 20, 1952, CBP.

19. Thanks to an anonymous reviewer for pointing this out.

20. Charles Brackett, "Niagara," January 19, 1953, 1, box 4, file 40, CBP.

21. By August 1952, Brackett was fully aware of the potential star power of Monroe. He wrote: "In this picture, we have two great stars—Marilyn Monroe and the mightiest waterfall on earth." Brackett to Zanuck, August 11, 1952, box 4, file 35, CBP. In December 1953, *Playboy*'s first issue featured Monroe on the cover, and by 1953, she was voted the top female box-office star by American film distributors.

22. Michael Abel to Zanuck, March 4, 1952, 1, TCF.

23. Brackett to Zanuck, November 8, 1952, box 4, file 35, CBP. Here Brackett is paraphrasing Zanuck.

24. The *Niagara Falls Evening Review*, January 27, 1953, published the eleven-page "Special Section Marking the Canadian Premier of 20th Century Fox Picture 'Niagara,'" which reported on all the events. Special prints of the film were flown to Buffalo and then to the Rainbow Bridge by helicopter, where Mayors Hawkins and Mirrington of the twin cities of Niagara Falls were on hand to deliver the film to their respective cities. Articles on various aspects of the film were included, many of which were provided by the studio's publicity department. Advertisements by the various businesses that sold props for the film and others that worked with the studio were also included, including the Jolley Construction Company, which built the Rainbow Motel for Twentieth Century Fox.

25. Abel to Zanuck, March 4, 1952, 1, TCF.

26. *The Adventurous Sex* (Gordon Douglas, 1925) and *Niagara Falls* (Gordon Douglas, 1941) deal with temporarily "decoupled" couples and end with sexually charged conclusions.

27. Brackett, "Niagara," January 19, 1953, 1, box 4, file 40, CBP.

28. John F. Sears, "Doing Niagara Falls in the Nineteenth Century," in *Niagara: Two Centuries of Changing Attitudes, 1697–1901*, ed. Jeremy Elwell Adamson (Washington, DC: Corcoran Gallery of Art, 1985), 106; McKinsey, *Niagara Falls,* 150.

29. Shields, *Places on the Margin*, 130.

30. Dubinsky, *The Second Greatest Disappointment*, 28; McKinsey, *Niagara Falls,* 35, 178.

31. Dubinsky, *The Second Greatest Disappointment*, 6.

32. This recipe was listed in *The Wonders of Niagara Scenic and Industrial* (New York: Shredded Wheat Company, 1915), n.p.

33. Notes from writer's conference on treatment of September 14, 1951, box 1228, TCF.

34. Treatment by Brackett, Richard Breen, and Walter Reisch, September 14, 1951, box 1228, TCF.

35. William R. Irwin, *The New Niagara: Tourism, Technology, and the Landscape of Niagara Falls, 1776–1917* (University Park: Pennsylvania State University Press, 1996), 182.

36. *The Wonders of Niagara Scenic and Industrial*, n.p.

37. Henry F. and Katharine Pringle, "Niagara Falls," *Saturday Evening Post*, October 30, 1948, 24; Wolfgang Langwiesche, "A New Look at Niagara Falls," *Reader's Digest*, August 1957, 159.

38. William H. Whyte Jr., *The Organization Man* (New York: Simon and Schuster, 1956). For more information about views on the midcentury executive, see my *Skyscraper Cinema: Architecture and Gender in American Film* (Minneapolis: University of Minnesota Press, 2009), 217–231.

39. Notes from writer's conference on treatment of September 14, 1951, box 1228, TCF.

40. The Rainbow Cabins was not a real motel. It was constructed by the Jolley Construction Company at a cost of $26,000. Special permission was obtained to have it built in Victoria Park so close to the falls.

41. Brackett, Reisch, and Breen, "Niagara," final shooting script, May 15, 1952, 9, obtained from Script Fly, Los Angeles, California.

42. The tunnel was also known as the Horseshoe Tunnel. The tour is currently known as the Journey behind the Falls.

43. Mark Twain, "The Earliest Authentic Mention of Niagara Falls," in *The Niagara Book: A Complete Souvenir of Niagara Falls* (Buffalo, NY: Underhill and Nichols, 1893), 96. At the turn of the century, H. G. Wells decried the "accumulation of human effort about Niagara" as "extremely defiling and ugly," conflating commercial signage, the haphazard arrangement of architecture, and industrial pollution. H. G. Wells, *The Future in America: A Search after Realities* (New York: Harper and Brothers, 1906), 54.

44. Dubinsky, *The Second Greatest Disappointment*, 6.

45. Brackett, Reisch, and Breen, "Niagara," final shooting script, May 15, 1952, 13.

46. Walter Reisch, "The Niagara Story," September 1, 1951, box 4, file 25, 1, TCF.

47. Gordon Donaldson, *Niagara! The Eternal Circus* (Toronto: Doubleday, 1979), 227–228.

48. Joseph Breen to Jason R. Joy, March 11, 1952, 15, box 4, file 44, Motion Picture Association of America, Production Code Administration Files, Margaret Herrick Library (hereafter PCA). Breen stipulated, "There should be no silhouette on Rose showing through the shower curtain," although his prohibition was partly ignored with the exposure of Monroe's upper torso.

49. André Bazin, "Niagara," in *Bazin at Work: Major Essays and Reviews from the Forties and Fifties*, trans. Alain Piette and Bert Cardullo (New York: Routledge, 1997), 127.

50. Cole Porter's "Night and Day" (1946) was the song originally selected for Rose. R. A. Klune to Zanuck, June 23, 1952. On June 6, 1952, Zanuck wrote a memo to Brackett and Hathaway, stating that he liked the song selection of Lionel Newman's "Kiss," which he believed would be "a hit" and "would fascinate the character that Marilyn Monroe is playing" (box 4, file 39, CBP).

51. David Douglas Duncan, *This Is War! A Photo-Narrative in Three Parts* (New York: Harper and Brothers, 1951); Marguerite Higgins, *War in Korea: The Report of a Woman Combat Correspondent* (Garden City, NY: Doubleday, 1951); Charles and Eugene Jones, *The Face of War* (New York: Prentice-Hall, 1951); *Faces of Korea* (New York: Museum of Modern Art, 1951).

52. Andrew J. Heubner, *The Warrior Image: Soldiers in American Culture from the Second World War to the Vietnam Era* (Chapel Hill: University of North Carolina Press, 2008), 97. For a general history of the Korean conflict, see David Halberstam, *The Coldest Winter: America and the Korean War* (New York: Hyperion, 2007).

53. Duncan, *This Is War!*, n.p.

54. Heubner, *The Warrior Image*, 101, 116; Susan Moeller, *Shooting War Photography and the American Experience of Combat* (New York: Basic Books, 1989), 296–297.

55. Heubner, *The Warrior Image*, 135–153; see also Paul M. Edwards, *A Guide to Films on the Korean War* (Westport, CT: Greenwood Press, 1997).

56. Ben Shephard, *A War of Nerves: Soldiers and Psychiatrists in the Twentieth Century* (Cambridge, MA: Harvard University Press, 2001), 242; Edgar Jones and Simon Wessely, *Shell Shock to PTSD: Military Psychiatry from 1900 to the Gulf War* (New York: Psychology Press, 2005), 121; Anthony Babington, *Shell Shock: A History of Changing Attitudes to War Neurosis* (London: Leo Cooper, 1997), 164. In *Shooting War*, Moeller reports that the incidence of battle fatigue varied over the years that the troops were in Korea (68). During the fiercest fighting in the first six months, the rate was ninety-nine per thousand. It dropped to eighty-nine per thousand during the following year, and to twenty-one per thousand in 1952.

57. Martin Deahl, "The Effect of Conflict on Combatants," in *Psychological Trauma: A Developmental Approach*, ed. Dora Black, Martin Newman, Jean Harris-Hendricks, and Gillian Mezey (Glasgow: Bell and Bain, 1997), 140.

58. After Glass's numerous interventions and expeditious treatment solutions, the incidence of protracted battle fatigue fell to thirty-seven per thousand, similar to its rate of occurrence during World War II. Edgar Jones, "Army Psychiatry in the Korean War: The Experience of 1 Commonwealth Division," *Military Medicine* 165, no. 4 (April 2000): 257.

59. Albert J. Glass, "Psychotherapy in the Combat Zone," *American Journal of Psychiatry* 110, no. 10 (1954): 730–731. See also Glass, "Preventive Psychiatry in the Combat Zone," *United States Armed Forces Medical Journal* 4, no. 3 (1954): 683–694.

60. Heubner, *The Warrior Image*, 100.

61. Pamela Robertson Wojcik points out that the phonograph is often used as a symbol of female transgression in "The Girl and the Phonograph; or The Vamp and the Machine Revisited," in *Soundtrack Available: Essays on Film and Popular Music*, ed. Pamela Robertson Wojcik and Arthur Knight (Durham, NC: Duke University Press, 2001), 433–453.

62. "Niagara," final shooting script, May 15, 1952, 20.

63. Ibid., 21.

64. *Psychoneurosis* was the term applied to the condition of sufferers during World War II. By the time of the Korean conflict, it was replaced by the term *battle fatigue*, which supposedly removed the stigma. *Let There Be Light* (John Huston, 1946) was suppressed by the army until 1981, although James Agee wrote about it in 1947 and 1948, suggesting that it was shown on a limited basis. See Vincent Canby, "'Let There Be Light': John Huston vs. the Army," *New York Times*, January 16, 1981; and Charles Morgan, "From *Let There Be Light to Shades of Grey:* The Construction of Authoritative Knowledge and Battle Fatigue (1945–48)," in *Signs of Life: Cinema and Medicine*, ed. Graeme Harper and Andrew Moor (London: Wallflower Press, 2005), 132–152.

65. Cotten had previously played a World War II battle-fatigued soldier in *I'll Be Seeing You* (William Dieterle, 1944).

66. Robert Eberwein, Armed Forces: *Masculinity and Sexuality in the American War Film* (New Brunswick, NJ: Rutgers University Press, 2007), 74. See also Jacqueline Noll Zimmerman, *People Like Ourselves: Portrayals of Mental Illness in the Movies* (Lanham, MD: Scarecrow Press, 2003).

67. "Niagara," final shooting script, May 15, 1952, 25.

68. Steven Jacobs, "Sightseeing Fright: Alfred Hitchcock's Monuments and Museums," *Journal of Architecture* 11 (2006): 593–601; Jacobs, *The Wrong House: The Architecture of*

Hitchcock (Rotterdam: 010 Publishers, 2007), 48–55. Although Hitchcock often made tourists of his viewers, and used grandiose architectural monuments in such films as *The Pleasure Garden* (1924), *Rich and Strange* (1932), and *The Man Who Knew Too Much* (1934), prior to 1953 he did not render a sense of place as a comprehensive character.

69. "Rainbow Bridge," *Architect and Engineer* (December 1943): 31–33, 36; "The Rainbow Tower Carillon" pamphlet, 1954; Joe Hvilivitzky, "Is There a Dire Secret Hidden in Niagara's Carillon Bells?," *Niagara Falls Review*, July 11, 1975, n.p., and "Ban on Bells Lifted," *Niagara Falls Review*, October 1, 1975, n.p., history and clipping files, Niagara Falls Public Library, Niagara Falls, New York (hereafter NFPL); George A. Seibel, *Bridges over the Niagara Gorge: Rainbow Bridge, 50 Years, 1941–1991: A History* (Niagara Falls, ON: Niagara Falls Bridge Commission, 1991).

70. John Fedor, "28-Year-Old Mistake Kept Bells from View," *Niagara Falls Review*, August 8, 1975, n.p., and "The Bell That Almost Cost Canada Its Prime Minister," *Niagara Falls Review*, May 18, 1989, n.p., NFPL. "Canada Erases Roosevelt, Churchill Names in Carillon Inscription to Remove 'Affront,'" *New York Times*, June 17, 1947. This article reports erroneously that all the names were removed.

71. The African American actor in this scene was an amateur selected by Hathaway.

72. "Niagara," final shooting script, May 15, 1952, 111.

15 | *Whose Future? "Star Wars," "Alien," and "Blade Runner"*

Peter Lev

Abstract: *Argues that George Lucas's film "Star Wars" creates an ideologically conservative future whereas Ridley Scott's "Alien" and "Blade Runner" create futures infused with liberal and socially critical ideas. Contrasts Lucas's film with Scott's films and argues that while "Star Wars" presents a future that is clean, wholesome, and morally clear, both of Scott's films present a future of oppressive institutions and continue the socially critical American cinema of "Chinatown" (1974) and "Nashville" (1975).*

The science fiction film, as a construction somewhat removed from everyday reality, is a privileged vehicle for the presentation of ideology. Because it is less concerned than other genres with the surface structure of social reality, science fiction can pay more attention to the deep structure of what is and what ought to be. In practice, this means that science fiction films vividly embody ideological positions, and that comparing science fiction films of the same era becomes an analysis of conflicting social visions. Such visions cannot, however, be reduced to a simple, discursive message. Instead, the total semiotic output of a film—images, sounds, textures, relationships—is a carrier of ideology.

As a test of this hypothesis, consider three popular films from the years around 1980: Star Wars (1977), Alien (1979), and Blade Runner (1982).[1] These films have much in common. All three are key moments in the renaissance of science fiction film stretching from the late 1970s to the present. And all three films are renowned for the quality of their visual design and special effects. However, Star Wars creates an ideologically conservative future, whereas Alien and Blade Runner create futures linked to liberal and socially critical ideas.

What factors account for Star Wars overwhelming success with the public? Certainly the film's narrative provides a partial answer. Star Wars is a modern quest narrative, blending such sources as Arthurian legend, Paradise Lost, Lord of the Rings, the Western, The Wizard of Oz, and the meta-discourse of Joseph Campbell's The Hero with a Thousand Faces.[2] Young, naive Luke Skywalker sets out on an adventure both physical and spiritual, which involves saving the princess, defeating the evil Empire, and establishing a more just government. The story has a mythic or fairytale dimension, but also a lightness of tone; Luke (Mark Hamill), Princess Leia (Carrie Fisher), and Han Solo (Harrison Ford) wisecrack their way

Reprinted by permission from *Literature/Film Quarterly* 26, no. 1.

through difficult situations. There are some weak points to the narrative. One would be a problem with character development, particularly apparent in the minor roles—e.g., Uncle Owen and Aunt Beru. Another would be the lack of emotional response to destruction of an entire inhabited planet! (Wyatt 609-10) However, the quest narrative of Star Wars has proved sufficiently compelling and resilient to support two film sequels (with more in process), numerous authorized novels, and a great deal of fan activity.

A second explanation is that Star Wars owes much of its popularity to a richness of audiovisual invention that is rare in science fiction or any other genre. Space ships, space wars, planetary ecology, alien beings (not one species of intelligent aliens, but perhaps a dozen) George Lucas and his collaborators deserve much credit for creating such a sweeping and detailed science fiction universe. John J. Pierce calls this level of invention "world creation," and notes that it is a prized aspect of science fiction novels but hard to find in science fiction films. Such worldbuilding requires a sweeping imagination that is also disciplined and thorough (Pierce 201, 209). An example from Star Wars would be the distinctively realized look, sound, and behavior of the two droids, R2D2 and C3PO. These two robots are original, detailed, and consistent; they may be the most interesting characters in the film. The created world in Star Wars is both packed with audiovisual information and given an imperfect, lived-in quality. For example, the sound effects generally start from complex natural sounds (e.g., a movie projector as the basis for the hum of the light sabers) rather than simpler, cleaner synthetic audio. Ben Burtt, the film's sound designer, explains that "The sounds of the real world are complicated and kind of dirty. They simply cannot be duplicated on a synthesizer" (Pollock 178).

John Seabrook, writing in the New Yorker, gives a more technical explanation of Star Wars' success. According to Seabrook, the film's "secret" is its control of the kinetic aspects of movie-making: "The first Star Wars movie is like a two hour image of raw speed." Lucas is not a particularly gifted director of actors, but his control of "editing and pace" creates a feeling of "pure kinetic energy which has become a part of the world's visual imagination." "Every time a studio executive tells a writer that his piercing and true story needs an "action beat" every ten minutes, the writer has George Lucas to thank" (45, 50).

This explanation seems to me far too simplistic. It leaves out Star Wars' most original use of kinetic filmmaking, which is genre-based: science fiction film can use the whole film frame to invent new kinds of motion. Lucas is very good at doing this, and he is a fine editor, but he does not deserve credit for singlehandedly changing the emphasis of American cinema. To take just one example from among Lucas's contemporaries, William Friedkin in The French Connection (1971) and The Exorcist (1973) is every bit as visual and kinetic as George Lucas in Star Wars. Yet no one would posit Friedkin as the sole inventor of contemporary film style. The increased emphasis on action and pace is undoubtedly a group creation, influenced as much by television (including commercials) as by film.

Star Wars is conservative, though not extreme right wing or Fascist, in its ideological underpinnings. Men are active heroes, Princess Leia is a damsel in distress, good and evil are clearly separated, and Luke is guided by the benevolent father figure Obiwan Kenobi. The film is very consciously a break from the anti-heroes and anti-genres of many films of the early 1970s. According to Dale Pollock's biography of Lucas, the film's return to family entertainment and traditional morality was a conscious decision by its writer-director. Lucas wanted to present positive values to the audience. In the 1970s traditional religion was out of fashion and the family structure was disintegrating. There was no moral anchor. Lucas remembered how protected he had felt growing up in the cocoonlike culture of the 1950s, a feeling he wanted to communicate in Star Wars. (143) Pollock lists the values of the film as "Hard work, self-sacrifice, friendship, loyalty, and a commitment to a higher purpose." Lucas himself comments, "I mean, there's a reason this film is so popular. It's not that I'm giving out propaganda nobody wants to hear" (140).

Star Wars has often been discussed as a harbinger of the renewed American conservatism of the Reagan presidency. It is certainly part of the move toward simple, optimistic genre films in the late 1970s. The clean-cut, well-spoken White youths of the film seem to come out of an idealized version of the 1950s, and the clear division between good and evil governments suggests the Cold War. Indeed, some phrases borrowed from the film became key ideological points of the Reagan years: "Star Wars" (meaning a futuristic missile defense system), "the Evil Empire" (meaning the Soviet Union). More recently, the name "Jedi Knights" was used by a U.S. Army group planning the Gulf War (Meyer 99). Lucas is not responsible for the uses politicians and governments make of his film. But the ease with which his ideas were put to political and military ends shows something about the Manichaean quality of the story.

Though Star Wars is part of a shift in film entertainment, away from socially critical work and toward optimistic genre films, that shift was neither simple nor complete. An alternate science fiction vision of the period can be analyzed in two films directed by Ridley Scott, Alien and Blade Runner. Both films are developments on George Lucas's combination of mythic storytelling and detailed "world creation" of the future in Star Wars. Ridley Scott is excellently suited for this type of science fiction filmmaking, because he is both a gifted director and a world-class art director.[3] In Alien, Scott takes on one part of the Star Wars legacy by creating an intricate and haunting portrait of a starship—the ancient Nostromo. He also develops a stunning variant on a 1950s science fiction cliche—the malevolent alien creature. In Blade Runner, Scott puts together a more complex version of Star Wars' worldbuilding project by creating a physically and emotionally convincing Los Angeles of the year 2019. Blade Runner, like Alien, draws on other influences as well, e.g., the look of 1940s film noir and the odd science fiction novels of Philip K. Dick.

The narrative premise of Alien is eminently simple: the monster attacks. Robbie Robertson has shown that the alien being with its savage survival logic has antecedents in science fiction literature, for example in the work of A.E. Van Vogt (175-76). Other antecedents would be science fiction films of the 1950s, including the Japanese Godzilla. Looking to mythology, the story relates to myths of the dragon, of the sea monster, of Jonah and the whale. In each case, human heroes are threatened by powerful, mysterious creatures which exaggerate the traits of known animals. In Alien, the monster designed by Surrealist artist H.R. Giger is reptilian, and thus related to fear of snakes, dinosaurs, and sea creatures.

Though simple, the premise of Alien is also trans-generic, a blend of science fiction and horror. One borrowing from the traditional horror film is a stretched-out anticipation of the monster's attack. Several scenes use silence and false cues to play with the moment of attack; this might be called the "haunted house" motif of horror film. As Scott Bukatman notes, Alien also presents a more contemporary (perhaps Postmodern) horror motif: the link between the monster and the human body (262-67). The alien creature in Alien does not merely kill humans, it uses them as hosts for a process of reproduction. This is terrifyingly shown in the scene where a small alien bursts from an astronaut's chest, killing him as a byproduct of "birth." Like the vampire, the werewolf, the zombie, the alien is thus a threat to the integrity of the human body. But in the 1979 film, the threat is more visceral, the body more subject to transformation than in classic horror films. The eruption of an alien from a human body could be seen as a disguised version of "monstrous" processes that are normally hidden, such as birth and sexuality.

Alien is unlike Star Wars and Blade Runner in that it deals with a restricted space. The main set is the human spaceship, with a few minutes spent on an uninhabited planet and in the alien ship. In the limited environment of the Nostromo, Ridley Scott and his collaborators present in a matter-of-fact way the organization and technology which make the ship work. Hibernation coffins, hospital room, airlock, gallery, control room, escape module, ship-controlling computer: all are presented simply and effectively. The ship also has a variety of hidden or "waste" spaces—vents, crawlways, corridors—and this becomes important in fighting a creature which exists apart from human spatial and conceptual logic. A particularly useful future technology invented by Scott and crew is a motion sensor that can indicate the distance of a moving object but not the direction or location.

In Star Wars the future is clean (though not shiny and new), wholesome, and morally clear. Alien reverses all three points. The starship in Alien is dank, dark, and messy. It is an old freighter owned by a large corporation, and therefore is maintained for utility rather than pride (compare the Millenium Falcon, Star Wars' version of a beloved hot rod). The unknown planet is a fiercely inhospitable environment, with strong winds and swirling gas clouds. The alien ship's scariest feature is an uncanny mixture of organic and inorganic forms. The walls and corridors of the ship seem also to be the skeleton of an organic creature, with spines and ribs and dripping mucous. Threat-as-body is thus part of the film's visual design in ways that go beyond the blatant threat of the monster itself.

Discussion of the ideological differences between Star Wars and Alien requires that we return for a moment to George Lucas's film. I have labeled Star Wars conservative, but it does present itself as a rebellious act. The rebels of the story have risen up against an oppressive Empire. Further, the main representative of the Empire is Darth Vader, a lightly disguised version of "Dark Father." So, Star Wars is a revolt against the father. However, the Rebel Alliance itself seems to be hierarchical and perhaps even authoritarian; it celebrates victory with an ending scene weirdly quoted from Leni Riefenstahl.[4] One should also remember that Star Wars' rebellion in no way challenges gender, race, or class relations. White male humans are "naturally" in positions of authority. The boy Luke grows up and takes his place as a responsible male leader. As Robin Wood says, the film's dominant tone is reassurance; things change so that they can return to a comfortable norm (162-65). Alien presents a more significant challenge to authority. In this film the "Company," boss and organizer of the crew, turns out to be an evil force, the malevolent twin of the monster.

The Company is represented on board by "Mother," the controlling computer; the nickname indicates the crew's dependence on the Company-programmed machine. The Company is also represented by Ash (Ian Holm), the science officer, who (unknown to other crew members) is an android. Ash's secret orders are to capture and bring back the alien; the crew is expendable. These orders are based on the commercial and military potentials of the alien creature. The Company responds to profit, and puts little value on human life. Superficially, the theme is reminiscent of The Poseidon Adventure (1972), where the ship owners have neglected needed repairs and put passengers and crew at risk. But in The Poseidon Adventure this theme seems perfunctory, a way to start the action; the film concludes with a powerful defense of patriarchal authority. In Alien, on the other hand, the Company's action is part of a pervasive pattern of oppression and paranoia. The film sympathizes with the outsiders on the crew, the proletarian engine mechanics and the independent-minded Ripley (Sigourney Weaver).

Blade Runner is designed around two intersecting myths. First, there is the film noir detective fighting crime and corruption in the decaying city. The detective is a version of the medieval knight, someone who embodies right values in the struggle between good and evil.[5] A complication of film noir is that good and evil may be hard to ascertain in the modern city. Further, the damsel-in-distress may not want to be saved. A second mythic plot in Blade Runner involves four "replicants"—androids of superior strength and intelligence who have made their way to earth. At one level, these replicants are the villains of the narrative. Deckard (Harrison Ford), the hero, is a "blade runner"—a specialized assassin hired to find and terminate replicants. But the replicants are also angels fallen to Earth; human-like beings with their own histories, needs, emotions, and morality. The link to angels is made explicit by a near-quote from William Blake uttered by Roy Batty (Rutger Hauer), leader of the replicants: "Fiery the Angels fell, while thunder roared around their shores, burning with the fires of Orc."[6]

As the conflict between the two myths suggests, Deckard's job as a blade runner is brought into question. Is he killing "skin jobs," i.e., non-human criminals? Or is he killing angels, i.e., human-like or more-than-human beings whose differences are to be respected? The film suggests that the replicants, despite differences of genesis and history, are emotionally and morally human. This point is made by the character of Rachael (Sean Young), a replicant who does not know her origins and is therefore completely human in behavior. It is reinforced when Roy Batty, who seems to be Blade Runner's arch-villain, ultimately saves Deckard's life in a Christ-like gesture of compassion. The theme of android and human mixing and merging in unforeseen ways has its roots in the source novel for Blade Runner, Philip K. Dick's Do Androids Dream of Electric Sheep?

In visual design, Blade Runner catapults us not into an idealized 1950s, but into the darkness of 1940s film noir. Fashions are part retro-1940s, and part futuristic. The chiaroscuro lighting of film noir mixes with enormous electronic billboards of the future. The film is set in an overpopulated, highly polluted Los Angeles in the year 2019. The climate has changed drastically, so that it rains all the time (convenient for film noir). Smoke and smog mask the city, and many residents wear gas masks outdoors. Asians, Hispanics, Blacks and Eastern Europeans swarm the streets; most Caucasian Americans seem to have departed for off-world colonies. A paramilitary police force maintains order, and enormous corporate head-quarters dominate the skyline. Clearly, this is not the best of all possible worlds.

Although Star Wars presents a dozen alien races, it assumes pre-eminence of humans. Both the Empire and the rebels are led by humans; most of the aliens are relegated to the "freak show" of the spacefarers' bar. Even Chewbacca, the one alien among the small group of heroes, is shown as Han Solo's sidekick. In this film, man is the measure of all things. Blade Runner, on the other hand, entertains ideas of "not-quite-human," "different-than-human," even "more-than-human." The elusive border between machine and human is shown visually in the scene where the replicant Pris (Darryl Hannah) hides among a bunch of animated toy figures maintained by the lonely J.R. Sebastian (William Sanderson). Sebastian's toys talk and move and seem to be emotionally attached to their owner. Though Pris can hide among the toys, she is different from them because of superior intelligence and strength plus an independent spirit, a will to live. In some ways replicants are superior to humans, not just to toys. But they are limited by a built-in four-year lifespan. Because of the short lifespan, replicants can be childlike at one moment, adult and philosophical the next (Morrison 3). The film ultimately affirms the validity of replicants as thinking, feeling beings, notably via the love affair between Deckard and Rachael. It thus makes an eloquent statement for acceptance of the Other. Part II

Both Alien and Blade Runner project a future of oppressive institutions, and therefore continue the socially critical American cinema of Chinatown (1974), Nashville (1975), and One Flew Over the Cuckoo's Nest (1976). They are far different in ideological hue from the optimistic, Norman Rockwellish vision of the future in Star Wars.[7] The first part of this essay has presented an overview of the films' conflicting approaches. The second part turns from this general exposition to discuss one aspect of the science fiction film: sex.

Vivian Sobchack, in her fine essay "On the Virginity of Astronauts," suggests that the American science fiction film is characterized by an absence of women and sexuality. Astronauts are primarily male, they wear unisex coveralls and spacesuits, their environment is technological and asexual. But, says Sobchack, if the signifiers of women and sex have been omitted from the science fiction film on the surface level, they return in the deep (subconscious) layer. Space travel is often presented as a penetration; both spaceship and space itself are wombs; alien threats are often sexual, and female.

Before applying Sobchack's model to the three film examples, I would like to consider an exception to Sobchack which proves the rule. The prize-winning science fiction writer C.J. Cherryh (Carolyn J. Cherryh) has paid considerable attention to how sex and reproduction could be handled in starship-based cultures. For example, in a culture of family-operated merchant space ships, where everyone on board is likely to be blood kin, both sex and the reproduction of the culture are made possible by "dockside sleepovers." Cherryh sketches out a pattern of sexual exchange and conventions protecting the greater social good. One example of the controlling social conventions is that children take the mother's name and stay with the mother's ship. The remarkable thing about Cherryh's approach to a spacefaring culture is that almost no one, in science fiction novels or films, has considered similar questions.[8]

Let us return to our film examples. In Star Wars there simply is no sex. The society of the film is primarily male, or technologically neuter (the droids). The one prominent female character, Princess Leia, does not appear in sexual terms. According to Sobchack, Leia is "simultaneously protected and desexed by her social position (princesses are to fight for, not to sleep with) and by her acerbic and pragmatically critical attitude" (106). Dale Pollock quotes Marcia Lucas (ex-wife of George Lucas) as saying that Star Wars was conceptualized as a movie that would appeal to ten-year-old boys (142). Star Wars is a movie coming out of the latency period, a movie which elides the adult problem of sexuality. This is curiously confirmed by the eventual revelation in the Star Wars trilogy that Leia is Luke's sister.

Star Wars does not, however, strongly support Sobchack's observation that sexuality repressed on the conscious level will return in subconscious symbolism. The film is not haunted by womb imagery or female monsters. Perhaps the pre-adolescent tone is so strong that it mutes such condensed or displaced signifiers. And, of course, audiences of all ages welcomed this tone, using it to escape current malaise and to return to a simpler, more conservative time. Only two scenes in Star Wars suggest to me the displaced sexuality described by Sobchack. First, there is an odd scene, peripheral to the main action, where several characters are caught in a disposal chute/compactor, and they are attacked by a tentacled creature. This scene, played for laughs in Star Wars, nevertheless presents the threat of bodily functions and unknown organic antagonists. It thus anticipates Alien. Second, in the final attack on the Death Star, the one-man fighters penetrating the sphere could certainly be a representation of human reproduction, with the combination of sexual and mechanical imagery recalling Dr Strangelove.

Unlike Star Wars, Alien is very specifically about a female, sexual threat. The alien creature is associated with darkness, rounded spaces, eggs, slime. Its temple-like ship has doors in the shape of vaginas. The alien's offspring may be male and phallic (e.g., the thing which springs into life from a male astronaut's chest), but the original threat is female. This is made even more explicit in Aliens (1986), the sequel to Alien, where the human expedition confronts an enormous, egg-laying alien Queen.

In a reversal of the common practice of science fiction films, the protagonist in Alien is a female. Ripley, one of two female astronauts, is the toughest, most suspicious, most resourceful of the Nostromo's crew. She, and not the captain or the male crew members, becomes the focus of audience hopes for human survival. Is this reversal incidental, or does it have important ideological consequences for the film? Sobchack notes that Ripley was originally scripted as a male, and that for most of the film "She is not marked as either a woman or sexual" (106). In other words, Ripley is an asexual astronaut among asexual astronauts. However, at the end of the film she strips down to her underwear (preparing for a mechanically aided hibernation), and becomes clearly and challengingly a human female. Sobchack comments as follows: "Ripley no longer represents a rational and asexual functioning subject, but an irrational, potent, sexual object—a woman, the truly threatening alien generally repressed by the male-conceived and dominated genre" (107). Here I partially disagree with Sobchack. I agree that this scene reveals the irrational and sexual side of the main character, but not that it suggests an equivalence with the alien monster. Rather, the revelation is that the primary conflict of Alien is not technological vs. primitive, or any variation on that theme, but rather species vs. species, irrational vs. irrational. The irrational side of Ripley's character is further brought out by her determination to save the cat—not a rational calculation, but a motherly instinct. The cat represents Ripley's animal nature, and her instinct for self-preservation and the preservation of those she loves.[9] In this film, such instincts are positive, whereas the rational calculations of the Company are shown as thoroughly negative. Ripley in her underwear is affirmed as a complex human individual, not presented as "the true threatening alien."

In Blade Runner, the representations of femaleness run all through the mise en scene. Los Angeles, 2019, is a dank, dark place, with smoke swirling and rain constantly falling. The Nostromo and the alien ship, both ancient and womblike, have as their equivalent an entire city. Only the occasional corporate headquarters (e.g., Tyrell Corporation) have the clean, clear lines of technological masculinity.

As noted earlier, Blade Runner combines elements of two male-oriented genres, science fiction and film noir. The combination is important to our current thread of discussion, because film noir commonly includes rather direct, though threatening, images of female sexuality, whereas science fiction represses such images. Blade Runner generally follows the film noir paradigm in presenting the three female replicants, Pris, Zhora (Joanna Cassidy), and Rachael. Zhora the snake-charmer has a threatening sexuality, and Pris, despite her childlike side, is threatening as well. Rachael, though she looks like the raven-haired fatal woman of film noir, is a little different. Raised in ignorance of her replicant status, she is a mediating character between the decaying human society and the new, artificially constructed super humans. The human hero Deckard's continuing love affair with Rachael is, despite her mediating status, a break with film noir and science fiction convention and a major statement about diversity. Blade Runner is film noir/science fiction with the woman as alien not repressed.

This theme of acceptance of diversity receives an added twist via the Director's Cut of Blade Runner, released in 1992 and now the most readily available version of the film. In this re-edited version, Ridley Scott provides a clue that points to Deckard himself being a replicant. In an added scene, Deckard, seated at the piano in his apartment, has a brief vision of a unicorn moving through a natural landscape. This links up with a moment late in the film when Gaff (Edward James Olmos), another blade runner, leaves an origami of a unicorn in front of Deckard's door. The suggestion is that Gaff knows Deckard's visions because Deckard is programmed, Deckard is a replicant. From one point of view, the message of humanness being defined by behavior rather than by external categories gets lost here, because Deckard is now no different than Rachael. But another point of view would be that the audience's identification with Deckard in itself proves that humanness is not a matter of categories such as natural/synthetic birth (or racial, sexual, national, or political identity).

Blade Runner's theme of replicant as more-than-human brings with it some other sexual/ideological possibilities. One, unfortunately, is the possible connection between large, blond Roy Batty, played by Rutger Hauer, and the Nazi theory of an Aryan master race (Wood 187). Another, far more positive line of speculation, is that a more-than-human character can break sexual boundaries. Roy, stronger and smarter than a human, is a fiercely burning Blakean angel with a maximum four year life span. He overrides human cultural limits in a variety of ways, one of which seems to be bisexuality. He kisses his creator, Tyrell, fully on the lips, and his final duel with Deckard has a strong sexual as well as violent content. Significantly, after Roy saves Deckard and dies himself, the original release version of Blade Runner concludes with a voiceover of affirmation: "They just wanted what everyone else wanted. Answers to the basic questions: Who am I? Where did I come from? Where am I going?" A violent/sexual combat here melds into understanding and empathy.

Alien and Blade Runner are clearly descendents of Star Wars, works which build on the revelation that audiences would support mythic, world-creating science fiction films. But the two Ridley Scott films do not follow George Lucas's political line. Whereas Star Wars advocates a return to heroism and traditional morality, the Ridley Scott films show a distrust of authority and an openness to characters outside traditional definitions of heroism (e.g., Ripley and the replicants). When looked at together, these three films present a kind of debate about the (imagined) future. George Lucas sees the future as a revision of the past, as a chance to get basic moral precepts right this time. The legend of King Arthur can be replayed in a possible future. For Ridley Scott and his collaborators, on the other hand, the future provides a way to look at other issues: the place of women in society, the threat of an unexamined rationalism, the acceptance of the Other, the merging of humanity and technology. In simple terms, George Lucas is backward-looking and traditional, i.e., conservative. Ridley Scott is forward-looking and accepting of diversity, i.e., liberal. Audiences drawn to these films are thus, among other things, experiencing an ongoing political dialogue.

Notes

1. Unless otherwise noted in the text, my analysis refers to the film Star Wars, not to the Star Wars trilogy. Similarly, I will be discussing the film Alien, and not its sequels, with any exceptions specifically noted in the text.

2. On the literary roots of Star Wars, see Wyatt and Collins.

3. See Sammon 71-75 for a description of how Ridley Scott's art direction skills transformed the script for Blade Runner.

4. Every army presents medals with pomp and ceremony, but the music used here recalls Triumph of the Will.

5. The connection between Raymond Chandler's literary detective and the chivalrous knight is outlined in Durham.

6. The lines from Blake begin "Fiery the angels rose" (America: A Prophecy, lines 115-16). For interpretation of this near-quote, see Wood and Morrison.

7. After writing these words, I learned that George Lucas collects Norman Rockwell's work! Rockwell's work! Rockwell's paintings hang prominently on the walls of the Skywalker Ranch, Lucas's business headquarters. See Seabrook 43. 8 See, for example, Cherryh's 1982 novel Merchanter's Luck. 9 Thanks to Rebecca Pauly for suggesting the importance of Jonesy the cat.

Works Cited

Bukatman, Scott. Terminal Identity. Durham: Duke UP, 1993. Cherryh, C.J. Merchanter's Luck. New York: Daw, 1982.

Collins, Robert G. "Star Wars: The Pastiche of Myth and the Yearning for a Past Future." Journal of Popular Culture 11:1 (1977): 1-10.

Durham, Philip. Down these mean streets a man must go. Chapel Hill: U of North Carolina P, 1963.

Meyer, David S. "Star Wars, Star Wars, and American Political Culture." Journal of Popular Culture 26:2 (1992): 99115.

Morrison, Rachela. "Casablanca meets Star Wars: The Blakean Dialectics of Blade Runner." Literature/Film Quarterly 18:1: 2-10.

Pierce, John J. "Creative Synergy and the Art of World Creation." Retrofitting Blade Runner. Ed. Judith B. Keman. Bowling Green: Bowling Green: Bowling Green Popular Press, 1991.

Pollack, Dale. Skywalking: The Life and Films of George Lucas. Hollywood: Samuel French, 1990.

Robertson, Robbie. "The narrative sources of Ridley Scott's Alien." Cinema and Fiction: New Modes of Adapting, 1950-1990. Ed. John Orr and Colin Nicholson. Edinburgh: Edinburgh UP, 1992.

Sammon, Paul M. Future Noir: The Making of Blade Runner. New York: HarperCollins, 1996.

Seabrook, John. "Why is the Force Still With Us?" New Yorker 6 January 1997.

Sobchack, Vivian. "On the Virginity of Astronauts." Alien Zone. Ed. Annette Kuhn. London: Verso, 1990.

Wood, Robin. Hollywood from Vietnam to Reagan. New York: Columbia UP, 1986.

Wyatt, David. "Star Wars and the Productions of Tune." Virginia Quarterly Review 58 (1982): 600-15.

16

Welcome to the Men's Club: Homosociality and the Maintenance of Hegemonic Masculinity

Sharon R. Bird

This study focuses on multiple masculinities conceptualized in terms of sociality, a concept used to refer to nonsexual interpersonal attractions. Through male homosocial heterosexual interactions, hegemonic masculinity is maintained as the norm to which men are held accountable despite individual conceptualizations of masculinity that depart from that norm. When it is understood among heterosexual men in homosocial circles that masculinity means being emotionally detached and competitive and that masculinity involves viewing women as sexual objects, their daily interactions help perpetuate a system that subordinates femininity and nonhegemonic masculinities. Nonhegemonic masculinities fail to influence structural gender arrangements significantly because their expression is either relegated to heterosocial settings or suppressed entirely.

To understand gender inequality, one must do more than study relations *between* genders. The nature of gender relations is such that asymmetries exist between men and women and among men and among women (Connell 1987, 1992). Recognition of masculinity as a social construct began only a couple of decades ago, and recognition of a power dynamic differentiating "normative" from "non-normative" masculinities began only a few years ago (Kimmel 1990). Investigation of the many possible types of masculinity conceptualizations has been rare (Connell 1987; Kimmel 1990). Connell's (1992) research on homosexual masculinities and their subordination to heterosexual masculinities is a notable exception. As Connell's work demonstrates, delineation of relations among masculinities is important because it facilitates a better understanding of how the structural order of gender is maintained. Hegemonic masculinity, which is "the maintenance of practices that institutionalize men's dominance over women" and is "constructed in relation to women and to subordinate masculinities"

Reprinted by permission from *Gender and Society* 10, no. 2 (April 1996).

(Connell 1987, 185–86), shapes the overall framework of gender relations. By problematizing masculinity, Connell challenges typically undisputed meanings associated with male dominance.

In this study, I focus on how meanings that correspond to hegemonic masculinity are maintained and how meanings that do not correspond to hegemonic masculinity are suppressed. Within the existing gender order, meanings associated with behaviors that challenge hegemonic masculinity are denied legitimation as *masculine;* such meanings are marginalized, if not suppressed entirely. Contradictions to hegemonic masculinity posed by male homosexuality, for example, are suppressed when homosexual masculinity is consistently rendered "effeminate" (Connell 1992).

The maintenance of hegemonic masculinity is explored here through investigation of male homosocial interactions. *Homosociality* refers specifically to the nonsexual attractions held by men (or women) for members of their own sex (Lipman-Blumen 1976). Homosociality, according to Lipman-Blumen, promotes clear distinctions between women and men through segregation in social institutions. I add, further, that homosociality promotes clear distinctions between hegemonic masculinities and nonhegemonic masculinities by the segregation of social groups. *Heterosociality,* a concept left untheorized by Lipman-Blumen, refers to nonsexual attractions held by men (or women) for members of the other sex.

Also critical to this analysis is an investigation of the relationship between sociality and the self-conceptualization of masculinity. As I argue here, homosocial interaction, among heterosexual men, contributes to the maintenance of hegemonic masculinity norms by supporting meanings associated with identities that fit hegemonic ideals while suppressing meanings associated with nonhegemonic masculinity identities. I focus specifically on the connection between individual masculinity and gender norms in small group interactions to capture subtle mechanisms of control. When personal conflicts with ideal masculinity are suppressed both in the homosocial group and by individual men, the cultural imposition of hegemonic masculinity goes uncontested (see Kaufman 1994).

The following meanings are crucial to our understanding of how homosociality contributes to the perpetuation of hegemonic masculinity: (1) *emotional detachment,* a meaning constructed through relationships within families whereby young men detach themselves from mothers and develop gender identities in relation to that which they are not (Chodorow 1978); (2) *competitiveness,* a meaning constructed and maintained through relationships with other men whereby simple individuality becomes competitive individuality (Gilligan 1982); and (3) *sexual objectification of women,* a meaning constructed and maintained through relationships with other men whereby male individuality is conceptualized not only as *different from* female but as *better than* female (Johnson 1988).

Conceptualizing Masculinities

Gender identity is distinguished from the heavily criticized concept of gender *role* in that the latter is used to refer to behavioral expectations associated with more or less static social positions, whereas the former refers to a continual *process* whereby meanings are attributed by and to individuals through social interaction. Gender, in other words, is relational. Gender identity originates in early interactions, becoming more stable through the accumulation of meanings attributed by and to the self over time (see Burke 1980; Burke and Reitzes 1981). Information received through interactions may be used either to reinforce existing self-notions of gender meanings or to weaken them. That is, mere socialization does not sufficiently explain how individuals conceptualize identity. Socialization provides the terms of social interaction but does not determine how individuals incorporate interactional meanings into their own conceptualizations of gender (Connell 1987).

The unique experiences of men, embedded within particular social institutions and subject to varying historical contexts, facilitate conceptualizations of masculinities that may differ considerably. Each male incorporates a variety of meanings into his gender identity, some of which are consistent with hegemonic masculinity and others of which are not (e.g., Connell 1992; Messner 1992b). The social ideal for masculinity, which in itself is a nonstatic notion, may be internalized (i.e., central to one's core self [see Chodorow 1980]) or simply interiorized (i.e., acknowledged by the self), enabling individuals to understand the gender norms to which they are held accountable. In either case, each male comes to understand both socially shared meanings of masculinity and the idiosyncratic meanings that comprise his unique gender identity. Internalization of hegemonic meanings provides a base of shared meanings for social interaction but also quells the expression of nonhegemonic meanings. The presumption that hegemonic masculinity meanings are the only mutually accepted and legitimate masculinity meanings helps to reify hegemonic norms while suppressing meanings that might otherwise create a foundation for the subversion of the existing hegemony. This presumption is especially prevalent in male homosocial interactions, which are critical to both the conceptualization of masculinity identity and the maintenance of gender norms.

Male Homosocial Interactions: Emotional Detachment, Competitiveness, and Sexual Objectification of Women

Three of the shared meanings that are perpetuated via male homosociality are emotional detachment, competition, and the sexual objectification of women. These meanings characterize hegemonic masculinity but are not always internalized as central to individual identity. First, emotional detachment (i.e., withholding expressions of intimacy) maintains both clear individual identity boundaries (Chodorow 1978) and the norms of hegemonic masculinity. To express feelings is to reveal vulnerabilities and weaknesses; to withhold such expressions is to maintain control (Cancian 1987). Second, competition in the male homosocial group supports an identity that depends not on likeness and cooperation but on separation and distinction (Gilligan 1982). Competition facilitates hierarchy in relationships, whereas cooperation suggests symmetry of relationships (Messner 1992a). Finally, the sexual objectification of women facilitates self-conceptualization as positively male by distancing the self from all that is associated with being female. The objectification of women provides a base on which male superiority is maintained (Johnson 1988), whereas identification with women (and what it means to be female) helps remove the symbolic distance that enables men to depersonalize the oppression of women.

Individual conceptualizations vary in the extent to which these meanings characterize one's masculinity. Masculinities that differ from the norm of hegemonic masculinity, however, are generally experienced as "private dissatisfactions" rather than foundations for questioning the social construction of gender (Thomas 1990; see also Kaufman 1994). Hegemonic masculinity persists, therefore, despite individual departures from the hegemonic form.

Method

The data collected for this study were gathered through personal interviews and field observations. Eight in-depth interviews were conducted in the fall of 1992 in a small northwestern city in the United States. Later, additional follow-up interviews were conducted with four new respondents to clarify how male homosocial and heterosexual interactions facilitate the perpetuation of hegemonic masculinity, on the one hand, but suppress nonhegemonic masculinity, on the other.

The men who participated in the interviews for this study were all selected from within the academic community of the city in which the study took place. Responses to questions, therefore, may reflect a level of education higher than that of the general population. The findings of this study, however, are consistent with findings of previous studies regarding the meanings associated with masculinity (e.g., Lehn 1992; Messner 1992a, 1992b; Phillips 1986). The men's educational level ranged from three years of undergraduate study to graduate level and post-Ph.D. The men ranged in age from 23 to 50 years. All but one of the interviewees were native-born Americans from various geographical regions of the country. The other male, a native of East Africa, had maintained residence in the United States for approximately two years before the time of the interview. Although the data received through the interview with this respondent were consistent with accounts offered by the respondents from the United States, this information was excluded from the analysis because of cultural differences that could contribute to misleading conclusions. Most of the men reported middle-class family origins, although three reported working-class backgrounds. Two of the men interviewed were Black, and the other nine were white. All of the men were raised primarily by female caretakers, and all were heterosexual.

The primary focus of the interviews was on the development of perceived consensual masculinity and the corresponding relationship between self-conceptualizations and hegemonic masculinity. Respondents were first asked questions about childhood. Each was asked to describe childhood memories of time spent with playmates, with siblings, and with parents. Responses to these questions provided general information from which more specific inquiries could be made regarding the meanings associated both with masculinity personally (i.e., identity) and with masculinity more generally (i.e., the beliefs, attitudes, and expectations of the group and of society).

To establish the parameters for the discussion during the interviews, each man was asked to consider the kinds of relationships he would find most desirable given non-work-related situations.[1] Each was then prompted to elaborate on his experiences within groups, especially those experiences within the male homosocial group. Although the men varied in how much they desired male homosocial group interaction, each explained that such groups have had a significant impact on their beliefs, attitudes, and behaviors. The men were asked to elaborate on what exactly would be considered appropriate or inappropriate, desirable or undesirable, for conversation among men and what interests were commonly or not commonly shared within their homosocial groups. The topics of sports, women, business, politics, and drinking were most commonly specified as desirable for conversation, while the topics of feelings and gossip were most frequently mentioned as undesirable. Each man was then asked to explain his views on the degree to which his personal interests corresponded to interests more generally shared by the group. I also made inquiries about why certain interests and topics are so prevalent among men in homosocial groups and whether they had experienced any repercussions when norms for male homosocial interaction were disregarded.

Additional data were collected during the fall of 1992 through field observations of male homosocial interactions in small-group contexts. Observations and interviews were conducted within the same academic community, but the men *observed* were not the same as the men *interviewed*. Approximately 25 hours of observations were conducted. The majority of the observations were made at a single location: a deli/bar frequented by men associated with the university but also visited regularly by men not associated with academia. Remaining observations were conducted at two coffee shops and three taverns, all located in the same academic community. The focus of the observations was on the interactions among male customers, including their conversations. Field notes were taken in one- to two-hour time periods at various times of the day and/or night and on various days of the week. Because the locations in which observations were made are consistently patronized by students and university faculty, the recording of observations went unnoticed. A running description was kept of interactions that transpired between men seated within hearing distance of the researcher (usually only a few feet away). Observations were made of groups ranging in size from two to eight men. Observations were also made of groups that were initially all male but were temporarily interrupted by a woman. Most of the conversations were recorded verbatim. Gestures, facial expressions, and the physical location of each group member were also noted.

The meanings described in the interviews and that emerged from the observations have been organized under the following subtopics: (1) emotional detachment, (2) competition, and (3) sexual objectification of women. The remainder of this article focuses on the processes through which these meanings are sustained and the processes through which alternative meanings are suppressed in male homosocial interaction.

Emotional Detachment: "We Were Masculine Little Kids!"

The rules that apply to homosocial friendships and to masculinity are so familiar that they are typically taken for granted by men and women alike. Rarely does anyone (other than the social scientist) seriously question the expectations associated with gender identity or gender norms. Instead, it is assumed that "boys will be boys" and will just naturally do "boy things." By the same token, "men will be men" and will continue to do "men things." Doing men things or "doing masculinity" is simply the commonplace activity of men's daily lives, recreated over and again, maintaining the norms of social behavior (West and Zimmerman 1987).

The men interviewed and those observed explained that being "one of the boys" is a key principle of symbolic and, in some cases, physical separation of "the boys" from "the girls." One man, for example, explained how, as a youngster, he and his pals "were rough and rugged . . . masculine little kids." He said,

> When you're a little boy, you hang out with other little boys and you do little boy things. You know, you burn ants and things like that. You just don't hang out with females because you don't want to be a wuss, you don't play with dolls, you don't whine, you don't cry . . . you do boy things, you know, guy stuff.

Being masculine, in other words, means being not-female. The masculinity ideal involves detachment and independence. The men interviewed indicated that emotions and behaviors typically associated with women were inappropriate within the male homosocial group. Among the emotions and behaviors considered most inappropriate, and most highly stigmatized, were those associated with feminine expressions of intimacy (e.g., talking "feelings"). As one of the men interviewed explained, "I usually talk about 'things' rather than getting into your head and asking, you know, that real intimate stuff."

This suppression of feminine emotions is more than merely a means of establishing individual masculinity. Emotional detachment is one way in which gender hierarchies are maintained. Expressing emotions signifies weakness and is devalued, whereas emotional detachment signifies strength and is valued (Cancian 1987).

In their discussions of feelings, the men hesitated; none of them made consistent use of the word *feelings*. Instead of feelings, they referred to "personal stuff," "those things," and "those matters," and when asked, many indicated that "ultimately you're doing it alone." The expectation is that "because you're going to be in situations where you're away from any support system . . . you're going to have to handle your stuff alone."

What these men explained was that within the male homosocial group, emotional detachment is viewed not only as desirable but as imperative. Those who do express their intimate emotions are excluded. On this point, the interviewees were quite clear: "If I was having a beer with a friend and they started crying, I would suspect that that person, if it were a male . . . I'd suspect that that person didn't have a very good definition of the social situation." If a guy did start crying, this interviewee was asked, where would that put him in relation to other guys? "Hmm, well, since . . . actually that would put him on the outs." The repercussion for violating the hegemonic meaning of emotional detachment, in other words, is to be "put on the outs," that is, to be ostracized from one's male homosocial group. Interviewees explained that violations of the norm of emotional detachment do not result in an alteration of the norm but instead result in the exclusion of the violator (see Schur 1984).

Data collected through observations clearly supported the pattern described by the men interviewed. Emotional detachment was exercised in even the most sensitive of topics. Two men observed, for example, appeared rather matter-of-fact as they discussed the marital problems that one of the men was experiencing: "Think of it this way, ya got a toothache. . . . You've got to have it taken out or you're gonna live with the bitch. Unless you bite the bullet and get the goddamn thing pulled out, you're gonna live with the pain." Feelings, as discussed by these two men, were something to "get over," not to experience—much less express. One man, when questioned about the possible repercussions for expressing feelings in the context of the male homosocial group, explained that feelings are "something for us all to joke about" because

> you certainly don't want to take things too seriously and have to deal with the heavy side, the heavy emotional side to it . . . Tears are a very extreme thing in these male circles, partly because it's messy . . . It has a lot to do with not looking soft and weak because if you do . . . it makes it difficult for men to have relationships with each other.

He explained that "developing emotional types of relationships with each other" is something men stereotypically do not do. Hegemonic masculinity is not expressed and maintained through excessive emotionality. This distinction separates the boys from the girls as well as the men who fit the hegemonic norm from those who do not. Through emotional detachment, the meanings formed in regard to masculinity are exaggerated so as to distinguish clearly that which all men are not, that is, female. The burden for demonstrating difference is on those trying to avoid the default meanings. Difference becomes an aspect of self in which men have a valued investment.

Departures from the norm of emotional detachment, however, do exist. Individual departures reflect an understanding of the dominant meanings but not necessarily an incorporation of them into one's self-concept. One man explained that although most men "do what the culture says and hide it" (i.e., hide their feelings), he had hoped to be able to express his feelings with other men: "A couple of times when I was hurting, uhm, I did kind of seek out a couple of male friends and I was really disappointed. . . . It was like they were embarrassed, you know, to talk about that shit, and so, uh, fuck it!" Five of the men who participated in the in-depth interviews and three of the four who participated in the follow-up interviews expressed discrepancies between hegemonic masculinity and their own masculinity. Each explained that although they knew they were *supposed* to separate themselves from things considered feminine, they did not assess their own identities to be as polarized as the hegemonic form would suggest.

> It was really unfortunate. As I grew older, I really wished that I wasn't so detached from my mom. I'm not that way now, though. After a while, I stopped caring about what everybody else thought. I mean, the intimate side got pushed aside for so long because that's not what "real" men are supposed to do. I got over it, though . . . I guess I'm not what "real" men are supposed to be.

The degree to which the masculinity meanings individuals hold for themselves correspond to the meanings of hegemonic masculinity may vary over time and from person to person. The point, however, is that although individual conceptualizations of masculinity depart from the hegemonic norm, nonhegemonic meanings are suppressed due to perceptions of "appropriate" masculinity. Even in a community where notions of the "new man" are common and where antisexist attitudes are often expected, hegemonic patterns of masculinity prevail. One whose masculinity conceptualization is nonhegemonic still understands himself as "not what 'real' men are *supposed* to be" (emphasis added).

The men who made the distinction between self-masculinity and hegemonic masculinity made three things clear. First, they explained that hegemonic masculinity was the form that prevailed in their interactions with other men throughout childhood and adolescence. Second, they asserted that when they found themselves in homosocial situations in the present, the expectation of emotional detachment continued to prevail. Third, they described themselves in the present as more heterosocially than homosocially oriented. These men explained that they did not prefer exclusively male social interaction groups. In sum, homosocial and heterosocial masculinity meanings are clearly differentiated. For these men, homosocial masculinity was characterized by emotional detachment, whereas heterosocial masculinity downplayed these factors.

Competition: "It's a Pecking Order Between Males"

Competition with other men provides a stage for establishing self both as an individual and as appropriately masculine. Competition also contributes to the perpetuation of male dominance. When asked to explain what competition meant to him, one interviewee replied,

> By nature I'm terribly competitive. I suppose one's ego gets wrapped around the things that you do. Its pretty important for me to win because I do have my ego wrapped up in that [games] and so, uhm, you know when I play a game at a party or whatever I kind of expect to win and play pretty fiercely.

To establish self as not female, young men seek out other men with whom to display "non-femaleness" (Johnson 1988). Homosocial group interactions provide feedback and support for masculinity self-conceptualization. In this sense, masculinity conceptualization is itself a form of competition. Four men described competition as a critical part of their self-conceptualizations and stressed that the competitions they preferred were those with men. Men, they believed, could understand the intensity and importance of competition, whereas women seemed less accepting and less understanding. When asked about participating in athletics with women, one interviewee responded that "women start getting angry at you and it gets ugly" when "you start getting really intense." Another added that "women typically don't want to play [basketball] or sort of want to but feel they'll be intimidated or whatever."

The men who described themselves as less competitive (or noncompetitive), on the other hand, explained that they considered the intensity with which other men engaged in competitions (especially sports) as relatively unimportant for themselves. At the same time, however, these men recognized the *expectations* of masculinity to be competitive. One man explained,

> Guys don't know what it means not to be competitive. Even those men who tell you that competition is silly know they have to [compete]. It's like otherwise you're gonna get walked on. Nobody appreciates that. I'm not as aggressive as most guys, but I can sure act it.

Again, the norms and expectations of hegemonic masculinity and individual conceptualizations do not necessarily fit; further, among the less competitive men, nonhegemonic masculinity and hegemonic masculinity meanings differ by sociality. Men whose conceptualizations of masculinity were nonhegemonic specified their lack of preference for homosocial interactions in both sporting and nonsporting activities. Men whose conceptualizations of masculinity were consistent with the hegemonic form specified a clear preference for homosocial interactions in sports. Homosociality corresponded with a focus on competitiveness, whereas heterosociality deemphasized competition. Homosocial and heterosocial meanings were clearly differentiated. In male homosocial groups, a man risks loss of status and self-esteem unless he competes. The meaning of competition is assumed under male homosocial circumstances, and violators of this norm are disadvantaged.

Sexual Objectification: "You Know, Women Were 'Othered' Early"

The competitions that support hegemonic masculinity continue throughout life in a variety of forms. Among the forms of competitions in which men engage are those that involve the objectification of women. Men often compete with one another in efforts to gain the attention and affections of women and in boasting about their sexual exploits. Observations revealed numerous stories about sexual objectification of women. In male homosocial conversations, references were made to women as "them," as clearly "other," as the nonthreatening "girl," and/or as objects to be used for sexual pleasure. While the use of these terms may or may not imply a conscious effort on the part of the speaker to objectify, they promote meanings that support hegemonic masculinity nonetheless.

The men not only explicated the objectification of women, they also explained and demonstrated the competition for objectified women. These competitions illustrate the interconnectedness of the meanings of emotional detachment, competition, and objectification. Conversations overheard at the deli/lounge, for example, shifted frequently from "shop talk" to competitive sex talk. Bantering sessions, in which one-upsmanship on stories of sexual exploits was the name of the game, were frequently overheard. For example, one man began,

> I've run across those kind. . . . I'll tell 'em, "I'll buy ya a beer." [And the hypothetical woman replies,] "Na, I'll buy you a beer." Then I'm thinkin' she's ready to get outa there with me. I just want one I can step out with, shoot up her, and get back in the bar in 5 or 10 minutes.

Another man then added his own story:

> Aw, shit, I had one down near Vegas. . . . Well, to make a long story short, when it was time to hit the rack we went back to her room. . . . We found a bucket of ice and a bottle of liquor at the door with a note from some other guy attached to it. . . . I just went ahead and drank the stuff and screwed her!

Not to be outdone, the remaining participant in the discussion followed with an account of his own:

> Yeah, one night I had a couple of beers, then went out to that country and western bar. . . . She was a bartender there. I'm tellin' ya, she was hanging all over me so much that the other bartender had to get on to her. Then later, she came knockin' on my trailer door. I thought, "What the hell, Judy won't find out, let's hop to it." She was a wicked thing.

Such conversations, according to the men interviewed, occur frequently but are less likely to be carried out with verbal explicitness when a woman or women actually join the interaction.

In this case, the conversation will likely shift; but, as my interviewees explained, the competition will continue. The question, "What happens if a woman enters the scene where you are engaging in a conversation with another man or men? prompted the following response: "Weird. Weird setup . . . because everybody is checking everybody else out. . . it's uncomfortable for everybody. You know, people are checking each other out. We'd see her as an issue of conquest." The men interviewed explained that men in homosocial groups both objectify and compete for women. When asked to describe the nature of interactions between men when an "available" woman is present among the group, one man explained, "It's competitive, you see, and it's a pecking order between men. If you do not peck, you get pecked. And so, one of the things over which there is a great deal of pecking is women."

To be "pecked" is an undesirable experience—to be avoided if a man wishes to maintain status within the male homosocial group. Objectification of women and men's competitiveness over objectified women constitute the very essence of what hegemonic masculinity means in this society (Connell 1992). Not all men view themselves in accordance with hegemonic masculinity, however, when it comes to objectifying women. Even so, men often go along with hegemonic norms to avoid being pecked. All of the men interviewed, when asked how an individual man avoids being pecked by other members of the group, explained that, on the one hand, they knew what the rules of the game were because

there's always an assessment going on in the group. Always. . . . Some guys will go along but wouldn't make a degrading comment about women themselves. But when some guy says something, because you want to be a member of the group, it becomes, "Yeah." You follow the lead.

Some men argued, however, that these hegemonic rules did not fit their own identities:

That stuff [sexual objectification of women] doesn't interest me terribly much because for the most part I don't really talk about those things and I don't hang out with men who do. It's a very nasty type of chat, and the goal seems to be to hurt somebody anyway.

Although the rules of hegemonic masculinity included sexual objectification, some individual conceptualizations minimized and/or disregarded its importance. Even among those men who rejected hegemonic masculinity for themselves, however, the hegemonic norm for sexual objectification prevailed in male homosocial groups. In fact, none of the men in the study, for example, mentioned ever verbally rejecting these hegemonic meanings in their all-male groups. The meanings of emotional detachment, competitiveness, and sexual objectification all were understood and behaviorally followed. Hegemonic masculinity was maintained despite individual departures from the norm, as individual departures were suppressed in homosocial settings. Nonhegemonic masculinity was subordinated through relegation to heterosocial settings. Emotional detachment, competitiveness, and the sexual objectification of women remained as the criteria to which men are held accountable, especially in all-male interactions.

Conclusions: Hegemonic Masculinity and the Gender Order

Hegemonic masculinity is consistently and continually recreated despite individual conceptualizations that contradict hegemonic meanings. Violations of the norms of hegemonic masculinity typically fail to produce alterations in the gender order; instead, they result in penalties to violators. With particular attention to the meanings that help sustain a pecking order among men, I have outlined some of the processes that pose barriers to gender equality in the United States, that is, the devaluation of meanings considered feminine, the suppression of these meanings in male heterosexual homosocial settings, and the relegation of non-hegemonic masculinity to heterosocial settings. Hegemonic masculinity, as demonstrated here, prevailed even in an academic community where ideals of gender equality are generally promoted. Reification of existing gender arrangements continues despite individual conflicts with hegemonic masculinity. The contradictions that nonhegemonic masculinity meanings (e.g., expression of intimate emotions, cooperation, and identification with women) potentially pose to dominant masculinity patterns are suppressed in male homosocial heterosexual interactions, inhibiting change. When individual departures from dominant masculinity are experienced as private dissatisfactions rather than as reason for contesting the social construction of masculinity, hegemonic patterns persist.

Because the barriers that distinguish appropriate from inappropriate masculinity generally are not accomplished through reconceptualization of individual masculinity alone, recasting the gender order in more favorable terms must also involve changes instigated at levels of social organization beyond that of social interaction. Subversion of widely accepted gender beliefs, attitudes, and expectations requires special attention to the processes that facilitate their *institutionalization*. That which must be continually challenged and ultimately eradicated in terms of masculinity, therefore, is the taken-for-granted assumption that being male means being emotionally detached, competitive, and supportive of the sexual objectification of women as well as the assumption that men whose identities do not embody these meanings are not true men. These changes must take place not only within heterosocial contexts but also within homosocial contexts and throughout all social institutions. In even broader terms, the goal yet to be accomplished is the *degenderization* of meanings. In other words, emotional detachment, competitiveness, and the sexual objectification of women must cease to exist as criteria by which being a man is measured. Indeed, the beliefs, attitudes, and expectations that decree the valuation and/or devaluation of distinctive masculine and feminine meanings in the first place must be deconstructed.

Author's Note: An earlier version of this article was presented at the 1993 annual meeting of the Pacific Sociological Association, Portland, OR. I thank Leslie Atkins, Kendal Broad, Peter Burke, Valerie Jenness, Lisa McIntyre, Margaret Andersen, Miriam Johnson, R. W. Connell, the reviewers at Gender & Society, and especially Lisa Broidy, Tim McGettigan, and Amy Wharton for their helpful criticisms and advice. Special thanks also to the men interviewed for this study.

Reprint Requests: Sharon R. Bird, Department of Sociology, Washington State University, Pullman, WA 99164-4020.

Note

1. Leisure situations, rather than work-related situations, were focused on to specifically highlight social interaction preferences.

References

Burke, Peter J. 1980. The self: Measurement requirements from an interactionist perspective. *Social Psychology Quarterly* 43:18–29.

Burke, Peter J., and Donald C. Reitzes. 1981. The link between identity and role performance. *Social Psychology Quarterly* 44:33–92.

Cancian, Francesca M. 1987. *Love in America: Gender and self-development.* Cambridge, UK: Cambridge University Press.

Chodorow, Nancy. 1978. *The reproduction of mothering.* Berkeley: University of California Press.

———. 1980. Gender, relation, and difference in psychoanalytic perspective. In *The future of difference,* edited by Hester Eisenstein and Alice Jardine. Boston: G. K. Hall.

Connell, R. W. 1987. *Gender and power: Society, the person, and sexual politics.* Stanford, CA: Stanford University Press.

———. 1992. A very straight gay: Masculinity, homosexual experience, and the dynamics of gender. *American Sociological Review* 57:735–51.

Gilligan, Carol. 1982. *In a different voice: Psychological theory and women's development.* Cambridge, MA: Harvard University Press.

Johnson, Miriam. 1988. *Strong mothers, weak wives.* Berkeley: University of California Press.

Kaufman, Michael. 1994. Men, feminism, and men's contradictory experiences of power. In *Theorizing masculinities,* edited by Harry Brod and Michael Kaufman. Thousand Oaks, CA: Sage.

Kimmel, Michael S. 1990. After fifteen years: The impact of the sociology of masculinity on the masculinity of sociology. In *Men, masculinities, and social theory,* edited by Jeff Hearn and David Morgan. London: Unwin Hyman.

Lehn, Gregory K. 1992. Homophobia among men: Supporting and defining the male role. In *Men's lives,* edited by Michael S. Kimmel and Michael A. Messner. New York: Macmillan.

Lipman-Blumen, Jean. 1976. Toward a homosocial theory of sex roles: An explanation of the sex segregation of social institutions. *Signs: Journal of Women and Culture and Society* 1:15–3 1.

Messner, Michael A. 1992a. Boyhood, organized sports, and the construction of masculinity. In *Men's lives,* edited by Michael S. Kimmel and Michael A. Messner. New York: Macmillan.

———. 1992b. *Power at play: Sports and the problem of masculinity.* Boston: Beacon.

Phillips, Gerald M. 1986. Men talking to men about their relationships. *American Behavioral Scientist* 29:321–41.

Schur, Edwin M. 1984. *Labeling women deviant: Gender; stigma, and social control.* New York: Random House.

Thomas, Alison. 1990. The significance of gender politics in men's accounts of their "gender identity." In *Men, masculinities, and social theory,* edited by Jeff Hearn and David Morgan. London: Unwin Hyman.

West, Candace, and Don H. Zimmerman. 1987. Doing gender. *Gender & Society* 1:125–51.

17

To Commend or To Critique?: The Question of Religion and Film Studies

John Lyden

Abstract

This paper examines two approaches to popular film to come out of religious studies. The first assumes popular culture is as valid as any culture, in which case "religious" analysis of films seeks to identify the iconography and mythology of film as expressive of a viable popular religion. The second method critiques popular film as a form of hegemonic discourse to be unmasked as supportive of classist, racist, and sexist ideologies. This paper accepts the validity of both methods and seeks to balance them by asserting that all films should be seen both as viable expressions of culture and also as ideology. Films are both to the extent that all contain multiple "texts" and multiple meanings, held together in an aporial and not entirely rational fusion. We do not need to decide which meaning is fundamental, as all are present in the film.

Article

The study of film from a religious studies vantage point has produced a broad consensus. Films include religious symbolism, consciously or unconsciously, and films may project a world-view which functions much like a religion in our culture.

Films are a creation and a reflection of the popular culture which produces and sustains them. They support this culture through creating myths, icons, and values which are celebrated and reinforced in a ritualized fashion. A variety of methods are used by religious scholars to study films. There are representative of the range of methods available within film studies generally: semiotics, textual or formalistic studies, psychoanalytic methods, ideological or political critiques, reader-response theories, genre and auteur studies, and so on.

There is a fundamental tension, however, between two basic approaches to the study of film as exemplative of a popular religious tradition. On the one hand, popular culture may be accepted as a culture which is as valid as any other, and which expresses its own values through media such as film. Even though the films are not produced by the people but by a technological industry, they are produced for the people and (in part) out of response to what people believe in and hope

Reprinted by permission from *Journal of Religion and Film* 1, no. 2 (October 1997).

for. An analysis of their religious impact will then seek to identify the mythology of popular film with the purpose of establishing how it contributes to the religion of popular culture, and will often (at least implicitly) celebrate the values expressed by this mythology.

On the other hand, the opposed method views films' presentation of popular culture and its religious aspects with great suspicion. The films are defined as a form of hegemonic discourse which ultimately supports the status quo of classist, racist, and sexist ideologies (to name the most significant). In this case, popular film is to be unmasked as this hegemonic discourse and deconstructed in order to reveal how it influences our society in negative ways. This method has been shaped by liberationist and feminist approaches to culture and religion.

Of course, this typology presents an oversimplification (as all typologies do), as there will be few interpreters of film who rigidly conform to either model. Most will "commend" the values of some films, and "critique" those of others. After all, like everybody else, religion scholars are prone to disagree about what constitutes a "good" or a "bad" movie. But my point here is that one's methodological assumptions may at the outset give one a bias either for or against popular film. As a result, one may either uncritically accept the values of the culture (arguing that they are as valid as any other), or uncritically reject those same values (arguing that nothing good can come out of Hollywood). And I do not think that one can avoid this question by claiming to bracket value judgments while one examines popular culture, as one's values will still affect how one views the phenomenon, implicitly or otherwise.

There is a parallel here with the study of non-Christian religions by western Christian scholars of religion. It is only recently that western theologians and historians of religion have been able to enter into genuine dialogue with other religions, listening to what they are saying rather than uncritically rejecting their views or uncritically accepting them (usually without really understanding them, in either case). I would argue that the study of popular film by religion scholars is at a similar place, as it is only very recently that they have begun to seriously examine how the whole range of popular films function, religiously and culturally. And yet the question still lurks in the background as to whether this popular filmic religion should be accepted in tolerance or torn down like an idol.

Many have tended towards the latter view; but I will argue it is too easy to condemn without analyzing the texts of popular film, and perhaps there is something to commend in them even as we critique them. I will argue that it is possible to balance the two approaches insofar as the films themselves can be considered both forms of viable religion, and ideology. We do not need to decide which "meaning" is fundamental, as many may exist in the same film in an aporial and not entirely rational fusion.

First let us examine those who "commend" popular film. In this view, one seeks to appreciate the values of popular film as a valid expression of the culture they mirror. As Catherine Albanese has observed in regard to the study of religion and American popular culture in general, no American scholar of popular culture can exist outside of the culture she or he describes, and so there are no "Olympian heights," of superior knowledge or taste, to which one might escape to level value judgments on the culture.[1] There is really no way to "bracket" value-judgments regarding one's own culture, so that the scholar (as participant/observer of it) will probably at least tacitly accept its values—unless he or she consciously rejects them.

In regard to the study of film, religious scholars have accepted some of what films do for the culture, as they have experienced some sense of the power of the movies to convey a distinctive religious vision of the world. Thus Darrol Bryant writes that "the profoundly spiritual significance of film lies not so much in content or subject matter as in our experience of the film itself—an experience of order and harmony that stands in counterpoint to our experience of the everyday world.[2]

Michael Bird has said that a film can be a "hierophany," a manifestation of the sacred in our midst, drawing on Paul Tillich's view of culture as "open" to the transcendent which it may symbolically reflect.[3] Even the earlier studies which were primarily interested in connections with Christianity mirrored this appreciation of the religious power of film. In 1970, Carl

Skrade wrote that "contemporary film-makers force their audiences not only to examine the structures of destruction and peer into the depths of the human predicament, but they also offer filmic forms of symbols of renewal."[4]

Recent studies of religion and film also evidence this approach. In *New Image of Religious Film*, editor John May notes that in viewing popular films as being worthy of theological consideration, the essays in the book acknowledge but regret the tendency of many theologians to "distrust" popular film. May, in contrast, argues that popular culture should be considered an "ally in the process of evangelization."[5] Further, the predominantly Roman Catholic authors in May's volume see film as expressing the sense of mystery and of the sacred to the modern world in an especially effective way. For example, Joseph Marty here claims that "cinema awakens *homo religious*" because

> *"It brings back to life the sense of mystery by making us love what is not immediately perceivable, what is beyond appearance and evidence. It suggests the invisible . . . Thus, cinema binds us again with the poetic and religious expression of humanity . . . Everything that is human, every relationship to the world and to nature, treated artistically by the cinema becomes a poem, a tale, a re-reading, a proposal of meaning, a celebration—in short, something that resembles a first religious step."[6]*

Another example of a collection of essays which includes some that "commend" the religious aspects of popular films is *Screening the Sacred: Religion, Myth, and Ideology in Popular American Film*, edited by Joel Martin and Conrad Ostwalt. In this volume there are a number of articles which indicate some appreciation for the "mythologies" of popular film. Thus Avent Childress Beck writes of *Platoon* that the film is: "a mythic reinvent of the war that displaces grand historical statement on the involvement of the United States with an assertion instead of the primacy of an individual's or a small group's religious or psychological experience of the war" so that "in dark theaters, we are treated to the balms of religious myth; in the case of *Platoon*, to the ordered familiarities and emotive comfort of the Christian narrative."[7]

Similarly, in the same volume, Caron Schwartz Ellis writes in regard to Science Fiction films which feature "saviors" from the sky that "our spacemen are important to us. They give us hope in a world in which our vision of the stars is obscured by pollution and the potential for nuclear holocaust."[8] And Andrew Gordon's essay, written in 1978, analyzes the mythological form of *Star Wars* (which George Lucas developed out of Joseph Campbell's work) and so argues that the film is a "myth for our times." He then concludes:

"The fact is that each generation must create its own myths and heroes or regenerate those of the past. We are in a period in which the heroes have been cast down through such national catastrophes as Vietnam and Watergate, when the lines between good and evil grow cloudy, and when sexual identities have been redefined by the women's movement. Meanwhile, we have created a machine world for ourselves, a world that seems drained of spiritual values, a world in which we feel impotent and alien. We desperately need a renewal of faith in ourselves as Americans, as good guys on the world scene, as men and women, as human beings who count, and so we return to the simpler patterns of the past."[9]

It is Gordon's remarks in particular which show the problematic nature of this sort of analysis. In being ready to applaud the fact that the film makes the viewer "feel good," he has concluded it is valuable precisely because it offers an easy dualism between good and evil, so avoiding the ambiguity of world politics and feminism. Americans fall into this sort of dualism easily enough in any case. Should one commend those films which encourage in our "popular culture" a dualistic attitude of "us versus them"? Are such films flawed in seeking to avoid any challenge to our hegemonic structures? It can be asked whether *Star Wars* really does this (or whether it only does this), but the question here is, are the values Gordon cites really the sort one should uncritically accept as an aspect of popular film?

This question leads to the other type of approach to the values of popular films, and it is probably the more common among scholars of religion. Drawing on liberationist and feminist critiques of hegemonic discourse, religious scholars trained in these approaches have viewed popular American films as a prime example of that which secures and perpetuates ideology in America. As scholars of religion, they have been able to identify the theological or mythological forms used to secure this ideology. This approach has also been able to draw on much in film studies proper, as ideological critique of popular film is a well-established method in that field. Again from *Screening the Sacred*, Joel Martin's treatment of *Rocky* engages in this sort of analysis by viewing the film as one which scapegoats blacks as the cause of America's economic problems. The film appealed to white working-class Americans precisely because it engages in this sort of racism which "aggressively and ideologically reinterprets recent history.[10] Similarly, Janice Hocker Rushing interprets *Aliens* as an antifeminist film which pits the "Good Mother/goddess" against the "Bad Mother/monster/goddess" and so reaffirms conservative visions of femininity which have bifurcated the feminine consciousness and so stigmatized certain types of women who do not accept their "proper" role in the patriarchy.[11]

Brandon Scott has also critiqued the ideology of popular films in his book *Hollywood Dreams and Biblical Stories*. His method is to establish a dialogue between the Bible and popular film and so he juxtaposes texts from both "canons" in regard to particular themes (e.g., gender, war, apocalyptic, etc.). He shows that the mythology transmitted by popular film works to legitimate (for example) violence and revenge (in the *Dirty Harry* films),[12] racism (in *The Birth of a Nation* and *Gone with the Wind*),[13] and female embeddedness (in *Mr. Mom* and *Fatal Attraction*).[14] In this sense, mythology functions as ideology, as it reinforces cultural hegemonies by suppressing conflict through an overarching narrative structure. Here Scott is drawing on the work of Roland Barthes (as expressed in his book, *Mythologies*,[15] which has influenced numerous film theorists). Scott also cites Claude Levi-Strauss' understanding of myth, which lies behind Barthes' application of the notion to popular culture. In Levi-Strauss' view, cited by Scott, "the purpose of myth is to provide a logical model capable of overcoming contradiction (an impossible achievement if, as it happens, the contradiction is real)."[16] We use myths to hide contradictions in the beliefs of our societies. As film genre analysis sees it, the film western, for example, mediates the contradiction between civilization and savagery in American society. That is, we approve of violence in our need to keep order. But the contradiction is overcome in film when the violence is evacuated from civilization after its occurrence: hence the need for the hero to leave after he saves the family in *Shane*, *The Searchers*, and innumerable other westerns.[17]

Although myth may be the dominant form in popular film, Scott also recognizes that popular films sometimes challenge and even subvert the myths of society. For example, he analyzes *Bronco Billy* as a myth-subverting western,[18] and *Private Benjamin* as a film which attacks the myth of female embeddedness[19]—though one might note that it does so by reinforcing myths about the military. John May has also noted that non-mythological films exist, and he draws a parallel between these and the form of parable (drawing on John Dominic Crossan's work), in that such films do not reassure us but challenge us to change our world-view.[20] He cites the work of Kubrick and Altman as examples of this form of parabolic cinema.[21]

Margaret Miles, in her book, *Seeing and Believing: Religion and Values in the Movies*, evidences yet another approach by a scholar of religious studies. She utilizes a cultural studies (rather than a textual-based) approach to assess the values projected by films within the socio-politico-cultural matrix in which the film is produced, distributed, and seen.[22] In doing so she seeks to avoid the automatic rejection of the values of the movies (which so often is the approach of conservative religion) as well as some of the assumptions of some ideological critics.[23] And yet, even though she claims she wishes to avoid "cultural pessimism,[24] her analysis draws considerably on ideological criticism in its rejection of the values of popular film. Out of all the films evaluated in her book, Miles seems able to approve the values only of one: *Daughters of the Dust* (1992).[25] And this one is hardly typical of popular films as it was an independent film made by an African-American woman.

Even films such as *Jesus of Montreal, Thelma and Louise,* and *Jungle Fever,* which could all be seen as challenging hegemonic structures, finally end up in Miles' analysis as films which make white males comfortable and do not deliver on the challenges they begin.[26] In her analysis, the cultural context in which such films are produced and received, as well as the content of the film images, disqualify them from being legitimate sources of values. "The many choices made in the production of a film," she writes in conclusion, "often undercut the radical topic filmmakers intended to present sympathetically," thus indicating the "profound conservativism" of Hollywood films.[27] The main value of popular films therefore lies merely in their ability to articulate the problems and anxieties of society, not to provide solutions.[28]

Miles' tendency to reject the values of almost all popular films and to embrace mainly independent films made outside the Hollywood system also mirrors a tendency of ideological criticism. Popular films tend to be lumped together as ideological, largely due to the fact that they are created by a major American capitalist industry which is more interested in profit and producing pleasing fantasies than in making challenging and subversive art films. This judgment can be traced to the analysis of "mass culture" developed by Theodor Adorno and Max Horkheimer, German intellectuals of the Frankfurt School who fled Nazi Germany only to come to Hollywood. Ready to see the seeds of totalitarianism everywhere, they viewed all Hollywood films as commodities of capitalism which injected their ideologies into passive audiences, discouraging thought or questioning of authority. In fact, Adorno and Horkheimer viewed all popular films as having basically the same plot and the same characters, as mass production eliminated any significant artistic individuality of the filmmakers.[29] The only films which could be viewed as legitimate were avant-garde art films made outside the Hollywood system, as these did not participate in its decadence but could critique it.

In spite of the fact that the study of film has developed beyond Adorno and Horkheimer's analyses, many film theorists have been unable to shake their view that popular film is by nature ideological and that only avant-garde cinema has value.[30] But Pierre Bourdieu has argued that this denigration of popular film is just another form of elitism, as cultural elites reject the taste of the "masses" in order to defend their own tastes, and hence secure their own cultural hegemony as the supposedly "legitimate" evaluators of culture.[31]

Besides being a not-too-subtle form of classism, this dualism between "popular" and "avant-garde" over-generalized about the content of films. If one is to evaluate popular film fairly, one cannot force a monolithic judgment on it without reference to individual films. Sometimes ideological film analysts are so certain of the content of the films they are discussing that they utilize a priori categories of interpretation which are in principle non-falsifiable and ignore details of the individual films; e.g., in Barbara Creed's psychoanalytic feminist analysis, all movie monsters are symbols of the feminine (because the female is defined as "monstrous" by our culture), even when the monsters are literally male in the film narrative.[32] This sort of analysis has determined what the film has said before ever examining the text, and so has identified all popular film with ideology rather than letting popular films speak for themselves.

This is not to say that all ideological film critics over-generalize in this way, nor to suggest that the religion scholars cited here have necessarily done so in every case. Rather, my purpose is to point out the danger present in ideological criticism if it is the primary method of interpretation. Just as Andrew Gordon's mythological analysis of *Star Wars* (see fn. 9, above) demonstrates the dangers of uncritical acceptance of the visions of popular film, so ideological critique may fall into an uncritical rejection of the worldview of popular film. Many interpreters have engaged in forms of both types of methods, and so have balanced them; but what principles should determine when one method is employed, and when the other? What criteria found in the films themselves might assist us in deciding whether to make peace or war on a particular film? Is it all just a matter of "taste" based on idiosyncrasies of our own worldviews, or are there principles that can guide the religious interpreter of film in regard to this question?

I would suggest that another look at the idea of "myth" may help solve this puzzle. Although mythology has been identified with ideology by some (e.g. Roland Barthes), even in following Levi-Strauss's basic definition of myth one need not conflate mythology with the original Marxist sense of ideology (as that which maintains hegemony). Myth holds together contradictions that cannot be mediated logically, but those contradictions are not always or merely accepted in order to conserve hegemonic structures. The Christian myth of the atonement holds together the aporia of a just-yet-loving God. How can God avoid sanctioning sin, and yet forgive it? The myth of God's Son dying for our sins is designed to overcome this aporia, but it does not do so in an entirely rational way. Though Anselm and others have tried to reduce the myth to a series of logical axioms, the effort has never been fully successful; one cannot logically explain how one person's death can pay for another's sins. There is something irreducible about the myth, the narrative of the story itself, which does not allow itself to be fully "explained" by any doctrine. Hence there has been no "authoritative" doctrine of the atonement in the history of Christian thought, and rival views have stood side by side.[33] This could be said of all religious myths, and the newer narrative theologies would support this non-rational mythological core of religion as essential to its nature. Indeed, it has been observed that there is something about classical narrative itself which contains a contradiction, as it seeks to resolve a conflict and so "end"—but in reality, there would be no end, as more events would transpire after the story finishes, upsetting the neat conclusion.[34]

All narrative then asserts a myth of wholeness which does not jar with our experiences in life. However, this does not in itself imply the reinforcement of hegemonic power structures; it only shows that we need the illusion of myth to make sense of our lives, which do not conform to the neatness of narrative. Myths can then exercise a positive function for societies by giving us a meaningful structure to live by, hopes to aspire to, ideas to believe in. *Star Wars*, for example, is not merely a movie that reinforces ideological dualism. It promotes a cosmic confidence in reality as governed by a higher power in which we can share, in spite of evidence to the contrary. Myths seek to reconcile the disparities and contradictions in our experience not by eliminating them, but by holding them together in a paradoxical and non-rationalizable fusion. And although myths may be inherently conservative of culture, cultures do need conserving and not simply critiquing.

Of course, there are times when popular film critiques itself, at least to some extent (as Scott and others have observed). At this level, the myth exposes some of its own aporial nature, even though this is usually suppressed by the end of the film. Still, in raising questions about itself, the myth grows and develops to incorporate the changing values of society. This also serves to conserve society (which myths do best) but in this case by allowing the myth to stretch with society as it seeks to develop its values. In this way, films of the 50's and 60's began to critique racism, even though the issues were dealt with in a carefully controlled fashion. For example, the harmonious liberal vision of interracial romance expressed in Stanley Kramer's *Guess Who's Coming to Dinner* (1967) is a far cry from the critique of the same in Spike Lee's *Jungle Fever* (1991), as Kramer's vision belittles racial tension through the myth of integration and assimilation. Yet Kramer's vision is also equally far from the overtly racist depiction of predatory black men attacking chaste white women in D. W. Griffith's *The Birth of a Nation* (1915). The values of films develop as society develops, and they reflect and encourage that development.

Affirming the importance of film as myth, however, should not erase the need to see film as ideology. In reality, films are both. As films already contain contradictory messages within them—as they both support and subvert established structures, or conserve society's values even while they critique them—so also the multiple texts within a film may be seen as conserving and developing society's values in a valid way, as well as illegitimately preserving power structures which ought to be dismantled. I would borrow a concept from my own Lutheran theological background to elucidate this, that of the Christian as "simul justus et peccator." According to this idea, the Christian has been justified by God even as and while a sinner, and so can be a subject and vehicle of God's grace in spite of human imperfection. Similarly, popular films may act as windows to transcendence which express messages seen as valuable by those of us in religious studies, as they open us to new visions or reassert what is valid in old ones—and films may also support class, race, and gender structures which deserve deconstruction. They may do both simultaneously, even within the same film, so that it is not a question of dichotomizing "good" vs. "bad" films, or "popular" vs. "avant-garde." The same film can convey both sorts of messages, and although some readers will be more sensitive to one than the other, neither can be discounted as present.

This does not mean all films are created equal. We may regard some as more or less valid than others. But we need at least to accept the possibility that any film can convey valid messages even while it contributes to ideology. And the presence of ideological content in a film does not somehow invalidate what the film might be said legitimately to accomplish as mythology of a popular religion which preserves values of society at least some of us might commend. Both the myth and the ideology are present in the film, and neither can be regarded as "the" fundamental meaning.

In evaluating a popular film, then, we should look at the ways in which it may provide not only an ideology, but a mythology which can provide the basis for meaningful life and action—in spite of, or even (like religion?) perhaps because of, its illusionism and idealism.

18

The Attack on "Jewish Hollywood": A Chapter in the History of Modern American Anti-Semitism

Harold David Brackman

As the United States became a magnet for mass Jewish emigration from Eastern Europe, the imprecation was born: "New York is not America." A continent away, with the advent of the movies a few decades later, the coda was added: "Neither is Hollywood." In tandem with the entry of emancipated Jews into the mainstream of modernity, traditional anti-Semitic images of Jews as economic parasites and moral polluters were complemented by a new image of Jews as corrupters of popular culture. First, in the nineteenth century, the new popular journalism was anointed as what Sander Gilman calls the "the secret language of the Jews." Then, in the twentieth century, the cinema supplanted the newspaper in the popular imagination as the magical source of the Jews' insidious power over culture. The Nazi purge of the Weimar film industry, deemed corrupted by "Jewish-Syrian influence"; Stalin's persecution of Yiddish filmmakers, pilloried for "the bourgeois cosmopolitanism in the motion picture arts," and Jewish performers, whose "Semitic features are blatantly obvious in close-ups"; and the more recent Muslim Fundamentalist assault on "satanic" American moviemakers, who are viewed as modern-day, secular "Crusaders" out to destroy Islamic culture as well as to promote Zionism—all are variations on the same theme. So, too, is America's own attack on "Jewish Hollywood."[1]

A vituperative ethnocultural critique of alleged Jewish domination and degradation of the entertainment industry has been a constant on the modern American scene. As we shall see, however, this attack on Jewish Hollywood has ebbed and flowed and evolved significantly over time. It began predominantly among old-stock white Protestants as a right-wing reflex that targeted African Americans as well as Jews. But in recent decades it has mutated increasingly among white leftists and black radicals into an enthusiasm that symptomizes deepening Black-Jewish estrangement.

The first of three waves of anti-Semitic-tinged animus against the film industry peaked in the 1920s. Virtually all European observers have viewed the Hollywood "dream factory" as quintessentially Ameri-

Reprinted from *Modern Judaism* 20, no. 1 (Feb. 2000), by permission of Oxford University Press.

can since its inception. But this is not the way it looked early in this century to culturally conservative Americans. They saw instead a nightmarish undermining of Victorian religious, racial, and sexual hierarchies. In their vision of American decline, white Anglo-Saxon Protestants were victims of typically Jewish popular-cultural entrepreneurs. Not least among the perceived sins of these Jewish entertainment merchants was their responsibility for unleashing libidinal impulses imagined as synonymous with African Americans. After World War I, former Progressives fearful that the movies were corrupting American youth shared anxieties with Ku Klux Klansmen who equated Jewish producers with big-city brothel owners. Ironically, American Catholics demonized by the Klan shared some of its concerns over moviedom's decadence. When in 1922 the New York Civic League's William Sheafe Chase asked, "What ground is there for thinking that the motion picture industry is in the despotic control of four or five Hebrews, such as Messrs. Lasky, Loew, Fox, Zukor and Laemmle?" his question answered itself in the minds of millions of anxious Americans.[2]

Characterizing Prohibition-era whiskey as "nigger gin" and jazz as "Yiddish moron music," Henry Ford's *Dearborn Independent* fused, crudely but effectively, the racism and anti-Semitism animating this antimodern critique. "As soon as the Jews gained control of the 'movies'," Ford observed, "we had a problem . . . . It is the peculiar genius of that race to create problems of a moral character in whatever business they achieve a majority." About producers "of Semitic origin," Ford's newspaper also observed that "many . . . don't know how filthy their stuff is— it is so natural to them." The movies deployed Jewish "cleverness" to "camouflage the moral filth" of "the monkey talk, jungle squeals, grunts and squeaks and gasps" of African American popular culture.[3]

During the 1920s Hollywood embraced the new liberated morality of the Jazz Age. Permissive screen images became all too real when the unconventional private lives of the movie colony spilled over into public scandals and even criminal prosecutions. The rise of Hollywood's Jewish moguls was coincidental rather than causative. Cecil B. DeMille, not one of the moguls, had taken the lead by making sophisticated sex comedies starring Gloria Swanson. Only later in the decade did he turn to movie epics that rendered sex respectable by clothing it in the robes of biblical and historical spectacle. Neither the comedian Roscoe "Fatty" Arbuckle, accused in a notorious rape case, nor the principal suspects in the era's other notorious scandals—the unsolved murder of director William Desmond Taylor and the suspicious death of producer Thomas Ince—were Jews. Adolph Zukor attributed his entry into the film industry to being "struck by the moral possibilities of the screen." Trying to neutralize criticism, he withdrew from release after some hesitation films costing $1 million to produce that starred Arbuckle, who was acquitted of any crime but had his career destroyed. Nevertheless, traditional moralists seized upon the Hollywood moguls as handy scapegoats while the less scrupulous, including associates of Boston's notorious Mayor Michael Curley, targeted them for blackmail. The Jewish movie producer, identified as a moral lecher who debauched innocent Christian girls much as Leo Frank was supposed to have corrupted Mary Phagan before he killed her, became a perfect symbol of Jazz Age decadence. And nothing was more decadent in the eyes of the moralists than the dynamic new popular music that gave the era its name and was associated with the threat to racial hierarchy posed by the Jazz Age's so-called "New Negroes."[4]

Ultimately Hollywood reassured middle-class moralists by forming the Hays Office, adopting the Production Code, and making its peace with the American Catholic Church. The price the moguls paid was surrender of significant power over film content to industry censors such as Joseph Breen of the Production Code Administration. Though not voiced in public, Breen's anti-Semitism was hardly distinguishable from Henry Ford's. Unlike Ford but like Father Coughlin in the 1930s, Breen was Catholic. Hollywood's golden age paid homage to his ethnic filiopiety with its glorification of Irish American priests, typically played by Pat O'Brien, Barry Fitzgerald, or Bing Crosby.[5]

Despite the rise of the Hollywood moguls, Jewish characters did not fare well. In 1927—coincident with the appearance of *The Jazz Singer*, the first talking picture in which Al Jolson sang in blackface—DeMille released *The King of Kings*, which still ranks as the most blatant film rendition ever made of the Jews-killed-Christ myth. For ethnic verisimilitude, DeMille raided the New York Yiddish theater for Rudolph and Joseph Schildkraut to play the chief villains, Caiaphus and Judas, and cast as extras in the mob scenes Orthodox Jews from the Boyle Heights neighborhood of Los Angeles. A devout Episcopalian who harbored grudges against his Jewish former partners both in the movie business and in the Julian Oil Scandal of the 1920s, DeMille was delighted rather than dismayed by the hackles his film raised in the Jewish community. On the other hand, he inoculated himself against Catholic criticism of his depiction of Jesus by having Jesuit Father Daniel Lord offer sunrise mass on the set every day.[6]

During the Depression and through the pre-Pearl Harbor debate over American involvement in World War II, attacks on Jewish Hollywood continued. On the political right, William Dudley Pelley, founder of the fascist Silver Shirts, claimed personal knowledge of the correspondence in the film industry between Jewish involvement and immoral practices:

> *The fleshpots of Hollywood. Oriental custodians of adolescent entertainment. One short word for all of it—JEWS! Do you think me unduly incensed about them? I've seen too many Gentile maidens ravished and been unable to do anything about it. They have a concupiscent slogan in screendom, "Don't hire till you see the whites of their thighs!" I know all about Jews. For six years I toiled in their galleys and got nothing but money.[7]*

The legend of the casting couch was evoked in Ben Hecht's novel, *A Jew in Love* (1931), whose protagonist, a New York publisher turned Broadway producer, was a forerunner of Philip Roth's sex-obsessed Portnoy. It became part of the broader legend of screendom's Jewish moguls, which entered America's mythic pantheon in 1941 with the simultaneous publication of F. Scott Fitzgerald's *The Last Tycoon* and Budd Schulberg's *What Makes Sammy Run?* Fitzgerald's unfinished novel sympathetically portrayed its hero, movie producer Monroe Stahr, as a Don Quixote questing after visions of cinematic greatness. But the novel by Schulberg (son of a film producer) mercilessly exposed its protagonist, Sammy Glick, as a vile Sancho Panza pursuing the lowest common denominator in both life and art. Schulberg's debunking novel made the greater impression.[8]

During the prewar debate over U.S. isolation, the fledgling House Committee on Un-American Activities (HUAC) took a political rather than a moral tack. It held hearings dramatizing the charge that the movie industry, because of Jewish influence, was subversively interventionist. Charles Lindbergh of America First fueled the fire by declaring that the Jews' "greatest danger to this country lies in their large ownership and influence in our motion pictures, our press, our radio, and our government." These attacks were effectively marginalized when the United States entered World War II. Not even American icon Lindbergh was able to reinject them into the political mainstream.[9]

But then the cold war incited a new red scare and a second highprofile attack on Jewish Hollywood. Congressman John Rankin of Mississippi accused filmmakers of "insidiously trying to spread subversive propaganda, poison the minds of your children, distort the history of our country and discredit Christianity." Responsible for "one of the most dangerous plots ever instigated for the overthrow of the government," Hollywood Jews presided over "the greatest hotbed of subversive activities in the United States."[10] Exploiting anti-Semitic prejudices as well as anticommunist fears, Rankin alleged that "Christian American actors and actresses" had been "virtually driven . . . from the film industry." Rankin buttressed this charge by exposing the Jewish "real names" behind the non-Jewish personas of film-industry leftists who had signed a petition in support of the Hollywood Ten:

They sent this petition to Congress and I want to read you the names.
One of the names is June Havoc. We found from the Motion Picture
Almanac *that her real name is June Hovick. Another name was Danny*
Kay, and we found out that his real name was David Daniel Kaminsky.
. . . Another one is Eddie Cantor, whose real name is Edward Isskowitz.
There is one who calls himself Edward Robinson. His real name is
Emanuel Goldenberg. There is another one who calls himself Melvyn
Douglas, whose real name is Melvyn Hesselberg. There are others too
numerous to mention. They are attacking the Committee for doing its
duty in trying to protect this country and save the American people
from the horrible fate the Communists have meted out to the unfortu-
nate Christian people of Europe.[11]

Ten of the nineteen people subpoenaed by the HUAC and six of the indicted Hollywood
Ten were Jews. This firestorm occurred while Hollywood attacked antiblack racism and anti-
Semitism in its first "message films." These included *No Way Out* (1950), Sidney Poitier's first
starring role. Rankin retaliated by playing the race card and accusing Jewish filmmakers of
"mongrelizing America." Producer and screenwriter Adrian Scott, one of the Hollywood Ten,
complained about "the 'cold war' now being waged . . . against the Jewish and Negro people."
Scott, a non-Jew whose credits included *Crossfire* (1946), Hollywood's first high-profile
exposé of anti-Semitism, soon found confirmation of his linkage of Jewish and black leftists as
victims of the new McCarthyism in the American Legion-orchestrated riot against Paul Robeson in Peekskill, New York.[12]

Forty years after the McCarthy period, the end of the cold war ironically ushered in a
third onslaught against Jewish Hollywood. Homefront America's moralizing spotlight once
again focused on the depravity of moviedom. As in the past, the white right played an instigat-
ing role. Though Jerry Falwell and Pat Robertson were avowedly philosemitic and pro-Israel,
the Moral Majority and the Christian Coalition nevertheless activated latent anti-Semitic
biases by stridently criticizing the secularism and permissiveness of the entertainment industry. Robertson, for example, warned that "the part that Jewish intellectuals and media activists
have played in the assault on Christianity may very possibly prove to be a grave mistake. . . .
For centuries, Christians have supported Jews in their dream of a national homeland. But
American Jews invested great energy in attacking these very allies. The investment may pay a
terrible dividend."[13]

Henry Ford's equation of the immorality of the movies with the Jewish backgrounds of
film producers was revived in the 1980s by Reverend R. L. Hymers of the Fundamentalist Bap-
tist Tabernacle in Los Angeles and Reverend Donald Wildmon of the American Family Association. Hymers warned that the alleged blasphemy of *The Last Temptation of Christ*, Martin
Scorsese's film based on Nikos Kazantzakis's novel, would "bring hatred on Jewish people"
because Lew Wasserman was chairman and Sidney Sheinberg president of the releasing company, MCA.[14] Wildmon threatened a boycott of television networks, whose sins he put at the
doorstep of the "59 percent of the people . . . responsible for network programs [who] were
raised in Jewish homes."[15] Even further to the right than Hymers and Wildmon, William
Pierce, author of *The Turner Diaries*, accused "Jews, with their 3,000-year history of nation-
wrecking" of using "Jewish television and Jewish films" to take "control of the minds and
souls of our children."[16] And Richard G. Butler of the Aryan Nations accused "hooked-nosed
anti-Christs in the line of Cain" of dominating the "Jewsmedia."[17]

Compared to the past, however, the white political right during the 1990s was not at the
forefront in giving anti-Hollywood discourse an anti-Jewish inflection. Conservatives like Dan
Quayle, Newt Gingrich, and William Bennett, who have politically mainstreamed the new
recoil against movie-industry sex and violence, have assiduously avoided any hint of anti-
Semitism. They also repudiated Pat Buchanan's overt appeal to anti-Jewish sentiment.
Though sometimes accused of using the term "Hollywood elite" as an ethnic euphemism or

code phrase, they have immunized themselves against charges of anti-Semitism sufficiently to win the support of religious Jews such as conservative movie critic Michael Medved, author of *Hollywood vs. America*, and centrist senator Joseph Lieberman. Even in the late-1990s climate of near hysteria over school shootings, conservative Republicans not beholden to Hollywood contributions and more critical of toxic media than lethal weapons show no inclination to play the anti-Jewish card the way it was played in the 1920s and the 1940s.[18]

Instead the renewed attack on Jewish Hollywood in the 1990s has been energized by white leftists and radical Black Nationalists. There is nothing new about black and white progressives uniting to protest racism in the entertainment industry. What's unprecedented is the growing popularity of an ostensibly antiracist gospel singling out Jews, past and present, as responsible for entertainment-industry racism. Jewish Hollywood, once viewed by the white right as complicit with African Americans in subverting racial hierarchy, now faces an antithetical indictment from the other end of the spectrum for reinforcing cultural repression and conspiring against black liberation. Golden-Age Hollywood, the presumed promised land of the Jewish moguls, has been recast as a prison house of racism. And Al Jolson, the Jew in blackface, is no longer viewed as a pied piper of Jazz Age permissive freedom but is pilloried as a cultural parasite and racist villain.

Not Jolson in blackface but Steven Spielberg, the adoptive father of two black children, has become a lightning rod for today's Black Nationalist attacks on Jewish Hollywood. This started in the 1980s when Spielberg began the transition from blockbuster adventure and fantasy films to socially portentous pictures focusing on the experience of African Americans and Jews. A protest against Spielberg's 1985 adaptation of Alice Walker's novel, *The Color Purple*, was the impetus for the organization of the Coalition Against Black Exploitation (CABE). CABE is the West Coast counterpart of New York's Committee to Eliminate Media Offensive to African People (CEMOTAP). Picketing the Hollywood premier of *The Color Purple*, CABE launched scattergun attacks on Jews who "with rare exceptions . . . have depicted black men as criminals, pimps, drug addicts, clowns and fools" and "black women . . . as fat, loud, bossy mammies who dominate their husbands and families . . . [or] as whores."[19] CABE's power base in metropolitan Los Angeles was the city of Compton, the black community where rap music was invented. Compton's mayor, Omar Bradley, blamed rap's unpalatable aspects not on black performing artists but on "lox and bagel eaters" in the music industry, whom he alleged were "having a bar mitzvah at the same time" they were destroying the black community. C. Delores Tucker of the Washington-based National Political Congress of Black Women also blamed rap excesses on "Jews in the suites" who produced the music rather than "blacks in the streets" who performed it.[20]

Attributing the most mercenary and malevolent motives to Spielberg, African American talk-show host and columnist Tony Brown in 1986 asked: "Did a Jew have to go into a gas chamber to understand Hitler's motives? I know what the 100 million dollars that 'Purple' has made at the box office means."[21] Essentially, Spielberg was caught in the crossfire between black feminists like Alice Walker and Oprah Winfrey and Black Nationalists like Tony Brown and sociologist Nathan Hare. Hare's 1984 book *The Endangered Black Family* argues that feminism is a genocidal Jewish conspiracy against African Americans that seeks to brainwash black women into emasculating their men and aborting their babies.[22] These attacks on Spielberg's movie version of *The Color Purple* set the stage for later Black Nationalist assaults on *Schindler's List*, which Louis Farrakhan's *Final Call* newspaper referred to as a "Swindler's List" designed to cause historical amnesia among African Americans about their own "slave trade Shoah." Nor were such critics appeased by Spielberg's recent movie *Amistad*, despite its glorified romantic portrayal of slave rebel Cinque teaching political philosophy to former president John Quincy Adams. They attacked *Amistad* as a conspiracy to cover up the Jewish role in slave dealing.[23]

In 1991 Professor Leonard Jeffries of the African American Studies Department of the City University of New York unveiled for a national audience this new Black Nationalist melodrama vilifying Jewish Hollywood. Though the headlines about Jeffries's speech at the Empire State Black Arts and Cultural Festival in Albany played up his charge that "rich Jews helped finance the slave trade," he actually devoted more time to attacking "a conspiracy planned and plotted and programmed out of Hollywood, with people named Greenberg and Weisberg and whatnot . . . for the destruction of black people."[24] Farrakhan compressed this libel into the compelling image of Hollywood Jews as "bloodsuckers of black people" and wielders of parasitic "control over black professionals, black intellectuals, black entertainers, [and] black sports figures." "What I represent is black suffering," Farrakhan intoned in 1994. "I don't own Hollywood. Who depicted black people?" he went on. "Who writes the books? Who writes the plays, the songs that make us look less than human? Do you mean to tell me that Jews have never done any evil to black people?"[25] In an interview with journalist Arthur Magida of the *Baltimore Jewish Times*, Farrakhan also promised or threatened that the Nation of Islam's book *The Secret Relationship Between Blacks and Jews*, which alleged "Jewish domination" of the slave trade, would be followed by a second volume that would "address such topics as Jewish control of Hollywood."[26]

In 1996, on the *Larry King Live* television program, Marlon Brando joined the new assault on Jewish Hollywood by accusing Jewish studio heads of defaming nonwhites while "drawing the wagons around" to protect their own kind from "kike" imagery. Brando's words echoed his comments in a 1979 *Playboy* magazine interview. However, they were given much more publicity the second time around, partly because of their synergy with similar attacks emanating from Black Nationalist circles. Of course, it is difficult to imagine a greater contrast than that between Farrakhan's puritanical, sexist, black separatist crusade and Brando's picaresque, hedonistic, Tahitian lifestyle. This was not the first time, however, that anti-Semitism made for strange bedfellows.[27]

Also in 1996 the scurrilous and crackpot accusations of Farrakhan and Brando were given the patina of academic respectability by the appearance of Berkeley political scientist Michael Rogin's *Blackface, White Noise: Jewish Immigrants in the Hollywood Melting Pot*. Heavily indebted for background to Neal Gabler's popular 1989 book *An Empire of Their Own*, on how "the Jews invented Hollywood," Rogin's study explores blackface minstrelsy and racial imagery in American films from the 1920s through the 1940s.[28]

In 1976 Irving Howe had sympathetically analyzed how, for performers such as Al Jolson, Eddie Cantor, George Jessel, and Sophie Tucker, and for composers such as Irving Berlin and George Gershwin, "black became a mask for Jewish expressiveness, with one woe speaking through the voice of another."[29] Rogin's book is a pejorative repackaging of Howe's thesis. "It was not just that antiblack racism was the badge of belonging in the United States," he asserts, "but that the badge was worn as blackface, and often by Jews," who in Rogin's eyes also wore a "stain of shame." Rogin is undeterred by the knowledge that his view of Jews as expropriators of "symbolic surplus value" from African American culture is uncomfortably close to Farrakhan's image of Jews as "bloodsuckers of black people."[30] There is no room in either Farrakhan's or Rogin's vision for the complex reality of two-way interaction and mutuality that historian Ann Douglas shows existed between Jews and African Americans at the center of American popular culture during the Jazz Age.[31] Jewish performers were inspired by black music, but the affinity was rooted partly in earlier borrowings from the Hebrew scriptures by African American slaves and freedmen.

The most virulent era of movie stereotyping of minorities—during which nickelodeon screens flickered with images of drunken Indians, violent Italians, and usurious Jews, as well as savage Africans—culminated in 1915 with D. W. Griffith's *Birth of a Nation*. The apotheosis of high cinematic art and low racial prejudice, Griffith's film, which President Wilson called "history written with lightning," glorified the post-Civil War Ku Klux Klan as saviors of the white South from newly freed African Americans.[32] It came at the end of the formative period in film history that predated the rise to dominance of Hollywood's legendary Jewish moguls, few of whom made the transition from East Coast movie distributors to West Coast moviemakers until after the outbreak of World War I. For example, when *Birth of a Nation* was made, Louis B. Mayer was still a Boston movie-house owner and former scrap metal dealer. Mayer did, however, make a tidy profit by buying the New England distribution rights to Griffith's film.[33]

The men who became the Hollywood moguls sometimes trafficked in cinematic bigotry demeaning not only other minorities but their fellow Jews. Zukor, for example, bought a European film version of the Oberammergau Passion Play for exhibition in the United States in 1910. But what distinguished them was an underlying uneasiness about the hard-core racism and anti-Semitism of the early silent-film era. This began to manifest itself as early as 1913, when the newly organized Anti-Defamation League started lobbying against a cycle of films that depicted Jews as sadistic misers exploiting Christian widows and as crafty arsonists burning down a clothing store for the insurance proceeds. Carl Laemmle, founder of Universal Pictures, responded with a low-key but persistent campaign to purge movie screens of the worst specimens of prejudice. In this spirit, the independent production *Birth of a Race* (1918), partly financed by Julius Rosenwald, sought to be an antidote to Griffith's cinematic racism.[34] In 1915—the year that juxtaposed the release of *Birth of a Nation*, the rebirth of the Ku Klux Klan, and the lynching of Leo Frank—Joel Spingarn, Lillian Wald, Jacob Schiff, and Rabbi Stephen S. Wise joined W.E.B. DuBois in picketing Griffith's film, which Rabbi Wise called an "incredibly foul and loathsome libel on a race of human beings."[35] These protests had limited immediate impact, but they set a precedent for more effective lobbying a generation later when Jewish rabbis and radicals joined the National Association for the Advancement of Colored People (NAACP) in persuading David O. Selznick to omit from the screenplay of *Gone With the Wind* (1939) the most objectionable aspects of the novel. "I feel so strongly about what is happening to the Jews of the world," Selznick averred, "that I cannot help but sympathize with the Negroes and their fears." Omitting the novel's portrayal of a black rapist, Selznick insisted that African American characters would be shown solely as "loveable, faithful, high-minded people." The film fell considerably short, however, of Selznick's stated intention "that the Negroes come out on the right side of the ledger" and that the film not serve as "an advertisement for intolerant societies in these fascist-ridden times."[36]

Arguably the most important film-industry development affecting African Americans occurred between the world wars, when the Jewish moguls consolidated their position behind the camera and a community of black actors and musicians appeared on screen for the first time.[37] This context helps explain why African American audiences joined Jewish audiences in applauding the story told by the film *The Jazz Singer*, in which an immigrant Jewish boy achieves American success by embracing black music. According to a Yiddish reviewer, Jolson in blackface proved that: "The son of a line of rabbis well knows how to sing the songs of the most cruelly wronged people in the world's history."[38] The equally positive African American reaction was summed up by a black newspaper that reported of Jolson that "every colored performer is proud of him." Looking for progress amidst frustrating paradox, African Americans saw in the white actor wearing burnt cork and singing black music a transitional step toward the day when African American performers, unencumbered by masks, would come into their own.[39]

Of course, for a generation after they began to appear on screen black actors played mainly butlers, maids, and plantation hands. During this same period, most Jewish characters were also relegated to comic relief. When Samuel Goldwyn put Montague Glass, creator of the hapless haberdashers Potash and Perlmutter, to work injecting coarse comedy into a screenplay adaptation of immigrant novelist Anzia Yezierska's *A Salome of the Tenements*, she broke down and cried.[40] But African American performers like Paul Robeson and Hattie McDaniel, who won a best supporting actress Oscar for her role in *Gone With the Wind*, conveyed an innate dignity that often triumphed over servile conventions.[41] During World War II a major fault line in Hollywood was between black actors like Lincoln Perry, stage name Stepin Fetchit, who played a comic buffoon and wanted to continue doing so, and civil rights organizations strongly supported by Jews, which wanted Hollywood to stop casting African Americans in such roles. By 1946 Walter White of the NAACP had suggested creation of a special organization—"something like the [Jewish] Anti-Defamation League"—to monitor minority portrayals in movies.[42]

White skin certainly gave Jews greater opportunities in front of the camera during Hollywood's golden age, but their advantage should not be exaggerated. The mythology that has grown up about Jews changing their names (and sometimes their noses) on the way to stardom is based on a handful of instances including those of John Garfield, Edgar G. Robinson, Paul Muni, Melvyn Douglas, and Paulette Goddard. Yet a study of the period 1932-1951 shows that less than five percent of the top box-office stars were Jews. The mythology is correct, however, in that the most successful Jewish actors specialized in empathetically playing every white ethnic group except their own.[43]

The campaign against anti-Jewish film prejudice bore fruit slowly, and then it took the perverse form of purging the screen not so much of anti-Semitism as of identifiable Jews. After *The Jazz Singer*, Jewish characters and themes—favorable and unfavorable—gradually disappeared, at the same time that Hollywood gradually destroyed the Yiddish film industry by stealing away its greatest talents.[44] By the Depression era, with *The Life of Emile Zola* (1937), about the Dreyfus case, the word *Jew* was left unsaid. Also in 1937, *They Won't Forget*, ostensibly based on Leo Frank's lynching, asked the audience to forget that Frank was a Jew.

Charlie Chaplin's comic but candid deflation of Nazi anti-Semitism in *The Great Dictator* (1940) raised the ire of isolationist senator Gerald Nye, who accused the film industry of having "its own foreign policy" and even of being "the most potent and dangerous fifth column in our country" and "the most gigantic engines of propaganda in existence to rouse the war fever in America and plunge this Nation to her destruction." Nye's Hollywood hall of shame, not surprisingly, was populated almost entirely by Jewish studio executives. Hollywood subsequently decided it was the better part of valor to fight World War II as if there were no Holocaust. That theme was not really engaged directly until *The Diary of Anne Frank* in 1959, but the Jewish content of the diary was so diluted by the film as well as by the play on which it was based that Meyer Levin sued.[45] Though MGM actually commissioned Leon Uris to write the novel that was the basis of the pro-Israel blockbuster *Exodus*, the 1960 film was delayed for years, partly by fears of an "Arab box office" backlash.[46] Three decades later, despite the recent spate of Holocaust films, a 1996 study showed the virtual disappearance from the wide screen of identifiable American Jewish characters and the proliferation on the narrow screen of culturally denuded Jews in the Seinfeld mold.[47]

In terms of preservation of group identity at least, Hollywood arguably has done better by African Americans than by Jews, whose ascriptive "whiteness," as Sander Gilman points out, poses the risk of making them, if not exactly invisible, culturally transparent. At or near parity as a percentage of Hollywood screen actors, blacks on the other hand are achieving gains as screenwriters and directors. Today the seriously underrepresented minority on screen is not African American but Hispanic.[48]

A new Hollywood is in the making that builds on the slow but real progress that has been made since the rise of the Jewish moguls. The future was portended almost sixty years ago in a scene in Fitzgerald's novel *The Last Tycoon*, in which producer Monroe Stahr, while walking on the beach at Malibu, encounters a black man who had been reading Ralph Waldo Emerson. The man tells Stahr that he never goes to the movies or lets his children go because movies aren't true to life. Stahr tells himself that the man "was prejudiced and wrong" and that "many pictures, a decade of pictures, must be made to show him that he was wrong." More than a half century later, Hollywood Jews are still trying to prove that African American wrong.[49]

In the new Hollywood some past paradoxes and moral contradictions are recapitulated in ironic guises at the same time that others are transcended. Hence, filmmaker Spike Lee personifies the film industry's heightened openness to African American talent. Yet, criticized for the crude stereotyping of Jewish nightclub owners in his film *Mo' Better Blues* (1990), he justified the portrayals as payback for "one hundred years of Hollywood cinema" racism. Lee's *Malcolm X* (1992), a $30-million project, was based on a screenplay by blacklisted writer Arnold Perl that had languished for twenty-five years. The resulting film can be viewed either as a triumphant collaboration by a young Black Nationalist filmmaker with the ghost of a Jewish radical or as a cynical ripoff of Perl by Lee, who took top billing for a script most of which Perl had written.[50]

In the new Hollywood white actor Ted Danson was harshly criticized for complying with the request of his then-girlfriend, Whoopi Goldberg, that he don blackface at a Friar's Club Roast in her honor. Yet African American star Eddie Murphy received no criticism for donning whiteface in one scene in the film *Coming to America* (1986) in order to play a comical elderly Jewish man. Nor did Murphy or his production company receive much blame in the media when writer Art Buchwald sued and won for their failure to give him appropriate credit and compensation for the idea upon which *Coming to America* was based. In contrast, Spielberg was pilloried as "Stealberg" when his production company was the target of an unmerited plagiarism suit in connection with the film *Amistad*.[51]

At a time when Hollywood and Hollywood's Jewish community are caught up in an ethnic succession process through which African Americans and other minorities have made strides but are impatient for more, the newest attack on Jewish Hollywood is bad history and no road map to a more inclusive future.

SIMON WIESENTHAL CENTER

Notes

1. Sander L. Gilman, *Jewish Self-Hatred: Anti-Semitism and the Hidden Language of the Jews* (Baltimore, 1986), pp. 145–46 and 229–34; John Weiss, *Ideology of Death: Why the Holocaust Happened in Germany* (Chicago, 1996), p. 246; Gennadi Kostyrencho, *Out of the Shadows: Anti-Semitism in Stalin's Russia* (Amherst [NY], 1995), p. 173; Arkady Vaksberg, *Stalin Against the Jews* (New York, 1994), p. 138; Daniel Pipes, *The Long Shadow: Culture and Politics in the Middle East* (New Brunswick, 1989), p. 13. See also David Welch, *Propaganda and the German Cinema* (New York, 1987), pp. 285–90.

2. Kevin Starr, *Inventing the Dream: California Through the Progressive Era* (New York, 1985), pp. 329–30; Lary May, *Screening Out the Past: The Birth of Mass Culture and the Motion Picture Industry* (Chicago, 1983), pp. 36–41 and 43–59; Hiram Wesley Evans, "The Klan's Fight for Americanism," *North American Review* (March 1926), p. 33; William Sheafe Chase, *Catechism on Motion Pictures in Inter-State Commerce*, 3d ed. (Albany, 1922), pp. 5–57.

3. "Baring The Heart of Hollywood: The Truth About the Motion Pictures," *Dearborn Independent*, 29 October–10 December 1921; *The International Jew* (Dearborn, 1920–22), Vol. 2, pp. 117–26; Vol. 3, pp. 64–87; and Vol. 4, pp. 7–41.

4. Robert Sklar, *Movie-Made America: A Cultural History of American Movies* (New York, 1975), pp. 78–83 and 91–92; Cecil B. DeMille, *Autobiography*, ed. Donald Hayne (Englewood Cliffs, 1959), pp. 219–20; Thomas Doherty, *Pre-Code Hollywood: Sex, Morality, and Insurrection in American Cinema, 1930-1934* (New York, 1999), p. 26; Stuart Oderman, *Roscoe "Fatty" Arbuckle: A Biography of the Silent Film Comedian, 1887–1933* (Jefferson [NC], 1994), pp. 138 and 196; Neal Gabler, *An Empire of Their Own: How the Jews Invented Hollywood* (New York, 1988), pp. 277–78; Jack Beatty, *The Rascal King: The Life and Times of James Michael Curley, 1874–1958* (Reading [MA], 1992), pp. 195–96; Thomas Cripps, *Slow Fade to Black: The Negro in American Film*, 1900–1941 (New York, 1993), pp. 117 and 134; Nancy MacLean, "Gender, Sexuality, and the Politics of Lynching: The Leo Frank Case Revisited," in *Under Sentence of Death: Lynching in*

the South, ed. W. Fitzhugh Brundage (Chapel Hill, 1997), pp. 168–169. Jazz Age scandals engulf the moguls in Andy Edmunds's anti-Semitic-tinged *Frame-Up!: The Untold Story of Roscoe "Fatty" Arbuckle* (New York, 1991), which portrays Adolph Zukor as a sexual hypocrite who engineered Arbuckle's undoing as a way of punishing the comedian for high salary demands, and in William Manus's recent play, *Last Laugh*, which instead places the blame on bigots in the Los Angeles District Attorney's Office.

5. Leonard J. Leff and Jerold L. Simmons, *The Dame in the Kimono: Hollywood, Censorship, and the Production Code from the 1920s to the 1960s* (New York, 1990), pp. 1–54; Gregory D. Black, *Hollywood Censored: Morality, Catholics, and the Movies* (New York, 1994), pp. 70–71 and 149–83; Doherty, p. 98.

6. Starr, pp. 331–33; Charles Higham, *Cecil B. DeMille* (New York, 1973), pp. 179–80; Black, p. 65; Les Keyser and Barbara Keyser, *Hollywood and the Catholic Church: The Image of Roman Catholicism in American Movies* (Chicago, 1984), p. 22.

7. Leo P. Ribuffo, *The Old Christian Right: The Protestant Right from the Great Depression to the Cold War* (Philadelphia, 1982). Pp. 43–47 and 61–63; Michael E. Birdwell, *Celluloid Soldiers: The Warner Bros. Campaign against Nazism* (New York, 1999), pp. 41–43; Quoted in Adam Parfrey, *Cult Rapture* (Portland, 1995), p. 366. Bill Kaufman, *America First! Its History, Culture, and Politics* (Amherst [NY], 1995), echoes the charges of the unAmericanism of Jewish Hollywood: "Beginning in 1939, the spectacle of our stateside Eisensteins, many of them foreignbred, urging American natives to sacrifice their sons for Winston Churchill, provoked a brief, sad, and futile protest by the pugnacious guardians of the Old Republic" (pp. 85–86).

8. Gabler, pp. 335–38; Ben Hecht, *A Jew in Love* (New York, 1931), pp. 45– 46 and 214–17; William MacAdams, *Ben Hecht: The Man Behind the Legend* (New York, 1990), pp. 137–40; John F. Callahan, "F. Scott Fitzgerald's Evolving American Dream: The 'Pursuit of Happiness' in *Gatsby, Tender is the Night,* and *The Last Tycoon,*" *Twentieth Century Literature*, Vol. 42 (September 1996), pp. 372–96; Budd Schulberg, *What Makes Sammy Run?* (New York, 1941).

9. Birdwell, pp. 154–171; Leonard Dinnerstein, *Antisemitism in America* (New York, 1994), pp. 129–30; Edward S. Shapiro, "The Approach to War: Congressional Isolationism and Anti-Semitism," *American Jewish History*, Vol. 74, No. 1 (March, 1984), pp. 47–49; Richard Maltby, "Made for Each Other: The Melodrama of Hollywood and the House Committee on Un-American Activities, 1947," in *Cinema, Politics and Society in America*, ed. Philip Davies and Brian Neve (Manchester [England], 1981), p. 82. Hollywood and the legendary aviator have come full circle, with Steven Spielberg reportedly planning a new film biography based on A. Scott Berg's *Lindbergh* (New York, 1998) downplaying its protagonist's anti-Semitism.

10. Howard M. Sachar, *A History of the Jews in America* (New York, 1992), p. 624; Edward S. Shapiro, "Anti-Semitism Mississippi Style," in *Anti-Semitism in American History*, ed. David A. Gerber (Urbana, 1986), pp. 144–45; Walter Goodman, *The Committee: The Extraordinary Career of the House Committee on Un-American Activities* (New York, 1968), pp. 167–89.

11. Victor S. Navasky, *Naming Names* (New York, 1980), pp. 113 and 369; Larry Ceplair and Steve Englund, *The Inquisition in Hollywood: Politics in the Film Community, 1930–1960* (Garden City, 1980), p. 289; Clancy Segal, "Hollywood During the Great Fear," *Present Tense*, Vol. 9 (Spring 1982), pp. 45–48.

12. Navasky, p. 113; Shapiro, pp. 138–39; Nancy Lynn Schwartz, *The Hollywood Writers' Wars* (New York, 1982), p. 273; Gordon Kahn, *Hollywood on Trial: The Story of the 10 Who Were Indicted* (New York, 1948), pp. 106–8; Martin Duberman, *Paul Robeson: A Biography* (New York, 1989), pp. 364–74.

13. Michael Lind, "Pat Robertson's Grand International Conspiracy Theory," *New York Review of Books*, Vol. 42 (2 February 1995), p. 23; Anti-Defamation League, *The Religious Right: The Assault on Tolerance and Pluralism* (New York, 1994).

14. Leo Noonan, "The Temptation of R. L. Hymers," *Jewish Journal* (Los Angeles), 29 July–4 August 1988, p. 6; John Dart, "2 Step Back From Film Protest Over Anti-Jewish Tone," *Los Angeles Times*, 23 July 1988, p. B1.

15. Steve Weinstein, "Religious Right May Be in for a Fight," *Los Angeles Times*, 20 May 1991, Calendar section, p. 1; Glenn R. Simpson, "Four Years Later, Buchanan's Advisers, Not His Words, Draw Criticism," *Wall Street Journal*, 22 February 1996, p. A20.

16. Leonard Ziskind, *The "Christian Identity" Movement: A Theological Justification for Racist and Anti-Semitic Violence* (Division of Church and Society of the National Council of the Churches of Christ in the U.S.A.; Atlanta, 1986), pp. 5–40; *National Vanguard Book Service Catalog*, No. 16 (William L. Pierce's National Alliance; November 1995).

17. Michael Barkun, *Religion and the Racist Right: The Origins of the Christian Identity Movement* (Chapel Hill, 1994), pp. 162–64; David H. Bennett, *The Party of Fear: From Nativist Movements to the New Right in American History*, rev. ed. (New York, 1995), p. 349.

18. William Bennett, *The De-Valuing of America: The Fight for Our Culture and Our Children* (New York, 1992); Dan Quayle and Diane Medved, *The American Family: Discovering the Values that Make Us Strong* (New York, 1996); M. J. Rosenberg, "Dan Quayle, Hollywood, and Anti-Semitism," *Jewish Journal* (Los Angeles), 25 September–1 October 1992, p. 28; Michael Medved, *Hollywood vs. America* (New York, 1993), pp. 313–19; Steven Levy, "Loitering on the Dark Side," *Newsweek*, 3 May 1999, p. 39.

19. Bruce Newman, "On Location: Spielberg's Children Inspired Him to Recount the Amistad Mutiny of 1839," *Los Angeles Times*, 9 November 1997, Calendar section, p. 8; Earl Walter and Legrand H. Clegg II, " 'The Color Purple': Another Bad Image," *Los Angeles Sentinel*, 5 December 1985, p. A12; Coalition Against Black Exploitation (CABE), "Why Do Jewish Producers Degrade Blacks in Hollywood?" (1989 mimeographed broadside); J. J. Goldberg, *Jewish Power: Inside the Jewish Establishment* (Reading [MA], 1996), pp. 288–89.

20. James Bolden, "Compton Mayor Omar Bradley's Comments Spark Anger Among Jews," *Los Angeles Sentinel*, 27 October 1993, p. 1; "The Rap on 'Gangsta Rap,'" *Final Call*, 2 August 1995, p. 8.

21. Tony Brown, "The Color Purple is White," *Los Angeles Herald-Dispatch*, 9 January 1986, p. A4.

22. Andrea M. Wren, "Rerunning 'The Color Purple' Controversy Over 1985 Movie Now Seems Unfathomable," *St. Louis Post-Dispatch*, 10 March 1996, p. C5; Nathan Hare and Julia Hare, *The Endangered Black Family: Coping with the Unisexualization and Coming Extinction of the Black Race* (San Francisco, 1984), pp. 33–37, 59, and 133; Abdul Allah Muhammad, "I Have A Scheme," *Final Call*, 2 March 1994, p. 10.

23. J. F. Moses, "Spielberg's Movie Answer to Jewish Slave Dealing?" *Blacks&Jews News* (available online at http: //www.blacksandjews.com/Amistad. html [cited May, 1999]).

24. The full text of Jeffries' speech is in *New York Newsday*, 18 August 1991, p. 1; and *New York Amsterdam News*, 31 August 1991, p. 1. See also Jim Sleeper, "The Battle for Enlightenment at City College," in *Blacks and Jews: Alliances and Arguments*, ed. Paul Berman (New York, 1994), pp. 239–53.

25. Louis Farrakhan, "Let My People Go!" *Final Call*, 23 September 1993, p. 16; Sylvester Monroe, "They Suck the Life From You," interview with Farrakhan, *Time*, 28 February 1994, p. 22; *Meet the Press*, interview with Farrakhan, 18 October 1998.

26. Arthur J. Magida, *Prophet of Rage: A Life of Louis Farrakhan and His Nation* (New York, 1996), pp. 139–72.

27. Abiola Sinclair, "Marlon Brando Blasts Hollywood Jews More Pointedly than Dr. Jeffries," *New York Amsterdam News*, 13 April 1996, p. 10; Rosalind Muhammad, "Brando Ignites Debate About Jewish Filmmakers," *Final Call*, 28 April 1996, p. 3.

28. Michael Rogin, *Blackface, White Noise: Jewish Immigrants in the Hollywood Melting Pot* (Berkeley, 1996). For critical reviews of Rogin's book, see Gabler, *Forward*, 24 May 1996; Lary May, *American Jewish History*, Vol. 85 (March 1997), pp. 115–19; Hasia Diner, *Commonquest* (Summer 1997), pp. 40–43; Cripps, *Journal of American History*, Vol. 83 (March 1997), pp. 1462–63; Harold Brackman, "Through the Prism of Race and Slavery," *AJS Review*, (in press).

29. Irving Howe with the assistance of Kenneth Libo, *World of Our Fathers* (New York, 1976), p. 561.

30. Rogin, pp. 11, 16–17, 64, and 68.

31. Ann Douglas, *Terrible Honesty: Mongrel Manhattan in the 1920s* (New York, 1995), p. 359.

32. Lester D. Friedman, ed., *Unspeakable Images: Ethnicity and the American Cinema* (Urbana, 1991); Daniel J. Leab, *From Sambo to Superspade: The Black Experience in Motion Pictures* (Boston, 1976), pp. 23–40.

33. Eileen Bowser, *The Transformation of Cinema, 1907–1915* (New York, 1990), p. 12; Diana Altman, *Hollywood East: Louis B. Mayer and the Origins of the Studio System* (New York, 1992), pp. 1–23 and 48–53.

34. Will Irwin, *The House That Shadows Built* (Garden City, 1928), pp. 145–47; Nathan C. Belth, *A Promise to Keep: A Narrative of the American Encounter with Anti-Semitism* (New York, 1979), p. 50; Patricia Erens, *The Jew in American Film* (Bloomington, 1984), pp. 31–37; Cripps, *Slow Fade to Black*, pp. 71–73 and 157; Cripps, "The Making of *Birth of a Race*: The Emerging Politics of Identity in Silent Movies," in *The Birth of Whiteness: Race and the Emergence of U.S. Cinema*, ed. Daniel Bernardi (New Brunswick, 1996), pp. 38–55.

35. Altman, p. 5l; Dinnerstein, *The Leo Frank Case* (New York, 1968), pp. 71–72 and 156–57; Joel Williamson, *A Rage for Order: Black/White Relations in the American South Since Emancipation* (New York, 1986), p. 244; Diner, *In the Almost Promised Land: American Jews and Blacks, 1915–1935* (Baltimore, 1977), p. 134.

36. David O. Selznick to Sidney Howard, 6 January 1937, in *Memo from David O. Selznick*, ed. Rudy Behlmer (New York, 1972), p. 151; Carlton Jackson, *Hattie: The Life of Hattie McDaniel* (New York, 1980), pp. 41–43; Cripps, *Slow Fade to Black*, pp. 361–64 and 430–31; Cripps, "Africans Americans and Jews in Hollywood," in *Struggles in the Promised Land: Toward a History of Black-Jewish Relations in the United States*, ed. Jack Salzman and Cornel West (New York, 1997), p. 265. Joseph Goebbels admired *Gone With the Wind* as a triumph of epic film technique but kept his opinion private because of Hitler's preference for the hard-core racism of Griffith's *Birth of a Nation*. See David Stuart Hull, *Film in the Third Reich: Art and Propaganda in Nazi Germany* (Berkeley, 1969), pp. 179–82 and 212.

37. Donald Bogle, *Toms, Coons, Mulattoes, Mammies, and Bucks: An Interpretive History of Blacks in American Films*, 3d ed. (New York, 1994), pp. 35–100; Cripps, *Slow Fade to Black,* pp. 94–114.

38. Diner, *In the Almost Promised Land*, p. 69. *The Jazz Singer* was one of many generational conflict dramas about the contradictory demands of tradition and ambition including the play and film, *Der vilner balebesl*, also about a cantor's son who has to choose between filial obedience and artistic success, not on Broadway in blackface, but at the Warsaw Opera House.

39. Cripps, *Slow Fade to Black*, p. 222; and "African Americans and Jews in Hollywood," in *Struggles in the Promised Land*, p. 263.

40. Montague Glass, *'I' Understand* (New York, 1925); Anna Yezierska, *Red Ribbon on a White Horse* (New York, 1950), p. 81; Mary V. Dearborn, "Anzia Yezierska and the Making of an Ethnic American Self," in *The Invention of Ethnicity*, ed. Werner Sollors (New York, 1989), pp. 113–14.

41. Cripps, *Slow Fade to Black*, pp. 361–62 and 366; Duberman, *Paul Robeson*, pp. 113–15, 203–4 and 604–5. Robeson eventually left Hollywood, frustrated by limited opportunities; but contrary to legend, he was eager to sing in the 1936 Hollywood film version of *Showboat* (though he preferred the word *darkey* to *nigger* in singing "Old Man River").

42. Cripps, *Making Movies Black: The Hollywood Message Movie from World War II to the Civil Rights Era* (New York, 1993), pp. 11, 32, 44–56, 81, and 180; Cripps, "Stepin Fetchit and the Politics of Performance," in *Beyond the Stars: Stock Characters in American Popular Film*, ed. Paul Loukides and Linda K. Fuller (Bowling Green, 1990), pp. 45–46.

43. Ian C. Jarvie, "Stars and Ethnicity: Hollywood and the United States," in *Unspeakable Images*, pp. 103–8; Gilman, *Creating Beauty to Cure the Soul: Race and Psychology in the Shaping of Aesthetic Surgery* (Durham, 1998), pp. 72–80.

44. Gabler, *An Empire of Their Own*, pp. 300–2; Friedman, *Hollywood's Image of the Jew* (New York, 1982), p. 130; David S. Lifson, *The Yiddish Theater in America* (New York, 1965), pp. 178–79; J. Hoberman, *Bridge of Light: Yiddish Film Between Two Worlds* (Philadelphia, 1995), pp. 113–22. Edgar Ulmer, a refugee from Hitler's Germany, bridged the gap between the Yiddish film industry and independent black film production before it, too, was absorbed by Hollywood. See George Lipsitz, *Time Passages: Collective Memory and American Popular Culture* (Minneapolis, 1990), pp. 194–200.

45. Friedman, *The Jewish Image in American Film* (Secaucus, 1987), p. 120; Wayne S. Cole, *Senator Gerald P. Nye and American Foreign Relations* (Minneapolis, 1962), pp. 186–88; Lawrence L. Langer, "The Americanization of the Holocaust on Stage and Screen," in *From Hester Street to Hollywood: The Jewish American Stage and Screen*, ed. Sarah Blacher Cohen (Bloomington, 1983), pp. 212–30; Judith E. Doneson, *The Holocaust in American Film* (Philadelphia, 1987), pp. 42–46 and 60–70; K. R. M. Short, "Hollywood Fights Anti-Semitism," in *Film and Radio Propaganda in World War II*, ed. K. R. M. Short (London, 1983), p. 159; Gilman, *Jewish Self-Hatred*, pp. 345–60.

46. Otto Preminger, *Otto Preminger: An Autobiography* (Garden City, 1977), pp. 165–66; Deborah Dash Moore, *To the Golden Cities: Pursuing the American Jewish Dream in Miami and L.A.* (New York, 1994), pp. 243–53.

47. Alan Spiegel, "Vanishing Act: A Typology of the Jew in Contemporary American Film," in *From Hester Street to Hollywood*, p. 275; David Porush, "Jews Don't Hitch: The American Religion in *Northern Exposure*," in *Representations of Jews Through the Ages*, ed. Leonard Jay Greenspoon and Bryan F. LeBau (Omaha, 1996), pp. 115–30; Frank Rich, "The 'Too Jewish' Question," *New York Times*, 3 March 1996, p. 15; Susan Kaplan, "From

'Seinfeld' to 'Chicago Hope': Jewish Men Are Everywhere; But . . . ," *Forward*, 29 November 1996, p. 1.

48. Gilman, *The Jew's Body* (New York, 1991), pp. 236–38; Claudia Puig and Greg Braxton, "Minorities Open Doors for Each Other in Hollywood," *Los Angeles Times*, 7 December 1995, p. D1; Cripps, "Film Industry," in *Split Image: African Americans in the Mass Media*, ed. Jannette L. Dates and William Barlow, 2d ed. (Washington, D.C., 1993), pp. 171–80; S. Robert Lichter and Daniel R. Amundson, *Distorted Reality: Hispanic Characters in TV Entertainment* (Washington, D.C., 1 September 1994), pp. 14–16. The most recent studies show representation of African American characters on television achieving parity in 1994 but dipping by 1998. See Paul Fahi, "It's a White, White World on Network TV," *Washington Post*, 13 July 1999, p. A1.

49. F. Scott Fitzgerald, *The Last Tycoon: An Unfinished Novel*, ed. Edmund Wilson (New York, 1941), pp. 92 and 95.

50. Ed Guerrero, *Framing Blackness: The African American Image in Film* (Philadelphia, 1993), pp. 197–204; Murray Friedman, *What Went Wrong?: The Creation and Collapse of the Black-Jewish Alliance* (New York, 1995), p. 109; Paul Buhle, "The Hollywood Left: Aesthetics and Politics," *New Left Review*, No. 212 (July/August 1995), p. 119.

51. Patricia J. Williams, "On Imagining Foes, Imagining Friendship," in *Struggles in the Promised Land*, p. 379; Nelson George, *Blackface: Reflections on African-Americans and the Movies* (New York, 1994), p. 96; Pierce O'Donnell and Dennis McDougal, *Fatal Subtraction: The Inside Story of Buchwald v. Paramount* (New York, 1992); Bruce Handy, "Steven Stealberg?" *Time*, 24 November 1997, p. 99.

19

Marriage, Moynihan, Mahogany: *Success and the Post–Civil Rights Black Female Professional in Film*

Miriam Thaggert

On June 4, 1965, President Lyndon B. Johnson gave the keynote commencement speech to the graduating class of Howard University, arguably America's most elite historically black college and university. Johnson's speech, titled "To Fulfill These Rights," informed the graduates about the new possibilities that would be open to them: the "rights" Johnson and other Americans intended to fulfill had recently been guaranteed through several forms of civil rights legislation, including the Civil Rights Act of 1964, which prohibited segregation in public facilities. The speech, the setting, and the audience were more than just symbolic: Johnson's address was an early public articulation of what would come to be known as affirmative action, and this group of college graduates would be members of the first generation of African Americans to take advantage of the hard-fought-for legislation and other fruits of the civil rights movement. As Johnson stated, the graduates would play active roles in this "next and more profound stage of the battle for civil rights."[1]

But the success of such legislation would prove elusive, for the overt racism of the 1960s and earlier decades evolved into the subtle racism of the 1970s. Defining success was particularly complex for African American women of the post–civil rights era. A few months after Johnson's appearance at Howard University, for example, a leaked government document explained why some African Americans failed to benefit from existing civil rights policies. Two problems, apparently, were the African American family and the woman's putative power within it, problems alluded to in the graduation speech. Johnson's commencement address was a shortened version of the Moynihan Report, written by Daniel Patrick Moynihan, which, since its appearance in 1965, has problematized the African American female worker and her role in the family.[2] The widely read report has now been well refuted, but I begin with one lesser-known incarnation of it in order to highlight an unseemly paradox—celebrating the civil rights legislation with an "inspiring" speech derived from a warning about black female aptitude.

Reprinted from *American Quarterly* 64, no. 4 (2012), by permission of Johns Hopkins University Press.

This essay examines the representation of the post–civil rights African American female professional by reading the 1975 film *Mahogany* in the context of the political, social, and racial dynamics of the United States in the early 1970s, for the film raises important questions about career-oriented black women, the black family, conventional conceptions of American "success" in the post–civil rights era, as well as the troubling shortcomings of civil rights initiatives and programs.[3] *Mahogany* stars Diana Ross as Tracy Chambers, a young African American woman from Chicago's South Side who aspires to be a clothing designer; Billy Dee Williams, as Brian, an African American lawyer and her love interest; and Anthony Perkins, as Sean McAvoy, an internationally known white photographer who wants Tracy to see him as a viable romantic suitor. All three characters contend with varying levels of personal and professional ambition, and all have lofty goals that they struggle to make tangible.

Throughout the film, however, the audience learns to oppose the illusory dreams of Tracy and Sean to the realistic and "important" dreams of Brian and to define "success" as, to use the film's most memorable line, "nothing without someone you love to share it with"—specifically, as dependent on a normative, heterosexual union in the United States. Although Brian is frequently an object of ridicule, by the end of the film he is the only one of the three characters who has the realistic opportunity to achieve his goals of a nuclear family and a politician's position. The film follows a woman's meteoric rise in a competitive industry as she reaches a long-desired goal only to renounce her version of "success" and make a decision that implicitly limits her professional path: she leaves her job as a model and designer in Italy and returns to the United States to pursue a relationship, implicitly a marriage, with Brian. Ultimately, a film that risks so much in its portrayal of a black woman with visual aptitude concludes by pathologizing her professional goals as abnormal and pushing her into the more acceptable but potentially stifling paradigms of the family and male achievement. "Visual aptitude," as I use it here, refers to Tracy's efficiency in *creating* images, such as her fashion designs, and to her talent in posing as image as a model, in short, Tracy's skills in producing and circulating images so that they have an effective reception by others.

My purpose here is to study how the film portrays this post–civil rights black female professional and her ideological dilemmas, to chart the film's narrative strategies in tempering Tracy's excessive drive to succeed and to examine the different responses to addressing the continued inequities in American cities in the wake of the civil rights movement. When examined from these multilayered perspectives, particularly through the lens of black women succeeding as professionals, *Mahogany* contradicts several powerful American mythologies such as the idea that unlimited social opportunities are available through sacrifice and ingenuity. Instead, the film invokes another powerful, national narrative: that of the family. Earlier feminist film scholars have read *Mahogany* as evidence of how black femininity disappears from universalized feminist theories or as a commentary on Hollywood's co-optation of the ideals of the American civil rights and feminist movements. Here I extend previous interpretations by analyzing more polemical issues, for *Mahogany* also reveals the post–civil rights dynamic between black men and black women and illustrates how visuality—a keen awareness of the power of images in various areas of American life—functions in the potent topic of the late-twentieth-century black female professional and the "problems" with her ambition.

As a tale of the career woman struggling to achieve a professional dream, *Mahogany* follows other cinematic narratives that portray working women and the dangers such women pose to their families and friends, especially the men and children in their lives. Such classic American films as *Blonde Venus* (1932), *Mildred Pierce* (1945), *All about Eve* (1950), and the various versions of *A Star Is Born* (1937, 1954, 1976) register society's acute anxiety about ambitious career women and the danger of letting such women work without being contained. Other films with predominantly black casts, such as Michael Roemer's *Nothing but a Man* (1964) and Ossie Davis's *Black Girl* (1972) prefigure *Mahogany*'s depiction of a black community's ambivalence for upwardly mobile black women.[4] *Mahogany*'s portrayal of the

African American working woman is unique in several ways from these earlier films: it illustrates both the promise and the limits of racial liberalism, and it demonstrates the white and black sexism that circumscribes American women of color —the very racialized and gendered dynamics that complicate America's celebrated myth of a meritocracy that rewards hard work and persistence and the unique intersections of racism and sexism that American women of color face. Revising Richard Dyer's interpretation, that the film paradoxically "both celebrates the American way of life and keeps [blacks] in their place," I argue that the film reconciles this paradox by employing a too-familiar strategy.[5] It celebrates the American way of life by keeping the black *woman* in her "place"—as a vital, but secondary, member of an American heterosexual family, an institution that functions in a larger political and social discourse as a metonym for the nation. The construction and replication of such a family were the goals of the Moynihan Report, one of several discourses that attempted to explain the successes and failures of a post–civil rights black America.

Mahogany demonstrates the dilemmas of the African American professional in the post–civil rights era, as well as the inherently visual nature of (African) American success during this period. In *Mahogany*, for example, the three characters' desires and ambitions are mediated by and through the visual: the film charts a line of success by detailing each character's skill at operating in the realm of visual knowledge. Achieving success means being able to harness both verbal and visual skills and performing for an increasingly visually inflected American society. Significantly, the director of *Mahogany* was Berry Gordy, the owner and president of Motown, a music company that became successful in the 1960s by appealing to mainstream white America with black talent rigorously groomed for public appearances.[6] *Mahogany* reflects and amplifies the performative skills Gordy harnessed at Motown, as well as his shrewd use of the image to fashion Diana Ross as a star.

Mahogany has unfortunately been dismissed as "a garish, garbled black version of outmoded kitsch."[7] But I suggest that the film deserves a much more critical, nuanced evaluation—and not only because of its influences on contemporary African American women.[8] Because *Mahogany* emphasizes image production and circulation, whether in politics, fashion, or advertising, it offers an opportunity to revisit early feminist film theory and analyses of the film. And because the film reflects specific historical, political, and cultural issues that confronted African American communities, and the nation as a whole, in the 1970s, it has much to teach us—through its narrative, its cinematic techniques, and its extradiegetic material—about how films of that era negotiate the frustrating persistence of inequalities in American society.

Mahogany, Moynihan, and Civil Rights

Arriving a decade after several pieces of major civil rights legislation, *Mahogany* summons the political and social uncertainty of the 1970s, an amorphous moment when the legal achievements of the previous decade were undermined by the unstated discrimination that lawmakers could not legislate away. The unprecedented successes—and unexpected disappointments—of the period are invoked in the film, sometimes explicitly, as when Brian dejectedly notes that "a couple of years ago, it seemed as if everything was going to change," and sometimes implicitly, as when a department store supervisor informs a photographer about the store's racially exclusive modeling policy, although, of course, the supervisor herself feels "*very* different." Both of these statements suggest how the Civil Rights Act of 1964, one of the three significant legislative acts of the 1960s that affected national racial politics, did not solve all of the problems of being African American. In fact, the act may have contributed to a complacency and an ambivalence among white and nonwhite Americans that made it harder for African Americans to achieve professionally.[9] For at the same time that Americans were questioning the day-to-day effects of the legal achievements of the 1960s, African Americans were being called on to pull themselves up by their "socks," apparently the 1970s version of boot-straps, and to take advantage of recent juridical advancements.[10] Other uncertainties concerned what, specifically, constituted "success" in a post–Civil Rights Act world. As with *Mahogany*'s theme song, Diana Ross's "Do You Know Where You're Going To?," the film posits questions that would become familiar to the young black American shaped by such legislation, the African American "cultural mulatto" of the 1970s and 1980s:[11] How hard are you willing to work to make your dreams come true? Are you willing to sacrifice personal happiness for professional achievement? And, once you and other African American individuals have advanced socially, how should you "give back" to your neighborhood or communities?

Two scholars who examine the film, Jane Gaines and Robyn Wiegman, situate their analyses within the context of feminist film theory and analyze how early academic feminism ignored, appropriated, or commodified the experiences of African American women. In "White Privilege and Looking Relations," Gaines actively questions her own position as a white feminist critic reading black cultural images, and she raises important concerns about the way that feminist film theory uses Marxist and psychoanalytic concepts in relation to women of color. The emphasis on class in one theory and gender in the other failed to account adequately for the experiences of the black female subject.[12] In "Black Bodies/American Commodities," Wiegman cautions against the complacency that may result if the spectator is seduced by the "good" cinematic images of African Americans. Examining black female representation from the 1930s to the 1980s, Wiegman demonstrates how films such as *Mahogany* and *Lethal Weapon* present positive images of black femininity primarily to provide a false appearance of a democratizing and egalitarian America; such images thus render obsolete the call for equality that was so central to the civil rights and feminist movements.[13] Both Gaines and Wiegman take issue with how *Mahogany* positions race against gender, privileging one aspect of identity over the other and denying the way these qualities, along with issues of class, intersect in the portrayal of black femininity. Thus Wiegman asserts that the film "veil[s] the black woman's complex positioning by casting her oppression solely within the symbolic register of white masculine desire." And Gaines argues that "we may not immediately see white man as the aggressor against Black woman. Other strategies encourage the viewer to forget or not notice racial issues."[14]

Gaines and Wiegman wrote their analyses during specific moments in the history of feminist film theory, and thus they invite a reexamination, particularly because, as Gaines herself notes, the discussions about the problems of psychoanalysis, a key element of early feminist film theory, and the specific concerns of women of color emerged contemporaneously.[15] Now that the complex issues raised by Gaines and Wiegman have been recognized, what previously unexplored issues of nonwhite female representation are located in a narrative so obviously constructed along the lines of "classical narrative cinema"?[16] Further, how does the examination of American politics in the film withstand more contemporary analyses of black political participation in the 1970s and the cinematic representation of such involvement?

A focus on Tracy's visual acumen and its role in fulfilling her goals highlights with remarkable clarity the issues of race, class, gender, and politics in *Mahogany*. The film problematically portrays a narrative of black female success and the (self-)policing of black women who venture either *outside* the bounds of ideal American family life or *into* the narratives of success that have previously been constructed by and restricted to white American men. Ironically, the potential threat of black female achievement intersects the theoretical concept of psychoanalysis that Gaines identifies as inadequate to address fully the historical dimensions of the black family and the development of black femininity. Briefly invoking psychoanalysis, the Moynihan Report is a post–civil rights document that attempts to explain the American work ethic, the opportunities enabled by civil rights legislation, and the cultural perceptions of black male and female achievement.

Officially titled *The Negro Family: The Case for National Action*, the report was initially a confidential analysis by Moynihan, then assistant secretary in the Department of

Labor, to explain the disparate levels of success among groups of African Americans. How to account for the perception, quite dramatically illustrated through charts and statistics, that some blacks had achieved a level of success equal to whites while others had not? Although the period from 1954 to 1964, from the Supreme Court's *Brown v. Board of Education of Topeka, Kansas* decision to the passage of the monumental Civil Rights Act, was the time of the "negro revolution," some African Americans did not benefit during this period, and Moynihan attributed this difference to the presence or absence of a stable family. Drawing on the work of several prominent African American scholars and activists, such as Kenneth Clark, E. Franklin Frazier, and Whitney Young, men who emphasized the problem of female-headed households in black families, Moynihan called the family unit the most important structure through which children are socialized into their environment and noted that, unlike the (assumed) norm of white American families, black families are usually headed by women. This difference demoralized the black father and negatively affected the black male child and his self-esteem, which in turn contributed to black male unemployment and the continuation of a vicious cycle.[17] According to Moynihan, the status of the black family would reach crisis proportions unless the government intervened.[18] Early in *The Negro Family*, Moynihan invokes psychoanalysis, writing that "[a] fundamental insight of psychoanalytic theory . . . is that the child learns a way of looking at life in his early years through which all later experiences [are] viewed and which profoundly shapes his adult conduct."[19] Although this single brief reference to psychoanalysis in *The Negro Family* is odd, cited mainly to bolster the report's general thesis that family is key to a child's development, Moynihan's invocation and use of it exemplifies larger cultural and patriarchal assumptions about the need for masculine authority in the family. Moynihan's analysis of the black family, during slavery and later, can best be described as a "distortion," attributing female-headed households as the cause and not the result of poverty and racial oppression. As numerous scholars have shown, constructions of the black family were much more diverse and complex than that portrayed in the Moynihan Report. Angela Davis notes, for instance, that within the slave family, men and women performed domestic work equally, "but to go further and maintain that [women] consequently dominated their men is to fundamentally distort the reality of slave life."[20] During reconstruction, marriage took on political, social, and economic significance among upwardly mobile African Americans. For women in such families, respectability and propriety were important not just to prove that black women could in fact be "ladies" but to challenge racial stereotypes of loose morality. Late-nineteenth and early-twentieth-century black women reflected ideas about the black family and, more generally, African Americans as a group. As the historian Michelle Mitchell argues, "Orderly marital relations [were] indicative of collective progress."[21] The public representation of women in black families continued to act as a metonym for blacks collectively throughout the twentieth century. During the black nationalist movement of the 1960s, activists appropriated the black matriarchy concept to assert a heterosexual, masculine dominance as a vital component to the black revolution. "[A]gree[ing] with Moynihan's thesis about the emasculating effects of black women and the need for black men to resume their roles as patriarchs," black nationalist groups, such as the Black Panther Party, employed masculinist rhetoric and encouraged women to accept secondary positions in organizations and familial units in order to fight the "larger" cause of racial inequality.[22]

It is in this historical context of the black family that we need to understand the late-twentieth-century gendered, familial imperative that ultimately constrains Tracy's career goals and later contributes to the significance of Tracy and Brian's union at the end of the film. Although *Mahogany* takes place during a moment of supposed social and economic opportunity for black women, it perceptively reveals a more entrenched and impalpable racism and a culture's resistance to an excess of success by black women. This resistance to black female success has most insidiously been invoked in the Moynihan Report. As Hortense Spillers notes, Moynihan "suggests that 'underachievement' in black males of the lower classes is primarily the fault of black females, who achieve out of all proportion, both to their numbers in the community and to the paradigmatic example before the nation."[23] Statistically, black women are too successful, even in programs that are designed to assist African Americans generally. Citing the government's hiring efforts in the Department of Labor, for example, Moynihan noted that "special efforts have been made recently to insure equal employment opportunity for Negroes . . . However, it may well be that these efforts have redounded mostly to the benefit of Negro women, and may even have accentuated the comparative disadvantage of Negro men."[24] The report implies that if the black woman would only use her ambition in the service of the family and the black man, the black family could more readily repeat the appearance of a white nuclear family, and the black man could, finally, take advantage of government programs, become a productive contributor to American society, and encourage future male generations. In this way, black men would not only "shar[e] in the responsibilities and rewards of citizenship" and support their wives and children without government assistance but also help the nation live up to its ideal of liberty, if not equality, for all. Moynihan's family narrative is not only a racial narrative but also a national one with significant political, economic, and gender implications. Throughout his analysis, Moynihan develops an interdependence between the African American family and America's lofty, and unfulfilled, ideals.[25]

Wiegman, Gaines, and, in a different context, Spillers have shown how psychoanalytic paradigms were inadequate to account for certain aspects of African American experience; Roderick Ferguson and Steve Estes have delineated how the Moynihan Report contributed to a rhetoric of gender, sexual, and familial normativity during the civil rights movement.[26] Building on their work, I aim to understand how *Mahogany* equates semiotic aptitude with performing (or failing to perform) "success," and how Tracy, in order to fulfill a post–civil rights national and racial narrative of the family like that posited by Moynihan, must either disavow this skill or use it to improve a male partner. At moments the film seems to be a cinematic retelling of the Moynihan Report, complete with a theme song that appears to paraphrase a line from it. (Compare, for example, Moynihan's injunction that African Americans must determine for themselves how they want "to move from where they now are to where they want, and ought to be" and the first few lines of *Mahogany*'s theme song.)[27] The message is that Tracy must redirect her ambition and creativity; she must use her visual and verbal skills not to further her own career in a foreign country but to advance the national political career of Brian, a man of quick temper who struggles to develop a recognizable (i.e., visible) political presence to "make [Chicago] a better place."

Visual knowledge—a savvy awareness about how images and the body create an elusive aura or celebrity presence—functions in *Mahogany* as a type of currency that can be exchanged, bartered for the unlimited success that seemed possible with the passage of multiple civil rights acts. To achieve in *Mahogany*'s post–Civil Rights Act world and in a consumer and political culture dominated by the visual, in order to take advantage of the affirmative action opportunities that others have rallied, marched, and sometimes even died for, one must be adroit in the visual signs of American life. Brian fails because he lacks visual knowledge and verbal prowess, a point the film makes repetitively. Instead, visual sophistication and oratorical skills are embodied in the black female character, a figure that has historically been the abject object of the gaze, visually naive about the effect or implications of appearances, or present merely to provide negative difference to the white female. "Achieving out of all proportion" as an international model and designer, Tracy must retreat professionally in order for "her man" to succeed in America. But until the end of *Mahogany*, Tracy refuses to be contained by the men in her life. In fact, no one in the film can contain her overwhelming professional ambition until she, quite savagely, does so herself. The film celebrates the potential that resides in a normative, heterosexual family, even as it denigrates Tracy's unusual ambition—facilitated in part by the profound social transformations wrought by the civil rights movement.

Motown's Visual Politics

In her cultural history of Motown, Suzanne Smith notes how important a public image was for Motown's "commodities," its musical acts. First organized as Tamla Records in 1959, Motown was incorporated as a music company one year later and achieved success with an "automated" method of creating and marketing black talent. Specific people in Motown were responsible for writing and developing the music and then crafting an act's image, and Motown's artist development section, or "the company 'charm school,'" became significant to a group's success. By mid-1964, artist development was an established division within Motown and the space where "performers learned etiquette, deportment, choreography, and stage presence" in order to bring the musical groups to "wider and whiter audiences."[28] During this period, one particular Motown group, the Supremes, began receiving "wider and whiter" public attention, appearing as part of Dick Clark's "Caravan of Stars" summer tour in 1964 and then performing at the elite Copacabana nightclub in 1965. Although the women who would form the Supremes arrived at Motown with an already well-developed fashion sense and social poise, Motown honed their skills, and Berry Gordy in particular developed and refined those abilities in the Supremes' lead singer, Diana Ross.[29]

Much about Ross's background is reflected in *Mahogany*, with Tracy's success in fashion replacing Ross's success in music. In his autobiography, Gordy reflects on his determination to make Ross a more versatile star by casting the singer in films. After the Supremes broke up and Ross began a solo career in 1970, Gordy planned to place her in movies and television to move her "to unparalleled heights."[30] Casting her in films with Billy Dee Williams, dubbed "the black Clark Gable," was central to this goal.[31]

The pairing of Ross and Williams served as an alternative to the African American cinematic representations available in the blaxploitation films of the 1970s, such as *Shaft* (1971) or *Foxy Brown* (1974), action films that presented sensational, crime-driven images of African Americans and reflected the more nationalist elements of the civil rights movement. For example, Melvin Van Peebles's *Sweet Sweetback's Baadasssss Song* (1971) reflected an assertive black nationalist theme, garnering an endorsement from Black Panther cofounder Huey Newton as "'the first truly revolutionary black film.'"[32] *Mahogany* also offered politics but a more mainstream and idealistic conception of the American political system. Like Motown's most successful musical acts, the union of Ross and Williams provided safe elements of blackness that could appeal to black audiences yet still attract white moviegoers. Gordy saw the coupling of Ross and Williams in terms of possible profit and payoff: "With the two as a romantic leading couple, I felt we could have a franchise—like Astaire and Rogers and Tracy and Hepburn."[33] First united in the 1973 film *Lady Sings the Blues*, Ross and Williams presented to America a black romantic couple in a mainstream film in which they were also the leading stars—a sight not seen by American filmgoers since Twentieth Century Fox's 1954 musical *Carmen Jones*.[34] Within the context of *Mahogany*, the pairing offered the promise of black upward mobility and stability—an African American romantic couple that reflected societal norms and a duo that could challenge prevalent images of dysfunctional black couples and families in America during that time.

The difficult political and economic landscape of 1970s black America resonates powerfully throughout the film. Although wage inequalities between blacks and whites decreased after the civil rights legislation of 1964 and 1965, black unemployment remained high, especially among black men.[35] As one unemployed black man states in the film to Brian campaigning to be an alderman, "I'll vote for anyone who can get me a job." But, notably, the political and economic stresses affect the two lead characters in differing ways. Brian, a former lawyer, has a middle-class status but working-class concerns, while Tracy refuses to let her working-class background stall her ambitiously upperclass dreams. The class stratification between Brian and Tracy highlights Brian's transformational community politics and Tracy's careerist individualism.[36] By identifying Brian with the very real dilemmas of urban

African Americans in the 1970s, such as high unemployment and urban renewal, the film portrays him as the more politically invested character, the one figure in the film who can redeem America's broken promises. But one of Brian's more challenging tasks will be to awaken Tracy to these important dilemmas confronting her neighborhood and, more expansively, the black urban class of which she is a part. How, the film asks, will her blind ambition to be a designer be brought under control to help her man and her people?

Declarations of Independence and Difference

Mahogany initially, and quite fervently, draws on America's celebrated myth of unlimited opportunities for those who are willing to work hard. Yet Tracy is constantly reprimanded for exceeding expectations. Indeed, in an early scene in a design class, Tracy struggles against simplicity. Her instructor asks the students to draw a simple cocktail dress, and Tracy's classmates have complied by sketching basic dresses. But when the camera pans over Tracy's shoulders, we see her designing an elaborate dress with long, flowing sleeves. The bold gold and brown design seems to take up the whole page of her sketchbook. Her teacher gives another assignment: "a basic swimsuit . . . no sequins, no rhinestones, no ostrich feathers," she warns Tracy, who responds by giving the teacher a dismissive, rather ominous look, a glare that she will frequently direct to those who underestimate or question her skills and ambition.

When the film begins, Tracy has been promoted from a saleswoman behind a counter in a Marshall Field's department store to an assistant in the display department. Explaining her late arrival for work one morning, Tracy blames her night classes. Although she attends the classes on her own time, her supervisor, Mrs. Evans, advises her to let her "promotion to the display department satisfy any creative urge you may *think* you have." Despite these reprimands, Tracy never gives up her dreams of designing and showing her own fashion line, even when she later becomes a successful model in Italy. To gain publicity as a designer, for example, she arrives at a fashion shoot wearing her own creations and later walks a runway for a charity event wearing her own flamboyant design. Never content with the status quo in her life, Tracy is a woman who may be the most ideal candidate for writing "A Plea for Color," a manifesto that, according to Helga in Nella Larsen's novel *Quicksand* (1928), would celebrate the dark body as a palette for vibrant clothing.[37] Unfortunately, *Mahogany* equates the development of Tracy's character and the resolution of the plot with her ability to subsume her ambition, to rein in her quest to stand out and be different, and to use her desire for originality in the service of Brian.

In answer to the theme song's questions, Tracy knows exactly what she wants: to be a fashion designer, to have her own line. One of the narrative's more interesting strategies is to reflect Tracy's career goals in her creations. Dismayed with the fashion knock-offs that populate the department store, Tracy wonders about her colleagues, "Why did all these people labor so mightily, fighting, scrambling, competing, stealing the best designs of Paris, Rome, London, Dublin—and yes, New York, and once having grasped these treasures, proceed to destroy them, cheapen them with subtle changes, reductions, substitutions?"[38] Tracy positions an American city as an afterthought to European spaces of fashion creativity and rebels against the discounted clothes that serve merely a utilitarian purpose instead of clothes that inspire women. Her own designs provide the best example of "couture" fashion. In one scene, she models one of her multicolored dresses, twirling around to achieve a rainbow effect, as if she were flying. Tracy wears this design, notably, during a scene in which she learns how her race and gender, as well as her reluctance to leave the United States, may prevent her from flying—prevent her, that is, from achieving her goals. If she remains in America, she will be limited by people like Mrs. Evans who practice a covert racism. The scene presents a delicate indictment of America, which cannot accommodate Tracy's dreams, despite the civil rights movement, the laws derived from them, and perhaps even the then recent policy of affirmative action.

It thus becomes apparent that the obstacles to Tracy's dreams are less institutional and more individual, and one of the primary individuals restricting her aspirations is, unfortunately, her romantic interest, Brian. Surrounded by an impoverished setting on Chicago's South Side, the two discuss their goals and dreams and, implicitly, the best way for African Americans to challenge the urban plight and improve their conditions and those of their less fortunate neighbors. Their disagreement about this issue mirrors the unanswerable issues raised by *The Negro Family*. One danger of the Moynihan Report was the statistical evidence it provided for the beliefs of disparate political groups. Depending on one's ideological inclinations, the report could be used either to advocate for more government programs to assist African Americans or to excoriate African Americans for failing to take advantage of the programs that already existed, a division that *Mahogany* replicates as well: Should the audience admire Tracy's desire to leave Chicago or root for her to stay in the United States with Brian as he improves existing government programs and develops new ones?[39] *Mahogany* presents this issue of black advancement in ways that, initially, evade easy solutions. As Tracy slowly gets closer to her dream—by assisting Sean in a photo shoot in an economically and physically distressed area of Chicago, by organizing her fashion designs for her collection, by pitching the designs to clothing manufacturers—Brian attempts to awaken her to the reality of her status in Chicago and the extraordinary nature of the goal she has set for herself.

The urban photo shoot scene demonstrates one of the primary ways to disparage Tracy's ambition: to portray her dream as outlandish and as opposed to the goals of the civil rights movement. Sean has organized a photo shoot on the South Side, with a dilapidated house as the backdrop. Well-dressed models are interspersed throughout the house, where they contrast with the rundown neighborhood and its African American residents. The scene dramatizes what the sociologist Ella Bell identifies as the "bicultural experience" of the professional black woman, which necessitates "a dynamic, fluid life structure" in which she maintains mobility between her personal and professional arenas.[40] This scene in the film literalizes Bell's metaphorical movement between a white and black world. Shuttling between Sean, photographing from the house, and Brian, stationed behind a wire fence, Tracy must divide her attention between the two men. Tracy's entire dialogue with Brian takes place through the fence that physically separates the couple who also disagree philosophically. While Tracy sees the shoot as a networking opportunity, Brian sees Sean's photography as exploiting the neighborhood's residents, including Tracy.

Not only is Tracy's goal apparently unrealistic, it is also individualized and personal: she has no explicit desire to bring her community along with her, wherever she goes. Yet even when the audience is presented with the stark contradiction between Tracy's elite aspirations and her surroundings, they can still hope that she will overcome this gap, if only to defy expectations. She responds passionately to Brian, emphatically stated in a close-up: "One thing I can't forget and that's how many times I've been told what I can't do and where I can't go and why I can't be different from anybody else. Because that's all I've had to keep track of all my life, from everybody." Tracy's declaration of independence and difference taps into the allure and hope that anyone can make it in America, a promise denied to African Americans by years of discrimination, rectified by civil rights legislation, yet still unfulfilled, as Moynihan noted in his report.

Additional obstacles to Tracy's dream derive from her status as a workingclass woman of color. Throughout the 1970s, political and legal gains by African Americans improved the economic conditions for black and white women. In addition to offering legal safeguards against segregation in public facilities, the Civil Rights Act of 1964 prohibited gender discrimination and led to more equitably based admission policies in U.S. educational institutions. The film, once again, calls into question the impact of such legal successes. For example, Tracy's aunt works as a seamstress in what appears to be a sweatshop filled mostly with other women, and Tracy has difficulty finding a paying job as a designer but can readily locate employment as a secretary. Moreover, the film repeatedly portrays the implications of Tracy's need for a job to pay the rent so her fashion dream can become reality, despite her recent promotion. Restricted by the temporal demands of a nine-to-five job, Tracy uses the excuse of a doctor's appointment to secure time to interview with a designer and get a better job. When she accidentally leaves her sketchbook in the designer's office, the designer calls Tracy at work and exposes her ruse. Mrs. Evans fires her, apparently as much for the deception as for being too ambitious, for too obviously hoping to leave her assistant job for one more in line with her professional goal. Also suggesting Tracy's financial predicament is her decision to take the subway and walk home alone rather than spend money on a taxi. Had she splurged on a taxi, Tracy could have avoided being harassed outside her subway stop. Finally, Tracy's economic concerns are revealed by the "bum check" she uses to get Brian out of jail. Rather than obscure class, the film demonstrates how much Tracy has to "hustle" to ensure that her working-class background does not prevent her from achieving her dream.

Economics also influence Tracy by continually placing her in the position of having to determine if and how she will "sell" her body or her designs. The film introduces this dilemma early in a brief, humorous moment when Tracy foils a potential assault. When she realizes she is being followed at night by a stranger, she turns around, confronts the man, and pretends to be a prostitute, asking "Wanna buy a piece of ass?" While the man stands there stunned by Tracy's surprise offer, she strolls away safely. The scene amusingly illustrates her street smarts and street knowledge, but raises a serious issue she will have to address throughout the film: will she indeed be bought? When she is finally head of Mahogany Creations, Inc., and thus in the position of reprimanding an employee, she is still not the one who pays that worker's salary, as she is reminded by Christian, a wealthy Italian count who is yet another love interest for Tracy. Her final success—the showing of her Asian-inspired fashion line that opens and closes the film—is mitigated by the fact that she has to "pay up" and complete, physically and sexually, her part of what Christian had earlier termed a business "deal," by having sex with him.[41]

Tracy's ability to navigate urban Chicago suggests her confidence and her refusal to be limited by obstacles, either those created by her specific circumstances as a single, working black woman or those that others attempt to impose on her. Hazel Carby has examined the social danger evoked by the black woman who refuses to regulate herself or to allow others to monitor her actions; she argues that the migrating black woman of the early twentieth century was a threat because "if a black woman can claim her freedom and migrate to an urban environment, what is to keep her from negotiating her own path through its streets?" Although Carby writes of an earlier era, elements in *Mahogany* exemplify several of her arguments. The Tracy Chambers of the 1970s could, like her earlier, migrating sisters, "be variously situated as a threat to the progress of the race; as a threat to the establishment of a respectable urban black middle class; as a threat to congenial black and white middle-class relations; and as a threat to the formation of black masculinity in an urban environment."[42]

Tracy's status as the potential social menace described by Carby is, notably, most evident in her interactions with Brian, "a handsome ghetto dude who could light up Tracy like a pinball machine."[43] Brian is an activist attempting to organize the Southside Block Association to prevent the demolition of apartments in the area. Although he has achieved some success as a lawyer before running for alderman, he is susceptible to the professional defects that have stereotypically been attributed to black men. Heckled by a group of white construction workers as he tries to give a speech outdoors, Brian has to be physically restrained by his campaign worker, Will, who warns him, "You know that's how we always blow it." Will implies that black male violence, or more generally a lack of self-control, has thwarted or compromised the achievements of black men. This scene also communicates how Tracy is a threat or a "disruptive presence."[44] She secretly pours milk into Brian's bullhorn, which then douses him when he places it near his face, to the delight of the white men standing nearby. Her practical joke reveals the various impediments a mobile and ambitious black woman creates as described by Carby, for the prank provokes a fight between black and white men, sends Brian to jail for a night, and prevents him from sharing information about government programs with black Chicago residents.

Tracy's threats appear even more disturbing in light of the Moynihan Report's assumptions about black femininity and masculinity. Again, Moynihan's incidental examples, apparently innocuous, present the most damaging and striking generalizations of black femininity and masculinity. According to Moynihan's narrative, discriminatory practices prevent a visual and performative machismo and restrict the black male's literal and metaphorical mobility. Drawing on an example from Reconstruction, Moynihan asserts that "the very essence of the male animal, from the bantam rooster to the four-star general, is to strut. Indeed, in nineteenth-century America, a particular type of exaggerated male boastfulness became almost a national style. Not for the Negro male. The 'sassy nigger' was lynched." Moreover, Moynihan argues that Jim Crow segregation had a harsher effect on the black man than the black woman, for the black male circulated more often in public spaces: "The male was more likely to use public facilities, which rapidly became segregated once the process began, and just as important, segregation, and the submissiveness it exacts, is surely more destructive to the male than to the female personality."[45] The types of male debasement cited here are, notably, forms in which Brian fails and Tracy succeeds: public, visual self-presentation and mobility.

As I discuss below, *Mahogany* continually presents female prowess and male embarrassment. The professional fields that Brian and Tracy choose, politics and fashion, demand performances before a public, commodity-producing gaze; as such, professional accomplishments in these fields are connoted and measured by visual signs. Both characters' visual aptitude contrasts with that of Sean, a former combat photographer. *Mahogany* presents the three major figures along a spectrum of visual and national morality and intelligence: the hapless Brian lacks visual knowledge and flounders in his campaign in America, while Tracy displays a greater level of knowledge and uses her skills to further her career goals outside the United States, and Sean artfully and malevolently manipulates his visual aptitude, in the United States and abroad.

Visualizing Success—and Failure

Mahogany shows a wide disparity between the visual competence of Brian and Tracy. Brian foreshadows the group of African American politicians active in the 1990s and early 2000s, including Barack Obama, Deval Patrick, Cory Booker, and Harold Ford Jr. As embodied antidotes to the Moynihan Report, these men have reaped the benefits of post–civil rights initiatives and programs.[46] Unlike the real African American politicians of the twenty-first century, however, Brian Walker lacks visual acumen. He is a poor performer without "pizzazz," Tracy's word for charisma. While it does so less overtly than the Robert Redford film *The Candidate* (1972), *Mahogany* does reveal the ineluctable marriage between politics and spectacle, primarily by suggesting that a union between Brian and Tracy could help him be more effective in his local campaign.[47] Brian would benefit from Tracy's most commodifiable attribute: performing in front of others and developing an image to sell to the public. Brian gives several speeches throughout the film. He haltingly plods through each one, earnestly describing the benefits of a government program or asserting his qualifications for city alderman. But his speeches are problematic: they consist of generalities and the empty, political rhetoric of campaign promises that fail to address the concrete realities of being black, poor, and unemployed in Chicago. He does not achieve a comfortable style of delivery until Tracy adopts a persona to tease Brian in public: "a widow from the South Side with six kids" (a persona that recalls the single-black-mother paradigm made familiar by the Moynihan Report). Though Tracy's banter is in fun, her jests in the middle of an unemployment office force Brian to address the day-to-day issues of the people he would like to represent and thereby make more compelling impromptu presentations to his constituency. By developing humorous campaign slogans for Brian and drawing the designs for his campaign posters, Tracy reveals how much Brian the candidate needs her, and she becomes particularly invaluable to him while she is unemployed. The unmarried Brian needs Tracy to attend functions and dinners with him, events where other politicians are accompanied by their wives. The difference between Tracy's visual and verbal successes and Brian's failures is most clearly revealed when Brian asks his campaign workers how the press is covering his campaign. One finds no coverage in the newspaper he is reading, and another reports that their party is doing poorly in the polls. At this moment a campaign worker hands Brian a magazine containing a glossy image of Tracy. The magazine is not a high-fashion, gossip publication but the politically relevant *Newsweek*. The picture confirms Tracy's transatlantic success while highlighting Brian's local failure. The message is that black male access to the world of political power and the media is blocked, but Tracy's unique combination of skills—her savvy about visual images and appearances and her ability to construct short, memorable campaign slogans—represents a promising "open door" for Brian. Tracy has knowledge and a flair for public presentations that Brian needs as an up-and-coming political figure. Brian must learn from Tracy how to use language and images, how to negotiate the verbal and the visual in a predominantly white American male culture and achieve "success." The film equates the mass duplication of one's image with personal and professional achievement; it seems to ask how to substitute Tracy's closeup for Brian's and how Tracy can replace her designs and images on billboards with posters and billboards featuring Brian.

At times the film is quite punishing in comparing Brian's relative lack of visual knowledge with Tracy's visual intelligence; in fact, the narrative briefly places Brian in the conventional role of the vulnerable, naive woman. Tracy moves successfully through the streets of Chicago as well as the boulevards of Rome. Discouraged when Brian dismisses her career plans, she travels fairly easily to Italy. Brian, however, is noticeably out of place when he visits Tracy in Rome. He is shocked that Tracy will spend "57,000" for his new Italian suit—and she has to tell him that the payment is in lire, not American dollars. After she buys the suit, Brian resorts to behavior traditionally associated with the unconfident woman: "I feel like a sissy walking around holding this thing. Everybody is looking at me." Yet Brian's unease only works to further validate an American heterosexual masculinity and becomes another strategy the film uses to devalue Tracy's ambitions. Tracy's party in Italy is a location where Brian, unable to communicate in a foreign language and caught in an unfamiliar space, needs labels to tell, in his derogatory words, "who from what." The film links a heterosexual masculinity to national identity—it confirms Brian's normative sexuality as more "American" here. Tracy is comfortable in a space where nonnormative sexuality and transgender identities are ordinary and unremarkable, but the celebration as seen through Brian's eyes is marked by what he will later call a "freakish" deviance.[48] Moreover, Tracy's reproductive capabilities—her potential to be a wife and a mother and thus satisfy a black familial imperative—will go unfulfilled in this place of exotic excess.[49]

As the representative of this location where gender categories are visually indeterminate, Sean McEvoy contrasts with Brian; together they provide a central dichotomy of the story, with Tracy as the physical prize for which the two men compete. Physically and philosophically, the two men are polar opposites. Whereas the handsome Brian tries to renovate Chicago's housing projects, the emaciated Sean aestheticizes poverty in order to produce a good photograph. Sean has a hyperconscious awareness of how to make the ordinary into fantasy, along with a keen sense of the boundary between truth and artifice and knowledge of how to exploit others' confusion over these distinctions. Sean continually poses people, either explicitly with commands or more manipulatively with a camera or a gun; these "inanimate objects" are "fiercely truthful" even when he is not, and he relies on them to control Brian and Tracy.

In the context of Tracy and her ambition, however, Brian's and Sean's differences are less important than their similarities. Both try to undermine Tracy's focus on her goals and both equate Tracy with inanimate objects; Sean, notably, renames Tracy to reflect an object that is "rich, dark, beautiful, and rare": mahogany. Perhaps most importantly, the one other trait Brian and Sean have in common is their experiences of crushing failures that prevent what Moynihan calls "an exaggerated male boastfulness."[50] We learn about one of Brian's several failures after the fact: when he visits Tracy in Italy, he tells her he lost the election for alderman. He has come to Italy to convince her to return to Chicago to help him win a much bigger political position: United States senator for the state of Illinois.[51] Sean fails when he is unable to "prove," sexually, how much he loves Tracy. Later, his impotence leads him to try to diminish Tracy's success: he rips the dress she wears to a photo shoot and humiliates her when she dares to wear her own dress at a charity fashion show.

Because she is unable to be contained by the two men, the film ultimately weakens Tracy by pathologizing her success as unnatural and abnormal; this pathology is articulated not by Sean, who becomes more unstable as the film progresses, but by the supposedly normal, and normative, Brian. Brian initially defines Tracy's success as "some kind of cartoon character that [Sean] made up—freak of the month." Notably, when Tracy finally achieves her goal—showing her own fashion line—she hears not the sounds of success and the applause of admiration but a voice of doubt: Brian whispering *Nothing!*" In a sequence of approximately five minutes near the end of the film, Tracy is either completely silent as Christian, the financier of her clothing line, complains of "being cold for weeks" or she resorts to uttering the childlike refrain: "I want to go home." She evolves from a confident, assertive woman who can clearly articulate her life goals to one who hears voices in her head. The film adopts an easy strategy to depict a woman suffering from questionable delusions, such as thinking she can operate her own clothing company.

Unfortunately, these strategies succeed not only in weakening Tracy but also in blunting the spectator's narrative, if not visual, pleasure. There is something quite pleasurable about seeing a woman persevere against latent racism, obvious sexism, and individual mediocrity. Thus when Tracy decides to return to Chicago for what is implied will be a marriage to Brian and perhaps a more quotidian career in the fashion industry, it brings, at least to this viewer, a level of disappointment. Earlier in the film, a designer rejects Tracy by stating, "This is Chicago, not Paris. You don't make it here, you end up here." One cannot help but feel that Tracy's ambition has been replaced by a forced complacency. Having indeed made it elsewhere, in Italy, Tracy gives up that success to settle in Chicago. The film seems to ask Tracy to choose the least of three evils: work with an emotionally unstable photographer, be a well-paid mistress to an older Italian, or use her creative intelligence in the service of her "ol' man" and the black residents of Chicago. Ironically, the film cannot envision "Diana Ross's dream come true"—of being successful, if not in her hometown then at least somewhere in her own country, of simultaneously having a career as a designer and a life as a married woman.[52]

By the end of the film, an intertwined racial, familial, and, more subtly, national, paradigm asserts itself. When the resolution is achieved and Brian and Tracy are reunited, their reunion is rendered in a form resembling a marriage ceremony. Brian asks several questions of Tracy in the final scene: "Are you prepared to stand by [your man] when the going gets rough? Would you be willing to put your imagination to work on behalf of the cause he's fighting for? Would you love, cherish him for the rest of your life? Madam, if you're willing to do all that, I'll guarantee you, I'll get you your ol' man back." The oaths Tracy affirms enact Brian's definition of success as "nothing without someone you love to share it with." The final scene of a campaign rally, then, is both a democratic and a matrimonial ceremony and perhaps most fully reflects the possibility of a patriotic, self-sustaining black family. Tracy has little possibility of creating a conventional family life in a foreign land with Sean or Christian, but Brian's (African) American vitality encourages one to assume he will be able to procreate with Tracy. The black man will be the head of the household, and, as Moynihan imagines in his report, traditional familial roles will be replicated in the black (sub)urban environment; they will be good citizens. For Brian will now not only be a husband and possibly a father; he will also contribute actively to the betterment of the country if he wins this second election. As with the

Moynihan Report, this heterosexual family narrative intersects with a national one. The report was not just a compendium of statistics and thoughts on the black family. It was also a tract to help engage blacks to be better participants, if not in the American political system then at least in the American dream, and to help the country "at last redeem the full promise of the Declaration of Independence."[53] Brian will contribute to the betterment of the government in one of the most elite forms possible in the country: service as a U.S. congressman.

One should not overlook the potential of the collaboration between Tracy and Brian. There is a promising transformative power in Brian and Tracy's alliance that may accomplish significant benefits for Chicago residents, the "cause that [Brian] is fighting for." The film thus speaks to the possibility that black male-female unions may be instrumental in changing social and economic injustices. This union, however, is predicated on Tracy subsuming her career interests. To see how differently the film could have ended, one need only view the previously mentioned *Nothing but a Man*, appearing independently eleven years before *Mahogany*. Both films conclude by affirming a black familial unit, but in the earlier film the stabilization of the black family does not involve the dilution of female self-sufficiency. Taking place in Alabama in 1963, *Nothing but a Man* obliquely references major events of the civil rights movement, such as the Emmett Till lynching in Mississippi eight years earlier and Martin Luther King Jr.'s desegregation efforts in nearby Birmingham.[54] Duff gives up a well-paying, nomadic job as part of a railroad section gang in order to marry the middle-class Josie, a teacher and the daughter of the town's conservative preacher. Although Josie demonstrates empathy for the specific challenges Duff faces as a black working-class man in a rural southern town, Duff still believes that Josie does not fully comprehend his frustrations. He leaves her in part because of these frustrations and his inabilities to maintain a job, but he returns when he realizes that, with Josie at his side, he can be a better father to his son than his own father was to him. Throughout the film, Duff maintains a rebellious spirit, and his relationship with Josie is important to sustaining this fighting mode, his commitment to "make trouble" in their small, segregated southern world.

In a cogent reading of the "male-female interdependency" exemplified in *Nothing but a Man*, Judith Smith argues that "despite the unequal power dynamics" between Duff and Josie, the film's "representation of gender and family mutuality . . . constitute a key resource enabling resistance." Brian and Tracy's relationship also consists of "unequal power dynamics," and the resolution of *Mahogany* requires that Tracy relinquish some of that power to ensure an effective bond. But Duff and Josie, by using "the resources of marital and familial reciprocity," will be able to survive in their town.[55] Both *Nothing but a Man* and *Mahogany* raise issues that will concern African American women writers of the 1970s—constructing gendered responses to covert racism and systematic inequities and questioning the strength of the union between black men and women joined in such battles. But *Nothing but a Man* is the more progressive, indeed radical, film, not only in its portrayal of middle-class black femininity but also in its unambiguous celebration of the fighting potential of black male and female love. This fight and its difficulties are signaled by Duff's final words, spoken over Josie's shoulder as the camera closes in on Josie's face: "It ain't gonna be easy. But it'll be alright. Baby, I feel so free inside." Duff's words demonstrate the collaborative potential between black men and black women during and after the civil rights movement.

After Tracy

Since *Mahogany*'s 1975 premiere, the cinematic representation of the successful black professional woman has increased—but not always for the better. Predominantly black-cast dramas such as *Love Jones* (1997) and *Soul Food* (1997) present multidimensional appraisals of the complex black female life, but a range of black urban comedies—from 1992's *Boomerang* to 2003's *Deliver Us from Eva*—often use the female professional as a standard source of humor.

Perhaps the best—or worst—image of professional black women appeared via the cinematic "event" for women in the late twentieth century, *Waiting to Exhale*. Premiering at number one in December 1995, *Waiting to Exhale* became an occasion, according to news media, for women of various ethnicities to attend the film in large blocks. Articles published in the *New York Times, Time,* and *Newsweek* celebrated the fact that black professional women could finally see themselves onscreen and watch successful black women deal with "real-life" relationship issues. Yet the film's complexity resided not in the portrayal of the four central characters but in their relationships with the men in their lives: Savannah is romantically involved with a married man, Gloria feels rejected by her gay ex-husband, Robin cannot perceive the obvious deception of her many lovers, and Bernadine must fight for money to support herself and her two children when her husband leaves her for another woman. Although these are incidents that many women may face, the characters' persistent concern with finding and keeping a man in order to feel "complete" undermined any narrative plot suggesting female sufficiency and aptitude. Although *Waiting to Exhale* was a commercially successful "crossover" film, it continued to deny a cinematic image of professional, happily partnered women of color in nonheteronormative relationships. Indeed, *Waiting to Exhale* presented yet another, albeit, new, stereotype of black women: "the young professional woman who can excel in a demanding job . . . yet who is abjectly clueless about defending herself from exploitative males."[56]

In his brief reading of the film, Richard Dyer notes that the myriad issues presented in *Mahogany* can only "tortuously be reconciled" by the end of the film.[57] But if *Mahogany* is filled with unsatisfyingly reconciled issues—the incessant demands of the fashion world, the stress of performing in a predominantly white culture, a desire for professional recognition, the difficulty of finding effective creative outlets, and a need for a fulfilling personal life with an admirable partner—it may speak to the continuing dilemmas of a post–civil rights black female life.[58]

Notes

I would like to thank the *American Quarterly* editorial collective for their astute suggestions and comments. I would also like to thank Corey Creekmur and Deborah Whaley for their helpful comments on an earlier draft of the essay.

1. President Lyndon B. Johnson, "The Howard University Address," in *The Moynihan Report and the Politics of Controversy*, ed. Lee Rainwater and William L. Yancey (Cambridge, Mass.: MIT Press, 1967), 126.

2. Ibid., 132. Johnson's speech was cowritten by Moynihan and Richard N. Goodwin. For a reading of the Moynihan Report and its construction of African American femininity, see Patricia Hill Collins, "A Comparison of Two Works on Black Family Life," *Signs* 14.4 (1989): 875–84.

3. *Mahogany*, directed by Berry Gordy (1975; Los Angeles, CA: Paramount, 2007), DVD.

4. *Nothing but a Man* portrays the middle-class Josie, a teacher, in love with Duff, who is frustrated by the accumulation of daily racist indignities. *Black Girl* showcases the troubling issue of competition and jealousy among black women. *Nothing but a Man*, directed by Michael Roemer (1964; US: Cinema V, 2004), DVD; *Black Girl*, directed by Ossie Davis (1974). *Black Camera* 3.2 (2012) devotes several essays to Roemer's important film.

5. Richard Dyer, "Mahogany," in *Films for Women*, ed. Charlotte Brunsdon (London: British Film Institute, 1986), 131.

6. As Suzanne Smith notes throughout *Dancing in the Street: Motown and the Cultural Politics of Detroit* (Cambridge, Mass.: Harvard University Press, 1999), Motown often had

an ambivalent relationship to the civil rights and black nationalist movements. Motown became a symbol of the possibilities of black-owned capitalism advocated by black nationalists, while its crossover black artists suggested the promise of black and white integration. Gordy directed the film after firing director Tony Richardson.

7. Pauline Kael, *5001 Nights at the Movies: A Guide from A to Z* (New York: Holt, Rinehart, and Winston, 1982), 354.

8. For brief discussions of the film's impact on African American women, see Derek Blasberg, "I Called Her Mahogany," *V Magazine*, September 2008, www.vmagazine.com/article.php?n=11319 (accessed February 10, 2009) and www.vmagazine.com/2010/05/v55-fall-2008/ and www.trendhunter.com/ trends/tyra-banks-i-called-her-mahogany-in-v-magazine#!/photos/41214/3 (accessed August 9, 2012). See also an interview with the film's producer, Rob Cohen, conducted by Scott Essman, "CinNews Interview with Rob Cohen," *Nuvein Magazine Online Edition, http://nuvein.net/index.php?option =com_co ntent&task=view&id=217&Itemid=40* (accessed February 10, 2009).

9. In *Still a Dream: The Changing Status of Blacks since 1960* (Cambridge, Mass.: Harvard University Press, 1975), Sar Levitan, William B. Johnston, and Robert Taggart analyzed the conditions of African Americans between 1964 and 1974 and detailed the effects of the civil rights acts. They concluded that the civil rights laws were not quite as effective as civil rights leaders had hoped: "Eliminating discrimination is not like building homes, providing medical services, creating jobs, or supplementing income. The problem is seldom obvious or well-defined. Most institutional arrangements or individual decisions are subtly discriminatory rather than obviously racist; the rules of the game are usually unstated and frequently flexible" (267–68).

10. Lee Rainwater and William L. Yancey, *The Moynihan Report and the Politics of Controversy* (Cambridge, Mass.: MIT Press, 1967), 135.

11. The term comes from Trey Ellis's essay on the late-twentieth-century black cultural producer: "Just as a genetic mulatto is a black person of mixed parents who can often get along fine with his white grandparents, a cultural mulatto, educated by a multi-racial mix of cultures, can also navigate easily in the white world" ("The New Black Aesthetic," *Callaloo* 12 [1989]: 235).

12. Jane Gaines, "White Privilege and Looking Relations: Race and Gender in Feminist Film Theory," in *Issues in Feminist Film Theory*, ed. Patricia Erens (Bloomington: Indiana University Press, 1990), 197–214.

13. Robyn Wiegman, "Black Bodies/American Commodities: Gender, Race, and the Bourgeois Ideal in Contemporary Film," in *Unspeakable Images: Ethnicity and the America Cinema*, ed. Lester D. Friedman (Urbana: University of Illinois Press, 1991), 308–28.

14. Ibid., 318; Gaines, "White Privilege and Looking Relations," 205; Dyer, "Mahogany," 132.

15. A version of Gaines's essay appeared in *Cultural Critique* 4 (1986). Wiegman's essay appeared in 1991.

16. As Wiegman points out, the film continually grants subject status to Tracy. Its seductive cinematic techniques—such as camera shots and point-of-view—glamorize Diana Ross as Tracy Chambers, particularly in the film's two central montages where she arrives in Italy and poses for Sean's camera. These methods contrast with conventional modes of representing African American women in Hollywood films in which black women function as other to privileged white femininity. I am concerned less with the looking relations between and among black and white characters in the film than with how the characters navigate their personal and professional spaces, work that requires visual skills. For a more specific, psychoanalytic reading of black and white femininity in the cinema, see Mary Ann Doane's analyses of *Birth of a Nation* and *Imitation of Life* in

"Dark Continents Epistemologies of Racial and Sexual Difference in Psychoanalysis and the Cinema," in *Femme Fatales: Feminism, Film Theory, Psychoanalysis* (New York: Routledge, 1991), 209–48.

17. James T. Patterson, *Freedom Is Not Enough: The Moynihan Report and America's Struggle over Black Family Life, from LBJ to Obama* (New York: Basic Books, 2010), 26–42.

18. Daniel Patrick Moynihan, *The Negro Family: The Case for National Action* (Washington, D.C.: Office of Policy Planning and Research, United States Department of Labor, 1965), 1, 29.

19. Ibid., 5.

20. Angela Davis, *Women, Race, and Class* (1981; repr. New York: Vintage, 1983), 17.

21. Michelle Mitchell, *Righteous Propagation: African Americans and the Politics of Racial Destiny after Reconstruction* (Chapel Hill: University of North Carolina Press, 2004), 115.

22. Roderick Ferguson, *Aberrations in Black: Toward a Queer Color Critique* (Minneapolis: University of Minnesota Press, 2004), 123.

23. Hortense Spillers, "Mama's Baby, Papa's Maybe: An American Grammar Book," in *Black, White, and in Color: Essays on American Literature and Culture* (Chicago: University of Chicago Press, 2003), 205.

24. Moynihan, *Negro Family*, 33.

25. Ibid., 32–33, 48.

26. Ferguson, *Aberrations in Black*; Steve Estes, *I Am a Man: Race, Manhood, and the Civil Rights Movement* (Chapel Hill: University of North Carolina Press, 2005), 107–29.

27. Moynihan, *Negro Family*, 4.

28. Smith, *Dancing in the Street*, 119. For a different reading of Motown's creative methods, see Jon Fitzgerald, "Motown Crossover Hits, 1963–1966, and the Creative Process," *Popular Music* 14.1 (1995): 1–11.

29. In her autobiography, Mary Wilson states that before they became famous as the Supremes, the members of the Primettes would spend hours discussing clothes and accessories and coordinate their appearance (*Dreamgirl: My Life as a Supreme* [New York: St. Martin's Press, 1986], 62).

30. Berry Gordy, *To Be Loved: The Music, the Magic, the Memories of Motown, an Autobiography* (New York: Warner Books, 1994), 310.

31. Judy Klemesrud, "'The Black Clark Gable' Branches Out," *New York Times*, September 19, 1976.

32. "Power to the Peebles," *Time*, August 16, 1971, 47.

33. Gordy, *To Be Loved*, 334.

34. *Lady Sings the Blues*, directed by Sidney J. Furie (1972; Los Angeles: Paramount, 2005), DVD.

35. For 1975 the average unemployment rate was 8.5 percent; the black unemployment rate was 10.5 percent, according to the U.S. Department of Labor (www.bls.gov/cps/prev_yrs.htm/ [accessed June 28, 2012]). The National Urban League used a different method to count unemployment and noted that black unemployment was 25.7 percent and married black male unemployment was 9.8 percent in 1975 ("Black Jobless Rate Put at 25.7% for Quarter by Urban League," *New York Times*, June 9, 1975).

36. As Dyer suggests, Brian's and Tracy's divergent class positions and identifications help the film appeal to multiple audiences ("Mahogany," 132).

37. Notably, Helga constructs this plea while reminiscing about "one of the loveliest sights [she] had ever seen," "a sooty black girl decked out in a flaming orange dress," an apt description of Tracy's design for the cocktail dress (Nella Larsen, *Quicksand*, ed. Deborah McDowell [New Brunswick, N.J.: Rutgers University Press, 1987], 18).

38. Burton Wohl, *Mahogany*, based on an original screenplay by John Byrum, story by Toni Ambler (New York: Bantam Books, 1975), 14–15. The mass market book was a promotional tie-in for the movie.

39. For a discussion of the contradictory readings of the report, see Rainwater and Yancey, *Moynihan Report*, 133–36.

40. Ella L. Bell, "The Bi-Cultural Life Experience of Career-Oriented Black Women," *Journal of Organizational Behavior* 11 (1990): 462.

41. This deal reflects how, for Tracy, her body is a commodity that she must exploit or allow to be exploited in order to achieve her aims, ironically a concern of the protagonists in other black female-centered films of the period such as *Coffy* (1973) or *Foxy Brown* (1974).

42. Carby, "Policing the Black Woman's Body in an Urban Context," in *Identities*, ed. Kwame Anthony Appiah and Henry Louis Gates Jr. (Chicago: University of Chicago Press, 1995), 123, 118.

43. The quote is from the novel's back cover. Brian is less visually naive in the novelization of *Mahogany*. For example, he wants Tracy to accompany him to a dinner with a congressman, because he knows professional networking "has to look social" (Wohl, *Mahogany*, 67).

44. Erica Edwards, "Black President Hokum," *American Quarterly* 63.1 (2011): 35.

45. Moynihan, *Negro Family*, 16.

46. All four men attended elite colleges and law schools, and they are members of the first generation of black politicians who did not receive political training within the trenches of the civil rights movement (Alec MacGillis and Perry Bacon Jr., "Obama Rises in New Era of Black Politicians," *Washington Post*, July 28, 2007). See also Gene Jarrett's description of "post-race politicians" in *Representing the Race: A New Political History of African American Literature* (New York: New York University Press, 2011), 203–4.

47. *The Candidate*, directed by Michael Ritchie (1972; Warner Home Video, 1997), DVD.

48. Sexual orientation is an understated aspect of the film *Mahogany* that is more explicit in the novel. It is implied in the film that one of the modeling executives is gay, and Sean, played by Anthony Perkins (who, as an actor, never fully escaped the role of Norman Bates in *Psycho*) seems to signify a queer aesthetic. The novel implies that Tracy's modeling agent, Carlotta Gavina, is a lesbian (Wohl, 100).

49. For more on how marriage and children were vital to African American uplift in the late nineteenth and early twentieth centuries, see Mitchell, *Righteous Propagation and Ann duCille, The Coupling Convention: Sex, Text, and Tradition in Black Women's Fiction* (New York: Oxford University Press, 1993). For a discussion of the significance of marriage and black reproduction during the late twentieth century, see Deborah Gray White, *Too Heavy a Load: Black Women in Defense of Themselves, 1894–1994* (New York: Norton, 1999).

50. Moynihan, *Negro Family*, 16.

51. Barack Obama occupied this same position three decades later, from 2005 to 2008.

52. Gaines, "White Privilege and Looking Relations," 206.

53. Moynihan, *Negro Family*, 1.

54. Judith Smith, "Civil Rights, Labor, and Sexual Politics on Screen in *Nothing but a Man* (1964)," *Black Camera: An International Film Journal* 3.2 (2012): 176.

55. Ibid., 180, 177.

56. Jack E. White, "Heavy Breathing—*Waiting to Exhale*," Time, January 15, 1996. Moreover, Rebecca Wanzo argues that within the past decade the media image of the "Unmarriageable Professional Black Woman" has gained traction, as illustrated by the numerous news stories focused on answering the dilemma "Why can't a successful black woman find a man?"—a question that she notes was the specific subject of a 2009 *Nightline* episode (Wanzo, "Black Love Is Not a Fairy Tale: African American Women, Romance, and Rhetoric," in *Sexing the Colorlines: Black Sexualities, Popular Culture, and Cultural Production*, Project on the Rhetoric of Inquiry [POROI] Online Journal 7.2 [2011], http:// ir.uiowa.edu/poroi/vol7/iss2/ [accessed December 15, 2011]).

57. Dyer, "Mahogany," 132. Dyer also inexplicably states that a shot of Diana Ross with her head thrown back resembles the well-known shot of Rita Hayworth in *Gilda*, except that Ross has "an unmistakably black mouth" (134).

58. Another African American female from Chicago's South Side mirrors the trajectory of Tracy's success and, perhaps, containment, First Lady Michelle Robinson Obama. Since President Barack Obama was elected in 2008, one component of Michelle Obama's image appears to resemble Tracy's: "motivator-inchief" for others' successes. Like Tracy, Mrs. Obama, a lawyer, relinquished a prominent and successful career to support a partner's electoral ambitions. Of course, this inspirational use of Mrs. Obama's image hides more problematic black female representations in American culture and is beyond the scope of this essay. See Rachel L. Swarns, "Mrs. Obama Visits Students as Motivator in Chief," *New York Times*, May 15, 2009.

20

From Margin to Centre? Images of African-American Women in Film

Sharon L. Jones

Introduction

Despite strides towards more realistic depictions of black woman-hood in American cinema, much progress still needs to be made. This study will examine recent films such as *The Color Purple, Waiting To Exhale* and *Jackie Brown* to critique how motion pictures transmit memorable images with the power to alter or reinforce popular concep-tions of black women. When these images are problematic or distor-tions of reality, it can have a detrimental effect on both the viewer and the individuals portrayed upon the screen.

Historically, the overwhelming majority of portrayals of African-American women in American cinema have perpetuated stereotypical ideas. Black women are often presented as decentralised, marginalised, and unempowered individuals. These depictions serve to reinforce the racial, class, and gender hierarchies in the United States, which places women of colour as socially, economically, and politically disenfranchised despite the Civil Rights Movement of the 1960s and the Women's Rights Movement of the 1970s. As Jacqueline Bobo (1995:36) notes: "fictionalized creations of black women are not innocent; they do not lack the effect of ideological force in the lives of those represented in that black women are rendered as objects and useful commodities in a very serious power struggle."

At any rate, there is an attempt, among some directors, writers, and producers, to bring black women from margin to centre. However, it is important to note that despite some progress, much more still must be made in the American cinema in terms of multidimensional portraits of black women of all ages, socioeconomic levels, sexual orien-tations, and professions.

In this study, I will examine characterisations of black women in three major Hollywood films, *The Color Purple, Waiting To Exhale*, and *Jackie Brown*, to analyse both the progressions and regressions in cine-matic portrayals of African-American women by placing the films within the context of historical representations of black females. I argue that while *The Color Purple* offers a scathing indictment of racial, class, and gender oppression by critiquing the institution of marriage, *Waiting To Exhale* obscures these issues while suggesting

Reprinted by permission from *Social Alternatives* (October 1998).

that the key to self-fulfilment for black women lies in heterosexual relationships culminating in marriage. The reasons for the conflicting messages of the two films may stem from their settings and the comfort of audiences in regards to issues of race, class, and gender oppression. Because the setting of the film *The Color Purple* takes place primarily in the American South from the early 1900s through the 1930s, audiences may have felt more comfortable viewing disturbing images of racism, class prejudice, and sexism when these images are set in the past, providing them with a sense of distance and removal from the problems presented on screen. In contrast, the commercial success of *Waiting To Exhale*, a film set during modern times, may be attributed in part to the movie's lack of emphasis on the tripartite racial, sexual, and gender oppression black women face.

Jackie Brown departs from both films in genre as a crime drama and in its focus on an unmarried African-American woman seeking economic independence as an ultimate goal rather than fulfilment through marriage or heterosexual relationships.

Background

Comprehending the problems associated with recent portrayals of African-American women in film requires a contextualisation of these earlier representations. A survey of major Hollywood productions from the 1930s through 1950s reveals a predominance of the "mammy" figure in terms of representations of African-American women, most notably in films such as *Gone With The Wind*, released in 1939 and set before, during, and after the American Civil War. Dark-skinned, heavy-set, and fiercely loyal despite her oppression, the "mammy" figure dominated screen representations of black women in American cinema for many years. Perhaps to a movie-going audience more interested in romanticism than realism (viewing film as a means of escape primarily during the Great Depression of the 1930s and World War II in the 1940s), a variety of images of black women in film would have been unappealing as they would have challenged the status quo and prevailing notions about the "proper" racial, class, and gender structure in American society, particularly at a period of time in which legal separation of the races existed in America.

With the advent of the Civil Rights Movement of the late 1950s and 1960s, coupled with the feminist movement of the 1970s, stronger and more multidimensional representations of African-American women appeared on the big screen. Films such as *Coffy*, a groundbreaking film released in 1973 which starred Pam Grier, featured a confident and assertive black woman. As Freydberg notes (1995:235): "[T]he Pam Grier movies exploited sex and women during the era of the contemporary women's liberation movement. The creation of this machismo character provided soft pornography for men and a vicarious pleasure and satisfaction for some feminists who believe these images were positive examples of equitable casting."

The film features much sex, violence, and nudity (Pam Grier frequently bares her breasts). The film functions alternately as an example of liberation in its focus on an assertive African-American woman and of exploitation in the gratuitous nudity, which muted the potential of the film to be an example of a black feminist heroine.

The Color Purple

By the 1980s, the scarcity of movies featuring African-American women as the primary focus led to much interest among movie-goers in *The Color Purple*. When the film *The Color Purple*, based upon Alice Walker's Pulitzer prize winning novel, appeared in 1985 it elicited much controversy, particularly among critics concerned that the film was anti-black male in its portrayal of chauvinism and violence against women. Nevertheless, the film attempts to portray a wider range of African-American female sexuality, empowerment, and creativity. Set in the rural South, the film focused on the lives of black women in an often racist, sexist, and class conscious society. Female characters include Celie, her sister Nettie (who later becomes a missionary in Africa), Shug Avery (a blues singer who teaches Celie about black female independence), and Sophia (a strong-willed black woman who resists racial and sexual oppression). The film's plot centres around the childhood and adulthood of Celie as she endures a loveless marriage and later discovers her self worth through her friendship with Shug and her reunion with her biological children, who had grown up in Africa while being reared by a minister, his wife, and her sister Nettie.

Admittedly, the exploration of black female sexuality proves problematic in the film. The film has received some criticism for not fully developing the lesbian overtones in the relationship between Shug Avery and Celie. Nevertheless, the film attempts to explore an aspect of black female sexuality many viewers may not have seen on screen before. As Donald Bogle notes (1988:61): "[I]n the past these women would have played maids, comic servants never to be thought about twice. But when Spielberg's camera moves in for loving close-ups—the camera treats the women with respect and concern—the visual statement itself moves and affects us, even while we may feel cheated by much else that goes on."

While the film received some criticism due to the fact that a white male filmmaker served as director, and the film strayed at times from the actual text of the book, the film's attempt to portray the lives of African-American women strongly enduring and ultimately transcending racial, sexual, and class oppression stands out in terms of the historical representations of African-American women in film.

The film addresses the sexual oppression of black women in the characterisation of Celie, who is raped by her stepfather as a teenager, and then forced by her stepfather to marry a man who seeks a wife to raise his children. The film portrays women as commodities unable to assume ownership of their own bodies and children. Celie's marriage in the film critiques the institution of marriage as it portrays the abuse and neglect she suffers at the hands of a husband who attempts to mute her voice. However, through female community with her sister Nettie and later Shug (her husband's mistress), Celie learns to assert her own voice and develop a sense of herself as a human being. In one pivotal scene, she reminds her husband that despite her status as a poor black woman, she does have self worth and her very existence proves that her life has meaning. Leaving the entrapment of her marriage, she flees her husband and the rural southern community she comes from and later returns to open her own business making unisex pants for men and women. She becomes economically independent, and makes a statement in regards to gender equity. Her subsequent reunion at the film's end with the children she bore due to the rape by her stepfather (children raised in Africa by Nettie) reveals a strong, empowered woman who has succeeded despite racial, class, and gender oppression.

The film succeeds in rendering a brutal depiction of tripartite oppression while celebrating the human spirit and will to survive.

Waiting to Exhale

Perhaps one of the most commercially successful films to focus on the lives of African-American women is the 1995 film *Waiting To Exhale*, based upon the best-selling novel by Terry McMillan. The film focuses on the lives of four black women of different ages, occupations, and educational backgrounds. While the film can be praised in its depictions of African-American professional women (a departure from many Hollywood films), the film tends to downplay or obscure the role sexism, class prejudice, and racism has on black women's lives in America. The film portrays the difficulty of obtaining satisfactory heterosexual relationships as the biggest obstacle in the women's lives. The film fails to adequately explore the real problems of social and economic injustice that African-American women face. bell hooks (1996:54) points out that:

> The film *Waiting To Exhale* took the novelistic images of professional black women concerned with issues of racial uplift and gender equality and turned them into a progression of racist, sexist stereotypes that feature happy darkies who are

all singing, dancing, fucking, and having a merry old time even in the midst of sad times and tragic moments.

By portraying the key to fulfilment for black women in terms of heterosexual relationships rather than in economic independence, female community, or a strong sense of racial identity, the film serves as a regression and not a progression in terms of Hollywood portrayals of black women despite its potential to be a groundbreaking film in its focus on black female friendship.

Set in Arizona, the plot of *Waiting To Exhale* centres primarily around the life of Bernadine (Angela Bassett), who sacrificed her career goals and ambitions to help her husband set up his own business. When he leaves her for another woman, she becomes distraught, and her friends, Robin, Gloria, and Savannah, provide her with emotional support. The film culminates in Bernadine winning a large settlement in the divorce from her husband and regaining her sense of self-respect. The film also focuses on the lives of her friends, who also face problems in their heterosexual relationships. Robin (Lela Rochon) is a young black woman working for an insurance company who desires to live the life of a suburban housewife with a husband and kids, yet she continually becomes involved with men who use and abuse her. Gloria (Loretta Devine) is a divorced woman with a teenage son who runs a beauty salon, but in the film she appears to be more concerned in finding a husband than operating her business. Savannah (Whitney Houston) is a television news producer involved in a relationship with a married man, but her career often takes a secondary place in relation to her quest for a romantic relationship. Bernadine (Angela Bassett), who possesses an MBA, helped her husband create a multimillion dollar business only to discover that he is having an affair and desires a divorce from her. Throughout much of the film, the character focuses more on seeking revenge against her husband than using her education and skills to create a new life and career for herself. The film implies that females lack the capacity to control their own economic and social development.

Another weakness of the film centres around its failure to adequately address racial, sexual, and class politics in America in relation to African-American women's lives. When *Waiting To Exhale* addresses issues of race, class, and gender, it places these issues within the context of heterosexual relationships. For example, in the film, Bernadine strikes the young white female her husband had an affair with, and she laments black men leaving black women for white women. Therefore, the film portrays racism in the context of black women and white women vying in sexual competition for black men, rather than in the terms of institutionalised racism in America which impacts black women socially and economically. The film's addressing of race downplays and obscures the real impact of race on black women's lives.

Admittedly, the film proves distinct from other major Hollywood releases in terms of its attempt to portray the lives of professional African-American females in comparison to early depictions of black women as "mammy" figures, yet *Waiting To Exhale* has received some criticism for glossing over the realities of racism, sexism, and class prejudice in America and presenting a distorted view of black womanhood. As bell hooks notes (1996:54): "When a film that's basically about the trials and tribulations of four professional heterosexual black women who are willing to do anything to get and keep a man is offered as a 'feminist' narrative, it's truly a testament to the power of the mainstream to co-opt progressive social movements and strip them of all political meaning through a series of contemptuous ridiculous representations."

The film proves problematic in its lack of an in-depth critique of race, class, and gender relations, and its focus on the importance of heterosexual relationships as leading to happiness and fulfilment for the women in the film.

Jackie Brown

Grier's most recent film, *Jackie Brown*, released in 1997, which was directed by Quentin Tarantino, casts the actress in a crime drama as an airline flight attendant who smuggles money into the United States given to her by a man who buys and sells firearms illegally. The plot centres around Jackie Brown (Pam Grier) agreeing to assist law enforcement officials in ending the criminal activities of her friend Ordell (Samuel L. Jackson) in exchange for having charges dropped against her for smuggling money into the country for Ordell. As Brian D. Johnson notes (1997:103): "By casting '70s blaxploitation star Pam Grier as Jackie Brown—and stacking the sound track with vintage soul music—Tarantino has coupled his love for Leonard's laidback style with an homage to the retro cool of 1970s black pop culture."

The film breaks ground in its depiction of a black woman as a centralised and empowered figure, signifying a continuation of the roles Pam Grier played in early blaxploitation films such as *Coffy*, yet Tarantino's achievement is also diminished by the fact that Jackie's involvement in smuggling money for an African-American man who deals illegally in selling firearms arguably functions as a stereotypical depiction of African Americans as criminals. Furthermore, by the end of the movie, Jackie Brown leaves Los Angeles in fear that the law enforcement officials will discover that she has kept nearly half a million dollars that she had smuggled out of the country for Ordell. Therefore, she remains marginalised from society despite her success in outwitting law enforcement officials and her criminal associate. Therefore, *Jackie Brown* illustrates the limitations that still exist in terms of recent portrayals of African-American women in film.

Conclusion

Analysing images of African-American women in film reveals both how prevailing myths and realities about the African-American female experience have been portrayed in cinema. For the most part, American cinematic history reveals a tendency to perpetuate distorted images of black womanhood in film. Both *The Color Purple* and *Waiting To Exhale* represent the strengths and weaknesses in these depictions. Films such as *Jackie Brown* illustrate possible new directions in portrayals of black women by featuring a black actress cast as the lead character in a crime drama, a genre primarily featuring white male protagonists. While some progress has been made in terms of representations of black women in film, it is vitally necessary that more dynamic representations of African-American women appear on the American cinematic landscape to explode and destroy the predominant notions and images that have promoted racial, sexual, and class stereotypes or obscured the impact that these misconceptions have upon the viewer.

Sharon Jones is an assistant professor of English at Earlham College in Richmond, Indiana where she teaches general humanities courses and African-American Literature.

References

Bobo, Jacqueline. 1995. *Black Women as Cultural Readers*. Columbia University Press: New York.

Bogle, Donald. 1988. *Blacks In American Films and Television*. Simon and Schuster: New York.

Freydberg, Elizabeth Hadley. 1995. "Sapphires, Spitfires, Sluts and Superbitches: Aframericans and Latinas in Contemporary American Film." In Kim Marie Vaz (ed.). *Black Women in America.* Sage: London.

hooks, bell. 1996. *Reel to Real: race, sex, and class at the movies.* Routledge: New York.

Johnson, Brian D. 1997. "Review of Jackie Brown" *Maclean's* 29 December: 103–105.

21 Manhunting: The Female Detective in the Serial Killer Film

Philippa Gates

In the 1980s, Hollywood film enacted a backlash against feminism that was evident in the detective film through the representation of troubled masculinity masquerading as tough and triumphant and through the representation of women as demonized or excluded from the center of the screen. Neo-noir films like Body Heat (Kasdan 1981) dealt with the female threat by offering women cinematic space only to present them as evil and destructive for the male hero; on the other hand, cop-action films like Lethal Weapon (Donner 1987) excluded them from the center of the narrative altogether through the focus on a buddy relationship and presenting women on the margins as damsels in distress that needed to be saved by the hero. Although each film offered a different response to the perceived masculine crisis incited by women, both relied on the highlighting of sexual difference with a focus on the female body as seductive and dangerous and the male body as empowered and heroic.

During the early 1990s, however, mainstream film saw a shift to "sensitive men" heroes[1] in a negotiation of changing social attitudes towards masculinity that was mirrored in the detective film by the appearance of protagonists defined by brains instead of brawn. Because detective-heroes no longer had to be gun-wielding, law enforcement types that embodied a heroism defined as white, muscular, working-class, and male—like Martin Riggs (Mel Gibson) in Lethal Weapon or John McClane (Bruce Willis) in Die Hard (McTiernan 1988)—the detective film explored new kinds of heroes who were a more realistic size, shape, and age. The detective-hero did not need to be tough so much as smart to bring the new highly intelligent criminals of the 1990s to justice and this included African-American men, for example Denzel Washington in The Bone Collector (Noyce 1999); older men, including Clint Eastwood in Blood Work (Eastwood 2002); and women, such as Sandra Bullock in Murder by Numbers (Schroeder 2002).

Following the success of The Silence of the Lambs (Demme 1991), Hollywood film saw an increasing presence of the female detective on screen. This shift away from white hypermasculinity would suggest a more liberal and feminist approach to the definition of law enforcement heroism. However, while the detective genre has brought

Reprinted by permission from Post Script—Essays in Film and the Humanities 24, no. 1 (fall 2004).

women to the center of the narrative with a seemingly greater degree of agency as the protagonists who drive the narrative action forward, this agency is tempered and contained. The male detective is empowered in the contemporary detective film through his identification with the serial killer—the man who has the desire and ability to inflict violence on women—while the female body remains a site of objectification and powerlessness. This is not, however, necessarily due to the cinematic serial killer's tendency to seek out female victims, but because the female detective succumbs to an over-identification with the killer's victims and often is a former or potential victim of violence perpetrated by men.

In the serial killer film, masculinity is still regarded as the embodiment of strength and heroism and the female body, weakness and victimization. Thus, the female detective is portrayed as competent and successful only as a masculinized or defeminized woman; when she exhibits feminine traits—usually emotional—she is branded as a professional failure. While The Silence of the Lambs was generally regarded as "a profoundly feminist movie" (Taubin, "Grabbing" 129), the reviews of 1995's Copycat expose the possibility of dual readings of the serial killer film with a female protagonist (or two in the case of this film). Lizzie Francke of Sight and Sound praised the casting of Holly Hunter and Sigourney Weaver as the film's protagonists—detective and the potential victim—as "enhancing its status an instant post-feminist classic" (51); conversely, Kenneth Turan of the L.A. Times argued that the casting led the filmmakers "to believe that they'[d] made a significant feminist statement, the movie's two hours-plus of almost continual sadistic abuse of women notwithstanding"[1].

Similarly, more recent serial killer films offer some of Hollywood's toughest and attractive female stars appearing repeatedly in the genre—for example, Ashley Judd and Angelina Jolie—offering strong female characters while, simultaneously, undermining their agency through casting them as the former or potential victims of male violence. While the male detective is given a position of stability and agency through his identification with the perpetrator of the crimes, the female detective is presented as objectified and victimized. The female body—of the detective as well as the victim—thus functions as a site of the working through of masculine anxieties incited by a female presence in the traditionally masculine profession of law enforcement.

A New Kind of Detective

Hollywood has been obsessed with murder for the last decade and even more so with serial murder. Films like The Silence of the Lambs (Demme 1991), Copycat (Amiel 1995), Citizen X (Gerolmo 1995), Seven (Fincher 1995), Just Cause (Glimcher 1995), Serial Killer (David 1995), Kiss the Girls (Fleder 1997), The Bone Collector (Noyce 1999), American Psycho (Harron 2000), Along Came a Spider (Tamahori 2001), Blood Work (Eastwood 2002), Insomnia (Nolan 2002), Red Dragon (Ratner 2002), Murder by Numbers (Schroeder 2002), Twisted (Kaufman 2004), and Taking Lives (Caruso 2004) focus on a detective's investigation of serial murders. The serial killer has captured the popular imagination because he—and the serial killer is most often male[2]—is the most violent, most gruesome, and most elusive of criminal types. He does not kill for the traditional motives of jealousy, greed, and power but because he is psychopathic—often resulting from a traumatic childhood experience related to a mother or other female figure—and cannot refrain from killing until he is stopped by the law. Hollywood may be obsessed with the serial killer as the perpetrator of contemporary crime; however, this is a misrepresentation of the reality of criminal behavior as serial killers account for only a fraction of the national murder rate: murder accounts for only 0.27% of felonies in the FBI's Index of Serious Crime (Livingstone 40).[3]

The crimes of the serial killer strike fear in the popular imagination because they appear motiveless; he does not necessarily choose people he knows as his victims but strangers—innocent people. The detective's investigation of the killer's crimes functions to demystify the seeming motiveless and random killings by attributing to them a pattern—and thus a motive.

The motivation for the killings is often attributed to an abusive childhood or major trauma that then has been repressed and resurfaces in the compulsive need to kill. The killer's pattern or MO (modus operandi) functions as a "signature" that can identify the seemingly invisible and elusive killer and, as Richard Dyer argues, the appeal of the serial killer for film audiences is the attempt to discern this pattern (16). However, the serial killer narrative is merely the formalization and simplification of a pattern established in classical detective fiction by authors like Agatha Christie: the killer only means to dispose of one victim but then is forced to kill others who stumble onto the truth of the crime and threaten to reveal the killer's identity. The pleasure for the viewer of the serial killer film is, thus, to identify the pattern and, therefore, the killer before the detective does. The detective narrative, however, also offers reassurance to its audience: the pattern of the killings, in a reflection of the killer's psychological state of mind, produces a motive so that even seemingly "motiveless" crimes can be understood and resolved. No matter how chaotic and dangerous contemporary society seems to be, the contemporary detective film assures audiences that there is a hero who can restore order or normalcy to the society disrupted by the killer by identifying and removing that "abnormality" through death or incarceration.

Real-life serial killers are often described as "abnormally normal" (Seltzer 10): in other words, they appear normal to those who know them but obviously are abnormal in their need to commit multiple murders. According to novelist Patricia Cornwell, "the most distinctive and profound characteristics of all psychopaths is that they do not feel remorse. They have no concept of guilt. They do not have a conscience" (27).[4] As a society, we label serial killers as pathological, insane, and abnormal in order to differentiate them from us and our supposed normalcy. The detection of the serial killer in the contemporary detective narrative, thus, functions to identify the abnormal that masquerades as normal so that it can be extracted from society and presumably contemporary crime with it. According to Patrice Fleck, the serial killer film is Hollywood's response to the national conversation about crime—a conservative discourse that points to a degeneration of morals as the cause of this kind of violent crime (35). As Woody Haut argues, contemporary crime fiction turns "the fear of violent death into a narrative subtext while investigating the society from which that fear derives" (207). Haut identifies that fear as an end-of-the-millennium obsession with personality disorders, sexual deviancy, and AIDS (209). The serial killer is a silent one—he is not easily recognizable and it takes the trained eye of the detective to identify him. As Steffen Hantke notes, the killer's evil is not written on his body (36); instead it is the body of the victim that becomes the abject one, written upon by the killer and thus becomes a text to be read by the detective—and a spectacle to be beheld by the audience.

It is also our increasing reliance on technology and the isolation of contemporary urban living, however, that makes us vulnerable to the anonymous killer. As Suzanne Hatty explains, films centered on serial killers can be regarded as a cinematic response to the contemporary fear and anxiety about victimization and public safety that has been evident since the 1980s (83). And as Gerard Collins discusses in relation to Patricia Cornwell's novels, serial killers are "the embodiment of a disease that permeates modern western society: isolation" (159). Our growing cities produce increasing proportions of crime and, at the same time, individuals are more isolated despite the burgeoning of electronic technology. While that technology may improve global and instantaneous communications, it deters interpersonal interactions especially with the people who we are surrounded by everyday: our increasing reliance on voice-mail, e-mail, cell phones, and text messaging decrease our face-to-face communications.

The serial killer plays on this fear of alienation by suggesting that the greatest threat to the individual is the anonymous "other" who may be a neighbor or a stranger but whose evil is imperceptible to us. However, the contemporary detective film assures us that, while science and technology may be responsible for our vulnerability to the serial killer, the detective has mastered the science and technology to track, identify, and stop him. These films rarely offer the "pleasure" of alignment with the killer in his perpetration of violence—as the horror film does—and, instead, focus on the post-mortem examination of the killer's violence and align audiences with the detective-hero and the pleasure of detection.

The serial killer is both incredibly intelligent and brutally violent, and what is needed to stop him is a very special kind of detective-hero: "the 'profiler,' the genius like investigator able, on the basis of clues at the scene of the crime, to narrow down the social and geographical location of the killer as well as his psychological make-up" (Dyer 17). Whether a forensic scientist, psychologist, medical examiner, or homicide detective, the hero of the contemporary detective film is the "criminalist." He/she must possess a diverse range of skills and specialized knowledge—an expert not only of forensic science, behavioral science, and profiling, but also culture in general. As the criminalist expert, Lincoln Rhyme, explains in the novel The Bone Collector:

> A criminalist is a renaissance man. He's got to know botany, geology, ballistics, medicine, chemistry, literature, engineering. If he knows facts—that ash with a high strontium content probably came from a highway flare, that faca is Portuguese for "knife," that Ethiopian diners use no utensils and eat with their right hands exclusively, that a slug with five land-and-groove rifling marks, right twist, could not have been fired by a Colt pistol—if he knows these things he may just make the connection that places the [unknown subject] at the crime scene. (Deaver 120)

The criminalist is an expert in analyzing "trace" evidence but, more importantly, an expert in human behavior and that is how he/she tracks down the killer: he/she is—as the title of Michael Mann's 1986 film suggests—a "manhunter." The appeal of the criminalist is his/her knowledge and use of science and technology in an era defined by information technology and there has been a proliferation of criminalists in all forms of the detective genre—fiction, film, and television.[5]

Although the fictional serial killer has become a popular trend in mainstream film since the early 1990s, America's obsession with serial killings is far longer than its dominance in mainstream film would suggest. The 1980s saw the proliferation of the serial killer narrative in fiction, most notably in the novels of Thomas Harris, at the same time as American society began to note the burgeoning of real serial killers. A fascination with real killers led to a barrage of TV movies beginning in the 1970s and snowballing in the 1980s as real-life cases became fodder for the mass audience.[6] What distinguishes the big screen version of serial killing since the early 1990s is that the majority of the serial killers on screen are fictional and the violence they commit exponentially increased. The TV-movies of the 1980s—whether dramatized accounts of the real-life killers or documentaries—offered the stories of brutal murder but not the image or violence of it because they were aimed at prime-time audiences. In contrast, the serial killer films from the 1990s on have relished in lingering close-ups of mutilated corpses whether at the scene, in autopsy, or in crime scene photos.

The Spectacle of the "Gross"

In her discussion of the "body genres" of porn and horror films, Linda Williams argues that there is a "system of excess" with a "gross display of the human body"[3]. Similarly, the serial killer film (as an offshoot of the horror genre) offers a visceral pleasure for the audience and something that the serial killer narrative in fiction can only achieve to a degree: a spectacle of the gross in relation to the representation of the human body. Mark Seltzer identifies this impulse as a product of our contemporary "wound" culture, "a culture centered on trauma (Greek for wound): a culture of the atrocity, exhibition, in which people wear their damage like badges of identity, or fashion accessories"[2]. Wound culture is evident in Western culture's obsession with the violence of death perpetrated on the human body—with the penetration of the body and the making visible of the inside of the body through wounds, violence, and autopsies. This obsession with bodily trauma is evident as passers-by rubberneck at car crashes and as people patronize controversial art exhibitions, such as the "Sensation" exhibit at the Brooklyn Museum in 1999, which included Damien Hirst's collection of dissected and preserved livestock displayed in glass cases. Even the public autopsy has made a reappearance recently: in London in 2002 Professor Gunther von Hagens of Germany invited 500 spectators to view the first public autopsy in Britain in 170 years (Wardell A16). The emphasis during the autopsy was less on the scientific or the medical and more on the performative as Professor von Hagens wore a black fedora and blue surgical gown; the autopsy was shown on giant screens inside the gallery; a television network said they would broadcast edited footage; and the organs of the deceased were passed amongst the spectators in trays. Similarly in film, violence is no longer merely shown exacted and somebody killed, but is lingered over in close-up as bodies are dissected and innards exposed in autopsies.

Our desire for trauma is manifested in our cultural texts through the spectacle of the gross. The visualization of death and mutilation has escalated in frequency and detail in the last decade or so in popular culture as our alignment—as spectators and consumers—has shifted from the perpetration of trauma to its investigation. The committing of the violence tends to be withheld, leaving such horrors up to the imagination of the viewer—for example, the atrocities committed by Hannibal Lecter in The Silence of the Lambs are not revealed; instead, the mutilated corpse and its relevance to the investigation of a crime have become the focus of cultural narrative. At the time when Seltzer was writing Serial Killers (1998), ER was the most popular series on television and the prime example of what Seltzer describes as "pure wound culture." The most popular show in 2003 and 2004 was CSI and, it too, is representative of the same impulse to indulge in the gross. ER offers its audiences "an endless series of torn and opened bodies and an endless series of emotionally torn and exposed bio-technicians" (Seltzer 22)—the spectacles that make up wound culture. Seltzer argues that the appeal of wound culture seems to be its spectacle where private desire and public fantasy intersect; because it offers a private motivation for public violence, for example childhood abuse, wound culture gives comfort to viewers that there is a reason for violent trauma (257-58).

Similarly, the criminalist narrative (including the serial killer film and shows like CSI) offers cadavers as spectacular bodies with gaping wounds that repulse and attract simultaneously. The cadaver is read as a text to determine what caused the body to pass from life into death and, on CSI this reading leads to an oral—accompanied by a visualized—reconstruction of the crime in which the cadaver is seen alive and then killed again. These sequences are done with digital and / or computer generated effects; for example, the camera / viewer follows the passage of a bullet through a wall and into the head of a sleeping child or witnesses the impact of an axe into a skull from beneath the blade.

In the serial killer film of the last decade, the horrors perpetrated by the killer that were hidden in films like The Silence of the Lambs are not only exposed but indulged in as cameras offer these extended and hypergraphic scenes of mutilation. In Murder by Numbers, the young killers in eerie, astronaut-like suits choke the life out of a panicked victim and blow the brains out of another; in Twisted, a victim's face is so viciously battered that the detective only recognizes the corpse by a tattoo on his hand; and in Taking Lives, the disfigured faces of the victims, their wrists sawn off at the hands, and the photos of the crime scenes are given lingering and detailed close-ups. As Amy Taubin notes, in The Bone Collector, the foregrounding of the investigation "allows director Phillip Noyce to display hideously mutilated corpses and to fetishize the details—skin carved, burnt, or bitten down to the bone—in giant digitized close-up. We've come a long way—technologically speaking—since Blow-Up" ("Death" 136). This embodies a kind of pornography of violence, a fetishization of the body—especially the female body—in death rather than sex. Rather than necessarily being offered as an erotic object, the female body becomes a text to be objectified, analyzed, and probed in order to identify the real enigma of the narrative—the male serial killer. While this spectacle of violence, death, and disfigurement of the female body as a victim of male violence facilitates a working through of contemporary anxieties about crime and law and order, its coupling with the representation of the female detective also allows a contemplation more specifically on gender roles in contemporary society.

The detective film of the 1990s saw a repositioning of the female body from fatal or absent to ever-present following a shift of the central relationship of the narrative. The neo-noir detective film, like Basic Instinct (Verhoeven 1992), focuses on the relationship that develops between the hero and a femme fatale, and the cop action film, like Lethal Weapon, on one between the hero and a buddy. On the other hand, the serial killer film with a male protagonist sees a focus on the relationship that develops between the detective and his adversary. The spectacular body of the neo-noir was that of the erotic and dangerous femme fatale, for example Sharon Stone in Basic Instinct; however, it is the white male—muscled, stripped off, and violent—that was the body of spectacle in the cop action film as the space for the expression and negotiation of masculine crisis. Whereas the neo-noir films of the 1980s cast the woman in the role of the criminal—as the desire but also potential demise of the male hero—the serial killer narrative reconfigures the female body as the victim—not unlike the horror film. Rarely is a romantic relationship the focus or conclusion of the serial killer film with a female investigator or her body presented as erotic spectacle; instead, the work of bodily spectacle is relegated to the female corpse.

The diegetic world of the film is one that is saturated with signs and, from a self-awareness of the text, it follows that those signs are loaded with meaning and should be read as such. As Walter Burket argues, human beings "create perceptible signs which act to stabilize the common world as it has been formed by language and cultural tradition" and one such system of signs to reveal meaning on the surface, at a visual level, is the marking of territory and the body (165). The main spectacle of the serial killer film is the "work" of the killer—a code or language—that, if analyzed and interpreted correctly, gives clues to the killer's identity and his moral project as exhibited through the body of his victim (Fleck 39). Just as the serial killer is almost always male, so too is his "work" almost always performed through the female body. The female body, thus, rather than offering a visual opposition to the manly physique of the hero or being a sexual object to be desired and dominated by him, functions as text. A "literacy" between the serial killer and the detective is established whereby the killer produces a system of symbols through his victims that the detective must decipher in order to stop and capture the killer (Fleck 35): the female body then becomes a mode of communication for the two men—one as author (the killer) and the other as reader (the detective). The detective's reading of the text, or profiling, is "an attempt to appropriate the text's language in order to identify the author" (Simpson, Psycho 80). In reading the text, the detective—like a semiotician—tries to discern the patterns of the author's "writing" and, through unraveling and recognizing those patterns, discern the identity of the killer.

Fans of the criminalist narrative are rewarded for their devotion to the genre as they are invited by the text to read the signs alongside the detective and to try to solve the mystery before he/she does; however, the genre has also reached a new level of self-consciousness due to audience familiarity with the conventions / signs of the genre as well as its increasing popularity in fiction, film, and television. The language, rules, and ritual of investigation in the criminalist film or show include the crime scene kit, the "Luminol" and ultraviolet light that exposes blood, the "cracked" chest and weighing of organs in the autopsy, the lifting of "partials" (fingerprints), the magnification of fibers and hair "tags" (skin on the end of the follicle), the killer's MO, and "unsubs" (unknown subjects) at the scene. The ritual is so familiar that more recent films like Murder by Numbers engage in a postmodern play with the audience who knows the language of the criminalist narrative.

The high school student killers in the film, Richard (Ryan Gosling) and Justin (Michael Pitt), plan the "perfect murder"—i.e. motiveless—to prove the "freedom" that Justin discusses in his in-class presentation, an allusion to Nietzsche's concept of the "Superman." In doing so, the film references Hitchcock's 1948 film Rope in which two young men kill simply to prove that they can get away with it. Hitchcock's film as well as two others—Compulsion (1959) and Swoon (1992)—were inspired by the real-life murder of Bobby Franks committed by Nathan Leopold and Richard Loeb in Chicago in the 1920s (Fuchs 117-18). Justin and Richard read up on forensics, plant false evidence, and attempt to construct an MO that will lead the police away from them as suspects. However, the detective on the case, Cassie (Sandra Bullock), recognizes the inconsistencies of the falsified MO and Richard and Justin's real or unconscious MO. In other words, the profile they try to establish through the killing and trace suggests an unorganized and impulsive killer while their own profile, as organized but inexperienced killers, is also apparent—to the trained eye. Where once the killer unintentionally left behind clues to his identity through his killings, now he often stages his "work" in order for it to be read in a specific way with its audience—the detective-hero—in mind. The popularity and familiarity of the genre with audiences has lead to new incarnations of the genre in order both to capitalize on its popularity and also to make individual films seem different and innovative.

It is this last point that is most likely the motive for the current trend of serial killer films starring female detectives. The younger white male detective gave way to the African-American male and older detectives and now to the young, white, female detective. While this would suggest that the genre is attempting to offer a feminist message, as Barry Keith Grant argues, film's presentation of black, female, or gay characters is often merely a substitution for the white, male hero and does "little or nothing to challenge the sexist or racist assumptions that inform the myths by which they operate" (196).

Victims in a Man's World

In terms of the representation of the female detective, some early serial killer films of the early 1990s—like Blue Steel (Bigelow 1990), The Silence of the Lambs, and Copycat—were praised for their feminist narratives that saw empowered women at the center succeeding in the male world of law enforcement and putting a stop to the violence perpetrated against women by the killer. While the female detective has remained a staple of the serial killer genre and the presence of a woman in the role of protagonist (or partner to a male detective) should articulate a positive image of women onscreen, the serial killer film tends to contain or overturn a feminist theme through two strategies: the over-identification between the heroine and the victim, and her "masculinization" (and related problematic relationships with men). The male detective tends to be presented as a stable and self-controlled individual—for example, Morgan Freeman's Detective Somerset in Seven or Alex Cross in Kiss the Girls—or, if presented initially as traumatized or in crisis—for example, Denzel Washington's Lincoln Rhyme in The Bone Collector, Al Pacino's Will Dormer in Insomnia, or Clint Eastwood's Terry McCaleb in Blood Work—then the hunt for the serial killer and his eventual demise at the hands of the detective function to restore and revitalize the hero's self-confidence and prove his masculinity.

On the other hand, the "problem" of the female detective is that she has had to become masculinized in order to succeed in the male sphere of law enforcement—a masculinization that occurs because of trauma stemming from her relationship with her father or to her previous victimization at the hands of a violent man. Her salvation—i.e., "re-feminization"—occurs by the end of the film, not so much through her pursuit and execution of the killer, but often through her acquiescence to a "healthy" / heteronormative relationship with a male love interest. Hillary Radner argues that the masculinized or de-feminized "psychofemme" of the 1990s—for example, Sarah Connor (Linda Hamilton) of Terminator 2: Judgment Day (Cameron 1991) and Margie Gunderson (Frances McDormand) of Fargo (Coen 1996)—offered a strong and independent model for women, one not dependent on sacrifice, acceptance, or re-education demanded in melodramas and comedies (248). In a continuation of this strong female model, the contemporary criminalist is also masculinized or de-feminized and offers a resistance to male violence by tracking and bringing to justice the male serial killer. While detective films with a male protagonist focus on investigating the masculinity of the hero, those with a female protagonist are concerned with examining their heroes struggle as women in a man's world trying to balance a professional and personal life—and losing.

The representation of the female detective in the 1990s and 2000s serial killer film follows on from the themes of the 1980s detective film with a female lawyer as a detective figure, including Jagged Edge (Marquand 1985), Suspect (Yates 1987), The Accused (Kaplan 1988), Class Action (Apted 1991), and Guilty as Sin (Lumet 1993). As Cynthia Lucia explains, the female lawyer appeared to be a feminist model—as a professional, powerful, central female character—but her representation was in truth a result of the glossing over of reactionary impulses to feminism. Despite her alliance with the law, the female lawyer—like the femme fatale—was presented as "dangerously ambitious"; however, this masculine trait and her independence were denied by her presentation as "personally and professionally deficient" (Lucia 33). In terms of her professional life, the female lawyer was not necessarily competent and was often forced to defer to male authority or was proven wrong by a male colleague; in terms of her personal life, she was not whole but flawed and tended to be married to her job, unable to attain happiness or fulfillment until she found a child and/or love interest.

Similarly, the contemporary female detective has risen through the ranks because she has sacrificed the traditional female roles of wife and mother to pursue a career in the male sphere of law enforcement. Rather than being a nurturer to a man, she is a threat to him as competition in his professional life. While she may excel at her job, she tends to dress like a man (or not in a feminine manner), is sexually aggressive, and has no desire for a committed relationship. Whether or not this is acceptable behavior for a woman in American society in the twenty-first century is beside the point as for Hollywood this can signify nothing other than that she is neurotic and unhappy even if she believes otherwise. In other words, the female detective can only succeed at her professional life if her personal life suffers. While this is not necessarily a new trope for the genre, it is certainly highlighted in the contemporary detective film as this representation of women seems out of date in today's climate of female advancement in professional circles.

Her struggle to operate in a man's world is more acute in the case of the serial killer narrative as the detective often has the potential to become a victim of the man she hunts. The films of the last decade with female detective-heroes explore two issues or conflicts related to her sex and her presence in two male dominated worlds: that of law enforcement where the majority of detectives are male, and that of the serial killer where the killer is male and the victims are almost always female.[7] The female detective appeared with increasing frequency along with the shift from the action-cop to the criminalist detective; however, the female detective presents a problem in the genre because of her appropriation of the male position in mainstream film. Linda Mizejewski argues that

> the "problem" of the female investigator is most easily resolved
> through familiar heterosexual strategies: the excessive fetishization
> and domesticization of the female detective in V.I. Warshawski (1991);
> the imposition of a romantic subplot [...] in The Stranger Among Us
> (1992); the glamorization in Impulse (1990); the heterosexual partner-
> ship in Rush (1992). An alternative resolution of the female dick prob-
> lem in cinema has been to represent her as a Hollywood version of the
> lesbian, thereby associating her with another kind of "illegitimacy."
> (6-7).

There seems to be a need in mainstream film to contain the representation of women in the same instance as giving her voice expression.[8] In the action and detective films of the late 1980s and early 1990s—for example, Blue Steel, The Silence of the Lambs, and Point of No

Return (Badham 1993)—the woman's fear is that, through the appropriation of the male position as detective (i.e., "dick") and male weapon of the gun (i.e., phallus), she suffers a loss of femininity—or at least the ability to perform it successfully. In Blue Steel, Megan (Jamie Lee Curtis) looks uncomfortable and out of place in her evening dress when out on a date compared to the confidence she exudes when in her masculine uniform; in Silence of the Lambs, Hannibal Lecter (Anthony Hopkins) undermines Clarice (Jodie Foster) and her self-confidence when he identifies her cheap shoes and perfume; and in Point of No Return, while Maggie (Bridget Fonda) is proficient in street-fighting and firing a gun, she needs lessons in how to walk, dress, and present herself convincingly as a woman. This construction of female heroism in the early 1990s through signifiers associated with established notions of male heroism may account for what Mizejewski sees as the "lesbianization" of the female hero—aligning her with "illegitimate" notions of femininity in order to mediate her accession to heroism.

The female body is constructed in mainstream cinema almost always in terms of sexual display for the male gaze, but, in many of the detective films of the 1990s, the female body is presented less as an erotic object and more as spectacular—either in death as the female corpse or in action as the female detective. The Bone Collector opens with a familiar scene: a woman sits at the window while a man is shown in bed and a police officer's uniform, gun, holster, and boots lay on the floor beside the bed. The implication is these tools of the law enforcement trade belong to the man in bed; however, in a reversal of gender roles, it is Amelia (Angelina Jolie) that is the cop and her lover who complains that she is commitment phobic. He accuses her of not being emotionally involved enough in their relationship and that the night they just spent together was "another slam bam thank you 'mam'—he being the one who has been used. This reversal establishes Amelia as masculinized, and, therefore, it is not surprising that she turns out to be a tough and competent cop who readily dispatches the killer when he attempts to kill the male detective, Rhyme. Similarly, in Murder by Numbers, Cassie (Sandra Bullock) is presented as more masculine than feminine: she wears gender non-specific clothes, most often a turtleneck or T-shirt with trousers and a black "pleather" jacket, little make-up, and her long hair is usually tied back for functionality. Cassie and her new partner, Sam (Ben Chaplin), represent a role reversal: she is the sexual predator in the relationship and he is the one who asks, "What about what I want?" Cassie's nickname given to her by her male colleagues on the force is "The Hyena"; the female hyena has a mock penis and Cassie acts as if she possesses a phallus.

In Kiss the Girls, Kate McTiernan (Ashley Judd) is originally one of the killer's captives but later becomes his hunter and is also somewhat masculinized. She is shown in kickboxing class: her muscles gleam and flex under the stress of her combat as her fists and feet find their marks; her body is revealed in a sports top and shorts during these sequences of action rather than stripped off or in feminine garb and in positions of passivity. In fact when she is held captive by the killer—drugged up and tied to the bed—her body is disguised beneath a baggy sweater. In Twisted, Judd plays a homicide detective, Jessica Shepard, who investigates a string of killings to which she is intimately involved—all the victims are men that she has had sexual relations with. Like Bullock's Cassie in Murder by Numbers, Jessica's uniform is jeans and turtleneck sweaters under a leather jacket. Her hair is short and she is presented as pretty—but also pretty tough. She is a sexual predator, roaming bars for passionate one-night stands with strangers. In Taking Lives, the film begins with Special Agent Illeana Scott (Angelina Jolie) portrayed as a smart and skilled behavioral scientist and her self-control and confidence is echoed in her put-together outfits—dark slim-fitting shirts, dark trousers, and a blazer or leather jacket—and her hair tightly wound back. Even her name—she answers her phone with her surname, "Scott"—and her cool handling of her black Mustang convertible in a car chase suggest she is masculine. Like, Jessica and Cassie, Illeana is a highly sexualized woman and she develops what she describes as a "favorable reaction" to the lead witness, Costa (Ethan Hawke)—eventually having a night of passion with him. Although she wears a wedding ring—suggesting that, unlike the majority of female detectives, she has found a balance between her professional and personal life—she confesses to Costa that it is a prop, worn to ward off male advances.

The female detective is often presented as a masculinized woman; however, the most effective strategy to contain the agency of the female hero is to place her in the position of victim, or potential victim, at the same time as that of hero. In Kiss the Girls, Kate is one of Casanova's victims: she was stalked, kidnapped, drugged, and would have been raped and / or killed if she had not escaped. She uses her strengths to gain not only her freedom from his dungeon, but also the ability to face him again. As such a strong and admirable character, Kate defies the traditional representation of a woman in this type of film where women tend to be the helpless victims; however, in her showdown with the killer, it is the male detective, Alex Cross (Morgan Freeman), who must come to her rescue and shoot the killer as Kate lies helpless on the floor. Kate—despite her strength and martial arts skills—is ultimately a victim rather than a successful "manhunter." Kate is also not a professional detective; she is a medical intern who gets involved in the case after being the only victim to escape and this allows greater latitude with her representation.

In Taking Lives, Illeana is introduced as a very successful and talented profiler from the F.B.I. The Montreal detectives—Duval and Paquette—to whom she has been assigned to assist find her, not at the airport, but in the grave where the victim was buried. One of the problems with the film is that it never fully develops or explains this and other aspects of what the film's official website identify as her "intuitive, unconventional approach" and "unorthodox methods" (takinglives.warnerbros.com), like the posting of crime scene photos above her bed, in the bathroom, and on the chair opposite her at dinner; however, the process of lying in the grave would suggest that Illeana is attempting to align herself with the victim. Similarly, at Martin's childhood home, Illeana discovers a basement room where it is implied Martin was confined and she lies in his bed. She tries to identify with Martin, whom she begins to regard as a victim himself—a victim of an obsessive and cruel mother—only to be attacked by Martin who is hiding under the bed. Her renowned abilities as a profiler are called into question by her fellow detectives and herself as, to her horror, Illeana discovers that the witness—and the man she has fallen for—is, in fact, the killer she seeks. With her realization that she has been seduced by the killer, she begins to unravel emotionally, a loss of confidence mirrored by her increasingly disheveled appearance with her long hair loose and in tangles, and her eyes red and rimmed with tears. Although the film begins with her as a strong character, her inability to identify the killer correctly and his ability to seduce her so easily portray Illeana as a woman successful in her profession but weak when it comes to men; it is her femininity that makes her vulnerable and almost one of Martin's unfortunate victims. However, the usual cause of the female detective's inability to be both professionally and personally successful in the serial killer film is most often cited as a past trauma involving violence perpetrated by men.

In Murder by Numbers, Cassie's single-minded pursuit of the killer and her abandonment of a personal life in favor of doing her job may mark her as a masculinized woman, but they are identified as a result of her past as she was once the near-victim of a killer herself. Her former abusive husband stabbed her seventeen times in an attempt to kill her and this attack haunts her life in every aspect. In her private life, she sabotages any relationship that brings any man too close—"That's Cassie's MO" her ex-boyfriend explains to her new partner Sam. In her professional life, she over-identifies with the victim and, as her boss explains, the detective must identify with the killer in order to catch him, not with the victim. Cassie's close alignment with the murdered woman (indicated by Cassie's referral to her by her first name) leads to her being pulled off the case. Cassie must deal with her own victimization in order to move on with her life, but she avoids it at all costs. When asked by Sam why she became a police detective, she lies and says it was because someone she knew was killed; and, when later she recounts her traumatic past, she refers to herself in the third person. She also uses a nickname and her maiden name, Cassie Mayweather, to differentiate herself as a detective from the victim she was as Jessica May Hudson. By meeting face to face with the killers in this case, fighting them, and bringing them to justice, Cassie is able to rewrite her past with a new sense of herself as a survivor. However, it turns out that her own experiences did cloud her judgment as she was convinced that Richard (the boy who reminds her of her husband) was the real villain, and killer, rather than the loner Justin with whom she self-identified. She concludes her rehabilitation by facing her former husband as a witness at his parole hearing and, when called as "Jessica May Hudson," Cassie answers.

Whereas Cassie used Sam for sexual gratification at the beginning of the film before literally kicking him out of bed, the film suggests that with her coming to terms with her past as victim, she will now embrace a normal relationship with Sam. This concern with "deviant" sexuality is also made explicit through the "unhealthy" relationship that emerges between Richard and Justin. The real-life killers, Leopold and Loeb, were rich, young men, and also lovers; while Murder by Numbers does not suggest that Richard and Justin engage in a homosexual relationship, it does imply that had Justin's teenage exuberance been channeled in the more usual direction of sexual interest girls, he would have never turned to murder as a hobby. He says suggestively to Lisa, the girl he likes, "If only I had met you first." She comforts him saying that, left to his own devices, he would not have killed—that Richard "seduced him" into it.

While Cassie is haunted by her near-fatal experience at the hands of her abusive husband, the masculinization of the heroines of The Silence of the Lambs, The Bone Collector and Twisted is blamed on the violent deaths of their policemen fathers at the hands of criminals. In The Silence of the Lambs, Clarice (Jodie Foster) successfully navigates the patriarchal men who test or challenge her presence in law enforcement, brings the killer that eludes the male police and agents to justice, and concludes the film without abandoning her career and / or taking a more socially prescribed role as the "significant other" of a man, a role that would lead to marriage and motherhood. In the classic horror movie, Diane Dubois notes, the female protagonist is often recovered through being "rescued" from her career by the hero through marriage and motherhood or through her "abandonment of career-based ambition," but that The Silence of the Lambs demands its protagonist does neither (305). On the other hand, The Bone Collector ends with Amelia recouped into this more traditional role. She effects Rhyme's emotional rehabilitation as he does not carry out his plans for his "final transition" (commit suicide) and is reunited with his long estranged friends and family by Amelia. More importantly, Amelia has suppressed her masculine sexual appetites apparent at the beginning of the film to be Rhyme's non-sexual companion. He is a quadriplegic and sexual intimacy between the two occurs only through the stroking of his finger that maintains feeling. The conclusion of Twisted also sees its heroine's femininity recovered as it is suggested that Jessica will embark on a meaningful and exclusive relationship with her police partner, Mike (Andy Garcia).

New Twists in the Genre

The more recent contributions to the genre, Taking Lives and Twisted, present a shift from the majority of serial killer films with female detectives that preceded them. Both films present a serial killer that preys on male rather than female victims and this, in turn, should present a shift in the representation of the female detective away from being the potential victim of the killer and male violence. In Twisted, Jessica is not a potential victim but a suspect in the case as the victims were men with whom she had intimate relations. The past trauma that haunts her is that her father—also a police detective—committed a series of murders that concluded with her mother's murder and his own suicide. It is revealed by the end of the film, however, that it was not her father that committed those atrocities when she was a child, but her seemingly benevolent guardian and police commander (Samuel L. Jackson). He did not like the men that her mother was pursuing and dispatched them; similarly, he does not like the men that Jessica sleeps with and is killing them. Jessica does not suffer from an unhealthy alignment with the victims—fearing that she may become one; instead she develops an unhealthy alignment with the killer—fearing that she may be the one committing the murders, not unlike her father. Once she discovers the truth that it is her guardian not herself or her father who is / was the murderer, Jessica is "cured" of her neurosis—and, thus, her masculinity. She is able to become feminized—i.e., vulnerable—and fall in love with Mike.

In Taking Lives, the victims of the killer are men because the killer wants to be someone else with a life different from his own; he, therefore, kills in order to take their place and live their lives like a hermit crab, as one of the detectives notes in the film. Illeana does not suffer from a childhood trauma; she appears to be confident and stable. She does not over-identify with the victims and remains professional in her following of the case; however, she does form an attraction to the killer—although unbeknownst to her. While she appears masculinized in the first half of the film, her traumatic realization that her lover is the killer sends her into a self-destructive spiral signaled by her increasingly "feminized" appearance. At the end of the film, she comes to embody hyperfemininity as she appears to be seven months pregnant with Costa/Martin's twins. He confronts her in her farmhouse hideaway and viciously attacks her—beating her, kicking her, strangling her, and ultimately stabbing her in the belly. What was interesting about this scene is the effect it had on the audience. At the screening I attended, the audience—myself included—was visibly and audibly disturbed at the sight of a heavily pregnant young woman being beaten so viciously. For Illeana/Jolie to engage in a fight with the killer seems to be acceptable to the audience only when she is masculinized; when she is feminized to this extreme degree, an incompatibility arises between her role as mother-to-be and "manhunter." However, this image of the detective as feminized—the horrifying image of a pregnant woman being attacked and beaten—is only a masquerade; Illeana is not pregnant but only pretends to be in order to lure Costa/Martin to her so that she may exact justice by killing him in self-defense. Thus, the disturbing nature of the scene dissipates with the realization that Illeana is still a masculine woman merely utilizing the masquerade of femininity to achieve her desire—to kill Martin outside the bounds of the law.

These more recent additions to the serial killer film offered new "twists" in order to attract viewers now familiar with the subgenre's conventions: Taking Lives and Twisted offer male killers who pursue male—rather than the usual female—victims. Twisted also attempts to surprise viewers by directing suspicion onto its female detective-hero who is, of course, revealed to be innocent of the crimes. One film of recent years, however, has broken with the conventions of the trend not only by presenting a serial killer who is a woman but also by making the killer—rather than a detective—the film's protagonist. Monster (Jenkins 2003) stars Charlize Theron as real-life killer Aileen Wuornos and, rather than having a detective's investigation as the driving force behind the narration, the film focuses instead of the desires and crimes of the female killer. The film's critical success—Theron won both the Golden Globe and Academy Award for Best Actress—and box-office success as an independent film— earning over $34 million (www.imdb. com)—may cause Hollywood to reconsider the focus and formulation of the recent serial killer film. However, much of the interest in the film, no doubt reflected by the awards the film won, was in the film's success at transforming the female body at the center of the narrative. Rather than the bodies of Wuornos's victims, the film offers Theron's as the spectacle of the narrative. Theron—hailed as one of Hollywood's most glamorous actresses—was successfully transformed into the Florida prostitute-turned-killer with the help of make-up, greasy hair, crooked teeth, thirty pounds of weight gain, and a dramatic change in her physical posturing to disguise her years of ballet training. In other words, Wuornos/Theron is masculinized not only because her inattention to her looks, her unfashionable clothes, and her physical carriage are non-feminine, but also because she commits what is traditionally male violence—i.e., serial murder—and engages in a non-heteronormative relationship with another woman. However, at the same time, the film presents its killer as sympathetic—and, to some extent, justifies her actions—because she is the victim of male violence herself. Thus, while Monster deviates from the current mainstream trend with its focus on the killer—and a female killer at that—it does retain an emphasis on the female body, the masculinization of the female protagonist, and depicting women as the victims of male violence.

Women Can't Have It All?

The female detective tends to be presented initially as extremely successful at her job: she is an intuitive and astute observer and tracker. Her failing tends to be in her personal life; she is unable to develop a satisfying and committed relationship with a man because she is married to her job or because she or her father was the victim of male violence. However, a shift occurs during the film whereby the female detective's inability to form a normal relationship with a man comes to impede her ability to perform her job—as in Murder by Numbers and Twisted—or she becomes the intended or potential victim of male violence—as in Kiss the Girls and Taking Lives. Her personal life intersects with the professional and leaves her vulnerable and/or unable to do her job well. In Murder by Numbers, Cassie is pulled off the case because she develops an unhealthy identification with the victim and dislike for Richard; in Twisted, Jessica is regarded as the most likely suspect as her father was a killer and she slept with all the victims; in The Bone Collector, Amelia is pulled off the case by the police chief as she attempts to play detective instead of keeping to her place as a beat patrol cop; in Kiss the Girls, Kate has escaped from the killer once but becomes his target again at the end of the film; and in Taking Lives, Illeana misreads the case and embraces the killer as a lover instead of recognizing him for the serial murderer he is. Like the female lawyer protagonist of the 1980s, the female criminalist is still plagued by the seeming inability to have both a healthy personal life as well as a strong professional one, most likely because her function in contemporary film is still to process and negotiate male anxieties centered on the proliferation of women in traditionally male spheres of public life.

The majority of Hollywood serial killer films that have populated the big screen for the last decade do not present a necessarily challenging message and, instead, tend to offer the serial killer as a sacrifice to the detective to restore order in society. As Philip Simpson explains,

> *While sensational depictions of violence can radically subvert cultural ideology, the latest serial killer films typically construct their sensationalism from a conservative political stance that allows for commercial success. Thus, while the films radically appear to transgress taboo, especially in their depiction of violence, they actually serve to uphold a patriarchal, law-and-order status quo derived in large measure from a repressively patriarchal heritage. ("Politics" 119)*

In the serial killer narrative, a sense of community and consensus is created by the sacrifice of a few victims when the abnormal element of the society—the killer—is identified and removed from that society—through death or imprisonment. The detective is also redeemed through the sacrifice of the victims as the male detective is able to validate his masculinity and/or competence as a detective through hunting and identifying the killer; the female detective, on the other hand, has the added pressure of having to be successful in both her private and professional lives—and is unable to do so. Through the tracking and killing or bringing to justice the serial killer, the female detective is able to prove her abilities as a detective and affect her own "cure" for her neurosis that has plagued her adult life, stemming from the childhood trauma of losing her father to violence or being the victim of male violence herself. The symptom that she is cured—or at least partly responsible for her cure—is that the female detective has given up her obsession with the loss of her father or the violent men of her past to pursue a healthy, normative relationship with a good man—often her partner from work.

The films leave the heroine at this moment of balance—success in both her professional and personal lives—i.e., a happy ending.

One cannot help, however, but suspect that having dealt with the traumatic past event that drove her to be a detective, our heroine may lose her ambitious—and "masculine"—drive in terms of work. Similarly, now that she has found romance and stability with her partner, the female detective will no longer be able to indulge in the single-minded pursuit of the killer. The lone male detective of the serial killer film remains unattached at the end of the narrative; like the Western hero, the detective must remain unencumbered by romantic and familial entanglements if he is to remain effective as the detective that operates on the margins of society—on the thin blue line between crime and the law. The female detective, on the other hand, is expected to give up her independence and work with the team—especially her partner. The sacrifice of the serial killer's victims—and ultimately the serial killer himself—functions to highlight and work through many contemporary anxieties of women in the traditionally male workplace. While the female detective may prove her abilities as a "manhunter," she is ultimately contained or her success devalued through a reinscribing and containment of her professional ambition and aggressive sexuality in the contemporary serial killer film.

The author gratefully acknowledges that financial support for this research was received from a grant partly funded by Wilfrid Laurier University (WLU) Operating funds and partly by the SSHRC Institutional Grant awarded to WLU.

Notes

1. For an in-depth discussion of this movement toward "sensitive men" heroes see Susan Jeffords, "Can Masculinity Be Terminated?" Screening the Male: Exploring Masculinities in Hollywood Cinema, Eds. Steven Cohan and Ina Rae Hark (London: Routledge, 1993), or Fred Pfeil, White Guys: Studies in Postmodern Domination and Difference (London: Verso, 1995).

2. As Christian Fuchs notes, the FBI assume that less than 5% of all serial killers are women, and those that are mainly kill direct relatives: Aileen Wuornos is "the great exception" (188). Similarly, the cinematic serial killer is almost always male and there are only a few exceptions, including Eye of the Beholder (Elliott 2002) starring Ashley Judd as a fictional serial killer and Monster (Jenkins 2003) starring Charlize Theron as real-life killer Wuornos.

3. For further discussion of the liberties taken in representing the fictional serial killer in film see Carl Goldberg and Virginia Crespo, "A Psychological Exaimination of Serial Killer Cinema: The Case of Copycat," Post Script 22.2 (2003): 55-63.

4. Emphasis in the original.

5. The criminalist is the protagonist in the fiction of authors like Thomas Harris, Patricia Cornwell, James Patterson, and Jeffrey Deaver; in films like Kiss the Girls and Blood Work; and on television with series like McCallum (1995 to present), Silent Witness (1996 to present), and Prime Suspect (1990 to 1996) in Britain, Da Vinci's Inquest (1998 to present) and Cold Squad (1998 to present) in Canada, and CSI: Crime Scene Investigation (2000 to present), CSI Miami (2002 to present), Crossing Jordan (2001 to present), and Law and Order: Criminal Intent (2001 to present) in the United States. Several documentary series have also cashed in on the popularity of the serial killing and forensic investigations, including IR: Cold Case Files (part of the Investigative Reports series [1991 to present]), American Justice (1992 to present), Medical Detectives (1998 to present), and City Confidential (1998 to present). Unlike the criminalist narrative in fiction and in film, the ones on television rarely present investigations of serial killers and

instead bring the contemporary fascination with forensic investigation to the traditional cop show.

6. These TV-movies include The Deadly Tower (Jameson 1975) about Charles Whitman, Helter Skelter (Gries 1976) about the Manson Family, Guyana Tragedy: The Story of Jim Jones (Graham 1980) about Jim Jones, The Executioner's Song (Shiller 1982) about Gary Gilmore, Out of the Darkness (Taylor 1985) about "The Son of Sam" killer David Berkowitz, The Deliberate Stranger (Chomsky 1986) about Ted Bundy, The Case of the Hillside Stranglers (Gethers 1988) about Kenneth Bianchi and Angelo Buono, Manhunt: Search for the Night Stalker (Green 1989) about Richard Ramirez, To Catch a Killer (Till 1992) about John Wayne Gacy, Murder in the Heartland (Markowitz 1993) about Charles Starkweather and Caril Fugate, and Citizen X (Gerolmo 1995) about the Russian killer, Andrei Chikatilo. For more details about these TV-movies, see Christian Fuchs's Bad Blood: An Illustrated guide to Psycho Cinema (New York: Creation Books, 2002).

7. In Twisted and Taking Lives the serial killer's victims are men. This seems to be the newest evolution of the genre and this gender twist enacts a shift in the relationship between the detective and the killer but also the victims and is a theme I will explore later in the paper.

8. This is a trend or need similar to that of containing black masculinity in the contemporary serial killer film. The black detective may outwit the evil serial killer, but his sexuality, race, and ability to perform heroic action—unlike those of the traditional white hero—are held in check or left undeveloped. For further discussion, see Philippa Gates, "Always a Partner in Crime: Black Masculinity and the Hollywood Detective Film" Journal of Popular Film & Television 32.1 (Spring 2004): 29.

Works Cited

Burket, Walter. Creation of the Sacred: Tracks of Biology in Early Religions. Cambridge, MA: Harvard UP, 1996.

Collins, Gerard. "Contagion and Technology in Patricia Cornwell's Scarpetta Novels." The Devil Himself." Villainy in Detective Fiction and Film. Eds. Stacy Gillis and Philippa Gates. Westport, CT: Greenwood Press, 2002. 159-69.

Cornwell, Patricia. Portrait of a Killer: Jack the Ripper Case Closed. New York: G. P. Putnam's Sons, 2002.

Deaver, Jeffrey. The Bone Collector. New York: Viking, 1997.

Dubois, Diane. "'Seeing the Female Body Differently': Gender Issues in The Silence of the Lambs." Journal of Gender Studies 10.3 (2001): 297-310.

Dyer, Richard. "Kill and Kill Again." Sight and Sound 7.9 (1997): 14-17.

Fleck, Patrice. "Looking in the Wrong Direction." Post Script 16.2 (1997): 35-43.

Francke, Lizzie. "Review of Copycat." Sight and Sound 6.5 (1996): 51-2.

Fuchs, Christian. Bad Blood: An Illustrated Guide to Psycho Cinema. Trans. by Otmar Lichtenwoerther. New York: Creation Books, 2002.

Goldberg, Carl and Virginia Crespo. "A Psychological Examination of Serial Killer Cinema: The Case of Copycat." Post Script: Essays in Film and the Humanities 22.2 (2003): 55-63.

Grant, Barry Keith. "Strange Days: Gender and Ideology in New Genre Films." Ladies and Gentlemen, Boys and Girls: Gender at the End of the Twentieth Century. Ed. Murray Pomerance. New York: State U of New York P, 2001. 185-99.

Hantke, Steffen. "Monstrosity Without a Body: Representational Strategies in the Popular Serial Killer Film." Post Script: Essays in Film and the Humanities 22.2 (2003): 34-54.

Hatty, Suzanne E. Masculinities, Violence, and Culture. Thousand Oaks, CA: Sage Publications, Inc., 2000.

Haut, Woody. Neon Noir: Contemporary American Crime Fiction. London: Serpent's Tail 1999.

Internet Movie Database (7 March 2005) <www.imdb.com /title/tt0340855/business> and <http://www.imdb.com/ titlett0340855/awards>

Livingstone, Jay. "Crime and the Media: Myths and Reality." USA Today 122:2588 (1994): 40-2.

Lucia, Cynthia. "Women on Trial: The Female Lawyer in the Hollywood Courtroom." Cineaste 19.2-3 (1992): 32-37.

Mizejewski, Linda. "Picturing the Female Dick: The Silence of the Lambs and Blue Steel." Journal of Film and Video 45.2-3 (1993): 6-23.

Radner, Hillary. "New Hollywood's New Women: Murder in Mind—Sarah and Margie." Contemporary Hollywood Cinema. Eds. Steve Neale and Murray Smith. London: Routledge, 1998. 247-62.

Seltzer, Mark. Serial Killers: Death and Life in America's Wound Culture. New York: Routledge, 1998.

Simpson, Philip L. "The Politics of Apocalypse in the Cinema of Serial Murder." Mythologies of Violence in Postmodern Media. Ed. Christopher Sharrett. Detroit: Wayne State UP, 1999. 119-144.

—. Psycho Paths: Tracking the Serial Killer through Con temporary American Film and Fiction. Carbondale: Southern Illinois UP, 2000.

Taking Lives Official Website (23 March 2004) <takinglives.warnerbros.com>

Taubin, Amy. "Death and the Maidens—A Series of Serial Killers: The Loss of Innocence, Mobility, and Air." [Review of Felicia's Journey, The Bone Collector, and Oxygen] Village Voice (16 November 1999): 136.

—."Grabbing the Knife: The Silence of the Lambs and the History of the Serial Killer Movie." Women and Film: A Sight and Sound Reader. Eds. Pam Cook and Philip Dodd. London: Scarlet Press, 1991. 123-131.

Turan, Kenneth. "Review of Copycat." Los Angeles Times (27 October 1995): Calendar 1.

Wardell, Jane. "London Audience Flocks to Public Autopsy." Toronto Star (21 November 2002): A16.

Williams, Linda. "Film Bodies: Gender, Genre, and Excess." Film Quarterly 44.4 (1991): 2-13.

Selected Filmography

Basic Instinct (1992) Dir. Paul Verhoeven. Perf. Michael Douglas and Sharon Stone. Prod. Carolco Pictures, Le Studio Canal+, and TriStar Pictures.

Blue Steel (1990) Dir. Kathryn Bigelow. Perf. Jamie Lee Curtis and Ron Silver. Prod. Lightning Pictures, Mack-Taylor Productions, and Precision Films.

Bone Collector, The (1999) Dir. Phillip Noyce. Perf. Denzel Washington and Angelina Jolie. Prod. Columbia Pictures and Universal Pictures.

Copycat (1995) Dir. John Amiel. Perf. Sigourney Weaver and Holly Hunter. Prod. New Regency Pictures, Regency Enterprises, and Warner Bros.

CSI: Crime Scene Investigation (2000 to present). Perf. William L. Petersen, Marg Helgenberger, et al. Prod. Alliance Atlantis Communications and CBS Productions (TV series).

Die Hard (1988) Dir. John McTiernan. Perf. Bruce Willis and Bonnie Bedelia. Prod. 20th Century Fox, Gordon Company, and Silver Pictures.

ER (1994 to present) Perf. Noah Wyle, Laura Innes, et al. Prod. Amblin Television, Constant C Productions, and Warner Bros. Television (TV series).

Fargo (1996) Dir. Joel Coen. Perf. Frances McDormand and William H. Macy. Prod. Gramercy Pictures, PolyGram Filmed Entertainment, and Working Title Films.

Kiss the Girls (1997) Dir. Gary Fleder. Perf. Morgan Freeman and Ashley Judd. Prod. Paramount Pictures and Rysher Entertainment.

Lethal Weapon (1987) Dir. Richard Donner. Perf. Mel Gibson and Danny Glover. Prod. Silver Pictures and Warner Bros.

Manhunter (1986) Dir. Michael Mann. Perf. William L. Petersen and Kim Greist. Prod. De Laurentiis Entertainment Group and Red Dragon Productions.

Monster (2003) Dir. Patty Jenkins. Perf. Charlize Theron and Christina Ricci. Prod. Media 8 Entertainment, DEJ Productions, K/W Productions, Denver and Delilah Productions, VIP 2 Medienfonds, MDP Worldwide, and Zodiac Productions.

Murder by Numbers (2002) Dir. Barbet Schroeder. Perf. Sandra Bullock and Ben Chaplin. Prod. Castle Rock Entertainment, Schroeder Hoffman Productions, and Warner Bros.

Point of No Return (1993) Dir. John Badham. Perf. Bridget Fonda and Gabriel Byrne. Prod. Art Linson Productions and Warner Bros.

Silence of the Lambs, The (1991) Dir. Jonathan Demme. Perf. Anthony Hopkins and Jodie Foster. Prod. Orion Pictures.

Taking Lives (2004) Dir. D.J. Caruso. Perf. Angelina Jolie and Ethan Hawke. Prod. Warner Bros., Village Roadshow Pictures, Atmosphere Pictures, and Taking Lives Films.

Terminator 2: Judgement Day (1991) Dir. James Cameron. Perf. Arnold Schwarzenegger and Linda Hamilton. Prod. Carolco Pictures, Le Studio Canal+, Lightstorm Entertainment, and Pacific Western.

Twisted (2004) Dir. Philip Kaufman. Perf. Ashley Judd and Samuel L. Jackson. Prod. Paramount Pictures, Blackout Productions, Intertainment AG, and Kopelson Entertainment.

22 Racial Microaggressions in Everyday Life: Implications for Clinical Practice

Derald Wing Sue, Christina M. Capodilupo, Gina C. Torino, Jennifer M. Bucceri, Aisha M. B. Holder, Kevin L. Nadal, and Marta Esquilin
Teachers College, Columbia University

Racial microaggressions are brief and commonplace daily verbal, behavioral, or environmental indignities, whether intentional or unintentional, that communicate hostile, derogatory, or negative racial slights and insults toward people of color. Perpetrators of microaggressions are often unaware that they engage in such communications when they interact with racial/ethnic minorities. A taxonomy of racial microaggressions in everyday life was created through a review of the social psychological literature on aversive racism, from formulations regarding the manifestation and impact of everyday racism, and from reading numerous personal narratives of counselors (both White and those of color) on their racial/cultural awakening. Microaggressions seem to appear in three forms: microassault, microinsult, and microinvalidation. Almost all interracial encounters are prone to microaggressions; this article uses the White counselor—client of color counseling dyad to illustrate how they impair the development of a therapeutic alliance. Suggestions regarding education and training and research in the helping professions are discussed.

Editor's note. Lillian Comas-Díaz served as the action editor for this article before Derald Wing Sue joined the *American Psychologist* Editorial Board as an associate editor on January 1, 2007.

Authors' note. Derald Wing Sue, Christina M. Capodilupo, Gina C. Torino, Jennifer M. Bucceri, Aisha M. B. Holder, Kevin L. Nadal, and Marta Esquilin, Department of Counseling and Clinical Psychology, Teachers College, Columbia University.

Aisha M. B. Holder is now at Fordham University.

Correspondence concerning this article should be addressed to Derald Wing Sue, Department of Counseling and Clinical Psychology, Box 36, Teachers College, Columbia University, 525 West 120th Street, New York, NY 10027. E-mail: dwingsue@aol.com

Although the civil rights movement had a significant effect on changing racial interactions in this society, racism continues to plague the United States (Thompson & Neville, 1999). President Clinton's Race Advisory Board concluded that (a) racism is one of the most divisive forces in our society, (b) racial legacies of the past continue to haunt current policies and practices that create unfair disparities between minority and majority groups, (c) racial inequities are so deeply ingrained in American society that they are nearly invisible, and (d) most White Americans are unaware of the advantages they enjoy in this society and of how their attitudes and actions unintentionally discriminate against persons of color (Advisory Board to the President's Initiative on Race, 1998). This last conclusion is especially problematic in the mental health professions because most graduates continue to be White and trained primarily in Western European models of service delivery (D. W. Sue & Sue, 2003). For that reason, this article focuses primarily on White therapist–client of color interactions.

Because White therapists are members of the larger society and not immune from inheriting the racial biases of their forebears (Burkard & Knox, 2004; D. W. Sue, 2005), they may become victims of a cultural conditioning process that imbues within them biases and prejudices (Abelson, Dasgupta, Park, & Banaji, 1998; Banaji, Hardin, & Rothman, 1993) that discriminate against clients of color. Over the past 20 years, calls for cultural competence in the helping professions (American Psychological Association, 2003; D. W. Sue, Arredondo, & McDavis, 1992) have stressed the importance of two therapist characteristics associated with effective service delivery to racial/ethnic minority clients: (a) awareness of oneself as a racial/cultural being and of the biases, stereotypes, and assumptions that influence world-views and (b) awareness of the world-views of culturally diverse clients. Achieving these two goals is blocked, however, when White clinicians fail to understand how issues of race influence the therapy process and how racism potentially infects the delivery of services to clients of color (Richardson & Molinaro, 1996). Therapists who are unaware of their biases and prejudices may unintentionally create impasses for clients of color, which may partially explain well-documented patterns of therapy underutilization and premature termination of therapy among such clients (Burkard & Knox, 2004; Kearney, Draper, & Baron, 2005). In this article, we describe and analyze how racism in the form of racial microaggressions is particularly problematic for therapists to identify; propose a taxonomy of racial microaggressions with potential implications for practice, education and training, and research; and use the counseling/therapy process to illustrate how racial microaggressions can impair the therapeutic alliance. To date, no conceptual or theoretical model of racial microaggressions has been proposed to explain their impact on the therapeutic process.

The Changing Face of Racism

In recent history, racism in North America has undergone a transformation, especially after the post-civil rights era when the conscious democratic belief in equality for groups of color directly clashed with the long history of racism in the society (Jones, 1997; Thompson & Neville, 1999). The more subtle forms of racism have been labeled *modern racism* (McConahay, 1986), *symbolic racism* (Sears, 1988), and *aversive racism* (Dovidio, Gaertner, Kawakami, & Hodson, 2002). All three explanations of contemporary racism share commonalities. They emphasize that racism (a) is more likely than ever to be disguised and covert and (b) has evolved from the "old fashioned" form, in which overt racial hatred and bigotry is consciously and publicly displayed, to a more ambiguous and nebulous form that is more difficult to identify and acknowledge.

It appears that modern and symbolic racism are most closely associated with political conservatives, who disclaim personal bigotry by strong and rigid adherence to traditional American values (individualism, self-reliance, hard work, etc.), whereas aversive racism is more characteristic of White liberals (Dovidio & Gaertner, 1996, 2000). Aversive racists, according to these researchers, are strongly motivated by egalitarian values as well as antiminority feelings. Their egalitarian values operate on a conscious level, while their antiminority feelings are less conscious and generally covert (DeVos & Banaji, 2005). In some respects, these three forms of racism can be ordered along a continuum; aversive racists are the least consciously negative, followed by modern and symbolic racists, who are somewhat more prejudiced, and finally by old-fashioned biological racists (Nelson, 2006).

Although much has been written about contemporary forms of racism, many studies in health care (Smedley & Smedley, 2005), education (Gordon & Johnson, 2003), employment (Hinton, 2004), mental health (Burkard & Knox, 2004), and other social settings (Sellers & Shelton, 2003) indicate the difficulty of describing and defining racial discrimination that occurs via "aversive racism" or "implicit bias"; these types of racism are difficult to identify, quantify, and rectify because of their subtle, nebulous, and unnamed nature. Without an adequate classification or understanding of the dynamics of subtle racism, it will remain invisible and potentially harmful to the well-being, self-esteem, and standard of living of people of color (U.S. Department of Health and Human Services, 2001). Ironically, it has been proposed that the daily common experiences of racial aggression that characterize aversive racism may have significantly more influence on racial anger, frustration, and self-esteem than traditional overt forms of racism (Solórzano, Ceja, & Yosso, 2000). Furthermore, the invisible nature of acts of aversive racism prevents perpetrators from realizing and confronting (a) their own complicity in creating psychological dilemmas for minorities and (b) their role in creating disparities in employment, health care, and education.

The Manifestation of Racial Microaggressions

In reviewing the literature on subtle and contemporary forms of racism, we have found the term "racial microaggressions" to best describe the phenomenon in its everyday occurrence. First coined by Pierce in 1970, the term refers to "subtle, stunning, often automatic, and non-verbal exchanges which are 'put downs'" (Pierce, Carew, Pierce-Gonzalez, & Willis, 1978, p. 66). Racial microaggressions have also been described as "subtle insults (verbal, nonverbal, and/or visual) directed toward people of color, often automatically or unconsciously" (Solórzano et al., 2000). Simply stated, microaggressions are brief, everyday exchanges that send denigrating messages to people of color because they belong to a racial minority group. In the world of business, the term "microinequities" is used to describe the pattern of being overlooked, underrespected, and devalued because of one's race or gender. Microaggressions are often unconsciously delivered in the form of subtle snubs or dismissive looks, gestures, and tones. These exchanges are so pervasive and automatic in daily conversations and interactions that they are often dismissed and glossed over as being innocent and innocuous. Yet, as indicated previously, microaggressions are detrimental to persons of color because they impair performance in a multitude of settings by sapping the psychic and spiritual energy of recipients and by creating inequities (Franklin, 2004; D. W. Sue, 2004).

There is an urgent need to bring greater awareness and understanding of how microaggressions operate, their numerous manifestations in society, the type of impact they have on people of color, the dynamic interaction between perpetrator and target, and the educational strategies needed to eliminate them. Our attempt to define and propose a taxonomy of microaggressions is grounded in several lines of empirical and experiential evidence in the professional literature and in personal narratives.

First, the work by psychologists on aversive racism (Dovidio & Gaertner, 1996; Dovidio et al., 2002), studies suggesting the widespread existence of dissociation between implicit and explicit social stereotyping (Abelson et al., 1998; Banaji et al., 1993; DeVos & Banaji, 2005), the attributional ambiguity of everyday racial discrimination (Crocker & Major, 1989), the daily manifestations of racism in many arenas of life (Plant & Peruche, 2005; Sellers & Shelton, 2003; Vanman, Saltz, Nathan, & Warren, 2004), and multiple similarities between microaggressive incidents and items that comprise measures of race-related stress/perceived discrimination toward Black Americans (Brondolo et al., 2005; Klonoff & Landrine, 1999; Utsey & Ponterotto, 1996) and Asian Americans (Liang, Li, & Kim, 2004) all seem to lend empirical support to the concept of racial microaggressions. Second, numerous personal narratives and brief life stories on race written by White psychologists and psychologists of color provide experiential evidence for the existence of racial microaggressions in everyday life (American Counseling Association, 1999; Conyne & Bemak, 2005; Ponterotto, Casas, Suzuki, & Alexander, 2001). Our analysis of the life experiences of these individuals and the research literature in social and counseling psychology led us to several conclusions: (a) The personal narratives were rich with examples and incidents of racial microaggressions, (b) the formulation of microaggressions was consistent with the research literature, and (c) racial microaggressions seemed to manifest themselves in three distinct forms.

Forms of Racial Microaggressions

Racial microaggressions are brief and commonplace daily verbal, behavioral, and environmental indignities, whether intentional or unintentional, that communicate hostile, derogatory, or negative racial slights and insults to the target person or group. They are not limited to human encounters alone but may also be environmental in nature, as when a person of color is exposed to an office setting that unintentionally assails his or her racial identity (Gordon & Johnson, 2003; D. W. Sue, 2003). For example, one's racial identity can be minimized or made insignificant through the sheer exclusion of decorations or literature that represents various racial groups. Three forms of microaggressions can be identified: microassault, microinsult, and microinvalidation.

Microassault

A microassault is an explicit racial derogation characterized primarily by a verbal or nonverbal attack meant to hurt the intended victim through name-calling, avoidant behavior, or purposeful discriminatory actions. Referring to someone as "colored" or "Oriental," using racial epithets, discouraging interracial interactions, deliberately serving a White patron before someone of color, and displaying a swastika are examples. Microassaults are most similar to what has been called "old fashioned" racism conducted on an individual level. They are most likely to be conscious and deliberate, although they are generally expressed in limited "private" situations (micro) that allow the perpetrator some degree of anonymity. In other words, people are likely to hold notions of minority inferiority privately and will only display them publicly when they (a) lose control or (b) feel relatively safe to engage in a microassault. Because we have chosen to analyze the unintentional and unconscious manifestations of microaggressions, microassaults are not the focus of our article. It is important to note, however, that individuals can also vary in the degree of conscious awareness they show in the use of the following two forms of microaggressions.

Microinsult

A microinsult is characterized by communications that convey rudeness and insensitivity and demean a person's racial heritage or identity. Microinsults represent subtle snubs, frequently unknown to the perpetrator, but clearly convey a hidden insulting message to the recipient of color. When a White employer tells a prospective candidate of color "I believe the most qualified person should get the job, regardless of race" or when an employee of color is asked "How did you get your job?", the underlying message from the perspective of the recipient may be twofold: (a) People of color are not qualified, and (b) as a minority group member, you must have obtained the position through some affirmative action or quota program and not because of ability. Such statements are not necessarily aggressions, but context is important. Hearing these statements frequently when used against affirmative action makes the recipient likely to experience them as aggressions. Microinsults can also occur nonverbally, as when a White teacher fails to acknowledge students of color in the classroom or when a White supervisor seems distracted during a conversation with a Black employee by avoiding eye contact or turning away (Hinton, 2004). In this case, the message conveyed to persons of color is that their contributions are unimportant.

Microinvalidation

Microinvalidations are characterized by communications that exclude, negate, or nullify the psychological thoughts, feelings, or experiential reality of a person of color. When Asian Americans (born and raised in the United States) are complimented for speaking good English or are repeatedly asked where they were born, the effect is to negate their U.S. American heritage and to convey that they are perpetual foreigners. When Blacks are told that "I don't see color" or "We are all human beings," the effect is to negate their experiences as racial/cultural beings (Helms, 1992). When a Latino couple is given poor service at a restaurant and shares their experience with White friends, only to be told "Don't be so oversensitive" or "Don't be so petty," the racial experience of the couple is being nullified and its importance is being diminished.

We have been able to identify nine categories of microaggressions with distinct themes: alien in one's own land, ascription of intelligence, color blindness, criminality/assumption of criminal status, denial of individual racism, myth of meritocracy, pathologizing cultural values/communication styles, second-class status, and environmental invalidation. Table 1 provides samples of comments or situations that may potentially be classified as racial microaggressions and their accompanying hidden assumptions and messages. Figure 1 visually presents the three large classes of microaggressions, the classification of the themes under each category, and their relationship to one another.

The experience of a racial microaggression has major implications for both the perpetrator and the target person. It creates psychological dilemmas that unless adequately resolved lead to increased levels of racial anger, mistrust, and loss of self-esteem for persons of color; prevent White people from perceiving a different racial reality; and create impediments to harmonious race-relations (Spanierman & Heppner, 2004; Thompson & Neville, 1999).

The Invisibility and Dynamics of Racial Microaggressions

The following real-life incident illustrates the issues of invisibility and the disguised problematic dynamics of racial microaggressions.

> I [Derald Wing Sue, the senior author, an Asian American] recently traveled with an African American colleague on a plane flying from New York to Boston. The plane was a small "hopper" with a single row of seats on one side and double seats on the other. As the plane was only sparsely populated, we were told by the flight attendant (White) that we could sit anywhere, so we sat at the front, across the aisle from one another. This made it easy for us to converse and provided a larger comfortable space on a small plane for both of us. As the attendant was about to close the hatch, three White men in suits entered the plane, were informed they could sit anywhere, and promptly seated themselves in front of us. Just before takeoff, the attendant proceeded to close all overhead compartments and seemed to scan the plane with her eyes. At that point she approached us, leaned over, interrupted our conversation, and asked if we would mind moving to the back of the plane. She indicated that she needed to distribute weight on the plane evenly.

Both of us (passengers of color) had similar negative reactions. First, balancing the weight on the plane seemed reasonable, but why were we being singled out? After all, we had boarded first and the three White men were the last passengers to arrive. Why were they not being asked to move? Were we being singled out because of our race? Was this just a random event with no racial overtones? Were we being oversensitive and petty?

Although we complied by moving to the back of the plane, both of us felt resentment, irritation, and anger. In light of our everyday racial experiences, we both came to the same conclusion: The flight attendant had treated us like second-class citizens because of our race. But this incident did not end there. While I kept telling myself to drop the matter, I could feel my blood pressure rising, heart beating faster, and face flush with anger. When the attendant walked back to make sure our seat belts were fastened, I could not contain my anger any longer. Struggling to control myself, I said to her in a forced calm voice: "Did you know that you asked two passengers of color to step to the rear of the 'bus'"? For a few seconds she said nothing but looked at me with a horrified expression. Then she said in a righteously indignant tone, "Well, I have never been accused of that! How dare you? I don't see color! I only asked you to move to balance the plane. Anyway, I was only trying to give you more space and greater privacy."

Attempts to explain my perceptions and feelings only generated greater defensiveness from her. For every allegation I made, she seemed to have a rational reason for her actions. Finally, she broke off the conversation and refused to talk about the incident any longer. Were it not for my colleague who validated my experiential reality, I would have left that encounter wondering whether I was correct or incorrect in my perceptions. Nevertheless, for the rest of the flight, I stewed over the incident and it left a sour taste in my mouth.

The power of racial microaggressions lies in their invisibility to the perpetrator and, oftentimes, the recipient (D. W. Sue, 2005). Most White Americans experience themselves as good, moral, and decent human beings who believe in equality and democracy. Thus, they find it difficult to believe that they possess biased racial attitudes and may engage in behaviors that are discriminatory (D. W. Sue, 2004). Microaggressive acts can usually be explained away by seemingly nonbiased and valid reasons. For the recipient of a microaggression, however, there is always the nagging question of whether it really happened (Crocker & Major, 1989). It is difficult to identify a microaggression, especially when other explanations seem plausible. Many people of color describe a vague feeling that they have been attacked, that they have been disrespected, or that something is not right (Franklin, 2004; Reid & Radhakrishnan, 2003). In some respects, people of color may find an overt and obvious racist act easier to handle than microaggressions that seem vague or disguised (Solórzano et al., 2000). The above incident reveals how microaggressions operate to create psychological dilemmas for both the White perpetrator and the person of color. Four such dilemmas are particularly noteworthy for everyone to understand.

Dilemma 1: Clash of Racial Realities

The question we pose is this: Did the flight attendant engage in a microaggression or did the senior author and his colleague simply misinterpret the action? Studies indicate that the racial perceptions of people of color differ markedly from those of Whites (Jones, 1997; Harris

TABLE I. EXAMPLES OF RACIAL MICROAGGRESSIONS

Theme	Microaggression	Message
Alien in own land When Asian Americans and Latino Americans are assumed to be foreign-born	"Where are you from?" "Where were you born?" "You speak good English." A person asking an Asian American to teach them words in their native language	You are not American. You are a foreigner.
Ascription of intelligence Assigning intelligence to a person of color on the basis of their race	"You are a credit to your race." "You are so articulate." Asking an Asian person to help with a math or science problem	People of color are generally not as intelligent as Whites. It is unusual for someone of your race to be intelligent. All Asians are intelligent and good in math/sciences.
Color blindness Statements that indicate that a White person does not want to acknowledge race	"When I look at you, I don't see color." "America is a melting pot." "There is only one race, the human race."	Denying a person of color's racial/ethnic experiences. Assimilate/acculturate to the dominant culture. Denying the individual as a racial/cultural being.
Criminality/assumption of criminal status A person of color is presumed to be dangerous, criminal, or deviant on the basis of their race	A White man or woman clutching their purse or checking their wallet as a Black or Latino approaches or passes A store owner following a customer of color around the store A White person waits to ride the next elevator when a person of color is on it	You are a criminal. You are going to steal/ You are poor/ You do not belong. You are dangerous.
Denial of individual racism A statement made when Whites deny their racial biases	"I'm not racist. I have several Black friends." "As a woman, I know what you go through as a racial minority."	I am immune to racism because I have friends of color. Your racial oppression is no different than my gender oppression. I can't be a racist. I'm like you.
Myth of meritocracy Statements which assert that race does not play a role in life successes	"I believe the most qualified person should get the job." "Everyone can succeed in this society, if they work hard enough."	People of color are given extra unfair benefits because of their race. People of color are lazy and/or incompetent and need to work harder.
Pathologizing cultural values/communication styles The notion that the values and communication styles of the dominant/White culture are ideal	Asking a Black person: "Why do you have to be so loud/animated? Just calm down." To an Asian or Latino person: "Why are you so quiet? We want to know what you think. Be more verbal." "Speak up more."	Assimilate to dominant culture.

Chapter Twenty-Two

TABLE I. EXAMPLES OF RACIAL MICROAGGRESSIONS (CONTINUED)

Theme	Microaggression	Message
Pathologizing cultural values/ communication styles (cont'd)	Dismissing an individual who brings up race/culture in work/school setting	Leave your cultural baggage outside.
Second-class citizen Occurs when a White person is given preferential treatment as a consumer over a person of color	Person of color mistaken for a service worker	People of color are servants to Whites. They couldn't possibly occupy high-status positions.
	Having a taxi cab pass a person of color and pick up a White passenger	You are likely to cause trouble and/or travel to a dangerous neighborhood.
	Being ignored at a store counter as attention is given to the White customer behind you	Whites are more valued customers than people of color.
	"You people ..."	You don't belong. You are a lesser being.
Environmental microaggressions Macro-level microaggressions, which are more apparent on systemic and environmental levels	A college or university with buildings that are all named after White heterosexual upper class males	You don't belong/You won't succeed here. There is only so far you can go.
	Television shows and movies that feature predominantly White people, without representation of people of color	You are an outsider/You don't exist.
	Overcrowding of public schools in communities of color	People of color don't/shouldn't value education.
	Overabundance of liquor stores in communities of color	People of color are deviant.

Poll commissioned by the National Conference of Christians and Jews, 1992). In most cases, White Americans tend to believe that minorities are doing better in life, that discrimination is on the decline, that racism is no longer a significant factor in the lives of people of color, and that equality has been achieved. More important, the majority of Whites do not view themselves as racist or capable of racist behavior.

Minorities, on the other hand, perceive Whites as (a) racially insensitive, (b) unwilling to share their position and wealth, (c) believing they are superior, (d) needing to control everything, and (e) treating them poorly because of their race. People of color believe these attributes are reenacted everyday in their interpersonal interactions with Whites, oftentimes in the form of microaggressions (Solórzano et al., 2000). For example, it was found that 96% of African Americans reported experiencing racial discrimination in a one-year period (Klonoff & Landrine, 1999), and many incidents involved being mistaken for a service worker, being ignored, given poor service, treated rudely, or experiencing strangers acting fearful or intimidated when around them (Sellers & Shelton, 2003).

Dilemma 2: The Invisibility of Unintentional Expressions of Bias

The interaction between the senior author and the flight attendant convinced him that she was sincere in her belief that she had acted in good faith without racial bias. Her actions and their meaning were invisible to her. It was clear that she was stunned that anyone would accuse her of such despicable actions. After all, in her mind, she acted with only the best of intentions: to distribute the weight evenly on the plane for safety reasons and to give two passengers greater privacy and space. She felt betrayed that her good intentions were being questioned. Yet considerable empirical evidence exists showing that racial microaggressions become automatic because of cultural conditioning and that they may become connected neurologically with the processing of emotions that surround prejudice (Abelson et al., 1998). Several investigators have found, for example, that law enforcement officers in laboratory experiments will fire their guns more often at Black criminal suspects than White ones (Plant & Peruche, 2005), and Afrocentric features tend to result in longer prison terms (Blair, Judd, & Chapleau, 2004). In all cases, these law enforcement officials had no conscious awareness that they responded differently on the basis of race.

Herein lies a major dilemma. How does one prove that a microaggression has occurred? What makes our belief that the flight attendant acted in a biased manner any more plausible than her conscious belief that it was generated for another reason? If she did act out of hidden and unconscious bias, how do we make her aware of it? Social psychological research tends to confirm the existence of unconscious racial biases in well-intentioned Whites, that nearly everyone born and raised in the United States inherits the racial biases of the society, and that the most accurate assessment about whether racist acts have occurred in a particular situation is most likely to be made by those most disempowered rather than by those who enjoy the privileges of power (Jones, 1997; Keltner & Robinson, 1996). According to these findings, microaggressions (a) tend to be subtle, indirect, and unintentional, (b) are most likely to emerge not when a behavior would look prejudicial, but when other rationales can be offered for prejudicial behavior, and (c) occur when Whites pretend not to notice differences, thereby

Figure 1
Categories of and Relationships Among Racial Microaggressions

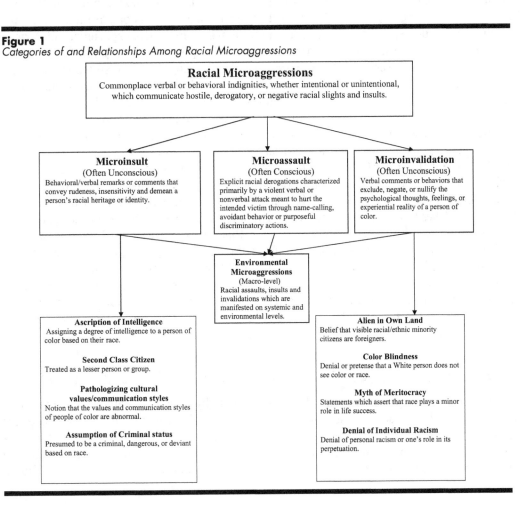

justifying that "color" was not involved in the actions taken. Color blindness is a major form of microinvalidation because it denies the racial and experiential reality of people of color and provides an excuse to White people to claim that they are not prejudiced (Helms, 1992; Neville, Lilly, Duran, Lee, & Browne, 2000). The flight attendant, for example, did not realize that her "not seeing color" invalidated both passengers' racial identity and experiential reality.

Dilemma 3: Perceived Minimal Harm of Racial Microaggressions

In most cases, when individuals are confronted with their microaggressive acts (as in the case of the flight attendant), the perpetrator usually believes that the victim has overreacted and is being overly sensitive and/or petty. After all, even if it was an innocent racial blunder, microaggressions are believed to have minimal negative impact. People of color are told not to overreact and to simply "let it go." Usually, Whites consider microaggressive incidents to be minor, and people of color are encouraged (oftentimes by people of color as well) to not waste time or effort on them.

It is clear that old-fashioned racism unfairly disadvantages people of color and that it contributes to stress, depression, shame, and anger in its victims (Jones, 1997). But evidence also supports the detrimental impact of more subtle forms of racism (Chakraborty & McKenzie, 2002; Clark, Anderson, Clark, & Williams, 1999). For example, in a survey of studies examining racism and mental health, researchers found a positive association between happiness and life satisfaction, self-esteem, mastery of control, hypertension, and discrimination (Williams, Neighbors, & Jackson, 2003). Many of the types of everyday racism identified by Williams and colleagues (Williams & Collins, 1995; Williams, Lavizzo-Mourey, & Warren, 1994) provide strong support for the idea that racial microaggressions are not minimally harmful. One study specifically examined microaggressions in the experiences of African Americans and found that the cumulative effects can be quite devastating (Solórzano et al., 2000). The researchers reported that experience with microaggressions resulted in a negative racial climate and emotions of self-doubt, frustration, and isolation on the part of victims. As indicated in the incident above, the senior author experienced considerable emotional turmoil that lasted for the entire flight. When one considers that people of color are exposed continually to microaggressions and that their effects are cumulative, it becomes easier to understand the psychological toll they may take on recipients' well-being.

We submit that covert racism in the form of microaggressions also has a dramatic and detrimental impact on people of color. Although microaggressions may be seemingly innocuous and insignificant, their effects can be quite dramatic (Steele, Spencer, & Aronson, 2002). D. W. Sue believes that "this contemporary form of racism is many times over more problematic, damaging, and injurious to persons of color than overt racist acts" (D. W. Sue, 2003, p. 48). It has been noted that the cumulative effects of racial microaggressions may theoretically result in "diminished mortality, augmented morbidity and flattened confidence" (Pierce, 1995, p. 281). It is important to study and acknowledge this form of racism in society because without documentation and analysis to better understand microaggressions, the threats that they pose and the assaults that they justify can be easily ignored or downplayed (Solórzano et al., 2000). D. W. Sue (2005) has referred to this phenomenon as "a conspiracy of silence."

Dilemma 4: The Catch-22 of Responding to Microaggressions

When a microaggression occurs, the victim is usually placed in a catch-22. The immediate reaction might be a series of questions: Did what I think happened, really happen? Was this a deliberate act or an unintentional slight? How should I respond? Sit and stew on it or confront the person? If I bring the topic up, how do I prove it? Is it really worth the effort? Should I just drop the matter? These questions in one form or another have been a common, if not a universal, reaction of persons of color who experience an attributional ambiguity (Crocker & Major, 1989).

First, the person must determine whether a microaggression has occurred. In that respect, people of color rely heavily on experiential reality that is contextual in nature and involves life experiences from a variety of situations. When the flight attendant asked the senior author and his colleague to move, it was not the first time that similar requests and situations had occurred for both. In their experience, these incidents were nonrandom events (Ridley, 2005), and their perception was that the only similarity "connecting the dots" to each and every one of these incidents was the color of their skin. In other words, the situation on the plane was only one of many similar incidents with identical outcomes. Yet the flight attendant and most White Americans do not share these multiple experiences, and they evaluate their own behaviors in the moment through a singular event (Dovidio & Gaertner, 2000). Thus, they fail to see a pattern of bias, are defended by a belief in their own morality, and can in good conscience deny that they discriminated (D. W. Sue, 2005).

Second, how one reacts to a microaggression may have differential effects, not only on the perpetrator but on the person of color as well. Deciding to do nothing by sitting on one's anger is one response that occurs frequently in people of color. This response occurs because persons of color may be (a) unable to determine whether a microaggression has occurred, (b) at a loss for how to respond, (c) fearful of the consequences, (d) rationalizing that "it won't do any good anyway," or (e) engaging in self-deception through denial ("It didn't happen."). Although these explanations for nonresponse may hold some validity for the person of color, we submit that not doing anything has the potential to result in psychological harm. It may mean a denial of one's experiential reality, dealing with a loss of integrity, or experiencing pent-up anger and frustration likely to take psychological and physical tolls.

Third, responding with anger and striking back (perhaps a normal and healthy reaction) is likely to engender negative consequences for persons of color as well. They are likely to be accused of being racially oversensitive or paranoid or told that their emotional outbursts confirm stereotypes about minorities. In the case of Black males, for example, protesting may lend credence to the belief that they are hostile, angry, impulsive, and prone to violence (Jones, 1997). In this case, the person of color might feel better after venting, but the outcome results in greater hostility by Whites toward minorities. Further, while the person of color may feel better in the immediate moment by relieving pent-up emotions, the reality is that the general situation has not been changed. In essence, the catch-22 means you are "damned if you do, and damned if you don't." What is lacking is research that points to adaptive ways of handling microaggressions by people of color and suggestions of how to increase the awareness and sensitivity of Whites to microaggressions so that they accept responsibility for their behaviors and for changing them (Solórzano et al., 2000).

Racial Microaggressions as a Barrier to Clinical Practice

In a broad sense, counseling and psychotherapy can be characterized as the formation of a deeply personal relationship between a helping professional and a client that involves appropriate and accurate interpersonal interactions and communications. For effective therapy to occur, some form of positive coalition must develop between the parties involved (D. W. Sue & Sue, 2003). Many have referred to this as the "working relationship," the "therapeutic alliance," or the "establishment of rapport" (D. W. Sue & Sue, 2003). A strong therapeutic relationship is often enhanced when clients perceive therapists as credible (trustworthy and expert) and themselves as understood and positively regarded by their therapists (Strong & Schmidt, 1970). Helping professionals are trained to listen, to show empathic concern, to be objective, to value the client's integrity, to communicate understanding, and to use their professional knowledge and skills to aid clients to solve problems (Grencavage & Norcross, 1990).

As a therapeutic team, therapist and client are better prepared to venture into problematic areas that the client might hesitate to face alone. Research suggests that the therapeutic alliance is one of the major common factors of any helping relationship and is correlated with successful outcome (Lui & Pope-Davis, 2005; Martin, Garske, & Davis, 2000). More important, however, are findings that a client's perception of an accepting and positive relationship is a better predictor of successful outcome than is a similar perception by the counselor (Horvath & Symonds, 1991). Thus, when clients do not perceive their therapists as trustworthy and when they feel misunderstood and undervalued, therapeutic success is less likely to occur. Oftentimes, the telltale signs of a failed therapeutic relationship may result in clients being less likely to self-disclose, terminating prematurely, or failing to return for scheduled visits (Burkard & Knox, 2004; Kearney, Draper, & Baron, 2005).

Although the task of establishing an effective therapeutic relationship applies to the entire helping spectrum, working with clients who differ from the therapist in race, ethnicity, culture, and sexual orientation poses special challenges. White therapists who are products of their cultural conditioning may be prone to engage in racial microaggressions (Locke & Kiselica, 1999). Thus, the therapeutic alliance is likely to be weakened or terminated when clients of color perceive White therapists as biased, prejudiced, or unlikely to understand them as racial/cultural beings. That racism can potentially infect the therapeutic process when working with clients of color has been a common concern voiced by the President's Commission on Mental Health (1978) and the Surgeon General's Report on *Mental Health: Culture, Race and Ethnicity* (U.S. Department of Health and Human Services, 2001). It has been postulated that therapist bias might partially account for the low utilization of mental health services and premature termination of therapy sessions by African American, Native American, Asian American, and Latino/Hispanic American clients (U.S. Department of Health and Human Services, 2001).

Yet research also reveals that most people in our nation believe in democracy, fairness, and strong humanistic values that condemn racism and the inequities that it engenders (Dovidio et al., 2002). Such a statement is arguably truer for mental health professionals, whose goals are to help rather than hinder or hurt clients of color. Both the American Psychological Association and the American Counseling Association have attempted to confront the biases of the profession by passing multicultural guidelines or standards that denounce prejudice and discrimination in the delivery of mental health services to clients of color (American Psychological Association, 2003; D. W. Sue et al., 1992). Like most people in society, counselors and therapists experience themselves as fair and decent individuals who would never consciously and deliberately engage in racist acts toward clients of color. Sadly, it is often pointed out that when clinician and client differ from one another along racial lines, however, the relationship may serve as a microcosm for the troubled race relations in the United States. While many would like to believe that racism is no longer a major problem and that the good intentions of the helping profession have built safeguards against prejudice and discrimination, the reality is that they continue to be manifested through the therapeutic process (Utsey, Gernat, & Hammar, 2005). This is not to suggest, however, that positive changes in race relations have not occurred. Yet, as in many other interactions, microaggressions are equally likely to occur in therapeutic transactions (Ridley, 2005).

The Manifestation of Racial Microaggressions in Counseling/Therapy

Microaggressions become meaningful in the context of clinical practice, as relational dynamics and the human condition are central aspects of this field. The often unintentional and unconscious nature of microaggressions (Dilemma 2: Invisibility) poses the biggest challenge to the majority of White mental health professionals, who believe that they are just, unbiased, and nonracist. Further, mental health professionals are in a position of power, which renders them less likely to accurately assess (Dilemma 1: Conflict of Racial Realities) whether racist acts have occurred in their sessions. Thus, the harm they perpetrate against their clients of color is either unknown or minimized (Dilemma 3: Minimal Harm). Microaggressions not only oppress and harm, but they place clients of color in the unenviable position of a catch-22 (Dilemma 4).

In clinical practice, microaggressions are likely to go unrecognized by White clinicians who are unintentionally and unconsciously expressing bias. As a result, therapists must make a concerted effort to identify and monitor microaggressions within the therapeutic context. This process is reminiscent of the importance of becoming aware of potential transference and countertransference issues between therapist and client and how they may unintentionally interfere with effective therapy (Woodhouse, Schlosser, Crook, Ligiero, & Gelso, 2003). The inherent power dynamic in the therapeutic relationship further complicates this issue, as therapists are in a position of power to make diagnoses and influence the course of treatment. The power dynamic between therapist and client also effects the catch-22 of responding to microaggressions because clients may be less likely to confront their therapists and more likely to question their own perceptions in the event of a microaggression.

Table 2 provides a few examples of microaggressions in counseling practice under each of the nine categories identified earlier. Under Color Blindness, for example, a client of color stresses the importance of racial experiences only to have the therapist reply, "We are all unique. We are all individuals." or "We are all human beings or the same under the skin." These colorblind statements, which were intended to be supportive, to be sympathetic, and to convey an ability to understand, may leave the client feeling misunderstood, negated, invalidated, and unimportant (especially if racial identity is important to the client). Moreover these statements presume that the therapist is *capable* of not seeing race and impose a definition of racial reality on the client (Neville et al., 2000).

Under Denial of Individual Racism, a common response by Whites to people of color is that they can understand and relate to experiences of racism. In Table 2, under this category, we provide the following anecdote: A client of color expresses hesitancy in discussing racial issues with his White female therapist. She replies, "I understand. As a woman, I face discrimination too." The message is that the therapist believes her gender oppression is no different from the client's experiences of racial/ethnic oppression. This response is problematic because such attempts by the therapist to explain how he or she can understand a person of color's experience with racism may be perceived by the client as an attempt to minimize the importance of his or her racial identity, to avoid acknowledging the therapist's racial biases, or to communicate a discomfort with discussing racial issues. Furthermore, the therapist excuses himself or herself from any blame or fault in perpetuating racism and the power of racism. This failure to acknowledge the significance of racism within and outside of the therapy session contributes to the breakdown of the alliance between therapist and client. A therapist's willingness to discuss racial matters is of central importance in creating a therapeutic alliance with clients of color (Cardemil & Battle, 2003).

Under the category "Alien in Own Land," many Asian Americans and Latino/Hispanic Americans report that they are commonly seen as perpetual foreigners. For example, a female Asian American client arrives for her first therapy session. Her therapist asks her where she is from, and when told "Philadelphia," the therapist further probes by asking where she was born. In this case, the therapist has assumed that the Asian American client is not from the United States and has imposed through the use of the second question the idea that she must be a foreigner. Immediately, a barrier is created in the helping relationship because the client feels invalidated by the therapist (she is perceived as a foreigner, not a U.S. citizen). Unfortunately, the Asian American client is unlikely to question her therapist or point out the bias because of the power dynamic, which causes her to harbor resentment and ill feelings toward the therapist.

We contend that clients of color are at increased risk of not continuing in the counseling/therapy session when such microaggressions occur. Worse yet, they will not receive the help they need and may leave the session feeling worse than when they first sought counseling. Because it is unlikely that clinicians intentionally create hostile and unwelcoming environments for their ethnic minority clients, it can be assumed that these biases are being expressed through microaggressions. Therapists can convey their bias to their ethnic minority clients in myriad ways, such as by minimizing symptoms for Asian Americans on the basis of a false belief in the "model" minority (D. W. Sue & Sue, 2003) or by placing greater emphasis on symptoms such as paranoid delusions and substance abuse in Native Americans and African Americans, who are believed to suffer from these afflictions (U.S. Department of Health and Human Services, 2001).

Last, White counselors and therapists can impose and value their own cultural worldview while devaluing and pathologizing the cultural values of their ethnic minority clients. Previous research has shown that pathologizing clients' cultural values has been a major determinant of clients of color discontinuing psychotherapy (S. Sue, Fujino, Hu, & Takeuchi, 1991). Many clients of color may feel misunderstood by their therapists because of a lack of cultural understanding. Asian American or Latino American clients who enter therapy to discuss family issues such as feeling obligated, stressed, or overwhelmed with excess family responsibilities may be encouraged by therapists to speak out against their families or to make decisions regardless of family support or expectations. Therapists may be unaware that they may be directly invalidating cultural respect for authority and imposing an individualistic view over a collectivist one.

Future Directions in the Understanding of Racial Microaggressions

With respect to racism, D. W. Sue (2004, p. 762) has stated that the greatest challenge society and the mental health professions face is "making the 'invisible' visible." That can only be accomplished when people are willing to openly and honestly engage in a dialogue about race and racism. In that respect, the education and training of mental health professionals must incorporate issues of race and culture. One would ordinarily expect that mental health professionals would be more willing than most to dialogue on this topic, but studies suggest that White clinicians receive minimal or no practicum or supervision experiences that address race and are uncomfortable broaching the topic (Knox, Burkard, Johnson, Suzuki, & Ponterotto, 2003). Many White trainees in therapy dyads experience anxiety in the form of poor articulation, faltering and/or trembling voices, and mispronunciation of words when directly engaged in discussions about race (Utsey et al., 2005). It is interesting that such nonverbal behaviors also serve as a form of racial microaggression. When helping professionals have difficulty addressing race issues, they cut off an avenue for clients of color to explore matters of bias, discrimination, and prejudice.

Education and Training and Racial Microaggressions

It is clear that mental health training programs must support trainees in overcoming their fears and their resistance to talking about race by fostering safe and productive learning environments (Sanchez-Hucles & Jones, 2005). It is important that training programs be structured and facilitated in a manner that promotes inquiry and allows trainees to experience discomfort and vulnerability (Young & Davis-Russell, 2002). Trainees need to be challenged to explore their own racial identities and their feelings about other racial groups. The prerequisite for cultural competence has always been racial self-awareness. This is equally true for understanding how microaggressions, especially those of the therapist, influence the therapeutic process. This level of self-awareness brings to the surface possible prejudices and biases

TABLE 2. EXAMPLES OF RACIAL MICROAGGRESSIONS IN THERAPEUTIC PRACTICE

Theme	Microaggression	Message
Alien in own land When Asian Americans and Latino Americans are assumed to be foreign-born	A White client does not want to work with an Asian American therapist because "she will not understand my problem." A White therapist tells an American-born Latino client that he/she should seek a Spanish-speaking therapist.	You are not American.
Ascription of intelligence Assigning a degree of intelligence to a person of color on the basis of their race	A school counselor reacts with surprise when an Asian American student had trouble on the math portion of a standardized test. A career counselor asking a Black or Latino student, "Do you think you're ready for college?"	All Asians are smart and good at math. It is unusual for people of color to succeed.
Color blindness Statements which indicate that a White person does not want to acknowledge race	A therapist says "I think you are being too paranoid. We should emphasize similarities, not people's differences" when a client of color attempts to discuss her feelings about being the only person of color at her job and feeling alienated and dismissed by her co-workers. A client of color expresses concern in discussing racial issues with her therapist. Her therapist replies with, "When I see you, I don't see color."	Race and culture are not important variables that affect people's lives. Your racial experiences are not valid.
Criminality/assumption of criminal status A person of color is presumed to be dangerous, criminal, or deviant on the basis of their race	When a Black client shares that she was accused of stealing from work, the therapist encourages the client to explore how she might have contributed to her employer's mistrust of her. A therapist takes great care to ask all substance abuse questions in an intake with a Native American client, and is suspicious of the client's nonexistent history with substances.	You are a criminal. You are deviant.
Denial of individual racism A statement made when Whites renounce their racial biases	A client of color asks his or her therapist about how race affects their working relationship. The therapist replies, "Race does not affect the way I treat you." A client of color expresses hesitancy in discussing racial issues with his White female therapist. She replies "I understand. As a woman, I face discrimination also."	Your racial/ethnic experience is not important. Your racial oppression is no different than my gender oppression.

TABLE 2. EXAMPLES OF RACIAL MICROAGGRESSIONS IN THERAPEUTIC PRACTICE (CONTINUED)

Theme	Microaggression	Message
Myth of meritocracy Statements which assert that race does not play a role in succeeding in career advancement or education.	A school counselor tells a Black student that "if you work hard, you can succeed like everyone else." A career counselor is working with a client of color who is concerned about not being promoted at work despite being qualified. The counselor suggests, "Maybe if you work harder you can succeed like your peers."	People of color are lazy and/or incompetent and need to work harder. If you don't succeed, you have only yourself to blame (blaming the victim).
Pathologizing cultural values/communication styles The notion that the values and communication styles of the dominant/White culture are ideal	A Black client is loud, emotional, and confrontational in a counseling session. The therapist diagnoses her with borderline personality disorder. A client of Asian or Native American descent has trouble maintaining eye contact with his therapist. The therapist diagnoses him with a social anxiety disorder. Advising a client, "Do you really think your problem stems from racism?"	Assimilate to dominant culture. Leave your cultural baggage outside.
Second-class citizen Occurs when a White person is given preferential treatment as a consumer over a person of color	A counselor limits the amount of long-term therapy to provide at a college counseling center; she chooses all White clients over clients of color. Clients of color are not welcomed or acknowledged by receptionists.	Whites are more valued than people of color. White clients are more valued than clients of color.
Environmental microaggressions Macro-level microaggressions, which are more apparent on a systemic level	A waiting room office has pictures of American presidents. Every counselor at a mental health clinic is White.	You don't belong/Only white people can succeed. You are an outsider/You don't exist.

that inform racial microaggressions. A first step for therapists who want to integrate an understanding of racism's mental health effects into the conceptualization of psychological functioning is to undergo a process of learning and critical self-examination of racism and its impact on one's life and the lives of others (Thompson & Neville, 1999). For White clinicians, it means addressing the question "What does it mean to be White?" and being fully cognizant of their own White racial identity development and how it may intrude on people of color (Helms, 1992, 1995). In addition, it has been suggested that articulating a personal theory of reality and of therapeutic change in the context of an environment of racism is one way to begin integrating knowledge of racism with the practice of psychotherapy (Thompson & Neville, 1999). Education and training must aid White clinicians to achieve the following: (a) increase their ability to identify racial microaggressions in general and in themselves in particular; (b) understand how racial microaggressions, including their own, detrimentally impact clients of color; and (c) accept responsibility for taking corrective actions to overcome racial biases.

Research on Racial Microaggressions

A major obstacle to understanding racial microaggressions is that research is in a nascent state. Researchers continue to omit subtle racism and microaggressions from their research agendas, and this absence conveys the notion that covert forms of racism are not as valid or as important as racist events that can be quantified and "proven." In fact, omitting microaggressions from studies on racism on the basis of a belief that they are less harmful encourages the profession to "look the other way." Moreover, the fact that psychological research has continued to inadequately address race and ethnicity (Delgado-Romero, Rowland, & Galvin, 2005) is in itself a microaggression. Pursuing a line of research examining how cross-racial dyadic compositions impact the process and outcome of counselor/client interactions would be a tremendous contribution to the field of counseling and clinical psychology. Helms and Cook (1999) noted that racial consciousness is a critical consideration in determining White therapists' ability to operate effectively in cross-racial dyads.

For mental health purposes, it would be useful to explore the coping mechanisms used by people of color to stave off the negative effects of microaggressions. The fact that people of color have had to face daily microaggressions and have continued to maintain their dignity in the face of such hostility is a testament to their resiliency (D. W. Sue, 2003). What coping strategies have been found to serve them well? A greater understanding of responses to microaggressions, both in the long term and the short term, and of the coping strategies employed would be beneficial in arming children of color for the life they will face. Such research is necessary because without documentation and analysis to help better understand microaggressions, the threats that they pose and the assaults that they justify can be easily ignored or downplayed (Solórzano et al., 2000). Studying the long-term impact that microaggressions have on mental health functioning, self-esteem, self-concept, and racial identity development appears crucial to documenting the harm microaggressions inflict on people of color. The taxonomy of microaggressions proposed here may make it easier to explore other social psychological questions as well.

First, it is highly probable that microaggressions vary in their severity and impact. As indicated, a microassault does not evoke a guessing game because the intent of the perpetrator is clear. However, the racist intent of microinsults and microinvalidations is less clear and presents different dilemmas for people of color. Some questions to ponder include the following: (a) Are the three forms of racial microaggressions equal in impact? Are some themes and their hidden messages more problematic than others? Although all expressions may take a psychological toll, some are obviously experienced as more harmful and severe than others. (b) Is there a relationship between forms of racial microaggressions and racial identity development? Recent research and formulations on White racial identity development and the psychosocial costs of racism to Whites (Helms, 1995; Spanierman, Armstrong, Poteat, & Beer, 2006) imply that forms of racial microaggressions may be associated with certain statuses or trait clusters. (c) Finally, is it possible that different racial/ethnic groups are more likely to encounter certain forms of racial microaggressions than others? A preliminary study suggests that Asian Americans are prone to be victims of microinvalidations with themes that revolve around "alien in one's own land" (D. W. Sue, Bucceri, Lin, Nadal, & Torino, 2007) rather than microinsults with themes of "criminality." Is it possible that Blacks are more likely to be subjected to the latter than to the former? What about Latinos and American Indians?

Second, the challenge in conducting research aimed at understanding microaggressions involves measurement. Adequate assessment tools need to be created to effectively explore the new and burgeoning field of microaggression research. Although there are several promising race-related stress and discrimination measures, such as the Perceived Ethnic Discrimination Questionnaire (PEDQ; Brondolo et al., 2005), the Color-Blind Racial Attitude Scale (COBRAS; Neville et al., 2000), the Index of Race Related Stress (IRRS; Utsey & Ponterotto, 1996), and the Schedule of Racist Events (SRE; Klonoff & Landrine, 1999), none of them is directly aimed at distinguishing between categories of racial microaggressions or their intentional or unintentional nature. The PEDQ uses four subscales that broadly measure stigmatization, harassment, workplace discrimination, and social exclusion; the COBRAS is specific to a person's minimization of race and racism; the IRRS uses Jones's (1997) framework to measure individual, institutional, and societal racism; and the SRE is aimed at measuring frequency of racist incidents. All contain examples of racial microaggressions that support our taxonomy, but none makes conceptual distinctions that allow for categorical measurements of this phenomenon. It seems imperative that specific instruments be developed to aid in understanding the causes, consequences, manifestations, and elimination of racial microaggressions.

Conclusion

Nearly all interracial encounters are prone to the manifestation of racial microaggressions. We have chosen mainly to address the therapeutic relationship, but racial microaggressions are potentially present whenever human interactions involve participants who differ in race and culture (teaching, supervising, training, administering, evaluating, etc.). We have purposely chosen to concentrate on racial microaggressions, but it is important to acknowledge other types of microaggressions as well. Gender, sexual orientation, and disability microaggressions may have equally powerful and potentially detrimental effects on women, gay, lesbian, bisexual, and transgender individuals, and disability groups. Further, racial microaggressions are not limited to White-Black, White-Latino, or White-Person of Color interactions. Interethnic racial microaggressions occur between people of color as well. In the area of counseling and therapy, for example, research may also prove beneficial in understanding cross-racial dyads in which the therapist is a person of color and the client is White or in which both therapist and client are persons of color. Investigating these combinations of cross-racial dyads would be useful, because it is clear that no racial/ethnic group is immune from inheriting the racial biases of the society (D. W. Sue, 2003). We encourage future research in these two areas because all forms of microaggressions have detrimental consequences.

References

Abelson, R. P., Dasgupta, N., Park, J., & Banaji, M. R. (1998). Perceptions of the collective other. *Personality and Social Psychology Review, 2,* 243–250.

Advisory Board to the President's Initiative on Race. (1998). *One America in the 21st century: Forging a new future.* Washington, DC: U.S. Government Printing Office.

American Counseling Association. (1999). *Racism: Healing its effects.* Alexandria, VA: Author.

American Psychological Association. (2003). Guidelines on multicultural education, training, research, practice, and organizational change for psychologists. *American Psychologist, 58,* 377–402.

Banaji, M. R., Hardin, C., & Rothman, A. J. (1993). Implicit stereotyping in person judgment. *Journal of Personality and Social Psychology, 65,* 272–281.

Blair, I. V., Judd, C. M., & Chapleau, K. M. (2004). The influence of afrocentric facial features in criminal sentencing. *Psychological Science, 15,* 674–679.

Brondolo, E., Kelly, K. P., Coakley, V., Gordon, T., Thompson, S., & Levy, E. (2005). The Perceived Ethnic Discrimination Questionnaire: Development and preliminary validation of a community version. *Journal of Applied Social Psychology, 35,* 335–365.

Burkard, A. W., & Knox, S. (2004). Effect of therapist color-blindness on empathy and attributions in cross-cultural counseling. *Journal of Counseling Psychology, 51,* 387–397.

Cardemil, E. V., & Battle, C. L. (2003). Guess who's coming to therapy? Getting comfortable with conversations about race and ethnicity in psychotherapy. *Professional Psychology: Research and Practice, 34,* 278–286.

Chakraborty, A., & McKenzie, K. (2002). Does racial discrimination cause mental illness? *British Journal of Psychiatry, 180,* 475–477.

Clark, R., Anderson, N. B., Clark, V. R., & Williams, D. R. (1999). Racism as a stressor for African Americans. *American Psychologist, 54,* 805–816.

Conyne, R. K., & Bemak, F. (2005). *Journeys to professional excellence: Lessons from leading counselor educators and practitioners.* Alexandria, VA: American Counseling Association.

Crocker, J., & Major, B. (1989). Social stigma and self-esteem: The self-protective properties of stigma. *Psychological Review, 96,* 608–630.

Delgado-Romero, E. A., Rowland, M., & Galvan, N. (2005). The continuing and evolving challenge of race and ethnicity in empirical counseling and counseling psychology research: A reply. *Counseling Psychologist, 33,* 559–564.

DeVos, T., & Banaji, M. R. (2005). American = White? *Journal of Personality and Social Psychology, 88,* 447–466.

Dovidio, J. F., & Gaertner, S. L. (1996). Affirmative action, unintentional racial biases, and intergroup relations. *Journal of Social Issues, 52,* 51–75.

Dovidio, J. F., & Gaertner, S. L. (2000). Aversive racism and selective decisions: 1989–1999. *Psychological Science, 11,* 315–319.

Dovidio, J. F., Gaertner, S. L., Kawakami, K., & Hodson, G. (2002). Why can't we all just get along? Interpersonal biases and interracial distrust. *Cultural Diversity and Ethnic Minority Psychology, 8,* 88–102.

Franklin, A. J. (2004). *From brotherhood to manhood: How Black men rescue their relationships and dreams from the invisibility syndrome.* Hoboken, NJ: Wiley.

Gordon, J., & Johnson, M. (2003). Race, speech, and hostile educational environment: What color is free speech? *Journal of Social Philosophy, 34,* 414–436.

Grencavage, L. M., & Norcross, J. C. (1990). Where are the commonalities among the therapeutic common factors? *Professional Psychology: Research and Practice, 21,* 372–378.

Helms, J. E. (1992). *A race is a nice thing to have: A guide to being a white person or understanding the white persons in your life.* Topeka, KS: Content Communications.

Helms, J. E. (1995). An update of Helms's White and people of color racial identity models. In J. G. Ponterotto, J. M. Casas, L. A. Suzuki, & C. M. Alexander (Eds.), *Handbook of multicultural counseling* (pp. 181–191). Thousand Oaks, CA: Sage.

Helms, J. E., & Cook, D. (1999). *Using race and culture in counseling and psychotherapy: Theory and process.* Needham Heights, MA: Allyn & Bacon.

Hinton, E. L. (2004, March/April). Microinequities: When small slights lead to huge problems in the workplace. *DiversityInc.* (Available at http://www.magazine.org/content/files/Microinequities.pdf)

Horvath, A. O., & Symonds, B. D. (1991). Relationship between working alliance and outcome in psychotherapy: A meta-analysis. *Journal of Counseling Psychology, 38,* 139–149.

Jones, J. M. (1997). *Prejudice and racism* (2nd ed.). Washington, DC: McGraw-Hill.

Kearney, L. K., Draper, M., & Baron, A. (2005). Counseling utilization by ethnic minority college students. *Cultural Diversity and Ethnic Minority Psychology, 11,* 272–285.

Keltner, D., & Robinson, R. J. (1996). Extremism, power, and imagined basis of social conflict. *Current Directions in Psychological Science, 5,* 101–105.

Klonoff, E. A., & Landrine, H. (1999). Cross-validation of the Schedule of Racist Events. *Journal of Black Psychology, 25,* 231–254.

Knox, S., Burkard, A. W., Johnson, A. J., Suzuki, L. A., & Ponterotto, J. G. (2003). African American and European American therapists' experiences of addressing race in cross-racial psychotherapy dyads. *Journal of Counseling Psychology, 50,* 466–481.

Liang, C. T. H., Li, L. C., & Kim, B. S. K. (2004). The Asian American Racism-Related Stress Inventory: Development, factor analysis, reliability, and validity. *Journal of Counseling Psychology, 51,* 103–114.

Locke, D. C., & Kiselica, M. S. (1999). Pedagogy of possibilities: Teaching about racism in multicultural counseling courses. *Journal of Counseling and Development, 77,* 80–86.

Lui, W. M., & Pope-Davis, D. B. (2005). The working alliance, therapy ruptures and impasses, and counseling competence: Implications for counselor training and education. In R. T. Carter (Ed.), *Handbook of racial-cultural psychology and counseling* (pp. 148–167). Hoboken, NJ: Wiley.

Martin, D. J., Garske, J. P., & Davis, M. K. (2000). Relations of the therapeutic alliance with outcome and other variables: A meta-analytic review. *Journal of Counseling and Clinical Psychology, 66,* 832–837.

McConahay, J. B. (1986). Modern racism, ambivalence, and the Modern Racism Scale. In J. F. Dovidio & S. L. Gaertner (Eds.), *Prejudice, discrimination and racism* (pp. 91–126). Orlando, FL: Academic Press.

National Conference of Christians and Jews. (1992). *Taking America's pulse: A summary report of the National Conference Survey on Inter-Group Relations.* New York: Author. (Available at http://eric.ed.gov/ERICDocs/data/ericdocs2/content_storage _01/0000000b/80/23/84/59.pdf)

Nelson, T. D. (2006). *The psychology of prejudice.* Boston: Pearson.

Neville, H. A., Lilly, R. L., Duran, G., Lee, R., & Browne, L. (2000). Construction and initial validation of the Color Blind Racial Attitudes Scale (COBRAS). *Journal of Counseling Psychology, 47,* 59–70.

Pierce, C. (1995). Stress analogs of racism and sexism: Terrorism, torture, and disaster. In C. Willie, P. Rieker, B. Kramer, & B. Brown (Eds.), *Mental health, racism, and sexism* (pp. 277–293). Pittsburgh, PA: University of Pittsburgh Press.

Pierce, C., Carew, J., Pierce-Gonzalez, D., & Willis, D. (1978). An experiment in racism: TV commercials. In C. Pierce (Ed.), *Television and education* (pp. 62–88). Beverly Hills, CA: Sage.

Plant, E. A., & Peruche, B. M. (2005). The consequences of race for police officers' responses to criminal suspects. *Psychological Science, 16,* 180–183.

Ponterotto, J. G., Casas, J. M., Suzuki, L. A., & Alexander, C. M. (2001). *Handbook of multicultural counseling.* Thousand Oaks, CA: Sage.

President's Commission on Mental Health. (1978). *Report of the President's Commission on Mental Health.* Washington, DC: U.S. Government Printing Office.

Reid, L. D., & Radhakrishnan, P. (2003). Race matters: The relations between race and general campus climate. *Cultural Diversity and Ethnic Minority Psychology, 9,* 263–275.

Richardson, T. Q., & Molinaro, K. L. (1996). White counselor self-awareness: A prerequisite for multicultural competence. *Journal of Counseling & Development, 74,* 238–242.

Ridley, C. R. (2005). *Overcoming unintentional racism in counseling and therapy* (2nd ed.). Thousand, Oaks, CA: Sage.

Sanchez-Hucles, J., & Jones, N. (2005). Breaking the silence around race in training, practice, and research. *Counseling Psychologist, 33,* 547–558.

Sears, D. O. (1988). Symbolic racism. In P. A. Katz & D. A. Taylor (Eds.), *Eliminating racism: Profiles in controversy* (pp. 53–84). New York: Plenum.

Sellers, R. M., & Shelton, J. N. (2003). The role of racial identity in perceived racial discrimination. *Journal of Personality and Social Psychology, 84,* 1070–1092.

Smedley, A., & Smedley, B. D. (2005). Race as biology is fiction, racism as a social problem is real. *American Psychologist, 60,* 16-26.

Solórzano, D., Ceja, M., & Yosso, T. (2000, Winter). Critical race theory, racial microaggressions, and campus racial climate: The experiences of African American college students. *Journal of Negro Education, 69,* 60–73.

Spanierman, L. B., Armstrong, P. I., Poteat, V. P., & Beer, A. M. (2006). Psychosocial Costs of Racism to Whites: Exploring patterns through cluster analysis. *Journal of Counseling Psychology, 53,* 434–441.

Spanierman, L. B., & Heppner, M. J. (2004). Psychosocial Costs of Racism to Whites Scale (PCRW): Construction and initial validation. *Journal of Counseling Psychology, 51,* 249–262.

Steele, C. M., Spencer, S. J., & Aronson, J. (2002). Contending with group image: The psychology of stereotype and social identity threat. In M. Zanna (Ed.), *Advances in experimental social psychology* (Vol. 23, pp. 379–440). New York: Academic Press.

Strong, S. R., & Schmidt, L. D. (1970). Expertness and influence in counseling. *Journal of Counseling Psychology, 17,* 81–87.

Sue, D. W. (2003). *Overcoming our racism: The journey to liberation.* San Francisco: Jossey-Bass.

Sue, D. W. (2004). Whiteness and ethnocentric monoculturalism: Making the "invisible" visible. *American Psychologist, 59,* 759–769.

Sue, D. W. (2005). Racism and the conspiracy of silence. *Counseling Psychologist, 33,* 100–114.

Sue, D. W., Arredondo, P., & McDavis, R. J. (1992). Multicultural competencies/standards: A call to the profession. *Journal of Counseling & Development, 70,* 477–486.

Sue, D. W., Bucceri, J., Lin, A. I., Nadal, K. L., & Torino, G. C. (2007). Racial microaggressions and the Asian American experience. *Cultural Diversity and Ethnic Minority Psychology, 13,* 72–81.

Sue, D. W., & Sue, D. (2003). *Counseling the culturally diverse: Theory and practice* (4th ed.). New York: Wiley.

Sue, S., Fujino, D. C., Hu, L., & Takeuchi, D. (1991). Community mental health services for ethnic minority groups: A test of the cultural responsiveness hypothesis. *Journal of Consulting and Clinical Psychology, 59,* 533–540.

Thompson, C. E., & Neville, H. A. (1999). Racism, mental health, and mental health practice. *Counseling Psychologist, 27,* 155–223.

U.S. Department of Health and Human Services. (2001). *Mental health: Culture, race, and ethnicity—A supplement to Mental Health: A Report of the Surgeon General.* Rockville, MD: U.S. Department of Health and Human Services, Substance Abuse and Mental Health Services Administration, Center for Mental Health Services.

Utsey, S. O., Gernat, C. A., & Hammar, L. (2005). Examining White counselor trainees' reactions to racial issues in counseling and supervision dyads. *Counseling Psychologist, 33,* 449–478.

Utsey, S. O., & Ponterotto, J. G. (1996). Development and validation of the Index of Race-Related Stress (IRRS). *Journal of Counseling Psychology, 43,* 490–502.

Vanman, E. J., Saltz, J. L., Nathan, L. R., & Warren, J. A. (2004). Racial discrimination by low-prejudiced Whites. *Psychological Science, 15,* 711–719.

Williams, D. R., & Collins, C. (1995). US socioeconomic and racial differences in health: Patterns and explanations. *Annual Review of Sociology, 21,* 349–386.

Williams, D. R., Lavizzo-Mourey, R., & Warren, R. C. (1994). The concept of race and health status in America. *Public Health Reports, 109,* 26–41.

Williams, D. R., Neighbors, H. W., & Jackson, J. S. (2003). Racial/ethnic discrimination and health: Findings from community studies. *American Journal of Public Health, 93,* 200–208.

Woodhouse, S. S., Schlosser, L. Z., Crook, R. E., Ligiero, D. P., & Gelso, C. J. (2003). Client attachment to therapist: Relations to transference and client recollections of parental caregiving. *Journal of Counseling Psychology, 50,* 395–408.

Young, G., & Davis-Russell, E. (2002). The vicissitudes of cultural competence: Dealing with difficult classroom dialogue. In E. Davis-Russell (Ed.), *The California School of Professional Psychology handbook of multicultural education, research, intervention, and training* (pp. 37–53). San Francisco: Jossey-Bass.

23 | The Destructive Power of Money

Karl Marx

Marx advances the thesis that money is the alienated form of labor process as well as a "disruptive power," which undermines all social relations. This argument is presented in the present selection, the first part of which is taken from Marx's notes of 1844 on James Mill's Treatise of Political Economy, *and the second part is from the* Third of the Economic and the Philosophical Manuscripts *of the same year.*

The essence of money is not primarily that it externalizes property but that the *mediating activity* or process—the *human* and social act in which man's products reciprocally complement one another—becomes *alienated* and takes on the quality of a *material thing,* money, external to man. By externalizing this mediating activity, man is active only as he is lost and dehumanized. The very *relationship* of things and the human dealings with them become an operation beyond and above man. Through this *alien mediation* man regards his will, his activity, and his relationships to others as a power independent of himself and of them—instead of man himself being the mediator for man. His slavery thus reaches a climax. It is clear that this *mediator* becomes an *actual god,* for the mediator is the *actual power* over that which he mediates to me. His worship becomes an end in itself. Apart from this mediation, objects lose their value. They have value only insofar as they *represent* it while originally it appeared that the mediation would have value only insofar as *it* represents *objects.* This inversion of the original relationship is necessary. The *mediation,* therefore, is the lost, alienated *essence* of private property, exteriorated and *externalized* private property, just as it is the *externalized exchange* of human production with human production, the *externalized* species-activity of man. All qualities involved in this activity are transmitted to the mediator. Man as separated from this mediator thus becomes so much the poorer as the mediator becomes *richer.* . . .

Reprinted from *Basic Writings on Politics and Philosophy*, edited by Lewis S. Feuer (1967), by permission of Robin Feuer Miller.

Why must private property end up in *money?* Because man as a social being must resort to *exchange* and because exchange—under the presupposition of private property—must end up in value. The mediating process of man making exchanges is no social, no *human process,* no human relationship; rather, it is the *abstract relationship* of private property to private property, and this *abstract* relationship is the *value* whose actual existence as value is primarily *money.* Because men making exchanges do not relate to one another as men, *things* lose the significance of being human and personal property. The social relationship of private property to private property is a relationship in which private property has alienated itself. The reflexive existence of this relationship, money, is thus the externalization of private property, an abstraction from its *specific* and personal nature. . . .

[. . . Money is] the *pander* between need and object, between human life and the means of subsistence. But *that which* mediates *my* life mediates also the existence of other men for me. It is for me the *other* person.

> *"Why, Zounds! Both hands and feet are, truly—*
> *And head and virile forces—thine:*
> *Yet all that I indulge in newly,*
> *Is't thence less wholly mine?*
> *If I've six stallions in my stall,*
> *Are not their forces also lent me?*
> *I speed along completest man of all,*
> *As though my feet were four-and-twenty*
> (Goethe, *Faust*—Mephistopheles)[1]

Shakespeare in Timon of Athens:

> *Gold? yellow, glittering, precious gold? No, gods,*
> *I am no idle votarist: roots, you clear heavens!*
> *Thus much of this will make black, white; foul, fair;*
> *Wrong, right; base, noble; old, young; coward, valiant.*
> . . . . *Why this*
> *Will lug your priests and servants from your sides;*
> *Pluck stout men's pillows from below their heads:*
> *This yellow slave*
> *Will knit and break religious; bless th' accurst;*
> *Make the hoar leprosy ador'd; place thieves,*
> *And give them title, knee, and approbation,*
> *With senators on the bench: this is it*
> *That makes the wappen'd widow wed again;*
> *She whom the spital-house and ulcerous sores*
> *Would cast the gorge at, this embalms and spices*
> *To th'April day again. Come, damned earth,*
> *Thou common whore of mankind, that putt'st odds*
> *Among the rout of nations, I will make thee*
> *Do thy right nature."*[2]

And later on:

> *"O thou sweet king-killer and dear divorce*
> *'Twixt natural son and sire! Thou bright defiler*
> *Of Hymen's purest bed! thou valiant Mars!*
> *Thou ever young, fresh, loved, and delicate wooer,*
> *Whose blush doth thaw the consecrated snow*
> *That lies on Dian's lap! thou visible god,*

That solder'st close impossibilities
And mak'st them kiss! that speak'st with every tongue,
To every purpose! O thou touch of hearts!
Think, thy slave man rebels; and by the virtue
Set them into confounding odds, that beasts
May have the world in empire!"[3]

Shakespeare portrays admirably the nature of *money*. To understand him, let us begin by expounding the passage from Goethe.

That which exists for me through the medium of *money*, that which I can pay for (i.e., which money can buy), that I *am*, the possessor of the money. My own power is as great as the power of money. The properties of money are my own (the possessor's) properties and faculties. What I *am* and *can do* is, therefore, not at all determined by my individuality. I *am* ugly, but I can buy the *most beautiful* woman for myself. Consequently, I am not *ugly*, for the effect of *ugliness*, its power to repel, is annulled by money. As an individual I am *lame*, but money provides me with twenty-four legs. Therefore, I am not lame. I am a detestable, dishonorable, unscrupulous and stupid man, but money is honored and so also is its possessor. Money is the highest good, and so its possessor is good. Besides, money saves me the trouble of being dishonest; therefore, I am presumed honest. I am *stupid*, but since money is the *real mind* of all things, how should its possessor be stupid? Moreover, he can buy talented people for himself, and is not he who has power over the talented more talented than they? I who can have, through the power of money, *everything* for which the human heart longs, do I not possess all human abilities? Does not my money, therefore, transform all my incapacities into their opposites?

If *money* is the bond which binds me to *human* life, and society to me, and which links me with nature and man, is it not the bond of all *bonds*? Is it not, therefore, also the universal agent of separation? It is the real means of both *separation* and *union*, the galvano-*chemical* power of society.

Shakespeare emphasizes particularly two properties of money: (1) it is the visible deity, the transformation of all human and natural qualities into their opposites, the universal confusion and inversion of things; it brings incompatibles into fraternity; (2) it is the universal whore, the universal pander between men and nations.

The power to confuse and invert all human and natural qualities, to bring about fraternization of incompatible, the *divine* power of money, resides in its *character* as the alienated and self-alienating species-life of man. It is the alienated *power of humanity*.

What I as a *man* am unable to do, and thus what all my individual faculties are unable to do, is made possible for me by *money*. Money, therefore, turns each of these faculties into something which it is not, into its *opposite*.

If I long for a meal, or wish to take the mail coach because I am not strong enough to go on foot, money provides the meal and the mail coach; i.e., it transforms my desires from representations into *realities*, from imaginary being into *real being*. In mediating thus, money is a *genuinely creative* power.

Demand also exists for the individual who has no money, but his demand is a mere creature of the imagination which has no effect, no existence for me, for a third party . . . and which thus remains unreal and without object. The difference between effective demand, supported by money, and ineffective demand, based upon my need, my passion, my desire, etc., is the difference between being, and thought, between the merely inner representation and the representation which exists outside myself as a real object.

If I have no money for travel I have no *need*—no real and self-realizing need—for travel. If I have a *vocation* for study but no money for it, then I have *no* vocation, i.e., no *effective, genuine* vocation. Conversely, if *I* really have *no* vocation for study, but have money and the urge for it, then I have an *effective* vocation. *Money* is the external, universal *means* and *power* (not derived from man as man or from human society as society) to change *representation* into *reality* and *reality* into *mere representation*. It transforms *real human and natural faculties* into mere abstract representations, i.e., *imperfections* and tormenting chimeras; and on the other hand, it transforms *real imperfections and fancies,* faculties which are really important and which exist only in the individual's imagination, into *real faculties and powers*. In this respect, therefore, money is the general inversion of *individualities,* turning them into their opposites and associating contradictory qualities with their qualities.

Money, then, appears as a *disruptive* power for the individual and for the social bonds, which claim to be self-subsistent *entities*. It changes fidelity into infidelity, love into hate, hate into love, virtue into vice, vice into virtue, servant into master, stupidity into intelligence and intelligence into stupidity.

Since money, as the existing and active concept of value, confounds and exchanges everything, it is the universal *confusion and transposition* of all things, the inverted world, the confusion and transposition of all natural and human qualities.

He who can purchase bravery is brave, though a coward. Money is not exchanged for a particular quality, a particular thing, or a specific human faculty, but for the whole objective world of man and nature. Thus, from the standpoint of its possessor, it exchanges every quality and object for every other, even though they are contradictory. It is the fraternization of incompatibles; it forces contraries to embrace.

Let us assume *man* to be *man,* and his relation to the world to be a human one. Then love can only be exchanged for love, trust for trust, etc. If you wish to enjoy art you must be an artistically cultivated person; if you wish to influence other people you must be a person who really has a stimulating and encouraging effect upon others. Every one of your relations to man and to nature must be a *specific expression,* corresponding to the object of your will, of your *real individual* life. If you love without evoking love in return, i.e., if you are not able, by the *manifestation* of yourself as a loving person, to make yourself a *beloved person,* then your love is impotent and a misfortune.

Notes

1. Goethe, *Faust*. Part I, Scene 4. This passage is taken from the translation by Bayard Taylor; the Modern Library, New York, 1950.—*Tr. Note*

2. Shakespeare, *Timon of Athens*. Act IV, Scene 3. Marx quotes from the Schlege-Tieck translation.—*Tr. Note*

3. *Ibid*.

24 | *The Thief of Time*

Caleb Crain

"**M**oments are the elements of profit," Karl Marx wrote in *Capital*, quoting from an 1860 report by one of the British government's factory inspectors. Marx believed that the uniformity of time underlay the fungibility of money; the time it took to make a commodity was, according to his theory, the basis of its value in the marketplace. If it takes ten hours to make an overcoat and ten to make a wheel of Stilton cheese, the coat and the cheese can be fairly traded. After all, a coat maker's ten hours mean as much as a cheesewright's. Or, as Thoreau put it, somewhat more poetically: "The cost of a thing is the amount of what I will call life which is required to be exchanged for it, immediately or in the long run."

Andrew Niccol's new movie *In Time* brings the labor theory of value to the big screen with bold literalness. In the future, thanks to genetic engineering, everyone's physical appearance ceases to develop or decline at age twenty-five, at which moment, with a silent, monitory thump, a stop watch on the left forearm—a cross between an Auschwitz serial number and a lime-green digital alarm clock—begins ticking down from one year. To get more time, one must beg, borrow, steal, or work, and with sufficient wealth, one can live forever. If one's clock runs out, though, there is a second thump, this time lethal, and the stopwatch fades from digital crispness to a blurry, inky string of thirteen zeroes, somewhat resembling the library due-date stamp of a twentieth-century childhood. In the meantime, time is currency, exchangeable by hand clasps or by chrome bracelets.

The notion of hours as dollars takes some getting used to. In an early scene, the movie's working-class hero, Will Salas (played by Justin Timberlake), is given thirty minutes by his mother so that he can have a nice lunch for himself. At first I thought that the gift meant that Will would be able to stay away from the assembly line for an extra half hour at midday; in fact his mother expects him to trade the half hour for a sandwich and eat it. One gets the hang of it soon enough. By the time a hotelier announced that "A night here costs two months," I found myself thinking, *Marx would love this shit*. Thoreau once famously asserted that he could walk as fast as a locomotive, so long as when you calculated the locomotive's speed you added to the denominator the time it cost to earn the money for the ticket, and Thoreauvians will particularly enjoy the scene where a character is asked to choose between a bus ride that costs two hours and a walk that will take a hundred and twenty minutes.

Reprinted by permission from *The Paris Review*, October 31, 2011.

The movie makes no effort to imagine how or why all of humanity came to accept such a modification to its genome. Surely, a viewer thinks, it must be obvious, even in a fantasized neoliberal future that has privatized education away, that no biological process, not even a genetically engineered one that produces immortality, could possibly require regular influxes of money, which is only an idea? It isn't obvious to them, though. Somewhat improbably, it comes as a revelation to Will that the austerity built into this system isn't really necessary. "The truth is, there's more than enough," reveals Henry Hamilton (played by Matt Bomer), a depressive 105-year-old who looks like a mildly sloshed J. Crew model. (Ages in the movie are given in a form that brings to mind cricket scores: Will is 25 for 3; his love interest, Sylvia [played by Amanda Seyfried] is 25 for 2.) But even though there's more than enough, some dark authority has been at pains to keep it from being spread around, for reasons that seem a bit nebulous. "Everyone can't live forever. Where would we put them?" Henry intones, just before surreptitiously donating to Will a century or so.

Neither Henry nor the movie quite seems to believe in the overpopulation objection, nor seems to expect Will to, and a further motive for things-as-they-are is also thrown in: Henry explains that the powers-that-be keep deliberately raising the cost of living to ensure that a sufficient number of people keep dying—thereby encouraging, or so the viewer infers, a sufficient number of others to keep working. "Four minutes for a cup of coffee," a character complains. "Yesterday it was three." If this movie were an economist, in other words, it would be the sort of economist who believes that the lower classes only take jobs when threatened with starvation, and that recessions and depressions occur because workers have been spoiled by welfare and have come to think of themselves as morally superior to the unpleasantness of toil. *Is this movie Marxist or isn't it?* I began petulantly to wonder. After all, Marx believed that "the determination of the magnitude of value by labour-time is ... a secret hidden under the apparent movements in the relative values of commodities." That is, if it takes three minutes to make a cup of coffee, the value of the cup of coffee will always be equivalent to three minutes of labor-time. (Periodically *The Economist* magazine takes advantage of this principle and checks currency strengths against what it calls the Big Mac index—the cost of a Big Mac, a uniform product around the world, in dollars, pounds, yen, renminbi, and so on.) If Marx is right, then if time *were* a currency, the cost of a cup of coffee in time shouldn't fluctuate, unless a productivity breakthrough were somehow to reduce the amount of time needed to brew a cup. In fact Marx gets very sniffy about economists who think that the value of an item has anything to do with the amount of money in circulation. On the other hand, though, Marx does also say that "price may diverge from the magnitude of value," so maybe if labor-time were itself to become fetishized as a money-form, it could diverge from ... itself?

Fortunately, whenever such speculation is provoked in the viewer's mind, a car chase supervenes. The cars look to be of 1950s vintage—black muscle cars for the police, who are known as "timekeepers," and boxy black limousines for the wealthy—except for a curvy silver item purchased by Will, which, to the flummoxing of a salesman, he declines to have shipped to a car collectors' storage facility and instead drives out of the showroom. (Shades of the red Ferrari of *Ferris Bueller's Day Off?*) As in his debut movie, *Gattaca,* Niccol has the wit to represent the future through style rather than mere CGI. Even in the slums, which are filled with empty but refuse-free postindustrial warehouses that Williamsburg would envy, one may find a cocktail dress of crushed velvet in a sort of auburn-plum color if one rummages through the right closet.

Niccol has imagined his conceit thoroughly enough to realize that if currency could be stored on one's person, there would be no banks in the poorer parts of town. Accordingly, when Will and Sylvia set out to rob from the rich and give to the poor, they don't knock over banks. They knock over lending shops—imagined as check-cashing storefronts run by a sort of credit-card-slash-subprime-loan conglomerate—which are ubiquitous. We see a character make a loan payment, but the movie is a little elliptical about the economics of this lending. I briefly found myself wishing it had been more fully explained. After all, even in a world where people die when broke, the real money wouldn't be made by hiring people desperate for a job. It would be made by offering credit at usurious rates to the same workers. So long as indebted workers keep making their minimum monthly payments, they're worth far more alive than dead, even if their net, off-the-forearm balances are negative—in fact, they're excellent investments, thanks to the backstop of their lethal stopwatches. Once I thought this through, though, it seemed that maybe this didn't really need to be explained at any great length to a contemporary movie audience: it's how we live now.

By the end of the movie, Will and Sylvia are being pursued by the police across rooftops—like figures out of *The Matrix*? like figures out of Dickens?—for stealing time from the usurers and distributing it to the workers, in an economic stimulus package as privatized by a high-fashion Bonnie and Clyde, as it were. Alas, it isn't clear if the movie has confidence in the revolution they propose. Once the stolen time begins to leak out to the masses, factories idle. Suddenly people have enough time on their hands to stand around, and they do. ("If the worker consumes his disposable time for himself, he robs the capitalist," Marx wrote.) "Too much time in the wrong hands can crash the market," warns the disembodied voice of an investor in the conglomerate behind the lending shops—is it the voice of one of Paul Krugman's "bond vigilantes"? The prices of bread and milk start to rise. In response, the hero and the heroine vow to steal and redistribute more and yet more, but will their campaign merely lead to a vicious circle? "In the end nothing will change," warns one of the bad guys. He explains that it's "because everyone wants to live forever," but the viewer nearly expects to hear the word "stagflation."

Caleb Crain is a writer living in Brooklyn.

25 | Dealing with Complexity in Research Processes and Findings: How Do Older Women Negotiate and Challenge Images of Aging?

Susan Hogan and Lorna Warren

The Representing Self—Representing Ageing initiative has been funded by the ESRC as part of the New Dynamics of Ageing cross–council research program. It has consisted of four projects with older women using visual research methods and participatory approaches to enable women to articulate their experiences of aging and to create alternative images of aging. Complex research processes were utilized. Innovative methods included the use of art elicitation, photo diaries, film booths, and phototherapy.

KEYWORDS women and aging, aging and popular culture, feminism and aging, images of aging, participatory arts, visual research methods

Framing Gender and Age: A Brief Review

Historically, a biomedical model of age, along with functionalist theory, has positioned aging as fundamentally problematic, and the biomedical model is still seen as the predominant one today within social gerontology (Maynard, Afshar, Franks, & Wray, 2008). This is despite the development of a critical gerontology, which introduced a political economy model approach in the 1980s, with greater emphasis on structural inequalities. As Phillipson (1998, p. 16) has astutely pointed out, much social-gerontological theory might be viewed as "colluding with a repressive and intolerant society" and reflecting its values about aging in the way the subject has been interrogated.

An emphasis on structural inequality has been useful for highlighting gender inequalities such as old age poverty for women (Arber & Ginn, 1995; Calasanti, 2010; Gilleard & Higgs 2000; Land, 1976; Rosenman, 1986). Furthermore, given increasing longevity in the UK,

Address correspondence to Susan Hogan, University of Derby, Britannia Mill, Mackworth Rd., Derby, DE22 3BL, United Kingdom. E-mail: s.hogan@derby.ac.uk

Reprinted by permission from *Journal of Women & Aging* 24, no. 4 (2012).

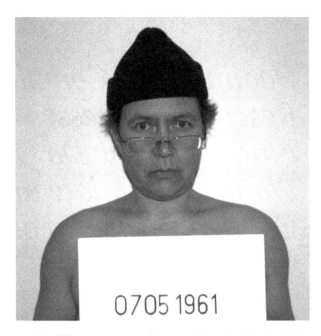

Figure 1 *I feel like a prisoner of the numbers* by Claudia B Kuntze.

some women are caring for aged parents or partners when old themselves.[1] Moreover, the focus on structural inequalities has illuminated disparities in levels of support forthcoming to men and women experiencing chronic illness late in life and applying for support to stay in their homes, for example.[2] Phillipson (1998) goes on to argue that a "political economy approach" should add a biographical and narrative perspective, which is also interested in symbols and "new rituals which help to enable changes through the life course," thus producing a more well rounded and sophisticated picture of how older age is actually experienced (p. 14). Calasanti (2010) makes the useful point that gender relations are *dynamic*, by which she means that they change over the life course, creating different pressures and constraints along the way; furthermore, that we should not overlook *agism* as a "devalued status" in our discussions, as this is still of importance (p. 721).

Maynard, Afshar, Franks, and Wray (2008)) appear to concur with Birren and Bengston's assertion (1988, p. 31), that social-gerontological studies of older women tend to be "data rich and theory poor," and who assert, in polemical fashion, that even studies by feminists "have largely failed to examine the interrelationship of sexism and ageism and how this affects women" (p. 37). This is a glib assertion, given that virtually all of the research that examines sexism and aging has been informed by feminist perspectives, many of which highlight women's heightened sensitivity to aging processes in a variety of ways: Burman, 1992; Chapakis, 1986; Copper, 1988; Cruikshank, 2003; Fishel, 2008; J. Fraser and Boffin, 1991; Greer, 1991; Gullette, 2004; Howson, 2005; Lock, 1993; Martin, 1999, 2003, & 2006; Oakley, 2007; Pearsall, 1997; Reichenberg-Ullman, 1992; Reinharz, 1997; Russell, 1987; Woodward, 1999; and Zita, 2003, for example, as well as the groundbreaking work of earlier feminists such as Sontag's *The Double Standard of Aging* (1978) and De Beauvoir's *Old Age* (1972). Though older women experience some of the constraints that younger women do, as Bernard and Meade (1993) point out, age profoundly alters the way this is experienced. Responding to the gauntlet thrown down by Phillipson, the need for rich qualitative research data that interrogates the narratives that older women create to understand their embodied experience of aging is apparent.

Look at Me! Visual Representations on Women and Aging

The Second World Assembly on Ageing in 2003 recognized a need to challenge stereo-typed images of aging and later life, particularly those related to older women. The use of visual methods as a means of allowing older women to articulate their experiences of aging is one way of doing this but, to date, "ordinary" older women have not had the opportunity either to comment on, or create, their own images of aging and old age. This was the aim of a successful research bid Representing Self–Representing Ageing, which we shall discuss (War-ren, Gott, & Hogan 2009).[3] Who is an "ordinary" older woman is one of a number of concepts that will require interrogating; nevertheless, this has been an important omission, given that the limited images that are popularly available typically present older people as either diminu-tive, dependent, and frail, or as aging "positively" and belying their physical age. Turner (1984) identifies a "new puritanism"—a tendency to attribute moral significance—indeed, to ascribe goodness of character to those who have a beautiful, healthy body. Critics of this emphasis on healthy well-regulated bodies and a movement towards "positive aging" (epitomized by seeing older bodies engaged in traditionally youthful pursuits) view such ideology and rhetoric as potentially "tyrannical," worrying that problems associated with biological aging may increas-ingly be viewed as deviant or pathological. Blaikie (1999, p. 209) asserts, "unless you work on being 'liberated' from chronological destiny, you are less than normal."

Representations of aging are particularly important to older women because their expe-riences of aging (and ageism) are deeply rooted in appearance (Bordo, 1993). In particular, the perception of their aged bodies makes them invisible in later life and can affect their social sta-tus and access to resources and opportunities (Shilling, 2011). For women especially, the transcendence of age requires constant vigilance over our bodies (Hockey & James, 2003, p. 214). Women's potential fertility is also of importance when they are looking for partners in so-called middle age; many men are not interested in women they cannot reproduce with, so such women may feel themselves subject to the affects of aging earlier than men.

Older women's invisibility is being explored and challenged by women both within pop-ular culture and through academic work, but still in limited ways: for example, television pro-grams uncritically buy into the antiaging industry and focus on heterosexual women. There have been a number of refreshing attempts to address this, such as the UK's Channel 4's *Com-ing of Age*, though how far the series moved beyond clichés is debatable.[4]

Using the Arts to Explore Older Identities

Female artists have produced new images resisting conventional stereotypes of older women: Martin's (2003) *Outrageous Agers*, for example, was challenging in its photographic depiction of older women. Practitioners and researchers are increasingly using visual meth-ods as a tool for personal empowerment and social critique (Ball & Smith, 1992; Banks, 2001; Banks & Morphy, 1997; Hogan, 2003; Hogan & Pink, 2010; Pink, 2001, 2006, 2012; Pink, Hogan, & Bird, 2011; Stanazak, 2007; Rose, 2007). Such approaches offer a way forward for older women's participation beyond their typical involvement in research as users of welfare services.

The Warren, Gott, and Hogan study, Representing Self—Representing Ageing asks how media and cultural representations of older people have conveyed ideas and expectations about age and gender. It aimed to enable older women, recruited in different ways, to create their own images of aging using a variety of visual and textual methods. In particular, the project has been keen to reflect upon the relationship between cultural and creative activity and later-life well-being and the contribution of visual "real-life methods" to participatory processes. Furthermore, the project (which is still ongoing) aims to demonstrate the contri-bution of arts and humanities to critical gerontology. However, there is a potentially "evangel-ical" strand, which perhaps requires explicit acknowledgement, which is to enhance recognition of the authority, wisdom, and productivity of older women. This was explicitly stated in the funding proposal.

What Is an Older Woman?

Feminist theorists often emphasize that women "become" women though a process of socialization (De Beauvoir, 1949) and reiterated practices (Butler, 1990) and challenge the notion of "woman" as an "immobile, stable, coherent, fixed, prediscursive, natural, and ahistorical" category of meaning (Moi, 1999, p. 4). Or, as the philosopher Wittgenstein (1958) put it, "The meaning of a word is its use in the language."[5] This poststructuralist turn in much feminist theory is an attempt to resist biological determinist and other reductive discourses that oppress women and limit our practical and conceptual potential.

"Woman" as a universal category is problematic, as there are many social distinctions that have an impact on women's lived experience of being women. As Reinharz (1997, p. 74) notes, "Feminist theorists have long recognized that women represent a highly diversified group with cross-cutting allegiances to work, family, race, class, religion, ethnic group, age group and more." Elam (1994) has made the point that "a feminism that believes it knows what a woman is and what she can do both forecloses the limitless possibilities of woman and misrepresents the various forms that social injustice can take" (p. 32). Furthermore, as Gillies and Alldred (2002, p. 35) point out, a focus on "the heterogeneity of women's experience dissolves many of the assumed commonalities that feminism was built on."

While women may generally be materially disadvantaged in relation to men in Britain today, and suffer from structural disadvantages (especially around the organization of childbirth and child-rearing, and pensions), Gillies and Alldred (2002) continue to avow that, "Even when specific experiences or identities are shared by the researcher and researched, affinity in itself cannot be regarded as an authoritative basis for representative research" (p. 40). Drawing on the work of Butler (1990), they suggest that "even when we do share identities, we cannot assume that common identities produce common political perspectives" (p. 42). They critique this idea thus (p. 40):

> *Paradoxically, when an emphasis is placed on sameness, power differences are highlighted in terms of whose version of the account is eventually told, even if the research is presented as a coconstruction. Foregrounding commonality at the expense of difference risks generating a falsely homogenized view of particular experiences and may result in an overrepresentation of issues that resonate with white, middle-class researchers. Thus, although sharing an experience or standpoint may generate empathy and a desire to speak on behalf of others, it can compromise critical reflexivity by encouraging a reliance on unchallenged assumptions and inferences.*

Further Ethical Dilemmas and the Reflexive Turn in Feminist Approaches

Edwards and Mauthner (2002, p. 14) note that, "Ethics concerns the morality of human conduct. In relation to social research, it refers to the moral deliberation, choice and accountability on the part of researchers throughout the research process." The ethical dimension of this project is important. Birch et al. (2002) "have identified the need in feminist qualitative research to combine universal ethical standards with a more reflexive model of ethics, especially in relation to participatory approaches involving sensitive topics and/or vulnerable groups."[6] But what does this really mean, and how should we apply this idea? Mauthner (1998) argues that reflexivity "is a central tenet of a feminist methodology whereby the researcher documents the production of knowledge and locates herself in the process" (p. 49).[7]

Birtch et al. (2002, p. 4) elaborate that this will include "an interest in the interplay between public, social knowledge and private and personal lived experience." Gillies and Alldred argue (2002, p. 32) that "the goals of feminist research" tend to be oriented toward better understanding or representing women's lived experience with "the explicitly political aim of challenging gender oppression and improving women's lives"—research in this model becomes a "political tool to be used strategically to make political interventions."[8] Given that this project aims to have social policy relevance, this is the project team's barely articulated agenda.

Gillies and Alldred (2002, p. 32) complain that research ethics has tended to focus on how well research participants are treated, but has not generally been "extended to encompass broader questions about the ethics of knowledge itself." It would seem appropriate that, in a project that seeks to explore the politics of representation, these processes form an integral part of the research analysis.

In her critique of sociological interviewing textbook advice, Oakley (1981) notes that a rather harsh, mechanistic description permeates many texts, in which the subject is seen as essentially passive:

> *For the contradiction at the heart of the textbook paradigm is that interviewing necessitates the manipulation of interviewees as objects of study/sources of data, but this can only be achieved via a certain amount of humane treatment. A balance must then be struck between warmth required to generate "rapport" and the detachment necessary to see the interviewee as an object under surveillance. (p. 48)*

She goes on eloquently to challenge the mythology of the "hygienic" research interview, arguing that personal involvement can greatly enrich the quality of the information proffered, especially regarding intimate subject matter. She argues for "the recognition that personal involvement is more than dangerous bias—it is the condition under which people come to know each other and to admit others into their lives" (Oakley, 1981, p. 58).

The contingent nature of analysis needs to be highlighted (Burman, 1992). Alldred and Gillies (2002, p. 146) point out that the research interview (and we do think that the ongoing art elicitation workshop, which will be discussed, can be viewed as a form of extended interview, as well as an opportunity to create imagery), "is not a clear window into the interviewee's experience, rather it is *the joint production of an account by interviewer and interviewee through the dynamic interaction between them*" (our italics). This, they assert, is now "widely accepted" among qualitative researchers, especially those with feminist convictions.

Gillies and Alldred (2002, p. 41) note that one strategy adopted by feminist researchers in relation to the issue of representing others has been for researchers to "put themselves in the picture," "so that the research account is not a disembodied 'view from nowhere'" (N. Fraser & Nicholson, 1990). As Birch and Miller (2002, p. 93) put it, "In gathering narratives . . . the researcher must acknowledge their own part as co-producer of such stories" and "it is this recognition of the dynamics and constituent nature of the research encounter in which data is generated that necessitates the need for *all participants to be visible in the research process*" (our italics).

Of course, detractors may claim "self-indulgence," or challenge the researcher's "objectivity" or even "professionalism." Nevertheless, a reflexive approach would seem to be definitively justified in a research project of this nature, which has aspirations to be "participatory."

> *First, the overall intention of specific representational research needs to be acknowledged and clarified in terms of what might be achieved by speaking for or about "others." Secondly, the researcher's position in relation to those whom she is representing needs to be thoroughly explored, in terms of her own social, political, and personal interests, and the assumptions she brings to her understanding of those she is researching (Gillies & Alldred, 2002, p. 42).*

Birch and Miller (2002) assert that if "participatory" research is to be more than a mere semantic shift, then those participating must be clear about the project's research aims. They assert that researchers must be clear about their research aims (p. 103) and open about the research process (p. 99).

> *To see full and active participation from our research participants—throughout a project—demands that not only we, but also those whose lives we research, share a common interest and understanding of the research enterprise. For many this would require a fundamental shift in ways in which research is conceptualized. . . . [This] depends upon negotiation of an active research relationship. (Birch & Miller, 2002, pp. 103–104).*

They also assert that research designs should identify "processes of participation" (Birch & Miller, 2002, p. 99). These remarks pertain to the project as a whole, but in relation to the miniprojects. This has led to facilitators keeping a reflective diary of the process and actually participating in some of the initial workshops.

For example, Susan joined in with the initial introductory sessions of the art elicitation group. Thus, she revealed something of herself and potentially put herself on more on an equal footing with participants than is often the case in experiential work. However, fuller participation was limited by the need to facilitate the group and ensure participant safety through her vigilant responsiveness.[9]

Alldred and Gillies (1992) assert, rather without evidence, that research interview practices suggest to participants that they "employ conventional modes of self-expression" and so perform in predictable ways (p. 146) and if there is any validity in their rather crude and unsubstantiated claim, then the potential iconoclasm and unpredictability of using art materials must be viewed as a potential asset. (Cameron [2001] identifies "saving face" and respondents interpreting what the researcher wants as potential problems; however, she also outlines many other ways that interview respondents can behave, pointing out that "resistances" and "contradictory accounts" can also yield important information that can be considered (pp. 148–157).

Research Methods

The Representing Self—Representing Ageing initiative has brought together a team of researchers from different disciplines, with a shared interest in aging and gender, and a cultural development agency (Eventus) that aims to use the transformative power of the arts "to make a difference to people and places," targeting the 23% of people identified by Arts Council England as not currently engaged in the arts (Ace Insight Report 2008).[10] The basic format of the project included using a variety of participatory methods and different art forms working with four separate groups of women.

All participants in the four groups were interviewed by our project researcher before and after the respective projects. The resulting work—images and text—has been exhibited in exhibitions held in several sites in Sheffield to date, entitled *Look at Me!*

The project as a whole was launched by a women-only film screening of Deirdre Fishel's "Still Doing It: The Intimate Lives of Women Over 65." Women from the audience had the opportunity after the screening to talk to a camera in a private booth about their views about late-in-life sexuality and how it is portrayed.

Two of the groups were organized through Eventus. A group of women volunteers at a historical site, located in a relatively deprived area of Sheffield, were identified. The Manor Lodge is managed by an environmental social enterprise called Green Estate. A photographer, Laura Pannack, well known for her powerful portraiture, was recruited to work with the women, with a brief that would be developed informally with the women. The Green Estate

Figure 2 *Elaine* by Laura Pannack (color figure available online).

Figure 3 *Elaine* by Laura Pannack (color figure available online).

women were photographed individually by Pannack in settings that they chose and in which they felt at ease.

These two photographs "read" well as a pair, as Elaine said she didn't like the first image as it makes her look as though she was living in an institution; this dissatisfaction led to the outdoor image (see Figures 2 and 3).

A further group was recruited from older women in an "extra care" scheme at the Guildford Grange sheltered-housing project. Monica Fernández, a fine-art photographer, was recruited to work with this group of women. Of her general approach, she wrote,

> *Without looking for an explanation or judgment, I frequently wonder and feel intrigued by people's behaviour, habits, dysfunctionalities, excesses, obsessions, orders and disorders. Through my photography I observe and artistically re-interpret these mundane scenes, when the ordinary becomes extraordinary and the grotesque and the beautiful might hug each other.[11]*

Some of the results of her work with women from Guildford Grange made for slightly uncomfortable viewing and divided opinion among exhibition attendees, and the project team, to the extent that Lorna and I have had difficulty agreeing on the precise wording of this section. Certainly, the juxtapositions created in some of the works are potentially disquieting. On the other hand, elements of her work capture a youthful flamboyance and playfulness in her subjects, which many exhibition attendees could identify with and said they had enjoyed. This work also garnered some extreme reactions: that the women were degrading themselves, for example. Such responses may point to societal ideals about age-appropriate behavior, and participant and audience responses will be explored in further detail in a forthcoming article. Audience feedback has been captured by questionnaires at two of the three exhibition venues to date (and by the film-crew). See Figure 4 for the most popular image in the audience survey.

A further set of art works emerged from an experiential art group, recruited largely via the launch film screening, project fliers distributed around the city center, and an advertisement in a local paper. The group met for 16 hours over an eight-week period and was facilitated by a registered art therapist (Susan Hogan), who is also trained in social science research methods. The group employed techniques from analytic art psychotherapy. The women used a wide variety of art media to explore aging and were active in interrogating their own very particular feelings about the process of aging. This included articulating their feelings about media and cultural representations of aging women.

Although not immediately legible, these images of a cervix were hung in the first exhibition venue, having been initially rejected by our curator. Susan argued to have the images included, as she was worrying that the exhibition might be too anodyne and wanted some intimate imagery to be included. This is what the woman who made the image had to say about it:

> *The two images in question are of a cervix. I made the drawings because they are views of women that are so very rarely discussed, even less frequently seen, in the media. Indeed a cervix is still an area of anatomy many women have not seen. It struck me recently, when I had some "investigations" in that area, and watched the camera images on-screen in the hospital, that it is a view I don't get even though it is a familiar sight to the (male in my case) gynaecologist who will see it with a medical mind rather than an aesthetic one. He seemed especially uninterested in how it looked and felt to me. Since the menopause hit, the skin of my vagina has become thinner and more delicate. . . .*
>
> *One of the cervix images has a small drip of blood—I no longer bleed periodically—it was a farewell to all that; the other image a kind of hello and welcome to none of that and a new set of hormonal/non-hormonal effects.*
>
> *I used oil pastels for the drawings—oil pastels give a lovely viscous quality to the work.... This quality seemed to lend itself to the fleshiness and viscosity of gynaecology.*[12]

Perhaps not surprisingly, these images drew mixed audience responses, with one attendee finding them "the most challenging work," and another finding it raw and painful and uncomfortable viewing (see Figure 5).

The most complex of the projects was perhaps Rosy Martin's six days of intense phototherapy workshops (constituting about 42 hours of group work) with a group of self-selected women who had responded to advertisements in the local paper or via a leaflet left in arts and other venues, including a local health club, which has a predominantly middle and older-aged clientele.

Martin works in an intense way and also required her participants to keep a photo diary to reflect on age and aging in between the first two sessions. Phototherapeutic techniques were used to enable the women to examine and then reframe their own narratives of age and aging. The technique involves women working in pairs and deciding on specific scenarios to explore, enact, and reinterpret. The women take turns being the photographer and the client/performer. Drawing on techniques from cocounseling and Gestalt psychotherapy, but

Figure 4 *Hermi* by Monica Fernandez (color figure available online).

using props to help the performance of her story, each woman had the opportunity to explore a narrative, which was photographed at various junctures. The control rests primarily with the person telling the story, with the photographer acting very much under her instruction. Martin explains the process:

> *Working in pairs, each woman performed her stories, using her chosen clothes and props and determined how she wanted to be represented. The woman being photographed asked for what she wanted, and the photographer was supportive, encouraging and was "there for" her partner as witness, advocate, and nurturer, whilst photographing the process. . . . It is a collaborative process both sitter/protagonist and photographer work together to make the images. (Martin, 2011, p. 2)*

Martin stresses the psychotherapeutic dimension of her work, and emphasizes that the woman in the role of photographer offers a "gaze of nurturance and permission" to the sitter. Each narrative ended with images of transformation: the process as a whole enabling each woman to find ways to transform aspects of her lived experience.

Reflecting on her work, Martin (2011) added,

> *The re-enactment phototherapy sessions produce an atmosphere of playful creativity. The roles are exchanged, so both have the opportunity to be in the picture, and to be the photographer. The resulting images challenge stereotypes of ageing. The whole process enabled each participant to find ways to transform her views of herself.*

Figure 5 *Cervix* (color figure available online).

At the Workstation exhibition, these images of Jen were "read" by some viewers as showing that motherhood had been particularly stressful, but actually the middle image represents multiple caring roles, and so it is interesting to see how easily the images can be read differently (see Figure 6). Of these, Jen said, "It's like a joy sandwich with some deep, dark, difficult stuff in the middle." Images are inherently polysemous and subject to a diversity of potential meanings. As Hogan (2011a, p. 274) has pointed out,

> *The producers of culture arguably never have absolute control over how the artifact is understood. . . . The "meaning" of a cultural artifact, or "text" broadly defined (be it an image, or written text, or case study which uses a range of media), is always open to interpretation. The "meaning" of an artifact is generated by the reader of the artifact; the audience is active in interpreting the material in relation to their existing knowledge and understanding, which is particular. Although the actual content of the artifact may suggest certain preferred readings. It is "read" and understood by the reader in "relation to its inter-textual space." (Cowie, 1977, p. 20)*

Hogan (2011a) argues,

> *Alternative meanings are generated not by new content or a changed "consciousness" but as a result of a different strategy for production of cultural knowledge in relation to the inter-textual space. . . . [This may result in the production of work that is] complex and perhaps uncomfortable viewing but it is multidimensional, not easily read, and perhaps actually resists, by its very complexity, reductive interpretation. (p. 275)*

Figure 6 Jen in collaboration with Barbara Harriott (color figure available online).

In the context of exhibitions, which images are selected and then how they are juxtaposed creates narratives perhaps not intended by the artist (creating particular challenges for those interested in participatory frameworks).

Four short documentary films have been produced on each of the projects by filmmaker Clair Allam, and at most of the events, including the exhibitions, a film crew has been on hand to capture participant and audience responses.

Exhibition Strategy—Some Further Musings

In a study about how older women feel about aging processes, and representations of aging in the mass media, is it appropriate and useful to use exhibition and installation as a format for the presentation of research results? Secondly, what are the advantages, if any?

A fairly traditional exhibition format could contain an installation space within it. One characteristic of an installation is that it uses the total space and invites the viewer to move within it. This physical moving into the discursive space is slightly different qualitatively to simply looking at something on a wall or plinth; it is a more bodily engagement with the artwork and offers a more immersive experience. It is potentially more challenging in its theatrical invitation to the viewer to engage with the subject matter in an embodied way.

How the narrative flow unveils itself depends on the participant's movement through the space; one perspective may necessarily cut off another, and new configurations are generated by being at different vantage points in the space. The format evokes uncertainty, anxiety perhaps, and the entire work cannot be viewed from any particular vantage point.

Older women are heterogeneous. The participants' "stories" can be told using a multiplicity of modalities: Text fragments and images can be juxtaposed in a myriad of ways, and film clips can be projected into the space.

How older women are depicted in society is a contested terrain and in constant flux; using an exhibition format that withholds overarching interpretation or meta-analysis, yet affords the opportunity for the stimulation of empathy in the viewer, would seem particularly appropriate, at a point when audience responses will be "captured" as part of the data collection and evaluation process.

Above all, the installation format invites the viewer to engage in a dynamic process of meaning making that doesn't necessarily offer any sort of closure with respect to the subject matter.

Given that we wish the audience to respond to the work on film, this more conceptually open format would seem particularly appropriate and may be used in future exhibition of the work. The initial exhibition in the Workstation took a more conventional format, though with some interesting juxtapositions between the different groups of work, and textual accompaniments, which took the form of quotations from participants, some of which were reproduced in large text on the walls; the result was arguably a good compromise between those in the project team who wanted the work to challenge and those who were more concerned to make the work accessible—though we all wanted both.

Dealing with Complex Research: Discussion

Qualitative research, with its emphasis on understanding the social world from the point of view of the research participants themselves, may now be, as Maynard, Ashar, Franks, and Wray (2008) assert, "accepted as legitimate" as a means of researching older people (p. 3). We have interrogated how problematic the notion of the "older women" is and mused on the implications of different exhibition strategies.

This study draws on analytical techniques and collaborative approaches developed within visual anthropology to enable individuals or communities to represent themselves or to challenge dominant representations. Guided by anthropologically informed theories of observation and visual representation (Banks, 2001; Pink, 2004; Ruby, 2005), practical documentary film may be used in a variety of ways, in conjunction with other art-making techniques, as a part of a case study in its own right, or to elicit further research materials. The latter includes visual elicitation methods in which visual data, which have been found or made by respondents, are used in conjunction with interviewing techniques to elicit responses (Newbury, 2005). From a research perspective, we might view the four separate projects as complementary, and as generating different perspectives, as well as bringing different issues for interrogation to the fore (Corden & Hirst, 2008; Hodgkin, 2008; Masson, 2006; Sale et al., 2002; Woolley, 2009).

The findings of the groups will be varied, complex, and contradictory (this is already evident even in initial analysis), so presentation strategies that allow for multiple readings are perhaps appropriate. Some text-based research findings will be produced, and Marcus Banks (2009) has talked about the value of using images in research projects to create "a parallel argument" or a "parallel discourse" to the written text.

In using this approach, we are rejecting the problematic metaphor of triangulation and regard contradictory findings as potential starting points generating new theoretical formulations (Erzberger & Prein, 1997; Masson, 2006). The advantage of running four different projects with four quite different populations of older women, using different visual research techniques, is that it affords the opportunity for the creation of multidimensional accounts; this approach may, in the final analysis, lead to an open exploration of tensions inherent in contradictory accounts between (and within) the groups, leading to "dialogic" explanations and analysis (Masson, 2006) rather than an "integrated" or "tidy" picture.

Future possibilities include the creation of an installation space, which invites the viewer to move within it, offering more bodily engagement with the art work and a more immersive experience.

Conclusion

Given the project's epistemological openness to producing polysemous research, using a multimethod approach should produce different types of data that can be contrasted, and juxtaposed, in interesting ways, to produce a "collage" of the areas under investigation. Taussig

(1987), for example, uses the analogy of a mosaic. Work from the projects has already been exhibited in a variety of spaces, including a contemporary gallery (Workstation), shop fronts, and in a hospital. These exhibitions were arranged by a professional curator (Alison Morton). Further funding may be pursued, so that some of the data may form part of larger installation-type exhibition pieces later on in the research and dissemination process. The short films have been screened at The Showroom Cinema and are available via the project Web site.[13]

Masson (2006) has suggested that "we should think more in terms of 'meshing' or 'linking' than 'integrating' data and method." She goes on to argue "for the development of 'multi-nodal' dialogic explanations that allow the distinctiveness of different methods and approaches to be held in creative tension" (p. 1).

Tensions were expressed within the research team between conflicting desires: the need to communicate clearly for social policy makers, the desire not to be condescendingly overintellectual to the extent that the result might alienate some of the actual participants, and the aspiration to produce something challenging and potentially iconoclastic. The decision to employ a professional curator for the initial exhibitions meant that the women participants did not have a hands-on role in the organization of the space, though they were consulted about the inclusion of their images, the statements that accompanied them, and whether they wanted to be named or not. This was partly pragmatic, as we had limited funding available (and had underbudgeted for the realities of full participation).

Cornwall and Jewkes (2000, p. 1) assert that the "key difference between participatory and conventional methodologies lies in the location of power in the research process." Participatory approaches are those that broadly recognize the "particular expertise" of people within particular circumstances (Bennett & Roberts, 2004); this could be because of local or particular knowledge (Breitbart, 2003). Some theorists conceptualize this as "active co-research" between researchers and participants (Wadsworth, 1998) who are active in defining research problems (Anyanwu, 1988) and that, furthermore, participatory research "must be sharply distinguished from conventional elitist research which treats people as objects of the research process" (Tilakaratna, 1990, p. 1). Certainly, this was one of the areas in which different members of the research team had different understandings of the term *participatory*, and how this would translate into concrete methods. Obviously, there are different levels of participation, and potentially women's involvement in a curatorial process might have provided further opportunities for learning and empowerment. How much control participants should retain over the final products of research is a complex topic in its own right. It is worth research teams spending time exploring concepts such as "participation" at the outset of projects and not assuming that there is a common understanding.

A quantitative and qualitative analysis of exhibition audience responses will follow. However, only a cursory view of the works produced will convince the viewer that this project had helped to enrich the range of images of older women on offer.

Acknowledgments

The Representing Self—Representing Ageing initiative has been funded by the ESRC as part of the New Dynamics of Ageing cross-council research programme (grant number RES.356 25-0040). Thanks to all the women who took part in the project and the project team members for their insights, commitment, and inspirational work: Claire Allam (filmmaker), Merryn Gott (coinvestigator), Clare McManus (Aventus), Alison Morton (curator), Naomi Richards (researcher), Judith Taylor (project administrator), and also the commissioned artists: Monica Fernández, Rosy Martin, and Laura Pannack.

Notes

1. Men are less able to maintain a dependent spouse in the home; thus, it is "predominantly women's labour that maintains aged couples in their own homes, with consequent savings to the public sector" (Gibson, 1998, p. 75). Gibson also challenges the concept of "interdependence," providing evidence that even disabled and frail elderly women continue to provide a proportionally larger share of domestic responsibilities, especially cooking (p. 84). Late-in-life poverty and links to women's responsibilities for childcare are more obvious (Calasanti, 2010). Other structural inequalities highlighted have been the devalued status of women's work and the tendency for women to be segregated into lowerpaying fields of work (Calasanti, 2010). What is defined as "woman's work" changes historically, but it is often relatively less well rewarded. Calasanti, in particular, is at pains to point out that a complex set of gender relations combine to result in late-in-life poverty for women, and that in Britain women are almost twice as likely as men to experience late-in-life poverty (Calasanti, 2010, p. 722).

2. "Social policy provisions for frail and disabled older people are predicated on the expectation that women will provide the vast majority of care at no fiscal cost to the state and that much of the remainder will be subsidised by unpaid female labour" (Gibson, 1998, p. 73). Gibson notes research that points to this being a pattern across diverse systems of health care, including Britain, Australia, North America, Canada, and Scandinavia.

3. Research Programme Proposal, ESRC New Dynamics of Ageing RES-356-25-0040 (Warren, Gott, Hogan, in collaboration with McManus & Martin, 2009).

4. *Coming of Age* was billed as "a week of programming dedicated to the over 60s in a bid to challenge some of the preconceptions and stereotypes surrounding the lives of older people" and was screened in November 2009 on Channel 4 in the U.K. Several of Channel 4's favorite programm turned their attention to the over 60s.

5. Wittgenstein as cited in Moi (1999, p. 7).

6. Research Programme Proposal, ESRC New Dynamics of Ageing (Warren, Gott, Hogan, in collaboration with McManus & Martin, 2009).

7. Reflexivity is an awareness of oneself in the field of action and one's role in creating that situation: "Reflexivity is thus distinct from reflectivity in its focus on the constitutive role of the self" (Bloor & Wood, 2006, pp. 145–146).

8. Certainly, Oakley (1981) notes that, in "departing from conventional interviewing ethics," she was concerned to give "the subjective situation of women greater visibility not only in sociology, but, more importantly, in society, than it has traditionally had" (p. 48).

9. There is considerable debate in psychotherapy literature on this point, and facilitators must vary. I personally find that if I muse about my own material too much in sessions, I can get distracted from my role as facilitator (this is even the case in scrutinizing my own emotional responses when I have not actively made a disclosure or image at all, and part of the role of an analytic psychotherapist is to reflect on her own feelings about what is happening in the group in an ongoing way), but in a feminist model it does feel *inappropriate* to maintain a completely "opaque" approach, revealing absolutely nothing of oneself, so participating during initial warm-up exercises before the group gets properly underway is a compromise.

10. From the mission statement: www.eventus.org.uk. Eventus is a Regularly Funded Organisation (RFO) of Arts Council England. It aims its work at the 23% of the population identified in Arts Council England's research (Arts Audiences: Insight, Arts Council

England, 2008) as "not currently engaged in the arts," primarily, though not exclusively, through partnerships with nonarts organizations.

11. http://www.representing-ageing.com/

12. The artist's commentary. Personal correspondence, Susan Hogan, 2010.

13. http://www.representing-ageing.com/

References

Alldred, P., & Gillies, V. (1992). Eliciting research accounts: Re/producing modern subjects. In M. Mauthner, M. Birch, J. Jessop, & T. Miller (Eds.), *Ethics in qualitative research* (pp. 146–165). London, England: Sage.

Anyanwu, C. N. (1998). The Technique of Participatory Research. *Community Development Journal, 23,* 11–15. Retrieved from http://cdj.oxfordjournals.org/ cgi/reprint/23/1/11

Arber, S., & Ginn, J. (1995). *Connecting gender and ageing: Changing roles and relationships. (Ageing & Later Life).* Buckingham, England: Open University Press.

Afshar, H., Franks, M., Maynard, M., & Wray, S. (2008). *Women in later life: Exploring race and ethnicity.* Berkshire, UK: Open University Press/McGraw Hill.

Ball, M. S., & Smith, G. W. H. (1992). *Analyzing visual data.* London, England: Sage.

Banks, M. (2001). *Visual methods in social research.* London, England: Sage.

Banks, M. (2009, September). *Slow research, or Letting the image breathe.* Paper presented at the 1st International Visual Methods Conference, ESRC Research Developer Initiative, University of Leeds, England.

Banks, M., & Morphy, H. (Eds.). (1997). *Rethinking visual anthropology.* New Haven, CT: Yale University Press.

Bennett, F. & Roberts, M. (2004). Participatory Approaches to Research on Poverty. Findings Report. Retrieved from http://www.jrf.org.uk/sites/files/jrf/334.pdf

Birch, M., & Miller, T. (2002). Encouraging participation: Ethics and responsibilities. In M. Mauthner, M. Birch, J. Jessop, & T. Miller (Eds.), *Ethics in qualitative research* (pp. 91–106). London, England: Sage.

Birrin, J. E., & Benston, V. L. (1988). *International perspectives on families, aging & social support.* New York, NY: Springer.

Blaikie, A. (1999). *Ageing and popular culture.* Cambridge, England: Cambridge University Press.

Bordo, S. (1997). The Reproduction of Feminity. In K. Conboy, N. Medina, & S. Stanbury (Eds.), *Writing on the body: Female Embodiment and Feminist Theory.* New York, NY: Columbia University Press.

Breitbart, M. (2003). Participatory Research. In Clifford, N. & Valentine, G. (Eds.), *Key Methods in Geography.* London, England: Sage.

Butler, J. (1990). *Gender Trouble: Feminism and the Subversion of Identity.* London, England: Routledge.

Burman, E. (1992). Feminism and discourse in developmental psychology: Power, subjectivity and interpretation. *Feminism & Psychology, 2*(1), 45–60.

Calasanti, T. (2010). Gender relations and applied research on aging. *The Gerontologist, 50*(6), 720–734.

Cameron, D. (2001). *Working with spoken discourse.* London, England: Sage.

Cattell, J., Hitchins, T., Mackie, A. (2009). Care Services Improvement Partnership. Ace Insight Report Dec 2009. Retrieved from http://webarchive. nationalarchives.gov.uk/+/http://www.cabinetoffice.gov.uk/media/342005/ ace231209final.pdf

Chapakis, W. (1986). *Beauty secrets: Women and the politics of appearance.* London, England: The Women's Press.

Copper, B. (1988). *Over the hill: Reflections on ageism between women.* Freedom, CA: Crossing Press.

Corden, A., Hirst, M., & Nice, K. (2008). Financial implications of death of a partner. North Yorkshire, UK: Social Policy Research Unit, University of York. Retrieved from http://php.york.ac.uk/inst/spru/pubs.

Cornwall, A., & Jewkes, R. (2000). The use of qualitative methods: What is participatory research? Department of Anthropology, SOAS, University of London, London WC1H 0XG, England. 10 March 2000.

Cowie, E. (1977).Women, Representation and the Image. *Screen Education, 23,* 15–23.

Cruikshank, M. (2003). *Learning to be old: Gender, culture, and ageing.* Oxford, England: Rowman & Littlefield.

De Beauvoir, S. (1949). *The Second Sex. Women as Other.* London, England: Jonathan Cape.

De Beauvoir, S. (1972). *Old age.* Trans. P. O'Brian, London, England: André Deutsch.

Edwards, R., & Mauthner, M. (2002). Ethics and feminist research: Theory and practice. In M. Mauthner, M. Birch, J. Jessop, & T. Miller (Eds.), *Ethics in qualitative research* (pp. 32–52). London, England: Sage.

Elam, D. (1994). *Feminism and deconstruction.* London, England: Routledge.

Erzberger, C., & Prein, G. (1997). Triangulation: Validity and empirically-based hypothesis construction. *Quality and Quantity, 31*(2), 141–154.

Fishel, D. (2008). *Still doing it: The intimate lives of women over 60.* New York, NY: Avery, Penguin.

Fraser, J., & Boffin T. (1991). *Stolen glances: Lesbians take photographs.* London, England: Pandora.

Fraser, N., & Nicholson, L. J. (1990). Social criticism without philosophy: An encounter between feminism and postmodernism. In L. J. Nicholson (Ed.), *Feminism/postmodernism* (pp. 19–38). London, England: Routledge.

Gibson, D. (1998). *Aged care: Old policies, new problems.* Cambridge, England: Cambridge University Press.

Gilleard, C. J., & Higgs, P. (2000). *Cultures of ageing: Self, citizen, and the body.* Harlow, England: Prentice Hall.

Gillies, V., & Alldred, P. (2002). The ethics of intention: Research as a political tool. In M. Mauthner, M. Birch, J. Jessop, & T. Miller (Eds.), *Ethics in qualitative research* (pp. 32–52). London, England: Sage.

Greer, G. (1992). *The Change: Women, Ageing and the Menopause.* London, England: Penguin.

Gullette, M. M. (2004). *Aged by culture.* Chicago, IL: The University of Chicago Press.

Hockey, J. & James, A. (2003). *Social Identities Across the Life Course.* Basingstoke, England: Palgrave Macmillan.

Hogan, S. (Ed.) (2003). *Gender issues in art therapy.* London, England: Jessica Kingsley Press.

Hogan, S. (2011a). Images of Broomhall, Sheffield: Urban violence and using the arts as a research aid. *Visual Anthropology, 24*(5), 247–266.

Hogan, S. (2011b). Postmodernist but not post-feminist! A feminist postmodernist approach to working with new mothers. In H. Burt (Ed.), *A postmodernist perspective* (pp. 70–82). London, England: JKP.

Hogan, S., & Pink, S. (2010). Routes to interiorities: Art therapy, anthropology and knowing in anthropology. *Visual Anthropology, 23*(2), 1–16.

Howson, A. (2005). *Embodying gender.* London, England: Sage.

Martin, R. (1999). Too close to home? *n.paradoxa, International Feminist Art Journal, 3,* 73–80.

Martin, R. (2003). Challenging invisibility—Outrageous agers. In S. Hogan (Ed.), *Gender issues in art therapy* (pp. 194–227). London, England: Jessica Kingsley.

Martin, R. (2006). Curating the museum of sources: Stilled lives, memory, morality and the domestic space. In K. Newton & C. Rolph (Eds.), *Stilled: Contemporary still life photography by women.* A special edition of *Ellipsis.* Vol. 3. Cardiff, Wales: Iris & Photogallery.

Martin, R. (2011, May). *Phototherapy workshop created and led by Rosy Martin.* Unpublished paper supplied by author.

Masson, J. (2006). Mixing methods in a qualitatively driven way. *Qualitative Research, 6*(1), 9–25.

Mauthner, M. (1998). Bringing silent voices into public discourse: Researching accounts of sister relationships. In J. Ribbens & R. Edwards (Eds.), *Feminist dilemmas in qualitative research: Public knowledge and private lives* (pp. 39–58). London, England: Sage.

Moi, T. (1999). *What is a woman? And other essays.* Oxford, England: Oxford University Press.

Newbury, D. (2005). Editorial: The challenge of visual studies. *Visual Studies, 20*(1), 1–3.

Oakley, A. (2007). *Fracture: Adventures of a broken body.* Bristol, UK: Policy Press.

Oakley, A. (1981). Interviewing women: A contradiction in terms. In H. Roberts (Ed.), *Doing feminist research* (pp. 30–62). London, England: Routledge.

Pearsall, M. (1997). *The other within us: Feminist explorations of women and aging.* Boulder, CO: Westview Press.

Phillipson, C. (1998). *Reconstructing Old Age: New Agendas in Social Theory and Practice.* London, England: Sage.

Pink, S. (2001). *Doing Visual Ethnography: Images, Media and Representation in Research.* London, England: Sage.

Pink, S. (2004). Applied visual anthropology: Social intervention, visual methodologies and anthropology theory. *Visual Anthropology Review, 20*(1), 3–16.

Pink, S. (2006). *Doing Visual Ethnography: Images, Media and Representation in Research* (2nd ed.). London, England: Sage.

Pink, S. (Ed.). (2012). *Advances in visual methods.* London, England: Sage.

Pink, S., Hogan, S. & Bird, J. (2011) Boundaries and intersections: Using the arts in research. *Inscape: International Journal of Art Therapy, 16*(1), 14–19.

Reichenberg-Ullman, J. (1992). Menopause naturally. *Natural Health, 22*(2), 75–80.

Reinharz, S. (1997). Friends or foes: Gerontological and feminist theory. In M. Pearsall (Ed.), *The other within us: Feminist explorations of women and aging* (pp. 73–94). Boulder, CO: Westview Press.

Rose, G. (2007). *Visual methodologies: An introduction to the interpretation of visual materials.* London, England: Sage.

Ruby, J. (2005). The last 20 years of visual anthropology—A critical review. *Visual Studies, 20*(2), 159–170.

Sontag, S. (1978). The double standard of aging. In M. Pearsall (Ed.), *The other within us: Feminist explorations of women and aging* (pp. 19–24). Boulder, CO: Westview Press.

Stanczak, G. C. (2007). *Visual Research Methods. Image, Society & Representation.* London, England: Sage.

Taussig, M. (1987). *Shamanism, colonialism, and the wild man: A study in terror and healing.* Chicago, IL: The University of Chicago Press.

Tilakaratna, S. (1990). A Short Note on Participatory Research. Retrieved from http://www.caledonia.org.uk/research.htm

Turner, B. S. (1984). *The body and society: Explorations in social theory.* Oxford, England: Blackwell.

Wadsworth, Y. (1998). What is Participatory Research? Action Research International. Retrieved from http://www.scu.edu.au/schools/gcm/ar/ari/pywadsworth98. html

Wittgenstein, L. (1958). *Philosophical investigations* (3rd ed.). Trans. G.E.M Anscombe. Upper Saddle River, NJ: Prentice-Hall.

Woodward, K. (Ed.). (1999). *Figuring age: Women, bodies, generations.* Bloomington, IN: Indiana University Press.

Zita, J. N. (2003). Heresy in the female body: The rhetorics of menopause. In J. Callahan (Ed.), *Menopause: A mid-life passage* (pp. 95–112). Bloomington, IN: Indiana University Press.

26

Gender as a Social Structure: Theory Wrestling with Activism

Barbara J. Risman

In this article, the author argues that we need to conceptualize gender as a social structure, and by doing so, we can better analyze the ways in which gender is embedded in the individual, interactional, and institutional dimensions of our society. To conceptualize gender as a structure situates gender at the same level of general social significance as the economy and the polity. The author also argues that while concern with intersectionality must continue to be paramount, different structures of inequality have different constructions and perhaps different influential causal mechanisms at any given historical moment. We need to follow a both/and strategy to understand gender structure, race structure, and other structures of inequality as they currently operate while also systematically paying attention to how these axes of domination intersect. Finally, the author suggests we pay more attention to doing research and writing theory with explicit attention to how our work can indeed help transform as well as inform society.

G ender has become a growth industry in the academy. In the years between my own college education and today, we have moved from not enough having been published in 1972 to justify my writing a literature review for an undergraduate course paper to more sociologists' studying and teaching about gender than any other single substantive area in American society. In 1998, I published *Gender Vertigo: American Families in Transition* (Risman 1998), which offered both a historical narrative about how the field of gender had developed and an integrative theoretical explanation for the tenacity of gender stratification in families. In this article, I briefly summarize my earlier argument that gender should be conceptualized as a social structure (Risman 1998) and extend it with an attempt to classify the mechanisms that help produce gendered outcomes within each dimension of the social structure. I then provide evidence from my own and others' research to support the usefulness of this theoretical schema. Finally, using gender structure as a starting point, I engage in conversation with ideas currently emerging about intersectionality and wrestle with how we might use theory in the service of social change.

Reprinted by permission from *Gender and Society* 18, no. 4 (August 2004).

Chapter Twenty-Six

Gender as a Social Structure

With this theory of *gender as a social structure,* I offer a conceptual framework, a scheme to organize the confusing, almost limitless, ways in which gender has come to be defined in contemporary social science. Four distinct social scientific theoretical traditions have developed to explain gender. The first tradition focuses on how individual sex differences originate, whether biological (Udry 2000) or social in origin (Bern 1993). The second tradition, perhaps portrayed best in Epstein's (1988) *Deceptive Distinctions,* emerged as a reaction to the first and focuses on how the social structure (as opposed to biology or individual learning) creates gendered behavior. The third tradition, also a reaction to the individualist thinking of the first, emphasizes social interaction and accountability to others' expectations, with a focus on how "doing gender" creates and reproduces inequality (West and Zimmerman 1987). The sex-differences literature, the doing gender interactional analyses, and the structural perspectives have been portrayed as incompatible in my own early writings as well as in that of others (Fuchs Epstein 1988; Kanter 1977; Ferree 1990; Risman 1987; Risman and Schwartz 1989). England and Browne (1992) argued persuasively that this incompatibility is an illusion: All structural theories must make assumptions about individuals, and individualist theories must make presumptions about external social control. While we do gender in every social interaction, it seems naive to ignore the gendered selves and cognitive schemas that children develop as they become cultural natives in a patriarchal world (Bern 1993). The more recent integrative approaches (Connell 2002; Lorber 1994; Ferree, Lorber, and Hess 1999; Risman 1998) treat gender as a socially constructed stratification system. This article fits squarely in the current integrative tradition.

Lorber (1994) argued that gender is an institution that is embedded in all the social processes of everyday life and social organizations. She further argued that gender difference is primarily a means to justify sexual stratification. Gender is so endemic because unless we see difference, we cannot justify inequality. Lorber provided much cross-cultural, literary, and scientific evidence to show that gender difference is socially constructed and yet is universally used to justify stratification. She wrote that "the continuing purpose of gender as a modem social institution is to construct women as a group to be subordinate to men as a group" (p. 33). I share this presumption that the creation of difference is the very foundation on which inequality rests.

Martin (forthcoming) extended Lorber's (1994) use of the term "institution" in her argument that gender should be conceptualized as such. She identified the criteria for a social institution as follows: (1) Characteristic of groups; (2) persists over time and space; (3) includes distinct social practices; (4) constrains and facilitates behavior/action; (5) includes expectations, rule/norms; (6) is constituted and reconstituted by embodied agents; (7) is internalized as identities and selves; (8) includes a legitimating ideology; (9) is contradictory, rife with conflict; (10) changes continuously; (11) is organized by and permeated with power; and (12) is mutually constituted at different levels of analysis. I build on this notion of gender as an institution but find the institutional language distracting. The word "institution" is too commonly used to refer to particular aspects of society, for example, the family as an institution or corporations as institutions. My notion of gender structure meets the criteria offered by Martin (forthcoming) as well. While the language we use may differ, our goals are complementary, as we seek to situate gender as embedded not only in individuals but throughout social life (Patricia Martin, personal communication).

I prefer to define gender as a social structure because this brings gender to the same analytic plane as politics and economics, where the focus has long been on political and economic structures. While the language of structure suits my purposes, it is not ideal because despite ubiquitous usage in sociological discourse, no definition of the term "structure" is widely shared. Smelser (1988) suggested that all structuralists share the presumption that social structures exist outside individual desires or motives and that social structures at least partially explain human action. Beyond that, consensus dissipates. Blau (1977) focused solely on the constraint collective life imposes on the individual. In their influential work, Blau and his colleagues (e.g., Blau 1977; Rytina et al. 1988) argued that the concept of structure is trivialized if it is located inside an individual's head in the form of internalized norms and values. Blau focused solely on the constraint collective life imposes on the individual; structure must be conceptualized, in his view, as a force opposing individual motivation. Structural concepts must be observable, external to the individual, and independent of individual motivation. This definition of "structure" imposes a clear dualism between structure and action, with structure as constraint and action as choice.

Constraint is, of course, an important function of structure, but to focus only on structure as constraint minimizes its importance. Not only are women and men coerced into differential social roles; they often choose their gendered paths. A social structural analysis must help us understand how and why actors choose one alternative over another. A structural theory of action (e.g., Burt 1982) suggests that actors compare themselves and their options to those in structurally similar positions. From this viewpoint, actors are purposive, rationally seeking to maximize their self-perceived well-being under social-structural constraints. As Burt (1982) suggested, one can assume that actors choose the best alternatives without presuming they have either enough information to do it well or the options available to make choices that effectively serve their own interests. For example, married women may choose to do considerably more than their equitable share of child care rather than have their children do without whatever "good enough" parenting means to them if they see no likely alternative that the children's father will pick up the slack.

While actions are a function of interests, the ability to choose is patterned by the social structure. Burt (1982) suggested that norms develop when actors occupy similar network positions in the social structure and evaluate their own options vis-a-vis the alternatives of similarly situated others. From such comparisons, both norms and feelings of relative deprivation or advantage evolve. The social structure as the context of daily life creates action indirectly by shaping actors' perceptions of their interests and directly by constraining choice. Notice the phrase "similarly situated others" above. As long as women and men see themselves as different kinds of people, then women will be unlikely to compare their life options to those of men. Therein lies the power of gender. In a world where sexual anatomy is used to dichotomize human beings into types, the differentiation itself diffuses both claims to and expectations for gender equality. The social structure is not experienced as oppressive if men and women do not see themselves as similarly situated.

While structural perspectives have been applied to gender in the past (Epstein 1988; Kanter 1977), there has been a fundamental flaw in these applications. Generic structural theories applied to gender presume that if women and men were to experience identical structural conditions and role expectations, empirically observable gender differences would disappear. But this ignores not only internalized gender at the individual level (which indeed purely structural theorists deny exists) but the cultural interactional expectations that remain attached to women and men because of their gender category. A structural perspective on gender is accurate only if we realize that gender itself is a structure deeply embedded in society.

Giddens's (1984) structuration theory adds considerably more depth to this analysis of gender as a social structure with his emphasis on the recursive relationship between social structure and individuals. That is, social structures shape individuals, but simultaneously, individuals shape the social structure. Giddens embraced the transformative power of human action. He insisted that any structural theory must be concerned with reflexivity and actors' interpretations of their own lives. Social structures not only act on people; people act on social structures. Indeed, social structures are created not by mysterious forces but by human action. When people act on structure, they do so for their own reasons. We must, therefore, be concerned with why actors choose their acts. Giddens insisted that concern with meaning must go beyond the verbal justification easily available from actors because so much of social life is routine and so taken for granted that actors will not articulate, or even consider, why they act.

This nonreflexive habituated action is what I refer to as the cultural component of the social structure: The taken for granted or cognitive image rules that belong to the situational context (not only or necessarily to the actor's personality). The cultural component of the social structure includes the interactional expectations that each of us meet in every social encounter. My aims are to bring women and men back into a structural theory where gender is the structure under analysis and to identify when behavior is habit (an enactment of taken for granted gendered cultural norms) and when we do gender consciously, with intent, rebellion, or even with irony. When are we doing gender and re-creating inequality without intent? And what happens to interactional dynamics and male-dominated institutions when we rebel? Can we refuse to do gender or is rebellion simply doing gender differently, forging alternative masculinities and femininities?

Connell (1987) applied Giddens's (1984) concern with social structure as both constraint and created by action in his treatise on gender and power. In his analysis, structure constrains action, yet "since human action involves free invention ... and is reflexive, practice can be turned against what constrains it; so structure can deliberately be the object of practice" (Connell 1987, 95). Action may turn against structure but can never escape it. We must pay attention both to how structure shapes individual choice and social interaction and to how human agency creates, sustains, and modifies current structure. Action itself may change the immediate or future context.

A theory of gender as a social structure must integrate this notion of causality as recursive with attention to gender consequences at multiple levels of analysis. Gender is deeply embedded as a basis for stratification not just in our personalities, our cultural rules, or institutions but in all these, and in complicated ways. The gender structure differentiates opportunities and constraints based on sex category and thus has consequences on three dimensions: (1) At the individual level, for the development of gendered selves; (2) during interaction as men and women face different cultural expectations even when they fill the identical structural positions; and (3) in institutional domains where explicit regulations regarding resource distribution and material goods are gender specific.

Advantages to Gender Structure Theory

This schema advances our understanding of gender in several ways. First, this theoretical model imposes some order on the encyclopedic research findings that have developed to explain gender inequality. Thinking of each research question as one piece of a jigsaw puzzle, being able to identify how one set of findings coordinates with others even when the dependent variables or contexts of interest are distinct, furthers our ability to build a cumulative science. Gender as a social structure is enormously complex. Full attention to the web of interconnection between gendered selves, the cultural expectations that help explain interactional patterns, and institutional regulations allows each research tradition to explore the growth of their own trees while remaining cognizant of the forest.

A second contribution of this approach is that it leaves behind the modernist warfare version of science, wherein theories are pitted against one another, with a winner and a loser in every contest. In the past, much energy (including my early work; Risman 1987) was devoted to testing which theory best explained gender inequality and by implication to discounting every alternative possibility.[1] While this is perhaps an effective technique for building academic careers, as a model for explaining complex social phenomena, it leaves much to be desired. Theory building that depends on theory slaying presumes parsimony is always desirable, as if this complicated world of ours were best described with simplistic monocausal explanations. While parsimony and theory testing were the model for the twentieth century science, a more postmodern science should attempt to find complicated and integrative theories (Collins 1998). The conceptualization of gender as a social structure is my contribution to complicating, but hopefully enriching, social theory about gender.

A third benefit to this multidimensional structural model is that it allows us to seriously investigate the direction and strength of causal relationships between gendered phenomena on each dimension. We can try to identify the site where change occurs and at which level of analysis the ability of agentic women and men seem able, at this historical moment, to effectively reject habitualized gender routines. For example, we can empirically investigate the relationship between gendered selves and doing gender without accepting simplistic unidirectional arguments for inequality presumed to be either about identities or cultural ideology. It is quite possible, indeed likely, that socialized femininity does help explain why we do gender, but doing gender to meet others' expectations, surely, over time, helps construct our gendered selves. Furthermore, gendered institutions depend on our willingness to do gender, and when we rebel, we can sometimes change the institutions themselves. I have used the language of dimensions interchangeably with the language of levels because when we think of gender as a social structure, we must move away from privileging any particular dimension as higher than another. How social change occurs is an empirical question, not an a priori theoretical assumption. It may be that individuals struggling to change their own identities (as in consciousness-raising groups of the early second-wave women's movement) eventually bring their new selves to social interaction and create new cultural expectations. For example, as women come to see themselves (or are socialized to see themselves) as sexual actors, the expectations that men must work to provide orgasms for their female partners becomes part of the cultural norm. But this is surely not the only way social change can happen. When social movement activists name as inequality what has heretofore been considered natural (e.g., women's segregation into low-paying jobs), they can create organizational changes such as career ladders between women's quasi-administrative jobs and actual management, opening up opportunities that otherwise would have remained closed, thus creating change on the institutional dimension. Girls raised in the next generation, who know opportunities exist in these workplaces, may have an altered sense of possibilities and therefore of themselves. We need, however, to also study change and equality when it occurs rather than only documenting inequality.

Perhaps the most important feature of this conceptual schema is its dynamism. No one dimension determines the other. Change is fluid and reverberates throughout the structure dynamically. Changes in individual identities and moral accountability may change interactional expectations, but the opposite is possible as well. Change cultural expectations, and individual identities are shaped differently. Institutional changes must result from individuals or group action, yet such change is difficult, as institutions exist across time and space. Once institutional changes occur, they reverberate at the level of cultural expectations and perhaps even on identities. And the cycle of change continues. No mechanistic predictions are possible because human beings sometimes reject the structure itself and, by doing so, change it. Much time and energy can be wasted trying to validate which dimension is more central to inequality or social change. Instead, the feminist project is better served by finding empirical answers to particular questions and by identifying how particular processes explain outcomes in need of change. If our goal is to do scholarship that contributes to transforming society, the identification of the processes that explain particular outcomes is the first step in effectively changing those processes and subsequently the outcomes themselves.

Social Processes Located by Dimension in the Gender Structure

When we conceptualize gender as a social structure, we can begin to identify under what conditions and how gender inequality is being produced within each dimension. The "how" is important because without knowing the mechanisms, we cannot intervene. If indeed gender inequality in the division of household labor at this historical moment were primarily explained (and I do not suggest that it is) by gendered selves, then we would do well to consider the most effective socialization mechanisms to create fewer gender-schematic children and resocialization for adults. If, however, the gendered division of household labor is primarily constrained today by cultural expectations and moral accountability, it is those cultural images we must work to alter. But then again, if the reason many men do not equitably do their share of family labor is that men's jobs are organized so they cannot succeed at work and do their share at home, it is the contemporary American workplace that must change (Williams 2000). We may never find a universal theoretical explanation for the gendered division of household labor because universal social laws may be an illusion of twentieth-century empiricism. But in any given moment for any particular setting, the causal processes should be identifiable empirically. Gender complexity goes beyond historical specificity, as the particular causal processes that constrain men and women to do gender may be strong in one institutional setting (e.g., at home) and weaker in another (e.g., at work).

The forces that create gender traditionalism for men and women may vary across space as well as time. Conceptualizing gender as a social structure contributes to a more postmodern, contextually specific social science. We can use this schema to begin to organize thinking about the causal processes that are most likely to be effective on each dimension. When we are concerned with the means by which individuals come to have a preference to do gender, we should focus on how identities are constructed through early childhood development, explicit socialization, modeling, and adult experiences, paying close attention to the internalization of social mores. To the extent that women and men choose to do gender-typical behavior cross-situationally and over time, we must focus on such individual explanations. Indeed, much attention has already been given to gender socialization and the individualist presumptions for gender. The earliest and perhaps most commonly referred to explanations in popular culture depend on sex-role training, teaching boys and girls their culturally appropriate roles. But when trying to understand gender on the interactional/cultural dimension, the means by which status differences shape expectations and the ways in which in-group and out-group membership influence behavior need to be at the center of attention. Too little attention has been paid to how inequality is shaped by such cultural expectations during interaction. I return to this in the section below. On the institutional dimension, we look to law, organizational practices, and formal regulations that distinguish by sex category. Much progress has been made in the post-civil rights era with rewriting formal laws and organizational practices to ensure gender neutrality. Unfortunately, we have often found that despite changes in gender socialization and gender neutrality on the institutional dimension, gender stratification remains.

What I have attempted to do here is to offer a conceptual organizing scheme for the study of gender that can help us to understand gender in all its complexity and try to isolate the social processes that create gender in each dimension. This is necessary before we can begin to imagine how to change these processes and thus to change the way we socially construct gender. Table 1 provides a schematic outline of this argument.[2]

Cultural Expectations during Interaction and the Stalled Revolution

In *Gender Vertigo* (Risman 1998), I suggested that at this moment in history, gender inequality between partners in American heterosexual couples could be attributed particularly to the interactional expectations at the cultural level: the differential expectations attached to being a mother and father, a husband and wife. Here, I extend this argument in two ways. First, I propose that the stalled gender revolution in other settings can similarly be traced to the interactional/cultural dimension of the social structure. Even when women and men with feminist identities work in organizations with formally gender-neutral rules, gender inequality is reproduced during everyday interaction. The cultural expectations attached to our sex category, simply being identified as a woman or man, has remained relatively impervious to the feminist forces that have problematized sexist socialization practices and legal discrimination. I discuss some of those processes that can help explain why social interaction continues to reproduce inequality, even in settings that seem ripe for social change.

Contemporary social psychological writings offer us a glimpse of possibilities for understanding how inequality is reconstituted in daily interaction. Ridgeway and her colleagues (Ridgeway 1991, 1997, 2001; Ridgeway and Correll 2000; Ridgeway and Smith-Lovin 1999)

Table 1 Dimensions of Gender Structure, by Illustrative Social Processes

		Dimensions of the Gender Structure	
	Individual Level	*Interactional Cultural Expectations*	*Institutional Domain*
Social Processes[a]	Socialization Internalization Identity work Construction of selves	Status expectations Cognitive bias Othering Trading power for patronage Altercasting	Organizational practices Legal regulations Distribution of resources Ideology

[a]These are examples of social processes that may help explain the gender structure on each dimension. They are meant to be illustrative and not a complete list of all possible social processes or causal mechanisms.

showed that the status expectations attached to gender and race categories are cross-situational. These expectations can be thought of as one of the engines that re-create inequality even in new settings where there is no other reason to expect male privilege to otherwise emerge. In a sexist and racist society, women and all persons of color are expected to have less to contribute to task performances than are white men, unless they have some other externally validated source of prestige. Status expectations create a cognitive bias toward privileging those of already high status. What produces status distinction, however, is culturally and historically variable. Thus, cognitive bias is one of the causal mechanisms that help to explain the reproduction of gender and race inequality in everyday life. It may also be an important explanation for the reproduction of class and heterosexist inequality in everyday life as well, but that is an empirical question.

Schwalbe and his colleagues (2000, 419) suggested that there are other "generic interactive processes through which inequalities are created and reproduced in everyday life." Some of these processes include othering, subordinate adaptation, boundary maintenance, and emotion management. Schwalbe and his colleagues suggested that subordinates' adaptation plays an essential role in their own disadvantage. Subordinate adaptation helps to explain women's strategy to adapt to the gender structure. Perhaps the most common adaptation of women to subordination is "trading power for patronage" (Schwalbe et al. 2000, 426). Women, as wives and daughters, often derive significant compensatory benefits from relationships with the men in their families. Stombler and Martin (1994) similarly showed how little sisters in a fraternity trade affiliation for secondary status. In yet another setting, elite country clubs, Sherwood (2004) showed how women accept subordinate status as "B" members of clubs, in exchange for men's approval, and how when a few wives challenge men's privilege, they are threatened with social ostracism, as are their husbands. Women often gain the economic benefits of patronage for themselves and their children in exchange for their subordinate status.

One can hardly analyze the cultural expectations and interactional processes that construct gender inequality without attention to the actions of members of the "dominant group." We must pay close attention to what men do to preserve their power and privilege. Schwalbe et al. (2000) suggested that one process involved is when superordinate groups effectively "other" those who they want to define as subordinate, creating devalued statuses and expectations for them. Men effectively do this in subversive ways through "politeness" norms, which construct women as "others" in need of special favors, such as protection. By opening doors and walking closer to the dirty street, men construct women as an "other" category, different and less than independent autonomous men. The cultural significance attached to male bodies signifies the capacity to dominate, to control, and to elicit deference, and such expectations are perhaps at the core of what it means for men to do gender (Michael Schwalbe, personal communication).

These are only some of the processes that might be identified for understanding how we create gender inequality based on embodied cultural expectations. None are determinative causal predictors, but instead, these are possible leads to reasonable and testable hypotheses about the production of gender. I offer them as part of a conceptual scheme to help us think about how different kinds of processes are implicated at each dimension of the gender structure. Martin's (2003) research on men and women workers in a corporate setting can help illustrate how such a conceptual scheme might work. She wrote about a male vice-president's asking his female counterpart to pick up a phone call, which she does unreflectively, but she soon thereafter identifies this request as problematic. Martin presented this as an example of how interactional status expectations attached to sex category create inequality within professional relationships. This empirical example supports the thesis that shared but routine cultural expectations re-create inequality even without the conscious intent of the actors. Gender structure theory does not presume that this man and woman do not bring gendered selves to the office to accept Martin's analysis. In fact, one might suggest that a vice-president who had more thoroughly internalized traditional femininity norms would not have noticed the inequity at all. Nor does one need to have a company that has purged all discriminatory practices from its policies to see the import of the cultural expectations that Martin identified. A meta-analysis that looks at the effects of gender inequality in the workplace should integrate findings about social processes at the level of individual identities, cultural expectations, and organizational practices. In the next section of this article, I provide empirical illustrations of this conceptual scheme of gender as a social structure.

Empirical Illustrations

I begin with an example from my own work of how conceptualizing gender as a social structure helps to organize the findings and even push forward an understanding of the resistance toward an egalitarian division of family work among contemporary American heterosexual couples. This is an area of research that incorporates a concern with nurturing children, housework, and emotional labor. My own question, from as early as graduate school, was whether men could mother well enough that those who care about children's well-being would want them to do so. Trained in the warfare model of science, my dissertation was a test of structural versus individualist theories (Kanter 1977) of men's mothering. As someone who considered herself a structuralist of some generic sort, I hypothesized (Risman 1983) that when men were forced into the social role of primary parent, they could become just like mothers: The parenting role (e.g., a measure of family structure) would wipe out the effects of individual gendered selves in my models. What I found was, alas, more complicated. At the time, I concluded that men could "mother" but did not do so in ways identical to women (Risman 1983). After having been influenced by studies showing that tokenism worked differently when men were the tokens (Williams 1992; Zimmer 1988) and that money could not buy power in marriage for women quite as it seemed to for men (Brines 1994; Ferree 1990), I came to the realization that gender itself was a structure and would not disappear when men and women were distributed across the variety of structural positions that organize our social world.

To ask the question, Can men mother, presuming that gender itself is a social structure leads us to look at all the ways that gender constrains men's mothering and under what conditions those change. Indeed, one of my most surprising, and unanticipated, findings was that single fathers who were primary caretakers came to describe themselves more often than other men with adjectives such as "nurturant," "warm," and "child oriented," those adjectives we social scientists use to measure femininity. Single fathers' identities changed based on their experiences as primary parents. In my research, men whose wives worked full-time did not, apparently, do enough mothering to have such experiences influence their own sense of selves. Most married fathers hoard the opportunity for leisure that frees them from the responsibilities of parenting that might create such identity change. My questions became more complicated but more useful when I conceptualized gender as a social structure. When and under what conditions do gendered selves matter? When do interactional expectations have the power to overcome previous internalized predispositions? What must change at the institutional level allow for expectations to change at the interactional level? Does enough change on the interactional dimension shift the moral accountability that then leads to collective action in social organizations? Could feminist parents organize and create a social movement that forces workplaces to presume that valuable workers also have family responsibilities?

These questions led me to try to identify the conditions that enable women and men to actually succeed in creating egalitarian relationships. My next research project was an in-depth interview and qualitative study of heterosexual couples raising children who equally shared the work of earning a living and the family labor of child care, homemaking, and emotion work. The first interesting piece of data was how hard it was to find such people in the end of the twentieth century, even when recruiting at daycare centers, parent-teacher associations, university venues, and feminist newsletters (all in the southeastern United States). Three out of four volunteer couples failed the quite generous criteria for inclusion: Working approximately the same number of hours in the labor force (within five hours per week), sharing the household labor and child care tasks within a 60/40 split, and both partners' describing the relationship as equitable. There are clearly fewer couples who live equal lives than those who wish fervently that they did so.

What I did find from intensive interviews and home observations with 20 such couples was that the conditions that enabled their success spread across each dimension of the gender structure. Although I would have predicted otherwise (having once been committed to a purely structural theory of human behavior), selves and personalities matter. The women in my sample were strong, directive women married to relatively laidback men. Given the overwhelming gendered expectations for men's privilege in heterosexual marriage, this should have been expected, but to someone with my theoretical background, it was not. Less surprising to me, the women in these couples also had at least the income and career status of their partners and often bettered them. But this is not usually enough to dent men's privilege, or we would have far more egalitarian marriages by now. In addition, these couples were ideologically committed to equality and to sharing. They often tried explicitly to create social relationships with others who held similar values, for example, by joining liberal churches to meet like-minded others. Atypical gendered selves and shared feminist-inspired cultural expectations were important conditions for equality, but they were not enough. Men's workplace flexibility mattered as well. Nearly every father in this sample was employed in a job with flexible working hours. Many women worked in jobs with flexibility as well, but not as uniformly as their male partners. These were privileged, educated workers for whom workplace flexibility was sometimes simply luck (e.g., a father who lost a corporate job and decided to sell real estate) but more often was a conscious choice (e.g., clinical psychologists choosing to teach at a small college to have more control over working hours despite decreased earning power). Thus, these couples experienced enabling contexts at the level of their individual selves, feminist ideology to help shape the cultural expectations in their most immediate environments (within the dyad and among at least some friends), and the privilege within the economy to have or find flexible jobs. By attending to each dimension of the gender structure, I amassed a more effective explanation for their ability to negotiate fair relationships than I could have without attention to selves, couple interaction, and their workplaces. The implications for feminist social change are direct: We cannot simply attend to socializing children differently, nor creating moral accountability for men to share family work, nor fighting for flexible, family-friendly workplaces. We must attend to all simultaneously.

The research on gender in occupational settings (Williams 1992; Zimmer 1988) and quantitative studies of household division of labor (Brines 1994; Greenstein 2000) also provide good examples of how using gender structure as a conceptual framework can help organize meta-analytic reviews of the literature to create cumulative knowledge. Kanter's (1977) early structural hypotheses presumed that tokenism per se was an important mechanism that explained women's and men of color's continued subordination in the labor force. But as research testing this tokenism hypothesis expanded to include men in women's jobs, it became clear that the theory was not indeed only about numbers. Tokenism did not work the same way for white men. Men tokens rode glass escalators while women and racial minorities hit glass ceilings (Reskin 1998; Williams 1992; Yoder 1991). Gender and race remained important; the cultural interactional expectations remained different even in integrated work settings. Status expectations (Ridgeway 1991; Ridgeway et al. 1998) favored men and devalued women, whatever their numbers. We can conceptualize this as the interactional cultural level impeding further changes that realignments on the institutional dimension would predict.

Similarly, quantitative research findings about the household division of labor have made it quite clear that even when women work outside the home full-time, they shoulder the majority of household and child care. Over time, researchers have tested a variety of theories for why, sometimes presuming that as time pressures and resources equalized between husbands and wives, so too would the burden of household labor (Bianchi et al. 2000; Coverman 1985; Pleck 1985; Presser 1994; Shelton 1992). Not so. The data are unequivocal. Even in dual worker families, women do considerably more work and retain the majority of responsibility, even if they do share (or perhaps delegate) some of the family work to husbands and children. Sociology has provided solid evidence (Fenstermaker Berk 1985; Greenstein 1996, 2000; Robinson and Milkie 1998; Twiggs, McQuillan, and Ferree 1999) that domestic work, whether cleaning toilets or changing diapers, is as much about the production and display of gender as it is about clean toilets and dry bottoms. But such information only gets us so far analytically. We can integrate such research by asking questions about when and how the different effects of the gender structure remain resistant to change and when some progressive feminist change has occurred. Do young women in the twenty-first century, raised by feminists, successfully negotiate fair families? Or does the moral accountability to do gender as mothers and wives combined with devalued status in the workplace still defeat even women socialized for equality? Does workplace flexibility for men allow feminist women more success in their negotiations at the family level? The conceptualization of gender as a structure, and attention to the mechanisms at work in each dimension of the gender structure, helps to frame the kind of research that might answer such queries.

Gender structure theory allows us to try to disentangle the "how" questions without presuming that there is one right answer, for all places, times, and contexts. It is easy to illustrate that a combination of gender wage gap and the organization of careers requiring inflexible hours and full-time commitment pushes married mothers outside the labor force and creates stressful lives for mothers who remain within it, married or not. But we must still ask why this is true for women but not men. Perhaps, under some conditions, women socialized for emphasized femininity do indeed hold themselves accountable for being personally responsible for more than good enough mothering and sparkling households. Research should identify under what conditions and to what extent gendered selves help to account for objective inequalities (e.g., women working more hours a day than their partners) and when other factors are more significant. My own hypothesis is that feminist women are often defeated in their attempt at egalitarian heterosexual relationships by cultural gendered interactional expectations. Within the past year, memoirs have been written by young feminists, academics, and daughters of famous women's movement leaders (Fox 2003; Hanauer 2002) bemoaning the impossible expectations facing career women who choose motherhood as well. Similarly, a recent feminist cyberspace conversation on the Listserve of Sociologists for Women in Society described the struggle to combine motherhood and career in the academy in nearly as despairing a tone as did Arlie Hochschild (1975) in her classic article first published three decades ago. I have yet to see recent memoirs, or hear of painful listserver conversations, among twenty-first-century fathers. Little cultural change has occurred around fathering. Most men are still not morally responsible for the quality of family life, and women have yet to discover how to avoid being held accountable.

Gender structures are even more complicated than my discussion suggests thus far because how gender identities are constructed on the individual and cultural dimensions vary tremendously over time and space. Even within contemporary American society, gender structures vary by community, social class, ethnicity, and race.

Gender Structure and Intersectionality

Perhaps the most important development in feminist thought in the last part of the twentieth century was the increasing concern with intersectionality (Andersen and Collins 1994; Baca Zinn and Thornton Dill 1994; Collins 1990). Women of color had been writing about intersectionality from nearly the start of the second wave of feminist scholarship. It was, however, not until several decades into the women's movement when they were heard and moved from margin closer to center (Myers et al. 1998). There is now considerable consensus growing that one must always take into consideration multiple axes of oppression; to do otherwise presumes the whiteness of women, the maleness of people of color, and the heterosexuality of everyone.

I concur with this consensus that gender must be understood within the context of the intersecting domains of inequality. The balkanization of research and theory into specializations of race or ethnicity or gender or stratification has undermined a sophisticated analysis of inequality (but see Reskin 2002; Schwalbe et al. 2000; Tilly 1999). I do not agree, however, with an operational strategy for scholarship that suggests the appropriate analytic solution is to only work within an intersectionality framework. While various axes of domination are always intersecting, the systems of inequality are not necessarily produced or re-created with identical social processes. The historical and current mechanisms that support gender inequality may or may not be those that are most significant for other kinds of oppression; whether this is the case is an empirical question. Gender research and theory can never again ignore how women's subordination differs within racial and ethnic communities or is constructed within class dynamics. Yet we should not therefore only study gender, race, and class simultaneously. There is a difference between an analysis of psychological, historical, or sociological mechanisms that construct inequality and the subjective experience of the outcomes of such mechanisms. There may be similarity of outcomes (e.g., experiences of oppression) along axes of oppression that arise from different causal mechanisms, but that is an empirical question, not a logical necessity. To focus all investigations into the complexity or subjective experience of interlocking oppressions would have us lose access to how the mechanisms for different kinds of inequality are produced. Feminist scholarship needs a both/and strategy (Collins 1998). We cannot study gender in isolation from other inequalities, nor can we only study inequalities' intersection and ignore the historical and contextual specificity that distinguishes the mechanisms that produce inequality by different categorical divisions, whether gender, race, ethnicity, nationality, sexuality, or class.

Calhoun (2000) exemplifies this both/and strategy in her argument that heterosexism cannot simply be understood as gender oppression and merged into feminist theory. She argued that we must study heterosexism as a separate system of oppression. While it is clearly the case that gender subordination and heterosexism support one another, and a gendered analysis of homophobia is critical, the two oppressions should not be conflated. It is often presumed that Rich's (1980) argument about "compulsory heterosexuality and lesbian existence" suggests that heterosexism is primarily a product of men's dominance, an attempt to ensure sexual access to women by men, and that this is a primary explanation for lesbian oppression.

While this is surely an important component of heterosexism, Calhoun argued that it is a mistake to presume that it is the whole of it. She suggested instead that challenging men's dominance is a necessary condition of ending the subordination of lesbians and gay men but not a sufficient condition to end such oppression. It is important for analytic clarity, and therefore to the scholarly contribution to social change, to identify causal mechanisms for heterosexism and gender oppression distinctly.

Other examples also illustrate the analytic usefulness of paying attention to the distinct properties of different axes of oppression. Gendered images support racial domination, but racial domination can hardly be attributed to gender inequality. For example, Black men's inferiority gets promoted through constructions of hyper-sexuality (Collins 2004), and Black women's inferiority gets promoted through sexualized images such as Jezebel or welfare queen (Collins 2000). Similarly, Asian American men's autonomy and even citizenship rights were abrogated by constructions of effeminacy (Espiritu 1997). Yet it is implausible to argue that racial domination is nothing but a product of gender oppression. While we must pay attention to how axes of oppression affect one another and how the experience of their oppressions are simultaneous, we must continue to study and work to transform each one independently as well as in conjunction with one another.

Each categorical inequality (Tilly 1999) that is deeply embedded in society can be conceptualized as a social structure. Bonilla-Silva (1997) has made this argument persuasively for conceptualizing race as a social structure. He argued that race is a social structure that influences identities and attitudes but is also incorporated into how opportunities and constraints work throughout every societal institution. According to Bonilla-Silva, to conceptualize race as a social structure forces us to move beyond seeing racial inequality as constructed simply by racist attitudes and to understand the ways in which our society embeds white privilege at every level of analysis. I hardly need to argue that class inequality should be conceptualized as a structure as the economic structure of society has long been a primary concern of social scientists. Similarly, political structures have long been studied both at the national and comparative level because here too, politics are routinely considered a basic component of human society. My argument is that race, gender, and sexuality are as equally fundamental to human societies as the economy and the polity. Those inequalities that are fundamentally embedded throughout social life, at the level of individual identities, cultural expectations embedded into interaction, and institutional opportunities and constraints are best conceptualized as structures: The gender structure, the race structure, the class structure, and the sexuality structure. This does not imply that the social forces that produced, nor the causal mechanisms at work in the daily reproduction of inequality within each structure, are of similar strength or type at any given historical moment. For example, gender and race structures extend considerably further into everyday life in the contemporary American context, at home and at work, than does the political structure.[3] I propose this structural language as a tool to help disentangle the means by which inequalities are constructed, recreated, and—it is hoped—transformed or deconstructed. The model for how gender structure works, with consequences for individuals, interactions/cultural expectations, and institutions, can be generalized to the study of other equally embedded inequalities such as race and sexuality. Each structure of inequality exists on its own yet coexists with every other structure of inequality. The subjective experience of actual human beings is always of intersecting inequalities, but the historical construction and contemporary reproduction of inequality on each axis may be distinct. Oppressions can be loosely or tightly coupled, can have both common and distinct generative mechanisms.

Theory Wrestling with Activism

Within any structure of inequality, perhaps the most important question a critical scholar must ask is, What mechanisms are currently constructing inequality, and how can these be transformed to create a more just world? If as critical scholars, we forget to keep our eye on social transformation, we may slip without intention into the implicitly value-free role of social scientists who study gender merely to satisfy intellectual curiosity (Risman 2003). The central questions for feminists must include a focus on social transformation, reducing inequality, and improving the status of women. A concern with social change brings us to the thorny and as yet too little explored issue of agency. When do subordinate groups collectively organize to challenge their oppression? When do superordinate groups mobilize to resist? How do we know agency when we see it, and how can we support feminist versions of it?

Feminist scholarship must seek to understand how and why gender gets done, consciously or not, to help those who hope to stop doing it. I end by focusing our attention on what I see as the next frontier for feminist change agents: A focus on the processes that might spur change at the interactional or cultural dimension of the gender structure. We have begun to socialize our children differently, and while identities are hardly postgender, the sexism inherent in gender socialization is now widely recognized. Similarly, the organizational rules and institutional laws have by now often been rewritten to be gender neutral, at least in some nations. While gender-neutral laws in a gender-stratified society may have short-term negative consequences (e.g., displaced homemakers who never imagined having to support themselves after marriage), we can hardly retreat from equity in the law or organizations. It is the interactional and cultural dimension of gender that have yet to be tackled with a social change agenda.

Cognitive bias is one of the mechanisms by which inequality is re-created in everyday life. There are, however, documented mechanisms for decreasing the salience of such bias (Bielby 2000; Reskin 2000; Ridgeway and Correll 2000). When we consciously manipulate the status expectations attached to those in subordinate groups, by highlighting their legitimate expertise beyond the others in the immediate social setting, we can begin to challenge the nonconscious hierarchy that often goes unnoticed. Similarly, although many subordinates adapt to their situation by trading power for patronage, when they refuse to do so, interaction no longer flows smoothly, and change may result. Surely, when wives refuse to trade power for patronage, they can rock the boat as well as the cradle.

These are only a few examples of interactive processes that can help to explain the reproduction of inequality and to envision strategies for disrupting inequality. We need to understand when and how inequality is constructed and reproduced to deconstruct it. I have argued before (Risman 1998) that because the gender structure so defines the category woman as subordinate, the deconstruction of the category itself is the best, indeed the only sure way, to end gender subordination. There is no reason, except the transitional vertigo that will accompany the process to dismantle it, that a utopian vision of a just world involves any gender structure at all. Why should we need to elaborate on the biological distinction between the sexes? We must accommodate reproductive differences for the process of biological replacement, but there is no a priori reason we should accept any other role differentiation simply based on biological sex category. Before accepting any gender elaboration around biological sex category, we ought to search suspiciously for the possibly subtle ways such differentiation supports men's privilege. Once two salient groups exist, the process of in-group and out-group distinctions and in group opportunity hoarding become possible. While it may be that for some competitive sports, single-sex teams are necessary, beyond that, it seems unlikely that any differentiation or cultural elaboration around sex category has a purpose beyond differentiation in support of stratification.

Feminist scholarship always wrestles with the questions of how one can use the knowledge we create in the interest of social transformation. As feminist scholars, we must talk beyond our own borders. This kind of theoretical work becomes meaningful if we can eventually take it public. Feminist sociology must be public sociology (Burawoy forthcoming). We must eventually take what we have learned from our theories and research beyond professional journals to our students and to those activists who seek to disrupt and so transform gender relations. We must consider how the knowledge we create can help those who desire a more egalitarian social world to refuse to do gender at all, or to do it with rebellious reflexiveness to help transform the world around them. For those without a sociological perspective, social change through socialization and through legislation are the easiest to envision. We need to shine a spotlight on the dimension of cultural interactional expectations as it is here that work needs to begin.

We must remember, however, that much doing gender at the individual and interactional levels gives pleasure as well as reproduces inequality, and until we find other socially acceptable means to replace that opportunity for pleasure, we can hardly advocate for its cessation. The question of how gender elaboration has been woven culturally into the fabric of sexual desire deserves more attention. Many of our allies believe that "viva la difference" is required for sexual passion, and few would find a postgender society much of a feminist utopia if it came at the cost of sexual play. No one wants to be part of a revolution where she or he cannot dirty dance.

In conclusion, I have made the argument that we need to conceptualize gender as a social structure, and by doing so, we can analyze the ways in which gender is embedded at the individual, interactional, and institutional dimensions of our society. This situates gender at the same level of significance as the economy and the polity. In addition, this framework helps us to disentangle the relative strength of a variety of causal mechanisms for explaining any given outcome without dismissing the possible relevance of other processes that are situated at different dimensions of analysis. Once we have a conceptual tool to organize the encyclopedic research on gender, we can systematically build on our knowledge and progress to understanding the strength and direction of causal processes within a complicated multidimensional recursive theory. I have also argued that our concern with intersectionality must continue to be paramount but that different structures of inequality have different infrastructure and perhaps different influential causal mechanisms at any given historical moment. Therefore, we need to follow a both/and strategy, to understand gender structure, race structure, and other structures of inequality as they currently operate, while also systematically paying attention to how these axes of domination intersect. Finally, I have suggested that we pay more attention to doing research and writing theory with explicit attention to how our work can come to be "fighting words" (Collins 1998) to help transform as well as inform society. If we can identify the mechanisms that create gender, perhaps we can offer alternatives to them and so use our scholarly work to contribute to envisioning a feminist utopia.

Author's Note: There are too many scholars who have read this work and helped to improve it to thank each and every one. I do owe a great deal to the feminist intellectual community of Sociologists for Women in Society. Special thanks are due to Shannon Davis, Patricia Yancey Martin, Michael Schwalbe, Donald Tomaskovic-Devey, and the students in my 2003 and 2004 graduate seminars in sociology of the family, sociology of gender, and feminist thought. All of them have helped improve my argument, but of course I alone remain responsible for the content, flaws and all.

Reprint Requests: Barbara J. Risman, North Carolina State University, Department of Sociology, Raleigh, NC 27695–8107.

Notes

1. See Scott (1997) for a critique of feminists who adopt a strategy where theories have to be simplified, compared, and defeated. She too suggested a model where feminists build on the complexity of each others' ideas.

2. I thank my colleague Donald Tomaskovic-Devey for suggesting the visual representation of these ideas as well as his usual advice on my ideas as they develop.

3. One can certainly imagine a case where political structures extend far into everyday life, a nation in the midst of civil war or in the grips of a fascist state. One can also envision a case when race retreats to the personal dimension, as when the Irish became white in twentieth-century America.

References

Andersen, Margaret, and Patricia Hill Collins. 1994. *Race, class, and gender: An anthology.* Belmont, CA: Wadsworth.

Baca Zinn, Maxine, and Bonnie Thornton Dill. 1994. *Women of color in U.S. society.* Philadelphia: Temple University Press.

Bern, Sandra. 1993. *The lenses of gender.* New Haven, CT: Yale University Press.

Bianchi, Suzanne M., Melissa A. Milkie, Liana C. Sayer, and John P. Robinson. 2000. Is anyone doing the housework? Trends in the gender division of household labor. *Social Forces* 79 (1): 191–228.

Bielby, William T. 2000. Minimizing workplace gender and racial bias. *Contemporary Sociology* 29 (1): 120–29.

Blau, Peter. 1977. *Inequality and heterogeneity.* New York: Free Press.

Bonilla-Silva, Eduardo. 1997. Rethinking racism: Toward a structural interpretation. *American Sociological Review* 62 (3): 465–80.

Brines, Julie. 1994. Economic dependency, gender, and the division of labor at home. *American journal of Sociology* 100 (3): 652–88.

Burawoy, Michael. Forthcoming. Public sociologies contradictions, dilemmas and possibilities. *Social Forces.*

Burt, Ronald S. 1982. *Toward a structural theory of action.* New York: Academic Press.

Calhoun, Cheshire. 2000. *Feminism, the family, and the politics of the closet: Lesbian and gay displacement.* New York: Oxford University Press.

Collins, Patricia Hill. 1990. *Black feminist thought: Knowledge, consciousness, and the politics of empowerment.* New York: Routledge.

———. 1998. *Fighting words: Black women and the search for justice.* Minneapolis: University of Minnesota Press.

———. 2004. *Black sexual politics: African Americans, gender, and the new racism.* New York: Routledge.

Connell, R. W. 1987. *Gender and power: Society, the person, and sexual politics.* Stanford, CA: Stanford University Press.

———. 2002. *Gender: Short introductions.* Malden, MA: Blackwell.

Coverman, Shelley. 1985. Explaining husbands' participation in domestic labor. *Sociological Quarterly* 26 (1): 81–97.

England, Paula, and Irene Browne. 1992. Internalization and constraint in women's subordination. *Current Perspectives in Social Theory* 12:97–123.

Espiritu, Yen Le. 1997. *Asian American women and men: Labor, laws, and love.* Thousand Oaks, CA: Sage.

Fenstermaker Berk, Sarah. 1985. *The gender factory: The apportionment of work in American households.* New York: Plenum.

Ferree, Myra Marx. 1990. Beyond separate spheres: Feminism and family research. *Journal of Marriage and the Family* 53 (4): 866–84.

Ferree, Myra Marx, Judith Lorber, and Beth Hess. 1999. *Revisioning gender.* Thousand Oaks, CA: Sage.

Fox, Faulkner. 2003. *Dispatches from a not-so-perfect Life: On how I learned to love the house, the man, the child.* New York: Harmony Books.

Fuchs Epstein, Cynthia. 1988. *Deceptive distinctions: Sex, gender, and the social order.* New Haven, CT: Yale University Press.

Giddens, Anthony. 1984. *The constitution of society: Outline of the theory of structuration.* Berkeley: University of California Press.

Greenstein, Theodore N. 1996. Husbands' participation in domestic labor: Interactive effects of wives' and husbands' gender ideologies. *Journal of Marriage and the Family* 58: 585–95.

———. 2000. Economic dependence, gender, and the division of labor in the home: A replication and extension. *Journal of Marriage and the Family* 62 (2): 322–35.

Hanauer, Cathi. 2002. *The bitch in the house: 26 women tell the truth about sex, solitude, work, motherhood, and marriage.* New York: William Morrow.

Hochschild, Arlie. 1975. Inside the clockwork of male careers. In *Women and the power to change,* edited by Florence Howe. New York: McGraw Hill. Repr. in *The commercialization of intimate life.* Berkeley: University of California Press, 2003.

Kanter, Rosabeth. 1977. *Men and women of the corporation.* New York: Basic Books.

Lorber, Judith. 1994. *Paradoxes of gender.* New Haven, CT: Yale University Press.

Martin, Patricia. 2003. "Said and done" versus "saying and doing": Gendering practices, practicing gender at work. *Gender & Society* 17:342–66.

———. Forthcoming. Gender as a social institution. *Social Forces.*

Myers, Kristen A., Cynthia D. Anderson, and Barbara J. Risman, eds. 1998. *Feminist foundations: Toward transforming society.* Thousand Oaks, CA: Sage.

Pleck, Joseph H. 1985. *Working wives/working husbands.* Beverly Hills, CA: Sage.

Presser, Harriet B. 1994. Employment schedules among dual-earner spouses and the division of household labor by gender. *American Sociological Review* 59 (3): 348–64.

Reskin, Barbara. 1998. *The realities of affirmative action in employment.* Washington, DC: ASA.

———. 2000. The proximate causes of employment discrimination. *Contemporary Sociology* 29 (2): 319–28.

———. 2002. How did the poison get in Mr. Bartlett's stomach? Motives and mechanisms in explaining inequality. Presidential address given at the 97th annual meetings of the American Sociological Association, Chicago, August.

Rich, Adrienne. 1980. Compulsory heterosexuality and lesbian existence. *Signs: Journal of Women in Culture and Society* 5 (4): 631–60.

Ridgeway, Cecilia L. 1991. The social construction of status value: Gender and other nominal characteristics. *Social Forces* 70 (2): 367–86.

———. 1997. Interaction and the conservation of gender inequality: Considering employment. *American Sociological Review* 62 (2): 218–35.

———. 2001. Gender, status, and leadership. *Journal of Social Issues* 57 (4): 637–55.

Ridgeway, Cecilia L., and Shelley J. Correll. 2000. Limiting inequality through interaction: The end(s) of gender. *Contemporary Sociology* 29:110–20.

Ridgeway, Cecilia L., Kathy J. Kuipers, Elizabeth Heger Boyle, and Dawn T. Robinson. 1998. How do status beliefs develop? The role of resources and interactional experience. *American Sociological Review* 63:331–50.

Ridgeway, Cecilia L., and Lynn Smith-Lovin. 1999. The gender system and interaction. *Annual Review of Sociology* 25:191–216.

Risman, Barbara J. 1983. Necessity and the invention of mothering. Ph.D. diss, University of Washington.

———. 1987. Intimate relationships from a microstructural perspective: Mothering men. *Gender & Society* 1:6–32.

———. 1998. *Gender vertigo: American families in transition.* New Haven, CT: Yale University Press.

———. 2003. Valuing all flavors of feminist sociology. *Gender & Society* 17:659–63.

Risman, Barbara J., and Pepper Schwartz. 1989. *Gender in intimate relationships.* Belmont, CA: Wadsworth.

Robinson, John P., and Melissa A. Milkie. 1998. Back to the basics: Trends in and role determinants of women's attitudes toward housework. *Journal of Marriage and the Family* 60 (1): 205–18.

Rytina, Steve, Peter Blau, Jenny Blum, and Joseph Schwartz. 1988. Inequality and intermarriage: Paradox of motive and constraint. *Social Forces* 66:645–75.

Schwalbe, Michael, Sandra Godwin, Daphne Holden, Douglas Schrock, Shealy Thompson, and Michele Wolkomir. 2000. Generic processes in the reproduction of inequality: An interactionist analysis. *Social Forces* 79 (2): 419–52.

Scott, Joan Wallach. 1997. Comment on Hawkesworth's "Confounding Gender." *Signs: Journal of Women in Culture and Society* 22 (3): 697–702.

Shelton, Beth Anne. 1992. *Women, men and time: Gender differences in paid work, housework and leisure.* Westport, CT: Greenwood.

Sherwood, Jessica. 2004. Talk about country clubs: Ideology and the reproduction of privilege. Ph.D. diss., North Carolina State University.

Smelser, Neil J. 1988. Social structure. In *Handbook of sociology,* edited by Neil J. Smelser. Beverly Hills, CA: Sage.

Staples, Robert. 1990. Social inequality and Black sexual pathology: The essential relationship. *Black Scholar* 21 (3): 29–37.

Stombler, Mindy, and Patricia Yancey Martin. 1994. Bring women in, keeping women down: Fraternity "little sister" organizations. *Journal of Contemporary Ethnography* 23: 150–84.

Tilly, Charles. 1999. *Durable inequality.* Berkeley: University of California Press.

Twiggs, Joan E., Julia McQuillan, and Myra Marx Ferree. 1999. Meaning and measurement: Reconceptualizing measures of the division of household labor. *Journal of Marriage and the Family* 61 (3): 712–24.

Udry, J. Richard. 2000. Biological limits of gender construction. *American Sociological Review* 65:443–57.

West, Candace, and Don Zimmerman. 1987. Doing gender. *Gender & Society* 1: 125–51.

Williams, Christine. 1992. The glass escalator: Hidden advantages for men in the "female" professions. *Social Problems* 39:253–67.

Williams, Joan. 2000. *Unbending gender: Why family and work conflict and what to do about it.* New York: Oxford University Press.

Yoder, Janice. 1991. Rethinking tokenism. *Social Problems* 5:178–92.

Zimmer, Lynn. 1988. Tokenism and women in the workplace: The limits of gender-neutral theory. *Social Problems* 35:64–77.

Barbara J. Risman is Alumni Distinguished Research Professor of Sociology at North Carolina State University. She studies gender in intimate and family relationships. She is the author of Gender Vertigo: American Families in Transition *(1998, Yale University Press). She also edits* The Gender Lens *book series with Judith Howard and Joey Sprague, designed to transform the discipline of sociology by mainstreaming a gender perspective throughout the curriculum. She is past president of Sociologists for Women in Society and is currently co-chair of the Council on Contemporary Families. Her current research focuses on gender and sexual ideology among teenagers.*

27 Introduction: Centering Sexual Orientation Politics

Cheshire Calhoun

This book is devoted to two different but interrelated questions about centering sexual orientation politics. The first is the question of the extent to which lesbian theorizing occupies the center of feminist theorizing about women. In raising this first question, my aim is to unsettle the comfortable assumption that because feminist thought is about women, and because so much of existing lesbian theorizing has been conducted within a feminist frame, lesbians are already securely at the center of feminist theory in a way in which women of color or poor and working class women have not been. I will suggest instead that the specifically lesbian features of lesbian lives persistently slip from view in feminist theory. In order to keep lesbian specificity in view, feminist theorizing needs to give up the idea that heterosexism is nothing but a byproduct of sexism; and it needs to work out the basic structure of lesbian and gay subordination.

The second question is the question of what the political center of lesbian and gay liberatory activity should be. In raising this second question, I aim to unsettle the common assumption that lesbian and gay politics should be centered first around combating the socio-legal structures that regulate sexual activity and second around securing protection against the material costs of discriminatory practices. Prioritizing challenges to sexual regulations makes sense if one assumes that gays and lesbians are primarily stigmatized for their sexual object choice. I will suggest instead that the stigma of being lesbian or gay emerges from a century's worth of constructing the identities 'lesbian' and 'homosexual' as types of persons whose deviancies are not limited to sexual object choice. Looking at the multiple deviancies attributed to lesbians and gays suggests that marriage and family issues need special priority in a lesbian and gay politics. The second standard goal of lesbian and gay politics—securing protection against the material costs of discriminatory practices—makes sense if one assumes that lesbian and gay subordination directly parallels race and gender oppression. I will argue that it does not because gays and lesbians can largely evade the material costs of discrimination. This does not necessarily mean that pursuing anti-discrimination protection should not be central to lesbian and gay politics. What it does mean is that we need a better account of why that protection is so important.

Reprinted from *Feminism, the Family, and the Politics of the Closet: Lesbian and Gay Displacement* (2003), by permission of Oxford University Press.

In this chapter, I simply want to lay out some of the groundwork for later chapters. Later chapters will focus on specific ways that feminist scholarship drops lesbians from view—even while talking about lesbians. Later chapters will also focus on the specific shape of lesbian and gay subordination. Here, I want to defend the general methodological strategy of treating lesbian and gay subordination as a distinct axis of oppression that intersects with gender, race, and class axes of oppression. Readers unfamiliar with lesbian feminist work may find this puzzling. Surely it is obvious that gays and lesbians are penalized specifically on the basis of their sexual orientation. Does this not imply that heterosexism differs from sexism and classism and racism? Well, yes and no. Lesbian feminist theorists recognize that lesbians (and gay men) suffer a distinctive set of social penalties; but they also typically trace those penalties back to gender oppression and regard homophobia and heterosexism as just one among many specific ways that sexism gets enacted. Section I of this chapter lays out the general arguments for *not* treating heterosexism as simply one among many byproducts of gender oppression.

Section II introduces what I take to be the two central features of lesbian and gay subordination. First, the principal, damaging effect of a heterosexist system is that it *displaces* lesbians and gays from both the public and private spheres of civil society so that lesbians and gays have no legitimated social location, not even a disadvantaged one. Second, the principal ideologies rationalizing lesbian and gay displacement are: (1) that there are two and only two natural and normal sex/genders, (2) that lesbian and gay sexuality is excessive, compulsive, and disconnected from romantic love, and (3) that for a variety of reasons lesbians and gays are fundamentally unfit for marital and familial life. Throughout this book, my analyses of lesbian and gay subordination include remarkably little mention of *sex*. This may strike readers as odd. Lesbianism and homosexuality are, after all, *sexual* orientations, and lesbians and gays are socially penalized because what they do sexually is thought by many to be pathological or immoral. Later chapters will, in quite specific ways, take issue with this idea that gay and lesbian subordination emerges straightforwardly out of cultural aversion to same-sex sexual activity and desires. Here, I simply want to introduce the idea that lesbianism and homosexuality are stigmatized sexualities because of the way that same-sex sexuality has been culturally connected to other, more deeply stigmatizing characteristics.

My approach throughout this book is a social constructionist one. That is, in order to understand the nature of lesbian and gay subordination, I think it is crucial to work from a detailed description of our dominant cultural understanding of what it means to have a lesbian or gay identity. I conclude this chapter, in Section III, with some general remarks on how this book fits into the essentialist-constructionist controversy.

I. Feminism and Lesbian Theory

Of all liberatory academic discourses, feminist thought has been the most self-critical. Feminists have been acutely and distinctively alive to the risk of producing theories that, while ostensibly about women generally, are in fact tacitly about only the most privileged women. Very early in the history of second wave feminism, black women objected to feminism's failure to problematize the relation between black and white women, to invoke the experience of black women as the ground of theory construction, and to orient feminist politics around anything except those issues that were most salient to middle class white women. Black feminists insisted that feminist theorizing, if it hoped to be genuinely about all women, needed to move issues of race and class from the margins to the center.[1] This required making a key shift in feminist methodology. First wave and early second wave feminism approached the analysis of women's situation through the lens of a single system of oppression—gender oppression. Because analyses that focused only on gender relations in fact dropped women of color and poor and working class women out of the picture, taking a different methodological tack seemed warranted. The most promising methodological strategy for bringing nonwhite and nonmiddle class women from the margins to the center was to move away from an exclusive focus on only one system of oppression—gender oppression—and to begin thinking in terms of multiple, interlocking systems of oppression. The key shift in feminist method, then, was to begin from the assumption that there are multiple, conceptually distinct systems of oppression that in actual social arrangements intersect to produce race and class-specific experiences of gender oppression. Theorizing that attends to the *intersections* of conceptually distinct systems of oppression became, and continues to be, at least the regulative ideal of contemporary feminist work even if race and class issues often continue in practice to occupy the margins of feminist work.

Lesbians of all races and economic classes could have voiced a parallel complaint and pushed a parallel methodological solution. Both first wave and second wave feminism were conducted from a specifically heterosexual viewpoint. The relation between heterosexual and nonheterosexual women was not problematized. Heterosexual women's experience, and not lesbians' experience, provided the ground for theory construction. And feminist politics were virtually exclusively centered around those issues that were most pressing for heterosexual women, such as educational and employment discrimination on the basis of sex, inadequate access to contraception and abortion, gender dominance within heterosexual intimate relations, and heterosexual pornography. The marginalization of lesbians within feminist thought might naturally have been thought to be a product of exactly the same problematic methodology that marginalized black women—the exclusive focus on gender oppression. And the solution might naturally have been thought to be the same—a shift to thinking about the ways that gender oppression intersects with a conceptually distinct system of lesbian and gay subordination. None of this in fact happened. This is not to say that lesbian feminists have never protested heterosexual bias in feminist work. It is, however, to say that that protest had a distinctively different character. Black feminists protested by emphasizing their *difference* from white, middle class feminists. Lesbian feminists, particularly of the 1980s, protested by emphasizing the potential *commonalities* or continuum between lesbians' and heterosexual feminists' experience, especially their valorization of woman-loving and their resistance to compulsory heterosexual interaction with men. Black feminists protested by underscoring the racial and class *biases* encoded in dominant feminist theorizing. Lesbian feminists protested by underscoring the *incompleteness* of dominant feminist theorizing's resistance to gender oppression when it failed to call into question heterosexuality itself. Black feminists took the problem with feminist theorizing to be both methodological and social. Methodologically, feminist theorizing was too narrowly focused on only one system of oppression; and the narrow focus was itself a product of many feminist theorists' racism and classism. Lesbian feminists took the problem to be neither methodological nor particularly social. If lesbians were at the margins of feminist theorizing it was only because feminists had not extended their analyses of gender oppression far enough; and it was not heterosexual feminists' heterosexism that barred them from doing so as much as it was simply an uncritical adoption of cultural ideology about the naturalness and immutability of one's sexual orientation. In short, the marginal position of lesbians was not taken to be problematic for feminism in the way that the marginal position of women of color and poor and working class women was.

I think this was a mistake. One of my central aims in this book is to argue that specifically lesbian oppression cannot be either adequately described or politically addressed without a shift in methodology. In particular, lesbian and gay subordination needs to be taken as a conceptually distinct axis of oppression that intersects with systems of gender, race, and class oppression. . . . If what is needed in order to bring lesbians from margin to center in feminist theorizing is attention to lesbian and gay subordination as a separate axis of oppression, then we will need an account of the basic contours of that axis of oppression.

Because so much of this book is devoted to the thesis that lesbian and gay subordination is not simply a byproduct of male dominance, but is itself a separate system of oppression, it is worthwhile saying a bit more about this claim. What do I mean when I refer to a 'separate' axis of oppression? Why has it generally been thought to be unnecessary to describe heterosexism (lesbian and gay subordination) as a separate axis? Why is it methodologically important to treat heterosexism as a separate axis?

What distinguishes oppression or subordination from merely unequal treatment in a particular sphere is by now fairly well articulated. 'Oppression' and 'subordination' refer to social systems. One cannot claim to be oppressed simply because one is treated in a disadvantagingly unequal way in a particular sphere of human activity. Men, for example, cannot claim to be oppressed simply because they are not given equal priority in child custody decisions. Nor can students claim to be oppressed simply because they are not granted equal academic freedom with professors. Both treatments may be wrong or unfair, but this fact by itself does not make the treatment oppressive or subordinating in the sense in which racist or sexist treatment is oppressive or subordinating. Oppression and subordination depend on the cultural articulation of basic social identities that are taken to be: (a) relatively or completely immutable features of persons, (b) determinative of their psychological, moral, physical, and intellectual capacities, and (c) in polar opposition to an Other identity where polarity of evaluation (good-bad, respectable-unrespectable, superior-inferior, natural-unnatural) is central. Such identities are basic in the sense that they serve as the basis for a systematic organization of social life and social relations. And it is organization of a particular sort. An interlocking set of practices based on the assumption that one social type is deficient in relation to its polar Other produces a pervasive reduction of one group's political status, self-determination, life chances, resources, physical safety, and control over cultural products.[2] These interlocking practices also produce pervasive and important benefits, privileges, and liberties for the other social group. For a variety of reasons, oppressive systems are extremely difficult to intervene in. One obvious reason is that they are systems. Men's right of sexual access to women, for instance, is encoded in dating and marital practices, advertising images, pornography, prostitution, women's responsibility for pregnancy, and the like. Piecemeal or quick-fix efforts to address oppression, such as censoring pornography, are thus unlikely to have a substantial effect. The importance and scope of benefits accruing to the dominant group also produce a vested, if often unconscious, interest in preserving the system. Thus, attempts to intervene in oppressive systems often result in oppression taking new forms rather than in an overall reduction of oppression itself. For instance, affirmative action policies aimed at increasing racial minorities' access to professional occupations, while in fact making those occupations more accessible, have also been used in cultural discourse to reaffirm basic social beliefs about black inferiority and inability to compete on their own merits. Finally, because oppression is connected to the way that we view our most basic social identities and most fundamental ways of organizing social life, oppressive systems generate ideologies about the naturalness, divine authorization, and scientific validity of differential treatment. This works both against seeing that oppression is taking place at all and against justifying alternative, less oppressive arrangements.

Although accounts of oppression along these lines are now commonplace, what is not commonplace are criteria for *individuating* systems of oppression.[3] That gender, race, and class are connected to separate systems of oppression is, more often than not, treated as an obvious fact. Their assumed separability provides the *starting* point for analyses that then look at their intersection. Once we move beyond these three systems, it becomes much less clear how we are to go about counting systems of oppression. Heterosexism occupies a particularly problematic place. On the one hand, heterosexism looks very much like a free standing system of oppression. Heterosexism is an interlocking set of practices built on the distinction between what appear to be basic identities—heterosexual versus gay and lesbian—whose effect is the pervasive reduction of lesbian and gay life chances, self-determination, political status, physical safety, and control over cultural products. On the other hand, heterosexism looks very much like a *component* of gender oppression. Heterosexism appears to be part of a broader array of interlocking practices built on the distinction between the identities 'man' and 'woman'. The social penalties visited upon lesbians and gay men for their gender and sexual deviance appear to be simply a special case of the systematic penalization of *anyone* who departs from the gender and sexual norms that support male dominance and female oppression. Are heterosexism and sexism two systems or one, the one being gender oppression?

I am not sure what a conclusive answer to this question would look like. I do, however, think there are good conceptual and pragmatic arguments for treating sexism and heterosexism as two separate systems.

One might begin with a thought experiment. Imagine a society that is not structured around male dominance. It might be a society that draws no gender distinctions but still emphasizes male–female sexual differences. Or it might be a society that draws masculine-feminine gender distinctions but either inverts our evaluative order (so that the society is female-dominant) or treats the two genders as equal though different. Could that society have a stringent taboo on homosexuality and lesbianism? Could social practices and social relations be systematically structured around heterosexuality? Could those practices work pervasively to the detriment of lesbians and gays and to the benefit of heterosexuals? It seems to me that the answer to all three questions is yes. Heterosexism would, of course, have to take a quite different form. The very notions of heterosexuality, lesbianism, and homosexuality would have to be socially constructed differently. In a gender-undifferentiated society, for example, gender deviance could not occupy a central role in what it means to be homosexual as it does in our society; and in a gender-inverted society, being lesbian would likely be more severely penalized than being gay. But in principle there seems to be no more reason to deny that one could have heterosexism in a gender-egalitarian society than to deny that one could have racism in a gender-egalitarian society.

What may make it tempting to say that there could not be heterosexism without sexism is that it is hard to see what the *point* of heterosexism would be if it were not aimed at preserving the gender distinctions and sexual relations that support male dominance. Gayle Rubin's early piece, 'The Traffic in Women,' is useful in clarifying what that point might be.[4] There, she argued that the sex/gender system gets off the ground when a society installs the male–female couple as the most basic economic unit. A sexual division of labor within the household makes the male–female couple more economically viable. That sexual division of labor, however, depends on producing differently gendered types of persons who are suited to assume their particular labor. Anatomical sex difference is thus turned into gender difference. A sex/gender system that depends on the male–female couple as the foundational social and economic unit will also need to construct strong taboos against lesbianism and homosexuality. Although Rubin adds to her account an explanation of how the sex/gender system comes to be male-dominant (namely, through the traffic in women to establish new kinship relations), the taboo on same-sex sexuality is, in her account, not *essentially* connected to male dominance. Thus, heterosexism is not essentially connected to sexism. *Any* society, even a gender-egalitarian one, that makes the male–female couple foundational will be one in which stigmatizing lesbianism and homosexuality has a point.

Heterosexism can, of course, have more than one point. I do not mean to deny that heterosexism plays a substantial role in sustaining male dominance. I do mean to assert that this is not the only possible point heterosexism might have. . . .

The possibility of heterosexism serving multiple points undercuts one very tempting argument against treating heterosexism as a separate system of oppression. That argument begins from the observation that heterosexism serves male dominance and concludes that heterosexism is *nothing but* a byproduct of male dominance. Consider, for example, Andrienne Rich's ground-breaking piece, 'Compulsory Heterosexuality and Lesbian Existence'. There, Rich argued that heterosexuality is not clearly a natural orientation for women.[5] It is, instead, systematically enforced through a wide variety of practices that make women sexually accessible to men and that conceal and penalize the lesbian option. It is thus a mistake for feminists, particularly heterosexual feminists, to treat a heterosexual orientation simply as a natural fact outside the scope of feminist political critique. Practices that enforce male right of sexual access to women, including the taboo on lesbianism, constitute the center of women's oppression. Given the central role that heterosexism plays in all women's oppression, including the specific subordination of lesbians, it is then tempting to conclude that heterosexism is nothing but a product of male dominance. The inference, however, does not follow. What Rich's argument shows is only that challenging male dominance is, in our own society, a *necessary* condition for eliminating the subordination of lesbians and gay men.[6] That is, lesbians and gay men cannot interrupt the system that subordinates them unless they adopt a broadly feminist agenda. The argument does not, however, show that eliminating gender oppression is *sufficient* for liberating lesbians and gays. This is because the male right of sexual access may not be the only driving force behind heterosexism. Thus, the claim that there is only one system of oppression (gender oppression) rather than two (gender and sexual orientation oppression) cannot be established simply by showing that heterosexism and male dominance are interconnected. To establish a single system one would have to show, in addition, that there is no other possible basis for the extensive social control of lesbians and gays. In particular, one would have to argue that heterosexual women and men, as a class, do not derive benefits from lesbian and gay subordination that are of sufficient magnitude to motivate the transformation, rather than elimination, of heterosexist practices were gender equality to be achieved.

Two analogies with feminist thinking about class and race are useful here. Consider, first, the history of specifically Marxist theorizing about women's oppression. Marx and Engels, and subsequently second wave Marxist feminists, tried to argue that women's oppression is a byproduct of oppressive economic class relations. Fairly early on in second wave feminism, the defects of this approach became apparent. Why think that women would automatically be liberated through the elimination of economic classes or that their oppression would be reduced in tandem with improved, more egalitarian worker conditions? After all, within a single class, women are subordinate to men. Moreover, the benefits to men of male dominance are sufficiently great that it seems more reasonable to suppose that male dominance is independently motivated and is more likely to simply undergo transformation rather than elimination were more egalitarian economic relations established. Finally, in fact, improved economic conditions, such as the family wage, worked in favor of male dominance rather than undercutting it.[7] Thus, as Heidi Hartmann has argued, even if capitalism and patriarchy often work together in such a way that one can show how capitalism contributes to male dominance, it does not follow that capitalism and patriarchy are not two separate systems. Just as it behooved feminists to ask whether their interests were being adequately advanced by Marxist class critiques, it behooves lesbians to ask whether their interests are being adequately advanced by feminist gender critiques. A central aim of this book is to open up the critical space for asking and beginning to answer that question.

Turning now to the second analogy, consider how inflected with gender the images and practices are that support racial dominance. Black men's inferiority, for example, gets promoted through constructions of black men as both hypersexual and thus threateningly excessive embodiments of masculinity and as emasculated within the family by unfemininely strong black women. Our conception of racial differences is so heavily inflected with images drawn from the domain of gender oppression that it is difficult to imagine what a construction of racial difference would look like absent gender-subordinating images. However, it seems obviously implausible to argue that because one can give a gender analysis of racially subordinating practices and stereotypes, racial oppression is *nothing but* a byproduct of gender oppression. Even if gender readings of racist practices are possible, those readings do not exhaust the content of racist practices. By the same token, it does not follow from the fact that much of lesbian and gay experience can be analyzed through the lens of gender oppression that one cannot also give an analysis through the lens of lesbian and gay subordination. It is thus methodologically important to resist 'nothing but' inferences of the form 'Lesbians and gay men are socially penalized for their gender insubordination, therefore heterosexism is nothing but a form of gender oppression'. This may be true. Its truth, however, is not established by the fact that one can give a gender analysis of lesbian and gay experience.

So far, I have been trying to establish one simple conceptual point. It is a negative one. The possibility that sexual orientation subordination is a separate axis of oppression cannot be ruled out simply by showing that heterosexism and male dominance are connected. Let me now turn to more positive methodological and pragmatic arguments for employing the assumption that lesbian and gay subordination and gender oppression are two separate axes of oppression. In particular, I want to forestall the objection that any attempt to isolate lesbian and gay subordination from gender oppression is methodologically a bad idea, because in social practice, different systems of oppression do not operate independently of one another; they are interpenetrating.

It is certainly true that in actual social practice and experience, different systems of oppression do not operate entirely separately. Racial dominance of east Asians, for example, gets played out via gender images of east Asian men as effeminate and thus inferior in relation to Caucasian men; it also gets played out via sexual orientation images of east Asian men as questionably heterosexual and thus deficient in relation to Caucasian men. Taunting east Asian men with the jeer 'faggot' thus simultaneously invokes systems of race, gender, and sexual orientation dominance.[8] Neither the specific experiences of oppression suffered by some particular people nor the full meaning of specific social practices can be adequately analyzed without bringing to bear an understanding of multiple systems of oppression. It would thus seem that it is methodologically a bad idea to try to specify lesbian and gay oppression in abstraction from race, gender, and class oppression. The particular experiences of particular people are not fully describable in terms of a single system of oppression.

At one level, this is absolutely right. An exhaustive socially critical analysis of any particular experience of oppression or any particular subordinating social practice cannot be done without invoking multiple systems of oppression. Some care, however, needs to be taken in what we infer from this. It does not mean that racial dominance has no specificity apart from class dominance or that heterosexual dominance could not have any specificity apart from gender dominance. That is, it does not follow from the fact that multiple systems of oppression converge to give particular practices a complex texture of meaning that one cannot *conceptually* distinguish racial dominance from gender dominance from sexual orientation dominance. Nor does it follow that there is no good methodological reason for doing so.

One might think about the possibility and point of conceptually distinguishing separate systems on analogy with that of distinguishing conceptually distinct features of good writing. A good piece of writing is one that at the least is grammatical, has no spelling errors, does not mix metaphors, is clear, and has some narrative or logical order. In any piece of writing, these desiderata do not occur separately. Any one paragraph is likely to satisfy a number of the criteria for good writing. The fact that this is so, however, does not make it impossible to point out which of the criteria are being satisfied where and how. Good grammar may be used in clear prose, indeed may be essential to it; but good grammar and clear prose remain conceptually separable features of a piece of writing.

By the same token, for any particular social practice or experience of oppression where multiple systems of oppression are at work, we can point out those features that make the experience or practice racist, sexist, classist, and so on. Consider, for example, what Patricia Hill Collins has called 'controlling images' of black women—the mammy, the matriarch, the Jezebel, and the welfare mother.[9] Without denying that these are racist images, we can say a lot about what makes these images gendered images, how they are connected across racial lines to other gendered images, and how they function in a general pattern of black and white women's oppression. The mammy image, for example, trades on broad cultural associations between women and domesticity, between women and self-sacrificing virtues, and between motherhood and asexuality. Similarly, without denying that these are sexist images, we can say a lot about what makes these images raced images, how they are connected across gender lines to other raced images, and how they function in a general pattern of racial oppression of both black women and black men. The mammy image, for example, trades on broad cultural associations between being black and failure to establish an adequate family of one's own and between being a good black and being a devoted, faithful servant of whites.

Not only *can* different systems of oppression be conceptually separated, but there is a good methodological reason for trying to tease out the basic structures of different systems of oppression. One cannot even begin to give a complex analysis of the interpenetration of race, sex, and class unless one has first attempted to delineate the basic structures of, say, racial oppression in abstraction from other forms of oppression. One might reasonably think, then, that one also cannot give a complex analysis of the interpenetration of lesbian and gay subordination with race, class, and gender oppression unless one has first attempted to delineate the basic structures of lesbian and gay subordination in abstraction from racism, sexism, and classism. The abstract concept of lesbian and gay subordination makes it possible to answer the question: 'What is specifically heterosexist about this practice or this experience?'

In Chapter 4, my primary aim will be to show how this point has been largely lost in feminist theorizing about lesbians that begins from the assumption that feminist analyses must attend to the intersections of race, class, and gender. Race, class, and gender get taken as the exclusive systems of oppression with the result that there is nothing specifically lesbian for them to intersect with. Although dropping lesbian and gay subordination from the list of intersecting axes might be justified by showing that heterosexism is nothing but a byproduct of male dominance, dropping lesbian and gay subordination out of the picture cannot be justified by a methodological appeal to the importance of attending to multiple axes of oppression. That method conceptually depends on there being separable axes to intersect. Thus, that method cannot be used as a rationale *not* to inquire whether heterosexism is itself a separate axis.

To my mind, the most compelling reason for treating lesbian and gay subordination as a separate axis of oppression is a straightforwardly pragmatic one. Here, it will be helpful to call back into view exactly why second wave feminists came under such pressure to thematize race and class. At the time that it was published, Betty Friedan's *The Feminine Mystique* was a pathbreaking feminist work.[10] So too was Mary Daly's *Gynecology*.[11] Both, however, in different ways seriously failed to address all women's oppression even while claiming to do so. Friedan's pinpointing 'the problem that has no name' resonated with middle class white women's experience of gender oppression. But it clearly presupposed that women were all located in a relatively moneyed family that could afford to keep the wife out of the paid labor force and in full-time child rearing and domestic labor. Moreover, it presupposed that absent male dominance, all women would have access to meaningful paid labor in the public sphere. From the point of view of black women who confronted a racial division of labor and from the point of view of poor and working class women who did not have the luxury of experiencing 'the problem with no name', but instead entered the paid labor force out of economic necessity, *The Feminine Mystique* was clearly not about their experience of gender oppression.

Taking a different tack from Friedan, Daly in *Gynecology* ruthlessly exposed the extent and nature of patriarchal ideology and invited women to free themselves from internalized gender oppression by reconceiving both social practices and scholarly production as lethal for women. Again, her emphasis on accurately naming the contours of social reality and engaging in a largely conceptual rebellion against patriarchy resonated with white, middle class women, particularly women connected with academia. But from the point of view of women for whom material rather than ideological barriers were most salient, a strategy of naming anti-woman practices, reconceiving women's experience, and transvaluing patriarchal values was clearly not addressed to solving their experiences of gender oppression.

What I want to note about both examples is that there was no *conceptual* reason why a feminist who set out to describe women's oppression using only the lens of gender oppression would necessarily fail to describe the forms that gender oppression takes for women of color and poor and working class women. After all, black women who complain that they are disproportionately placed in the division of labor as domestic workers are pointing out a fact about the *gender* division of labor. Poor and working class women who complain that they lack the material resources of male peers and are inadequately positioned to care for and support their children are pointing out a fact about the *gendered* distribution of income and responsibility for children. Race and class are certainly relevant to the complete explanation of why different women end up being differently located in patriarchal systems; and understanding the structure of racial and class oppression makes it possible to diagnose the specifically racist and classist dimensions of some women's experience of gender oppression. But even without appeal to race and class as separate axes of oppression, a straightforward gender analysis should not have dropped women of color and poor and working class women out of the picture. Had those feminist writers who were later charged with race- and class-biased accounts begun with a broad base of empirical information about *all* women it would have been clear from the onset that not all women suffered from the problem with no name, that paid labor was not liberating for all women, and that much of women's oppression is a function of their material conditions rather than ideology. The problem of bias to which the method of using separate but intersecting axes of oppression was introduced as a solution was *not* largely methodological. The problem was a practical one. Those producing feminist accounts were almost exclusively white and middle class. The temptation to use their own social location as the vantage point for viewing all women was enormous. The familiarity of white, middle class women's experience, combined with the fact that in a racist and classist culture white, middle class women are constructed as the norm for women, made it highly likely that women of color and poor and working class women would drop out of the picture even though there is nothing about a gender analysis that necessitates the equation of women's oppression with white, middle class women's oppression. Adopting a different method that begins from a set of axes of oppression was in this case primarily a pragmatic move. For the purposes of targeting the variety of factors that sustain women's oppression, the lenses of race and class were not *conceptually* necessary. But for practical reasons deriving from who was producing theories, using those lenses was *pragmatically* necessary as an antidote to the accidental importation of race and class bias into feminist theorizing.

In short, even were it not possible to show that racial dominance and class dominance are separate axes of oppression, there would nevertheless be good pragmatic reasons for adopting a methodological strategy that treats them as separate axes. Lesbians have also tended to drop out of the feminist picture even in work that is ostensibly about lesbian experience. For example, in the 1980s, heterosexual women's experience of woman-loving was installed as the norm for all woman-loving, including that of lesbians. And throughout the 1980s and 1990s, heterosexual women's experience of gender deviance from the category woman was installed as the norm for all gender deviance, obscuring lesbians' historical relation to a third gender category, the not-womanly invert. Because being heterosexual, like being white and middle class, are socially constructed as the norm for women, there is a real danger that lesbian specificity will drop out of feminist theorizing unless some methodological strategy is adopted that compels attention to lesbian versus heterosexual difference. Thus, even if one remains skeptical that heterosexism is anything more than a byproduct of male dominance, there is nevertheless pragmatic reason to adopt the methodological strategy of treating lesbian and gay subordination as a separate axis of oppression.

II. Lesbian and Gay Politics

I said at the beginning of this chapter that this book is devoted to two different questions about centering sexual orientation politics. The first is the question of whether and how lesbian theorizing can be centered in a feminist frame.

The second question, which is equally thematic, is the question of which political issues belong at the center of a lesbian and gay political agenda and why they belong there. Two strategies are commonly used both to locate which issues are politically important and to explain why addressing them would improve the standing of lesbians and gays.

The first strategy for locating central political issues is to look for the most serious *effects* of lesbian and gay subordination and then target policies and practices that produce those effects. So, for example, it is commonly claimed that anti-gay employment policies have the serious effect of diminishing lesbian and gay access to income and status by comparison to heterosexuals' access to these same things. If the material costs of discrimination are sufficiently pervasive and serious to constitute an injustice), then securing anti-discrimination protection belongs on a lesbian and gay political agenda. Just how central securing anti-discrimination protection should be to a lesbian and gay politics would depend on how serious one takes the effects of discrimination to be when compared to other policies and practices that also have detrimental effects on gays and lesbians as a group.

The second strategy for locating those issues that belong on a lesbian and gay political agenda is to begin by determining what *ideological representations* of lesbians and gays are used to rationalize the subordinating treatment of lesbians and gays. Policies and practices predicated on those ideologies can then be targeted for political challenge. For example, gay men (and to a lesser extent lesbians) are commonly stereotyped as having poorly controlled sexual desires. Some youth organizations like the Boy Scouts of America use this stereotype to rationalize barring gay men from youth leadership positions. Family courts have also used this stereotype to rationalize not awarding custody to divorcing parents who are gay or lesbian. A gay and lesbian politics should challenge such policies and practices that are based on ideological representations, because it is unfair to treat members of a social group differently on the basis of merely alleged, but in fact nonexistent, differences. In addition, one of the most direct ways of disrupting stigmatizing ideological is to eliminate the policies and practices that reflect and reinforce that particular mistaken representation.

I will be using both of these strategies to argue that anti-discrimination protection, same-sex marriage, and opposition to policies that restrict lesbians' and gay men's access to children belong at the center of a lesbian and gay politics. These are not novel conclusions. However, in reaching those conclusions I will be arguing that we need to rethink *which* effects of subordination and *which* rationalizing ideologies belong at the center of lesbian and gay political arguments. It is generally taken for granted that the relevant serious effects of lesbian and gay subordination are broadly *material* effects (in terms of income, status, education, housing, health care, and the like), and thus that a liberatory political agenda needs to be centered on remedying the material costs of subordination. Arguments for laws protecting lesbians and gays against discrimination, are consequently centered on documenting the material costs of discrimination. It is also generally taken for granted that the primary ideological representations used to rationalize the unequal treatment of lesbians and gays are ones that stigmatize lesbian and gay sexuality. As a result, discussions of sexuality and critiques of sexual regulations, particularly anti-sodomy laws, end up at the center of lesbian and gay political arguments; and historians, anthropologists, and sociologists who aim to produce scholarship that will have a liberatory effect end up focusing on other cultures and time periods that have not stigmatized same-sex sexual practices.

One of my main aims in this book is to challenge the pervasive assumption that the principal serious effect of discriminatory policies is that they undermine lesbians' and gays' material welfare. Centering political concern on the material costs of discriminatory treatment obscures its most serious effect—the displacement of lesbian and gay identities from the public sphere and the displacement of lesbians and gays from a protected private sphere. A second main aim of this book is to challenge the pervasive assumption that gays and lesbians are stigmatized exclusively or primarily for their sexual object choice. Centering political concern around the stigmatizing of same-sex sexuality obscures what I think are more damaging ideological representations—namely, the multiple representations of lesbians and gays as outlaws to the family. In this chapter, I simply want to lay some introductory groundwork for later arguments by, first, briefly introducing the notion of displacement that will be central throughout this book, and second, describing the ideological representations of lesbians and gays which I think, in fact, motivate and rationalize the subordinating treatment of lesbians and gays.

Gender and race oppression impose serious material costs on women and racial minorities. If one assumes that lesbian and gay subordination is directly analogous to gender and race oppression, it makes sense to assume that lesbian and gay subordination also imposes material costs. But, lesbian and gay subordination is *not* analogous to gender and race oppression. Lesbian and gay identities can be closeted. One's gender or race typically cannot. Because lesbian and gay identities can be closeted, lesbians and gay men can often evade the material costs of discriminatory policies in a way that those who have more visible identities cannot. Thus, if there is a good reason for insisting that lesbians and gays not be treated discriminatorily, that reason is *not* that nondiscriminatory treatment would equalize lesbians' and gays' material position. I will argue that, unlike race and gender oppression, the primary serious effect of lesbian and gay subordination is not material disadvantage so much as it is the *displacement* of lesbians and gays from civil society.[12] Discriminatory policies that penalize openly lesbian and gay persons have the effect of requiring everyone to present themselves as heterosexual if they are to have full access to the public sphere. Discriminatory policies thus have the effect of displacing lesbian and gay identities from the public sphere. In addition, lesbians and gay men are displaced from the private sphere through anti-sodomy laws and policies that impose barriers to the formation of lesbian and gay marriages and families.

In contrasting being *disadvantagingly placed* in a way that produces material costs with being *displaced*, I am not suggesting that lesbian and gay subordination has no material costs or that securing anti-discrimination coverage does not belong on a lesbian and gay political agenda. Nor am I suggesting that race and gender oppression never involve the displacement of raced or gendered identities from the public sphere. Minority raced images *are* quite often displaced from cultural visibility. Nor am I suggesting that there are no other forms of oppression characterized more by displacement than by being disadvantagingly placed. Anti-Semitism is very much like lesbian and gay subordination in the sense that it requires the closeting of Jewish identity as a condition of full access to the public sphere. What I am suggesting is that if our interest is in determining which issues belong at the *center* of lesbian and gay politics and why they belong there, it is important not to assume uncritically that a lesbian and gay politics should be centered on the same equity issues that have been central to gender and race politics or that the reasons for stressing these equity issues are the same.

Let me turn now to the question of which rationalizing ideologies should be of central concern in lesbian and gay political arguments. The idea that stigma attaches directly to same-sex object choice is a natural enough thought. After all, the defining trait of the identities 'lesbian' and 'gay' seems obviously to be the orientation of desire and activity toward members of the same sex. Lesbian and gay subordination appears, then, to be the direct result of systematically organizing social life around the division of people into two, differently evaluated types—those whose sexual desire and activity is oriented toward members of the opposite sex and those whose sexual desire and activity is oriented toward members of the same sex. The stigmatizing of same-sex sexual object choice as unnatural, pathological, and morally abhorrent produces a set of regulations aimed at controlling or eliminating same-sex sexual interaction and the persons whose defining trait is the desire to engage in same-sex sexual interaction. If one assumes that hostility to same-sex sexual object choice is the primary factor motivating lesbian and gay subordination, it makes sense to put challenges to sexual regulations, especially to anti-sodomy laws, at the center of lesbian and gay politics and to do so for the purpose of legitimating same-sex sexual object choice.

I think this view is mistaken. I suggest that same-sex sexual object choice comes to be stigmatized only because same-sex sexuality is culturally interpreted as inherently connected to *other* more fundamentally stigmatizing characteristics of lesbian and gay identity—three, in particular. First, we as a culture assume that there are two and only two natural, normal, nonpathological sex/gender categories—'woman' and 'man'. . . . Gays' and lesbians' sexual orientation toward members of the same sex dislocates them from these two sex/gender categories. Lesbians are not-women. Gays are not-men. It is this latter ideology that explains why same-sex sexuality is so stigmatizing. Engaging in same-sex sexual activity marks one out as an inferior sort of person only if raises doubts about one's manhood or womanhood. Heterosexuals, for example, can often engage in same-sex sexual activity without similar stigma because their heterosexual orientation links them securely to the category 'woman' or 'man'. Lesbians and gays who engage in exactly the same sexual activity are vulnerable to being stigmatized because that activity is culturally read as a sign of their failure to be either real women or real men.

Lesbian and gay sexuality is also stigmatized because it is culturally interpreted as being *qualitatively* different from heterosexual sexuality. Since the popularization of psychoanalytic theories in the mid 1900s, lesbians and gays have been culturally imagined to be prone to pathological sexual excess and a neurotic obsession with sexual gratification. Once lesbians and gays are thought to be psychologically incapable of romantic and marital love, it then makes sense to *reduce* lesbian and gay identities to purely sexual identities that have nothing to do with romance, marriage, family, and parenting. Heterosexuality, by contrast, retains a very strong cultural connection with the most esteemed forms of intimate relationships. What makes same-sex sexuality so stigmatizing, then, is not the sheer fact that desire is focused on a same-sex partner. Rather, lesbian and gay sexuality comes to be deeply stigmatizing because it is culturally construed as a kind of sexuality that consumes one's psychology, driving out ennobling emotional attitudes like romantic and marital love.

Finally, taken together, lesbians' and gay men's failure to occupy a nonpathological sex/gender category and their possession of an excessive sexuality makes them fundamentally unfit to participate in the foundational institution of society—the family. Lesbianism and homosexuality represent, in the cultural imagination, a threat to family life. Being neither fully men nor women, gay men and lesbians cannot be counted on to raise properly gendered children. Possessing excessive sexual desires, gay men and lesbians cannot sustain stable marital relationships, nor can they be counted on to refrain from seducing children. These ideological representations of lesbians and gay men as outlaws to the family are what make same-sex sexuality so stigmatizing.

In sum, a lesbian and gay politics needs to be centered on challenging policies and practices that are predicated on the assumptions that: (1) there are only two natural, normal, non-pathological sex/gender categories, (2) lesbian and gay sexuality differs qualitatively from heterosexual sexuality in being more excessive and compulsive, and (3) lesbians and gays are fundamentally unfit for marriage and family.

Implicit in what I have just said is a rejection of the view that gay and lesbian identities are properly defined simply in terms of the orientation of sexual desire and activity. This narrow or 'simple' definition drops from view too much of the culturally elaborated content of the identities 'lesbian' and 'gay'. As a result, this narrow definition invites a mislocation of lesbian and gay politics. In particular, narrowly defining lesbian and gay identity in terms of sexual object choice makes it seem politically reasonable to focus on legitimatizing same-sex *sex*. Gay historical and anthropological work, for example, often seems to take its political task to be showing that other cultures and time periods have not stigmatized sexual activity between men or between women. But if the contemporary stigma of lesbianism and homosexuality attaches in part to lesbians' and gays' presumed unfitness for participation in the family, then gay historians and anthropologists need to question whether their narratives of cultures that have not penalized same-sex *sexual* activity—but have nevertheless organized marriage and parenting around heterosexuals—are as liberatory as they take them to be. They also need to question whether their narratives of cultures that assume that there are only two (normal) sex/gender categories and that tolerate same-sex sex in 'real' men are as liberatory as they take them to be. Finally, the popular assumption that pursuing same-sex marriage rights is less radical and thus less critical to lesbian and gay politics than pursuing liberalized legal and educational policies with respect to same-sex sex needs to be critically reassessed.

In addition, the assumption that being sexually oriented toward members of the same sex is the defining trait of lesbians and gay men, has obscured the politics of theorizing about lesbians within a feminist frame that takes its subject to be women. Feminists have been able to assume uncritically that lesbians and heterosexual women are equally *women*, differing only in their sexual object choice.

My point, of course, is not that same-sex sexual object choice is irrelevant to lesbian and gay identity. It is, rather, that the orientation of sexual desire and activity does not exhaust the content of the identities 'lesbian' and 'homosexual' as they have been socially constructed over the past century. Locating the ideologies that rationalize lesbian and gay subordination requires a more expansive account of the cultural content of these identities.

III. Identity, Essentialism, Constructionism

The term 'identity' is ambiguous. 'Identity' can refer to the social category that people take themselves to occupy, or are taken by others to occupy (e.g., a lesbian, a professor, a woman). Identity in this sense can be contested. We can dispute whether or not an individual really does occupy a particular social category. Questions about identity in this sense sometimes take a normative form, for example: 'Who counts as a *real* lesbian?' 'Identity' can also refer to the subjective experience of living with a particular identity and to the subjective meaning that that identity has for oneself. In this case, questions about identity are typically questions about what it has meant to the individual to live life, say, as a lesbian and how she interprets what having a lesbian identity does and does not involve. Lesbian autobiographies and narrative-based studies of lesbians are about identity in this sense.[13] They give us detailed accounts of the multiplicity of experiences of being lesbian and conceptions of lesbianism, including descriptions of how lesbian identity is differently inflected by one's class, race, religious, and ethnic identities.

In this book, I am not concerned with 'identity' in either of these senses. My concern is with the *culturally authorized* conception of how lesbianism and homosexuality differ from heterosexuality. Although lesbians and gays have influenced that conception, they have not been in a position to authorize or culturally disseminate their own developed understandings of what it means to be lesbian or gay. The culturally authorized conception has instead emerged largely from within medical, psychiatric, and scientific work. Government policy, laws and legal reasoning, literature, the media, and religion have also had a hand in constructing the culturally authorized conception of lesbianism and homosexuality. That conception shapes and is reinforced by routine social practices, such as the practices of closeting lesbian and gay identity and of discriminating against lesbians and gays. . . .

My concern with the cultural content of our conceptions of lesbianism and homosexuality as it has developed since the end of the 1800s places me squarely in the social constructionist camp. Social constructionists take sexuality to be a social fact about persons, not a natural fact. On this view, there is no such thing as sexuality *simpliciter*. Rather, cultures create the possibility of being sexual by supplying 'sexual' with a culture-specific meaning; and different cultures may construct substantially different scripts for being sexual. Homosexuality and lesbianism, too, are social, not natural facts, about persons. By supplying meaningful content to a concept of homosexuality, and a script for enacting a homosexual identity, a culture creates the opportunity for individuals to be homosexual in much the same way that a culture can create the opportunity for individuals to be a peasant or a Democrat. Understanding what it means to be sexual or to have a sexual orientation, then, is always a matter of understanding how a particular culture or a particular time period understands those possibilities. Capturing the complex cultural content of 'sexual' or 'sexual orientation' requires complex definitions of these notions. Essentialists, by contrast, assume that sexuality and sexual orientations are natural facts about persons. So, for example, if a person is lesbian, she would be lesbian no matter which culture or time period she were transported to. And, since having a sexual orientation, on the essentialist view, does not depend on whether or not the culture has a conception of homosexuality or heterosexuality, there may in fact have been homosexuals in all cultures and all time periods. Since what it means to have a sexual orientation is not culture-specific, a simple definition such as 'persistent desire for persons of the same sex/gender' may suffice.[14]

My approach in this book is a constructionist one with one qualification. While constructionists contest, as I do, the utility of using narrow definitions of lesbians' and gays' identity, they have not always contested essentialists' narrow focus on *sex*. David Halperin, for example, does not reject essentialist definitions because they drop from view lesbians and gays different sex/gender categorization or their construction as outlaws to the family. He objects because, in his view, the very concept of a sexual orientation is a modern, western invention.[15] Medical and psychiatric discourses beginning in the late nineteenth century invented the idea of a sexual orientation that constitutes a deep feature of one's personality. The invention of distinct personality types connected to sexual object choice, he argues, provided the cultural opportunity to *be* lesbian or homosexual. By contrast, as I suggested in the previous section, I want to challenge the assumption underlying both essentialist and some constructionist views that sexual object choice is *the* defining feature of lesbian and gay identities.

The constructionist approach to lesbian and gay identity has often seemed to pose an insuperable barrier to doing lesbian and gay history and anthropology. It entails that if a culture does not share our detailed conception of lesbian and gay identity there are no lesbians and gays in that culture. Absent real lesbians and gays to study, no lesbian and gay history or anthropology can be done. As a result, key players in standard gay history and anthropology must be eliminated. For example, it would seem that on a constructionist view the sexual man–boy relationships of Ancient Athens should *not* be described as homosexual relationships. This is because, as Morris Kaplan puts it: 'Athenians of the fifth century did not understand themselves as defined by their desires for objects of a specific gender or biological sex. What mattered was the political and social status and age of the object of desire, as well as the sexual practices in which the citizen engaged'.[16] Nor are the Native American *berdache*, who function as members of the opposite sex, obvious players in a constructionist history, since their gender difference from their sexual partners disqualifies them from being culturally read as different from ' heterosexuals'. Indeed, it may turn out that there are no lesbians or gays at all outside western society since the late nineteenth century.

This unfortunate upshot of the constructionist approach makes essentialism more appealing. As I said above, essentialists assume that there really is some natural fact about persons that makes them oriented toward same-sex sexual activity even if that natural fact is not cross-culturally recognized and elaborated. Historical and anthropological records might then be searched for evidence of the existence of persons who have this natural property, just as we might search for evidence of hemophilia or epilepsy in cultures that do not recognize these medical conditions.

While invoking the essentialist's narrow definition of lesbian and gay identity may get us around the main problem with constructionism, it leaves in place the very problem that motivated constructionism in the first place. There is certainly something odd about subsuming under the identity categories, 'lesbian' and 'gay', people who, from their own culture's perspective did not differ from (what we would call) heterosexuals in their culture. Cultures simply do not always attach significance to the fact that a sex partner is anatomically similar. In some cultures, for example, the fact that males have sex with other males does not mark them out as sexually different from males who do not, provided that they occupy the dominant position and do not permit penetration of themselves. In others, they are not marked out as different so long as one is a man and one is a boy. In others, lack of difference from 'heterosexual' males is preserved by adopting a masculine gender role in relation to a femininely gendered male. In our own culture, some men claim that they are heterosexual because they are only occasionally having sex with other men or because the males they are having sex with are drag queens who are 'real women'. Thus, what one does while having sex, how often one has sex with anatomically similar people, what the relative ages of the two people are, and what the gender roles of the two people are may be the significant factors distinguishing sexual actors—*not* the fact that a person is regularly having same-sex sex.

The solution to this particular dilemma over whether essentialism or constructionism is the preferred basis for doing history and anthropology is, I think, to rethink what the point of doing lesbian and gay history is. It is a political one. When we look across cultures and time periods at persons who, if transported to *our* culture would qualify as lesbian or gay, we discover a politically significant fact. There has never been a universal taboo on same-sex desire as we understand it. Many cultures regard sexual interaction between men as compatible with being heterosexual. Some cultures, notably ancient Greece have valorized what *we* see as man–boy homosexuality, ranking it over what *we* see as heterosexuality. Other cultures, for example in New Guinea and Melanesia, have prescribed sexual interaction between men and boys as a necessary transition to heterosexual adulthood. Similarly, there has never been a universal taboo on same-sex romantic intimacies. Native American and some African cultures have institutionalized what to *our* eyes look like same-sex marriages. The nineteenth-century Boston marriages institutionalized what to *our* eyes look like lesbian partnerships. What studies like Kenneth Dover's history of Greek homosexuality[17] or histories of same-sex marriage underscore is the parochialism, and from a global point of view arbitrariness, of our culture's obsessive aversion to sexual interaction and intimate partnerships between men or between women. Seen in this light, contemporary sodomy laws, proscriptions on gays and lesbians in the military, bars to same-sex marriage, and legal toleration of discrimination against gays and lesbians seem insupportable. They cannot be justified by appeal to the naturally abhorrent nature of same-sex sex. The historical and cross-cultural record suggests that there is nothing natural at all in our culture's intolerance.

Gay history and anthropology thus serve as valuable political tools when they begin from our contemporary, western, complex definition of lesbian and gay identity and then search the historical and cultural records for people who, if transported to our culture, would be categorized as lesbian or gay. What matters is not, for example, whether the Greeks regarded man–boy sexual interaction as homosexual. What matters is that we do. Only by looking at how people that we 'read' as lesbian or gay were treated can gay history and anthropology reveal the arbitrariness of our contemporary hostility to lesbianism and homosexuality. Deciding whom to include in gay and lesbian history and anthropology by asking: 'Whom can *we* read as gay or lesbian?' need not distort the historical or anthropological record so long as we are self-conscious about what we are doing. That individuals get into gay and lesbian histories and anthropologies because we read them as gay or lesbian does not entail that historians and anthropologists should not also attend to how these individuals would have been categorized and complexly described from their own culture's perspective. In short, constructivists can do history and anthropology. Doing so, however, requires adopting the fiction that our own categories can be applied across cultures and across time periods to determine who is gay or lesbian. That is, it requires treating our identity categories as though they pick out a transtemporal and transcultural essence. In doing so, we employ *fictional essences,* since the persons picked out may well not be read by their own culture and time period as bearing the traits that we attribute to lesbians and gays.

Notes

1. That image was crystallized in the subtitle of bell hooks' widely read book, *Feminist Theory: From Margin to Center* (Boston: South End Press, 1984).

2. For an enormously helpful discussion of the forms that oppression takes see Iris Young's 'The Five Faces of Oppression', *Justice and the Politics of Difference* (Princeton: Princeton University Press, 1990).

3. I owe this point to Ann Ferguson, 'Cheshire Calhoun's Project of Separating Lesbian Theory from Feminist Theory'. *Hypatia* 13 (1998): 214–22.

4. Gayle Rubin, 'The Traffic in Women', in *Toward an Anthropology of Women,* ed. Rayna Reiter (New York: Monthly Review Press, 1975),157–210. For a somewhat more extended discussion of Rubin, see my 'Taking Seriously Dual Systems and Sex', *Hypatia* 13 (1998): 224–31.

5. Adrienne Rich, 'Compulsory Heterosexuality and Lesbian Existence', in *The Signs Reader: Women, Gender, and Scholarship,* ed. Elizabeth Abel and Emily K. Abel (Chicago: University of Chicago Press, 1983), 139–68.

6. Ann Ferguson clarifies this distinction between necessary and sufficient conditions for lesbian and gay liberation in 'Cheshire Calhoun's Project of Separating Lesbian Theory from Feminist Theory'.

7. Heidi Hartmann, 'The Unhappy Marriage of Marxism and Feminism', in *Feminist Frameworks,* 2nd ed., ed. Alison M. Jaggar and Paula S. Rothenberg (New York: McGraw-Hill, 1984), 172–89.

8. The example is drawn from Cynthia Peterson, 'Envisioning a Lesbian Equality Jurisprudence', in *Legal Inversions: Lesbians, Gay Men, and the Politics of Law* (Philadelphia: Temple University Press, 1995). 118–37, 122.

9. Patricia Hill Collins, *Black Feminist Thought: Knowledge, Consciousness and the Politics of Empowerment* (New York: Routlege, 1990).

10. Betty Friedan, *The Feminine Mystique* (New York: Norton, 1963).

11. Mary Daly, *Gynecology* (Boston: Beacon, 1978).

12. I have been using the term 'subordination' rather than 'oppression' to refer to lesbians' and gay's political position precisely in order to avoid implying a strong analogy between lesbians and gays on the one hand, and women and racial minorities on the other. Because sexual identity can be closeted, and thus the force of discriminatory policies evaded, 'oppressed' seems the wrong description. In Marilyn Frye's classic description, '[t]he experience of oppressed people is that the living of one's life is confined and shaped by forces and barriers which are not accidental or occasional and hence avoidable, but are systematically related to each other in such a way as to catch one between and among them and restrict or penalize motion in any direction'. *The Politics of Reality* (Freedom, CA: Crossing Press, 1983), 4.

13. Kath Weston's *Render Me, Gender Me,* for example, is about identities in this sense (New York: Columbia University Press, 1996).

14. For very helpful overviews of the essentialism-constructionism debate, see Daniel R. Ortiz, 'Creating Controversy: Essentialism/Constructivism and the Politics of Gay Identity', *Virginia Law Review* 79 (1993): 1833–57; Edward Stein, 'The Essentials of Constructionism and the Construction of Essentialism', *Forms of Desire: Sexual Orientation and the Social Constructionist Controversy*, ed. Edward Stein (New York: Routledge, 1992); Edward Stein, *The Mismeasure of Desire: The Science, Theory, and Ethics of Sexual Orientation* (Oxford University Press, 1999).

15. David Halperin, 'Is There a History of Sexuality?' in *The Lesbian and Gay Studies Reader*, ed. Henry Abelove, Michele Aina Barale, and David M. Halperin (New York: Routledge, 1993), 416–31. See also Jonathan Katz, *The Invention of Heterosexuality* (New York: Dutton, 1995).

16. Morris B. Kaplan, *Sexual Justice: Democratic Citizenship and the Politics of Desire* (New York: Routledge, 1997), 54.

17. Kenneth Dover, *Greek Homosexuality* (New York: Vintage, 1980).

28 | *Treat Students Right by Valuing Their Diversity*

Matthew Meuleners

The human body has more than 200 different types of cells. Each cell develops to maturity differently, just as each person grows up in a different environment. Cells work towards different goals, just as each of us does.

Some cells tell us we are hungry, while others help us digest the food we eat. They deal with different challenges—stomach cells adapt to resist the harsh acidic environment around them, while muscle cells maintain a delicate chemical balance to create motion.

Each cell looks very different, just as every human being is distinctive. A human egg cell is the size of the period at the end of this sentence, while some nerve cells stretch the length of your leg. Millions of unique cells are working together to make it possible for you to read this article right now.

Yet, even the great diversity of cells in the human body is nothing when it is compared to the diversity of background, thought, experience, and expression which exists in the minds of just one classroom of students. This variety is a wonderful thing when we respond to it in ways which are appropriate, but we can cause serious problems if we deal with diversity in the wrong way.

Picture a ladder with three rungs on it. Each of these rungs is spaced widely from the next, making it impossible to reach one without first reaching the one directly below it. Rising to the next rung requires a big stretch that would be difficult for someone who is stiff and inflexible, while someone who is limber could more easily make the ascent. The way we each deal with diversity develops in a progression like this ladder.

The first stage is recognition, when we make contact with "it" and compare "it" to ourselves. In this first stage, we don't understand what "it" is, and we are often afraid. The next stage is tolerance. In this stage, we understand "it" better, but are still uncomfortable. We often try to distance ourselves from "it." In the final stage, which is called celebration, we accept "it" fully and acknowledge that "it" adds value to our life.

This progression is not determined by our age or by our intelligence, but by our attitude and our experience. Some people spend all their lives in the recognition stage, growing stiff and locked in their

Reprinted by permission from *Education Digest* 67, no. 4 (2001).

ways. Others arrive at the stage of celebration while still very young, developing open, limber minds in an environment where diversity is the norm.

Where on the ladder are you located? How can you help guide your school to climb to higher levels?

1. Recognition. "Racist," "bigot," and "ignorant" are some of the words which are aimed at those who are locked in the stage of recognition. These are people who respond negatively when they come in contact with someone they don't understand or who is different from them. The problem here is a lack of information. This ignorance can cause trouble in two ways.

First, when we don't have any knowledge of something that is new, our brain will often use our past experiences of something that is similar to fill in the gaps. Psychologists call this a schema reaction. A schema is a blueprint for how we see the world.

When a new experience fits with this blueprint for how we see the world, then that new experience is added to memory, but when something new disagrees with the blueprint, it is rejected and replaced with data from a past experience. Does this sound familiar? This is how a stereotype is formed.

For example, if the only Hispanic person you ever met had stolen from you, you might tend to be less trusting of the next Hispanic person you meet. These stereotypes can build into a vicious cycle, and, unfortunately, a person's schema doesn't even have to be based upon his or her own experiences.

Attitudes are often passed down from parents, peers, and other role models. Advisers and student leaders are role models, whether they realize it or not. For this reason it is important for them to be conscious of the actions and the attitudes which they are passing on to others.

The second way in which it is possible for ignorance to cause trouble is by creating fear. People are sometimes afraid of what they don't understand. Too often, this terror transforms into feelings of anger and hate. These powerful emotions can lead people to do things that they wouldn't even consider doing if they were in other circumstances.

Everything from verbal harassment to physical hate crimes can result from the discomfort and fear of the unknown. In middle-level and high schools, this often takes the form of rejection and verbal abuse between cliques. Encouraging an open-minded attitude within your school organization can indirectly create a more tolerant attitude in your school community by setting a model for others to follow.

2. Tolerance. Remember that what keeps people locked in the recognition stage is a lack of information. So, in order for one to move on to the second stage, that of tolerance, one must ask questions. As we learn about the unknown, it becomes easier to accept as reality, like adjusting the focus control on a camera. When we make the effort, we can see details that we might otherwise have missed.

For people who are in the tolerance stage, the different people are accepted, but they are not welcomed. A good way to describe it might be respectful distance. They respect the other person's right to exist as long as they keep their distance.

People in the tolerance stage don't want to be directly affected by diversity. These are the people who create policies like the military department's "Don't ask, don't tell." The government tells people, "It's okay to be gay as long as nobody ever knows." In high school, people in the tolerance stage include the guy who doesn't have anything against black people, but avoids making black friends or taking black lab partners.

This attitude can be just as destructive as direct confrontation. Those who are stuck in the tolerance stage often miss many opportunities for friendship, growth, and fresh ideas. By making a real effort to go outside of your comfort zone and to interact with people who make you feel uncomfortable, you can push yourself away from this stage.

People in the tolerance stage have to overcome difficult obstacles in order to move on to the stage of celebration. They have to learn to see the qualities about each person that are worthy of praise and attention. They also have to realize the value of true synergy, and the path to take in order to achieve it.

No matter how a person looks on the surface, or how they view the world, it is important to realize that we are all connected by our heritage as human beings. Each one of us brings value to the equation, and each one of us is worthy of love and praise.

True synergy is a state of being where a community, family, or team works together to create more than they could create if each was working alone. The only way in which to accomplish this state of smooth, enhanced interaction is to utilize each person's unique talents, nurture the reduction of their unique limitations, and empower them to reach their full potential.

3. Celebration. Imagine that your school organization is making plans for a year-end celebration banquet. Kris is an organizational whiz, and Montel is the best speaker in the group. Obviously, each is going to work more on their area of specialty than they will be working on the rest of the planning which is to be done. This utilization of unique talents will make your event planning more efficient and more effective, but the celebration still won't quite reach its full potential.

What about when Kris has to tell the rest of the organization about your progress? She isn't exactly the best communicator. Montel could deliver the information beautifully, but he can't keep all of it straight in his head. Everyone has shortcomings, skills that could be improved.

As a team, it is important to nurture the reduction of individual limitations by teaching and learning from each other. When Montel gives Kris a few tips on eye contact and provides her with a pep talk, she can do the briefing in a clear, concise way. Kris could also help Montel to organize his speech notes for the purpose of ensuring that the presentation flows through the agenda smoothly.

Celebrating diversity is the equation for true synergy, whether you happen to be a smooth-talking student leader or a well-organized adviser. By acknowledging that every member of your community, organization, or family has something to contribute and recognizing that his or her contributions add value to your life, you are moving toward the stage of celebration.

When you celebrate the many differences in those around you, you will be able to utilize, nurture, and empower others to achieve more than ever before. But how do you empower?

You start the process by being flexible. Remember that the ladder is difficult to climb if you are stiff and intolerant. However, when you are flexible—and you adapt to other people's preferences, opinions, and needs—this allows them to create at their full potential. This is often the most difficult barrier for people to cross because it means thinking about your life as cooperation rather than competition.

Modern American society pushes individual strength and independence. We are taught not to rely on or help other people, but rather that we will be less successful if others are more so. We must unlearn these attitudes if we are to ever achieve real synergy in our society by empowering those around us.

To return to the analogy from the introduction, the human body is an example of synergy that has been amazing scientists for centuries. Vastly dissimilar cells work in teams to form tissues and organs that carry out the functions of life.

If you think of each person around you as being like a cell, you can imagine that your entire organization makes up an organ that provides some of the functions which are necessary for the lift of our society. Each of the groups that are in your school works together to support the human race like organ systems which are cooperating to support a single body.

The near perfection of the human body's synergy is what makes us the most advanced creatures on the planet. Nerve cells trigger muscle cells to fire. Muscle cells contract in the heart to keep our blood cells circulating. Blood cells carry essential nutrients to cells in our glands that release protective immune cells to fight disease. Hundreds of systems cooperate and sustain each other for the purpose of achieving a common goal. If our society were to run like that, just imagine what we would accomplish.

What happens when the synergy in our bodies fails? What happens when, for some reason, one system stops working with another system? Sometimes in our society, two or more cultures of communities stop working together.

What if, like a group of older people who refuse to interact with today's "crazy" youth, our brain's reflex reaction center stopped working with our muscles? The next time our hand touched a hot burner on a stove, we wouldn't move it off until we smelled smoke!

What about when our fellow human beings attack each other, through hate crimes and ridicule, destroying the lives of innocent people just because they are different? This is like when our own body cells turn against each other, invading, reprogramming, and destroying healthy cells around them. This is a virus called AIDS, and it is no less frightening and destructive when applied to our model of society.

The virus invades the protective barriers of healthy cells, like a bigot who breaks down someone's self-esteem through taunts and abuse. Then the virus reprograms the cell's DNA to produce copies of the AIDS virus itself. In the same way, a victim of prejudice and intolerance can sometimes believe that their abusers are right, that they deserve that treatment because they are lesser human beings.

Finally, the virus causes the once-healthy cell to destroy itself, releasing thousands of copies of the disease to attack other healthy cells. Remember that intolerance and false schemas are easily passed on to those who are close to us—like children, friends, and organization members.

As of today, there is no cure for AIDS, just as there is no cure for the intolerance of diversity. Both of these diseases are reaching epidemic proportions across the world. The only way to restrict the growth of these outbreaks is by carefully regulating our own behavior and encouraging others to do the same.

Challenge yourself to ascend the ladder. Ask questions to help you understand the unknown. Keep a flexible mind that is open to new ideas and opinions. Utilize the talents of others while nurturing the reduction of the problem areas where they need help. Empower each other by cooperating instead of competing.

Remind yourself every day of the consequences of intolerance and work to celebrate the powerful strength that comes from the diversity of thought, experience, and expression in those around you.

29

A Revolution of Values

The Promise of Multi-Cultural Change

bell hooks

Two summers ago I attended my twentieth high school reunion. It was a last minute decision. I had just finished a new book. Whenever I finish a work, I always feel lost, as though a steady anchor has been taken away and there is no sure ground under my feet. During the time between ending one project and beginning another, I always have a crisis of meaning. I begin to wonder what my life is all about and what I have been put on this earth to do. It is as though immersed in a project I lose all sense of myself and must then when the work is done rediscover who I am and where I am going. When I heard that the reunion was happening, it seemed just the experience to bring me back to myself, to help in the process of rediscovery. Never having attended any of the past reunions, I did not know what to expect. I did know that this one would be different. For the first time we were about to have a racially integrated reunion. In past years, reunions had always been segregated. White folks had their reunion on their side of town and black folks had it on ours.

None of us was sure what it would be like to have an integrated reunion. Those periods in our adolescent lives of racial desegregation had been full of hostility, rage, conflict, and loss. We black kids had been angry that we had to leave our beloved all-black high school Crispus Attucks and be bussed halfway cross town to integrate white schools. We had to make the journey and thus bear the responsibility of making desegregation a reality. We had to give up the familiar and enter a world that seemed cold and strange, not our world, not our school. We were certainly on the margin, no longer at the center, and it hurt. It was such an unhappy time. I still remember my rage that we had to awaken an hour early so that we could be bussed to school before the white students arrived. We were made to sit in the gymnasium and wait. It was believed that this practice would prevent outbreaks of conflict and hostility since it removed the possibility of social contact before classes began. Yet once again the burden of this transition was placed on us. The white school was desegregated, but in the classroom, in the cafeteria, and in most social spaces racial apartheid prevailed. Black and white students who considered ourselves progressive

Reprinted from *Teaching to Transgress: Education as the Practice of Freedom* (1994), by permission of the author.

rebelled against the unspoken racial taboos that were meant to sustain white supremacy and racial apartheid even in the face of desegregation. The white folks never seemed to understand that our parents were no more eager for us to socialize with them than they were to socialize with us. Those of us who wanted to make racial equality a reality in every area of our life were threats to the social order. We were proud of ourselves, proud of our willingness to transgress the rules, proud to be courageous.

Part of a small integrated clique of smart kids who considered ourselves "artists," who believed we were destined to create outlaw culture where we would live as bohemians forever free, we were certain of our radicalness. Days before the reunion, I was overwhelmed by memories and shocked to discover that our gestures of defiance had been nowhere near as daring as they had seemed at the time. Mostly they were acts of resistance that did not truly challenge the status quo. One of my best buddies during that time was white and male. He had an old gray Volvo that I loved to ride in. Every now and then he would give me a ride home from school if I missed the bus—an action which angered and disturbed those who saw us. Friendship across racial lines was bad enough, but friendship across gender was unheard of and dangerous. We found out one day just how dangerous when grown white men in a car tried to run us off the road. Ken's parents were religious. Their faith compelled them to live out a belief in racial justice. They were among the first white folks in our community to invite black folks to come to their house, to eat at their table, to worship with them. As one of Ken's best buddies, I was welcome in their house. After hours of discussion and debate about possible dangers, my parents agreed that I could go there for a meal. It was my first time to eat together with white people. I was sixteen years old. I felt then as though we were making the new history of America, that we were in the process of living the dream of democracy, of creating a culture where equality, love, justice, and peace would be the values that would shape and form our nation's destiny.

After graduation I lost touch with Ken even though he always had a warm place in my memory. I thought of him when meeting and interacting with liberal white folks who believed that having a black friend meant that they were not racist, who sincerely believed they were doing us a favor by extending offers of friendly contact for which they felt they should be rewarded. I thought of him during years of watching white folks play at unlearning racism but walking away when they encountered obstacles, rejection, conflict, pain. Our high school friendship had been forged not because we were black and white but because we shared a similar take on reality. Racial difference meant that we had to struggle to claim the integrity of that bonding. We had no illusions. We knew there would be obstacles, conflict, and pain. In white supremacist capitalist patriarchy, words we never used then, we knew we would have to pay a price for this friendship, that we would need to possess the courage to stand up for our belief in democracy, in racial justice, in the transformative power of love. We valued the bond between us enough to meet the challenge. Remembering the sweetness of our friendship days before the reunion, I felt humbled by the knowledge of what we give up when we are young, believing either that we will find something just as good or better someday only to find that not to be so. I wondered just how it could have been that Ken and I could ever have lost contact with one another. Along the way I had not found white folks who understood as well the depth and complexity of racial injustice, who were as willing to practice the art of living a nonracist life as folks were then. In my adult life I have seen few white folks who are really willing to go the distance to create a world of racial equality—white folks willing to take risks, to be courageous, to live against the grain. I went to the reunion hoping that I would have a chance to see Ken face to face, to tell how much I cherished all that we shared, to tell him in words which I never dared to say to any white person back then, simply that I loved him.

Remembering this past, I am most struck by our passionate commitment to a vision of social transformation that was rooted in the fundamental belief in a radically democratic idea of freedom and justice for all. Our notions of social change were not fancy. There was no elaborate postmodern political theory shaping our actions. We were simply trying to change the way we went about our everyday lives so that our values and habits of being would reflect our commitment to freedom. Then our major concern was ending racism. That concern was coupled with other concerns for freedom: we wanted sexual freedom, we wanted an end to gender boundaries. As I grew up politically, I placed alongside the struggle to end racism a commitment to ending sexism and sexism oppression, to eradicating systems of class exploitation. Aware that we are living in a culture of domination I ask myself now as I did more than twenty years ago as I go about my daily life: what values and habits of being reflect my/our commitment to freedom?

In retrospect I see that in the last twenty years of my life I have encountered many folks who say they are committed to freedom and justice for all even though the way they live, the values and habits of being they institutionalize in public and private rituals daily help maintain the culture of domination, help create an unfree world. With prophetic insight Martin Luther King, in the book entitled *Where Do We Go from Here: Chaos or Community*, told the citizens of this nation that we would be unable to go forward if we did not experience a "true revolution of values." He assured us that "The stability of the large world house which is ours will involve a revolution of values to accompany the scientific and freedom revolutions engulfing the earth. We must rapidly begin the shift from a 'thing'-oriented society to a 'person' oriented society. When machines and computers, profit motives and property rights are considered more important than people, the giant triplets of racism, materialism, and militarism are incapable of being conquered. A civilization can flounder as readily in the face of moral and spiritual bankruptcy as it can through financial bankruptcy." Today we live in the midst of that floundering. We live in chaos, uncertain about the possibility of building and sustaining community. The public figures who speak the most to us about a return to old-fashioned values embody the evils King describes. They are most committed to maintaining systems of domination—racism, sexism, class exploitation, and imperialism. They promote a perverse vision of freedom that makes it synonymous with materialism. They teach us to believe that domination is "natural," that it is right for the strong to rule over the weak, the powerful over the powerless. What amazes me is that so many people claim not to embrace these values and yet our collective rejection of them cannot be complete as they prevail in our daily lives.

These days I am compelled to consider what forces keep us from moving forward, from having that revolution of values that would enable us to live differently. King taught us to understand that if "we are to have peace on earth," "our loyalties must transcend our race, our tribe, our class, and our nation." Long before the word multi-culturalism became fashionable, he encouraged us to "develop a world perspective." Yet what we are witnessing today in our everyday life is not an eagerness on the part of neighbors and strangers to develop a world perspective but a return to narrow nationalisms, isolationisms, and xenophobia. These shifts are usually explained in New Right and neo-conservative terms as attempts to bring order to chaos, to return to an idealized past. The notion of family evoked in these discussions is one in which sexist defined roles for males and females are upheld as stabilizing traditions. Not surprising, this idealized vision of family life is coupled with a notion of security and safety that suggests we are always most safe with people of our own group, who are of the same race, class, religion, etc. No matter how many statistics on domestic violence, homicide, rape, child abuse, etc. indicate that in fact the idealized patriarchal family is not a "safe" space; that those of us who experience any form of assault are more likely to be victimized by those who are like us rather than by some mysterious strange outsiders, these realities are denied. Considering these circumstances, it becomes apparent that one of the primary reasons for not having experienced a revolution of values is that a culture of domination necessarily promotes addiction to lying and denial.

That lying takes the presumably innocent form for many white people (and even some black folks) to suggest that racism does not exist anymore and that conditions of social equality are solidly in place that would enable any black person who works hard to achieve economic self-sufficiency. Forget about the fact that capitalism requires the existence of a mass underclass of surplus labor. It takes the form of mass media creating the myth that the feminist movement has completely transformed society, so much so that the politics of patriarchal power have been inverted and that men, particularly white men, like emasculated black men, have become the victims of dominating women, so that all men, white and black in particular, must pull together (e.g., the Clarence Thomas hearings) to support and reaffirm patriarchal domination. Add to this the widely held assumption on the part of many people that blacks, other minorities, and white women are taking jobs from white men, that people are poor and unemployed because they want to be, and it becomes most evident that part of our contemporary crisis is created by a lack of meaningful access to truth. When this collective cultural consumption of and attachment to misinformation is coupled with the layers of lying individuals do in their personal lives, our capacity to face reality is severely diminished as is our will to intervene and change unjust circumstances.

When we critically examine the traditional role of the university in the pursuit of truth and the sharing of knowledge and information, it becomes painfully clear that biases that uphold and maintain white supremacy, imperialism, sexism, racism, etc. have distorted education so that it has not been about the practice of freedom. The call for a recognition of cultural diversity, a re-thinking of ways of knowing, a deconstruction of old epistemologies, and the concomitant demand that there be a transformation in our classrooms, in how we teach and what we teach, has been a necessary revolution—one that seeks to restore life to a corrupt and dying academy. When everyone first began to speak about cultural diversity it was exciting. For those of us on the margins (many of us people of color, folks from working-class backgrounds, and/or gay), who had always felt ambivalent about our presence in institutions where knowledge was shared in ways that re-inscribed colonialism, domination, it was thrilling to think that the vision of justice and democracy that was at the very heart of the civil rights movement would be realized in the academy. At last there was the possibility of a learning community, a place where difference could be acknowledged, where we would finally all understand, accept, and affirm that our ways of knowing are forged in history and relations of power. Finally we were all going to break through collective academic denial and acknowledge that the education most of us had received and were giving was not and is never politically neutral. Though it was evident that change would not be immediate, there was tremendous hope that this process we had set in motion would lead to a fulfillment of the dream of education as the practice of freedom.

Initially, many of our colleagues were reluctant participants in this change. Yet many of them tried, and are still trying, to open their minds, to shift their paradigms. The greatest motivating catalyst for professorial change was and is the joy in our students, who for the most part sincerely desire a liberatory education. Change is difficult—particularly when we are called to uproot familiar ways of thinking and behaving and replace them with new thought and action.

Many folks found that as they tried to respect "cultural diversity" they had to confront the limitations of their training, knowledge, and possible loss of "authority." Indeed, exposing certain truths and biases in the classroom often created chaos and confusion. The idea that the classroom should always be a "safe" harmonious place was challenged. It was hard for individuals to fully grasp the idea that recognition of difference might also require of us a willingness to see and experience the classroom change, to allow for shifts in relations between students. A lot of people panicked. What they saw happening was not the comforting "melting pot" idea of cultural diversity, the rainbow coalition where we would all be grouped together, in our difference, but wearing the same "have a nice day" smile. This was the stuff of colonizing fantasy, a perversion of the progressive vision of cultural diversity. Critiquing this longing in a recent interview entitled "Critical Multiculturalism and Democratic Schooling," Peter McLaren asserts: "Diversity that somehow constitutes itself as a harmonious ensemble of benign cultural spheres is a conservative and liberal model of multiculturalism that, in my mind, deserves to be jettisoned because, when we try to make culture an undisturbed space of harmony and agreement where social relations exist within cultural forms of uninterrupted accord, we ascribe to a form of social amnesia in which we forget that all knowledge is forged in histories that are played out in the held of social antagonisms."[1] Many professors lacked strategies to deal with antagonisms in the classroom. When this fear joined with the refusal to change that characterized the stance of an old, predominantly white male guard, it created a space for disempowered collective backlash.

All of a sudden professors who had taken issues of multiculturalism and cultural diversity seriously were backtracking, expressing doubts, casting votes in directions that would restore biased traditions or prohibit changes in faculty and curriculum that were to bring diversity of representation and perspective. Joining forces with the old guard, previously open professors condoned senior colleagues using tactics of ostracization, belittlement, etc. to dissuade junior faculty members from making paradigm shifts that would lead to changes in curriculum, scholarly research, writing, and teaching practices. This week in my Toni Morrison seminar, as we went around our circle voicing critical reflections on Morrison's language, a sort of classically white, blondish J Crew kinda coed shared that one of her other English professors, an older white man (whose name none of us wanted her to mention) confided that he was so pleased to find a student still interested in reading literature—words—the language of texts and "not that race and gender stuff." Somewhat amused by the assumption he had made about her, she was disturbed by his conviction that conventional ways of critically approaching a novel could not co-exist in classrooms that also offered new perspectives.

I shared my recent experience of being at a Halloween party where a new white male colleague with whom I was chatting for the first time at the mere mention of my Toni Morrison seminar went on a tirade emphasizing that *Song of Solomon* was a weak re-write of Hemingway's *For Whom the Bell Tolls*. Passionately full of disgust for Morrison, being a Hemingway scholar, he seemed to be covertly sharing the often heard concern that black women writers/thinkers are just poor imitations of "great" white men. Not wanting at that moment to launch into Unlearning Colonialism, Divesting of Racism and Sexism 101, I opted for the strategy taught to me by that in-denial-of-institutionalized-patriarchy self-help book *Women Who Love Too Much*. I just said, Oh! Later, I assured him that I would read again *For Whom the Bell Tolls* to see if I would see the same connection. Both of these seemingly trivial incidents reveal how deep-seated the fear is that any de-centering of Western civilization, of the white male canon, is really an act of cultural genocide.

Some folks think that everyone who supports cultural diversity wants to replace one dictatorship of knowing with another, changing one set way of thinking for another. This is perhaps the gravest mis-perception of cultural diversity. Even though there are those overly zealous among us who hope to replace one set of absolutes with another, this perspective does not accurately represent progressive visions of the way commitment to cultural diversity can constructively transform the academy. In all cultural revolutions there are periods of chaos and confusion, times when grave mistakes are made. If we fear mistakes, doing things wrongly, having to be constantly evaluating, introducing new ideas and strategies, we will never transform the academy into a culturally diverse place with scholars and curriculum addressing every dimension of that difference.

As backlash swells, as budgets are cut, as jobs become even more scarce, many of the few progressive interventions that were made to change the academy, to create an open climate for cultural diversity are in danger of being undermined and/or eliminated. These threats should not be ignored. Nor should our collective commitment to cultural diversity change because we have not yet devised and implemented perfect strategies that would enable smooth transformation. To create a culturally diverse academy we must commit ourselves fully. Learning from other movements for social change, from civil rights and feminist liberation efforts, we must accept the protracted nature of our struggle and be willing to remain both patient and vigilant. To commit ourselves to the work of transforming the academy into a place where cultural diversity informs every aspect of our learning, we must embrace struggle and sacrifice. We cannot be easily discouraged, we cannot despair when there is conflict. Our solidarity must be affirmed by shared belief in a spirit of intellectual openness that celebrates diversity, welcomes dissent, and rejoices in collective dedication to truth.

Drawing strength from the life and work of Martin Luther King, I am often reminded of the profound inner struggle that took place within him when he felt spiritually called by his religious beliefs to oppose the war in Vietnam. Fearful of alienating conservative bourgeois supporters, of alienating the Black Church, King meditated on a passage from the Book of Romans which reminded him of the necessity of dissent, challenge, and change. That passage begins: "Be not conformed to this world but be ye transformed by the renewal of your minds. . . ." All of us in the academy and in the culture as a whole are called to renew our minds if we are to transform educational institutions and society, so that the way we live, teach, and work can reflect our joy in cultural diversity, our passion for justice, and our love of freedom.

Oberlin College

Endnote

1. Shirley Steinberg, "Critical Multiculturalism and Democratic Schooling: An Interview with Peter McLaren and Joe Kincheloe," International Journal of Educational Reform 1.4 (October 1992): 399.

30 | *National Identity and the Politics of Multiculturalism*

Henry A. Giroux

Global changes have provided the conditions for the emergence of new theoretical discourses that pose a powerful challenge to modern assumptions regarding the unity of nationalism and culture, the state and the nation, and national identity and the universal imperatives of a common culture. The changes that have, in part, produced new forms of theorizing about globalization, the politics of diaspora, immigration, identity politics, multiculturalism, and postcolonialism are as profound intellectually as they are disruptive politically. Judith Squires captures the scope of these changes, while expressing some reservations about what they have come to mean as they are rapidly absorbed into new theoretical discourses:

> The global economy is a given in our life now: transnational corporations cross borders to maximize productivity and transnational intellectuals cross academic boundaries to maximize knowledge. The academic discipline, along with the national state, is subject to powerful forces of change. And, as we might acknowledge the failings of the old model of state sovereignty and hegemonic nationalism but nonetheless remain deeply skeptical about the gains to be had from the free movement of international capital around the globe in pursuit of profit, so we must be attuned to the benefits of jettisoning the status of empirical area studies, the constricting patriarchal academic canons and oppressive hierarchical department structures, but also the pitfalls. (v)

The pitfalls to which Squires refers are the lack of specificity and theoretical blurriness that sometimes accompany the scholarly rush to take up issues of the politics of globalization, diaspora, multiculturalism, and postcolonialism (see also Grewal and Kaplan, Ien, Calhoun, "Nationalism," and Parry). I am particularly concerned here with a position that does not differentiate among radical, liberal, and conservative forms of multiculturalism within the politics of the nation state. Such generalizations often recycle or reproduce colonialist discourse. What must be resisted is the assumption that the politics of national identity is necessarily complicitous with a reactionary discourse of nationalism and has been superseded by theories which locate identity politics squarely within the discourses of postnational, diasporic globalism, or what Arjun Appadurai calls the "search for nonterritorial principles of solidarity" (417).

This is not to suggest that diverse nationalisms can be addressed outside of their transnational links, or that the mechanisms of a dominant and oppressive politics of assimilation can be abstracted from the pain, anguish, and suffering experienced by those diasporic groups who define themselves through "nonnational identities and aspirations" (Appadurai 418). What I am resisting is the claim that nationalism can only be associated with ethnic conflict, that nationalism is witnessing its death knell, or that the relationship between nationalism and national identity can only be framed within a transnational discourse. The importance of such arguments must be acknowledged, but at the same time it is important to recognize in the context of the current conservative ideological offensive in the United States that it is crucial for critical educators and others to "locate our theorizing in the grounded sites of cultural and political resistance" within the United States, on the one hand, and to guard against the tendency to "overgeneralize the global current of so-called nomadic, fragmented and deterritorialized subjectivity" (Squires vi).

Nationalism is crucial to understanding the debates over identity and multiculturalism in the United States. As important as the discourse of globalization might be, it cannot be used to overlook how national identity reasserts itself within new discourses and sites of learning. More specifically, I want to argue that rather than dismissing the politics of identity as another essentialist discourse, progressives need to address how the politics of identity and difference are being constructed around new right wing discourses and policies. Central to the construction of a right wing nationalism is a project of defining national identity through an appeal to a common culture that displaces any notion of national identity based upon a pluralized notion of culture with its multiple literacies, identities, and histories and erases histories of oppression and struggle for the working class and minorities. Stuart Hall is right in arguing that the 1990s is witnessing the return of recharged nationalism in big and small societies that serves to restore national culture as the primordial source of national identity ("Culture" 353). But this should not suggest that the relationship between nationalism and culture manifests itself exclusively in terms of oppression or domination or that any attempt to develop an insurgent multiculturalism through an appeal to radical democracy necessarily assumes or leaves intact the boundary of the nation as an unproblematic historical, political, and spatial formation. At stake here is the need to acknowledge the existence of the nation state and nationalism as primary forces in shaping collective identities while simultaneously addressing how the relationship between national identity and culture can be understood as part of a broader struggle around developing national and postnational forms of democracy.

The relationship between culture and nationalism always bears the traces of those historical, ethical, and political forces that constitute the often shifting and contradictory elements of national identity. To the degree that the culture of nationalism is rigidly exclusive and defines its membership in terms of narrowly based common culture, nationalism tends to be xenophobic, authoritarian, and expansionist. The latter reflects the most commonly cited example of a nationalism steeped in the practices of ethnic cleansing, genocide, or imperialist aggression. On the other hand, nationalism moves closer toward being liberal and democratic to the degree that national identity is inclusive and respectful of diversity and difference. And yet, a civic nationalism that makes a claim to respecting cultural differences does not guarantee that the state will not engage in coercive assimilationist policies. In other words, democratic forms of nationalism cannot be defended simply through a formal appeal to abstract, democratic principles. How nationalism and the nation state embrace democracy must be determined, in part, through the access diverse cultural groups have to shared structures of power that organize commanding legal, economic, and cultural institutions on the local, state, and national level (see Kymlicka).

Cultural differences and national identity stand in a complex relationship to each other and point to progressive as well as totalitarian elements of nationalism that provide testimony to its problematic character and effects. On the negative side, recent history bears witness to the second world war steeped in forms of national identity that mobilized racial hatred and supported right wing, anti-democratic governments in Germany, Italy, and Japan. Following 1945, one of the most flagrant legacies of such a poisonous nationalism is evident in the long-standing apartheid regime that, until recently, dominated South African politics as well as in the continuing attempt on the part of Turkey to deny the Kurds any status as a national group.

Representations of national identity constructed through an appeal to racial purity, militarism, anti-semitism, and religious orthodoxy have once again surfaced aggressively in Western Europe and can be seen in the rise of neo-nazi youth movements in Germany, the neo-Fascist political parties that won the recent election in Italy, and the ethnic cleansing that has driven Serbian nationalism in the former Republic of Yugoslavia. This highly selective list merely illustrates how national identity can be fashioned around appeals to a monolithic cultural identity that affirms intolerance, bigotry, and an indifference to the precepts of democratic pluralism. Needless to say, these forms of demagogic nationalism emerge from a diverse set of conditions and circumstances, the roots of which lie in a complex history of racial conflict, the unstable economic conditions that have gripped Europe, and the dismantling of the Soviet Union and its empire. As a social construction, nationalism does not rest upon a particular politics; it takes its form within, rather than outside of, specific historical, social, and cultural contexts.

The more positive face of nationalism has emerged in a number of countries through a legacy of democratic struggles and can be seen not only in various anti-colonialist struggles in Asia and Africa, but also in diverse attempts on the part of nation-states to mobilize popular sentiment in the interest of expanding human rights and fighting against the encroachments of undemocratic social forces. While many of these movements of national struggle are far from unproblematic, particularly during periods in which they assume state control, they do provide credibility to the emancipatory power of nationalism as a defining principle in world politics.[1] A progressive notion of nationalism requires the coordination of a democratic politics of difference and multiculturalism with a notion of border crossing, diasporic politics, and postnationalism that recognizes the transits, flows, and social formations being produced on a global scale. It is precisely in the interaction of the national and global that a borderline space exists for generating new forms of transnational literacy, social relations, and cultural identities that expand the meaning of democratic citizenship beyond national borders.

Mythic National Identity

For many Americans, questions of national identity seem to elude the complex legacy of nationalism and take on a mythic quality. Informed by the powerful appeal to assimilation and the legitimating discourse of patriotism, national identity often operates within an ideological register untainted by the historical and emerging legacies of totalitarianism. Rather than being viewed cautiously as a potential vehicle for undermining democracy, national identity in the United States has been defined more positively in commonsensical terms as deeply connected to the mythic march of progress and prosperity at home and the noble effort to export democracy abroad. Hence, national identity has all too often been forged within popular memory as a discourse that too neatly links nation, culture, and citizenship in a seamless and unproblematic unity. Invoking claims to the past in which the politics of remembering and forgetting work powerfully to legitimate a notion of national belonging that "constructs the nation as an ethnically homogeneous object" (Gilroy 3), national identity is rewritten and purged of its seamy side. Within this narrative, national identity is structured through a notion of citizenship and patriotism that subordinates ethnic, racial, and cultural differences to the assimilating logic of a common culture, or, more brutally, the "melting pot." Behind the social imaginary that informs this notion of national identity is a narrowly defined notion of history that provides a defense of the narratives of imperial power and dominant culture and legitimates an intensely narrow and bigoted notion of what it means to be an American.

In an era of recharged nationalist discourse in the United States, the populist invocation of national identity suggests that social criticism itself is antithetical to both the construction of national identity and the precepts of patriotism. Of course, national identity, like nationalism itself, is a social construction that is built upon a series of inclusions and exclusions regarding history, citizenship, and national belonging. As the social historian Benedict Anderson has pointed out, the nation is an "imagined political community" that can only be understood within the intersecting dynamics of history, language, ideology, and power. In other words, nationalism and national identity are neither necessarily reactionary nor necessarily progressive politically. They give rise to communities which, as Anderson points out, are "to be distinguished, not by their falsity/genuineness, but by the style in which they are imagined" (6).

The insight that national identity must be addressed according to the ways in which it is imagined signals for me the importance of pedagogical practices that are central to the current debates around questions of identity characterizing much political debate in the United States. It is the pedagogical processes at work in framing the current debates on national identity that interest me most. More specifically, the questions I want to raise are: what forms of address, images, texts, and performances are being produced and used in popular discourses to construct what it means to be an American, and what are the implications of these dominant representations for extending or undermining a substantive plural democracy?

The current debate over national identity represents not only a conservative backlash fueled by the assumption that "those common values and consensual freedoms that have defined the 'American' way of life, circa Norman Rockwell" (Bhabha, "A Good Judge" 233) are now under attack by racial, sexual, and political minorities. Moreover, the current conservatism produces a new nationalism rooted in an imaginary construction of national identity that is dangerous to any viable notion of democracy. This is not meant to suggest that the discourse of national unity voiced through an appeal to shared language of difference (not the assimilationist language of a common culture) should be summarily dismissed as Eurocentric, racist, or patriarchal. The vision of national identity steeped in a shared vision of social justice and a respect for cultural differences is to be applauded. At the same time, the healing grace of a national identity based on a respect for "lived cultures in the plural" (Graff and Robbins 434) should not be confused with a politically reactionary notion of national identity whose primary purpose is to restrict the terms of citizenship and community to a discourse of monoculturalism and nativism. National identity in the service of a common culture recognizes cultural differences only to flatten them out in the conservative discourse of assimilation and the liberal appeal to tolerance (see Ien, Hage). However, the relationship between national identity and nationalism is not bound by any particular politics, and by definition is not intrinsically oppressive. Hence, it is both important and necessary as part of a progressive politics of national identity to provide a theoretical space to address the potential of both a pedagogy and politics that can pluralize cultural differences within democratic relations of power as part of an effort to develop an emancipatory politics of national identity and nationalism. This is especially important at a time in the United States when the discourses of nationalism and national identity have taken a decidedly reactionary political turn.

The appropriation of national identity as a vehicle to foster racism, nativism, and political censorship is not specific to the 1990s, but has a long history in the United States. What is somewhat new are the conditions, contexts, and content through which the discourse of national identity is being produced and linked to virulent forms of nationalism. For example, media culture with its new cable technologies coupled with the proliferation of radio and television talk channels has created a public sphere that vastly expands the intrusion into daily life of mainstream discourses that greatly restrict the possibility for real debate, exchange, and diversity of opinions. These electronic media, largely driven by corporate conglomerates, have no precedent in American life in terms of their power both to disseminate information and to shape how national identity is configured, comprehended, and experienced as part of everyday life. Secondly, popular culture has become a powerful site for defining nationalism and national identity against diversity and cultural differences, the latter rendered synonymous with disruption, disunity, and separatism. In this populist discourse, there is a theoretical slippage that equates national identity with a common identity and the assertion of cultural pluralism with an assault on the very character of what it means to be an American. At issue here is a politics of forgetting that erases how disparate social identities have been produced, legitimated, and marginalized within different relations of power. But there is more at stake than the erasure of social memory; there is also the emergence of a racially saturated discourse that mobilizes national identity as the defining principle for a national community that is under siege. Similarly, the new nationalism in foreign policy employs the chauvinistic bravado of the marketplace with its call for the United States to be number one in the world while simultaneously stigmatizing internal social criticism as unpatriotic and a threat to American culture and civility.

Media Culture and the Populist Construction of Nationalist Identity

I want to examine briefly some populist examples of the new nationalism that speak from different places in the cultural apparatuses that shape public opinion. In different ways, these populist voices advocate a pedagogy and politics of national identity that serve to reproduce some reactionary elements of the new nationalism. For example, expressions of the new nationalism can be found in several sites: in the backlash against multiculturalism in the public schools and universities; in the rise of the English Only movement; in the notion of the state as a "stern parent" willing to inflict harsh measures on welfare mothers; and in educational reforms demanding a national curriculum. Ideological signposts pointing to the new nationalism can be found in analogies invoking metaphors of battle, invasion, and war, which increasingly shape the debates over immigration in the United States, as in the passing of anti-immigration legislation such as California's Proposition 187. Crime is represented in the dominant white media as a black issue, implying that race can only be understood through a reductionist correlation of culture and identity. Representations of black men appear ad nauseam on the covers of magazines such as *Newsweek, The New York Times Sunday Magazine,* and *Time* whenever a signifier is needed to mobilize and draw upon the general public's fear of crime and urban decay. Recent Hollywood films abound with racist representations that link criminality to skin color. Some of the most popular examples include *Pulp Fiction* (1994) and *Just Cause* (1995) (see Giroux). All of these examples underscore how nationalism is currently being shaped to defend a beleaguered notion of national identity read as white, heterosexual, middle-class, and allegedly threatened by contamination from cultural, linguistic, racial, and sexual differences.

The power of the new nationalism and its centrality to American political life can also be seen in its growth and popularity in a number of popular and public spaces. One example can be found in the written and television commentaries of Republican presidential hopeful Patrick Buchanan on shows such as CNN's *Crossfire.* Buchanan represents a new version of the public intellectual speaking from such critical public sites as the news media, especially the growing number of news programs on cable television that are largely dominated by right-wing commentary. For Buchanan, the new nationalism is defined through a bellicose nativism that views cultural differences as a threat to national unity. Buchanan argues that the reality of cultural difference, with its plurality of languages, experiences, and histories, poses a serious threat to both national unity and what he defends as Judeo-Christian values. According to Buchanan, calls for expanding the existing potential of political representation and self-determination are fine in so far as they enable white Americans to "take back" their country. In this reactionary discourse, difference becomes a signifier for racial exclusivity, segregation, or, in Buchanan's language, "self determination." For Buchanan, public life in the United States has deteriorated since 1965 because "a flood tide of immigration has rolled in from the Third World, legal and illegal, as our institutions of assimilation . . . disintegrated." Ushering in the discourse of nativism, Buchanan asks: "Who speaks for the Euro-Americans? Is it not time to take America back?" (qtd. in Krauthammer A4). Similarly, populist right-wing conservative Rush Limbaugh, who describes himself as the "Doctor of Democracy," rails against the poor and disadvantaged minorities because they do not act like "real" Americans who "rely upon their own resources, skills, talents, and hard work" (26). Limbaugh has become the populist equivalent of Beavis and Butt-Head. Combining humor, unrestrained narcissism, and outright buffoonery with a virulent and mean-spirited attack on progressive causes, Limbaugh accentuates the current appeal of the talk-show that is part of a broader reactionary, conservative offensive through popular media. Perhaps the only thing interesting about Limbaugh is that he exemplifies how right wing conservatives no longer limit their political agenda to the traditional channels of policy, news, and information. They have now extended their influence to the more populist cultural realms of radio and television talk shows, the world of stand-up comics, and other texts of media culture.

Rush Limbaugh, Howard Stern, Andrew Dice Clay, and other popular media figures represent a marriage of media culture and the lure of extremist attacks in what appears as a legitimation of a new form of public pathology dressed up as entertainment.[2] Limbaugh echoes the increasingly popular assumption that an "ethnic upsurge" threatens both the American model of assimilation and the unity of America as a single culture. Extending rather than challenging the ideological assumptions that buttress the old racism and Social Darwinism, Limbaugh and others echo a view of cultural unity less as an overt marker for racial superiority than as a discourse for privileging a white "minority." Within this populist discourse, racism is couched in the critique of the welfare state but serves primarily as a signifier for cultural containment, homogeneity, and social and structural inequality. Just as Charles Murray and Richard Herrnstein warn in *The Bell Curve* against the effects of immigration on the gene pool of white, middle-class Americans, and the religious right calls for a "holy war" to be waged in the schools to preserve the identity of the United States as a "Christian" nation, right wing populist commentators add a twist to the new nationalism and its racial coding by appealing to a nostalgic, romanticized view of history as the "good old days" in which white men ruled, blacks knew their place in the social and political hierarchy, and women attended to domestic work. The appeal is no longer simply to racial supremacy but also to cultural uniformity parading as the politics of nationalism, national identity, and patriotism. These anti-multicultural attacks organize themselves around a view of nationalism that eschews any disagreement by simply labelling critics as "America-bashers."

In the world of TV spectacles and mass entertainment, the Buchanans and Limbaughs represent the shock-troops of the new nationalism. On the academic front, a more "refined" version of the new nationalism has been advanced. Two examples will suffice, though they are hardly inclusive. In the first instance, public intellectuals writing in conservative periodicals such as *The New Republic, The New Criterion,* and *The American Spectator* increasingly put forth an argument for the new nationalism in terms that both dismiss multiculturalism and reproduce the discourse of assimilation and common culture. Rather than analyzing multiculturalism as a complex, legitimate, and necessary "ongoing negotiation among minorities against assimilation" (Bhabha, "Beyond the Pale" 15), the new nationalists see in the engagements of cultural difference less a productive tension than a debilitating divisiveness. John B. Judis and Michael Lind echo this sentiment in their own call for a new nationalism:

[T]here is a constructive and inclusive current of American nationalism that runs from Alexander Hamilton through Abraham Lincoln and Theodore Roosevelt. It emphasizes not the exclusion of foreigners, but rather the unification of Americans of different regions, races and ethnic groups around a common national identity. It stands opposed not only to nativism, but also to today's multiculturalism and economic or strategic globalism. (21)

Nationalism in this discourse becomes the marker of certainty; it both affirms monoculturalism and restores the racially coded image of "Americanness" as a beleaguered national identity (Hall, "Culture" 357). The new nationalism also posits national identity against the ability of different groups to articulate and affirm their histories, languages, cultural identities, and traditions through the shifting and complex relations in which people imagine and construct national and postnational social formations. This is evident in the attack being waged by the right and the Republican Congress on affirmative action, quotas, immigration, bilingualism, and multiculturalism in the public schools. But the new nationalism is not confined to right wing conservatives and evangelical Christians.

A more moderate version of the new nationalism can be found in the work of writers like Richard Rorty, a prominent liberal philosopher from the University of Virginia. While Buchanan, Limbaugh, and their followers might be dismissed as simply populist demagogues, public intellectuals such as Rorty command enormous respect from the academic community and the established press. Moreover, such intellectuals travel between academic and popular public spheres with enough influence to bring professional legitimacy to the new nationalism as it is taken up in television and talk radio programs, the electronic media, and in the major newspapers and magazines in the United States. Hence, it is all the more important that arguments that reinforce the logic of the new nationalism and parade under the banner of a "tough" or "patriotic" liberalism be critically engaged, especially for individuals who find in such arguments a semblance of reason and restraint.

Richard Rorty, Liberalism, and the Problem of National Identity

Writing in the Op-Ed section of *The New York Times,* Rorty has argued under the headline, "The Unpatriotic Academy," that left-wing academics who support multiculturalism are "unpatriotic." For Rorty, the litmus test for patriotism is not to be found in social criticism that holds a country up to its professed ideals, but in a refusal on the part of "this left . . . to rejoice in the country it inhabits. It repudiates the idea of a national identity, and the emotion of national pride." Speaking for an unspecified group of "patriotic" Americans, Rorty, in this instance, insists that "We take pride in being citizens of a self-invented, self-reforming, enduring constitutional democracy" (E15). One wonders: for whom do intellectuals such as Rorty speak? Have they appointed themselves as spokespersons for all Americans who disassociate themselves from the left? And does this generalization further suggest that one gives up respect and love of one's country if one engages in criticism that can be conveniently labeled as left-wing? Does a public assertion of patriotism, as ritualistically invoked by all manner of demagogues, suggest that such rhetoric provides a certified stamp of legitimacy regarding one's own politics?

Of course, Limbaugh and Buchanan consistently engage in the rhetoric of love for their country while simultaneously baiting gays, blacks, feminists, and others. Moreover, one must consider the implications of Rorty's attack on the left social critics in light of the ways in which the United States engaged in red-baiting during the 1920s and the McCarthy witchhunts of the 1950s. Is he suggesting that left-wing theorists (as if they could be grouped homogeneously) should be policed and punished for their lack of patriotism? There is a recklessness in Rorty's charges that places him squarely in the camp of those who would punish dissenters rather than support free speech, especially if it is speech that one disagrees with. Maybe Rorty was simply being rambunctious in his use of the term "unpatriotic," but given the way in which the term has been used historically in this country to squelch social criticism, such a lapse of historical memory seems unlikely. So what is the point?

Rorty seems to be caught between liberal guilt and the appeal of a rabid conservatism that equates cultural differences with a threat to national unity, a threat that has to be overcome. Equating the politics of difference with a threat to national unity, Rorty then takes the extraordinary step of identifying all those academics who support some version of multiculturalism as posing a threat to the social order. For Rorty, there is no contradiction in feeling one's heart swell with patriotism and "national hope" and feeling "shame at the greed, the intolerance and the indifference to suffering that is widespread in the United States" (E15). In this theoretical sweep, multiculturalism is not addressed in its complexity as a range of theoretical positions that run the ideological gamut extending from calls for separatism to new forms of cultural democracy. Multiculturalism for Rorty is simply a position that exists under some absolute sign. In this reductionistic perspective, there are no theoretical differences between multicultural positions espoused by academic leftists such as Hazel Carby, Guillermo Gomez-Pena, June Jordan, and bell hooks, on the one hand, and liberals such as James Banks, Gregory Jay, or Stanley Fish on the other. But there is more at stake here than Rorty's suspect appeal to patriotism. Social criticism is not the enemy of patriotism, it is the bedrock of a shared national tradition that allows for many voices to engage in a dialogue about the dynamics of cultural and political power. In fact, national identity must be understood within a broader concern for the expansion and deepening of democratic public life itself.

I believe that Rorty's notion of national identity closes down, rather than expands, the principles that inform a multicultural and multiracial democracy. However, Rorty is important in terms of exemplifying the limits of the reigning political philosophy of liberalism. Rorty's gesture towards tolerance "presupposes that its object is morally repugnant, that it really needs to be reformed, that is, altered" (Goldberg, *Racist Culture* 7). As David Theo Goldberg points out:

> Liberals are moved to overcome the racial differences they tolerate and have been so instrumental in fabricating by diluting them, by bleaching them out through assimilation or integration. The liberal would assume away the difference in otherness maintaining thereby the dominant of a presumed sameness, the universally imposed similarity in identity. (Racist Culture 7)

National identity cannot be constructed around the suppression of dissent. Nor should it be used in the service of a new fundamentalism by appealing to a notion of patriotism that equates left-wing social criticism with treason, and less critical forms of discourse with a love of nationalism or national identity. It is precisely this type of binarism that has been used, all too frequently throughout the twentieth century, to develop national communities that make a virtue of intolerance and exclusion. Moreover, this kind of logic prevents individuals and social groups from understanding and critically engaging national identity not as a cultural monument but as a living set of relations that must be constantly engaged and struggled over.

Rorty's facile equating of national identity with the love of one's country, on the one hand, and the dismissal of forms of left social criticism that argue for various forms of multiculturalism, on the other, are simply an expression of the new nationalism, one which views cultural differences and the emergence of multiple cultures as a sign of fragmentation and a departure from, rather than an advance toward, democracy. Rorty's mistake is that he assumes that national identity is to be founded on a single culture, language, and history when in fact it can't. National identity is always a shifting, unsettled complex of historical struggles and experiences that are cross-fertilized, produced, and translated through a variety of cultures. As such, it is always open to interpretation and struggle. As Hall points out, national identity "is a matter of 'becoming' as well of 'being.' . . . [It] is never complete, always in process. . . . [It] is not eternally fixed in some essentialized past [but] subject to the continuous 'play' of history, culture, and power" ("Cultural Identity" 225).

The discourse of multiculturalism represents, in part, the emergence of new voices that have generally been excluded from the multiple histories that have defined our national identity. Far from being a threat to social order, multiculturalism in its various forms has challenged notions of national identity that equate cultural differences with deviance and disruption. Refusing a notion of national identity constructed on the suppression of cultural differences and social dissent, multiculturalism, especially its more critical and insurgent versions, explores how dominant views of national identity have been developed around cultural differences constructed within hierarchical relations of power that authorize who can or cannot speak legitimately as an American. Maybe it is the insertion of politics and power back into the discourse on difference that threatens Rorty so much that he responds to it by labelling it as unpatriotic.

Pitting national identity against cultural difference not only appeals to an oppressive politics of common culture, but reinforces a political moralism that polices "the boundaries of identity, encouraging uniformity and ensuring intellectual inertia" (Rutherford 17). National identity based on a unified cultural community suggests a dangerous relationship between the ideas of race, intolerance, and the cultural membership of nationhood. Not only does such a position downplay the politics of culture at work in nationalism, but it erases an oppressive history forged in an appeal to a common culture and a reactionary notion of national identity. As Will Kymlicka points out, liberals and conservatives often overlook the fact that the American government "forcibly incorporated Indian tribes, native Hawaiians, and Puerto Ricans into the American state, and then attempted to coercively assimilate each group into the common American culture. It banned the speaking of Indian languages in school and forced Puerto Rican and Hawaiian schools to use English rather than Spanish or Hawaiian" (132).

What is problematic about Rorty's position is not simply that he views multiculturalism as a threat to a totalizing notion of national identity. More important is his theoretical indifference to counter-narratives of difference, diaspora, and cultural identity that explore how diverse groups are constructed within an insurgent multiculturalism, which engage the issue both of what holds us together as a nation and of what constitutes our differences from each other. Viewing cultural differences only as a problem, Rorty reveals a disturbing lacuna in his notion of national identity. It is a view that offers little defense against the forces of ethnic absolutism and cultural racism that are so quick to seize upon national identity as a legitimating discourse for racial violence. There is an alarming defensiveness in Rorty's view, one that reinforces rather than challenges a discourse of national community rooted in claims to cultural and racist supremacy.

Pedagogy, National Identity, and the Politics of Difference

Critical educators need a notion of national identity that addresses its political, cultural, and pedagogical components. In the first instance, national identity must be addressed as part of a broader consideration linking nationalism and postnational social formations to a theory of democracy. That is, the relationship between nationalism and democracy must address not only the crucial issue of whether legal rights are provided for all groups irrespective of their cultural identity, but also how structures of power work to ensure that diverse cultural communities have the economic, political, and social resources to exercise "both the capacity for collective voice and the possibility of differentiated, directly interpersonal relations" (Calhoun, "Nationalism" 311). Rather than waging war against the pluralization of cultural identities and the crucial spheres in which they are nurtured and engaged, educators must address critically how national identity is constructed in the media, through the politics of state apparatuses, and through the mobilization of material resources and power outside of the reach of the state (see Goldberg, "Introduction"). As part of a broader politics of representation, this suggests the need for progressive cultural workers to provide the pedagogical conditions and sites "open to competing conceptualizations, diverse identities, and a rich public discourse" necessary to expand the conditions for democracy to flourish on both a national and global level (Calhoun, "Nationalism" 327).

Secondly, national identity must be inclusive and informed by a democratic pluralization of cultural identities. If the tendency towards a universalizing, assimilative impulse is to be resisted, educators must ensure that students engage varied notions of an imagined community by critically addressing rather than excluding cultural differences. While the approach toward such a pedagogy is culturally inclusive and suggests expanding the varied texts that define what counts as knowledge in public schools and institutions of higher education in the United States, there is also a need to create institutionalized spaces obligated to transdisciplinarity and multicultural studies. But such pedagogical spaces must be firmly committed to more than a politics of inclusive representation or simply aimed at helping students to understand and celebrate cultural difference (Martin Luther King, Jr. Day, for example). The politics of cultural difference must be a politics of more than texts: it must also understand, negotiate, and challenge differences as they are defined and sustained within oppressive networks of power. Critically negotiating the relationship between national identity and cultural differences, as Homi Bhabha has pointed out, is a negating activity that should be valued for *making a difference* in the world rather than merely reflecting it ("Beyond" 22).

What educators need is a pedagogy that redefines national identity not through a primordial notion of ethnicity or a monolithic conception of culture, but as part of a postmodern politics of cultural difference in which identities are constantly being negotiated and reinvented within complex and contradictory notions of national belonging. A collective dialogue over nationalism, national identity, and cultural differences is not going to be established by simply labelling certain forms of social criticism as unpatriotic or national identity as a shared tradition that exists outside of the struggles over representation, democracy, and social justice. If American society is to move away from its increasing defensiveness about cultural differences, it will have to advocate a view of national identity that regards bigotry and intolerance as the enemy of democracy and cultural differences as one of its strengths. However, even where such differences are acknowledged and affirmed, it is important to recognize that they cannot be understood exclusively within the language of culture and identity, but rather as a part of an ethical discourse that contributes to a viable notion of democratic public life. In part, this suggests a pedagogy and language through which values and social responsibility can be discussed not simply as a matter of individual choice, reduced to complacent relativism, but as a social discourse and pedagogical practice grounded in public struggles. Goldberg is right in arguing that educators need a "robustly nuanced conception of relativism underpinning the multicultural project [one that] will enable distinctions to be drawn between more or less accurate truth claims and more or less justifiable values (in contrast to absolute claims to the truth or the good)" ("Introduction" 15). The issue here is not merely the importance of moral pragmatism in developing a pedagogy that addresses national identity as a site of resistance and reinvention. Equally important is the political and pedagogical imperative of developing a postmodern notion of democracy in which students and others will be attentive to negotiating and constructing the social, political, and cultural conditions for diverse cultural identities to flourish within an increasingly multicentric, international, and transnational world.

In short, if national identity is not to be used in the service of demagogues, it must be addressed pedagogically and politically to unravel how cultural differences have been constructed within the unequal distribution of resources, how such differences need to be understood around issues of power and struggle, and how national identity must be taken up in ways that challenge economic and cultural inequality.

Giroux is Waterbury Chair Professor of Education at Penn State. He writes in the fields of critical pedagogy, cultural studies, and popular culture. His most recent books include *Border Crossings, Living Dangerously, Disturbing Pleasures*, and his forth-coming *Fugitive Cultures: Race, Violence, and Youth* (Routledge).

Notes

1. The literature on nationalism and national identity is much too voluminous to cite here, but excellent examples can be found in Anderson; Chatterjee; Bhabha's *Nation and Narration;* Said; Parker, Russo, Sommer, and Yaeger; and Balibar and Wallerstein. Some recent sources can be found in Calhoun's *Social Theory and the Politics of Identity.*

2. For a brilliant analysis of this phenomenon, especially the marketing of Beavis and Butt-Head, see Kellner.

References

Anderson, Benedict. *Imagined Communities.* 2nd ed. London: Verso, 1991.

Appadurai, Arjun. "Patriotism and Its Futures," *Public Culture* 5.3 (1993): 411–29.

Balibar, Etienne, and Immanuel Wallerstein. *Race, Nation, Class: Ambiguous Identities.* London: Verso, 1991.

Bhabha, Homi K. "Beyond the Pale: Art in the Age of Multicultural Translation." *Kunst and Museum Journal* 5.4 (1994): 15–23.

———. "A Good Judge of Character: Men, Metaphors, and the Common Culture." *Race-ing Justice, En-Gendering Power: Essays on Anita Hill, Clarence Thomas, and the Construction of Social Reality.* Ed. Toni Morrison. New York: Pantheon, 1992.

———. ed., *Nation and Narration.* New York: Routledge, 1990.

Calhoun, Craig. "Nationalism and Civil Society: Democracy, Diversity, and Self-Determination." Calhoun, ed. 304–35.

———. ed., *Social Theory and the Politics of Identity.* Cambridge: Blackwell, 1994.

Chatterjee, Partha. *The Nation and Its Fragments.* Princeton: Princeton UP, 1993.

Gilroy, Paul. *The Black Atlantic: Modernity and Double Consciousness.* Cambridge: Harvard UP, 1993.

Giroux, Henry A. "Racism and the Aesthetic of Hyper-Real Violence: *Pulp Fiction* and Other Visual Tragedies." *Social Identities* 1.2 (forthcoming).

Goldberg, David Theo. "Introduction: Multicultural Conditions." *Multiculturalism: A Critical Reader.* Ed. Goldberg. Cambridge: Blackwell, 1994.

———. *Racist Culture.* Cambridge: Blackwell, 1993.

Graff, Gerald, and Bruce Robbins. "Cultural Criticism." *Redrawing the Lines.* Ed. Stephen Greenblatt and Giles Gunn. New York: MLA, 1992.

Grewal, Inderpal, and Caren Kaplan. "Introduction: Transnational Feminist Practices and Questions of Postmodernity." *Scattered Hegemonies.* Ed. Grewal and Kaplan. Minneapolis: U of Minnesota P, 1994. 1–33.

Hage, Ghassan. "Locating Multiculturalism's Other: A Critique of Practical Tolerance." *New Formations* 24 (Winter 1994): 19–34.

Hall, Stuart. "Cultural Identity and Diaspora." Rutherford, ed.

———. "Culture, Community, Nation." *Cultural Studies* 7.3 (Oct. 1993).

Ien Ang. "On Not Speaking Chinese: Postmodern Ethnicity and the Politics of Diaspora." *Social Formations* 24 (March 1995): 1–18.

Judis, John B., and Michael Lind. "For A New Nationalism." *New Republic* 27 (Mar. 1995): 19–27.

Kellner, Douglas. *Media Culture: Cultural Studies, Identity, and Politics—Between The Modern and the Postmodern.* New York: Routledge, forthcoming.

Krauthammer, Charles. "The Real Buchanan is Surfacing." *Cincinnati Enquirer* 3 Mar. 1990: A4.

Kymlicka, Will. "Misunderstanding Nationalism." *Dissent* (Winter 1995): 130–37.

Limbaugh, Rush H., III. *See, I Told You So.* New York: Pocket, 1993.

Parker, Andrew, Mary Russo, Doris Sommer, and Patricia Yaeger, eds. *Nationalisms and Sexualities.* New York: Routledge, 1992.

Parry, Benita. "Signs of Our Times: A Discussion of Homi Bhabha's *The Location of Culture*." *Third Text* 28/29 (Autumn/Winter 1994): 5–24.

Rorty, Richard. "The Unpatriotic Academy." *New York Times.* Op-Ed Section, Sunday (13 Feb. 1994): E15.

Rutherford, Jonathan, ed. *Identity, Community, Culture, Difference.* London: Lawrence and Wishart, 1990.

———. "A Place Called Home: Identity and the Cultural Politics of Difference." Rutherford, ed.

Said, Edward. *Culture and Imperialism.* New York: Knopf, 1993.

Squires, Judith. "Editorial." *New Formations* 24 (Winter 1994): v–vi.

Bibliography

Alpert, Robert. "*The Social Network*: The Contemporary Pursuit of Happiness Through Social Connections." *Jumpcut: A Review of Contemporary Media* 53 (2011).

Althusser, Louis. "Ideology and Ideological State Apparatuses (Notes: toward an Investigation)." *Lenin and Philosophy and Other Essays*. New York: Monthly Review Press, 1991.

Anderson, Benedict. "Introduction." *Imagined Communities*. New York: Verso Books, 2006.

Andre, Judith. "Stereotypes: Conceptual and Normative Considerations." *Racism and Sexism: An Integrated Study*. Ed. Paula S. Rothenburg. New York: St. Martin's Press, 1998.

Bird, Sharon R. "Welcome to the Men's Club: Homosociality and the Maintenance of Hegemonic Masculinity." *Gender and Society* 10.2 (1996): 120–132.

Brackman, Harold David. "The Attack on 'Jewish Hollywood': A Chapter in the History of Modern American Anti-Semitism." *Modern Judaism* 20.1 (2000): 1–19.

Calhoun, Cheshire. "Introduction: Centering Sexual Orientation Politics." *Feminism, the Family, and the Politics of the Closet: Lesbian and Gay Displacement*. Oxford University Press, 2000; 1–24.

Crain, Caleb. "The Thief of Time." *The Paris Review*. 31 October 2011.

Gates, Philippa. "Manhunting: The Female Detective in the Serial Killer Film." *Post Script-Essays in Film and the Humanities* 24.1 (2004): 42–61.

Giroux, Henry A. "National Identity and the Politics of Multiculturalism." *College Literature* 22.2 (1995): 42–57.

Hall, Stuart. "Representation, Meaning and Language." *Representation: Cultural Representations and Signifying Practices*. London: Sage, 1997.

Hogan, Susan & Lorna Warren. "Dealing with Complexity in Research Processes and Findings: How Do Older Women Negotiate and Challenge Images of Aging?" *Journal of Women and Aging* 24.4 (2012): 329–50.

hooks, bell. "A Revolution of Values: The Promise of Multi-Cultural Change". *The Journal of the Midwest Modern Language Association* 26.1 (1993): 4–11.

Jones, Sharon L. "From Margin to Centre? Images of African-American Women in Film." *Social Alternatives* 17.4 (1998): 35–39.

Kellner, Douglas. "Cultural Studies, Multiculturalism, and Media Culture." *Gender, Race, and Class in Media*. Eds. Gail Dines and Jean M. Humez. Thousand Oaks, CA: Sage, 2003. 9–20.

Lev, Peter. "Whose Future? "Star Wars," "Alien," and "Blade Runner"." *Literature/Film Quarterly* 26.1 (1998): 30–7.

Lull, James. "Hegemony." *Media, Communication, Culture: A Global Approach*. New York: Columbia University Press, 1995.

Lyden, John. "To Commend or To Critique? The Question of Religion and Film Studies." *Journal of Religion and Film Studies* 1.2 (1997).

Marx, Karl. "The Destructive Power of Money." *Marx's Concept of Man*. Ed. Erich Fromm. Trans. T.B. Bottomore. New York: F. Ungar Publishing, 1963.

McNamee, Stephen and Robert K. Miller, Jr. "The Meritocracy Myth." *Sociation Today* 2.1 (2004).

Mueleners, Matthew. "Treat Students Right By Valuing Their Diversity." *The Education Digest* (2001): 46–51.

Place, Janey. "Women in Film Noir." *Women in Film Noir*. Ed. E. Ann Kaplan. London: BFI, 1989. 35–68.

Risman, Barbara J. "Gender as a Social Structure: Theory Wrestling with Activism." *Gender and Society*. Thousand Oaks, CA: Sage, 2004.

Schleier, Merrill. "Fatal Attractions: 'Place,' the Korean War, and Gender in *Niagara*." *Cinema Journal* 51.4 (2012): 26–43.

Schrock, Douglas and Michael Schwalbe. "Men, Masculinity, and Manhood Acts." *Annual Review of Sociology* 35 (2009): 277–95.

Shaheen, Jack G. "Reel Bad Arabs: How Hollywood Vilifies a People." *Annals of the American Academy of Political and Social Science*. 588 (2003): 171–193.

Smith, Stacy L. and Crystal Allene Cook. "Gender Stereotypes: An Analysis of Popular Films and TV." The Geena Davis Institute on Gender in Media, 2008.

Sue, Derald Wing, Christina M. Capodilupo, Gina C. Torino, Jennifer M. Bucceri, Aisha M. B. Holder, Kevin L. Nadal, and Marta Esquilin. "Racial Microaggressions in Everyday Life: Implications for Clinical Practice." *American Psychologist* 62.4 (2009): 271–86.

Thaggert, Miriam. "Marriage, Moynihan, *Mahogany*: Success and the Post-Civil Rights Black Female Professional in Film." *American Quarterly* 64.4 (2012): 715–40.

Weber, Lynn. "A Conceptual Framework for Understanding Race, Class, Gender and Sexuality." *Psychology of Women Quarterly* 22.1 (1998): 13–32.